fine Cooking 2007

The Taunton Press
Inspiration for hands-on living®

©2007 by The Taunton Press, Inc.

All rights reserved.

Printed in the United States of America
ISBN: 978-1-60085-019-6

Fine Cooking, The Taunton Press, Inc.,
63 South Main Street, PO Box 5506,
Newtown, CT 06470-5506
e-mail: fc@taunton.com
www.finecooking.com

fine Cooking

Dear *Fine Cooking* reader,

The wait is over. Here it is, our ninth annual volume of *Fine Cooking* issues, gathered together in one handsome hardback edition. The year 2007 was a rich one for us—in fact, we published more recipes than ever, including three beautiful pull-out sections on Favorite Winter Pastas (February/March), Grilling for a Crowd (June/July) and Breakfast Basics (December). But that's not all. Take a look at some of the other highlights of 2007 that we're proud to share with you:

- An indispensable primer on **knife sharpeners** (April/May) — Finally, here's all the information you need on the different kinds of knife sharpeners available on the market and how to determine which one is right for you. As a bonus, we offer links to great **videos on Finecooking.com** showing how to steel and sharpen your knives.

- A delicious adventure in **Bistro Cooking** (February/March) — Contributing editor and French cooking expert Molly Stevens shows us how to make three bistro classics: Braised Lamb Shanks with Garlic & Vermouth, Chicken with Vinegar & Onions, and Beef Stew with Red Wine & Carrots.

- Valuable **equipment reviews** to take to the store with you — This year we evaluated large saucepans, ice cream scoops, garlic presses, and mortars & pestles.

- A brand new department called **Ask the Expert,** introduced in December — Our first two experts answered our questions on serving cheese and storing wine.

- **Classic articles** that will never go out of date — The Essential Guide to Roasting Vegetables (October/November), The Art of Making Green Salads (June/July), How to Make Flaky, Buttery Biscuits (April/May), The Secrets to Fluffy and Flavorful Rice Pilaf (February/March), to name a few.

- More of our **signature technique articles,** including two great "Cooking Without Recipes" articles on making fruit cobblers (June/July) and making hearty bean and vegetable soups (October/November.)

In addition to all of this great content, our big news this year was the launch of our newly expanded Web site, Finecooking.com. This means you'll find links throughout these pages to helpful videos, bonus recipes, and extra tips that will bring the articles to life in your kitchen. And there's no easier or better way to enjoy cooking than with *Fine Cooking* by your side.

So please enjoy!

Maria Taylor
Publisher

The Taunton Press, 63 S. Main St., PO Box 5506, Newtown, CT 06470-5506 (203) 426-8171 E-mail: fc@taunton. com

ew favorites: artisan cheeses, olive oils, wine, dark chocolate

fine
Cooking

JANUARY 2007 NO. 83

FOR PEOPLE WHO LOVE TO COOK

ow to:

fast flavor
or weeknight
dinners

nake-ahead
neat ragùs

ast 2
hickens,
et 4 great
neals

rispy
otatoes

ne best
ound cake

w.finecooking.com

95 CAN $7.95

01

7 44470 56529 1

**give pasta a quick boost with
shrimp, garlic & chorizo**

fine Cooking

JANUARY 2007 ISSUE 83

38

44

ON THE COVER

82a **Quick & Delicious**

Seven dishes for weeknight suppers or weekend company

Linguine with Shrimp & Chorizo

HOST A TASTING PARTY

50

Discover your favorite cheeses, chocolates, and olive oils.

UP FRONT

6 Index

8 Menus

10 Letters

14 Links

16 Contributors

18 Great Finds
American cheeses

20 In Season
Cauliflower

22 Q&A

24 Artisan Foods
Sea-salt caramels

26 Enjoying Wine
Break out of
your wine rut

28 Equipment
❖ Silicone update
❖ Palm peeler
❖ Crêpe pans
❖ Rice cookers

32 Food Science
Melting cheese

36 Readers' Tips

26

18

30

28

20

32

The Taunton Press
Inspiration for hands-on living®

visit our web site: **www.finecooking.com**

46   55   58   62

FEATURES

38   COOKING AHEAD
Roast Chicken for Today and Tomorrow
Roast two chickens; serve one on Sunday and turn the other into terrific weeknight meals
by Tony Rosenfeld

44   Crowd-Pleasing Crispy Potatoes
With a short ingredient list and a mostly make-ahead technique, these potatoes are perfect for parties
by Susie Middleton

70

46   Indian-Style Vegetable Stir-Fries
A few sassy spices and a simple one-pan technique are all you need to create these flavorful side dishes
by Suvir Saran

50   How to Host a Tasting Party
Get to know your palate and discover the chocolates, cheeses, and olive oils you love
by Dina Cheney

55   A Sweet Treat That's Easy to Make
This delicious apple dessert will make you feel like a brilliant pastry chef when you serve it
by Kimberly Y. Masibay

58   The Best Ragùs
The secret? Braise the meat on the bone first, then shred it, chop it, and mix it back into the rich sauce
by Biba Caggiano

62   COOKING WITHOUT RECIPES
Frittata: An Italian Omelet
Make dozens of different frittatas with the ingredients you like the best
by Joyce Goldstein

66   Pound Cake, Perfected
A couple of little tweaks make this classic butter cake moister, richer, and better than ever
by Nicole Rees

IN THE BACK

70   From Our Test Kitchen
❖ Indian spices
❖ Boiling eggs
❖ Shredding cabbage
❖ Sherry vinegar
❖ Following recipes

74

74   Tasting Panel
Prepared pesto

76   Where To Buy It

82   Nutrition Information

BACK COVER

Make It Tonight
Stir-fried cauliflower

71

index

◆ QUICK
Under 45 minutes

◆ MAKE AHEAD
Can be completely
prepared ahead but
may need reheating
and a garnish to serve

◆ MOSTLY MAKE AHEAD
Can be partially
prepared ahead but will
need a few finishing
touches before serving

◆ VEGETARIAN
May contain eggs
and dairy ingredients

recipes

Cover Recipe
◆ Linguine with Shrimp & Chorizo, 82a

Appetizers
◆◆◆ Smoky Eggplant & White Bean Dip
with Pita Crisps, 82a

Salads
◆ Lemony Chicken Caesar Salad with
Garlic-Parmesan Toasts, 42
◆ Steak, Egg & Blue Cheese Salad, 82a

Soups
◆◆◆ Curried Lentil Soup, 82a
Tuscan Peasant Soup with Rosemary
& Pancetta, 10

Pasta & Rice
◆ Coconut Rice with Chicken & Snow Peas, 40
◆ Linguine with Shrimp & Chorizo, 82a

Meat, Poultry & Sausage
◆ Buttermilk Country Fried Chicken with
Cucumber Salad, 82a
◆ Chinese Five-Spice-Crusted Duck Breasts,
82a
◆ Coconut Rice with Chicken & Snow Peas,
40
◆ Frittata with Kale, Onions & Chorizo, 62
◆ Frittata with Sausage, Mushrooms &
Onions, 62
◆ Lamb Shank & Sweet Pepper Ragù, 61
◆ Lemony Chicken Caesar Salad with
Garlic-Parmesan Toasts, 42
◆ Linguine with Shrimp & Chorizo, 82a
◆ Neapolitan Rib & Sausage Ragù, 59
Roast Chicken with Rosemary-Lemon Salt,
39

82a *Seared Tuna with Fennel Seeds
& Caper Brown Butter*

◆ Short Rib & Porcini Mushroom Ragù, 60
◆ Soft Chicken Tacos with the Works, 42
◆ Steak, Egg & Blue Cheese Salad, 82a

Seafood
◆ Linguine with Shrimp & Chorizo, 82a
◆ Seared Tuna with Fennel Seeds & Caper
Brown Butter, 82a

Egg Main Dishes
◆◆ Frittata with Asparagus, Herbs & Scallions,
62
◆ Frittata with Kale, Onions & Chorizo, 62
◆◆ Frittata with Mushrooms, Leeks & Goat
Cheese, 62
◆ Frittata with Potatoes, Onions & Pancetta,
62
◆ Frittata with Sausage, Mushrooms
& Onions, 62
◆ Steak, Egg & Blue Cheese Salad, 82a

Side Dishes
◆◆ Browned Cauliflower with Anchovies,
Olives & Capers, 21
◆◆ Cabbage & Carrot Stir-Fry with Toasted
Cumin & Lime, 47
◆◆ Crispy Smashed Roasted Potatoes, 45
◆◆ Green Bean Stir-Fry with Shredded
Coconut, 49
◆◆ Mushroom Stir-Fry with Onions
& Tomatoes, 48
◆◆ Potato Stir-Fry with Mint & Cilantro, 49
◆◆ Stir-Fried Cauliflower with Green Peas
& Ginger, back cover

Sauces
◆ Lamb Shank & Sweet Pepper Ragù, 61
◆ Neapolitan Rib & Sausage Ragù, 59
◆ Short Rib & Porcini Mushroom Ragù, 60

Spices & Vinaigrettes
◆◆◆ Garam Masala, 70
◆◆◆ Honey-Mustard Sherry Vinaigrette, 72

Cakes & Desserts
◆◆ Apple Brown-Butter Jalousie, 56
◆◆ Brandy & Rum Glazed Pound Cake, 68
◆◆ Butter Pound Cake, 67
◆◆ Chocolate Chip Pound Cake, 69
◆◆ Lemon-Coconut Pound Cake, 69
◆◆ Mixed-Berry Jalousie, 56

42 *Lemony Chicken Caesar Salad
with Garlic-Parmesan Toasts*

67 *Butter Pound Cake*

Photos: Scott Phillips

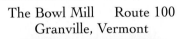

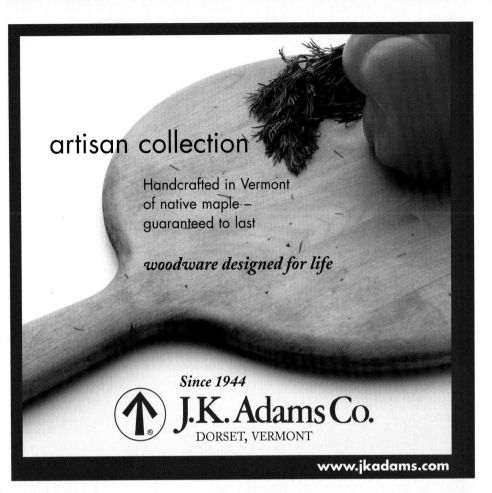

Keep It Casual & Comforting

You've just come through a long season of feasts and celebrations, so after ringing in the New Year, why not slow down and take it a bit easy. We're not suggesting you give up entertaining entirely—after all, there's no better cure for the post-holiday blues than an invitation to dinner—but when you do have people over, keep things low-key. Instead of multi-course extravaganzas, opt for comforting family-style meals. A delicious dish or two is really all you need to serve, but if you have the time and energy, go ahead and round out the meal with an easy appetizer, a simple salad, or a do-ahead dessert. To get you started, here are two entertaining menus with planning strategies to help you pull them together, plus four duos for weeknight dinners.

Before you cook, be sure to check the yield of every recipe, as you might need to double or triple a recipe if you're cooking for a crowd.

4 weeknight duos

These pairings are perfect for family meals yet special enough for impromptu entertaining. If you want to finish a meal with something sweet, any of the pound cakes on pp. 66–69 would be a good choice; they can be made from 3 to 7 days in advance, so you can bake on the weekend and have cake on hand for weeknight desserts.

1 Seared Tuna with Fennel Seeds & Caper Brown Butter, p. 82a

Browned Cauliflower with Anchovies, Olives & Capers, p. 21

2 Tuscan Peasant Soup with Rosemary & Pancetta, p. 10

Arugula salad with toasted almonds and Honey-Mustard Sherry Vinaigrette, p. 72

3 Buttermilk Country Fried Chicken with Cucumber Salad, p. 82a

Crispy Smashed Potatoes, p. 45

4 Potato, Onion & Pancetta Frittata with Basil & Parmigiano, p. 62

Romaine lettuce with Caesar Salad Vinaigrette, p. 42

Almost-fancy roast chicken dinner

You can salt the chicken and make the lentil soup up to a day ahead (though when you reheat the soup you may need to adjust its consistency by adding a little water). About 90 minutes before your guests arrive, pop the chicken into the oven to roast, wash and dry your salad greens, and start prepping the ingredients for the potato side dish (don't cook it until about 20 minutes before serving time, though). While the roast chicken rests, put the nuts you'll be using for dessert in the hot oven to toast.

Curried Lentil Soup, p. 82a

Roast Chicken with Rosemary-Lemon Salt, p. 39

Potato Stir-Fry with Mint & Cilantro, p. 49

A simple green salad

Vanilla ice cream topped with toasted nuts and honey

To drink: A young, fruity Beaujolais or a crisp Sauvignon Blanc from France

A slow-cook Sunday supper

Make the jalousie early in the day and let it rest until supper-time. You can make the eggplant dip up to a day ahead and chill—just be sure to bring it to room temperature before serving and garnish at the last minute—but if you're spending a leisurely afternoon in the kitchen, you'll have ample time to prepare the dip while the ragù simmers in the oven.

Smoky Eggplant & White Bean Dip with Pita Crisps, p. 82a

Lamb Shank & Sweet Pepper Ragù, p. 61, with fresh pappardelle pasta

Apple Brown-Butter Jalousie with whipped cream, p. 56

To drink: A medium-bodied French Syrah or Grenache blend

A promise to cook more,

Normal people make New Year's resolutions like "Lose 10 pounds," "No more sweets," "Never eat bread again." Here at *Fine Cooking,* we make resolutions about food, too; they're just a little different.

"This year, I want to learn to make a perfect loaf of crusty artisan bread," one editor told me. "I want to master the art of Thai cooking," another said. And, "I want to entertain more," from a third.

But aside from these ambitious cooks, everyone else—I discovered after taking an informal poll—has a seemingly simple wish: to just plain cook more, especially on the weekends. Everyone wants to cook great stuff over the weekend so they can have delicious (and quick) homemade meals throughout the week. Of course, the big bugaboo is finding the weekend time to do the cooking.

While we can't unplug your phone or run your errands for you, we can offer you an issue packed with make-ahead inspiration. Hopefully, inspiration equals motivation—if this January *Fine Cooking* doesn't get you in the kitchen, I don't know what will.

Here are a few great candidates for Sunday afternoon simmering (or baking or roasting):

❖ The delicious **meat ragùs** on pp. 58–61. Divide these into small portions and freeze them to use for quick and hearty pasta dinners later.

❖ Any of the **butter pound cakes** on pp. 66–69. Well-wrapped, they keep for a few days, but they can be frozen, too.

❖ The recipe for **two roast chickens** on pp. 38–43. Eat one for Sunday supper and save the other to make tacos, salads, or stir-fries over the next few days.

Lots of other recipes—like the crispy potatoes on pp. 44–45, the frittatas on pp. 62–65, and my Tuscan soup, below—can be mostly or completely made ahead. So, no excuses, anyone (and this includes you, FC staffers, and me). Don't worry, though; if your weekends are just too busy right now for leisurely cooking, we've still got

Tuscan Peasant Soup with Rosemary & Pancetta

Yields 3½ qts.; serves six to eight.

5 Tbs. extra-virgin olive oil
1¼ cups small-diced pancetta (about 6 oz. or 6 thick slices)
4 cups large-diced Savoy cabbage (about ½ small head)
2 cups medium-diced onion (10 to 12 oz. or 2 small)
1½ cups medium-diced carrot (about 4 medium carrots)
½ tsp. kosher salt; more as needed
2 Tbs. minced garlic
1 Tbs. plus 1 tsp. minced fresh rosemary
1 tsp. ground coriander
1 28-oz. can diced tomatoes, drained
7 cups homemade or low-salt canned chicken broth
2 15½-oz. cans small white beans, rinsed and drained (about 2½ cups, drained)
1 to 2 tsp. fresh lemon juice
Freshly ground black pepper
1 cup fresh breadcrumbs, toasted
1 cup grated Parmigiano-Reggiano

Heat 2 Tbs. of the olive oil in a 4- to 5-qt. Dutch oven over medium heat. When hot, add the pancetta and cook, stirring frequently, until quite shrunken, golden brown, and crisp (the oil will also be golden brown), about 6 minutes. Remove the pan from the heat and with a slotted spoon or strainer carefully transfer the pancetta to a paper-towel-lined plate. Pour off and discard all but 2 Tbs. of the fat from the pan.

Return the pot to medium-high heat and add the chopped cabbage. Cook the cabbage, stirring occasionally, until limp and browned around the edges, about 3 minutes. Remove the pot from the heat again and transfer the cabbage to another plate.

Put the pot back over medium heat and add 2 Tbs. more of the olive oil. When the oil is hot, add the onions, carrots, and salt. Cook, stirring occasionally, until the onions are softened and the vegetables are browned around the edges and beginning to stick to the bottom of the pan, 8 to 9 minutes. Add the last 1 Tbs. of olive oil, the garlic, 1 Tbs. of the fresh rosemary, and the ground coriander and cook,

eat better

plenty of quick dishes in this issue that you can pull together after work (see the recipe index on p. 6). And like the pasta on the cover, they all have that boost of *Fine Cooking* flavor you've come to expect.

—*Susie Middleton, editor*

P.S. It's true, this regular issue of *Fine Cooking* is packed with make-ahead recipes. But if you really get into cooking (and entertaining) on the weekend, you'll want to be sure to check out our new 2007 *Weekend Cooking*. This special collection of *Fine Cooking* recipes is on sale at newsstands now and is also available to purchase through our Web site at www.FineCooking.com.

stirring, until the garlic is fragrant, about 1 minute. Add the tomatoes, stir together, and cook the mixture 2 to 3 more minutes.

Return the cabbage to the pan and add the chicken broth. Stir well, bring to a boil, and reduce to a simmer. Cook for 10 to 15 minutes to infuse the broth with the flavor of the vegetables. Add the beans, bring back to a simmer, and cook for a minute or two. Remove the pan from the heat, stir in the remaining 1 tsp. fresh rosemary, and let rest a few minutes.

Taste the soup and add lemon juice to brighten it—you'll want at least 1 tsp. Season with more salt if necessary and a few grinds of fresh pepper. Serve the soup hot, garnished with the reserved pancetta crisps, the toasted bread-crumbs, and the grated Parmigiano.

from our readers

Two good reasons *not* to microwave dishes.

Heating dinner plates or other dishes in the microwave (a tip in *Fine Cooking* #81) is contraindicated if the dishes being heated have any metallic—gold or silver—trim. Even my Rosenthal Ascot pattern, with just a simple gold rim, caused arcing when I attempted to warm some soup in a bowl. Luckily, I was standing right by the microwave and was able to hit the Cancel button before harm was done to the bowl or the microwave.

—*Charles Chapman,
London, Ontario*

In *Fine Cooking* #81, a reader recommended using the microwave to heat dinner plates. If I'm not mistaken, the fact that an empty plate "heats" in the microwave is an indication that it is not microwave-safe. I learned that lesson the hard way when a stoneware plate exploded in my microwave.

—*Sally Geyer, Richardson, Texas*

Editors' reply: To help sort out the confusion over safe microwaving, we talked with Allison Eckelkamp, a public relations representative for GE appliances. She gave us some great guidelines:

"Microwave-safe" is a determination made by the cookware or utensil manufacturer. However, from the standpoint of an oven manufacturer like GE, "microwave-safe" means that the cookware will not heat up, or cause arcing, or soften, or melt, when used in accordance with the microwave manufacturer's instructions.

If you put a microwave-safe dish in the oven without food, it should not get any warmer than room temperature. That said, it's never a good idea to run the microwave empty or even with just a dish inside. For safe operation, there must be food in the oven to absorb the microwave energy. Running the microwave without food can damage the oven's components.

If you want to test the microwave safety of a dish, GE's "Use and Care" manual and Web site explain how to go about it (see paragraph below). Once you've determined that your dish is microwave-safe, go ahead and use it in the microwave—with food on or in it.

If you are not sure if a dish is microwave-safe, use this test: Place in the oven both the dish you are testing and a glass measuring cup filled with 1 cup of water—set the measuring cup either in or next to the dish. Microwave 30 to 45 seconds at high. If the dish heats, it should not be used for microwaving. If the dish remains cool and only the water in the cup heats, then the dish is microwave-safe.

Cooking smart

I am a subscriber to *Fine Cooking*, and I love it. I canceled all my other cooking magazines and use just this one. Your tips and ideas have helped me become a more spontaneous cook; I'm able to think of the lessons learned from the magazine and then create my own dishes using those principles.

One issue from a few years ago (*Fine Cooking* #51, June–July 2002) was so full of wonderful ideas and recipes that I use it almost every week. The grilled pork ("Foolproof Grilled Pork Tenderloin" by Pam Anderson) in that issue is my stand-by main course. Honestly, I fed it to every group I had over for dinner one summer (and I entertain once or twice a week) and just varied the sauce and glaze. The more times I grilled it, the better I got with it. I would stress to readers that to get the most out of a recipe you have to prepare it at least three times. Then you know its characteristics and feel in control of the situation.

—*Ann Jones, Columbus, Ohio*

Correction

Schott Zwiesel, maker of the Tritan Forté wine glasses mentioned on p. 27 of *Fine Cooking* #82, is a German company, not Austrian, as stated. It's located in Zwiesel, Bavaria, Germany (www.schott-zwiesel.com). ◆

Fine Cooking

EDITOR **Susie Middleton**

EXECUTIVE EDITOR
Sarah Jay

ART DIRECTOR
Steve Hunter

TEST KITCHEN MANAGER/RECIPE EDITOR
Jennifer Armentrout

SENIOR EDITOR **Kimberly Y. Masibay**

ASSOCIATE EDITOR **Rebecca Freedman**

ASSOCIATE WEB EDITOR **Sarah Breckenridge**

ASSISTANT EDITOR **Laura Giannatempo**

SENIOR COPY/PRODUCTION EDITOR
Enid Johnson

ASSOCIATE ART DIRECTOR **Annie Giammattei**

TEST KITCHEN ASSOCIATE/FOOD STYLIST
Allison R. Ehri

EDITORIAL ASSISTANT **Kim Landi**

EDITOR AT LARGE **Maryellen Driscoll**

TEST KITCHEN INTERNS
Noriko Yokota, Safaya Tork

CONTRIBUTING EDITORS
Pam Anderson, Abigail Johnson Dodge, Tim Gaiser, Tony Rosenfeld, Molly Stevens

PUBLISHER **Maria Taylor**

SENIOR MARKETING MANAGER
Karen Lutjen

CIRCULATION DIRECTOR
Dennis O'Brien

SINGLE COPY SALES MANAGER
Mark Stiekman

ASSOCIATE ADVERTISING SALES MANAGER
Linda Petersell

CORPORATE ACCOUNTS MANAGER
Judy Caruso

NATIONAL ACCOUNTS MANAGERS
Patricia Coleman, Linda Delaney

ASSOCIATE ACCOUNTS MANAGER
Chris Dunham

ADVERTISING SALES ASSOCIATE **Stacy Purcell**

Fine Cooking: (ISSN: 1072-5121) is published seven times a year by The Taunton Press, Inc., Newtown, CT 06470-5506. Telephone 203-426-8171. Periodicals postage paid at Newtown, CT 06470 and at additional mailing offices. GST paid registration #123210981.

Subscription Rates: U.S. and Canada, $29.95 for one year, $49.95 for two years, $69.95 for three years (GST included, payable in U.S. funds). Outside the U.S./Canada: $36 for one year, $62 for two years, $88 for three years (payable in U.S. funds). Single copy, $6.95. Single copy outside the U.S., $7.95.

Postmaster: Send address changes to *Fine Cooking*, The Taunton Press, Inc., 63 South Main St., P.O. Box 5506, Newtown, CT 06470-5506.

Canada Post: Return undeliverable Canadian addresses to *Fine Cooking*, c/o Worldwide Mailers, Inc., 2835 Kew Drive, Windsor, ON N8T 3B7, or email to mnfa@taunton.com.

Printed in the USA.

What's New at FineCooking.com

Visit our home page at FineCooking.com to see what's "On the Front Burner." This month, our special Web collections include a culinary passage to India and a celebration of olive oil.

ON THE FRONT BURNER
Exploring Indian Food

Break out of the winter doldrums with the warm, complex flavors of Indian cuisine. Whether you want to recreate an authentic dish or just add some subcontinental spice to your weeknight repertoire, we've got the recipes, techniques, and tools you need.

BONUS DOWNLOAD
The Essential Indian Pantry Checklist

TIPS, TOOLS & TECHNIQUES

Review: The best spice grinder

Technique Class: How to make samosas

Great Finds: Our favorite Indian cookbooks

RECIPES

Naan Bread from Your Own Oven

Indian Spiced Shrimp

Tandoori Chicken

Peppery Pink Lentil Soup

Eggplant with Fragrant Spices

And much more

ON THE FRONT BURNER
All About Olive Oil

Of course, it's a healthy cooking fat and great for dressings, but that's just the beginning. In this collection, we're celebrating the warm, sun-drenched flavor of olive oil when it takes a starring role in a dish.

TIPS, TOOLS & TECHNIQUES

Top olive oil picks

Great Finds: Stylish ways to serve and pour olive oil

Choosing the right oil for every occasion

RECIPES

Goat Cheese & Olives Marinated in Olive Oil

Tuna Poached in Olive Oil

Spinach with Pine Nuts & Raisins

Plum & Blueberry Upside-Down Cake

And lots more

MENU
An Olive Oil Tasting Party

FEATURE ARTICLES
Olive Oil: The Secret to Moist Cakes

How Olives Get From Tree to Bottle

Free email newsletter!

Subscribe at FineCooking.com to get great recipes, tips, techniques, and videos delivered directly to your inbox twice a month.

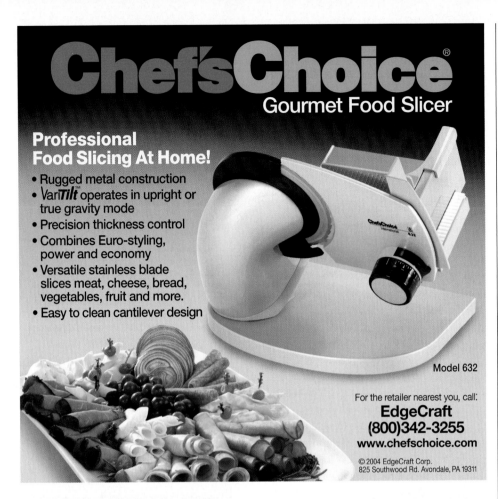

contributors

Tony Rosenfeld ("Roast Chicken," p. 38) had plenty of opportunities to refine his chicken-roasting technique while writing his first cookbook, *150 Things to Make with Roast Chicken and 50 Ways to Roast It,* which will be published by Taunton Press this spring. (And he's not done with the subject yet—look for his story on crisp coatings for chicken breasts in our next issue.) Tony is a food writer and restaurant consultant who lives on Boston's North Shore.

Fine Cooking editor **Susie Middleton** ("Crispy Potatoes," p. 44) says, "When I worked at Al Forno restaurant in Providence, R.I., the smashed red potatoes were the most popular thing on the menu. And during my stint as a chef in a gourmet market, I made hundreds of pounds of classic potato salad. These days, while the crowds at my house are a little smaller, I find anything potatoey will please just about everyone."

Suvir Saran

Born in New Delhi, **Suvir Saran** ("Indian Stir-Fries," p. 46) came to the United States in 1993 to study art. But it soon became apparent that what he really wanted to do was turn people on to the cooking of his native India. He opened a catering business, began to teach, wrote a book, *Indian Home Cooking,* and became executive chef at Dévi restaurant in New York City. Suvir's next book, *American Masala,* is due out in the fall, and he plans to open several more restaurants this year, all under the name American Masala.

Biba Caggiano

Dina Cheney ("Tasting Party," p. 50) is a cooking teacher, tasting host, and freelance writer. While teaching classes and leading tasting events, she met countless students who wanted to develop their palates but didn't know where to begin. That's what inspired her to

Dina Cheney

write her book, *Tasting Club,* which walks readers through all the steps of hosting at-home tasting parties.

In her article, senior editor **Kimberly Masibay** ("A Sweet Treat," p. 55) shares her secrets for making an apple jalousie. Kim trained as a pastry chef in Germany, studied journalism at Columbia University, and worked as a newspaper reporter and magazine editor in New York City before joining *Fine Cooking.*

Biba Caggiano ("The Best Ragùs," p. 58) was born and raised in Emilia-Romagna, the land of prosciutto, Parmigiano, lasagne, and, of course, ragù. "I've been making ragù for as long as I can remember," says Biba. She is the chef and owner of Biba Restaurant in Sacramento, California, host of the syndicated show *Biba's Italian Kitchen,* and author of eight cookbooks. Her latest is *Biba's Italy.*

As a busy cooking instructor, **Joyce Goldstein** ("Frittata," p. 62) is on the road a lot. When she gets home from a trip and needs a fast and tasty supper, she often reaches for eggs, cheese, and some leftover vegetables or a slice of bacon and whips up a frittata. Also a chef and cookbook author, Joyce is one of the foremost experts on Italian cooking in this country. Her many cookbooks include *Italian Slow and Savory, Enoteca,* and her latest, *Antipasti.*

Nicole Rees ("Pound Cakes," p. 66) has been developing cake recipes since the age of nine. She co-wrote the revised edition of *Understanding Baking,* a book on the science and technique of baking, as well as its companion recipe book, *The Baker's Manual.* A food scientist and frequent contributor to *Fine Cooking,* Nicole lives in Portland, Oregon. ◆

The Taunton Press
Inspiration for hands-on living®

INDEPENDENT PUBLISHERS SINCE 1975

TAUNTON, INC.
Founders, **Paul and Jan Roman**

THE TAUNTON PRESS
President & Editor In Chief **Suzanne Roman**
Executive Vice President & Chief Financial Officer **Timothy Rahr**
Executive Vice President & Publisher, Magazine Group **Jon Miller**
Publisher, Book Group **James Childs**
Chief of Operations **Thomas Luxeder**

DIRECTORS
Creative & Editorial Director **Susan Edelman**
Human Resources Director **Carol Marotti**
Controller **Wayne Reynolds**
Advertising Director **David Gray**
Consumer Marketing Director **Diana Allwein**
Fulfillment Director **Patricia Williamson**
Financial Analysis Director **Kathy Worth**

THE TAUNTON PRESS

Books: *Marketing:* Melissa A. Possick, Meg Day, Audrey Locorotondo. *Publicity:* Nicole Radder, Janel Noblin. *Editorial:* Helen Albert, Kathryn Benoit, Peter Chapman, Steve Culpepper, Robyn Doyon-Aitken, Pamela Hoenig, Carolyn Mandarano, Nicole Palmer, Jennifer Peters, Amy Reilly, Jennifer Russell, Erica Sanders-Foege, Kathleen Williams. *Art:* Chris Thompson, Alison Wilkes, Nancy Boudreau, Amy Griffin, Kathy Kelley, Sandra Mahlstedt, Wendi Mijal, Lynne Phillips, Carol Singer. *Manufacturing:* Thomas Greco, Laura Burrone.

Business Office: Holly Smith, Gayle Hammond, Patricia Marini. *Legal:* Carolyn Kovaleski. *Magazine Print Production:* Philip Van Kirk, Nicole Anastas, Jennifer Kaczmarcyk.

Circulation: Dennis O'Brien, Director; Andrew Corson, Catherine Hansen.

Distribution: Paul Seipold, Walter Aponte, Frank Busino, David DeToto, Leanne Furlong, Deborah Greene, Frank Melbourne, Reinaldo Moreno, Raymond Passaro, Ulysses Robinson, Alice Saxton, Nelson Wade.

Finance/Accounting: *Finance:* Brett Manning, David Pond. *Accounting:* Patrick Lamontagne, Lydia Krikorian, Judith O'Toole, Shannon Marrs, Elaine Yamin, Carol Diehm, Dorothy Blasko, Susan Burke, Lorraine Parsons, Larry Rice, James Tweedle, Priscilla Wakeman.

Fulfillment: Diane Goulart. *Fulfillment Systems:* Jodi Klein, Kim Eads, Nancy Knorr, Dawn Viglione. *Customer Service:* Ellen Grassi, Michelle Amoroso, Kathleen Baker, Bonnie Beardsley, Deborah Ciccio, Katherine Clarke, Alfred Dreher, Monica Duhancik, Eileen McNulty, Patricia Parks, Deana Parker, Patricia Pineau, Betty Stepney. *Data Entry:* Melissa Dugan, Anne Champlin, Mary Ann Colbert, Maureen Pekar, Debra Sennefelder, Andrea Shorrock, Marylou Thompson, Barbara Williams.

Human Resources: Linda Ballerini, Christine Lincoln, Dawn Ussery.

Information Technology Services: *Applications Development:* Heidi Waldkirch, Frank Miller, Robert Neilsen,

Photos, from top: Tanya Braganti, Ron Schwager, Scott Phillips

TAUNTON MAGAZINES

Fine Woodworking • Fine Homebuilding Threads • Fine Gardening • Fine Cooking

Our magazines are for people who are passionate about their pursuits. Written by practicing experts in the field, Taunton Press magazines provide authentic, reliable information supported by instructive and inspiring visuals.

TAUNTON BOOKS

Our books are filled with in-depth information and creative ideas from the finest authors in their fields. Whether you're practicing a craft or engaged in the creation of your home, Taunton books will inspire you to discover new levels of accomplishment.

WWW.TAUNTON.COM

Our website is a place where you can discover more about the interests you enjoy, converse with fellow enthusiasts, shop at our convenient on-line store or contact customer service.

EMPLOYMENT INFORMATION

To inquire about career opportunities, please e-mail us at tauntonjobs@taunton.com or visit our website www.taunton.com. You may also write to The Taunton Press, Human Resources, 63 S. Main St., Box 5506, Newtown, CT 06470.

CUSTOMER SERVICE

We are here to answer any questions you might have and to help you order our magazines, books and videos. Just call us toll-free at 800-477-8727.

American Originals

Four uniquely American cheeses and a beautiful board to show them off

BY LAURA GIANNATEMPO

1. An earthy, nutty blue

Bayley Hazen Blue is a lovely cow's milk blue cheese from Vermont's Jasper Hill Farm. We like its firm, crumbly texture, which turns slightly creamier in the mouth. It delivers the pungent sharpness you'd expect from a blue, balanced by a subtle floral note and hints of nuts. *Jasper Hill Farm Bayley Hazen Blue, $18.99 a pound at MurraysCheese.com. For information, visit JasperHillFarm.com.*

2. Perfect for nibbling or cooking

Faarko, a creation of Cedar Grove Cheese in Wisconsin, is a mild semisoft mixed milk cheese (*får* is Danish for sheep and *ko* means cow) that gets richer with every bite, developing a nice complex flavor. This is a great cheese for snacking or cooking. (Grilled cheese sandwich, anyone?) *Faarko, $10.99 a pound. To order, visit CedarGrove Cheese .com or call 800-200-6020.*

3. Parmigiano meets farmhouse Cheddar

Carr Valley's Gran Canaria is a delightful hard cheese made from cow, sheep, and goat milk, with a rind that is periodically rubbed with olive oil. Aged a minimum of two years, this cheese is intensely sharp, like Parmigiano, yet buttery and a little sweet, too, with hints of honey and fruit. *Carr Valley Gran Canaria, $16 a pound at CarrValleyCheese.com.*

4. A tangy heart with a soft, buttery rind

Another great one from Jasper Hill Farm, Constant Bliss is a buttery, bloomy-rind raw cow's milk cheese with a dense, tangy heart that becomes soft and nutty closer to the rind. It has an intense flavor that continues to develop in the mouth, leaving you with a pleasantly pungent back-of-the-throat kick. *Jasper Hill Farm Constant Bliss, $8.99 each (about a quarter pound) at MurraysCheese.com.* ◆

5. No ordinary cheese board

This natural olivewood board is a striking surface for setting out these special cheeses. Handcrafted in Italy, each board has a different shape and its own personality. *Olivewood cheese board, $60 at ArtisanalCheese.com.*

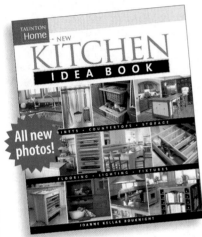

Cauliflower

Discover the hidden talents of this winter gem

BY RUTH LIVELY

When I was a child, we ate cauliflower only one way: boiled and coated with cheese sauce. I can't say I was crazy about it. The cauliflower was cooked too long, at least by today's standards, and back then I didn't like cheese very much. It was only years later, when I experienced perfectly cooked cauliflower topped by a delicate, citrusy hollandaise-type sauce, that I discovered its wonderfully sweet nuttiness and came to love this winter vegetable. Now, I serve it often—roasted or sautéed, as a side dish for hearty braises and roasts; puréed in soups; or even as an appetizer, along with a brightly flavored sauce or dip.

The secret to getting the most flavor from cauliflower is to not overcook it. It should be just tender—when a metal skewer inserted in the stem meets the faintest resistance, it's done. I prefer high-heat cooking methods like roasting or pan-searing (see the recipe opposite), because they brown the cauliflower and add a lovely caramelized sweetness. But cauliflower is also delicious steamed or boiled.

Besides the familiar combo with anchovies, cauliflower is great with other strong partners like olives, capers, soy sauce, and curry, as well as with rich pork products like bacon and prosciutto. At the other end of the spectrum, cauliflower plays nicely with cream, butter, eggs, and nuts. Potatoes and beans blend well with it, too, softening its flavor a bit.

How to cut cauliflower for any dish

Always start by trimming away the leaves and the base of the stem.

Whole florets

Simply cut the florets away from the central stem with a knife. Pay close attention during cooking and remove smaller ones as they're cooked through. Whole florets are great steamed, boiled, or roasted.

QUICK IDEA:
Lightly steam florets and serve them with a dip or sauce, such as a pungent anchoiade or bagna cauda (both anchovy-based), a garlic-basil mayonnaise, or a citrus-spiked soy dipping sauce.

Halved or quartered florets

Smaller cut-up florets are wonderful sautéed or roasted. Try to cut them into relatively even sizes so they cook at the same rate. (See the recipe opposite for more cutting details.)

QUICK IDEA:
Toss halved or quartered florets with olive oil, salt, and paprika, and roast at 375°F until tender and browned around the edges. Halfway through the cooking, add grated lemon zest and chopped fresh oregano. Squeeze on some lemon juice, toss, and serve warm.

Slices

For something a little different, cut whole florets lengthwise into thin, elegant slices that are perfect for deep frying or baking in gratins. You can also blanch them lightly and add them to salads for crunch.

QUICK IDEA:
Dip ¼-inch-thick slices in beaten egg, coat with breadcrumbs, and fry in 365°F peanut oil until golden outside and crisp-tender inside. Season with salt and serve with lemon wedges or a bowl of spicy marinara sauce.

A head of a different color

We're all familiar with white cauliflower, but nowadays you can also find a beautiful deep-golden variety and a stunning purple one. Then there's the exotic and weirdly gorgeous lime-green Romanesco, with conical, spiral florets that look like seashells. Despite their different appearances, all types of cauliflower have a similar sweet, assertive flavor that pairs well with both rich, pungent ingredients and more delicate ones.

Browned Cauliflower with Anchovies, Olives & Capers

Serves four.

Anchovies and cauliflower are a sublime pairing. If you think six filets are too much, trust me: You'll get a delicious suggestion of anchovy, not an overpowering punch. This is one of those dishes that improves greatly if allowed to sit for several hours before eating. Serve at room temperature or warm it gently on the stove or in the oven.

1 medium-small head cauliflower (about 2 lb.)
1 large clove garlic, peeled
Pinch coarse sea salt or kosher salt
6 oil-packed anchovy filets, drained
¼ cup extra-virgin olive oil
15 black olives (such as Kalamata or niçoise), pitted and roughly chopped
1 Tbs. fresh lemon juice; more to taste
2 tsp. capers, roughly chopped
1 tsp. finely grated lemon zest
Large pinch of crushed red pepper flakes or ⅛ tsp. Aleppo pepper

Trim the leaves and stem from the cauliflower head. Working from the bottom of the head, cut off individual florets until you reach the crown, where the florets are small

In a mortar, crush the garlic and the salt with a pestle until you obtain a paste. Add the anchovies and pound them to a paste as well. (If you don't have a mortar, you can mince the garlic, salt, and anchovies very finely and then mash them with the flat side of the knife until they become a paste.) Scrape this mixture into a large shallow bowl. Add 1 Tbs. of the oil, the olives, lemon juice, capers, lemon zest, and red pepper flakes. Stir well.

Heat 2 Tbs. of the olive oil in a heavy 10-inch skillet over medium-high heat. When the oil is hot, add half the cauliflower pieces in a single layer, flat side down. Cook the cauliflower until well browned on the bottom, 2 to 4 minutes, and then transfer to a plate. Add the remaining 1 Tbs. oil to the pan and repeat with the remaining cauliflower, but don't transfer it to the plate. Return the first batch of cauliflower to the pan, turn the heat down to low and carefully add ⅔ cup water. Cover and let steam until the stems are just tender, 6 to 8 minutes.

With a slotted spoon, transfer the cooked cauliflower to the bowl with the anchovy mixture. Add 1 Tbs. of the cooking liquid. Let sit 1 minute to warm and loosen the mixture, and then turn gently to coat the cauliflower and evenly dis-

I love the glossy sheen that a chocolate ganache glaze gives to cakes. But how can you retain the shine after refrigeration?

—Danya Goerig, via email

Alice Medrich responds: Ganache is a mixture of cream and chocolate, which, when poured warm over cakes, makes the ultimate rich chocolate glaze. Ganache naturally loses its shiny appearance as it cools and sets, and even more so when refrigerated, but there are several simple tricks you can use to preserve its attractive sheen.

If your cake requires refrigeration, be sure that it's refrigerator-cold (not frozen) *before* you glaze it, and return it immediately to the refrigerator (not the freezer) to set. Do this even if you plan to remove the cake from the fridge before serving to soften the texture. For the best sheen, let the ganache cool to a tepid temperature—90° to 100°F—and stir it before pouring it on the cake. If the ganache is too thick to pour at this temperature, thin it with warm cream. Once the ganache is poured over the cake, use as few spatula strokes as possible to spread the glaze; too much spatula work will dull the ganache as well.

Three more tricks for greater gloss:

❖ For 1 to 1½ cups ganache, add 2 to 3 teaspoons corn syrup to the glaze.

❖ Remove the dessert from the fridge 30 to 60 minutes before serving to bring back some of the sheen.

❖ And as a desperate measure, you can temporarily make a dull glaze shiny again with the help of a hair dryer set on low heat. Very carefully, starting from a conservative distance of at least 3 feet, aim the warm air at the glaze, moving the dryer constantly to avoid melting the glaze in a single spot, and moving closer to the cake as necessary. Stop when the cake looks shiny and don't overdo it. Serve the dessert shortly thereafter, since there's no telling how the ganache will look later, when it hardens again.

One last note: If the dessert doesn't require refrigeration, don't chill it. Glaze it and let it sit at room temperature. This will give you the best-looking ganache of all.

Alice Medrich, a chocolate expert, has written several books on the subject, including the award-winning cookbook, Bittersweet: Recipes and Tales from a Life in Chocolate.

Have a question of general interest about cooking? Send it to Q&A, Fine Cooking, PO Box 5506, Newtown, CT 06470-5506, or by email to fcqa@taunton. com, and we'll find a cooking professional with the answer.

Why does a green ring sometimes form around the yolk of a hard-cooked egg?

—Doris Gochal, via email

Elisa Maloberti responds: The gray-green discoloration you sometimes see on the surface of a hard-cooked yolk is caused by a reaction between the sulfur and the iron in the egg, but it affects neither the egg's flavor nor its nutritional content.

This chemical reaction is usually brought on by overcooking, but it can also be caused by water that's high in iron (hard water, for example). If your problem is hard water, try cooking your eggs in bottled water. But if it's not the water, then the solution is to avoid overcooking the eggs. (Editors' note: To find out how to boil an egg perfectly, see From Our Test Kitchen, p. 71.)

Elisa Maloberti is the consumer information coordinator for the American Egg Board.

When I make vinaigrette, it sometimes breaks very easily. Why does this happen and can it be fixed?

—Caroline DeGrazia, Santa Cruz, California

Molly Stevens responds: A vinaigrette is an emulsion, which is the technical term for a combination of two incompatible liquids, such as oil and vinegar. In the kitchen, there are two types of emulsions—stable and temporary. Stable emulsions, like mayonnaise, contain a binder (egg yolks in the case of mayonnaise) that combines the incompatible liquids and helps them stay blended.

A simple vinaigrette, on the other hand, is a temporary emulsion, so the two liquids (oil and vinegar) remain combined for only a brief time after whisking or shaking. Without a binder present, the dressing will always break, or separate, as it sits.

You can remedy this by vigorously whisking or shaking the vinaigrette (in a lidded jar) at the last minute before dressing your salad. Or you can stabilize the vinaigrette by adding a binder (for example, mustard, mayonnaise, cream, sour cream, or even a little vegetable or herb purée), thus transforming a temporary emulsion into a more stable one. This approach, however, overlooks one of the great qualities of a simple vinaigrette: Its lightness perfectly dresses fresh salad greens without weighing them down.

Molly Stevens is a contributing editor to Fine Cooking.

I'm pregnant and am concerned about the listeria risk in cheese. I've been told that if it's pasteurized, it's safe. But I've also heard that listeria could develop after pasteurization. Is this true?

—Alexandra Cerf, via email

A Catherine Donnell

only in certain cheeses. Listeria is an environmental pathogen, which means that it can be found in the environment in which a cheese is produced and pasteurized; therefore, the bacteria could potentially contaminate a cheese after it's been pasteurized but before it's been packaged. The good news for pregnant women is that most pasteurized, aged semihard or hard cheeses—for example, hard Swiss, Parmigiano-Reggiano, and Cheddars—simply do not support the growth of listeria, making them safe to consume.

But some other types of cheese can allow listeria to grow if they're contaminated after pasteurization. These include bloomy-rind cheeses like Brie and Camembert, feta, blue cheeses, and soft cheeses like ricotta, queso fresco, fresh goat cheese, and even cottage cheese. In a well-maintained production facility, the risk of contamination is very low, but because listeriosis can be devastating for a fetus, it's probably best for pregnant women to avoid these soft and fresh cheeses, even if they've been pasteurized. And of course, they should also avoid any unpasteurized cheeses.

There is one way for pregnant women to safely eat any cheese, regardless of type or pasteurization: Just cook it. By heating any cheese to 160°F or higher for at least two minutes, listeria will be ͏͏͏

Cathe͏͏͏

Little Flower Candy Company's sea-salt caramels are addictively delicious.

Christine makes the caramel by simmering milk, heavy cream, sugar, and corn syrup until the mixture reaches 248°F, or hard ball stage. She adds a mild gray French sea salt halfway through the cooking.

She carefully pours the hot caramel into a tray and lets it harden for 24 hours.

Handmade sea-salt caramels

BY LAURA GIANNATEMPO

Christine Moore first sunk her teeth into a Brittany sea salt caramel when she was training as a pastry chef in France in the early '90s. She was smitten by its delicacy—by the faint trace of salt that emerged from its chewy sweetness.

When, in 1999, she quit her pastry job in Los Angeles to take care of her first daughter, she found those caramels haunting her. Could she recreate them at home? After experimenting with 10 types of sea salt and a dozen recipes, she finally came up with a satisfyingly chewy caramel that struck just the right balance between salty and sweet.

She began selling these caramels to local stores, working out of her home. As word of her delicious candies spread and business grew, she rented a small professional kitchen in Hollywood and started the Little Flower Candy Company.

With the help of her staff of two, Christine makes and wraps her caramels by hand, packages them in small plastic bags bearing labels she designed herself, and personally delivers them to 40-odd stores around L.A. (She also sells them online.) "Business is brisk," she says. "We can barely keep up with demand." Although her offerings now include vanilla and lemon caramels as well as homemade marshmallows, it's her sea-salt caramels that sell the best. She's planning to open a store in Los Angeles but has no intention of changing her approach. "I'll keep making caramels by hand," she says.

To order, visit LittleFlowerCandyco.com or call 323-551-5948. ◆

The hardened caramel is transferred to a work surface, where Christine cuts it into little squares that are then ready to be wrapped.

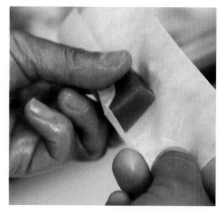

Christine is particular about her wrapping technique so that the waxed paper doesn't tear.

Breaking Out of Your Wine Rut

The wines you love can lead you to a whole world of exciting new varietals

BY TIM GAISER

When you find a wine variety you like, it's all too easy to fall into a comfortable rut, opening bottles of Chardonnay, say, or Pinot Noir over and over again. But the fact is, it's almost just as easy to break out of your rut—because your favorite wines can help you discover new varietals that you'll like as much if not more than ones you usually drink. Here's a rundown of six popular wine varietals and some delicious alternatives to them.

If you like Chardonnay, you may love Viognier

Chardonnay is still the most popular white wine and for good reason: The combination of ripe apple/pear fruit with notes of butter, spice, and oak make Chardonnay a pleasant sipping wine that's also tasty with a range of foods, from hearty grilled chicken and fish to lighter pasta dishes. Viognier (vee-oh-NYAY), a grape that originated in France's northern Rhône Valley, delivers exotic floral aromas and delicious peachy fruit flavors that are often highlighted by a touch of spicy oak, much like Chardonnay. The wine is a good accompaniment to any food with which you drink Chardonnay. Look for Viognier from California and Australia.

Bottles to try

2004 d'Arenberg The Hermit Crab Marsanne Viognier, McLaren Vale, Australia, $15

2005 Cold Heaven Viognier, Santa Rita Hills, California, $19

If you like Cabernet Sauvignon, you may love Malbec

Cabernet, the king of red wines, is beloved for its concentrated black cherry/currant fruit with notes of green olives and herbs and its firm, slightly bitter tannins. Like Cabernet, Malbec grapes originated in Bordeaux, France, but these days, the best Malbec wines hail from Argentina, where the mild climate, long growing season, and high altitude yield wines with ripe fruit, soft tannins, and high natural acidity. If you're a fan of California Cab, you'll be delighted to learn that Argentine Malbec is often aged in American oak barrels and offers the same spicy flavors and texture at a fraction of the price. And like Cabernet, Malbec is a perfect mate for red meat, especially beef and lamb.

Bottles to try

2004 Ñandú Malbec, Mendoza, Argentina, $12

2005 Alamos Selección Malbec, Argentina, $17

If you like Merlot, you may love Tempranillo

Merlot is the comfort food of red wines; its lush, plummy fruit flavor, herbal notes, and soft, velvety texture pair well with foods like burgers and meatloaf, barbecued chicken, even macaroni and cheese. Tempranillo is an important Spanish grape varietal and the primary grape in wines from Spain's Rioja region. Wines from this region are often referred to as "Riojas," and they're known for their ripe cherry/plum fruit, herbal notes, and soft, dusty tannins. And best of all, they're just as easy as Merlot to pair with food.

Bottles to try

2003 Campo Viejo Rioja, Spain, $12

2000 La Rioja Alta Alberdi, Spain, $19

If you like Red Zinfandel, you may love Shiraz

California Zinfandel and Australian Shiraz are like twins separated by an ocean. With its unbridled ripe, jammy fruits and pepper/spice notes, Zinfandel (red, not white) is the ultimate barbecue wine. You'll find a very similar combination of flavors and textures in Australian Shiraz but with added brightness and nuances of flowers and green fruits. Like Zin, Aussie Shiraz is deliciously fruity and easy to drink.

Bottles to try

2004 Penfolds Thomas Hyland, Australia, $13

2003 Peter Lehmann Shiraz, Barossa, Australia, $18

If you like Sauvignon Blanc, you may love Albariño

Sauvignon Blanc's vibrant citrus fruits, herbal notes, and mouth-watering acidity make it one of the most versatile and food-friendly white wines to be found. Like Sauvignon Blanc, Albariño from the Rias Baixas region of northwestern Spain is all about vibrant grapefruit/lime fruit, with green herb notes and tart acidity. You'll find these wines to be just as food friendly as your favorite Sauvignon Blanc.

Bottles to try

2005 Vionta Albariño, Rias Baixas, Spain, $12

2005 Valminor Albariño, Rias Baixas, Spain, $14

If you like Pinot Noir, you may love Cabernet Franc

With its bright red fruits, spice notes, and soft tannins, Pinot Noir pairs easily with either grilled fish or meats and is also a delight on its own. If you're a big fan of Pinot Noir, chances are you'll enjoy Cabernet Franc wines from France's Loire Valley, especially those from the village of Chinon. (Wines labeled Chinon are generally made with the Cabernet Franc grape; your wine merchant can help you confirm this.) These wines offer the bright red fruits and soft tannins that you love in Pinot but with an added herbal element.

Bottles to try

2004 Pierre Ferrand Château de Ligré, Chinon, France, $14

2003 Domaine de la Noblaie Les Chiens-Chiens, Chinon, France, $16

Fine Cooking *contributing editor Tim Gaiser is a master sommelier and wine educator who's always on the lookout for a new favorite wine.* ◆

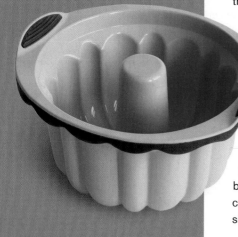

equipment

Palm peeler	28
Silicone updates	28
Crêpe pans	29
Convertible refrigerator	29
Review: rice cookers	30

BY KIMBERLY Y. MASIBAY

does it work?

A handy peeler

We're pretty particular about our peelers around here, and when we find one we like, we tend to stick with it. But this little peeler was so unusual—it's a mere 2 inches square, contoured to nestle in the palm of the hand—that we just had to give it a whirl.

Does it work? Absolutely, though it's not perfect for every peeling task. The stainless-steel blade is good and sharp, the peeler is very comfortable, and we loved using it to peel long vegetables like carrots, cucumbers, and asparagus. But because the blade is tucked into your palm, you can't really see what you're doing, which is awkward when you're trying to peel something small, round, and slippery like an apple or a potato. For those, a traditional peeler with a handle seems to provide better control.

The Chef'n Palm Peeler sells for $6.95 at ChefsResource.com.

update

The next generation of silicone kitchenware

In recent years, loads of silicone kitchenware has flooded the marketplace, and already, some manufacturers have begun to tweak their product lines, correcting flaws found in the first generation of silicone tools. Here are two updates we really like:

Better brushes

In the clean-up department, silicone basting and pastry brushes have an edge over natural-bristle brushes, which tend to get gunky and stay that way. But silicone bristles don't sop up liquid quite as well as natural bristles do. This new brush from Oxo, however, delivers the best of both worlds. It holds liquid, thanks to its uniquely absorbent center bristles, and it's easy to wash clean.

The pastry brush (shown) sells for $6.99, and the basting brush for $8.99 at Oxo.com.

A sturdier silicone Bundt pan

When I first put silicone Bundt pans to the test (see *Fine Cooking* #74, p. 21), I liked their lightness, flexibility, and nonstick qualities, but I was disappointed that the pans' sides bulged when filled with heavy cake batter, resulting in lopsided cakes. Still, I felt that a silicone Bundt pan could potentially be a great thing—removing cakes from deeply fluted metal pans can be tricky —if only someone would design one that didn't lose its shape.

And now, someone has. The new Bundt pan, left, from Silicone Zone's New Wave line, is plenty supple, but the wave around the pan's lip lends quite a bit of stability. When I poured rich, heavy pound cake batter into the pan, it held its shape, and the resulting cake released cleanly and wasn't at all lopsided.

Silicone Zone's 10-cup New Wave Bundt pan sells for $22.99 at LaprimaShops.com.

Photos: Scott Phillips, except refrigerator, courtesy of the manufacturer

tool vs. tool

Crêpe Pans

Crêpes are a delicious alternative to Sunday morning pancakes, and when you have the right tool, they're really not very difficult to make at home. But what is the right tool for the job? To find out, I put two options to the test: World Cuisine's 7-inch carbon-steel pan (below left) and Villaware's 7-inch electric crêpe maker.

In the end, both performed well, but the experience of using them is very different, and so are the results.

Traditional carbon-steel crêpe pan

Making crêpes in this pan involves pouring batter into the hot pan, swirling the pan to spread the batter into a thin layer, and cooking the crêpe briefly on both sides.

This pan needs to be seasoned before the first use—which takes just a few minutes—but once seasoned, the surface releases crêpes like a charm. The key to turning out perfect crêpes lies in mastering your timing and technique. When you pour batter into the hot pan, it sets in a matter of seconds, so you've got to swirl the batter very quickly into a nice thin circle or you'll end up with an oddly shaped crêpe.

Once you get the rhythm of pouring and swirling, though, the process feels natural and fun. Crêpes made in this pan turn out tender yet nicely browned on both sides; if you use about 1½ ounces of batter, the crêpes will be about 2.5 mm thick.

Pros: Crêpes are attractively browned on both sides and tender; mastering the technique is rewarding; pan is slim and easy to store.

Cons: If the pan isn't well seasoned, the crêpes will stick; swirling the batter into perfectly round crêpes takes some practice.

Pictured above: A 7-inch carbon-steel crêpe pan costs $10.99 at Fantes.com.

Electric crêpe maker

The learning curve with this crêpe maker is short. To use it, you simply dip the hot nonstick plate into the batter, flip the pan upright, and let the crêpe cook on one side for a few moments. (The instructions say that the crêpes don't need to be cooked on both sides, which is fine if you plan to roll them around a tasty filling, but if you're serving them flat, I think it would be nicer to brown both sides.)

It might take a few tries before you can dip the pan into the batter just so: too deep and the batter curls over the edges of the pan; too shallow and the crêpe will be small or elliptical. But once you get a feel for it, using this machine is very easy. I was making perfectly round crêpes in no time. Because such a thin layer of batter sticks to the hot plate when you dip it, the crêpes are exceptionally thin (just 1 mm thick) and crisp around the edges, which is different from what I'm used to but not unpleasant.

Pros: Short learning curve; lets you make perfectly round, impressively thin crêpes with very little effort.

Cons: The crêpes' crisp edges may not be to everyone's taste; somewhat awkward to store.

Pictured above: Villaware's 7-inch crêpe maker costs $29.95 at SurLaTable.com.

review

High-Tech Rice Cookers

BY MARYELLEN DRISCOLL

I've always followed standard stovetop procedure with rice: simmer gently, never peek, never stir. And the results have been perfectly fine. But when I made rice in some of the top fuzzy-logic rice cookers on the market, I realized that my stovetop method was no match.

And what is a fuzzy-logic rice cooker? Basically, it's an intelligent version of a no-frills rice cooker. Instead of just an on/off button, a fuzzy-logic rice cooker has a micro-computer that lets the machine regulate time and temperature according to the type of rice being cooked (brown rice, for example, cooks at a lower temperature than white rice). It can cook more kinds of rice than you've ever heard of—including sweet and germinated brown—and some models can even cook oatmeal or polenta, steam vegetables, and make stew. But what really sold us on the cookers was how well they handle the white and brown rice we use every day.

Such sophistication comes at a price, though. Even our Best Buy costs more than $100. And these cookers will also cost you time: Expect to wait 45 to 50 minutes for white rice to cook, more for brown.

Test results

All but one of the cookers we tried made excellent white rice. But in tasks beyond cooking white rice, the models showed their true colors. Our favorites (shown here) had special settings and guidelines for cooking finicky brown rice and did a better job than cookers without those special settings.

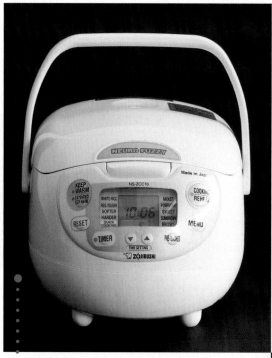

Best buy

Sanyo Micro-Computerized Rice Cooker & Steamer
model ECJ-F50S
$114.95 at Cooking.com

This 5-cup cooker has all the features almost anyone would need. Its only quirk: Brown rice must be washed and left to soak for an hour before cooking, or it will come out undercooked. If you can remember this step, though, you'll be rewarded with perfect brown rice.

Settings & features: quick cook, mixed, porridge, keep warm; settings to cook stew and dol sot bi bim bab (a classic Korean rice dish in which the bottom layer of rice gets toasted and crisp); steamer insert and removable inner lid for easy cleaning.

Best all-around

Zojirushi Neuro Fuzzy Rice Cooker & Steamer
model NS-ZCC10-WZ
$179.99 at EverythingKitchens.com

This 5½-cup cooker is as versatile as it is precise. A chime or tune (your choice) tells you when the cooking cycle is complete, which is especially handy with brown rice because it degrades in flavor and texture if held in the keep-warm setting. It also has a memory setting, which lets the cooker remember how you like a certain type of rice.

Settings & features: quick cook, mixed, porridge, keep warm, extended keep warm, reheat, timer-controlled cooking; removable inner lid for easy cleaning.

The other rice cookers in our tests were the Aroma Sensor-Logic rice cooker, model ARC-896, and the Elite Pro Fuzzy Logic rice cooker, model B601T.

There's no need to memorize water-to-rice ratios with these cookers. Lines etched on the inside of the cookpot tell you exactly how much water to add for the rice you're cooking.

tip: Don't throw away your cooker's cup

The plastic measuring cup that comes with your cooker isn't a standard 1-cup measure. It holds about 180 ml versus 240 ml for a standard U.S. cup. To ensure that your rice cooks properly, measure the rice with the cooker's plastic cup and then pour in water until it reaches the appropriate etched line inside the cooking bowl.

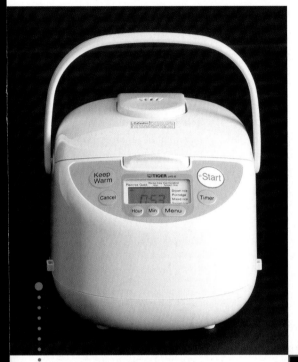

A whiz with white rice

Tiger Electric Rice Cooker

model JAG-B10U
$119.99 at Costco.com
(5% more for nonmembers)

This 5½-cup cooker lets you customize white rice's consistency, gives you the option to "scorch" it, meaning it can toast the bottom layer in the pot for a subtle nutty flavor and lightly crisped texture, and beeps when the cooking cycle is complete. Brown rice cooked unevenly in our tests: fluffy toward the top of the pot, pasty towards the bottom. Also, it's inconvenient that the inner lid isn't removable for in-sink cleaning.

Settings & features: quick cook, mixed, porridge, keep warm, reheat, scorch, timer-controlled cooking.

How we tested

We tested five manufacturers' top-of-the-line fuzzy-logic rice cookers with capacities between 5 and 6 cups uncooked rice. With each cooker, we cooked long-grain white rice at the cooker's maximum capacity and also with just 1 cup uncooked rice; we made brown rice with 3 cups uncooked rice; we tested the quick-cook cycle of those cookers that offered it, using 2 cups uncooked long-grain white rice; and, if cookers offered a harder or softer cooking mode or a cooking cycle for sushi or sweet rice, we tested it.

In each test, we evaluated the entire pot of rice for evenness in consistency and texture.

Menu settings, defined

Fuzzy-logic rice cookers have lots of menu settings and features. Here are definitions of some that you'll see.

Quick cook: cooks white rice 10 to 15 minutes quicker than the normal cycle but with some sacrifice in quality.

Mixed: for instances when you're cooking rice with ingredients other than just water, such as spices or broth.

Porridge: developed for rice porridge, an Asian staple, but also works for oatmeal, polenta, rice pudding, and the like.

Keep warm: use to keep rice warm for up to 12 hours after the cooking cycle; most manufacturers recommend using this only with white rice.

Reheat: for rice that's been sitting in the keep-warm cycle, this feature makes it hot for eating in 5 to 10 minutes; can't be used to reheat cold rice.

Timer controlled: lets you program the cooker in advance to cook rice at a set time.

Maryellen Driscoll is Fine Cooking's editor at large. ◆

The Rules of
Melting Cheese

BY ROBERT L. WOLKE

Melted cheese has given us many beloved dishes. From Italy, Switzerland, Mexico, and Great Britain we have inherited our lasagnes, fondues, quesadillas, and Welsh rabbits. America is nothing if not a melting pot—of cheeses, as well as ethnicities. But melted cheese has also given cooks many headaches. Sometimes it just doesn't melt the way you want it to. You'd like it to be smooth and saucy, and instead it turns stringy, or it separates, or maybe it won't melt at all.

Getting your desired results isn't always easy because cheese doesn't melt in quite the same way that simpler substances do (for an explanation, see the sidebar "What happens when cheese melts?" on p. 34). But by following three simple rules you can increase your odds of success.

Rule No.1
Use the cheese the recipe calls for, if you can.

This might sound obvious, but I mention it because I know how tempting it is to substitute a little bit of this for a little bit of that when you're cooking. With cheese, that's not always a good idea.

There are well over a thousand distinguishable cheeses, and it's no exaggeration to say that they are made by a thousand different methods. This embarrassment of variables guarantees that no two cheeses will have exactly the same properties—they'll differ in appearance, flavor, and texture; and, alas, they'll differ in their melting behavior, too.

The Melting Categories of Cheese

The names of the cheeses in this table are generic, because cheeses go by many names and may have many variations. One farmer's artisanal Swiss may not be the same as the Swiss made by another farmer on the Alp down the road.

Stretchy & stringy melters

These are the cheeses we love on pizza, in panini, and stuffed into croquettes. They stay pretty much where we put them, without running all over the place, and they can form extremely long strings when pulled.

Mozzarella (aged and fresh)
Queso Oaxaca
Scamorza
Provolone
String cheese
Fresh cheddar cheese curds

Sources: Dr. Carol Chen and Dr. Dean Sommer of the Wisconsin Center for Dairy Research

Smooth & flowing melters

This category claims the largest number of cheeses. Some are viscous when melted, while others have little body. These cheeses are great for making toasted sandwiches; topping soups or vegetable tarts; stuffing into vegetables; adding richness to baked pasta dishes; and folding into biscuit, scone, and bread dough. They also blend smoothly into other dishes, such as polenta, mashed potatoes, risotto, and soufflés.

Asiago
Cheddar
Emmentaler
Fontina
Gruyère
Havarti
Monterey Jack
Muenster
Gouda

Blue cheeses
(they melt around the mold)

Soft-ripened cheeses
like Brie & Camembert (the rind will not melt)

***Parmigiano-Reggiano**

Nonmelters

Some of these cheeses can be grilled, fried, or baked; though they may soften when heated, they won't lose their shape and flow. There are a few possible reasons that some cheeses don't melt: The cheese might be extremely high in salt. Or it might be low or high in acid, or it might contain high levels of whey proteins (during the cheese-making process, whey is removed from most cheese).

Halloumi
Fresh Mexican cheeses
such as queso blanco, queso fresco, ranchero, cotija

Indian paneer
Cottage cheese
Ricotta
Fresh goat cheese
Feta
***Parmigiano-Reggiano**

Over time, various cultures have created dishes that show off the unique qualities of their local cheeses. (For a list of the cheeses most commonly used in several traditional dishes, see the bottom box on p. 34.) You're better off sticking to the tried and true—you'll never be able to make a saucy Swiss fondue from a stringy Italian mozzarella (just try to dip a piece of bread into it).

But what if you don't have the exact cheese specified in a recipe or what if you just want to throw together a cheese toast, a vegetable gratin, or a quesadilla? You've been cooking for at least (fill in the blank) years, and you know your way around the kitchen. So, is there room for creativity instead of the unquestioning use of every recipe's chosen cheese? Sure there is, if you follow my second rule:

Rule No. 2
Choose a cheese that's known to melt the way you want it to.

The problem is, when you're shopping for cheese, you can't necessarily predict its melting behavior by scrutinizing its appearance or the nutrition information label. Cheeses melt in lots of ways, and you can't depend on seemingly similar cheeses to melt identically. One semisoft cheese might behave quite differently from another for reasons that are as complex as the cheeses themselves.

But there's no need to plow through dozens of scientific research papers on the properties of melted cheese. All you really need to know is that cheeses fall into three broad melting categories: stretchy and stringy, smooth and flowing, and non-melting. When you want to get creative, look at the table at left, choose a cheese that has the melting characteristics you want, and you won't go far wrong.

*What about Parmigiano?

Very hard, aged cheeses like Parmigiano don't fit cleanly into these categories. If you finely grate them and add them to a sauce or a dish with moisture, they will melt smoothly, but due to their own lack of moisture, they won't melt very well alone.

(continued on p. 34)

Now, one more rule:
Rule No. 3
Be gentle with the heat.

Choosing the right cheese is important, but that's not the only secret to success. You must also treat the cheese kindly during cooking. Even if you're using the perfect cheese for a dish, too high a temperature or too much heating time can make its proteins tighten up, squeezing out both water and fat. Result: rubbery globs of protein awash in a pool of grease. When this happens to pizza (and it often does because pizza is baked in such a hot oven), it's not the worst thing in the world, but when it happens to a cheese fondue, you've got a flop on your hands. And, unfortunately, these changes aren't reversible. But there are a few steps you can take to keep your cheese from meeting this sad fate:

Shred it. By shredding cheese, you increase the surface area that's in contact with the heat source, which reduces the amount of time the cheese will take to melt.

Give it a head start. Bringing cheese to room temperature before you hit it with heat also lessens the amount of time the cheese needs to be exposed to heat before it melts.

Use low heat. Although not all recipes call for it, cheese prefers low heat. At higher temperatures, the proteins in the cheese are more likely to seize up and squeeze out fat and moisture. So if you need to finish off a cheese topping under the broiler, keep a watchful eye on it and take care to expose it to the heat only long enough for the cheese to melt.

What happens when cheese melts?

Cheese is a complex network of milk proteins with globules of butterfat and water dispersed throughout, and it doesn't melt the way simpler substances do. Ice melts at precisely 32°F; sugar melts at 365°F; even salt will melt abruptly if we heat it to 1474°F. But cheeses don't really melt in the same sense, transforming tidily from solid to liquid. When cheese is heated, the butterfat starts to melt at around 90°F, and the cheese softens. Then, as the temperature enters the 105° to 120°F range, the cheese's protein structure changes, and depending on what kind of cheese it is, it may begin to flow slowly like lava (think of the oozing Jack cheese in a quesadilla), or it might become stringy and elastic (think of the stretchy mozzarella on a pizza), or it might appear outwardly unchanged. On further heating, the water evaporates from the cheese, it starts to resolidify as the proteins tighten, and, if the heating continues, the cheese becomes brown, blisters, and eventually burns.

Robert L. Wolke, professor emeritus of chemistry at the University of Pittsburgh, writes the award-winning syndicated Food 101 column for the Washington Post. *He is the author of several books, the latest of which is* What Einstein Told His Cook 2. ◆

Classic cheeses for classic dishes

❖ **Cheese fondue:** Emmentaler, Gruyère, Vacherin Fribourgeois, Appenzeller

❖ **Cheese toast and grilled cheese:** Cheddar, Fontina, American, Emmentaler, Gruyère, Jarlsberg

❖ **Eggplant or veal parmesan:** Mozzarella, Parmigiano

❖ **Lasagne:** Mozzarella, Ricotta, Parmigiano

❖ **Pizza:** Mozzarella, Fontina, Parmigiano, Asiago

❖ **Quesadilla:** Chihuahua, Monterey Jack, Queso Quesadilla

❖ **Welsh rabbit:** Cheshire, Cheddar, Colby, Emmentaler, Gruyère

❖ **Macaroni & cheese:** Sharp Cheddar, Colby, Emmentaler, American

Winning tip

Make "day old" bread in minutes

Sometimes I want to make French toast or bread pudding but don't have any "day-old" bread. So I place one oven rack in the center of the oven and another rack in the slot right beneath it. I put a baking sheet on the lower rack, insert bread slices through the slots of the upper rack so they stand up, and toast the bread on very low heat with the oven door slightly ajar. The bread dries out evenly on both sides with no need for turning.

—Mary Woosypiti, Cherokee, Oklahoma

A prize for the best tip

We want your best tips—we'll pay for the ones we publish—and we'll give a prize to the cleverest tip in each issue. Write to Tips, *Fine Cooking*, PO Box 5506, Newtown, CT 06470-5506 or email fctips@taunton.com.

The prize for this issue's winner: A Bonjour 12-cup Maximus French press and a Bonjour Zen glass teapot with stainless steel infuser; value $100.

Soak large batches of dried beans and freeze them

When a recipe calls for only 1 or 2 cups of presoaked dried beans, I often don't feel like going to the trouble for such a small amount.

Instead, I soak a large batch of dried beans overnight and then drain and freeze them in several small zip-top bags, each containing 1 cup. This way, when I need, say, 2 cups presoaked beans, all I have to do is grab two bags from the freezer and defrost them. If you have enough space, you can freeze several types of beans this way. Just make sure you label each bag to avoid confusion.

—Michelle Hoffman, via email

A hair dryer dries food quickly

I always keep a small travel hair dryer in a kitchen cabinet. I use it to dry a variety of foods, such as water-soaked potatoes for French fries before they go in the hot oil. It's quick and saves a lot of paper towels. Make sure to use it on the cool setting.

—Rick Morrison, Bloomfield Hills, Michigan

Clean mushroom caps with a melon baller

When I'm stuffing mushrooms, I use a melon baller to dig out the stem and gills, creating perfectly round, unbroken caps for stuffing. I use the smaller scoop of my melon baller for button mushrooms and cremini and the larger scoop for portabella and other large-stemmed mushrooms.

—Cheryl L. Beauchamp, Scotia, New York

A clear bowl lets you see the water when double-boiling

When I set up a double boiler, I use a heat-proof clear bowl (such as Pyrex), so I can monitor the simmering through the glass and make sure there's always enough water in the pot.

—*Tizi Young, San Francisco*

Get every last bit off a food processor blade safely

Here's how to get the last sticky remnants off a food processor blade without endangering your fingers or fussing with a rubber scraper. First, empty the contents of the work bowl, but don't worry about getting it all. Reassemble the processor (with the blade) and pulse several times. The remainder of the ingredients will now be up against the side of the bowl—not on the blade—so you won't have to scrape it. Take the blade out to make it easy to scrape down the sides of the work bowl.

—*Georgene Hawkins-Kunz, Fircrest, Washington*

Grind dried mushrooms to make seasoned dredging flour

If I have leftover dried mushrooms, I grind them to a fine powder in a coffee grinder. I then mix the powder with flour and other seasonings, such as smoked paprika, ground fennel seeds, or chopped fresh herbs, and dredge meats or fish in this seasoned flour before pan-searing or braising. It adds great flavor.

—*Bruce Wood, Ottawa, Ontario*

Gel ice keeps fish fresh

Instead of keeping fish and shellfish on watery, messy ice in the refrigerator, I use packets of gel ice (the kind used to ship perishable goods). I always keep a couple in the freezer. When I buy fish that I need to store in the refrigerator, I place an ice packet on a glass or ceramic dish, cover it with plastic wrap, lay the fish on top, and store it, covered, in the fridge. Once I've cooked the fish, I give the ice packet a thorough rinse and put it back in the freezer for later use.

—*Diane McCann, Flower Mound, Texas*

Plastic bins keep the freezer organized

I use small plastic bins with lids (the relatively inexpensive ones you find at housewares stores) to organize my small freezer. I label each bin according to the food type it holds: meat, fish, doughs, etc. I never have to dig around for things in the freezer, and I can fit more in it.

—*Jennifer Grobe, Burlington, Ontario*

Protect knives with potholders

I don't have a knife block in my kitchen, so I use pot handle holders to protect my knives in the drawer.

—*Patty Rowles, Pawleys Island, South Carolina* ◆

A pot lid can serve as a plate

When cooking a braised dish, you often have to brown the meat first and set it aside on a plate while you cook the aromatics. Instead of dirtying a plate, I use the lid of the braising pot and set it upside down on a burner or inside another pot so it sits level. A bonus: You get every last bit of juice back into the braise.

—*Steve Hunter, art director*

Roast Chicken for Today and Tomorrow

BY TONY ROSENFELD

Until relatively recently, I thought of roast chicken as nothing more than one great dinner. Any leftovers that resulted from the bird were just, well, leftovers—something I would try, often unsuccessfully, to use up in subsequent meals. I would like to be able to say that all this changed because something dramatic happened—like the birth of a child or a breakthrough in chicken technology. But the truth is that an editor called me up and asked me to write a book on how to roast chicken *and* cook with the leftovers. Now, a couple of years and many, many roast birds later, I've become a preacher of the leftover chicken gospel. All that roasting has convinced me that chicken on the second go-round is a very convenient and versatile addition to all sorts of weeknight dinners, from Caesar salad and tacos to quick stir-fries and pastas. With a roast chicken in the fridge, you have a head start on getting a delicious meal on the table fast.

Here's how it works: Roast two chickens when you have a little time. Serve one of them that night for dinner, and use the second one (plus any remaining meat from the first one) in lively dishes in the following few days. Just remember to plan your leftover meals ahead so that when you're at the market, you can pick up the ingredients you'll need.

Planning for leftovers. *After serving the first roast chicken for supper, you can look forward to more great meals from the second one. From top: stir-fried chicken and snow peas with coconut rice, chicken tacos, and chicken Caesar salad.*

Roast two chickens; serve one on Sunday and turn the other into delicious weeknight meals

Roast Chicken with Rosemary-Lemon Salt

One whole chicken serves four for dinner; the second yields enough to make two additional meals.

For a very flavorful roast chicken, I like to liven up plain old kosher salt by mixing it with some fresh rosemary and lemon zest. I use the food processor because it helps release the flavorful oils from the zest and the rosemary.

**2 medium lemons
2 Tbs. plus 1 tsp. kosher salt
2 Tbs. chopped fresh rosemary
1 tsp. freshly ground black
 pepper
2 4-lb. chickens, giblets and
 excess fat discarded
¼ cup unsalted butter, melted**

Finely grate the zest from the lemons. In a food processor or mini chopper, combine the zest with the 2 Tbs. salt, the rosemary, and black pepper. Pulse several times to combine.

Sprinkle each chicken with this salt mixture both inside and outside the cavity and between the skin and the breast meat (use your fingers to gently open up a pocket between the two). Cut 1 of the lemons in half and stuff a half in the cavity of each bird. Reserve the remaining lemon for another use. Set the chickens on a wire rack atop a rimmed baking sheet, and refrigerate uncovered for at least 4 hours and up to 24 hours.

About 30 minutes before you're ready to roast the chickens, set an oven rack in the middle position and heat the oven to 425°F. Take the chickens out of the refrigerator and brush the butter uniformly over the skin. Sprinkle each chicken with ½ tsp. salt. Set each chicken, breast side up, on 1 or 2 racks (preferably a large nonadjustable V-rack) in a large roasting pan. Let the chickens sit at room temperature while the oven heats.

Roast the chickens until the breasts are nicely browned and crisp, about 40 minutes. Gently flip each chicken (I like using tongs to clutch the inside of the cavity and the side of the bird) and roast until an instant-read thermometer inserted into the thickest part of the thigh registers 165°F to 170°F, about 20 minutes more. Let rest for 5 minutes before carving one of the chickens into pieces.

Tips for moist meat & crisp skin

A few techniques distinguish my roast chicken method from others you may have tried.

Salt the chicken ahead. Salting seasons the bird, of course, but if you can do it a day, or even a few hours, ahead, you'll get more flavorful meat and crisper skin. You can also flavor the salt with herbs and zest.

Use a rack. A V-shaped roasting rack cradles the chicken and allows its juices to drip away, leaving even the bottom skin crisp.

Start breast side up and flip halfway through. Starting with the breast up ensures brown, crispy skin. Turning the bird over keeps the breast moist while the slower-cooking legs finish roasting.

Leftover basics—getting the most from chicken #2

Handling tips

After serving the first chicken for dinner, wrap the leftovers in plastic wrap. Let the second chicken cool to room temperature and wrap in plastic as well. I've found that if it's well wrapped and refrigerated, the chicken will stay relatively moist and tender for up to 4 days. Here are a few more pointers for making the most of your leftover chicken.

DON'T CARVE UNTIL YOU HAVE TO. Sliced, diced, and otherwise cut-up chicken dries out and spoils faster than a whole one, so keep the chicken whole or in big pieces.

DISCARD THE SKIN. The crisp skin of a warm roast chicken is wonderful, but once it's cold, the skin tends to become unpleasantly rubbery. For this reason, I don't use it in my leftover dishes.

MATCH THE MEAT TO THE PREPARATION. Dark-meat leftovers tend to have a richer flavor and retain their moisture, so they're perfect for cooked dishes. White-meat leftovers are more apt to dry out when reheated, so their delicate flavor and texture do better in sandwiches and salads.

KEEP THE COOKING TO A MINIMUM. As leftover chicken is already cooked (and as chicken is lean to start with, particularly the breast), it's best to avoid further cooking. Whenever possible, I try to fold the chicken in at the end just to warm it up.

How much meat from a 4-lb. bird?

You can expect one roast chicken to serve four people nicely for dinner. A whole second bird should yield about 5 cups of meat, enough to make two of the three recipes on these pages.

LEFTOVER AMOUNT	YIELD (sliced or diced)
1 whole chicken	5 cups
½ chicken	2½ cups
1 breast	1 cup
1 leg (thigh and drumstick)	1 cup

How to carve

Because leftover chicken is generally cold when you work with it, it's a lot easier to carve. I like to use a paring knife and my fingers to feel for the breastbone and pry off the breast meat, making sure to pick off any meat that remains behind on the bones. I then slice to the bone on the drumsticks and thighs, peel off the meat, and sort through and discard any fatty patches or gnarly tendons.

As good as the wings are when they're hot, they're not well suited to picking for leftovers—there's little yield for all that work. So if they haven't been eaten on the first go-round, I usually just sprinkle them with some salt and eat them cold while I work on my leftover dish.

Coconut Rice with Chicken & Snow Peas
Serves four.

The rich coconut rice is the perfect counterpoint to a quick chicken stir-fry in a soy-jalapeño sauce. For color, add some red bell pepper to the stir-fry. You could also sprinkle with some toasted coconut as a finishing touch.

1½ cups jasmine rice or long-grain white rice
3 Tbs. minced fresh ginger
¼ cup canola oil
¾ cup unsweetened coconut milk (preferably not "lite")
¾ tsp. kosher salt
3 Tbs. soy sauce

shortcut

ROTISSERIE CHICKEN WORKS WELL, TOO

If you'd like to make some of these chicken dishes but don't have the time to roast the bird yourself, store-bought rotisserie chickens are a good option. In addition to their convenience, these prepared birds are flavorful and affordable.

2 Tbs. rice vinegar

1 Tbs. light brown sugar

2 tsp. cornstarch

2 large green or red jalapeños, cored, seeded, and finely diced

½ lb. snow peas (about 3 cups), trimmed

2½ to 3 cups diced leftover roast chicken (preferably dark meat); see recipe, p. 39

⅓ cup chopped fresh cilantro

Rinse the rice in three changes of cold water, or until the water becomes only slightly cloudy from the rice. Drain well in a sieve.

Heat 1½ Tbs. of the ginger with 2 Tbs. of the oil in a small (2-qt.) saucepan over medium-high heat until it begins to sizzle steadily

and becomes fragrant, 1 to 2 minutes. Add the rice and cook, stirring, until the grains and ginger start to brown in places, about 2 minutes. Stir in the coconut milk, 1¾ cups water, and the salt. Bring to a boil and then reduce to a simmer. Cook until the liquid has reduced to about the same level as the top of the rice, 5 to 7 minutes. Cover, reduce the heat to low, and cook without disturbing the rice until the liquid is absorbed and the rice is tender, 15 minutes.

Meanwhile, whisk together the soy sauce, rice vinegar, brown sugar, and cornstarch in a small bowl. Stir in ½ cup water and set aside.

In a large skillet over medium-high heat, cook the jalapeños and the remaining 1½ Tbs. ginger in the remaining 2 Tbs. oil until they sizzle steadily for about 30 seconds. Add the snow peas and cook until bright green and browned in places, about 1 minute. Whisk the soy mixture to recombine and add it and the chicken to the skillet. Cook, stirring, until the sauce thickens and the chicken just heats through, about 2 minutes. Stir in half of the cilantro, reduce the heat to low, and cook for another 2 minutes.

Fluff the rice with a fork and serve with the chicken and snow peas, sprinkled with the remaining cilantro.

Serves four to six as a main course.

This take on Caesar salad is lighter and brighter than most. Lemon juice and zest punch up the vinaigrette, while a little mascarpone, instead of the traditional raw egg yolks, imparts richness.

FOR THE VINAIGRETTE:
1 lemon
¼ cup freshly grated Parmigiano-Reggiano
2 Tbs. mascarpone (or cream cheese)
2 tsp. Dijon mustard
1 small clove garlic, chopped, sprinkled with a pinch of kosher salt, and mashed to a paste
¼ tsp. Worcestershire sauce
½ cup extra-virgin olive oil
1 tsp. chopped fresh thyme
Couple dashes of Tabasco
Kosher salt and freshly ground black pepper

Soft Chicken Tacos with the Works

Serves four to six.

Look for chipotles en adobo in the Mexican food section of the grocery store.

2 large ripe avocados, pitted
2 limes, 1 juiced and 1 cut into wedges
1½ tsp. kosher salt; more as needed
¼ tsp. freshly ground black pepper; more as needed
2 Tbs. extra-virgin olive oil
1 small yellow onion, finely diced
1 tsp. chili powder
Scant ⅛ tsp. ground cinnamon
1 14½-oz. can petite-diced tomatoes, drained

1 medium chipotle chile, finely diced, plus 1 to 2 Tbs. adobo sauce (from a can of chipotles en adobo)
2½ to 3 cups leftover roast chicken, shredded or cut into thin strips; see recipe, p. 39
12 small corn tortillas, warmed
6 oz. queso fresco or feta, crumbled (1⅓ cups)
3 cups thinly sliced red cabbage (about 6 oz.)
⅔ cup fresh cilantro leaves, washed and patted dry

Mash the avocados with the lime juice in a medium bowl. Season with about 1 tsp. of the salt and the pepper, or to taste.

Set a large, heavy-based skillet over medium heat. Add the oil and onion, sprinkle with the remaining ½ tsp. salt, and cook, stirring, until softened and translucent, about 6 minutes. Add the chili powder and cinnamon and cook, stirring, for 30 seconds. Add the tomatoes, chipotle, and adobo sauce and cook, stirring, for 5 minutes, mashing the tomatoes with a wooden spoon. Stir in the chicken, cover, reduce the heat to low, and cook until the chicken heats through, about 10 minutes. Taste, and season with salt and pepper if needed.

Let diners assemble their own tacos by spreading the warm tortillas with the avocado and then topping with the chicken, cheese, cabbage, cilantro, and a squeeze of juice from the lime wedges.

FOR THE SALAD:

2 Tbs. extra-virgin olive oil

1 small clove garlic, chopped, sprinkled with a pinch of kosher salt, and mashed to a paste

⅛ tsp. crushed red pepper flakes

½ baguette, cut into eight ½-inch-thick slices on the extreme diagonal so they're about 6 inches long

¾ cup freshly grated Parmigiano-Reggiano

2 cups thinly sliced leftover roast chicken; see recipe, p. 39

1 lb. romaine hearts (about 2 medium), cored, washed, spun dry, and cut in 2-inch pieces

Make the vinaigrette: Finely grate about 1 Tbs. zest from the lemon. Squeeze the lemon to get 2 Tbs. juice. In a blender or mini chopper, purée (as much as possible) the lemon juice, Parmigiano, mascarpone, mustard, garlic, and Worcestershire sauce, scraping the sides as needed. While puréeing, drizzle in the oil, slowly at first and then in a more steady stream as the mixture thickens and emulsifies. Thin the vinaigrette with water if needed. Add the lemon zest, thyme, and Tabasco and purée. Taste and season generously with salt and pepper (about 1 tsp. of each) and more lemon juice if you like.

Prepare the salad: Heat the oven to 425°F. In a small bowl, mix the oil, garlic, and red pepper flakes. Set the baguette slices on a baking sheet and brush them with the oil mixture. Sprinkle with ¼ cup of the Parmigiano. Bake until browned, 10 to 12 minutes.

In a small bowl, toss the chicken with about ¼ cup of the dressing. In a large bowl, toss the romaine and ¼ cup of the Parmigiano with enough dressing to coat lightly (you might not need it all). Add salt and pepper to taste.

Put the dressed greens on plates and top with the chicken and a drizzle of dressing, if any remains. Sprinkle with the remaining ¼ cup Parmigiano and some black pepper and serve immediately with the toasts.

And for next time, try one of these ideas

Leftover roast chicken is good in countless dishes. Here are a few more suggestions.

Pasta

Sauté canned artichokes with garlic, lemon, and black olives. Fold in shredded chicken and toss with fettuccine. For a home-style lo mein, stir-fry chicken with fresh Chinese noodles, bean sprouts, cabbage, and minced garlic and ginger.

Soups & stews

Create a flavorful soup by jazzing up chicken broth with some vegetables, spices, and herbs. Add the leftover shredded chicken towards the end of cooking. For a stew, use heartier ingredients, like sausage, potatoes, bacon, and tomatoes.

Casseroles

Toss diced chicken with a béchamel sauce and asparagus or broccoli, sprinkle with Parmigiano, and bake until golden brown. Or toss sliced chicken with feta, olives, and sun-dried tomatoes, top with a layer of phyllo or puff pastry, and then bake until crisp and golden brown.

Salads

Punch up a creamy chicken salad with sliced apple, toasted walnuts, and cilantro, and add some curry powder to the mayo. Or try substituting chicken for the tuna in a niçoise salad and toss with blanched green beans, black olives, halved cherry tomatoes, and a mustardy vinaigrette.

Sandwiches

Of all the things I make with roast chicken, I turn to sandwiches most often.

Grilled cheese with chicken & fresh herbs: Stack chicken, a couple of slices of cheddar and tomato, and fresh herbs on some good multigrain bread and grill until the cheese melts.

Chicken Reuben: Layer thinly sliced chicken, Swiss cheese, sauerkraut, and Thousand Island dressing on rye bread and grill until browned and melted.

Sesame chicken with cucumbers & scallions: Toss sliced chicken with soy sauce, hoisin sauce, sesame oil, and toasted sesame seeds. Pair with sliced cucumber and scallions and wrap with lavash.

Southwestern chicken sandwich with avocado & tomato: Purée a canned chipotle chile with a little balsamic vinegar, olive oil, and Dijon mustard and toss with leftover chicken. Layer with mashed avocado, red onion, tomato, and cilantro on toasted ciabatta.

Tony Rosenfeld is a contributing editor to Fine Cooking *and the author of Taunton's 150 Things to Make with Roast Chicken, due out this spring.* ◆

Crowd-Pleasing

BY SUSIE MIDDLETON

It's a little embarrassing to admit that I have certain recipes I use over and over again for casual entertaining. You'd think the editor of *Fine Cooking* could wow her guests with something new and fresh every time. But when you discover a dish that's truly easy and so delicious that absolutely everyone loves it, it's hard not to get hooked on it.

Not so much a recipe, these potatoes are more of a technique. It's really a double-cooking method. You first boil little red or yellow potatoes to get them tender. While they're still warm, you gently flatten them into patties. (You can do this hours ahead.) While your party guests are arriving, you crank up the heat in your oven (convection's even better) and douse the patties in lots of olive oil and kosher salt. In the hot oven, the potato patties sizzle and roast and quickly get crisp around the edges. But because they were first cooked with moist heat, they stay moist and tender inside.

That's really all there is to it. Turn the potatoes out onto a serving platter and let your guests dig in. For a crowd, you can keep doubling the recipe at right as much as you like, as long as you have sheet pans and room in the oven. Of course, you don't have to have a party to make these. They're just as nice served as a side dish with roast chicken or even meatloaf. And garnished with a bit of sour cream and chives, they make a nice starter.

Crispy Potatoes

With a simple ingredient list and a mostly make-ahead technique, these delicious potatoes are perfect for parties

Crispy Smashed Roasted Potatoes

Serves four as a side dish.

12 to 15 baby red or yellow
potatoes (about 1½ oz. each;
1½ to 2 inches in diameter)
2¾ tsp. kosher salt
½ cup extra-virgin olive oil

1. Boil

Put the potatoes in a large saucepan (preferably in one layer) and cover with at least an inch of water. Add 2 tsp. kosher salt to the water. Bring the water to a boil over high heat, reduce to a simmer, and cook the potatoes until they are completely tender and can be easily pierced with a metal or wood skewer. Make sure they are cooked through but don't overcook. The total cooking time will be 30 to 35 minutes.

While the potatoes are cooking, set up a double layer of clean dishtowels on your countertop. As the potatoes finish cooking, remove them individually from the water, and let them drain and sit for just a minute or two on the dishtowels.

2. Flatten

Fold another dishtowel into quarters, and using it as a cover, gently press down on one potato with the palm of your hand to flatten it to a thickness of about ½ inch. Repeat with all the potatoes. Don't worry if some break apart a bit; you can still use them.

MAKE AHEAD TIP:
Do the busy work—boiling and flattening the potatoes—up to 8 hours ahead. Let the potatoes cool completely, and store them on the pan, lightly covered, in the fridge. Then all you have to do at the last minute is Step 4: coat with oil and salt and roast.

3. Cool

Cover a large rimmed baking sheet with aluminum foil; put a sheet of parchment on top of the foil. Transfer the flattened potatoes carefully to the baking sheet and let them cool completely at room temperature.

If making ahead, cover loosely with plastic wrap and refrigerate. Otherwise, continue on to the roasting directions.

4. Roast

Remove the pan of potatoes from the refrigerator, if prepared ahead. Heat the oven to 450°F. Alternatively, if you have a convection function, turn it on and set the temperature at 400°F. Sprinkle the potatoes with about ¾ tsp. salt and pour the olive oil over them. Lift the potatoes gently to make sure some of the oil goes underneath them and that they are well coated on both sides. Roast the potatoes until they're crispy and deep brown around the edges, about 30 minutes if using a convection oven, 30 to 40 minutes if roasting conventionally, turning over once gently with a spatula or tongs halfway through cooking. Serve hot.

Susie Middleton is the editor of Fine Cooking. ◆

Spice Up Your Vegetable

A few sassy spices and a simple one-pan technique are all you need to create these flavorful side dishes

BY SUVIR SARAN

I n India, there is a Hindi saying that goes something like this: Lentils and beans are our spines, but vegetables make up our bodies. No matter what the occasion, we always have a few vegetable dishes, called *sabzis*, on the table. Here in America, I serve a lot of these dishes at my restaurant, and they're usually the foundation of the meals I cook for friends at home. Because they're so nourishing and warming, I think of them as Indian comfort food. They may be a little spicier or have one or two more exotic ingredients than the vegetable side dishes you're used to, but they're just as versatile and nutritious, and they're loaded with flavor.

Slower and spicier than a Chinese stir-fry. I refer to *sabzis* as Indian stir-fries because, like Chinese stir-fries, they're easy to prepare, with all of the vegetables cooked in one pan. But unlike Chinese stir-fries, which rely on flash cooking and added sauces and thickeners, Indian *sabzis* employ more spices and aromatics and a slower cooking method to develop deep flavor and tender texture.

You can learn the basic steps for creating an Indian stir-fry by making any of the recipes on these pages. Then you can improvise your own dishes with my lists of suggested spices and vegetables on p. 48, and by following the general method shown at right.

A wide, sloped pan is great for this kind of cooking. In India, we use a wok-like vessel called a *kadai* to cook these vegetables, but any pan with a generous girth (12 inch diameter is good) and rounded sides works well. You could use a large skillet or wok, a Dutch oven, or a brazier (for sources, see p. 76). The width is important because you want the liquids released from the vegetables to reduce quickly, and the rounded sides make stirring easier.

Layering on flavor, one step at a time

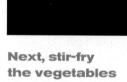

First, cook the spices & aromatics
Start by heating any long-cooking spices with oil in a wide, shallow pan over medium-high heat. When they're fragrant and sizzling, after just 2 to 3 minutes, add any short-cooking spices. Give them a minute or two to get fragrant and sizzle. Then add any delicate aromatics (garlic, ginger, etc.) and cook, stirring vigorously so nothing burns, again just until fragrant, no more than a minute. (For lists of spices and aromatics, turn the page.)

Next, stir-fry the vegetables
Add the vegetables in two phases (turn the page for vegetable options). The first to go in are the longer-cooking vegetables. When they've started to soften, add any quicker-cooking vegetables, occasionally stirring and scraping the bottom of the pan as they cook. (Denser vegetables, such as cauliflower, potatoes, and broccoli, do better if covered; low-moisture vegetables like green beans might need a little water to help them along.)

Stir-Fries, Indian Style

Cabbage & Carrot Stir-Fry with Toasted Cumin & Lime
Serves six.

This is really versatile—you can serve it as a side dish, as a chilled salad (like coleslaw), or use it as a filling for enchiladas.

1½ tsp. cumin seeds
2 Tbs. canola oil
¾ tsp. ground coriander
½ tsp. freshly cracked black peppercorns
½ jalapeño (seeds and ribs removed if you prefer a milder flavor), finely chopped
6 cups thinly sliced green cabbage (about ⅔ medium cabbage)
2 cups julienned or grated carrots (about ¾ lb.)
2½ tsp. kosher salt; more to taste
1½ tsp. granulated sugar
½ cup loosely packed fresh cilantro sprigs, finely chopped
3 Tbs. fresh lime juice

Toast 1 tsp. of the cumin seeds in a small skillet over medium-high heat, stirring frequently, until deeply browned and beginning to smoke, 3 to 5 minutes. Transfer to a bowl to cool. Grind to a fine powder in a spice grinder.

Heat the oil with the remaining ½ tsp. cumin seeds, the coriander, and peppercorns in a large wok, Dutch oven, or 12-inch skillet over medium-high heat, and cook until the cumin is browned, about 2 minutes. Add the jalapeño and cook until sizzling and just starting to soften, 30 to 60 seconds, and then add the cabbage and carrots. (If using a skillet, the pan will be crowded at first.) Cook, stirring occasionally until the cabbage has wilted yet is still al dente, 3 to 4 minutes. Stir in the freshly ground cumin, salt, and sugar, and cook for 30 seconds. Remove the skillet from the heat. Stir in the cilantro and lime juice and taste for seasoning. Serve warm, at room temperature, or cold.

Then, stir in delicate spices & seasonings
When the vegetables are tender, stir in the delicate finishing spices like cayenne or garam masala. These can turn bitter if heated too long, so cook for just 1 minute and then remove from the heat. This is also when you season with salt and perhaps a little sugar to balance the flavors.

Finally, finish with herbs & citrus
For an extra layer of fresh flavor, stir in fresh herbs like cilantro or mint, and squeeze lemon or lime juice on top. If you like, you can serve the dish with extra lemon or lime wedges or some reserved chopped fresh cilantro on the side.

tip: Seasoning with salt at the end of the cooking process may seem unconventional, but it actually works better in these stir-fries. Salt encourages vegetables to break down and release water, and that is not the goal in these dishes.

Improvise your own Indian stir-fries

Pick from the lists of vegetables and spices here, and then follow the general method shown on pp. 46–47 to bring the dish together.

Choose your vegetables

For these dishes, I like to classify vegetables by cooking time. You can include both shorter- and longer-cooking vegetables in your stir-fry; simply add the longer-cooking ones to the pan first to give them a headstart. Unless otherwise noted, you should chop, slice, or dice the vegetable into bite-size pieces.

LONGER COOKING

Broccoli (cut into florets)

Carrots

Celery root

Hearty greens like collards, kale, and mustard greens

Mushrooms

Onions, red or yellow

Potatoes

Radishes

Sweet potatoes

Tomatoes

Turnips

Winter squash like butternut and acorn

SHORTER COOKING

Asparagus

Baby spinach

Bell peppers

Cabbage, white or red (shredded)

Carrots (grated)

Cauliflower (cut into florets)

Coconut, unsweetened (shredded)

Fresh corn kernels

Green beans

Green peas

Summer squash like zucchini, pattypan, and yellow

Swiss chard

Tomatoes

tip: Add tomatoes with the longer-cooking vegetables for a jammy, saucy consistency or with the shorter-cooking vegetables so they retain more body and texture.

tip: Coconut can be added with the short-cooking vegetables for a toasty flavor, or at the end of cooking for a lighter note.

Pick spices & aromatics

Here's where you give your stir-fry its personality. As with the vegetables, I add these to the pan in stages, depending on how much heat they need to open up their flavors.

LONGER COOKING

Bay leaves

Cardamom seeds

Cinnamon sticks

Fenugreek seeds

Mustard seeds

Nigella seeds

Whole cloves

Whole peppercorns

SHORTER COOKING

Coriander, seeds or ground

Cumin seeds

Curry leaves

Dried red chiles, whole or flakes

Fenugreek leaves

Freshly ground pepper

Turmeric, ground

AROMATICS
(add after the spices)

Garlic

Ginger

Jalapeño

DELICATE SPICES
(add at the end of cooking)

Cayenne

Garam masala

Ground cumin, toasted

Mushroom Stir-Fry with Onions & Tomatoes
Serves six.

If you can find fenugreek leaves, by all means, use them—their bitterness nicely counters the sweetness of the caramelized onions. This would be lovely with steak or chicken.

3 Tbs. canola oil
¼ cup dried fenugreek leaves or ½ cup finely chopped fresh fenugreek (optional); see From Our Test Kitchen, p. 70
2 small whole dried red chiles (optional)
1 Tbs. cumin seeds
2 tsp. ground coriander
1 tsp. ground cumin
½ tsp. ground turmeric
2 lb. cremini (baby bella) mushrooms, cleaned, stems trimmed, and sliced ¼ inch thick (8 cups)
2 medium red onions, peeled, halved lengthwise and thinly sliced crosswise into half-moons (3 cups)
2 medium tomatoes, finely chopped (about 2½ cups)
1 tsp. homemade or store-bought garam masala; see p. 70
¼ tsp. cayenne (optional)
2 tsp. kosher salt; more to taste
¼ cup fresh cilantro, chopped
1 to 2 Tbs. fresh lemon juice

Heat the canola oil with the fenugreek leaves and chiles (if using), cumin seeds, coriander, ground cumin, and turmeric in a large wok, Dutch oven, or 12-inch skillet over medium-high heat. Cook, stirring occasionally, until the cumin is browned and the chiles darken, 2 to 3 minutes. Add the mushrooms, onions, and tomatoes, mix them into the spices, and cook, stirring occasionally, until the liquid has evaporated and the vegetables look evenly browned, softened, and dry, 15 to 20 minutes; there will be a lot of liquid in the beginning— just keep cooking, stirring more frequently as the vegetables become drier.

Add the garam masala, cayenne (if using), and salt, and cook 1 minute longer. Stir in the cilantro and lemon juice, taste for seasoning, and serve.

Green Bean Stir-Fry with Shredded Coconut

Serves six.

Instead of green beans, you could make this with another vegetable cut into bite-size pieces—try zucchini or cabbage, two of my favorites.

¼ cup canola oil
1 Tbs. yellow mustard seeds
24 curry leaves, roughly torn (optional); see From Our Test Kitchen, p. 70
1¼ tsp. cumin seeds
2 lb. green beans, trimmed and cut into bite-size pieces (about 7 cups)
¾ cup unsweetened shredded coconut
1½ tsp. kosher salt; more to taste

Heat the oil and the mustard seeds in a large wok or skillet over medium-high heat until the mustard seeds start to sizzle and pop, about 1 minute (use a splatter screen, if you have one, so the seeds don't pop out of the pan). Add the curry leaves (if using) and the cumin seeds and cook, stirring often, until the cumin becomes fragrant and browned, 1 to 2 minutes. Add the green beans and cook for 5 minutes, stirring occasionally. Stir in the coconut and 1 cup water and bring to a simmer. Cover the pan, reduce the heat to medium low, and cook until the green beans are tender, 8 to 10 minutes. Uncover, increase the heat to medium, and cook until all of the water has evaporated, stirring often, 2 to 5 minutes. Stir in the salt, taste, and add more salt if needed.

Suvir Saran is the executive chef at Dévi restaurant in New York City and the author of Indian Home Cooking. ◆

Find more Indian recipes plus tips, tools, and a guide to Indian ingredients at
finecooking.com

Potato Stir-Fry with Mint & Cilantro

Serves six.

This would go well with a roasted chicken or even scrambled eggs.

2 lb. red potatoes (about 6 medium), peeled and cut into ¾-inch cubes (about 5 cups)
3 Tbs. canola oil
1 Tbs. yellow mustard seeds
24 curry leaves (optional); see From Our Test Kitchen, p. 70
1 small whole dried red chile
2 tsp. ground coriander
2 tsp. cumin seeds
½ tsp. ground turmeric
2 medium cloves garlic, minced
1 jalapeño (seeds and ribs removed if you prefer a milder flavor), finely chopped
1 medium red onion, finely chopped
2 tsp. kosher salt; more to taste
½ tsp. cayenne (optional)
⅔ cup fresh mint leaves, finely chopped
½ cup loosely packed fresh cilantro sprigs, finely chopped
Juice of ½ lemon (1 to 2 Tbs.)

Put the potatoes in a medium bowl, cover with cool water, and set aside.

Heat the canola oil and the mustard seeds in a large wok or 12-inch skillet over medium-high heat until the mustard seeds start to sizzle and pop, 1 to 2 minutes (use a splatter screen, if you have one, so the seeds don't pop out of the pan). Add the curry leaves (if using), chile, coriander, cumin seeds, and turmeric and cook, stirring occasionally, until the cumin browns and the curry leaves are crisp, 1 to 1½ minutes. Stir in the garlic and jalapeño and cook until the garlic is fragrant, about 30 seconds.

Drain the potatoes and add them to the pan along with the onions. Cook, stirring occasionally, until the potatoes are translucent around the edges, 2 to 3 minutes. Cover, reduce the heat to medium-low, and cook, stirring and scraping the bottom of the pan every 5 minutes, until the potatoes are just tender, 12 to 15 minutes. (Reduce the heat to low if the potatoes seem to be burning.)

Add the salt and cayenne (if using) and cook for 30 seconds. Stir in the mint, cilantro, and lemon juice, cover the pan, and let the potatoes sit off the heat for 10 minutes. Scrape up the browned bits and stir them into the potatoes. Taste, add more salt if needed, and serve.

How to Host

Get to know your palate and discover the chocolates, cheeses, and olive oils you love

BY DINA CHENEY

When I teach cooking classes, students often ask me, "How much salt should I add to this dish?" or "Which chocolate should I use?" And I always reply, "It's up to you. You should prepare food that you—not I—will love."

But when it comes to matters of the palate, how do you go about learning what you love? The answer is simple: Just keep tasting. One of the most effective and enjoyable ways to get in touch with your flavor preferences is to organize a tasting party for your friends. It's easy. Simply gather several food or drink products—it could be cheese, honey, apples, balsamic vinegar, tea, ale, almost anything really—and then taste them side by side.

At such structured tastings, you'll learn how you react to different flavors, and you'll broaden the repertoire of ingredients you can use in your cooking. For example, if you taste several different plain dark chocolate bars at the same time, you might discover that you prefer bitter and intense, rather than mild, varieties; consequently, you may end up using chocolates with higher cacao content when you bake. Through a honey tasting, you might discover chestnut and acacia honeys. Or by tasting cheeses, you might find that you favor washed-rind varieties.

In this article, I'll provide general guidelines for putting together a tasting party and walk you through three sample tastings: of sharp Cheddar, chocolate, and extra-virgin olive oil. From there, you can explore other possibilities on your own.

How to taste

Tasting is different from eating. When you taste, you slow down, pay attention, and savor the food in a structured fashion, evaluating the samples' appearance, aroma, flavor, texture, and finish. Then you ask yourself, Did I enjoy this product? Would I buy it again?

1

Select a category. Choose a food or drink you and your guests enjoy and would like to learn more about, such as extra-virgin olive oil, chocolate, cheese, or something else you're curious about.

2

Narrow your focus. Research your topic and do a little pre-tasting. Choose a theme to help you tie your choices together. (It's important to compare apples to apples: Don't include flavored chocolate bars, flavored truffles, semisweet chocolate bars, and white chocolate bars in the same tasting.) Then, narrow the field to six samples—enough to experience a lot of tastes but not so many that you'll fatigue your palate.

a Tasting Party

3

Shop for all the samples and palate cleansers, plus food and drink for serving before and after the tasting, if you want. If you can't find what you're looking for locally, visit online specialty food merchants, such as Zingermans.com, Igourmet.com, or Agferrari.com. (For more sources, see p. 76.)

4

Organize everything, from tableware to paper and pens (you can download tasting sheets at FineCooking.com). Set your table and arrange the samples in tasting order, moving from more mildly flavored items to those with stronger flavors. If you try extremely flavorful samples first, you won't be able to fully experience the milder products. Also, it's a good idea to provide background information about each sample, including price and where to buy.

5

Conduct the tasting. Introduce the first sample and lead your guests through the tasting steps, encouraging them to take time to focus and jot down their thoughts. Then discuss the sample. Have everyone cleanse their palates with water and mild bread (I like baguette slices) or crackers to prepare for the next sample.

Download printable tasting sheets at finecooking.com

Blind vs. open

In blind tastings, the samples are disguised so that your preconceived notions don't color your assessments. That's fine for professional events, but for home parties I prefer open tastings, in which the samples are identified. Open tastings are easier to organize and more relaxed, yet they're still very educational.

Tasting:
Sharp Cheddar Cheese

Theme:
From supermarket to farmhouse

First, some definitions: Cheddar refers to cheeses in which the curds have been cut, stacked, drained, restacked, milled, salted, and pressed. Within this category, sharp Cheddars are those that have been aged for enough time to allow strong flavors to develop—in general, longer aging equals sharper flavor. Among sharp Cheddars, differences abound, especially between supermarket and farmhouse varieties. The former tend to be milder and less complex than the latter, which are typically produced in small batches right on the dairy farm. In this tasting, you'll experience the differences for yourself.

If you'd rather try another theme, you could compare Cheddars that have been aged for different lengths of time, resulting in increasing amounts of sharpness, or sample American, British, Irish, and Canadian products.

How to taste cheese:

Initially, you'll want to taste the cheeses alone. After that first round, though, it's fun to try them with accompaniments, such as mango chutney and pecans.

Cleanse your palate between samples by drinking cool (not cold) water and eating bread or crackers.

How to select varieties:

Purchase six sharp Cheddars, including both artisanal (farmhouse) and mass-produced (from the supermarket). Since farmhouse Cheddars are generally long-aged and thus extra sharp, buy the longest-aged supermarket products you can find to even things out a bit.

Here are some you might include: Keen's Cheddar (British farmhouse, raw milk, aged about two years), Fiscalini Bandaged Cheddar (American farmhouse, raw milk, aged about 16 months), Montgomery's Cheddar (British farmhouse, raw milk, aged up to two years), Cabot Extra Sharp (American, pasteurized milk, aged up to 18 months), Grafton Village 2-Year Extra Aged (American, raw milk), and Tillamook Sharp Cheddar (American, pasteurized milk, aged more than nine months). (For sources, see p. 76.)

Tasting steps:

First look at the cheese and assess its color. Rub a small piece between your fingers and consider its texture—is it very hard or semihard? Is it at all crumbly or buttery?

Hold the cheese in front of your nose and inhale. What are the aromas (for example, nutty or grassy)?

Now place the cheese on your tongue and press it to the roof of your mouth. Start chewing, and evaluate the mouthfeel and flavor notes (for example, strong, nutty, caramel).

Swallow the cheese and evaluate its finish. What flavors remain in your mouth? How long do they linger?

Finally, ask everyone whether they enjoyed the cheese.

Tasting:
Dark Chocolate

Theme:
From semisweet to unsweetened

A chocolate bar's personality depends largely on how much cacao, as opposed to other ingredients like sugar and vanilla, it contains. A higher percentage of cacao means a more intense chocolate flavor. In this tasting, you'll become familiar with the different flavor profiles of semisweet, bittersweet, and unsweetened chocolate. Bittersweet chocolate contains 35% or more cacao content, while unsweetened chocolate is 100% cacao. "Semisweet" chocolate is a more informal classification but generally refers to bars with 15% to 35% cacao content.

Other themes you might consider: only 70% cacao bars from around the world; only French dark chocolate; or French versus Belgian dark chocolate.

How to select varieties:

For this tasting, include six plain bars, each with a different cacao percentage. Keep in mind that bars labeled "semisweet" are often produced by mass-market companies, which may not include percentages on their labels.

Possible chocolates to include: Rapunzel semisweet chocolate bar, Chocolove 55% cacao bar, Santander 65% bar, Scharffen Berger 70% cacao bittersweet chocolate, Valrhona 85% cacao dark chocolate bar, and Ghirardelli 100% cacao unsweetened chocolate. (For sources, see p. 76.)

How to taste chocolate:

Taste the chocolate alone. Cleanse your palate between samples by drinking cool (not cold) water and eating bread or crackers.

Tasting steps:

Look at the chocolate: Is it shiny? Does it break cleanly?

Hold it in front of your nose and inhale its aromas. Does it remind you of nuts, coffee, tobacco, fruit? Is it mild or strong?

Now place the chocolate on your tongue and let it melt for several seconds. Consider its flavor notes (for example, floral, smoky, acidic, red fruit, caramel, or raisins) and texture (for example, dry and chalky, creamy, smooth). Then, bite down—how do the flavor and texture change?

Next, swallow the chocolate and evaluate its finish—does it dissipate quickly or linger? (A long finish is considered positive.)

Finally, did you enjoy the chocolate?

Tasting:
Extra-Virgin Olive Oil for Drizzling

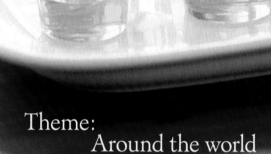

Theme:
Around the world

As with wine, provenance is a huge factor with extra-virgin olive oils. The terroir, or the nature of the land on which the olives grow, is important, and so too are the olive varieties used and how they're processed in that production area. For example, Tuscan olive oils are usually green and peppery, largely because Tuscan olives are picked when young, green, and pungent. Provençal olive oils, on the other hand, are often nutty and buttery, due to the later picking of the olives, when they're ripe and fattier. In this tasting, you'll learn which area's extra-virgin olive oils are to your liking—for drizzling over bread, vegetables, cheeses, meats, and fish.

Alternatively, you could opt for another tasting theme, such as single varietals (oils made with a single variety of olive) or regional comparisons (all from a specific region, such as Tuscany or Provence).

Dina Cheney, author of the book Tasting Club, is a freelance food writer and cooking instructor. ◆

How to select varieties:
For this tasting, purchase six bottles of high-quality, unflavored extra-virgin olive oil, each from a different country. Consider products representing France (especially Provence), Italy (Tuscany, Liguria, or Sicily), the United States (California), Greece, Spain, and Chile.

Some recommended brands are Lucini (Italy), McEvoy Ranch (California), Olave (Chile), Terra Medi (Greece), Nicolas Alziari (France), and 34° (New Zealand). (For sources, see p. 76.)

How to taste olive oil:
Taste the extra-virgin olive oil alone, using shot glasses or disposable pill cups, and then on a piece of neutral-flavored bread. Cleanse your palate between samples by drinking cool (not cold) water and eating bread or crackers; some professional tasters use green-apple slices as well.

Tasting steps:
First, what color is the oil? Is it cloudy or clear?

Swirl it around in the glass, then hold the vessel up to your nose and inhale. Describe its aromas (for example, green apple or grass).

Take a sip and swirl it around in your mouth. Evaluate its flavor notes (for example, bitter, fruity, spicy, earthy) and body (for example, buttery, round, silky).

Swallow the oil and evaluate the finish—how long does it last?

Finally, ask everyone whether they enjoyed the oil. If desired, try the oil again, this time with bread.

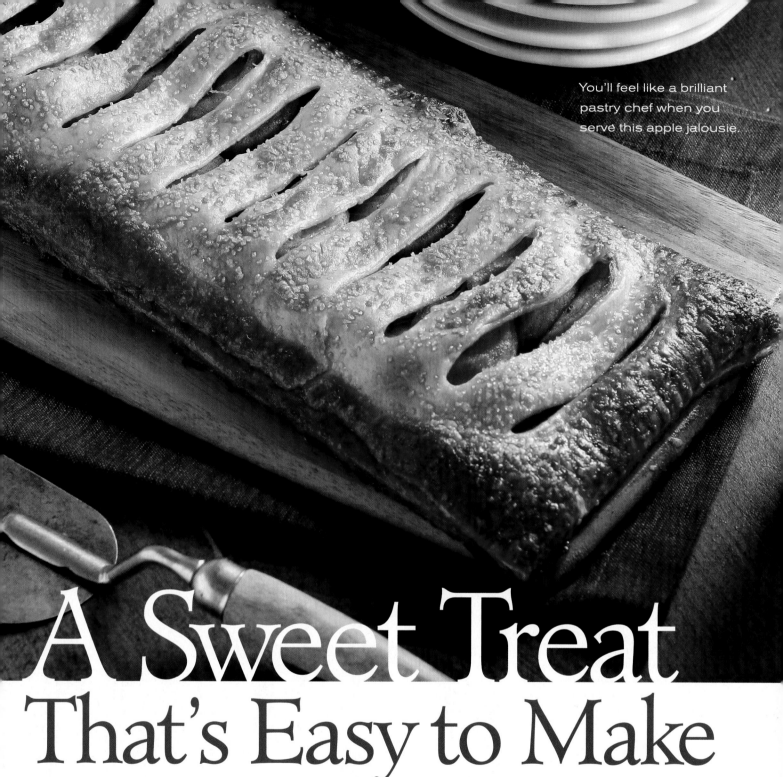

You'll feel like a brilliant pastry chef when you serve this apple jalousie.

A Sweet Treat
That's Easy to Make

BY KIMBERLY Y. MASIBAY

The last time I visited Paris, all I really wanted to do was wander from one pastry shop to the next and feast on all things sweet and buttery. The way I saw it, it was now or never again—I doubted I had the skills (or the patience) to recreate any of those exquisite pastries in my own kitchen. But I was wrong.

Not so long ago, inspired by a persistent craving more than anything else, I decided to attempt one of my French pastry-shop favorites: a jalousie. Made with light, flaky puff pastry and any fruit your heart desires, a jalousie (zhah-loo-ZEE) is sort of like a strudel, sort of like a turnover, but with its slatted top crust, it's far more elegant.

It's also not nearly as difficult to make as I'd expected. The secrets are to use store-bought frozen puff pastry instead of trying to make your own and to precook the fruit filling so it doesn't sog out the crust. Using these tricks, I very quickly mastered the method and began turning out professional-looking pastries from my own home oven.

And you can do it, too—even if you've never made a pastry before. Simply make a fruit filling (I've provided an apple brown-butter filling and an easy mixed-berry variation), assemble the pastry (I show you how on the next page), and pop it into the oven. Voilà! You've made a classic French pastry as pretty and delicious as any you'd find in Paris.

Apple Brown-Butter Jalousie

Yields one 6x14-inch jalousie pastry; serves eight.

For this pastry, the fruit filling shouldn't be very juicy or the bottom crust will become soggy. The solution is to precook the apples and reduce their juices. The filling can be made and stored in a covered container in the refrigerator for up to 2 days.

1¼ to 1½ lb. Granny Smith apples (about 3 medium), peeled, halved lengthwise, cored, and sliced crosswise into ½-inch-thick slices
¼ cup packed light or dark brown sugar
3 Tbs. granulated sugar
1 tsp. fresh lemon juice
¾ tsp. ground cinnamon
¼ tsp. kosher salt
Pinch freshly grated or ground nutmeg
3 Tbs. unsalted butter
1 vanilla bean, split and seeds scraped out with the back of a knife
1 large egg
1 sheet frozen packaged puff pastry (Pepperidge Farm brand), thawed overnight in the fridge or according to package instructions
Flour for rolling out the dough
1 tsp. demerara, turbinado, or granulated sugar
Crème fraîche, lightly sweetened whipped cream, or vanilla ice cream for serving (optional)

Make the filling: In a large mixing bowl, toss together the apples, brown sugar, granulated sugar, lemon juice, cinnamon, salt, and nutmeg.

In a 12-inch skillet, melt the butter over medium heat until the milk solids turn golden brown, 1 to 2 minutes. Remove from the heat, add the vanilla seeds, and stir. Carefully add the apple mixture to the skillet; with a heatproof rubber spatula, scrape all the sugar and spices from the bowl into the skillet. Stir the apples to coat them with the butter and then spread them in a fairly even layer. Return the pan to medium heat and cook, stirring gently with the spatula every few minutes (try not to break the apple slices), until the apples are tender but not mushy (taste one) and still hold their shape, and the juices have cooked down to a fairly thick, brown, bubbling syrup, 10 to 13 minutes. Scrape the apples into a wide shallow dish or onto a baking sheet to cool completely before assembling the jalousie.

Assemble the jalousie: Follow steps 1 through 4 at right.

Bake the jalousie: Right before baking, brush the top of the jalousie with a very light coating of the remaining egg wash (you won't need it all) and sprinkle with the demerara, turbinado, or granulated sugar.

Bake for 15 minutes and then rotate the baking sheet. Continue baking until the pastry is puffed, deep golden brown on top, and light golden brown on the bottom—use a spatula to gently lift the jalousie so you can peek underneath—10 to 15 minutes more. Immediately transfer the jalousie from the baking sheet to a wire rack to cool for at least 45 minutes. (Instead of trying to move the hot jalousie with a spatula, lift the parchment paper to move the jalousie to the rack and then carefully slide the paper out from under the pastry.)

Serve the jalousie slightly warm or at room temperature with crème fraîche, lightly sweetened whipped cream, or vanilla ice cream, if you like. I prefer to eat it the day it's made, but the jalousie will keep, wrapped well in aluminum foil, for 3 days. You can reheat it in a 325°F oven for 5 minutes before serving.

How to assemble a

1 Line a large rimmed baking sheet with parchment.

In a small bowl, make an egg wash by beating the egg with 1 Tbs. water until well combined.

Unfold the puff pastry dough on a floured surface, and gently pinch together any seams that have split. With a floured rolling pin, roll the dough into a 12x14-inch rectangle. With a sharp knife, cut the rectangle in half lengthwise to form two 6x14-inch rectangles. Use a long spatula to help you move one of the dough rectangles onto the parchment-lined baking sheet.

A bumble-berry jalousie is even easier

Mixed-Berry Filling

Yields about 1¼ cups filling; enough for one jalousie.

To keep this filling from being overly juicy, I cook the berries to release their juices and then thicken them with cornstarch. You may refrigerate the filling in a covered container for 2 days before using.

14 oz. frozen mixed berries (a mix of blueberries, raspberries, strawberries, and blackberries)
¼ cup granulated sugar; more to taste
1 tsp. fresh lemon juice; more to taste
¼ tsp. finely grated lemon zest

Photos: Scott Phillips

beautiful jalousie

2 Use a pastry brush to brush a 1-inch border of egg wash around the perimeter of the dough. (Save the remaining egg wash.) Arrange the fruit in a 4-inch-wide strip down the length of the dough. (I like to shingle the apple slices in a thick herringbone pattern down the length of the dough; you may need to make a double layer of apples.) Some syrupy apple juices will likely remain in the dish; spoon 2 to 3 Tbs. over the apples. If some of the liquid seeps onto the egg-washed border, don't worry about it.

3 Lightly dust the remaining piece of puff pastry with flour and then gently fold it in half lengthwise; don't crease the fold. Using a sharp knife, cut 1½-inch-long slashes at 1-inch intervals along the folded side of the dough; leave at least a 1-inch border on the remaining three sides. Do not unfold the dough. Using a long spatula, gently lift the folded strip and position it over the fruit-filled dough rectangle, matching up the straight edges.

4 Gently unfold the top piece of dough and stretch it over the filling, matching the straight edges all the way around the perimeter of the dough. Press the edges gently with your fingertips to seal the dough, and then, with a fork, very gently crimp the edges of the dough all the way around the pastry.

Chill the assembled jalousie for 15 to 20 minutes. Meanwhile, position a rack in the lower third of the oven and heat the oven to 400°F. Follow the baking instructions in the recipe at far left.

Generous pinch cinnamon
Pinch kosher salt
1½ Tbs. cornstarch

In a medium (3 qt.) saucepan, stir together the frozen berries, sugar, lemon juice, lemon zest, cinnamon, and salt. Heat over medium high until the berries start to release their juices and those juices bubble, 1 to 2 minutes. Reduce the heat to medium and simmer, stirring gently from time to time, until the berries release more juices and soften but still hold their shape for the most part (raspberries will probably break down, though, and blackberries might too), 7 to 9 minutes. Remove from the heat.

With a slotted spoon, scoop out the berries, letting as much juice as possible drain through the spoon, and put them into a small heat-proof bowl.

Dissolve the cornstarch in 3 Tbs. cold water. Whisk into the juices in the pan. Bring to a boil over medium-high heat. Boil, stirring with a wooden spoon, until the mixture is very thick, a full 2 minutes. Scrape the sauce into the bowl with the berries. Fold them together. Taste. If too tart, add a little more sugar; if too sweet, add a little more lemon juice. Let the filling cool completely before using. Assemble the jalousie as directed above, spreading the filling evenly down the length of dough.

Kimberly Y. Masibay is senior editor at Fine Cooking. ◆

The Best Ragùs

The secret? Braise the meat on the bone first, then shred it, chop it, and mix it back into the rich sauce

BY BIBA CAGGIANO

Ragù is a legendary long-simmered meat sauce that, once upon a time, Italian mothers and grandmothers prepared ritually every Sunday, filling the house with rich, comforting aromas. Some of my favorite ragùs are the ones my mother-in-law, who was from the southern-Italian city of Salerno, and my Roman aunt used to make. Instead of simmering ground or chopped meat, as in traditional Bolognese ragù, they braised short ribs, baby back ribs, shanks, and other meats on the bone to create a thick, deeply flavored sauce. Then they shredded the cooked meat and added it back into the sauce before tossing it with pasta. It is these sumptuous ragùs that have inspired the sauces you'll find here.

While they share the same braising technique and a similar flavor foundation, each of these ragùs has a unique personality that comes both from the different types of meat I use and from a few other ingredients that help boost flavor. In the short rib ragù, for instance, I add dried porcini mushrooms to the braise because they lend a lusty earthiness, and I toss pancetta in with the aromatics for a little flavor punch. The baby back rib ragù (at right) benefits from the addition of sausage, which gives the sauce more depth and complexity. And, borrowing from a traditional ragù made in the southern-Italian region of Abruzzi, I add bell peppers to my lamb shank ragù, because their sweetness provides a perfect counterpoint to the gaminess of the shanks.

When I'm ready to toss the ragù with pasta, I add a pat of butter and some grated Parmigiano-Reggiano, which help round out the flavors and give the sauce extra richness (see p. 60 for tips on the best pastas to use and how to combine them with the ragù).

baby back ribs and sausage
make a deeply satisfying sauce

Neapolitan Rib & Sausage Ragù
(Ragù di Costicine e Salsiccia alla Napoletana)

Yields about 5 cups ragù.

2 28-oz. cans imported Italian plum tomatoes, preferably San Marzano
2 lb. baby back pork ribs, trimmed of excessive fat (about 11 ribs)
½ cup extra-virgin olive oil
Kosher salt and freshly ground black pepper
1 medium yellow onion, finely chopped (about 1¼ cups)
2 medium cloves garlic, finely chopped
2 Tbs. chopped fresh flat-leaf parsley
½ tsp. crushed red pepper flakes; more to taste
2 links mild Italian sausage (about ½ lb.), casings removed, meat broken into small pieces
1 cup dry white wine
½ cup tomato paste diluted in ½ cup water

Position a rack in the lower third of the oven and heat the oven to 300°F.

Put one can of tomatoes and their juices in a food processor and process until puréed. Using a spatula or the back of a ladle, press the purée through a medium-mesh sieve set over a bowl to remove the seeds. Purée and strain the other can of tomatoes.

Cut the ribs into 2 or 3 pieces so they fit in a 7- to 8-qt. Dutch oven. Heat ¼ cup of the oil in the Dutch oven over medium-high heat. Season the ribs with kosher salt and pepper and add them to the hot oil, fatty side down. Cook until the ribs turn a light golden brown, propping them up as needed against the sides of the Dutch oven to brown them evenly, about 6 minutes. Turn the ribs over and brown them on the other side, about 2 minutes. Transfer the ribs to a large plate, discard the fat, and clean the pan with paper towels.

Heat the remaining ¼ cup oil in the pan over medium heat. Add the onion, garlic, parsley, and red pepper flakes and cook, stirring occasionally, until the onion just begins to color, about 5 minutes. Add the sausage and cook, stirring and breaking up the sausage with a wooden spoon until it's lightly browned, 3 to 4 minutes.

Return the ribs to the pan and stir them around with the savory base. Raise the heat to high and add the wine. Cook, stirring occasionally, until the wine is reduced approximately by half, about 5 minutes. Add the tomatoes and the diluted tomato paste. Season with ½ tsp. salt and ¼ tsp. pepper. Stir until the liquid begins to simmer.

Turn off the heat, cover the pan tightly with a lid or heavy-duty aluminum foil, and put it in the oven. Simmer very gently, turning the ribs every half hour, until the sauce has a medium-thick consistency and the meat begins to fall off the bone, about 2½ hours.

Remove the pan from the oven and transfer the ribs and any meat that has fallen off the bone to a cutting board. Use a ladle to skim the fat off the surface of the sauce. When the ribs are cool enough to handle, pull the meat off the ribs. Discard the bones and any fat and connective tissue. Finely chop the meat. Stir the meat back into the sauce and simmer on the stovetop over medium heat, stirring occasionally, to allow the flavors to meld and the sauce to thicken slightly, about 10 minutes. Adjust the seasoning with salt, pepper, and crushed red pepper to taste.

To pair the ragù with pasta, see the box on p. 60.

To pair the ragù with pasta, see the box on p. 60.

wine choices

Look for a youthful, intensely fruity Zinfandel such as the 2004 Bogle "Old Vine" Zinfandel, California ($14), or the 2004 Ravenswood "Zen of Zin" Zinfandel, California ($18).

porcini and pancetta give
a boost to short rib ragù

The last step:
Toss it with pasta

Once you've made your rich ragù, all that's left is to combine it with pasta. To serve four to six people, you'll need:

4 cups ragù
1 Tbs. unsalted butter
1 lb. dried or fresh pasta, cooked and drained
½ cup freshly grated Parmigiano-Reggiano or
Pecorino Romano

Heat the ragù (either in the Dutch oven you used to cook it or in a 12-inch skillet, if reheating) over medium-high heat. Add the butter and then pour in the pasta and Parmigiano or pecorino. Toss over medium-high heat until the pasta and sauce are well combined. Serve immediately.

Choosing the best pasta

Short, full-bodied dried pastas like rigatoni and orecchiette work great with these ragùs, because their nooks and ridges capture the sauce. If you want to use fresh pasta, a wide shape like pappardelle can stand up to a hearty sauce. And a ragù is a good excuse to cook gnocchi, too.

Short Rib & Porcini Mushroom Ragù
(Ragù di Manzo e Funghi Porcini)

Yields about 8 cups ragù.

1 oz. dried porcini mushrooms (about 1 cup)
2 28-oz. cans imported Italian plum tomatoes, preferably San Marzano
½ cup extra-virgin olive oil
2 lb. bone-in beef short ribs, trimmed of excess fat
1 lb. boneless beef chuck, trimmed of excess fat
Kosher salt and freshly ground black pepper
1 small yellow onion, finely chopped (about 1 cup)
1 small carrot, finely chopped (about 1 cup)
1 small celery stalk, finely chopped (about ½ cup)
1 medium clove garlic, finely chopped
2 oz. thickly sliced pancetta, finely chopped
1 Tbs. chopped fresh flat-leaf parsley
1 cup dry white wine

Position a rack in the lower third of the oven and heat the oven to 300°F.

Soak the mushrooms in 2 cups of warm water for 20 to 30 minutes. With a slotted spoon, transfer the mushrooms to a cutting board and chop them finely. Line a strainer with a coffee filter or two layers of paper towels and strain the mushroom-soaking water into a bowl to get rid of any grit. Set aside both mushrooms and liquid.

Put one can of tomatoes and their juices in a food processor and process until puréed. Using a spatula or the back of a ladle, press the purée through a medium-mesh sieve set over a bowl to remove the seeds. Purée and strain the other can of tomatoes.

Heat ¼ cup of the oil in a 7- to 8-qt. Dutch oven over medium-high heat. Season the ribs and beef chuck with kosher salt and pepper and add them to the hot oil. Cook, turning as necessary, until the meat is golden brown on all sides, about 10 minutes. Transfer to a large plate, discard the fat, and clean the pan with paper towels.

Heat the remaining ¼ cup oil in the pan over medium heat. Add the onion, carrot, celery, garlic, and pancetta and cook, stirring frequently, until the vegetables are lightly golden and soft, 7 to 8 minutes. Add the mushrooms and parsley and stir for about 1 minute to blend the ingredients.

Return the meat to the pan and stir to coat with the savory base. Raise the heat to high and add the wine. Cook, stirring occasionally, until the wine is reduced approximately by half, about 5 minutes. Add the tomatoes and ½ cup of the reserved mushroom-soaking water. Season with ½ tsp. salt and ¼ tsp. pepper. Stir until the liquid begins to simmer.

Turn off the heat, cover the pan tightly with a lid or heavy-duty aluminum foil, and put it in the oven. Cook, turning the meat every half hour, until the meat is fork tender and the ribs begin to fall off the bone, about 2½ hours.

Remove the pan from the oven and transfer the meat (including any that has fallen off the bone) to a cutting board. Use a ladle to skim the fat off the surface of the sauce. When the meat is cool enough to handle, pull the meat off the ribs. Discard the bones and any fat and connective tissue. Finely chop all the meat. Stir the meat back into the sauce and simmer on the stovetop over medium heat, stirring occasionally, to allow the flavors to meld and the sauce to thicken slightly, about 10 minutes. Adjust the seasoning with salt and pepper to taste.

To pair the ragù with pasta, see the box at left.

wine choices

The earthiness, intense fruit, and bright acidity of an Italian Barbera would be a good match for this ragù. Try the 2004 Michele Chiarlo Barbera d'Asti ($14) or the 2004 Moccagatta Barbera d'Alba ($19).

Lamb Shank & Sweet Pepper Ragù
(Ragù di Stinco d'Agnello con Peperoni)

Yields 6 to 7 cups ragù.

- **1 28-oz. can imported Italian plum tomatoes, preferably San Marzano**
- **4 lb. lamb shanks (about 2 large or 3 medium), trimmed of excess fat**
- **Kosher salt and freshly ground black pepper**
- **½ cup all-purpose flour**
- **½ cup extra-virgin olive oil**
- **1 medium yellow onion, finely chopped (about 1½ cups)**
- **2 medium cloves garlic, finely chopped**
- **1 bay leaf**
- **Pinch crushed red pepper flakes**
- **2 medium red bell peppers, seeded and cut into small dice (about 2½ cups)**
- **1 cup dry white wine**
- **¾ to 1½ cups homemade or low-salt canned beef broth**

Position a rack in the center of the oven and heat the oven to 300°F.

Put the can of tomatoes and their juices in a food processor and process until puréed. Using a spatula or the back of a ladle, press the purée through a medium-mesh sieve set over a bowl to remove the seeds.

Pat the lamb shanks dry with paper towels and season generously with salt and pepper. Spread the flour in a wide, shallow dish and dredge the shanks lightly in the flour.

Heat ¼ cup of the oil in a 7- to 8-qt. Dutch oven over medium-high heat. Add the shanks and cook, turning a few times, until they are golden brown on all sides, 8 to 10 minutes. Transfer the shanks to a large plate, discard the fat, and clean the pan with paper towels.

Heat the remaining ¼ cup oil in the pan over medium heat. Add the onion and cook, stirring frequently, until it's pale gold and soft, about 5 minutes. Add the garlic, bay leaf, and pepper flakes, stir for about 1 minute, and add the bell peppers. Cook, stirring frequently, until the peppers begin to color and soften a little, 4 to 5 minutes.

Return the shanks to the pan and stir them around with the pepper mixture. Increase the heat to high, add the wine, and stir until the wine is reduced approximately by half, 1 to 2 minutes. Add the tomatoes, ¾ cup of broth, and ½ tsp. salt. Stir until the liquid begins to simmer.

Turn off the heat, cover the pan tightly with a lid or heavy-duty aluminum foil, and put it in the oven. Cook, turning the shanks every half hour or so, until the meat begins to fall off the bone, 2 to 2½ hours.

Remove the pan from the oven and transfer the shanks to a cutting board. When the shanks are cool enough to handle, pull the meat off the bones, discarding any fat and connective tissue. Cut the meat into bite-size pieces. Stir the meat into the sauce and bring it back to a gentle simmer. Cook, stirring a few times, until the sauce has a medium-thick consistency and a rich, reddish color, 5 to 10 minutes. If the sauce seems too dry, stir in some or all of the remaining broth. Discard the bay leaf, adjust the seasoning with salt, and turn off the heat.

To pair the ragù with pasta, see the box at far left.

Biba Caggiano is the author of many cookbooks and the chef and owner of Biba Restaurant in Sacramento, California. Her latest book is Biba's Italy. ◆

wine choices

A Grenache blend would pair well with this braised lamb ragù. Try the 2004 Bonny Doon Clos de Gilroy ($12) or the 2004 Domaine de la Maurelle Gigondas ($18).

Make it ahead

You'll probably have leftovers after the first meal, or you might want to make the whole dish ahead. These ragùs keep for up to 5 days in the fridge and up to 1 month in the freezer.

Here's what to do: Transfer the hot ragù to a large bowl and refrigerate it, uncovered, stirring well every 20 minutes until it's completely cool. Cover the bowl tightly with plastic and refrigerate it, or freeze the ragù in small containers or zip-top bags.

bell peppers add a hint of sweetness to a rustic lamb sauce

Versatile Frittata,
for Breakfast, Lunch, or Dinner

Follow this method to make dozens of different frittatas with the ingredients you like best

BY JOYCE GOLDSTEIN

I f you asked me to list my favorite dishes to make on a weeknight (or a weekend, for that matter), a frittata would certainly be at the top of the list. It's tasty, relatively quick, and incredibly versatile. It can be served warm, at room temperature, or even cold. Not only is it great for breakfast or brunch, but I also serve it with a tossed salad or soup for a satisfying lunch or supper. And when I cut it up in elegant little squares, it turns into a tasty hors d'oeuvre that's perfect for a slightly more formal occasion.

But the greatest thing about a frittata is that once you learn how to make it (see the simple method on pp. 64–65), you can customize it any way you like using your favorite ingredients. And if that weren't enough, it's really easy to make—certainly easier than its French cousin, the omelet. When you make a frittata, there's no fussy folding of the eggs over the filling and no risk of the dish falling apart in the process.

All my frittatas start out the same way: I loosely beat eggs with a little milk or cream and flour. The dairy provides a bit of extra moisture and richness and keeps the frittata light. The flour bolsters the eggs' setting and thickening properties and helps incorporate the added milk or cream.

Then, I add all the other ingredients into the bowl of beaten eggs. There are no hard-and-fast rules for what to put in your creation. Almost any type of vegetable works (see some of my favorites on p. 64) and, if you want to make it a little heartier, add bacon, pancetta, or sausage. Just think of what goes well together, and don't go crazy adding too

many things—a combination of three vegetables and meats is plenty. Frittatas are also a great way to use up leftovers, whether they're roasted or sautéed vegetables from yesterday's dinner or a link of sausage that's been lingering in the fridge. Just be sure to cut everything into small pieces.

Cheese and herbs are optional

You can't go wrong with adding cheese to eggs. Sharp cheeses, such as Parmigiano, pecorino, and feta deliver a pungent, pleasantly salty flavor. Goat cheese adds a nice creamy tang, while ricotta creates little pockets of moisture and sweetness. But you can skip cheese entirely and let the other ingredients shine. My favorite thing to add to frittatas is fresh herbs. I use them copiously because they lend a fresh, subtle flavor note (sometimes I'll even make an herb-only frittata that's wonderfully light and perfumey), but a frittata without herbs can be good, too.

Make sure your pan is hot but not *too* hot. Before you pour in the egg mixture, your pan should be warm enough to set the frittata on the bottom but not so hot that the bottom will brown too quickly and become tough. That's why I heat the oil gently over medium heat and keep a close eye on the pan (you don't want the oil to start smoking).

Some people cook frittatas entirely on the stovetop, flipping them halfway through the cooking. But the flip can be tricky, so I finish my frittatas in the oven, instead. It's foolproof and eliminates the risk factor. To promote faster and more even cooking, I start on the stovetop with the pan covered for the first 10 minutes or so to help the eggs set, then I uncover it and transfer it to the oven.

5 great combos

Make one of these tasty frittatas or create your own following the steps on pp. 64–65.

- ❖ **Asparagus with mint, parsley, scallions, and a pinch of nutmeg**
- ❖ **Italian sweet sausage, mushrooms, and red onions with marjoram and pecorino**
- ❖ **Mushrooms and leeks with mint and goat cheese**
- ❖ **Potatoes, onions, and pancetta with basil and Parmigiano**
- ❖ **Kale, onions, and chorizo with Spanish paprika (pimentón)**

For the perfect hors d'oeuvre, cut a frittata into 1- to 1½-inch squares.

Chorizo and kale make a classic Mediterranean combination that works beautifully in a frittata.

Four easy steps to a delicious frittata

Serves four to six as a main dish, eight to twelve as an appetizer.

1 Get ready

Read the method from start to finish and choose your ingredients from Steps 2 and 3. Cook any add-ins that need cooking. Heat the oven to 350°F.

Ingredients you'll need

8 large eggs
½ cup whole milk, half-and-half, or heavy cream
1 Tbs. all-purpose flour
1 to 1½ tsp. kosher salt
Freshly ground black pepper
Up to 3 vegetables & meats (for a total of 2 cups)
1 or 2 fresh herbs (for a total of ¼ cup; optional)
1 or 2 aromatics & spices (optional)
1 or 2 cheeses (for a total of ½ cup; optional)
2 Tbs. extra-virgin olive oil; more as needed

2 Beat the eggs

In a bowl, lightly whisk 8 eggs with your choice of dairy from the list below, 1 Tbs. flour (don't worry if the flour forms small lumps), 1 to 1½ tsp. salt, and several grinds of pepper. **Note:** If using a salty cheese (such as pecorino or feta) or other salty ingredients (such as bacon or pancetta), use only 1 tsp. salt; otherwise, use 1½ tsp.

Dairy choices
Choose one, ½ cup

Milk
Half-and-half
Heavy cream

3 Stir in your add-ins

Combine your choice of add-ins from the lists at right with the egg mixture, folding them in gently. Allow any cooked ingredients to cool a bit before you add them to the eggs. They can be warm but not piping hot.

Vegetables & meat

Choose up to 3 in any combination, for a total of 2 cups

(The quantities given below all yield about 1 cup, unless otherwise noted.)

Asparagus — ½ to ⅔ lb., steamed, cut into 1½-inch pieces

Bell peppers — 1 lb. (about 2 large), roasted, peeled, cut into ¼-inch strips

Chorizo — ½ lb., cut into small dice, browned (yields about 1¼ cups)

Potatoes — 6 oz. (1 medium), peeled, boiled, cut into ¼-inch-thick slices

Fresh mushrooms — ½ lb., cut into ¼-inch-thick slices, sautéed

Hearty greens (such as collards or kale) — ½ lb., trimmed, cooked until tender in salted water, drained and squeezed to remove excess liquid, coarsely chopped

Italian Sausage — ½ lb., removed from its casing, crumbled, browned

Leeks — 2 medium (white and light green parts only), thinly sliced, sautéed

Onions — 1 large, thinly sliced, sautéed

Pancetta or bacon — ¼ lb., cut into ¼-inch dice, sautéed (yields ½ cup pancetta; ¼ cup bacon)

Spinach or Swiss chard — 1 lb., trimmed, sautéed, drained and squeezed to remove excess liquid, coarsely chopped

Zucchini — 6 to 7 oz. (about 1½ medium), cut into ¼-inch-thick slices, sautéed

Fresh herbs (optional)

Choose 1 or 2, for a total of ¼ cup

Basil — cut into thin strips

Chives — thinly sliced

Marjoram — chopped (use 1 Tbs. maximum)

Mint — cut into thin strips

Parsley — chopped

You can make a simple herb frittata using only fresh herbs and cheese. In this case, choose 3 herbs for a total of ½ cup.

Aromatics & spices (optional)

Choose 1 or 2

Crushed red pepper flakes — up to ½ tsp.

Garlic — minced, 1 tsp. (1 medium clove), sautéed

Lemon zest — finely grated, 1 tsp.

Nutmeg — finely grated or ground, a pinch

Scallions — thinly sliced, ¼ cup, sautéed

Spanish paprika (pimentón) — ½ tsp. added to any sautéed ingredients at the end of cooking

Cheeses (optional)

Choose 1 or 2, for a total of ½ cup

Feta — crumbled

Fontina — shredded

Fresh goat cheese — crumbled

Fresh ricotta — in dollops

Parmigiano-Reggiano — grated

Pecorino Romano — grated

4 Cook the frittata

Start on the stovetop. Heat 2 Tbs. olive oil in a 10-inch ovenproof anodized aluminum or nonstick skillet over medium heat. When the oil is hot, add the egg mixture, spreading everything evenly. Reduce the heat to low, cover, and cook until the eggs are set about 1 inch in from the sides of the pan, 8 to 12 minutes.

Transfer to the oven. Uncover the pan and finish the frittata in the oven until the top is puffed and completely set, 15 to 25 minutes longer.

Slide onto a cutting board. Remove from the oven and run a rubber spatula around the sides of the pan to loosen the frittata. Slip it out of the pan and onto a cutting board. Let the frittata cool for 10 minutes before cutting and serving. Or let it cool completely to room temperature.

Joyce Goldstein, the former chef-owner of Square One, in San Francisco, teaches and writes about cooking. Her latest book is Antipasti. ◆

Pound Cake, Perfected

A few little tweaks make this classic butter cake moister, richer, and better than ever

BY NICOLE REES

Once upon a time, the recipe for pound cake was a simple ratio that everyone knew by heart: a pound of butter creamed with a pound of sugar, beaten with a pound of eggs, and finished with a pound of flour. Easy, yes, but a tender cake it does not make. I've discovered that most traditional pound cake recipes—and I've tried many—yield a cake that's both too sturdy and too dry for modern tastes.

My updated version tweaks the classic formula to produce a cake that's soft and moist yet still has the classic's buttery flavor and springy texture. Though I've strayed from the traditional ratio of ingredients, this modern pound cake is remarkably simple, and it remains true to my idea of what a pound cake should be—a moist, fluffy, buttery slice of heaven.

A few new ingredients

To start, I use more sugar than flour by weight. Sugar inhibits the development of gluten, the protein responsible for the structure of the cake. Less gluten means a moister and more tender crumb. Using too much egg adds a lot of structure-forming proteins to the cake, which can make it seem hard and dry, so I reduce the number of eggs usually called for, substituting milk instead (the milk also makes the cake taste more buttery). Though I reduce the number of eggs overall, I keep the number of yolks high to preserve that rich, eggy flavor associated with pound cakes.

When I make this cake, I use cake flour because I like a light, tender crumb. I discovered, though, that with this particular recipe, all-purpose flour works wonderfully, too. This is unusual—generally, you'll run into trouble if you don't use cake flour in a recipe that calls for it. (For more information on using cake flour, see the sidebar on p. 69.)

Butter Pound Cake

Yields one 12-cup Bundt cake; serves twelve to sixteen.

10 oz. (1¼ cups) unsalted butter, softened at room temperature; more for the pan
10¼ oz. (2½ cups) cake flour or 11 oz. (2⅓ cups) unbleached all-purpose flour; more for the pan
1½ tsp. baking powder
½ tsp. table salt
1¾ cups granulated sugar
2 large egg yolks, at room temperature
3 large eggs, at room temperature
⅔ cup whole milk, at room temperature
1½ tsp. pure vanilla extract

Position a rack in the center of the oven and heat the oven to 350°F. Butter a 12-cup Bundt pan, dust the pan with flour, and tap out the excess. In a small bowl, whisk together the flour, baking powder, and salt until evenly combined.

In the bowl of a stand mixer fitted with the paddle attachment, beat the butter and the sugar at medium speed until light and fluffy, about 2 minutes. On low speed, beat in the yolks until smooth. Stop the mixer and scrape the bowl and the paddle. With the mixer running on medium-low speed, add the whole eggs, one at a time, mixing for at least 20 seconds after each addition. Stop the mixer and scrape the bowl and paddle again.

With the mixer running on the lowest speed, add half of the flour mixture and mix just to combine, add the milk and mix until combined, and then add the remaining flour mixture and mix just until combined. Scrape the bowl one last time, add the vanilla extract, and mix at medium speed until the batter is smooth and fluffy, 20 to 30 seconds.

Scrape the batter into the prepared pan and spread it evenly. Run a knife through the batter and tap the pan against the counter to dislodge trapped air. Bake until golden brown and a toothpick inserted in the center comes out with only moist crumbs clinging to it, 45 to 55 minutes.

Cool in the pan for 10 to 15 minutes and then invert onto a wire rack to cool completely. The cake will keep at room temperature for 3 days.

A new batter needs a new pan

Three easy variations

Here are three flavor variations that are perfect for winter: Brandy & Rum Glazed, Lemon-Coconut, and Chocolate Chip. The first two of these cakes are glazed, which keeps them fresh longer and also gives them an extra boost of flavor. The third has finely chopped chocolate mixed into the batter, which adds real richness. Don't hesitate to experiment with other mix-ins. In summer, I like to add fresh blueberries to the batter, and in fall, I stir in chopped cranberries.

Traditionally, pound cakes are baked in loaf pans, in which they rise slowly and form a high peak. My modern pound cake batter has more moisture and less protein structure than the original batter, so it will not rise as high or form that distinctive camel-back hump if baked in a loaf pan. To help the batter along, I bake it in a Bundt pan instead of a loaf pan. The Bundt shape gives the batter better support, and the hole in the center of the pan increases the total surface area that's exposed to heat, so the batter bakes more efficiently. This means the edges won't be dry by the time the center of the cake is set.

Brandy & Rum Glazed

Stir ½ tsp. freshly grated nutmeg into the completed batter. Then proceed with scraping it into the Bundt pan as directed on p. 67.

While the cake bakes, make a glaze by mixing 1¼ cups confectioners' sugar with 3 Tbs. brandy and 3 Tbs. rum until smooth. After the baked cake has cooled for 15 minutes, turn the warm cake onto a serving plate. Using a skewer, poke holes all over the cake. Brush the cake—every visible inch of it—with the glaze, until the glaze is gone. When the cake is completely cool, the glaze will form a protective crust over the cake, keeping it moist for 5 to 7 days.

Lemon-Coconut

Reduce the milk in the recipe to ½ cup, and when you add it to the batter, add ¼ cup fresh lemon juice as well. Then stir 1 Tbs. finely grated lemon zest and 1 cup loosely packed sweetened flaked coconut into the batter, breaking up any coconut lumps. Then proceed with scraping it into the Bundt pan as directed on p. 67.

While the cake bakes, make a glaze by mixing 1¼ cups confectioners' sugar with 6 Tbs. fresh lemon juice until smooth. After the baked cake has cooled for 15 minutes, turn the warm cake onto a serving plate. Using a skewer, poke holes all over the cake. Brush the cake—every visible inch of it—with the glaze, until the glaze is gone. When the cake is completely cool, the glaze will form a protective crust over the cake, keeping it moist for 5 to 7 days.

Chocolate Chip

Fold 4 oz. very finely chopped semisweet chocolate or ⅔ cup mini semisweet chocolate chips into the completed batter. Then proceed with scraping it into the Bundt pan as directed on p. 67.

If desired, sprinkle the cake with confectioners' sugar before serving. The cake will keep at room temperature for 3 days.

Frequent Fine Cooking *contributor Nicole Rees is a food scientist, cookbook author, and baker based in Portland, Oregon.* ◆

food science

What a difference the flour makes

It's your choice. *All-purpose flour makes a dense, moist pound cake, while cake flour delivers a taller, fluffier cake.*

The flour you use can noticeably affect the appearance and texture of the finished cake. To see for yourself, try this tasty little experiment: Make one of my pound cakes with cake flour and another with all-purpose and compare them side by side. The cake-flour version rises higher in its pan as it bakes, so it's a taller cake with a fluffier texture. The cake made with all-purpose flour, on the other hand, is denser, moister, and closer to a quick bread in texture.

Cake flour really is different from other flours. It's specially milled and processed to have finer granules, lower protein, and higher starch. The flour is bleached, which weakens its gluten and makes baked goods more tender.

If you use cake flour, check the cake on the early side of the doneness window to prevent overbaking—cake flour has a lower pH, which can help the batter set faster.

Indian spices	70
How to shred cabbage	71
Cooking poultry safely	71
Perfect boiled eggs	71
Sherry vinegar	72
Creminis	73
Chopping sticky food	73
Greasing a Bundt pan	73
Following recipes	73

BY JENNIFER ARMENTROUT

New flavors from the
Indian spice pantry

Curry leaves, fenugreek leaves, and the warming spice blend called garam masala are listed as optional ingredients in the Indian vegetable stir-fries on pp. 46–49, but they're worth seeking out and getting to know because they add a special, authentic touch to each dish. If you don't have an Indian grocery store near you, see p. 76 for a mail-order source.

Curry leaves

These dark-green spear-shaped leaves are highly aromatic and pleasantly bitter. As the name suggests, they smell like curry, but they are not an ingredient in curry powder, which is a multispice blend. Indian cooks generally fry curry leaves in cooking oil (often with other spices) before adding other ingredients. They look a little like bay leaves, but unlike bay, curry leaves can be eaten.

Curry leaves are available both fresh and dried; fresh are more flavorful. The fresh leaves are usually sold on the stem —strip the leaves off to use them. Fresh curry leaves in a zip-top bag will keep for about two weeks in the refrigerator. They may also be frozen for up to three months, though they'll lose some potency.

Fenugreek leaves

Both the leaves and the seeds of the fenugreek (FEN-yoo-greek) plant are used in Indian cooking, but the recipes on pp. 46–49 call for just leaves, which are herbal and bitter. Fresh fenugreek leaves are eaten as a vegetable in India. The dried leaves, called *kasuri methi,* are used to flavor savory dishes, especially vegetables and curries.

Fresh leaves wrapped in dry paper towels in a zip-top bag will keep for about two weeks in the refrigerator. Store dried leaves in a sealed jar in a cool, dark cupboard; use within four months.

Garam masala   *Yields about ¾ cup*

Garam masala, which means hot spice, is the Indian equivalent of the French herbes de Provence or the Chinese five-spice powder. The recipe changes from region to region in northern India, with each household adding its own touch. As a rule, garam masala is added at the last step of cooking, almost like a fresh herb. If cooked too long, it tends to become bitter.

Garam masala is available on some grocery store spice racks as well as in Indian markets, but for the best flavor, toast and grind your own.

1 cinnamon stick (2½ to 3 inches long), broken into pieces
2 bay leaves
¼ cup cumin seeds
⅓ cup coriander seeds
1 Tbs. green cardamom pods
1 Tbs. whole black peppercorns
2 tsp. whole cloves
1 small dried red chile, stemmed
¼ tsp. nutmeg (preferably freshly grated)
⅛ tsp. ground mace

Heat the cinnamon, bay leaves, cumin seeds, coriander seeds, cardamom pods, peppercorns, cloves, and chile in a medium skillet over medium-high heat, stirring often, until the cumin seeds darken to a deep, toasty brown color, 2 to 3 minutes —the spices may crackle and smoke a bit. Immediately transfer to a plate or bowl to cool. Add the nutmeg and mace, and grind the spices in a spice grinder to a fine powder, working in batches if necessary. Store in an airtight container for up to 4 months.
—*Suvir Saran is the author of* Indian Home Cooking.

Photos: Scott Phillips

Save $9.95 on gift subscriptions

Give a gift of *Fine Cooking* or renew at the regular price of $29.95 for seven issues. Then pay only $20.00 for each additional gift subscription you give – a savings of $9.95 each. We will announce your gifts with a card in your name.

YOUR INFO

N508360 Z N

Please complete the following to renew or give a gift(s) of *Fine Cooking*.

NAME _____

BILLING ADDRESS _____ APT. # _____

CITY _____ STATE _____ ZIP _____

Renewal or gift subscription

☐ **RENEW** my subscription at $29.95 and send it to the address above,

☐ **OR SEND FIRST GIFT** at $29.95 to the recipient below.

RECIPIENT'S NAME _____

ADDRESS _____ APT. # _____

CITY _____ STATE _____ ZIP _____

SIGN GIFT CARD FROM _____

Gift subscription

ADDITIONAL GIFT at $20.00 – a savings of $9.95.

RECIPIENT'S NAME _____

ADDRESS _____ APT. # _____

CITY _____ STATE _____ ZIP _____

SIGN GIFT CARD FROM _____

Gift subscription

ADDITIONAL GIFT at $20.00 – a savings of $9.95.

RECIPIENT'S NAME _____

ADDRESS _____ APT. # _____

CITY _____ STATE _____ ZIP _____

SIGN GIFT CARD FROM _____

Payable in U.S. funds. Prices for U.S. and Canadian residents (GST included). Outside the U.S. and Canada: $36/year; $62/2 years; $88/3 years. Order by 12/15/06 for holiday delivery of card. Offer expires 12/31/06.

Special Savings on *Fine Cooking*

Give the perfect gift to people who love to cook

Fine Cooking is the magazine for people who love to cook. Every issue is packed with all the ingredients to get great results every time, including:

- recipes that work
- classics with a fresh twist
- tips from the pros
- proven techniques from experts
- Quick & Delicious recipes
- tool and equipment reviews
- make-ahead menus
- timelines for entertaining
- bonus fold-out section and more!

Use the reverse side to order and save today!

(And don't forget to treat yourself – renew or start your subscription now.)

fine
Cooking
FineCooking.com

Shredding cabbage

Whether you're preparing cabbage for a sauté, a salad, or a soup, more often than not you'll be shredding it. For large quantities, use a food processor fitted with a slicing blade, but for small amounts, it's quick to shred by hand.

Quarter and core the head of cabbage. Thinly slice each quarter crosswise, keeping the fingertips of your guiding hand curled under so you don't cut them. If the quarter gets too awkward to hold, flip it onto another side and finish slicing.

A new doneness temperature for poultry

We aim for juicy white meat in our poultry recipes. That's why we've always advised you to cook poultry to a temperature of 165° to 170°F, even though the USDA recommended 180°F.

If the discrepancy ever made you uneasy, you can now relax. The USDA recently lowered the safe cooking temperature for all poultry to 165°F. At this temperature, salmonella and other pathogens will be destroyed, and the meat will be safe to eat and definitely juicy, but it may still have a pink tinge. If that's not to your liking, you might want to cook the meat to a slightly higher temperature.

As always, the best way to check the temperature is to insert an instant-read thermometer into the thickest part of the thigh.

—*Kimberly Y. Masibay, senior editor*

How to **boil an egg perfectly** every time

Boiling an egg may not be rocket science, but timing is important. Here are some guidelines.

Getting started

Put the eggs in a saucepan and add enough cold water to cover them by about 1 inch. Set the pan over medium-high heat and as soon as the water reaches a brisk simmer, start timing. As the eggs cook, adjust the heat as needed to maintain a brisk simmer. (Though we talk about hard-boiled eggs—and we're using that term here—the fact is that cooking eggs in boiling water cracks the shell and makes the eggs tough and rubbery. A simmer works much better.)

Peeling eggs

When the eggs are cooked, carefully pour out most of the hot water, leaving the eggs in the pan. Set the pan in the sink under cool running water for a few minutes until the eggs are barely warm. If the shells are stubborn, try peeling them under running water. The fresher the egg, the more attached the shell, so for boiling, older eggs are preferable.

Soft boiled: 2 minutes

The white is solid, but the yolk is still runny. Serve in an egg cup for breakfast. Use the side of a small spoon to crack and remove the pointed end of the egg, making a hole in the shell large enough to fit the spoon. Or use egg scissors, if you have them.

Medium boiled: 4½ minutes

The yolk is solid but still dark orange-yellow, moist, and dense in the middle. Beautiful and delicious quartered on a salad.

Hard boiled: 8 minutes

The yolk is completely solid, light yellow, and crumbly, with no sign of the telltale green or gray ring around the yolk that's caused by overcooking. Perfect for egg salad or deviled eggs.

The boil-and-walk-away method

For another way to hard-boil eggs, begin as directed at left with the eggs in cold water, but once the water reaches a brisk simmer, turn off the heat and let the eggs sit uncovered in the hot water for at least 10 minutes and up to 30 minutes—the water cools gradually, preventing the eggs from overcooking. This is a great method when you're multitasking and can't pay careful attention to the eggs.

—*Allison Ehri, test kitchen associate*

Sherry Vinegar

A long-time favorite of ours, Spanish sherry vinegar has been hovering in the wings of the world culinary stage for years, and we're wagering that it'll soon become as familiar as Italian balsamic vinegar, which was practically unknown in North America not so long ago.

What it is:

Sherry vinegar is made from sherry wine, which is produced in the Jerez (Xérès or Sherry) denomination of origin in south-western Spain. The unusual thing about the vinegar (and the wine) is that it's blended and aged using a special *solera* system. Imagine a pyramid of wooden barrels, each one containing vinegar. The bottom row of barrels (the *solera* level) holds the oldest vinegar; the top row holds the youngest. When the solera vinegar is ready for bottling, only a third of the vinegar from each barrel is drained and bottled, and then the void is filled with younger vinegar from the next row up, which is then replenished from the third row up, and so on. In this fashion, the younger vinegar picks up the characteristics of the older vinegar: complex, harmonious, deep, rich, nutty, slightly sweet, and very sharp.

Where to find it:

Look for sherry vinegar in gourmet shops and high-end supermarkets, as well as some large chain supermarkets. As this vinegar becomes more popular, it should begin to show up in smaller chain and independent markets. If you don't see it, ask the store manager about carrying it, and in the meantime, see p. 76 for a mail-order source.

see p. 76 for a mail-order source.

When buying sherry vinegar, look on the label for the symbol shown at right to verify that the vinegar was produced by registered bodegas (cellars) in the Jerez denomination of origin. There are two types of sherry vinegar: *vinagre de Jerez,* which is aged at least six months, and *vinagre de Jerez reserva,* which must be aged for at least two years but is often aged much longer, sometimes as many as 30 years.

How to use it:

Use sherry vinegar as you would any other wine vinegar. Add a splash to sautéed vegetables, soups (particularly gazpacho), stews, and sauces to brighten them and give them that certain something. Use it in a marinade or vinaigrette (like the one below), try it in a homemade mayonnaise, or turn it into a brine for pickling vegetables.

Honey-Mustard Sherry Vinaigrette

Yields about ¼ cup dressing, enough to dress a salad for four people; recipe may be doubled.

This subtly sweet vinaigrette is terrific with any combination of salad greens and vegetables, but I especially like it on a very simple salad of Boston lettuce and toasted sliced almonds.

4 tsp. sherry vinegar; more to taste
1 tsp. honey
½ tsp. Dijon mustard
¼ tsp. finely chopped fresh thyme (optional)
⅛ tsp. kosher salt
Pinch freshly ground black pepper
3 Tbs. extra-virgin olive oil

In a small bowl, whisk together the vinegar, honey, mustard, thyme (if using), salt, and pepper. Slowly add the olive oil, whisking constantly and vigorously as you go.

Alternatively, combine all the ingredients in a small jar, such as an empty mustard jar, close the lid tightly, and shake like crazy until well combined.

Taste and add a little more vinegar if you prefer a sharper vinaigrette.

A cremini one day, a portabella the next

You might be surprised to learn that creminis and portabellas are the same variety of mushroom—they look pretty different, after all. The cremini is actually an immature portabella, and that's why creminis are sometimes marketed as "baby bellas." It takes only two or three days for a cremini to blossom into a portabella.

Although they're botanically the same, they don't have the same flavor. The cremini tastes like a more flavorful version of its cousin, the white button, and the two can be used interchangeably. The portabella has a deeper, more robust flavor and a meaty texture.

A better way to grease a Bundt pan

Fancy fluted tube pans, popularly called Bundt pans, turn out gorgeous cakes—as long as the cake doesn't stick to the pan, that is. To make sure your Bundt cakes never stick, try greasing the pan with melted butter and a pastry brush instead of softened butter. The pastry brush lets you get the butter down into the crevices of the pan. Softened butter, on the other hand, tends to coat these pans unevenly—thickly in some spots and missing others entirely. For extra anti-stick insurance, flour the pan after buttering it.

Chopping sticky stuff

Crystallized ginger and dried fruit like apricots and figs can be frustrating to chop—as soon as you cut into these sticky-on-the-inside ingredients, they tend to mass together and cling to your knife like glue. Here are a few tips to make the chopping go more smoothly:

Make your knife nonstick. Coat the knife with a light film of vegetable oil or cooking spray.

Chop only small amounts at a time. Things will be less likely to clump together.

Dice rather than chop. Cut the ingredient lengthwise into thin strips and then cut across the strips into fine dice—you'll get less clumping and sticking than if you chop willy-nilly.

Trust your senses

In the *Fine Cooking* test kitchen, one of our main goals is to pack our recipes with as much detail as we can to help you get the same results we do. The catch is that everyone has different stoves and ovens and cookware—and ingredients differ, too. That's why, in addition to giving cooking times, almost every step in our recipes has a sensory clue that tells you what should happen. So when you follow one of our recipes, treat the time ranges as an estimate and pay more attention to phrases like "toast the spices until the seeds pop" or "simmer until the potatoes are tender."

Trust your instincts, too. If a recipe says to cook something over medium-high heat until golden brown, but the food seems to be burning rather than browning, your stove is probably hotter than ours or your cookware isn't as heavy-duty. Go ahead and follow your instinct to turn down the heat a bit. ◆

Rating Prepared Basil Pesto

BY LAURA GIANNATEMPO

Although fresh basil is in short supply at this time of year, I still crave the vibrant flavors of homemade pesto once in a while. So what's a pesto lover to do? It's tempting to reach for a container of prepared pesto. But is it any good? To find out, we invited 10 *Fine Cooking* staffers to a blind tasting of widely available prepared pestos, both in jars and in small tubs (these are found in the refrigerated section of supermarkets).

One thing was immediately clear: We didn't like any of the jarred pestos and wouldn't recommend using them. Most tasted overly acidic and processed, and many contained citric acid and other added preservatives. And the basil was, well—where *was* the basil? Instead of its bright, fresh flavor, we got a lot of brininess, too much salt, or too much cheese.

The fresher varieties we tasted (ranked here) fared much better. Overall, they had a creamier texture and a sweeter, more pleasant flavor than the jarred pestos. In a pinch, we'd toss them with pasta or add them to a dressing on a busy weeknight. But even these weren't in the same league as the homemade stuff. Capturing those bright summer flavors is harder than we thought. ◆

Top pick

TRADER JOE'S
$2.99 (7 ounces)

Trader Joe's pesto, labeled Trader Giotto, was our hands-down favorite. We found that its bright, sweet basil flavor with a good balance of garlic, cheese, and nuts came the closest to homemade. Some tasters weren't crazy about its chunky texture, with big pieces of pine nuts and garlic floating in oil, but overall, it was the best of the bunch.

Runners-up Fresh pestos are numbered in order of preference; prices will vary.

2
CIBO NATURALS
$5.99 (6 ounces)

This pesto (available at Whole Foods and other select grocery stores) had an appealing creamy texture and a decent fresh basil flavor. It did have a shortcoming, though: a slightly bitter aftertaste, which grew more pronounced with every bite.

3
BUITONI
$3.79 (7 ounces)

Tasters were divided on Buitoni's widely available pesto: Some liked its smooth, paste-like texture and pleasantly pungent flavor. Others thought it was too gummy, a bit salty, and heavy on the cheese.

4
BEAR POND FARM
$6.19 (6.3 ounces)

This herby pesto made with organic basil was a tad too garlicky for most tasters. It also contained oregano, which muddied the basil flavor a bit. We didn't love its dense, pasty texture, but we thought it might work tossed with pasta and diluted with a little cooking water. (Bear Pond Farm is available only in the Northeast and in some midwestern cities.)

We also tasted Amore's tubed pesto and the following jarred pestos (in alphabetical order): Alessi, Bertolli, Candoni, Classico, DeCecco, Racconto, Roland, Saclà.

Statement of Ownership, Management, and Circulation

1. Publication title: *Fine Cooking*. **2.** Publication no. 1072-5121. **3.** Filing date: September 29, 2006. **4.** Issue frequency: Bimonthly. **5.** No. of issues published annually: 7. **6.** Annual subscription price: $29.95. **7.** Complete mailing address of known office of publication: 63 S. Main St., PO Box 5506, Newtown, Fairfield County, CT 06470-5506. **8.** Complete mailing address of headquarters or general business office of publisher: 63 S. Main St., PO Box 5506, Newtown, CT 06470-5506. **9.** Publisher: Maria Taylor, address same as 8. Editor: Susie Middleton, address same as 8. Managing Editor: Sarah Jay, address same as 8. **10.** Owner: The Taunton Press, Inc., address same as 8. Stockholders owning or holding 1% or more of total amount of stock: Taunton, Inc., address same as 8. **11.** Known bondholders, mortgagees, and other security holders: None. **12.** Not applicable. **13.** Publication title: *Fine Cooking*. **14.** Issue date for circulation data below: August/September 2006. **15.** Extent and nature of circulation:

	Average number copies of each issue during preceding 12 months	Actual number copies of single issue published nearest to filing date
A. Total number copies (net press run)	446,842	448,382
B. Paid and/or requested circulation		
1. Mail subscriptions	135,332	138,376
2. Paid in-county subscriptions	0	0
3. Sales through dealers and carriers, street vendors, and counter sales	99,876	106,620
4. Other classes mailed through USPS	0	0
C. Total paid and/or requested circulation	235,208	244,996
D. Free distribution by mail (samples, complimentary, other free copies)		
1. Outside-county	6,774	9,605
2. In-county	0	0
3. Other classes mailed through USPS	0	0
E. Free distribution outside the mail	16,118	7,088
F. Total free distribution	22,892	16,693
G. Total distribution	258,100	261,689
H. Copies not distributed	188,742	186,693
I. Total (sum of 15G, 15H)	446,842	448,382
Percent paid and/or requested circulation	91.1%	93.6%

16. This statement of ownership will be printed in the January 2007 issue of this publication. **17.** I certify that all information on this form is true and complete. I understand that anyone who furnishes false or misleading information on this form or who omits material or information requested on the form may be subject to criminal sanctions (including fines and imprisonment) and/or civil sanctions (including multiple damages and civil penalties). Signature: Maria Taylor, Publisher.

Roast Chicken, *p. 38*
Roasting two chickens requires a large, heavy-duty roasting pan. A few that we like are KitchenAid's ($149 at ShopKitchenAid.com; 800-541-6390), Mauviel Cook Style's ($199.95 at Cooking.com; 800-663-8810), and Viking's ($274.95 at ChefsResource.com; 866-765-2433).

You'll also need a large roasting rack that will hold both birds. If you don't have one, try Calphalon's large rack (15x10½ inches) for $12.63 at Amazon.com.

Jalousie Pastry, *p. 55*
A giant spatula makes it easier to move the puff pastry rectangles from the countertop to the baking sheet. Look for one at BakersCatalogue.com (800-827-6836), where they're $19.95. Vanilla beans are usually available in supermarkets, but if you'd like to mail order them, visit Penzeys.com (800-741-7787); prices start at $6.29 for three beans.

Indian Vegetable Stir-Fries, *p. 46*
Most of the spices that Suvir Saran recommends are available in well-stocked supermarkets. However, if you're looking for dried or fresh fenugreek or curry leaves, you may need to visit or order from an Indian grocery. Suvir's favorite mail-order source for these items is Foods of India (212-683-4419). You'll also find dried and fresh fenugreek and dried curry leaves at Kalustyans.com (800-352-3451). Suvir likes to use Emile Henry's 3.25-quart black flameproof ceramic brazier pan for these stir-fries ($124.95 at Cooking.com).

Artisan Foods, *p. 24*
To order the sea-salt caramels from Little Flower Candy Company or for more information, visit LittleFlowerCandyCo.com or call 323-551-5948.

Meat Ragùs, *p. 58*
A 7- to 8-quart Dutch oven is ideal for the meat ragùs. We like Staub and Le Creuset brands, both available at ChefsResource.com (866-765-2433). Look for San Marzano canned tomatoes in some supermarkets, specialty shops, or for $4.50 per 28-ounce can at CyberCucina.com (800-796-0116).

Pound Cake, *p. 66*
You'll find an assortment of 12-cup Bundt pans (also known as "bundform" pans) at both Nordicware.com (877-466-7342) and KaiserBakeware.com (800-966-3009).

From Our Test Kitchen, *p. 70*
Look for good-quality sherry vinegar in a range of prices at Zingermans.com (888-636-8162) or Tienda.com (800-710-4304). Despaña Brand Foods carries three brands at their stores in Jackson Heights, Queens, New York (718-779-4971) and in Soho, New York (212-219-5050).

For information on fenugreek and curry leaves, see the source under Indian Vegetable Stir-Fries at left.

Tasting Party, *p. 50*

Dina Cheney recommends the following products
for a tasting party:

Extra-virgin olive oil

❖ 34° New Zealand reserve
extra-virgin olive oil, 375 ml for
$26.51 at 1800gourmet.com
(800-468-7638).

❖ Lucini Premium extra-virgin
olive oil is available in supermarkets (500 ml bottle for
$11.99 to $14.99), or for other
sources, visit Lucini.com
(888-558-2464).

❖ McEvoy Ranch extra-virgin
olive oil, 375 ml for $20 at
McEvoyRanch.com
(866-617-6779).

❖ Nicholas Alziari extra-virgin
olive oil, 1 liter for $36.99 at
Citarella.com (212-874-0383).

❖ Olave extra-virgin olive oil,
500 ml for $25 at Zingermans.
com (888-636- 8162).

❖ Terra Medi extra-virgin olive oil,
17 oz. for $12.95 at CrateAnd
Barrel.com (800-967-6696).

You'll find more olive oils at
Igourmet.com (877-446-8763),
DeanAndDeluca.com (800-221-
7714), and ChefShop.com.

Cheddar cheese

❖ Cabot Private Stock Cheddar,
8 ounces for $4.75 at Shop
Cabot.com (888-792-2268). It's
also available in supermarkets.

❖ Fiscalini Bandaged Cheddar,
1 pound for $18 to $24 at
FiscaliniCheese.com
(800-610-3276).

❖ Grafton Village 2-year
Extra-Aged Cheddar,
two 1-pound bricks for $17
at GraftonVillageCheese.com
(800-472-3866).

❖ Keen's Cheddar, 1 pound for
$24.99 at DiBruno.com
(888-322-4337).

❖ Montgomery's Cheddar,
1 pound for $30.50 at
ArtisanalCheese.com
(877-797-1200).

❖ Tillamook Sharp Cheddar is
available in supermarkets;
for a source near you, visit
TillamookCheese.com.

For more cheese sources,
try MurraysCheese.com
(888-692-4339) and
Cheese.com.

Dark chocolate

❖ **Ghirardelli** 100% cacao unsweetened baking bars are available in supermarkets; for more
information on store locations,
visit Ghirardelli.com.

❖ **Rapunzel** 85% organic semisweet chocolate, $3.69 per bar
at EFoodPantry.com
(866-372-6879).

❖ **Santander** 53% semisweet
chocolate, $1.80 per bar, and
Scharffen Berger 70% bittersweet chocolate, $4.15 per bar,
at Chocosphere.com
(877-992-4626).

❖ **Chocolove** 55% pure dark
chocolate, $2.99 per bar,
and **Valrhona** 85% dark
chocolate, $4.49 per bar, at
WorldwideChocolate.com
(800-664-9410).

ChocolateSource.com
(800-214-4926) also has
a vast selection of good-quality
chocolates. ◆

advertiser**shopping**guide A directory of our advertisers' products and services

Appliances

Art Culinaire *p.81* Lacanche professional ranges, handcrafted in France.
800-570-CHEF
www.frenchranges.com

Chef's Choice *p.15* Woo 'em with waffles! Prepare the world's most delicious waffles in 90 seconds! The Chef's Choice® unique Quad® baking system lets you choose the ideal flavor, texture, and color.
800-342-3255
www.chefschoice.com

Earthstone Wood-Fire Ovens *p.81* Wood-fired brick ovens for indoor and outdoor use. Can double as a fireplace. Great for baking, grilling, and roasting.
800-840-4915
www.earthstoneovens.com

Bakeware

A Cook's Wares *p.11* We have what you need for your kitchen: The finest cookware, bakeware, cutlery, utensils and small appliances. Since 1981.
800-915-9788
www.cookswares.com

Emile Henry *p.15* Beautiful, scratch-proof, naturally nonstick, and easy to clean. French-made Emile Henry® ovenware and bakeware heats evenly for perfect cooking. It does more, so you do less.™
www.emilehenry.com

House on the Hill *p.81* Over 400 molds for springerle, speculaas, gingerbread, marzipan, fondant and cake decorating. Order now for holiday cookie baking. Catalog on request.
www.houseonthehill.net

LaPrima Shops *p.11* LaPrimaShops.com is your on-line source for the finest products from Bialetti Cookware, Espresso and Cappuccino Makers to over 90 of SiliconeZone's Bakeware and Kitchen tools.
www.laprimashops.com

Lekue *p.7* Since 1957, Harold Import Company has been a leading supplier of kitchenware products to the specialty retail trade, offering almost 3000 items. Our products are available in thousands of stores worldwide. What can HIC offer your business?
www.lekueusa.com

Nordic Ware *p.17* Nordic Ware is America's favorite manufacturer of bakeware, cookware, and kitchenware. Our famous Bundt® pans are found in well-equipped kitchens all around the world.
www.nordicware.com

The Pepper Mill *p.81* The world's first kosher gourmet kitchenware store, with brand-name cookware and bakeware, kosher gourmet foods and baking ingredients.
866-871-4022
www.thepeppermillinc.com

Pillivuyt USA, Inc. *p.3* Over 400 porcelain items for cooking and serving. Virtually nonstick with easy-to-clean impenetrable glaze. Durable, versatile, and a joy to use.
www.pillivuytus.com

Silicone Zone *p.23* SiliconeZone, offering nonstick, high-temperature silicone bakeware, kitchen tools, and gadgets. SiliconeZone bakeware can go from 58°F to 500°F, from freezer to oven.
212-997-9591
www.siliconezoneusa.com

Silpat by Demarle *p.25* Makers of Silpat®, the original nonstick baking sheet, used by professional chefs and bakers around the world. Silpat: It's not just for cookies!
www.demarleusa.com

Books

Cookbook Publishers *p.80* Custom community fundraising cookbooks. Free kit.
800-227-7282
www.cookbookpublishers.com

Edward Hamilton Bookseller *p.13* Shop America's largest Bargain Book catalog. Save up to 80%! Thousands of titles in each catalog: cookbooks, fashion, gardening, 67 subject areas. Free catalog.
www.erhbooks.com/gmg

The Good Cook *p.18a* The Good Cook: We carry books for every cook. Remember, behind every great meal there is a great cookbook!
www.jointhegoodcook.com

Morris Press Cookbooks *p.80* Proven fundraisers for your church, school, or organization.
800-445-6621, 9706
www.morriscookbooks.com

Cookware

Beyond Pots and Pans *p.81* For the finest in culinary supplies. We also offer cooking classes. Call for more information.
www.BeyondPotsAndPans.com

Chefsresource.com *p.3, 33* Serious tools for serious chefs! The Chef's Resource offers the highest-quality hand-picked items for the serious home chef.
www.chefsresource.com

DeBuyer Industries *p.23* French manufacturer since 1830, de Buyer offers professional high-quality cooking and pastry utensils for lovers of flavor and gastronomy.
www.debuyer.com

Falk Culinair *p.25* Fine cookware for fine cooks. Stainless lined, solid copper cookware from Belgium. No other cookware conducts heat more efficiently or evenly than Falk.
www.copperpans.com

Kuhn-Rikon Corporation *p.75* Kuhn Rikon offers the finest in pressure cookers, specialty cookware, and distinctive kitchen tools to make a cook's life easier.
800-924-4699
www.kuhnrikon.com/fine

Scanpan USA, Inc. *p.19* Scanpan USA, Inc. is the importer and wholesaler of Scanpan cookware in the U.S. For details on products, technology, pricing, and retail sources, please visit our web site.
www.scanpan.com

Swiss Diamond Cookware *p.13* Swiss manufacturer of patented diamond reinforced non-stick cookware, up to 200,000 real diamonds per pan. Diamonds guarantees lifetime non-stick performance, oven, dishwasher, metal utensil safe.
www.swissdiamondusa.com

The Water Broiler Pan *p.80* Drannan Cookware Inventive Stainless Water-Broiler® - WaterRoaster™ Pan surprisingly eliminates smoke, splatter, flare-ups, and scrubbing. "Works wonderfully." (Pierre Franey, NY Times). "I love it." (Retired Chef).
www.waterbroiler.com

Cutlery

Japanese Chefs Knife *p.81* Top-brand Japanese chef's knives.
www.japanesechefsknife.com

Just Knives101 *p.11* At JustKnives.com, we stock it, ship it, and guarantee it for life. Featuring Global, Henckels, Kai Shun, and specialty Asian imports.
www.JustKnives101.com

Norton Professional Sharpening Solutions *p.3* Norton, the leading worldwide manufacturer of professional culinary sharpening stones for over a century, offers cutlery sharpening kits for home cooks that are easy to use and store.
800-848-7379
www.nortonstones.com

Gourmet Foods

Avocado of the Month Club *p.81* Your online source for delicious, premium avocados delivered straight to your front door.
805-277-7452
www.aotmc.com

Divine Delights *p.25* Your premium source for artisan petits fours. Delightful holiday assortments of hand-decorated bite sized cakes and confections. Shipped fresh nationwide.
www.divinedelights.com

La Tienda.com *p.81* Quality Spanish food selected by a dedicated family.
888-472-1022
www.latienda.com

Ladd Hill Orchards *p.81* Premium, Oregon-grown fresh or dried chestnuts and chestnut flour. Certified organic by guaranteed organic certification agency.
www.laddhillchestnuts.com

Magic Seasoning Blends *p.17* Chef Paul Prudhomme's all-natural magic seasoning blends, sauces and marinades, pepper sauce, smoked meats, cookbooks, gift packs, sweet potato pecan pie, and much more!
800-457-2857
www.chefpaul.com

Millie's Pierogi *p.80* Handmade pierogi, made fresh and shipped fresh to your door! Cabbage, potato-cheese, cheese, prune, or blueberry fillings.
www.milliespierogi.com

Paramount Caviar *p.11* Offering a large variety of domestic and imported caviar and gourmet gift items for the discriminating. Personal or Corporate gifts are accepted.
www.paramountcaviar.com

The Pepper Mill *p.81* The world's first kosher gourmet kitchenware store, with brand-name cookware and bakeware, kosher gourmet foods and baking ingredients.
866-871-4022
www.thepeppermillinc.com

Petaluma Coffee and Tea Co. *p.81* Since 1989, fair-trade coffees and gourmet teas.
800-929-JAVA
www.petalumacoffee.com

Sunnyland Farms *p.81* The widest selection of top-quality nuts, dried fruits and other specialty foods for creating delicacies at home, or for giving to friends.
www.sunnylandfarms.com

Trois Petits Cochons, Inc. *p.7* Artisanal charcuterie. By using all-natural, high-quality ingredients, and by crafting small, handmade batches, the excellent quality of our pates, terrines, and mousses is guaranteed.
www.3pigs.com

Upton Tea Imports *p.81* 380+ varieties of garden-fresh tea, plus accessories.
800-234-8327
www.uptontea.com

Ingredients

Bulk Foods *p.81* Offering a wide selection of spices, nuts, dried fruits, and other ingredients.
www.bulkfoods.com

Colavita USA *p.2* Extra-virgin olive oil unmatched for flavor and freshness, vinegars, pastas, and sauces. Colavita's authentic Italian products are available at food stores everywhere and visit our web site, where Fine Cooking readers receive a 10% discount with the code.
www.colavita.com

Magic Seasoning Blends *p.11* Chef Paul Prudhomme's all-natural magic seasoning blends, sauces and marinades, pepper sauce, smoked meats, cookbooks, gift packs, sweet potato pecan pie, and much more!
800-457-2857
www.chefpaul.com

Nestle Chocolatier *p.9* This baking chocolate is not kid stuff. Dark chocolate with 53% cacao for devoted spoon lickers. Bittersweet chocolate with 62% cacao for dedicated dessert fanatics. New Nestle Chocolatier baking chocolate. Rated R for Richness.
www.nestle-chocolatier.com

Rafal Spice Co. *p.81* Spices, herbs, teas, coffees, and food specialties.
800-228-4276
www.rafalspicecompany.com

San Francisco Herb Co. *p.81* Quality spices and herbs by the pound.
800-227-4530
www.sfherb.com

Sugarcraft, Inc. *p.81* Baking, cake decorating, candy, and cookie supplies.
www.sugarcraft.com

Kitchen Design & Tableware

The Bowl Mill *p.7* One-piece hardwood bowls made on 19th-century lathes in Vermont, ranging from 8" to 20" in diameter featuring maple, yellow birch, and cherry.
800-828-1005
www.bowlmill.com

Green River Stone Company *p.3* Green River Stone Company offers hand quarried 50 million years old fossil fish of exquisite quality and stunning detail for backsplashes, countertops and murals.
435-753-4069
www.greenriverstone.com

Plum Pudding Kitchen *p.25* Your online source for "irresistibly Italian" Vietri dinnerware, flatware, glassware, and much more. Let us help you set a special table!
888-940-7586
www.plumpuddingkitchen.com

Replacements, Ltd. *p.80* World's largest inventory: old and new china.
800-REPLACE
www.replacements.com

Kitchen Tools & Utensils

Bella Copper *p.81* The world's leading heat diffuser/defroster plate provides superior heat conduction for more even cooking and faster defrosting. Available in solid copper or pure silver. A gourmet kitchen essential.
805-215-3241
www.bellacopper.com

Beyond Pots and Pans *p.81* For the finest in culinary supplies. We also offer cooking classes. Call for more information.
www.BeyondPotsAndPans.com

Chefsresource.com *p.75* Serious tools for serious chefs! The Chef's Resource offers the highest-quality handpicked items for the serious home chef.
www.chefsresource.com

Component Design Northwest *p.7* CDN offers more than 60 different cooking thermometers and timers for the casual or gourmet chef. Find CDN products at gourmet specialty stores or online.
800-338-5594
www.cdn-timeandtemp.com

DeBuyer Industries *p.23* French manufacturer since 1830, de Buyer offers professional high-quality cooking and pastry utensils for lovers of flavor and gastronomy.
www.debuyer.com

House on the Hill *p.81* Over 400 molds for springerle, speculaas, gingerbread, marzipan, fondant and cake decorating. Order now for holiday cookie baking. Catalog on request.
www.houseonthehill.net

J.K. Adams Company *p.7* J.K. Adams, has been the premiere Vermont manufacturer of handcrafted, heirloom-quality, woodware for the kitchen and table since 1944.
www.jkadams.com

Kerekes *p.81* Your complete online source for professional chef tools, cookware, bakeware, and cake decorating supplies used by top chefs at the finest restaurants and kitchens.
www.bakedeco.com

Lekue *p.7* Since 1957, Harold Import Company has been a leading supplier of kitchenware products to the specialty retail trade, offering almost 3000 items. Our products are available in thousands of stores worldwide. What can HIC offer your business?
www.lekueusa.com

Let's Gel *p.11* STAND IN COMFORT! Let's Gel was started with one simple goal, to make the time you spend standing in your kitchen more comfortable.
866-GEL-MATS
www.letsgel.com

Silicone Zone *p.23* SiliconeZone, offering nonstick, high-temperature silicone bakeware, kitchen tools, and gadgets. SiliconeZone bakeware can go from 58°F to 500°F, from freezer to oven.
212-997-9591
www.siliconezoneusa.com

Silpat by Demarle *p.25* Makers of Silpat®, the original nonstick baking sheet, used by professional chefs and bakers around the world. Silpat: It's not just for cookies!
www.demarleusa.com

William Bounds, Ltd. *p.19* William Bounds Ltd.—known since 1963 for its high-quality pepper mills, salt mills, and spices—is now available online. Order today!
800-473-0504
www.wmboundsltd.com

Schools, Travel & Organizations

Culinary Business Academy *p.13* Extensive and comprehensive personal chef business knowledge and training from the world's recognized leader in the personal chef industry. Nobody offers what we offer.
800-747-2433
www.culinarybusiness.com

Institute of Culinary Education *p.80* NYC cooking classes, tours, tastings, and parties.
www.iceculinary.com

La Villa Bonita *p.75* La Villa Bonita offers a delicious immersion in the culinary joys of Mexico, with its culinary vacation packages in a 16th-century mansion in Cuernavaca.
800-505-3084
www.lavillabonita.com

Le Cordon Bleu *p.3* Master the culinary arts. Earn the Grand Diplome in approximately nine months. Three- to five-week intensive courses and online hospitality programs are also available.
800-457-2433
www.cordonbleu.net

Wines, Beverages & Accessories

International Wine Accessories *p.33* IWA is the ultimate source for Riedel and Spiegelau stemware and decanters, wine cellars, redwood racking, cooling units and much more! Call or log on to request our free catalog.
www.iwawine.com/fc

Monin Gourmet Flavorings *p.15* The world's largest and best-known producer of premium flavorings for beverage and culinary applications. Visit our website for more information or to place an order.
www.moninstore.com

Woodbridge Winery *p.83* For 25 years, we have aged our wines in small oak barrels and handcrafted each vintage. Woodbridge: Taste our small winery tradition™.
www.woodbridgewines.com

For direct links to all these advertiser websites in one place, please go to **finecooking.com/shopping**

cook's market

nutrition**information**

Recipe	Page	Calories		Protein	Carb	Fats (g)				Chol.	Sodium	Fiber	Notes
		total	from fat	(g)	(g)	total	sat	mono	poly	(mg)	(mg)	(g)	
Letters	10												
Tuscan Peasant Soup with Rosemary & Pancetta		370	160	17	37	18	4.5	10	2	20	1010	8	based on 8 servings
In Season	20												
Browned Cauliflower with Anchovies, Olives & Capers		340	210	23	9	24	4	15	3.5	55	2810	4	based on 4 servings
Roast Chicken	38												
Roast Chicken with Rosemary-Lemon Salt		570	310	59	0	35	12	13	7	205	1160	0	based on 8 servings
Coconut Rice with Chicken & Snow Peas		660	360	34	39	40	14	15	8	100	1300	3	based on 4 servings
Soft Chicken Tacos with the Works		510	250	29	40	28	7	15	4.5	75	1010	9	based on 6 servings
Lemony Chicken Caesar Salad with Garlic Toasts		490	310	20	26	35	8	20	4	60	750	2	based on 6 servings
Crispy Potatoes	44												
Crispy Smashed Roasted Potatoes		270	180	2	20	20	3	15	2	0	520	2	based on 4 servings
Indian Stir-Fries	46												
Cabbage & Carrot Stir-Fry with Toasted Cumin & Lime		80	45	2	10	5	0	3	1.5	0	510	3	based on 6 servings
Mushroom Stir-Fry with Onions & Tomatoes		140	70	5	16	8	0.5	4.5	2.5	0	390	4	based on 6 servings
Potato Stir-Fry with Mint & Cilantro		220	70	4	35	8	0.5	4.5	2.5	0	390	5	based on 6 servings
Green Bean Stir-Fry with Shredded Coconut		190	140	4	12	16	6	6	3	0	290	6	based on 6 servings
Jalousie Pastry	55												
Apple Brown-Butter Jalousie		250	120	3	30	13	5	6	1	25	190	1	based on 8 servings
Mixed-Berry Jalousie		190	80	3	24	9	2.5	4.5	1	15	170	2	based on 8 servings
Ragùs	58												
Neapolitan Rib & Sausage Ragù		350	230	16	9	26	7	15	2.5	50	530	2	per ½ cup serving
Short Rib & Porcini Mushroom Ragù		190	100	12	5	11	3	6	1	35	320	1	per ½ cup serving
Lamb Shank & Sweet Pepper Ragù		230	130	13	6	15	3.5	9	1.5	45	290	1	per ½ cup serving
Frittatas	62												
Frittata with Asparagus, Herbs & Scallions		130	70	10	5	7	2.5	2.5	1	285	390	1	based on 6 servings
Frittata with Kale, Onions & Chorizo		240	140	16	6	17	6	7	2	305	700	1	based on 6 servings
Frittata with Mushrooms, Leeks & Goat Cheese		190	100	14	8	11	5	3.5	1	295	450	1	based on 6 servings
Frittata with Potatoes, Onions & Pancetta		190	110	12	8	12	4	4.5	1.5	295	540	1	based on 6 servings
Frittata with Sausage, Mushrooms & Onions		200	120	14	6	13	5	4	1.5	300	560	1	based on 6 servings
Pound Cake	66												
Butter Pound Cake		310	140	3	37	16	10	4.5	1	105	130	0	based on 16 servings
Brandy & Rum Glazed Pound Cake		350	150	3	46	16	10	4.5	1	105	130	0	based on 16 servings
Lemon-Coconut Pound Cake		360	160	4	49	18	11	4.5	1	105	140	1	based on 16 servings
Chocolate Chip Pound Cake		340	160	4	41	18	11	4.5	1	105	130	1	based on 16 servings
Test Kitchen	70												
Honey-Mustard Sherry Vinaigrette		100	90	0	2	10	1.5	7	1	0	50	0	based on 4 servings
Quick & Delicious	82a												
Linguine with Shrimp & Chorizo		570	180	34	63	20	5	10	2.5	170	940	4	based on 6 servings
Curried Lentil Soup		330	100	19	43	11	6	3	1	25	320	14	based on 4 servings
Smoky Eggplant & White Bean Dip with Pita Crisps		270	130	7	31	15	2	9	3	0	430	8	based on 6 servings
Buttermilk Country Fried Chicken with Cucumber Salad		320	120	37	10	14	2	7	3.5	95	960	1	based on 2 servings
Steak, Egg & Blue Cheese Salad		600	420	37	7	48	12	28	4.5	285	1130	2	based on 4 servings
Seared Tuna with Fennel Seeds & Caper Brown Butter		600	290	72	2	33	16	10	5	220	400	1	based on 4 servings
Chinese Five-Spice-Crusted Duck Breasts		260	130	31	1	14	3.5	7	2	175	320	0	based on 4 servings
Back Cover													
Stir-Fried Cauliflower with Green Peas & Ginger		160	70	7	20	8	0.5	4	2.5	0	470	9	based on 6 servings

The nutritional analyses have been calculated by a registered dietitian at Nutritional Solutions in Melville, New York. When a recipe gives a choice of ingredients, the first choice is the one used in the calculations. Optional ingredients and those listed without a specific quantity are not included. When a range of ingredient amounts or servings is given, the smaller amount or portion is used. When the quantities of salt and pepper aren't specified, the analysis is based on ¼ teaspoon salt and ⅛ teaspoon pepper per serving for entrées, and ⅛ teaspoon salt and 1/16 teaspoon pepper per serving for side dishes.

Curried Lentil Soup

Yields about 1 quart;
serves four.

1 large clove garlic
1 piece (⅓ inch long) peeled
fresh ginger
½ small bulb fennel, cored
and cut into large chunks,
or 1 small rib celery, cut
into large chunks
1 small carrot, peeled and cut
into large chunks
1 small parsnip, peeled and
cut into large chunks
1 large shallot, cut in half
3 Tbs. unsalted butter
2 tsp. curry powder
1 cup brown lentils, picked
over and rinsed
1 qt. homemade or low-
salt canned chicken or
vegetable broth
¼ tsp. kosher salt; more as
needed
¼ tsp. freshly ground black
pepper; more as needed

Pulse the garlic and ginger
in a food processor until
chopped. Add the fennel or
celery, carrot, parsnip, and
shallot and pulse until
coarsely chopped.

Melt 2 Tbs. of the butter
in a 4-qt. saucepan over
medium-high heat. Add the
chopped vegetables and

cook, stirring, until softened,
about 3 minutes. Add the
curry powder and cook, stirring, until the curry powder is
fragrant, about 30 seconds.
Add the lentils, broth, salt,
and pepper. Bring the soup
to a boil over high heat,
reduce the heat to maintain
a brisk simmer, cover, and
cook until the lentils are
tender, 25 to 30 minutes.

Transfer 1½ cups of the
soup to a blender or a food
processor and purée until
smooth. Stir the purée back
into the soup along with the
remaining 1 Tbs. butter. Season to taste with salt and
pepper, and adjust the consistency with water, if you like.

Serving suggestion:

Garnish with a dollop of
plain whole-milk yogurt
and chopped fresh mint
or cilantro, or both.

Smoky Eggplant & White Bean Dip with Pita Crisps

Yields 1½ cups dip; serves
four to six.

5 Tbs. extra-virgin olive oil;
more for the pan
1½ lb. small eggplant (2 to 3
small), trimmed and cut in
half lengthwise
¾ tsp. plus a generous pinch
kosher salt
¼ tsp. freshly ground black
pepper
2 anchovy fillets (optional)
1 small clove garlic
1 cup canned cannellini
beans, drained and rinsed
3 pitas (preferably pocketless),
each cut into eight wedges
2 Tbs. fresh lemon juice;
more to taste
1 Tbs. chopped fresh mint,
plus 1 Tbs. small leaves
for garnish
2 tsp. chopped fresh oregano
2 Tbs. pine nuts, toasted

Position a rack 4 inches from
the broiler element and heat
the broiler to high. Line a
rimmed baking sheet with foil
and grease lightly with oil.
Rub the eggplant all over with
2 Tbs. of the oil and sprinkle
the flesh side with ½ tsp. of the
salt and the ¼ tsp. pepper.
Arrange the eggplant, flesh
side down, on the baking sheet
and broil until the skin is charred
and the eggplant flesh is very
tender, 20 to 30 minutes.

Meanwhile, if using anchovies, mash them into a paste

with the side of a chef's knife.
Roughly chop the garlic, sprinkle it with a generous pinch of
kosher salt, and mash it into a
paste with the side of a chef's
knife. Transfer the anchovy
and garlic pastes to a food
processor and add the beans,
2 Tbs. of the oil, and 1 Tbs.
water. Purée until smooth.

When the eggplant is done,
set it aside to cool briefly.
Meanwhile, in a medium bowl,
toss the pita wedges with the
remaining 1 Tbs. oil and ¼ tsp.
salt. Arrange in a single layer
on a baking sheet. Lower the
rack so it's 6 inches from the
broiler. Broil the pita wedges
until golden brown on both
sides, 1 to 2 minutes per side.

Scrape the eggplant flesh
from the skin and add the
flesh to the puréed beans in
the food processor, along
with the lemon juice, chopped
mint, and oregano. Pulse
briefly to form a chunky dip.
Adjust the seasoning with
more salt, pepper, or lemon
juice to taste. Serve sprinkled
with the pine nuts and mint
leaves, with the toasted pita
crisps on the side for dipping.

Serving suggestion:

This is also great with
crudités, especially bell
peppers and fennel.

Buttermilk Country Fried Chicken with Cucumber Salad

Serves two.

¼ cup halved and very thinly sliced red onion
1 very small clove garlic
Kosher salt
1 Tbs. canola or vegetable oil, plus 1 to 1¼ cups for frying
¾ cup plus 2 Tbs. buttermilk
1½ tsp. fresh lemon juice
1 Tbs. chopped fresh dill
Freshly ground black pepper
½ English cucumber, halved lengthwise, seeded, and thinly sliced crosswise (about 1 heaping cup sliced)
¾ cup all-purpose flour
2 boneless, skinless chicken breast halves (about ¾ lb. total), pounded to an even thickness (about ½ inch thick)

Put the onion in a small bowl, cover it with very hot water, and let it sit for 15 minutes. Roughly chop the garlic, sprinkle it with a generous pinch of salt, and mash it into a paste with the side of a chef's knife. In a medium bowl, whisk the mashed garlic, 1 Tbs. oil, 2 Tbs. buttermilk, the lemon juice, dill, ¼ tsp. salt, and a few grinds of pepper. Toss the cucumber in the bowl with the dressing. Drain the onion, toss it with the cucumber

salad, and let sit to allow the flavors to meld.

Put the flour in a shallow bowl and, in another shallow bowl, mix the remaining ¾ cup buttermilk with 1 tsp. salt. Season the chicken with ¾ tsp. salt and ¼ tsp. pepper. Dip the chicken in the buttermilk and then dredge it in the flour. (You can let the chicken sit in the flour while the oil heats; gently shake off excess flour before cooking.)

Choose a skillet (preferably cast iron) that's large enough to fit the chicken. Pour in oil to a depth of ¼ inch (about 1 cup for a 10-inch skillet or 1¼ cups for an 11-inch skillet). Heat over medium-high heat. When the oil is shimmering and the chicken sizzles briskly when a corner is dipped in the oil, cook the chicken until golden brown on both sides, 2 to 3 minutes per side. Transfer the chicken to paper towels and pat lightly to absorb excess oil. Sprinkle the chicken with a pinch of salt and serve it with the cucumber salad.

Steak, Egg & Blue Cheese Salad

Serves four.

1 small clove garlic
Kosher salt
3 Tbs. red-wine vinegar
1½ tsp. Dijon mustard
½ cup plus 1 Tbs. extra-virgin olive oil
Freshly ground black pepper
1 lb. beef sirloin steak tips
2 heads Boston lettuce, washed, spun dry, and torn into bite-size pieces (about 6 cups loosely packed)
4 medium- or hard-cooked eggs (see p. 71), peeled and quartered lengthwise
¾ cup crumbled blue cheese (about 4 oz.)
1 medium carrot, peeled and very thinly sliced crosswise
6 medium red radishes, thinly sliced
¼ cup 1-inch-long sliced fresh chives

Roughly chop the garlic, sprinkle it with the generous pinch of salt, and mash it into a paste with the side of a chef's knife. Transfer the garlic to a small bowl and whisk in the vinegar and mustard. Whisk in the ½ cup oil in a thin, steady stream. Season the vinaigrette to taste with salt and pepper. Drizzle the sirloin tips with 2 Tbs. of the vinaigrette and let sit while preparing the other salad ingredients. Reserve the remaining vinaigrette for dressing the salad.

Season the meat all over with 1 tsp. salt and ½ tsp. pepper. Heat the remaining 1 Tbs. oil in a 10-inch skillet (preferably cast iron), over high heat. When the oil is shimmering hot, add the meat and sear on both sides until cooked to your liking, about 3 minutes per side for medium rare. Let the meat rest briefly on a cutting board while assembling the salad.

Put the lettuce in a large serving bowl. Whisk the vinaigrette and toss the lettuce with just enough of the vinaigrette to coat. Slice the sirloin tips on the diagonal into ½-inch-thick medallions. Scatter the meat (and any accumulated juices), eggs, cheese, carrot, radishes, and chives on top of the lettuce. Drizzle the toppings with some of the remaining vinaigrette to taste (you may not need it all) and toss gently at the table. Serve any remaining vinaigrette on the side.

Note: If you're willing to brave the elements, this steak is also delicious cooked on the grill.

Tip: If you have a mandoline, use it to cut the carrots and radishes into very thin slices.

Seared Tuna with Fennel Seeds & Caper Brown Butter

Serves four.

- 1½ Tbs. fresh lemon juice
- 1 Tbs. capers, drained, coarsely chopped if large
- 6 Tbs. unsalted butter, cut into six pieces
- ¼ cup heavy cream
- 4 1-inch-thick tuna steaks (6 to 8 oz. each)
- 1 Tbs. fennel seeds, crushed
- ¾ tsp. kosher salt
- ½ tsp. freshly ground black pepper
- 2 Tbs. vegetable oil

Put the lemon juice and capers in a 1-qt. heatproof measuring cup. Bring the butter and cream to a brisk simmer in a small saucepan over medium heat, whisking often. The mixture will look homogenous at first and then will separate and begin to turn golden brown. Continue to whisk until it turns a dark rust color, about 10 minutes total. Carefully pour the brown butter mixture into the lemon juice; the butter will boil up and sputter. Whisk to combine and return to the saucepan, off the heat.

Sprinkle the tuna on both sides with the fennel seeds, salt, and pepper. Heat the oil in a 10- to 12-inch heavy skillet (preferably cast iron) over medium-high heat until shimmering hot. Sear the tuna on both sides until done to your liking, about 2 minutes per side for medium rare (still raw in the middle) or 3 minutes per side for medium (just pink in the middle). Transfer the tuna to plates. If necessary, quickly reheat the sauce. Serve the tuna drizzled with the sauce.

Serving suggestion:

This tuna is delicious sprinkled with fresh parsley, and it pairs well with roasted fennel.

Chinese Five-Spice-Crusted Duck Breasts

Serves four.

- 4 boneless duck breast halves with skin (2 to 2½ lb.)
- 1½ tsp. Chinese five-spice powder
- ¾ tsp. kosher salt
- ¼ tsp. freshly ground black pepper

Trim the visible fat and silverskin from the flesh side of the duck. If the tenderloins are still on the breasts, leave them on. Don't trim the skin side; simply score the duck skin in a crosshatch pattern to allow the fat to cook out. Mix the five-spice powder with the salt and pepper in a small bowl. Gently rub the duck all over with the mixture.

Heat a 12-inch skillet over medium-low heat and put the duck, skin side down, in the skillet. Slowly render the fat from the skin without moving the duck breasts. After 15 minutes, tilt the pan and carefully spoon off as much fat as possible. Cook until the skin is dark golden brown and crisp, about 25 minutes total.

Flip the breasts with a metal spatula (carefully loosen the skin if it's stuck to the pan). Increase the heat to medium and finish cooking the duck until the second side is golden and the duck is done to your liking, another 3 to 7 minutes, depending on thickness. (An instant-read thermometer should register 135°F for medium doneness, which will still be pink and juicy.)

Transfer the duck breasts to a cutting board and let rest, skin side up, for about 5 minutes before serving either whole or sliced on an angle into medallions.

Serving suggestion:

This duck goes nicely with a wild rice pilaf with toasted almonds and sautéed Asian greens seasoned with a touch of sesame oil.

Allison Ehri is Fine Cooking's test kitchen associate and food stylist. ◆

BY ALLISON EHRI

I keep an eclectic assortment of easy recipes tucked up my sleeve so that I can cook up something delicious for anyone who drops by, be it my vegetarian friends or my meat-and-potatoes father. These dishes are versatile: fast enough to pull together on a weeknight but special enough to serve for a planned—or improvised—dinner party. To put some of these dishes together into an entertaining menu, try serving the eggplant and white bean dip as an appetizer, the curried lentil soup as a starter, and the tuna or the duck as an entrée.

cover recipe

Linguine with Shrimp & Chorizo

Serves four to six.

Kosher salt
2 Tbs. extra-virgin olive oil; more as needed
6 oz. chorizo, sliced ⅛ inch thick (1⅓ cups)
1 lb. large shrimp (31 to 40 count), peeled and deveined
1 small onion, finely diced
4 medium cloves garlic, thinly sliced
1 26-oz. box Pomi brand chopped tomatoes (or 2 14-oz. cans petite-cut diced tomatoes)
¼ to ½ tsp. crushed red pepper flakes
1 lb. dried thin linguine
¼ cup roughly chopped fresh flat-leaf parsley

Bring a pot of generously salted water to a boil. Heat the olive oil in a 12-inch skillet over medium-high heat. Cook the chorizo, stirring occasionally, until browned, 2 to 3 minutes. Add the shrimp and cook, stirring occasionally, until it curls up and just begins to turn pink, about 2 minutes; don't cook it through. Off the heat, use a slotted spoon to transfer the chorizo and shrimp to a bowl.

Pour off all but 2 Tbs. of the fat from the skillet (or add more oil so you have 2 Tbs. fat in the pan) and set the skillet over medium heat. Add the onion and garlic and cook until softened, about 3 minutes. Stir in the tomatoes with their juices and the pepper flakes, scraping the bottom of the pan, and simmer briskly for 5 minutes to blend the flavors.

Meanwhile, cook the linguine in the boiling water until barely al dente, 4 to 6 minutes. Reserve ½ cup of the pasta water and drain the pasta in a colander.

Add the shrimp and chorizo to the sauce and simmer until the shrimp is just cooked through, another 1 to 2 minutes. Season the sauce to taste with salt. Toss the pasta, sauce, and parsley in the pasta pot over medium-low heat for 2 minutes. The sauce should just coat the pasta; add some of the pasta water to moisten if necessary. Drizzle each serving with a little oil.

"**Growing grapes is like any marriage.
The more you give, the more you get.**"

– Stanton Lange, grower, Woodbridge Winery

www.woodbridgewines.com

When Robert Mondavi founded Woodbridge Winery twenty-five years ago, he knew great grapes don't grow all by themselves. You need the right land, the perfect climate, and a whole lot of love. That's why we care for our vineyards with small winery techniques, and you can taste it in our crisp, delicious Chardonnay. (As you can tell, I get a little wrapped up in my work.)

WOODBRIDGE
BY ROBERT MONDAVI

TASTE OUR SMALL WINERY TRADITION.™

An Indian twist on a cauliflower sauté

Sometimes a little spice is all you need to liven up weeknight side dishes. Ginger and chiles give this quick stir-fry a jolt of heat, making it great paired with plain yogurt, alongside roasted chicken or pan-seared lamb chops.

Some like it hot (and some maybe not)

You can dial down the heat in this dish in two ways: by omitting the spicy dried red chiles entirely and by removing the ribs and seeds from the jalapeño. Use a small spoon to scoop out both seeds and ribs in one quick swipe and give the chile a quick rinse before chopping it.

For more Indian vegetable stir-fry recipes, turn to p. 46.

Stir-Fried Cauliflower with Green Peas & Ginger
Serves six.

Freshly ground coriander seeds have a beautiful citrusy essence and really make a difference in this dish. Grind the whole seeds in a spice grinder or mortar and pestle right before cooking. Pre-ground coriander works here but will be far less aromatic, especially if it's more than a few months old.

3 Tbs. canola oil
¼ cup dried fenugreek leaves or ½ cup fresh fenugreek leaves, chopped (optional); see From Our Test Kitchen, p. 70
1 to 3 small dried whole red chiles (optional)
1 Tbs. ground coriander, preferably freshly ground
1 tsp. cumin seeds
3 Tbs. minced fresh ginger
1 medium jalapeño (seeds and ribs removed if you prefer a milder flavor), finely chopped
2½- to 3-lb. head cauliflower, cored and cut into medium florets 1 to 1½ inches wide and 1½ inches long (6 to 8 heaping cups)
2 cups (about 10 oz.) frozen green peas (do not thaw)
2 tsp. kosher salt; more to taste
¼ tsp. homemade or store-bought garam masala (optional); see p. 70

Heat the oil with the fenugreek leaves, chiles (if using), coriander, and cumin seeds in a large wok or 12-inch skillet over medium-high heat. Cook, stirring occasionally, until the cumin browns and becomes fragrant, 2 to 3 minutes. Add the ginger and jalapeño and cook, stirring and scraping the bottom of the pan to prevent the ginger from burning, until the ginger is fragrant and sizzling, 30 seconds to 1 minute.

Add the cauliflower and stir to coat with the spices. Cover and reduce the heat to medium. Cook for 5 minutes and then stir in the frozen peas and salt. Cover and cook until the cauliflower is tender and the peas are very tender, 5 to 8 minutes more. Uncover the pan, increase the heat to high and cook, stirring occasionally, for 2 minutes. Add the garam masala (if using) and, if necessary, cook until any remaining liquid in the pan evaporates, 1 to 2 minutes longer. Taste and add more salt if needed before serving.

Suvir Saran is the executive chef of Dévi in New York City and Veda in New Delhi and the author of Indian Home Cooking. ◆

Photos: Scott Phillips

fine
Cooking

MARCH 2007 NO. 84

FOR PEOPLE WHO LOVE TO COOK

crispy chicken
from the oven

braising
rich
beef stew

perfecting
rice pilaf

easy sauces
for great fish

new
vegetable
side dishes

www.finecooking.com

$5 CAN $7.95

how to add crunch and flavor
for the best crumb coatings

The Rebirth of a Legend.

Introducing **TWIN® Four Star II**
from Zwilling J.A. Henckels, the
dramatic successor to the
FOUR STAR, the world's
most popular fine knives
for 30 years.

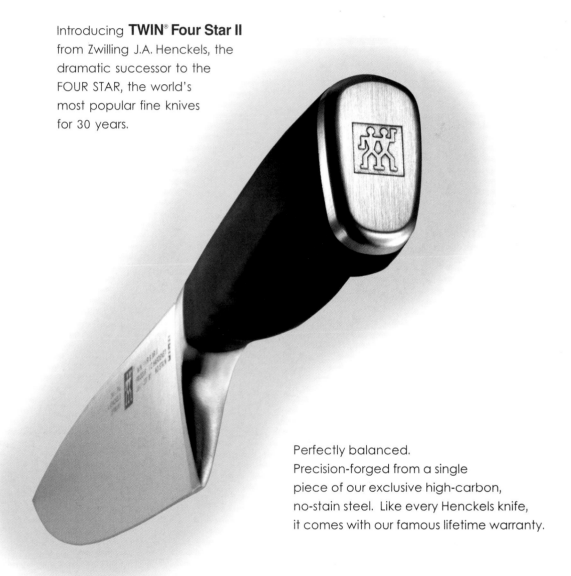

Perfectly balanced.
Precision-forged from a single
piece of our exclusive high-carbon,
no-stain steel. Like every Henckels knife,
it comes with our famous lifetime warranty.

ZWILLING
J.A.HENCKELS

PASSION FOR THE BEST. SINCE 1731.

jahenckels.com   The leading independent product testing organization ranks Henckels TWIN knives #1 and #2 among all brands.

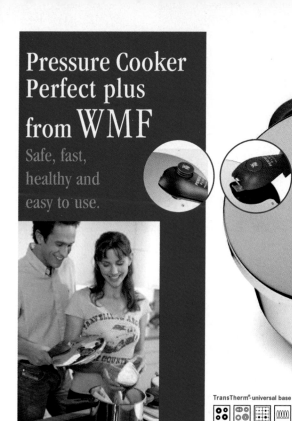

fine Cooking®

FEBRUARY/MARCH 2007   ISSUE 84

33   40

RECIPE FOLDOUT

26A **Favorite Winter Pastas**
**Seven hearty dishes to get
you through the cold months**

ON THE COVER

48 **Crispy Coated Chicken**

UP FRONT

6   Index

8   Menus

10   Letters

14   Links

15   Q&A

16   Contributors

18   In Season
     Parsnips

20   Enjoying Wine
     Wine lingo

22   Equipment
     ❖ **Powerful blender**
     ❖ **Brownie pan**
     ❖ **Hands-free faucet**
     ❖ **Review:**
       Garlic presses
     ❖ **Small-scale**
       appliances

28   Readers' Tips

30   Book Reviews
     **Cozy up to a
     new cookbook**

30

24

22

23

26

![The Taunton Press logo] **The Taunton Press**
Inspiration for hands-on living®

visit our web site: **www.finecooking.com**

45

53

58   62

FEATURES

33   Bistro Cooking at Home
Call up a few friends and settle in for a casual
dinner of braised lamb shanks, rustic beef
stew, or a saucy chicken sauté
by Molly Stevens

40   The Secrets to Fluffy and
Flavorful Rice Pilaf
Start with long-grain white rice and then
layer on the flavors
by Ris Lacoste

45   CLASSIC
Crème Brûlée
These luxurious custards topped with crisp
caramel are surprisingly simple to make
by Kimberly Y. Masibay

48   WEEKNIGHT COOKING
A New Take on
Crispy Coated Chicken
Bold flavors and extra-crunchy crumbs make this
oven-crisped chicken the best you've ever had
by Tony Rosenfeld

53   Getting to Know Asian Vegetables
You see them at the market, you eat them in
restaurants—now here are some tempting
ways to cook them
by Andrea Reusing

58   Quick-Braised Fish
A one-pan meal that's fast enough for
weeknights and fancy enough for company
by Allison Ehri

62   Playful Desserts
These clever and delicious desserts are easy
to put together and fun to eat
by Gale Gand

71

RECIPE FOLDOUT
78a   Quick & Delicious
Around the world in seven
quick recipes

IN THE BACK

66   From Our
Test Kitchen
❖ Hot chiles
❖ Choosing chuck
❖ Lamb "pizzas"
❖ Filleting fish
❖ Mexican crema

71   Tasting Panel
Champagne
vinegar

72   Where To Buy It

78   Nutrition
Information

BACK COVER

Make It Tonight
Warm lentil salad

66

67

index

◆ **QUICK**
Under 45 minutes

◆ **MAKE AHEAD**
Can be completely prepared ahead but may need reheating and a garnish to serve

◆ **MOSTLY MAKE AHEAD**
Can be partially prepared ahead but will need a few finishing touches before serving

◆ **VEGETARIAN**
May contain eggs and dairy ingredients

39 *Beef Stew with Red Wine & Carrots*

57 *Stir-Fried Snow Peas with Shiitakes & Ginger*

recipes

Cover Recipe

Crispy Chicken Breasts with Lemon & Capers, 50

Salads

◆ Colossal Shrimp with Watercress & Tomato Salad, 78a

◆ Tuna Teriyaki with Scallion Salad, 78a

Warm French Lentil Salad with Smoked Sausage, back cover

Rice

Rice Pilaf with Sage, Parmigiano & Prosciutto, 44

◆ Rice Pilaf with Spiced Caramelized Onions, Orange, Cherry & Pistachio, 42

◆ Saffron Rice Pilaf with Red Pepper & Toasted Almonds, 41

◆ Southwestern Rice Pilaf, 43

Pasta

◆ Baked Fettucine with Asparagus, Lemon, Pine Nuts & Mascarpone, 26a

◆ Baked Rigatoni with Cauliflower in a Spicy Pink Sauce, 26a

Baked Ziti with Tomato, Mozzarella & Sausage, 26a

◆ Campanelle with Broccoli Raab, Sausage & Olives, 26a

Cavatappi with Roasted Peppers, Capocollo & Ricotta, 26a

◆ ◆ Classic Macaroni & Cheese, 26a

◆ ◆ Spaghetti with Portabellas, Sage & Walnuts, 26a

Chicken

◆ Chicken with Vinegar & Onions, 37

Crispy Cheddar & Jalapeño Coated Chicken Breasts, 51

Crispy Chicken Breasts with Lemon & Capers, 50

Crispy Orange-Sesame Chicken Breasts, 52

Herbed Chicken Breasts with a Crispy Black Olive & Parmigiano Crust, 52

◆ Jerk Chicken Drumsticks, 78a

◆ Lime Chicken with Poblano Sour Cream, 78a

Beef, Lamb, Pork, Sausage

◆ Asian-Style Beef Barbecue in Lettuce Packages, 78a

◆ Beef Stew with Red Wine & Carrots, 39

◆ Braised Lamb Shanks with Garlic & Vermouth, 35

◆ Deviled Pork Chops, 78a

◆ Lamb Chops with Lemon, Thyme & Mustard Butter, 78a

◆ Middle Eastern Style Lamb Pita "Pizza," 68

Warm French Lentil Salad with Smoked Sausage, back cover

19 *Roasted Parsnips with Cinnamon & Coriander*

Seafood

Braised Cod with Fennel, Potatoes & Littlenecks, 61

◆ Braised Red Snapper Puttanesca, 59

◆ Colossal Shrimp with Watercress & Tomato Salad, 78a

Salmon Braised in Pinot Noir, 60

◆ Tuna Teriyaki with Scallion Salad, 78a

Side Dishes

◆ Braised Bok Choy with Sherry & Prosciutto, 54

Rice Pilaf with Sage, Parmigiano & Prosciutto, 44

◆ Rice Pilaf with Spiced Caramelized Onions, Orange, Cherry & Pistachio, 42

◆ ◆ Roasted Eggplant with Chiles, Peanuts & Mint, 55

◆ Roasted Parsnips with Cinnamon & Coriander, 19

◆ Saffron Rice Pilaf with Red Pepper & Toasted Almonds, 41

◆ Southwestern Rice Pilaf, 43

◆ Stir-Fried Napa Cabbage with Garlic, Fresh Chile & Basil, 56

◆ ◆ Stir-Fried Snow Peas with Shiitakes & Ginger, 57

Warm French Lentil Salad with Smoked Sausage, back cover

Condiments

◆ ◆ Homemade Crema (Mexican Sour Cream), 70

◆ ◆ ◆ Toasted Breadcrumbs, 48

Desserts

◆ ◆ Classic Crème Brûlée, 46

◆ ◆ Free-Form Pear Tarts with Almond & Cinnamon, 64

◆ ◆ Fried Chocolate-Hazelnut Wontons with Orange Dipping Sauce, 65

◆ ◆ ◆ Phyllo "Chips" with Vanilla Ice Cream & Strawberry Mash "Dip," 63

Photos: Scott Phillips

Simmer away the winter blues

If the weather has you down, chin up. The nastier it gets outside, the more excuses we have to stay inside, indulging our cravings for the rich, soul-satisfying fare we love. The bistro menu below is the perfect antidote to the winter doldrums. And when the cold temperatures break, look to the weeknight inspirations here for fast meals with fresh flavor.

Note: Before you start cooking, be sure to check the yield of every recipe; you might have to double or halve a recipe.

A comforting bistro supper

If you have time, make the entrée and crème brûlée a day ahead, but don't caramelize the brûlée topping until just before serving.

Warm French Lentil Salad with Smoked Sausage, *back cover*

Chicken with Vinegar & Onions (Poulet au Vinaigre), *p. 37*

Roasted Parsnips with Cinnamon and Coriander, *p. 19*

Classic Crème Brûlée, *p. 46*

WINE: A bright, crisp red like the 2004 Borgogno Barbera d'Alba ($18)

Saturday night dinner party

Early in the day, assemble the tarts and prep the ingredients for the rice pilaf and salmon. Pop the pear tarts in the oven when the salmon comes out (remember to increase the oven temperature), and they'll be ready to serve once you've cleared the table.

Salmon Braised in Pinot Noir, *p. 60*

Saffron Rice Pilaf with Red Pepper & Toasted Almonds, *p. 41*

Free-Form Pear Tarts with Almond & Cinnamon, *p. 64*

WINE: A supple, fruity Pinot Noir like the 2005 Edna Valley ($16)

Intimate Valentine's evening

Dinner with your special someone calls for something beyond the every-day, but with the holiday falling on a weeknight, that can be challenging. This quick and do-ahead menu makes it easy—the lamb chops broil in less than 15 minutes, and the dessert can be mostly made ahead.

Arugula salad with toasted hazelnuts, goat cheese, and a lemony vinaigrette

Lamb Chops with Lemon, Thyme & Mustard Butter, *p. 78a*

Rice Pilaf with Sage, Parmigiano & Prosciutto, *p. 44*

Phyllo "Chips" with Vanilla Ice Cream & Strawberry Mash "Dip," *p. 63*

WINE: A Cabernet blend like the 2005 Penfolds Rawson's Retreat Cabernet Shiraz ($9)

Four global weeknight pairings

Mexican

Lime Chicken with Poblano Sour Cream, *p. 78a*

Southwestern Rice Pilaf, *p. 43*

Japanese

Tuna Teriyaki with Scallion Salad, *p. 78a*

Roasted Eggplant with Chiles, Peanuts & Mint, *p. 55*

Mediterranean

Crispy Chicken Breasts with Lemon & Capers, *p. 50*

Braised Bok Choy with Sherry & Prosciutto, *p. 54*

Chinese

Asian-Style Beef Barbecue in Lettuce Packages, *p. 78a*

Stir-Fried Snow Peas with Shiitakes & Ginger, *p. 57*

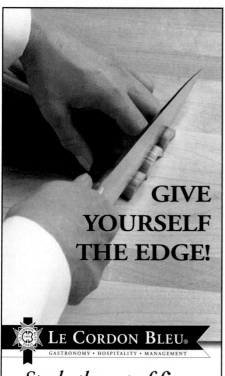

Get Your Mess in Place
...or how to prep like the pros

On my first day of culinary school, I learned how to wield a big knife and still keep all 10 fingers intact. The next day (or maybe it was the next hour), I learned to gather all my ingredients before starting to cook. OK, I remember thinking, my mother taught me this years ago; this cooking school thing isn't going to be so hard. This being a French cooking school,

though, they used a fancy name—*mise en place*—for getting organized. This is a phrase my mother definitely did not use. Pronounced MEEZ ahn plahs (and "mess in place" by my husband), it means "put everything in its place."

It turns out that having your "mise" done (as you'll hear restaurant chefs say) is about much more than just gathering your ingredients; it's about getting ready to cook so that when you start, your recipe will hum along like a well-choreographed num-

ber. You won't have to stop to run down to the basement for a special pot or to the neighbors for a forgotten ingredient. You won't have to let your fluffy egg whites deflate while you butter your ramekins, or let your breaded chicken get soggy while the oven heats.

It's not hard to get in the habit of doing your mise; in fact, if you put on your favorite CD, pour a sip of your favorite libation, and get into the groove, prepping can be one of the most pleasurable aspects of cooking. Even your weeknight cooking will come together a little more smoothly if you follow a few of our prep tips below:

Buy several sets of measuring spoons (instead of just one) and break them apart into individual measures. Keep them out in a cup or jar so that you can access them easily. Do the same with measuring cups and liquid measures—have several in each size and store them near your prep area.

Lay in a stash of little prep bowls. Sets of stainless-steel bowls in all sizes are good bargains at restaurant supply stores, but ceramic or melamine bowls work just fine, too. You'll use these again and again for minced garlic, diced vegetables, and chopped herbs. If you're prepping for several dishes at once (before a big dinner party, say), set the prep bowls on trays or sheet pans and label them with scraps of paper to remind you which dish the prep is for.

In your prep area, set up a tray of the ingredients you use most frequently, like kosher salt, good-quality olive oil, red pepper flakes, a black pepper grinder, a basic vinegar, a bowl of sugar.

Designate a convenient location for knife storage and cutting board storage. Keep your knives and boards close to your sink and trash area. Always start your prep by setting up a large cutting board (secure it in place by putting a damp towel underneath) with one or two of your most-used knives nearby. Set out a mixing bowl to use for scraps, and a dishtowel or two on the side.

Don't forget to dress comfortably. If it gets you in the zone, put an apron on (my mother can't cook without one); whatever you do, take thirty seconds to change into comfortable shoes before you start to cook. The favorite shoes of restaurant chefs are sturdy clogs, like those made by Dansko (for sources, see p. 72). They're slip resistant, and their good support means fewer back aches. Running sneakers are a good option, too.

Read first, then prep. While I know it seems obvious, our test kitchen manager would kill me if I didn't implore you to read the recipes thoroughly before starting. Yes, make sure you've got all your ingredients, but also be sure to prep them exactly as the ingredient list states. Dice your onions, peel and grate your ginger, plump your raisins in wine, and slice your pork into ½-inch medallions.

From the bistro favorites on p. 33 to the playful desserts on p. 62 , the delicious recipes in this issue of *Fine Cooking* are fun to both prep and cook. It's a great time of year to be in the kitchen, so get your mess in place and start cooking.

—*Susie Middleton, editor*

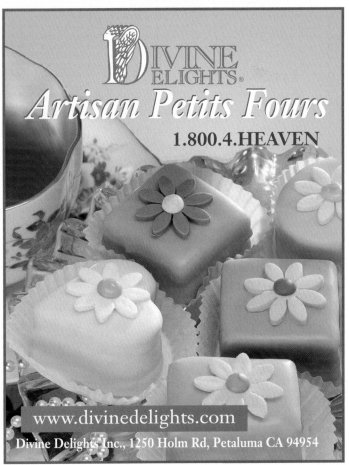

A salty story

A quick note to congratulate you on a great magazine. I look forward to each issue and always find recipes to try. In your December 2006 issue (*Fine Cooking* #82), however, I do question the Green Beans with Mustard-Tarragon Vinaigrette ("Green Beans on the Side," by Ris Lacoste). Why in the world did you recommend using ¼ cup salt for boiling the 1½ pounds of beans? I'm used to salting water to cook fresh vegetables—but ¼ cup? I used far less salt, 1 tablespoon, for the recipe, and also needed only half the amount of vinaigrette suggested. The results were excellent.

—*Marion Dunham, via email*

Ris Lacoste replies: First, let me assure you that the beans don't absorb all of that salt. *Fine Cooking*'s recipe testers used the amount of salt I specified through several rounds of testing, and the beans were delicious every time, never too salty. That said, you can certainly use any amount of salt you wish.

But to answer your question: The reason I use ¼ cup salt is mainly because I cook a relatively small amount of beans in a copious amount of water (4 quarts); less salt just wouldn't add the amount of flavor I desire. The large amount of water is important because it ensures that the beans cook evenly and also helps them retain their bright green color. During cooking, green beans release acids into the water, which can cause their color to change from brilliant green to olive-gray. By using more water, the acidity is diluted so the beans stay nice and bright.

What, no *Holiday Baking*?

I have just realized that I am not going to get a *Fine Cooking Holiday Baking* issue this year. I can't tell you how disappointed—and frustrated—I am by this. The holiday baking issue has always been the highlight of the year. As a Canadian, I have to say that getting a *Fine Cooking* with half of the content dedicated to cooking turkey every November is getting a bit tedious. So I'm feeling doubly frustrated: more and more Thanksgiving but no holiday baking? Why? I love this magazine but this imbalance is making me grumpy.

—*Allison Tom, via email*

Editors' reply: We certainly didn't mean to make you grumpy. We understand your frustration with Thanksgiving. We've cooked a lot of turkeys, too, though we know there are plenty of new cooks every year who haven't. That's why we made a special effort this year to ensure that nearly all of our Thanksgiving content did double duty. In other words, we included recipes that were seasonally appealing and practical for lots of different kinds of cooking, not just that one holiday. And we tried to have something for everyone; even our turkey feature included a delicious roast chicken and a stuffed turkey breast as alternatives to the big bird.

We also understand your disappointment about the *Holiday Baking* issue. But when we turned that issue into a regular, seasonal issue of *Fine Cooking* (to deliver more of the mix of different types of recipes and techniques that readers ask for), we made a conscious decision to devote a lot of space to baking. The holiday dessert party menu, the shortbread bar cookie story, and the cookie foldout deliver 22 baking recipes. So we thought we had met readers' needs for the season pretty well, but we realize it's not the same as an all-baking issue.

We want to make sure you know that you can now find more great baking recipes, tips, techniques, videos, and articles on our redesigned Web site. If you visit our homepage, www.finecooking.com, you'll see special features called "On the Front Burner." Many of these rich collections are dedicated to baking—from cookies to apple desserts to chocolate—and each has the kind of detailed recipes and in-depth information you're used to finding in the magazine. ◆

fine Cooking

EDITOR **Susie Middleton**

EXECUTIVE EDITOR **Sarah Jay**

ART DIRECTOR **Steve Hunter**

SPECIAL ISSUES EDITOR **Joanne McAllister Smart**

TEST KITCHEN MANAGER/RECIPE EDITOR **Jennifer Armentrout**

SENIOR EDITOR **Kimberly Y. Masibay**

ASSOCIATE EDITORS **Rebecca Freedman, Lisa Waddle**

ASSOCIATE WEB EDITOR **Sarah Breckenridge**

ASSISTANT EDITOR **Laura Giannatempo**

SENIOR COPY/PRODUCTION EDITOR **Enid Johnson**

ASSOCIATE ART DIRECTOR **Annie Giammattei**

TEST KITCHEN ASSOCIATE/FOOD STYLIST **Allison R. Ehri**

EDITORIAL ASSISTANT **Kim Landi**

EDITOR AT LARGE **Maryellen Driscoll**

TEST KITCHEN INTERNS **Noriko Yokota, Safaya Tork**

CONTRIBUTING EDITORS **Pam Anderson, Abigail Johnson Dodge, Tim Gaiser, Tony Rosenfeld, Molly Stevens**

PUBLISHER **Maria Taylor**

SENIOR MARKETING MANAGER **Karen Lutjen**

CIRCULATION DIRECTOR **Dennis O'Brien**

SINGLE COPY SALES MANAGER **Mark Stiekman**

ASSOCIATE ADVERTISING SALES MANAGER **Linda Petersell**

CORPORATE ACCOUNTS MANAGER **Judy Caruso**

NATIONAL ACCOUNTS MANAGERS **Patricia Coleman, Linda Delaney**

ASSOCIATE ACCOUNTS MANAGER **Chris Dunham**

ADVERTISING SALES ASSOCIATE **Stacy Purcell**

Fine Cooking: (ISSN: 1072-5121) is published seven times a year by The Taunton Press, Inc., Newtown, CT 06470-5506. Telephone 203-426-8171. Periodicals postage paid at Newtown, CT 06470 and at additional mailing offices. GST paid registration #123210981.

Subscription Rates: U.S. and Canada, $29.95 for one year, $49.95 for two years, $69.95 for three years (GST included, payable in U.S. funds). Outside the U.S./Canada: $36 for one year, $62 for two years, $88 for three years (payable in U.S. funds). Single copy, $6.95. Single copy outside the U.S., $7.95.

Postmaster: Send address changes to *Fine Cooking,* The Taunton Press, Inc., 63 South Main St., P.O. Box 5506, Newtown, CT 06470-5506.

Canada Post: Return undeliverable Canadian addresses to *Fine Cooking, c/o* Worldwide Mailers, Inc., 2835 Kew Drive, Windsor, ON N8T 3B7, or email to mnfa@taunton.com.

Printed in the USA.

HOW TO CONTACT US:

Fine Cooking

The Taunton Press, 63 S. Main St., P.O. Box 5506,
Newtown, CT 06470-5506   203-426-8171
www.finecooking.com

Editorial:

To submit an article proposal, write to *Fine
Cooking* at the address above or:

Call: **800-309-0744**

Fax: **203-426-3434**

Email: **fc@taunton.com**

Customer Service:

For subscription inquiries, you can:

• Visit our subscriber service section at:

  www.finecooking.com

• Email us: **fcservice@taunton.com**

• Call our customer support center:

  To report an address change, inquire about
  an order, or solve a problem, call:

  800-477-8727

  To subscribe, purchase back issues, books
  or videos, or give a gift, call:

  800-888-8286

Advertising:

To find out about advertising:

Call: **800-309-8940**

Email: **fcads@taunton.com**

Member Audit
Bureau of Circulation The Audit Bureau

Retail:

If you'd like to carry *Fine Cooking* in your store,
call the Taunton Trade Company at:

866-505-4674

Mailing List:

Occasionally we make our subscribers'
names and addresses available to responsible
companies whose products or services we feel
may be of some interest to you. Most of our
subscribers find this to be a helpful way
to learn about useful resources and services.
If you don't want us to share your name with
other companies, please contact our Customer
Service Department at:

800-477-8727

The Taunton Guarantee:

If at any time you're not completely satisfied with
Fine Cooking, you can cancel your subscription
and receive a full and immediate refund of the
entire subscription price. No questions asked.

What's New at FineCooking.com

Visit our home page often at FineCooking.com to see what's "on the front burner." This month, we have special Web collections of quick weeknight seafood dinners and warming bistro classics.

ON THE FRONT BURNER

Bistro Classics

Nothing's more satisfying on a cold winter day than comfort food with a French flair. We've collected some of our favorite bistro recipes all in one place, with the right tools and techniques to make them foolproof.

ON THE FRONT BURNER

Quick Seafood

When you need to get dinner on the table in a hurry, quick-cooking shrimp, scallops, or fish fillets are a natural. Try one of our techniques or recipes for a new twist on your favorites.

Bonus Download

Top 10 Quick Shrimp Recipes

Video

Wrap fish in parchment for quick steaming

Tips & Techniques

How to pick the best-quality fish, shrimp, scallops, and more

A faster way to thaw shrimp

Is it really done? How to tell

Recipes

Perfectly Seared Scallops

Seared Tuna with Citrus, Tomato & Olive Sauce

Grilled Salmon with Wasabi-Ginger Mayonnaise

Tilapia with Tarragon-Scallion Stuffing and Butter Sauce

And much more

Menu

A hearty bistro dinner starring braised lamb shanks

Bonus Download

10 Delicious Ways with Potatoes

Feature Articles

Making duck confit

The ultimate boeuf bourguignon

Equipment Review: Picking the best enameled Dutch oven

And dozens of recipes, including

Classic Coq au Vin

Leek & Potato Soup

Honey-Roasted Pears

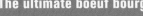

Free email newsletter!

Subscribe at FineCooking.com to get great recipes, tips, techniques, and videos delivered directly to your inbox twice a month.

My local market is selling "organic" salmon. Is there such a thing?

—*Celia LePage, Kensington, California*

Valerie Craig responds: There is such a thing as organic salmon. The biggest producers are based in Scotland, Canada, Ireland, and Chile, and the fish you saw at your local market is probably from one of these countries. Quite a few other countries are also raising organic salmon, though the United States is not yet one of them (by definition, organic salmon is farmed, not wild). While the standards for organic salmon vary somewhat among countries, there are some common elements, including the following:

❖ Hormones, antibiotics, or appetite stimulants cannot be used.

❖ The feed must meet certain requirements. Vegetable and grain feed must be organic; where fish is the feed, regulations vary, from requiring 100% fish trimmings (in other words, no additives) to using fish from sustainable fisheries.

❖ The number of fish per unit area (called stocking density) is lower for organic salmon than for conventionally farmed salmon.

The USDA has not yet created its own set of standards for organic salmon, or for organic fish in general, but a task force is working on it. Over the next couple of years, as these standards are developed, you can expect organic-salmon producers to appear in North America and as a result, you will see more organic salmon at your local fish market.

Valerie Craig is a representative at the Seafood Choices Alliance, a trade association for the sustainable seafood industry.

Have a question of general interest about cooking? Send it to Q&A, Fine Cooking, PO Box 5506, Newtown, CT 06470-5506, or by email to fcqa@taunton.com, and we'll find a cooking professional with the answer.

I'm in the market for a wine decanter, but I'm not sure what qualities make a good one. What should I look for?

—*Augustus Samson, New York City*

Tim Gaiser responds: Decanters are used to aerate wine. They range in price from $15 to more than $100, but you can find a good, all-purpose decanter for between $25 and $50 that will serve you well for years.

Decanters can take a variety of shapes, from simple carafes, to bottle shapes, to those with wider bases. I'd suggest avoiding ones with overly wide bases and lips, as it's difficult to pour all of the wine from them without spilling. Also, look for decanters made of clear glass without any decorative etching, which can detract from the appearance of the wine. And though some decanters come with glass stoppers, you shouldn't store any wine in the decanter long enough to need a stopper.

Tim Gaiser is a contributing editor to Fine Cooking *and a master sommelier.*

Why do some pot roast recipes tell you to place a sheet of parchment under the lid of the Dutch oven?

—*Lisa Lyons, via email*

Molly Stevens responds: Placing a sheet of parchment under the lid of a Dutch oven while cooking pot roast (or any other braise) serves three purposes:

First, the parchment tightens the seal between the pot and the lid, filling any gap that may occur between the two. This helps trap moisture in the pot, so whatever you're cooking will stay juicy.

Second, the parchment lessens the headroom in the pot (I crumple and push the paper downward so it almost touches the top of the ingredients in the pot), which helps keep the roast enveloped in moisture. In braising, there's an endless cycle of evaporation of pan juices and condensation as the steam hits the underside of the lid, turns back into liquid, and drips back into the pot, basting the food as it cooks. By adding the paper, you allow less space between the meat and the lid, intensifying this cycle.

Finally, the parchment helps baste the braise more evenly. The lids of most braising pots are dome shaped, which causes much of the condensation to drip down the sides of the pot, missing the food in the center. A sheet of parchment can create a flat or even convex ceiling so the condensation concentrates toward the center, allowing the drips from the condensed steam to baste the food more directly.

Molly Stevens, a contributing editor to Fine Cooking, *is the author of* All About Braising. ◆

In this issue, contributing editor Molly Stevens ("Bistro Cooking at Home," p. 33) shares her favorite bistro recipes—simple but satisfying dishes that taste authentically French. Molly has written and edited several books, including *All About Braising*, winner of both a James Beard award and an International Association of Culinary Professionals award. When she's not writing and developing new recipes, Molly is traveling around the country giving cooking classes; she won the IACP Cooking Teacher of the Year award in 2006. Classically trained as a chef in France, Molly has taught at the French Culinary Institute, New England Culinary Institute, and l'Ecole de Cuisine La Varenne in France and Italy.

Ris Lacoste ("Rice Pilaf," p. 40) has been a professional chef for nearly 25 years. She worked at several Massachusetts and D.C. restaurants, finally landing at 1789 Restaurant in Georgetown, where she was executive chef for 10 years. She recently left 1789 to open her own restaurant.

Fine Cooking senior editor Kimberly Masibay ("Crème Brûlée," p. 45) says, "I used to work as a pastry chef, so everyone who comes to dinner at my house expects an amazing dessert. Crème brûlée is my secret weapon. It's super easy and it never fails to impress, particularly if you fire up the blowtorch and caramelize the sugar at the table." Kim trained as a pastry chef in Germany and went to culinary school in Chicago.

In this issue, our tireless contributing editor Tony Rosenfeld ("Crispy Chicken," p. 48) lets us in on his clever technique for making crisp-coated chicken without the muss and fuss of deep frying.

Andrea Reusing

Kimberly Masibay

Gale Gand

Between his numerous projects for *Fine Cooking*, Tony somehow finds the time to watch over his growing restaurant empire in Boston. He also just finished writing his first cookbook, *150 Things to Make with Roast Chicken*, to be published by The Taunton Press this spring.

At her pan-Asian restaurant, Lantern, in Chapel Hill, North Carolina, Andrea Reusing ("Asian Vegetables," p. 53) offers authentic Asian food using seasonal, local ingredients. Andrea started her cooking career in New York City and moved to North Carolina in 1996. There, she ran a catering company and then became the chef at Enoteca Vin in Raleigh. She left in 2001 to open Lantern.

Fine Cooking's test kitchen associate and food stylist, Allison Ehri ("Quick-Braised Fish," p. 58), is a big fan of fish, which she cooks in every possible way. But come winter, her favorite method is to braise it in the oven in a flavorful sauce. "Braising fish preserves the integrity of its moist, tender flesh and its clean, delicate flavor," she says. In this story she shares three of her favorite braised fish recipes. Before joining the staff of *Fine Cooking*, Allison worked as a freelance recipe tester, developer, and writer for several food magazines.

Gale Gand ("Playful Desserts," p. 62) is well known for her creative desserts and humorous plays on classic American sweets. Gale is the executive pastry chef and partner at four restaurants in Chicago, including Tru and Gale's Coffee Bar. She's also the host of the Food Network's *Sweet Dreams* and has written six cookbooks, including *Gale Gand's Short + Sweet* and her latest, *Chocolate*

The Taunton Press
Inspiration for hands-on living®

INDEPENDENT PUBLISHERS SINCE 1975

TAUNTON, INC.
Founders, **Paul and Jan Roman**

THE TAUNTON PRESS

President & Editor In Chief **Suzanne Roman**

Executive Vice President & Chief Financial Officer **Timothy Rahr**

Executive Vice President & Publisher, Magazine Group **Jon Miller**

Publisher, Book Group **James Childs**

Chief of Operations **Thomas Luxeder**

DIRECTORS

Creative & Editorial Director **Susan Edelman**

Human Resources Director **Carol Marotti**

Controller **Wayne Reynolds**

Advertising Director **David Gray**

Consumer Marketing Director **Diana Allwein**

Fulfillment Director **Patricia Williamson**

Financial Analysis Director **Kathy Worth**

THE TAUNTON PRESS

Books: *Marketing:* Melissa A. Possick, Meg Day, Audrey Locorotondo. *Publicity:* Nicole Radder, Janel Noblin. *Editorial:* Helen Albert, Kathryn Benoit, Peter Chapman, Steve Culpepper, Pamela Hoenig, Carolyn Mandarano, Nicole Palmer, Jennifer Peters, Amy Reilly, Jennifer Russell, Erica Sanders-Foege, Kathleen Williams. *Art:* Chris Thompson, Alison Wilkes, Nancy Boudreau, Amy Griffin, Sandra Mahlstedt, Wendi Mijal, Lynne Phillips, Carol Singer. *Manufacturing:* Thomas Greco, Laura Burrone.

Business Office: Holly Smith, Gayle Hammond, Patricia Marini. *Legal:* Carolyn Kovaleski. *Magazine Print Production:* Philip Van Kirk, Nicole Anastas, Jennifer Kaczmarcyk.

Circulation: Dennis O'Brien, Director; Andrew Corson, Catherine Hansen.

Distribution: Paul Seipold, Walter Aponte, Frank Busino, David DeToto, Leanne Furlong, Deborah Greene, Frank Melbourne, Reinaldo Moreno, Raymond Passaro, Ulysses Robinson, Alice Saxton, Nelson Wade.

Finance/Accounting: *Finance:* Brett Manning, David Pond. *Accounting:* Patrick Lamontagne, Lydia Krikorian, Judith O'Toole, Shannon Marrs, Elaine Yamin, Carol Diehm, Dorothy Blasko, Susan Burke, Lorraine Parsons, Larry Rice, James Tweedle, Priscilla Wakeman.

Fulfillment: Diane Goulart. *Fulfillment Systems:* Jodi Klein, Kim Eads, Nancy Knorr, Dawn Viglione. *Customer Service:* Ellen Grassi, Michelle Amoroso, Kathleen Baker, Bonnie Beardsley, Deborah Ciccio, Katherine Clarke, Alfred Dreher, Monica Duhancik, Eileen McNulty, Patricia Parks, Deana Parker, Patricia Pineau, Betty Stepney. *Data Entry:* Melissa Dugan, Anne Champlin, Mary Ann Colbert, Maureen Pekar, Debra Sennefelder, Andrea Shorrock, Marylou Thompson, Barbara Williams.

Human Resources: Linda Ballerini, Christine Lincoln, Dawn Ussery.

Information Technology Services: *Applications Development:* Heidi Waldkirch, Jun Lu, Frank Miller, Robert Nielsen, Linda Reddington, John Vaccino,

Photos, from top: Natalie Ross, Scott Phillips, Jeff Kauck

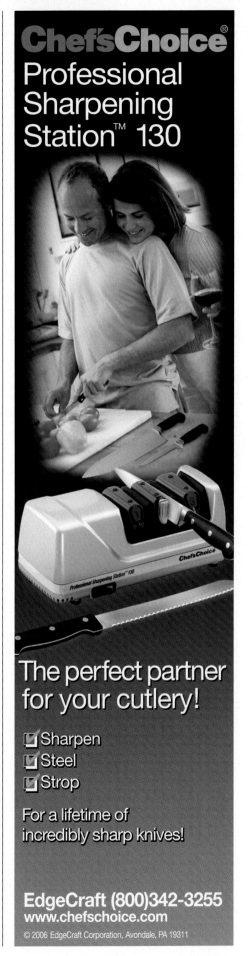

Sweet & Peppery Parsnips

BY RUTH LIVELY

While eating at a restaurant not so long ago, my order of lamb came with a delicious parsnip and apple gratin. The waiter told me that only recently had the chef been bold enough to describe it accurately on the menu. Before, he'd called it a "turnip and apple gratin," because he worried that parsnips might scare people off. (The idea that turnips might have more appeal than parsnips amused me a little.) In another dish, parsnips were snuck in as "white carrots."

I think the lowly parsnip deserves better than that. Yes, parsnips do look like overgrown white carrots (they're related to carrots, after all), but their flavor is more complex. They're wonderfully sweet like carrots—maybe more so—but they're also rich, earthy, faintly peppery, and a little nutty, too. It's an acquired taste for some, but to me, it's one worth having. I also love parsnips' versatility. They're good roasted or sautéed, braised, and even puréed for soups and mashes—and they make great side dishes with rich, wintery meat courses, such as braised short ribs, lamb shanks, pot roasts, and roasted duck.

Parsnips come into season in fall but are at their best smack in the middle of winter. They're sold either loose or in 1-pound plastic bags. Either way, look for roots that are firm and heavy for their size. Size itself doesn't matter, but larger parsnips often have a tough, fibrous core, which should be removed, at least from the thick upper half of the root. Store parsnips in a loosely closed plastic bag (don't tie it; you want some air to circulate) in the crisper drawer of the fridge. They'll keep for several weeks.

Parsnips are especially good with fruits and vegetables harvested in the same season, such as apples and pears, as well as with potatoes, carrots, turnips, and beets. Sometimes I play up their natural sweetness with brown sugar, maple syrup, or apple cider; other times, I add a counterpoint with a good sherry, cider, or wine vinegar. Balsamic works well, too, lending flavors both sour and sweet.

prepping tips

Simply trim away the tops and bottoms and peel them, just as you would with carrots. Parsnips have a core that can be tough and fibrous, especially in the thick upper part of the root. It's best to cut out that inner core.

In the garden

Parsnips need a loose, deeply worked, fertile soil and a full season of growth to come to maturity. As with carrots, sow the seed directly in the garden in spring and keep it moist until it sprouts, which may take up to three weeks. Late in the fall, cut the tops back, leaving just enough to see where the plants are, and begin harvesting. The flavor will improve as the weather gets colder and frosts convert some of the parsnips' starch to sugar.

Roasted Parsnips with Cinnamon & Coriander

Serves four.

The cooking method and the spices play up parsnips' sweetness, counterbalanced by last-minute additions of lemon juice and chopped fresh cilantro, which add brightness. If cilantro isn't to your liking, use parsley.

1½ lb. parsnips (about 10 medium)
¼ cup extra-virgin olive oil
½ tsp. ground cumin
½ tsp. ground coriander
½ tsp. sweet paprika (or a mix of mostly sweet and some hot)
½ tsp. kosher salt; more to taste
¼ tsp. ground cinnamon
2 Tbs. chopped fresh cilantro
2 tsp. fresh lemon juice

Position a rack in the center of the oven and heat the oven to 375°F. Peel the parsnips and cut each into 1-inch pieces crosswise, then cut the thicker pieces into halves or quarters to get chunks of roughly equal size. (Don't try to match the skinny tail-end pieces.) If the core seems tough or pithy, cut it out. You'll have about 4 cups.

Arrange the parsnips in a single layer in a 9x13-inch baking dish. Drizzle with the olive oil and toss to coat evenly. Combine the cumin, coriander, paprika, salt, and cinnamon in a small bowl and stir to mix. Sprinkle the spices evenly over the parsnips and toss until the parsnips are well coated.

Roast until completely tender and lightly browned on the edges, 35 to 45 minutes, stirring once or twice during cooking. Sprinkle with the cilantro and lemon juice and toss well. Taste and adjust the seasoning if necessary before serving.

3 ways to cook parsnips

Parsnips are so versatile they can be cooked almost any way you want. Here are some quick ideas for mashing, roasting, and braising.

Mashed or puréed

I usually start with boiled parsnips, but roasted parsnips are also delicious for these mashes and purées.

Mash boiled parsnips with cream, milk, and butter. Season with salt and pepper and a spoonful or two of sherry or Madeira. Transfer to a shallow baking dish, scatter chopped walnuts or pecans over the top, if you like, and bake until lightly browned on top.

Purée boiled parsnips and carrots with a bit of cream, season with salt and a little white pepper, and stir in some finely chopped crystallized ginger.

For a twist on applesauce, boil and mash together parsnips and tart apples. Add butter, freshly grated nutmeg, and a little lemon juice and zest. Serve with roast chicken, turkey, duck, or goose.

Roasted

Typically, I reach for olive oil when I'm roasting vegetables, parsnips included. (Follow general time and temperature guidelines in the recipe above.) You can roast them halved, cut into matchsticks, or in chunks, as in the braises at right.

Toss a blend of parsnips and carrots in olive oil, salt, and pepper and roast until tender and lightly caramelized. Stir in some cilantro pesto.

For a colorful mélange, toss parsnips, turnips, beets, and sweet potatoes with oil and season with salt, pepper, and a little cayenne. Roast until almost tender. Stir in lots of chopped parsley, some minced garlic, and lemon zest and finish roasting.

Toss the parsnips in oil, salt, and pepper and roast them with whole shallots until almost tender. Drizzle with a blend of maple syrup and fresh orange juice, toss with some chopped rosemary, and finish roasting.

Braised

When braising, I like to cut parsnips crosswise into 1-inch pieces; then I cut the thicker pieces in halves or quarters to get chunks of roughly equal size. I start by browning the pieces in a fat—I like butter, but olive or vegetable oil works well, too.

As the parsnips brown, season with a healthy sprinkle of chopped fresh sage. Then simmer in apple cider until the parsnips are tender and the cider boils away to a brown glaze.

Brown the parsnips, season with salt and pepper, toss in a few thyme sprigs, and braise in chicken broth until tender.

Combine parsnips with 2-inch chunks of leek and brown. Add salt and pepper, deglaze the pan with white wine or dry vermouth, and let it boil away. Add a little water, cover, and cook until tender.

Ruth Lively cooks, writes, and gardens in New Haven, Connecticut. ◆

Wine Lingo, Demystified

BY TIM GAISER

So you're shopping at your favorite wine shop, trying to pick out a good bottle for dinner. As you amble down the aisles, you pause to read a rave review taped to the shelf by some well-meaning shop clerk, and you suddenly realize you don't understand half of what you're reading. Well, take comfort: You're not alone.

Wine is potentially a very complex subject—and the language we wine geeks use probably just adds to the confusion—but it becomes a lot less intimidating once you're familiar with the basic jargon. Here's a glossary of many commonly used wine terms with easy-to-understand definitions.

Wine label jargon

You'll frequently encounter these terms on a wine label or when reading about wine. They don't describe a wine's taste, per se, but offer details about the wine's origin and the way it was made, both of which affect the quality and character of the wine.

Appellation tells you where the grapes were grown and the wine produced. The appellation is especially important in French wines that are known by place names and rarely list grape varieties.

Cru is a French term denoting a vineyard or estate of exceptional merit. The concept of cru is especially important for Burgundy and Champagne, where the best vineyards are labeled premier cru and grand cru.

Cuvée means blend; a wine labeled "cuvée" is a blend of many different base wines, which may themselves be blends.

Estate-bottled wines come from grapes grown on a winery's own vineyards.

Meritage is a marketing term developed to describe California Cabernet Sauvignon blends that are modeled after the great reds of Bordeaux.

Reserve is the most abused term in the world of wine. Theoretically, it should be used by a winemaker only to designate his best product, but you'll see the term slapped on the labels of cheap, mass-produced wines.

Barrels & bottles

Barrel- or stainless-steel-fermented are the winemaker's two fermentation options. The choice depends on the style of wine and the specific grape variety. Stainless-steel-fermented wines emphasize bright, youthful fruit; barrel-fermented wines offer rich, creamy aromas and flavors.

Barrel- or bottle-aged tells you whether wine is aged in oak barrels or in the bottle. Oak-aging adds aromas or flavors of vanilla, baking spices, and toast to the wine. Bottle-aging (also called bottle-maturation) implies aging in a cellar, which should increase the complexity of the wine and make it smoother.

Varietal wines are made from a single grape variety and bear the grape's name on the label. To bear a varietal name, such as Merlot, Riesling, or Chardonnay, on the label, the wine must contain at least 75% of that grape, according to United States law.

Vintage denotes the year the grapes were harvested and the wine made. Most wines state a vintage year on the label, but there are also nonvintage (NV) wines, which are blends of wines from several years.

Tasting terms

These words are used to describe how wine tastes. Understanding them will help you make sense of the descriptions you read in reviews and wine-buying guides. They'll also help you evaluate the wines you drink by giving you specific aspects to focus on and words to describe what you taste.

Acidity refers to the tartness of a wine. A wine can be described as crisp or soft, depending on the amount of acidity. High-acidity wines might be described as crisp or racy, while those with low acidity are called soft, and wines too little acidity are often described as flat. In addition to balancing and enlivening wine's flavor, acidity is a key element in successful food-and-wine pairing. Generally, the most food-friendly wines have moderate alcohol balanced by crisp acidity.

Alcohol refers to the amount of alcohol in a wine, which for table wines usually ranges between 13% and 15%. The amount of alcohol determines a wine's richness, body, and to a great extent, the intensity of flavor. Wines with low alcohol feel light-bodied, while wines with too much alcohol often taste overripe and imbalanced.

Balance describes the harmony (or lack thereof) among all the elements in a wine. A balanced wine is a seamless progression of fruit, acids, alcohol, and tannins, with nothing too prominent.

Body describes how weighty a wine feels in the mouth. Wines that feel heavy and rich are full-bodied (the word "big" is often used to describe these types of wines). Feathery wines with little weight are light-bodied. Medium-bodied wines fall in between.

Complexity refers to the aromas and flavors in a wine and how they interact with each other. The more layers of flavor and aroma, the more complex the wine and the higher its quality.

Corkiness, the most common flaw in wine, is caused by a tainted cork. Corked wines smell and taste of wet, musty, or mildewed cardboard.

Finish describes a wine's aftertaste, be it fruit, acidity, oak, or tannins. Generally, the longer the flavor lasts after you swallow, the better quality the wine. However, there are also bad wines with regrettably long finishes.

Legs (or tears) are the trickles of wine that run down the inside of a glass after you swirl it. The legs are clues to how much alcohol or residual sugar the wine contains; thicker, slower legs indicate a wine with more alcohol or residual sugar.

Malolactic fermentation is a process by which some of the sharp malic acid in a young wine is converted to softer, smoother lactic acids. The process also causes the wine to develop a buttery flavor compound, which you'll find in many Chardonnays.

Sweetness or dryness levels refer to the presence or lack of sugar in wine. Wines range from bone dry, with no residual sugar, all the way to dessert sweet in style. Off-dry wines have just a hint of sweetness. Most table wines are dry to off-dry.

Tannins, which come from the skins, seeds, and stems of the grapes and also from the barrels, are usually found in red wine. Tannins taste bitter and make your palate feel fuzzy, velvety, puckery, or even dry if there's a good deal of tannin. Wines high in tannins are often described as firm or chewy, and those without a lot of tannins are called soft or supple.

Texture refers to a wine's mouth-feel. The texture of a wine may be described as silky or astringent or dense.

Name that style

Brawny/muscular wines are big, robust reds with lots of tannins.

Earthy describes a wine whose aromas and flavors are either minerally or evocative of rich soil. European wines tend to be earthier than their New World counterparts. Earthy wines are often described as having a sense of terroir (pronounced teh-RWAHR), a French term that refers to the specific region or vineyard where the wine was made. A sense of terroir lends complexity and interest to any wine.

Fruit-forward wines are dominated by the flavors of fresh fruit—berries, apples, cherries, and so on.

Jammy wines taste of very ripe, almost overripe berries. Zinfandels are often described as "jammy."

Oaky wines have a toasty, vanilla flavor that comes from aging in oak barrels. It can be wonderful, but too much oak can throw a wine out of balance.

Contributing editor Tim Gaiser is a master sommelier and wine educator. ◆

Laser probe thermometer   22

KitchenAid blender   22

Baker's Edge pan   22

Care of nonstick surfaces   23

Mango splitter   23

Infrared faucet   23

Review: Garlic presses   24

Small-scale appliances   26

BY KIMBERLY Y. MASIBAY

what's new

A better laser thermometer

When we first tried Bonjour's handheld laser thermometer (see *Fine Cooking* #74), we didn't find it particularly useful because it couldn't take a roast's internal temperature and help you gauge its doneness; it could read only surface temperatures. Well, Bonjour has improved the design. Its new model has a retractable stainless-steel probe that you can insert into food for an instant digital temperature reading. And it still has the infra-red thermometer for quickly checking the surface tempera-tures of pans, ovens, grills, and whatnot.

The Bonjour Chef's Laser Probe Combo is $89.95 at SurLaTable.com.

A new and improved blender

KitchenAid's new five-speed blender may have an ultra-light polycarbonate pitcher, but there's nothing else lightweight about this machine. Sure, it can blend tomato sauces and purée vegetable soups with ease, but what's most impressive is how well it pulverizes the tough stuff: ice cubes, frozen fruit, nuts, chunks of Parmigiano. Whenever I made pesto or thick smoothies in my old blender, I would have to reach in several times to prod the ingredients into the blades. With this blender that wasn't necessary.

The two keys to its success seem to be the power-ful motor and the roomy 56-ounce pitcher, which has a wide base and a contoured design that funnels ingredi-ents toward the blade for fast and thorough blending.

The KitchenAid five-speed blender comes in white, red, cinnamon, chrome, and black. It sells for $99.95 at Cooking.com.

Edge-lovers, rejoice

When this unusual baking pan, designed for edge-lovers by 31-year-old inventor Matt Griffin, arrived in the mail, I couldn't help wondering, Does anyone really need this? Shortly thereafter, at a brownie tasting in the *Fine Cooking* test kitchen, I noticed several *FC* staffers vying for the chewy edge pieces and suddenly I understood that, yes, some people really do need the Baker's Edge pan.

When I tried this heavy-duty cast-aluminum pan, I discovered at least three good reasons to like it:

❖ **Chewy edges on every piece.** The pan's patented design guarantees that every piece will have at least two chewy edges.

❖ **Even cooking.** The maze-like interior of the pan conducts heat efficiently, so whatever you bake in it cooks more evenly than it does in a rectangular pan.

❖ **No recipe adaptation required.** I baked a few batches of bar cookies, and it seems that recipes created for 9x13-inch pans will work in this pan, too, though the baking time may be a bit shorter or longer.

The Baker's Edge pan sells for $32.50 at BakersEdge.com.

Nonstick cookware needs TLC

Nonstick sauté pans and skillets can take the anxiety—and the mess—out of cooking eggs, fish, and other prone-to-sticking foods, but if you want that nonstick coating to last, you need to treat it right. Since many of our recipes call for a nonstick pan, here's a little refresher in nonstick maintenance:

1. Don't let it get too hot. High heat (500°F+) weakens nonstick coatings, so never blast the heat as you might with a cast-iron or stainless-steel skillet. It's all right to heat an empty pan on medium heat for a couple of minutes before adding your ingredients—to make sure the pan isn't overheating, put a little oil or butter in it; if the fat smokes, the pan is getting too hot—but wait until the pan is full of food before increasing the heat to medium high.

2. Avoid nonstick cooking spray. In addition to ruining the nonstick coating, overheating can cause cooking oil to form a hard film on the pan's surface. This difficult-to-remove film causes pans to stop releasing food well. Because nonstick cooking spray goes on in such a thin layer, it can overheat very quickly, forming an invisible layer of this pesky film.

3. Clean it gently but well. Nonstick pans make cleanup a breeze, but don't take it too easy when you're washing up. Use hot soapy water, a sponge, and a bit of elbow grease to remove any cooked-on oils. If you use a scouring pad, make sure it's safe for nonstick surfaces.

4. Use the right utensils. When it comes to the enemies of nonstick coatings, utensil abrasion is right up there with high heat. Avoid metal utensils; use wood or silicone instead.

No more mangled mangos

We've tried all sorts of gadgets for slicing, splitting, and coring fresh fruit, but generally we don't consider them essential—a knife is really the only tool we need. Mangos, however, are different. Trying to remove the pit can feel like a guessing game, and separating the oddly shaped thing from the clutches of the fruit is a sticky, slippery, and sometimes precarious procedure. That's why we were thrilled to discover Oxo's ingenious mango splitter. This is one gadget we'll take over a knife any day. Just set a mango on end and press down on the splitter. In one quick motion, the sharp blades slice the fruit down the middle, cleanly excising the pit from the two succulent halves of fruit.

You can buy the Oxo Mango Splitter for $11.99 at Oxo.com.

Hands-free faucet

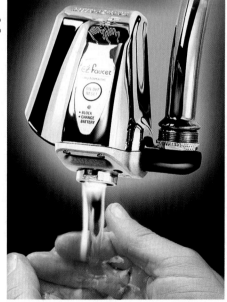

If you've ever handled raw chicken and then struggled to turn on the tap without contaminating the faucet, the EZ Faucet by iTouchless offers a solution. It's an infrared adapter that lets you convert any standard faucet into a touch-free tap without breaking the bank or calling the plumber.

I attached the adapter to my kitchen faucet (all by myself) and used it happily for several months. I was especially impressed with the unit's responsiveness. Whenever I held my hands under the tap, the water instantly flowed; when I moved my hands away, the water stopped. No water wasted and no worries about spreading germs all over the faucet's handle. And when I wanted to let the water run for an extended length of time to fill a stockpot or my dogs' bowl, I simply pressed a button on the front of the unit to override the automatic feature.

As much as I loved the convenience of the EZ Faucet, there was one cosmetic matter I wasn't crazy about: the faux-chrome plastic housing, which felt a little chintzy. But, considering the product's reasonable price, this is a minor quibble. What matters most is that the faucet performed reliably day after day in my busy kitchen.

The EZ Faucet, which unfortunately doesn't fit onto spray-head faucets, runs on four AAA batteries, which the manufacturer claims will last for up to 18 months. You can order the EZ Faucet for $59.95 at Itouchless.com.

review

Garlic Presses

BY MARYELLEN DRISCOLL

When there's garlic to be minced, many cooks reach for their garlic presses. Some cooks like the convenience—with just a squeeze of the handle, a single clove of garlic (or more) is reduced to a fine mash. Other cooks use presses because they want to avoid getting the pungent smell of garlic on their hands. Yet, after working with 18 different presses for a day, we found only three that really offered both advantages.

Plenty of garlic presses have obvious failings—poor leverage, shoddy hinges, uncomfortable grip, or chambers that are too cramped to fit a whole garlic clove—but after crushing clove after clove and interviewing a number of garlic press users and nonusers, we discovered that the most pervasive problem seemed to be cleanup. Nobody likes to dig mashed garlic out of a space slightly larger than a thimble. The pronged cleaning attachments that come with (or are built into) some presses help marginally. And pressing a clove unpeeled minimizes the mess to some extent. But either way, there's still stuff to scrape out, be it with the tip of a finger, a paring knife, or a toothpick. Now what's convenient about that?

In an attempt to solve this problem, a number of brands have begun making presses with removable sieves that are meant to be easier to clean. In some of these presses the sieves look like tiny, re-movable rectangular baskets. It's an improvement, but these presses aren't perfect: Cleaning them still requires a bit of digging, and then there's the risk of misplacing the loose parts. Our winners, the Kuhn Rikon and Rösle presses, took another approach. These have flat sieves that swing out on a hinge, making them refreshingly easy to swipe clean without the risk of lost parts. This innovation might cost you more than you'd expect to spend on a garlic press, but if you use one often, you'll appreciate the time and trouble saved when it comes to the real dirty work—cleaning.

Winners

Kuhn Rikon Epicurean garlic press
$34.95 at Hugthecook.com

We like that the roomy stainless-steel sieve on this press is a hinged plate that swings up for simple cleaning with a sponge. An interior thumb rest holds the sieve in place when you open the press to load with garlic. The arched handles offer real ergonomic advantages and are friendly to small hands; you just have to be careful not to pinch your skin as the handles meet. The only disadvantage to this clever design is that a small amount of pressed garlic can seep around the sides of the chamber. Kuhn Rikon makes another "easy-clean" model with a scraper on the face of the sieve, but we like this one better.

How we tested

For this review, we crushed garlic—small, medium, and large cloves, peeled and unpeeled—through 18 models of garlic presses. These were the other brands we tested: Amco, Anolon, Chantal, Cuisinart, Dalla Piazza, KitchenAid, Leifheit, Messermeister, MIU France, Pedrini, Progressive International, RSVP Z-Gadgets, Wüsthof, and Zyliss.

Rösle
garlic press
$34.95 at Cutleryandmore.com

Very similar in design to the Kuhn Rikon press, this sturdy model is strong and has nice balance. The handles provide good leverage once you begin to crush the clove, but if you have small hands, you may have to use both of them to get started because the handles are spaced far apart. Once shut, the brushed stainless-steel handles stay agreeably in place for storage. As with the Kuhn Rikon model, pressed garlic can seep around the edges of the chamber.

Minced vs. pressed:
Can you taste a difference?

Garlic presses aren't for everyone. Some cooks find it simpler to mince garlic with a knife; others argue that pressed garlic has inferior flavor. We've long wondered whether minced and pressed garlic actually taste any different. So to find out, we held a blind taste test, serving two versions of a quick marinara, sautéed Swiss chard, and gremolata (a garnish of minced garlic, lemon zest, and parsley). For each dish, we made one batch with minced garlic and one with garlic crushed in a press. Almost everyone found that garlic crushed in a press gave dishes a more aggressive garlic flavor. Many tasters found the pungency offensive in the gremolata, which featured raw garlic, but acceptable in the marinara, which was cooked.

Runner-up

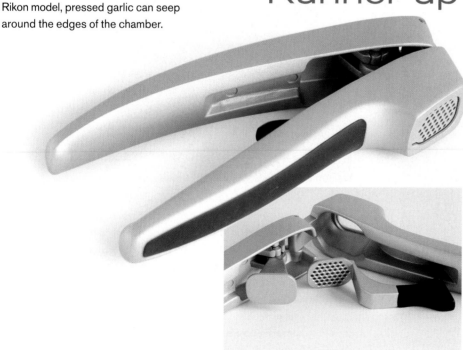

Oxo i-Series
garlic press
$16.95 at Lascosascooking.com

This garlic press is strong, comfortable to grip, and innovative. A small handle cleverly tucked inside the lower handle makes it easy to lift out the sieve plate for cleaning. The garlic chamber isn't as long as Rösle's or Kuhn Rikon's, but it's plenty deep, and the sieve plate fits snugly in place, so pressed garlic doesn't seep out. The plate, however, is thick, and some garlic does get stuck in the tapered holes; although the sieve mostly rinsed clean, we resorted to a toothpick to poke out those last few specks.

Maryellen Driscoll is Fine Cooking's *editor at large.*

equipment

Incredible
Shrinking
Appliances

In the world of major appliances, bigger isn't necessarily better, particularly if you're trying to outfit a small kitchen with top-of-the-line gear or you're putting in a second appliance for ancillary use. Well, here's good news: It seems top appliance manufacturers are becoming increasingly space conscious, as they've launched an array of high-performance models with diminutive dimensions. Here's a sampling of several noteworthy space-savers.

Liebherr 24-inch Premium no-frost refrigerator (CS1350)

German refrigerator manufacturer Liebherr is a newcomer to the American market, and this tall, narrow fridge (80 inches high by 24 inches wide by 25 inches deep) is but one of its space- and energy-efficient designs. In fact, this model is the most energy-efficient bottom-freezer refrigerator on the market. It features stainless-steel construction, dual silent compressors that allow independent control of the fridge section and the frost-free freezer. The retail price is about $2,800. To find dealers near you, visit LiebherrAppliances.com.

Bosch Integra 800 Series 18-inch dishwasher (SRV53C03UC)

This compact 18-inch built-in dishwasher is big on features: five wash cycles plus power scrub, glass, quick, economy, enviro, and many other settings. And the stainless steel interior is roomier than you might think; it has two adjustable racks, can handle 24 place settings, and has a special spray tower for extra-tall items. Expect to pay about $1,100. For more information visit BoschAppliances.com.

Danby Silhouette 27-bottle wine cooler (DWC276BLS)

Danby's svelte under-the-counter wine cooler is just 12 inches wide by 34 inches tall, so it can squeeze into even the smallest undercounter space. But it has the capacity to store 27 wine bottles. The suggested retail price is $700. For more information visit Danby.com.

24-inch Aga Companion

This 24-inch-wide dual-fuel range is meant to be a companion to a larger Aga range, but there's no reason why it couldn't be your one and only. It boasts four high-power gas burners, two electric ovens (one conventional oven with a broiler and one convection oven), and the classic Aga design. Made of cast iron and available in 15 appealing colors, it retails for about $4,350. For dealers visit www.Aga-Ranges.com. ◆

Other manufacturers are also making small-scale appliances. Visit their Web sites for information: DelonghiMajorAppliances.com; FiveStarRange.com; Gaggenau-usa.com; Miele.com; SummitAppliance.com; VikingRange.com.

Favorite Winter Pastas

COMPILED BY SARAH BRECKENRIDGE

On a blustery evening, there are few dishes as comforting as a hearty, hot pasta. So what better time, we thought, to offer you some of our favorite cold-weather pastas from past issues of *Fine Cooking*. As you might expect, we've included several baked pastas, like a gratin of macaroni and Cheddar and a baked ziti with sausage and tomatoes. But winter pastas can also be as quick as spaghetti tossed with the earthy flavors of mushrooms and sage, or campanelle with sausage and broccoli raab. In fact, you may just be tempted to make one of them for dinner tonight.

Baked Rigatoni with Cauliflower in a Spicy Pink Sauce

Serves six to eight.

3 Tbs. olive oil
2 28-oz. cans whole tomatoes
1 lb. yellow onions, halved and thinly sliced (about 3 medium)
1¼ tsp. kosher salt
2 cloves garlic, minced
½ cup heavy cream
¼ cup chopped fresh flat-leaf parsley
½ tsp. crushed red pepper flakes
1 lb. rigatoni
1 lb. 1- to 1½-inch cauliflower florets (about 4 cups)
10 oz. shredded Fontina (about 2½ cups)
2 oz. freshly grated Parmigiano-Reggiano (about ¾ cup)

Position a rack in the center of the oven and heat the oven to 450°F. Bring a pot of well-salted water to boil in a large pot with a pasta insert. Grease a 9x13-inch baking dish with 1 Tbs. olive oil.

Pour off 1 cup of juice from one of the cans of tomatoes and discard it. In a blender or food processor, purée both cans of tomatoes with their remaining juice and set aside.

Heat the remaining 2 Tbs. olive oil in a 6- to 8-qt. Dutch oven or heavy-based pot over medium-high heat. When the oil is shimmering, about 1 minute, add the onions and ¼ tsp. of the salt and cook, stirring occasionally, until nicely browned,

5 to 10 minutes. Push the onions to the side of the Dutch oven with a wooden spoon and add the garlic. Cook until it just starts to sizzle and becomes fragrant, about 10 seconds.

Add the puréed tomatoes and cream (be careful; it will splatter), plus the remaining 1 tsp. salt. Bring to a boil over medium-high heat, reduce to a gentle simmer, and cook for 10 minutes, stirring occasionally, so that the sauce thickens slightly. Add the parsley and the red pepper flakes, and cook until the flavors are melded, about 5 minutes more. Taste for salt and pepper and remove from the heat.

Meanwhile, when the salted water comes to a boil, cook the rigatoni until it's al dente, about 10 minutes. Drain the pasta by lifting out the insert and leaving the water in the pot. Add the pasta to the sauce. Return the water to a boil (with the pasta insert in the pot) and cook the cauliflower until barely tender, about 2 minutes. Drain and add it to the sauce.

Add 1½ cups of the shredded Fontina to the pasta mixture and toss well. Transfer to the prepared baking dish and spread evenly. Top the pasta with the remaining 1 cup Fontina and then the Parmigiano-Reggiano. Bake uncovered until the cheese is golden brown, about 15 minutes. Let the pasta rest for 10 minutes before serving.

—*Tony Rosenfeld,*
Fine Cooking #69

Baked Fettuccine with Asparagus, Lemon, Pine Nuts & Mascarpone

Serves four.

Mascarpone is a rich Italian cream cheese. It usually comes in a plastic tub and is available at most supermarkets. Grana Padano is a hard Italian grating cheese similar to Parmigiano but with a milder flavor and a lower price.

2 Tbs. olive oil; more for the baking dish
2 lb. medium-thick asparagus, ends trimmed, cut into 1-inch pieces on an angle
8 scallions, whites and tender greens cut into thin rounds
Finely grated zest from 2 lemons
Juice from 1 lemon (about 4 Tbs.)
A few sprigs fresh thyme or savory, leaves chopped
Kosher salt and freshly ground black pepper to taste
1 Tbs. unsalted butter
1 Tbs. all-purpose flour
1 cup whole milk
1 cup mascarpone
1 cup freshly grated Grana Padano
Small pinch cayenne
Generous pinch ground allspice
¾ cup coarse fresh breadcrumbs
1 lb. fresh fettuccine
½ cup pine nuts, lightly toasted

Heat the oven to 450°F. Lightly coat a large shallow baking dish with olive oil. Bring a large pot of salted water to a boil. Add the asparagus pieces and blanch until crisp-tender, about 2 minutes. With a large slotted spoon, transfer them to a colander, and run under cold water to preserve their green color. Drain well. Keep the water boiling for the pasta.

In a large skillet, heat the olive oil over medium heat. Add the scallions and sauté for 1 minute to soften. Add the asparagus and sauté briefly, about 1 minute. Take the skillet off the heat and add half of the zest, the lemon juice, and the thyme or savory. Season with salt and pepper, mix well, and reserve.

In a medium saucepan, heat the butter and flour over medium heat, whisking until smooth. Cook for 1 minute, whisking constantly, to cook away the raw taste of the flour. Add the milk and cook, whisking all the while, until it comes to a boil. Lower the heat a bit and cook until smooth and slightly thickened (to about the consistency of heavy cream), 3 to 4 minutes.

Turn off the heat and add the remaining lemon zest, the mascarpone, and ½ cup of the Grana Padano, whisking until the mixture is fairly smooth (there will be a slight grainy texture from the cheese). Season with the cayenne, the allspice, and more salt and pepper.

In a small bowl, combine the breadcrumbs and the remaining Grana Padano. Season with salt and pepper and add a drizzle of olive oil. Mix well.

Return the cooking water to a full boil and cook the fettuccine, leaving it slightly underdone. Drain well. Return the fettuccine to the cooking pot. Add the pine nuts, the mascarpone sauce, and the asparagus mixture. Toss and taste for seasoning.

Pour into the baking dish and sprinkle the breadcrumb mixture evenly over the top. Bake uncovered until bubbling and golden, 15 to 20 minutes. Serve right away.

—*Erica DeMane,*
Fine Cooking #37

Don't skimp on the salt

When you bring a pot of water to a boil to cook pasta, be sure to add a generous amount of salt. Well-salted water seasons the pasta internally as it absorbs liquid and swells. If the pasta is sufficiently salted during boiling, the pasta dish may even require less salt overall.

For one pound of pasta, use 4 quarts of water and 2 Tbs. of kosher salt: the water should taste as salty as seawater.

Campanelle with Broccoli Raab, Sausage & Olives

Serves three to four.

Kosher salt
1 lb. broccoli raab, thick stems trimmed, leaves and florets rinsed well
6 oz. campanelle pasta (2 cups)
3 Tbs. extra-virgin olive oil
¾ lb. sweet Italian sausage (bulk sausage or links removed from casing)
3 cloves garlic, minced
¼ tsp. crushed red pepper flakes
¾ cup homemade or low-salt chicken broth
½ cup pitted Kalamata olives, quartered
2 tsp. finely grated lightly packed lemon zest
⅓ cup freshly grated Pecorino Romano

Bring a large pot of well-salted water to a boil over high heat. Have a bowl of ice water ready. Add the broccoli raab to the boiling water and cook until bright green and tender, 2 minutes (the water doesn't have to come back to a full boil once the broccoli raab has been added). With tongs or a slotted spoon, transfer the broccoli raab to the bowl of ice water to stop the cooking. Drain well and gently squeeze the broccoli raab to remove excess water.

Return the pot of water to a boil, add the pasta, cook according to package directions, and drain.

While the campanelle cooks, heat the oil in a 12-inch skillet over medium-high heat. Add the sausage and cook, stirring and breaking it into smaller pieces with a wooden spoon until it's browned and almost cooked through, 4 to 6 minutes. Add the garlic and red pepper flakes and cook until the garlic is lightly golden, about 1 minute. Pour in the broth and bring to a boil; cook, scraping the pan with a wooden spoon occasionally, until the broth is reduced by about half, 3 to 4 minutes.

Add the broccoli raab, olives, and lemon zest and cook, stirring, until hot, 1 to 2 minutes. Add the pasta and cheese to the skillet and toss well. Season to taste with salt and serve immediately.

—*David Bonom,*
Fine Cooking #71

Baked Ziti with Tomato, Mozzarella & Sausage
Serves four.

Try to find freshly made ricotta and mozzarella to see how good this rustic dish can be.

Olive oil
1 large onion, cut into small dice
¾ lb. sweet Italian pork sausage, removed from its casing and crumbled
2 cloves garlic, minced
Kosher salt and freshly ground black pepper
¼ cup dry red wine
1 35-oz. can whole plum tomatoes, chopped, with their juice
¼ cup chopped fresh marjoram or oregano (from about 6 large sprigs)
1 cup fresh ricotta
1 cup freshly grated mild Pecorino Romano
⅓ cup chopped fresh flat-leaf parsley
Pinch nutmeg, preferably freshly grated
1 lb. ziti
½ lb. mozzarella, preferably fresh, cut into small cubes

Heat the oven to 375°F. Lightly oil a large, shallow baking dish. Bring a large pot of salted water to a boil.

In a large skillet, heat about 2 Tbs. of olive oil over medium heat. Add the onion and sauté until soft, about 5 minutes. Add the crumbled sausage and garlic and sauté until the sausage starts to brown. Season with salt and pepper. If the sausage gives off a lot of fat, pour off most of it, but leave a little to add flavor to the sauce. Add the red wine and let it boil until it's almost gone. Add the tomatoes with all of their juice and cook, uncovered, at a lively simmer for about 10 minutes. The sauce will thicken slightly. Add the marjoram or oregano and taste for seasoning.

In a large bowl, mix the ricotta, about half the Pecorino, the parsley, and the nutmeg. Season with salt and pepper.

Meanwhile, cook the ziti in the boiling water until al dente. Drain well and toss it with the ricotta mixture until well coated. Add the sausage sauce and mix again. Add the mozzarella and toss gently. Pour everything into the baking dish and sprinkle the remaining Pecorino on top. Bake uncovered until lightly browned and bubbling, about 20 minutes. Serve right away.

—Erica DeMane,
Fine Cooking #37

Spaghetti with Portabellas, Sage & Walnuts
Serves four.

Sage and mushrooms are one of those perfect culinary combinations. Another plus for this recipe is that the portabellas make it feel substantially "meaty," although the dish itself is meatless. Scraping out the gills of the portabellas keeps them from turning the pasta a grayish color.

Kosher salt
¾ lb. spaghetti
3 Tbs. extra-virgin olive oil
½ cup unsalted butter
3 large portabella mushroom caps, gills scraped out and discarded, caps thinly sliced and cut into 2-inch pieces
Freshly ground black pepper
⅔ cup loosely packed fresh sage leaves
⅓ cup toasted walnuts, coarsely chopped
½ cup freshly grated Parmigiano-Reggiano

Bring a large pot of salted water to a boil. Add the spaghetti and cook until al dente, about 9 minutes. Reserve 1 cup of the pasta cooking water and then drain the pasta and set aside.

Meanwhile, heat the olive oil and 2 Tbs. of the butter in a 12-inch skillet over medium-high heat until the butter is melted. Add the mushrooms, season with salt and pepper, and cook, stirring occasionally, until they're brown and tender, 4 to 5 minutes. Transfer the mushrooms to a bowl and set aside.

In the same skillet, melt the remaining 6 Tbs. butter over medium heat. Add the sage leaves and cook, stirring occasionally, until they darken and crisp and the flecks of milk solids in the butter are golden brown, 3 to 5 minutes. Return the mushrooms to the pan and pile in the walnuts, the cooked pasta, and ½ cup of the pasta water. Toss the pasta continuously with tongs to coat well, adding more water as needed so the pasta is moist, 1 to 2 minutes. (If your skillet isn't big enough, you can toss everything together in the pasta pot.) Season with salt and pepper, mound into bowls, and sprinkle generously with the Parmigiano. Serve immediately.

—Arlene Jacobs
Fine Cooking #57

Oil & pasta water don't mix

If you're in the habit of adding a little oil to the cooking water to keep the pasta from sticking, here's a good reason to stop: Pasta that's cooked in oily water becomes oily itself, and as a result, the sauce slides off, doesn't get absorbed, and you have less flavorful pasta. You can avoid sticking by stirring the pasta often at the start of cooking.

And while adding oil may keep the pasta water from boiling over, you can also prevent this problem by making sure you use a large pot and by reducing the heat a little (but still maintaining a boil).

Classic Macaroni & Cheese

Serves six to eight.

This dish will taste best if you assemble it ahead of baking time so the pasta can soak up the sauce. But sprinkle on the crumb topping just before baking. The recipe calls for a 9x13-inch baking dish, but it's also nice to use individual ramekins.

1 lb. macaroni
14 Tbs. (7 oz.) unsalted butter
6 Tbs. all-purpose flour
½ medium onion, thinly sliced
1 bay leaf
1 sprig fresh thyme
9 black peppercorns (optional)
4½ cups whole milk
2 tsp. table salt
1 tsp. freshly ground black pepper
Pinch nutmeg
6 cups (1 lb.) finely grated sharp Cheddar
1¼ cups coarse fresh breadcrumbs

Heat the oven to 375°F and butter a 9x13-inch baking dish. Bring a large pot of salted water to a boil and add the macaroni; cook according to package directions until just tender and drain well.

Melt 12 Tbs. of the butter in a heavy-based medium saucepan over medium heat. Add the flour, onion, bay leaf, thyme, and peppercorns; reduce the heat to medium low and cook for 2 to 3 minutes, stirring constantly, to make a roux. Slowly whisk the milk into the roux until smooth and blended. Raise the heat to medium high; whisk constantly until the mixture boils. Cook for 3 to 4 minutes, stirring constantly, until thickened. Lower the heat and continue simmering for about 10 minutes, stirring constantly.

Strain the sauce into a large bowl, removing the onion, herbs, and peppercorns. Add the salt, pepper, nutmeg, and Cheddar, stirring until the cheese is just melted. Toss the pasta with the cheese sauce and pour the mixture into the baking dish.

Melt the last 2 Tbs. butter and toss with the breadcrumbs. Spread the buttered crumbs over the casserole. Bake until sizzling and lightly browned, about 40 minutes, less time for individual dishes (cover with foil if the top browns too quickly).

—*Mary Pult & Rebecca Fasten,*
Fine Cooking #23

Cavatappi with Roasted Peppers, Capocollo & Ricotta

Serves four.

Capocollo is a lightly aged pork sausage usually flavored with white wine and nutmeg. If you can't find it, an excellent substitute is prosciutto di Parma.

Olive oil
5 medium red bell peppers
1 large onion, thinly sliced
Kosher salt and freshly ground black pepper
5 plum tomatoes, seeded and chopped (or one 14.5-oz. can diced tomatoes, drained)
⅓ lb. very thinly sliced capocollo, chopped
A few large sprigs fresh thyme, leaves chopped
1½ cups fresh ricotta
1½ cups heavy cream, preferably not ultrapasteurized
1 to 2 tsp. finely grated orange zest
Pinch nutmeg, preferably freshly grated
1 lb. cavatappi (or fusilli or penne)
¼ cup freshly grated Pecorino Romano
⅓ cup coarse fresh breadcrumbs

Bring a large pot of salted water to a boil. Lightly coat a large shallow baking dish with olive oil.

Roast the peppers by turning them over the flames of a gas burner until the skins are charred or by putting them under a broiler, turning until all sides are well blistered. When they're cool enough to handle, peel off the skins, core and seed the peppers, and cut the flesh into thin strips.

Heat the oven to 425°F. In a large skillet, heat about 3 Tbs. of olive oil over medium heat. Add the onion and cook, stirring occasionally, until it begins to soften. Add the peppers, season with salt and pepper, and sauté until soft and fragrant, about 5 minutes. Add the tomatoes and cook another 5 minutes. Turn off the heat and add the capocollo and thyme. Mix and set aside.

In a medium bowl, combine the ricotta, cream, orange zest, and nutmeg. Season with salt and pepper and whisk until smooth (you can do this in a food processor if you like).

Cook the cavatappi in the boiling water until al dente. Meanwhile, in a small bowl, toss the Pecorino with the breadcrumbs. Season with salt and pepper and add a drizzle of olive oil. Mix well.

Drain the pasta well and return it to the pot. Add the pepper mixture and toss. Add the ricotta mixture, toss again, and taste for seasoning.

Pour the pasta into the baking dish. Top with an even coating of the breadcrumb mixture and a drizzle of fresh olive oil. Bake uncovered until browned and bubbling, 15 to 20 minutes. Serve right away.

—*Erica DeMane,*
Fine Cooking #37

Use box wine for cooking

I used to buy regular bottles of wine for cooking, but I often couldn't use it all before it went bad. Now I use box wine instead. The airtight bag inside the box keeps oxygen out, so the wine lasts longer, and the spigot makes it easy to measure the amount I need. There are several good-quality box wines now, most of which are moderately priced.

—*Linda Simmerson, Sanford, North Carolina*

A little oil helps reopen bottles with sticky contents

Bottles with sticky contents, such as corn syrup, honey, and maple syrup, can be hard to open. So after I open the bottle the first time, I coat the threads lightly with oil. The oil keeps the cap from sticking and makes it a breeze to unscrew the next time. You might have to re-coat the threads every so often.

—*Erica Little, via email*

A cheese knife makes a clean cut on cheesecakes

I was recently slicing a cheesecake using the laborious technique of heating a knife under hot water and wiping it dry after every slice or two. It occurred to me to try my cheese knife, which has holes meant to prevent cheese from sticking. It made clean cuts and did not require any wiping between slices.

—*Jennifer Goldbeck, Cedarburg, Wisconsin*

Use sticky notes for shopping lists at the ready

When I decide to cook a recipe from a magazine, I write a list of all the ingredients on a sticky note. I stick the note onto my grocery list, putting a pencil mark next to the ingredients I need, and do the shopping. Then I use it as a bookmark in the magazine. The next time I want to make that recipe, I already have a shopping list prepared.

—*Wilma Cohrs, Kingston, Ontario*

A prize for the best tip

We want your best tips— we'll pay for the ones we publish—and we'll give a prize to the cleverest tip in each issue. Write to Tips, *Fine Cooking*, PO Box 5506, Newtown, CT 06470-5506 or email fctips@taunton.com.

The prize for this issue's winner: A Norton IM200 professional knife sharpener with how-to DVD; value, about $100.

Improvise a cake platter with cardboard and foil

When I bake a cake to bring to a friend's house, I want to be able to leave without bothering the host to claim my cake platter. So I create one from cardboard and foil. While the cake is cooling on the rack, I invert a platter that fits the cake size onto a piece of cardboard—usually cut from a box—and trace a circle around it. Then I cut out the cardboard circle and wrap it in foil to get a perfectly functional "silver" platter for my cake.

—*Irene Ong, Madison, Wisconsin*

Marbles warn when boiling water is too low

I'm prone to burning pots when steaming vegetables because I let the water completely evaporate. To prevent this, I place four or five glass marbles on the bottom of my stainless-steel pot. Then I add water, bring it to a boil, and steam my vegetables. When the water is low, the marbles start moving around on the bottom of the pot, making a racket, which tells me that I need to add more hot water.

—*Susan Bedsole, via email*

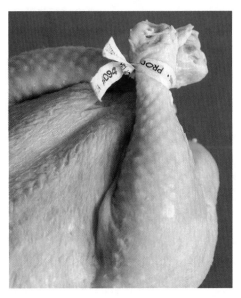

A slotted spatula removes ramekins from a water bath

I always found it tricky to remove crème brûlée ramekins from a hot-water bath. I've tried tongs, with little success. Then I bought a flat, slotted spatula, which works like a charm. I just slide it under each ramekin, allow the water to drain, and transfer the ramekin to my work surface. It's easy and safe.

—*Mary Vierra, Grants Pass, Oregon*

TOO GOOD TO FORGET
from *Fine Cooking* #11

Pinning down parchment

When I cut parchment from a roll, it curls up and slips around as I try to line a baking sheet with it. To prevent this from happening, I clip the parchment to the rim of the baking sheet with a spring-loaded clothespin at each corner. As soon as the item to be baked is safely on the baking sheet, whether it's a batch of cookies or a couple of loaves of bread, the item itself will hold the paper down, and the clothespins can be removed before putting the baking sheet in the oven.

—*James Hunter,
Traverse City, Michigan*

Wrap a bottle to catch the drips

Before I open a new bottle of oil, I fold a paper towel around the middle of the bottle and secure it with tape or an elastic band. The towel keeps the oil from running down the sides of the bottle, so my countertops stay clean, as do my hands. You may have to change the paper towel as it deteriorates with use.

—*Marilyn Quon,
San Diego, California*

Use a wire twist-tie to truss chicken legs

I often find myself without butcher's twine when I need to truss chicken or turkey legs before roasting. As an alternative, I use those large paper-covered wire twist-ties used to wrap lettuce and other produce in grocery stores. I save these twist-ties, rinse them to remove any dirt, and stash them in a drawer, ready to use. I throw them away after I've roasted the chicken or turkey.

—*Mary Ann Palchikoff,
Fairbanks, Alaska*

Mix flavored butter in a plastic bag

When making flavored (or compound) butter, instead of mixing the softened butter with the other ingredients in a bowl, I put all the ingredients in a zip-top bag, seal it tightly, and knead until well mixed. Then I lay the bag on a work surface and gently push the butter toward the bottom with a dough scraper or the back of a knife. I snip off a corner of the bag and pipe the butter onto a piece of parchment to form a log, which I wrap and store in the fridge. I find this method neater and easier, and there's no bowl to wash.

—*Eileen Godfrey,
Simi Valley, California* ◆

Cozy Up with a New Cookbook

Winter is a wonderful time to retreat to the kitchen and cook up something delicious. Whether you want to delve into uncharted culinary territory or stick to the classics, these new books will get you started.

BY LAURA GIANNATEMPO

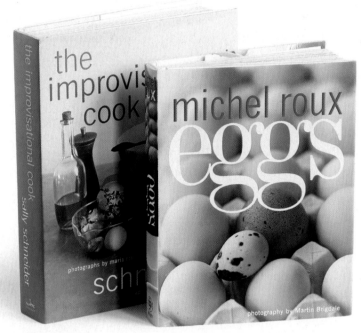

Inspiration in the kitchen

If you like to take liberties with recipes and wander off on your own path, you'll love *The Improvisational Cook* (William Morrow, $34.95). And even if you're a strict recipe follower, author Sally Schneider will give you the confidence and know-how to be more creative: "Once you understand how a basic technique or recipe works, you can start to improvise on it," says Schneider. She believes that what keeps most people from improvising in the kitchen is their unfamiliarity with specific techniques and with the way ingredients interact. So for each recipe, Schneider provides an "Understanding" section, a sort of guide to improvisation where she explains the logic behind the recipe and gives practical ideas for making it your own. Then she gives four or five examples of her own "Improvisations," offering valuable insight into a cook's creative process.

The main recipes are divided into seven categories and range from flavored oils and caramelized onions to a Rustic Root Vegetable Soup, Crisp Pan-Fried Fish Fillets, and an Ever-Improvisational Meat Loaf. Her guide to classic flavor affinities and sections about understanding flavor combinations and the importance of seasoning are also useful improvisational tools. With this book at your side, you're bound to see recipes in a whole new light—as springboards for tasty dishes of your own creation.

Eggs (Wiley, $24.95) is chef Michel Roux's delightful homage to the genius of the egg—an often underappreciated (and sometimes downright maligned) component of so many recipes. Roux expertly guides us through various techniques of egg cooking, from boiled, scrambled, and fried eggs to making omelets, soufflés, and custards. He even includes chapters on fresh egg pasta and ice cream. And for each technique, he shares several tempting recipes—some traditional, others a bit more adventurous. With dishes ranging from Eggs Benedict and Ham and Eggs to Thai-Style Rolled Omelet, Scrambled Eggs Masala, and Vanilla and Mango Soufflé, there's something here for everyone.

I was particularly intrigued by the deep-fried egg technique—and a little skeptical, too. But when our test kitchen gave it a spin, we loved the results: The eggs were crispy on the outside and oozing with yolky richness inside. Graced with stunning photographs, including step-by-step technique shots, this beautiful little book manages to be both inspirational and very practical.

Across the oceans

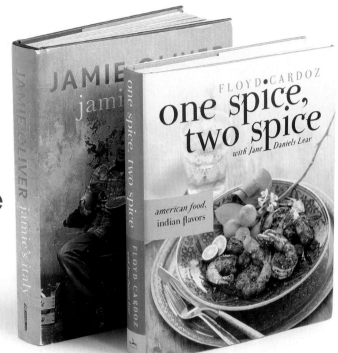

I n *Jamie's Italy* (Hyperion, $34.95), British celebrity chef Jamie Oliver takes on Italian cooking, inviting us on a whirlwind trip around the boot to explore the food of the "real" Italy, as he puts it, from antipasti to desserts. While in substance this book is not that different from other well-researched collections of traditional Italian recipes, Oliver's infectious energy and obvious passion for the food drew me in and sent me straight to the kitchen. Oliver's recipes are simple to follow, most can be made with easy-to-find ingredients, and the ones I've tried—including a delicious fennel risotto with ricotta and dried chiles—were quite tasty. His headnotes and introductory chapters also pack a lot of useful information, helping to put the recipes in context. And the book is a beauty to behold. It's filled with gorgeous, atmospheric photographs of inviting dishes as well as of Jamie Oliver himself roaming around the back streets of Italy, making pasta with Italian matrons, and sharing wine with craggy-faced shepherds (though I must admit that the photos seem a little contrived at times).

In so many ways, this is my kind of Italian cookbook: It's honest to the food yet fresh and inspiring. And it exudes charm right down to the intentional imprecision of the ingredient lists ("a pinch of ground fennel seeds" or "4 large handfuls of fresh basil"), which remind me of the way my Italian mother writes her own recipes.

Tabla, the acclaimed Indian-fusion restaurant in New York City, is easily one of my favorites in town. So as soon as I got a copy of chef Floyd Cardoz's first cookbook, *One Spice, Two Spice: American Food, Indian Flavors* (William Morrow, $34.95), I eagerly took it home and spent a glorious weekend in the kitchen cooking my way through a feast of Goan Spiced Crab Cakes and Avocado Salad, Lemon Chive Raita, and Shrimp Curry. Everything tasted amazing, almost as if it came straight from Tabla's kitchen, and his subtle use of spices translates surprisingly well in his recipes.

Cardoz's eclectic culinary background, which took him from Bombay and the island of Goa to France, and then New York City, makes for a distinctive and enticing collection. A useful introductory section offers valuable tips on buying and storing spices as well as on grinding and toasting them.

The recipes don't always feel accessible, though. Several call for ingredients that can be hard to come by, such as curry leaves and kokum (the fruit of the gamboge tree, impossible to find anywhere but at an Indian market), and others seem to belong strictly to a restaurant menu—I don't know many people who would tackle Black Spice-Rubbed Poussin with Kokum Jus at home. But the adventurous cook can learn a lot about how spices are used in Indian cuisine through Cardoz's unique interpretations.

A new *Joy*

America's most popular cookbook is back with a brand-new edition to celebrate 75 years of joyful cooking. *The Best Loved and Brand New Joy of Cooking* (Scribner, $30), released last November, replaces the controversial 1997 edition, which was accused by some of betraying the author's original quirky, first-person voice in favor of a more contemporary—and impersonal—approach. This new *Joy* is based largely on the beloved 1975 edition, and, indeed, such vintage recipes as Shrimp Wiggle and Quick Tuna Casserole are back (along with lots more that require opening a cream-of-something can). But while clearly bowing to nostalgia, this *Joy* sneaks in a few new sections that address more recent trends, like a grains cooking chart, a "cook for a day, eat for a week" section, and a list of 30-minute recipes.

—*L.G.*

For the dessert lover in all of us

Dorie Greenspan's *Baking, from My Home to Yours* (Houghton Mifflin, $40) is one of those books you know you must have as soon as you lay eyes on it. It's an attractive tome with lots of big photographs and yummy recipes that make you want to tie on an apron and get baking. And it's got weight, too. By that I don't just mean that it feels nice and heavy; it also has an impressive encyclopedic breadth. The book covers everything from muffins, scones, and other breakfast sweets to cookies, cakes, pies, tarts, and "spoon desserts" (puddings, custards, crisps, and ice creams). There's room in it for classics, such as Tarte Tatin, Pound Cake, and an All-American Apple Pie, as well as for more-unusual creations like Espresso Cheesecake Brownies and Fluted Polenta and Ricotta Cake. But Greenspan's tone is anything but academic. She gives recipes happy titles like Chocolate Chunkers and Cranberry Upside-Downer, and along the way, she serves up a wealth of baking pointers—from how to get perfect pie dough to

instructions for frosting layer cakes—with an amiable, reassuring voice that makes you feel that you have a baker friend at your side.

Tish Boyle's lovely *The Cake Book* (Wiley, $39.95) contains everything you need to know about baking cakes, whether it's a straightforward, single-layer carrot cake or a complicated, multilayered, frosted, and decorated chocolate dacquoise. A thorough and easy-to-follow introductory section covers the basics: from flours and fats to sugars, eggs, stabilizers, and leaveners, as well as cake-baking equipment, tips, and techniques (like measuring ingredients and preparing pans). And the recipes I made delivered great results. I can vouch for Boyle's Devilishly Moist Chocolate Cake, which uses safflower oil instead of butter. Quick enough to bake on a weeknight, it was easy and absolutely delicious.

Another jewel of a book, Emily Luchetti's *A Passion for Ice Cream* (Chronicle Books, $35) makes you want to get a spoon and dig into one of her

tempting frozen treats. Sure, you need to invest in an ice-cream maker (a requirement for most of the book's recipes), but once that's taken care of, you too can turn out meltingly soft, delicious creations like Dulce de Leche Frozen Yogurt, Lime Ice Cream, Tangerine Creamsicle Sodas, and Walnut Cookie and Caramel Ice-Cream Sandwiches. The recipes, which include sundaes, floats, sorbets, Popsicles, ice-cream cakes, and frozen desserts to eat with your fingers (think ice-cream sandwiches and bonbons) are all fun, imaginative, and totally doable. In addition, there are ideas for a variety of toppings and decorations. With this book at hand, you can easily say good-bye to the ice-cream man.

Laura Giannatempo is an assistant editor for Fine Cooking. ◆

Bistro Cooking at Home

Call up a few friends and settle in for a casual dinner of braised lamb shanks, rustic beef stew, or a saucy chicken sauté

BY MOLLY STEVENS

There's something about a real French bistro that makes you want to pull up a chair, tuck a napkin into your lap, and see what's on the menu. Warm and inviting, a bistro is the ultimate neighborhood restaurant, a place where, if you were lucky enough to live around the corner, you could happily eat three or four nights a week, even though the menu might offer nothing more than a few entrées, a couple of salads, and a

Braised Lamb Shanks

single house dessert. Bistro food is French home cooking at its best—simple but satisfying dishes, presented without fanfare or flourish, often lovingly prepared personally by the proprietor.

It would be impossible to name all the timeless classics that qualify as bistro fare—everything from steak frites and roast chicken to steamed mussels and braised rabbit—but three of my all-time favorites are braised lamb shanks, beef stew, and a chicken sauté with vinegar. These are the dishes I can't resist when I spot them on a menu, and since my visits to France aren't nearly frequent enough to satisfy my appetite for these wonderful meals, I've come up with my own versions. Like most bistro food, the recipes on these pages aren't fussy; and best of all, they taste really authentic. So next time you get a craving for that bistro atmosphere, here's what you do: Make one of these dishes, call up a few good friends, set a casual table, and put on an Edith Piaf or Jacques Brel CD, or just your favorite jazz music. And then enjoy the little French bistro you've created in the comfort of your own home.

Find more bistro recipes, tips, and cooking techniques, at finecooking.com

Serving suggestion: Fill out the meal with a potato gratin and a refreshing heap of green beans that you've blanched and then sautéed in a little butter and minced shallot. For recipes, visit FineCooking.com.

Photos: Scott Phillips

with Garlic & Vermouth
Souris aux Aulx

About the only place you'll see whole lamb shanks on a French menu is in a bistro. Perhaps the primitive appearance of the meaty shanks is considered too boorish for fine dining, I don't know. But what I do know is that nothing matches slow-cooked lamb shanks for tenderness and depth of flavor. The inspiration for my recipe comes from Richard Olney's *Simple French Food,* where the shanks and garlic are cooked with nothing more than a bit of water. I've updated Olney's version by adding dry white vermouth and a few bay leaves to give the braising liquid an elusive, herbaceous flavor that permeates the meat and intensifies the dish.

A few points: Lamb throws off a considerable amount of fat as it cooks, so be sure to take the time to thoroughly skim the sauce before serving. Better yet, braise the shanks a day or two before you plan to serve them, and store them and the braising liquid in the refrigerator. When it comes time to reheat and serve, simply lift the solidified fat from the surface of the sauce. The dish will have even more flavor after a day or two.

Braised Lamb Shanks with Garlic & Vermouth

Serves six.

6 lamb shanks (¾ to 1 lb. each)
Kosher salt and freshly ground black pepper
2 Tbs. extra-virgin olive oil
1 cup dry white vermouth, preferably Vya or Noilly Pratt
2 bay leaves
2 heads garlic, separated into cloves (unpeeled)
2 tsp. fresh lemon juice; more as needed
¼ cup chopped fresh herbs, preferably a mix of mint and parsley (chervil and chives are also good)

Position a rack in the lower third of the oven and heat the oven to 325°F. If necessary, trim any excess fat from the lamb shanks, but don't trim away the thin membrane that holds the meat to the bone. Season the shanks all over with salt and pepper.

Heat the oil over medium heat in a large Dutch oven or other heavy braising pot large enough to accommodate the lamb shanks in a snug single layer. When the oil is shimmering, add half the shanks and brown them on all sides, 12 to 15 minutes total. Set the browned shanks on a platter. Repeat with the remaining shanks. When all the shanks are browned, pour off and discard the fat from the pan.

Set the pan over medium-high heat and add the vermouth. As it boils, stir with a wooden spoon to dissolve any drippings. Return the shanks to the pan, arranging them as best you can so they fit snugly. Tuck the bay leaves in between the shanks and scatter the garlic over them. Cover and braise in the oven, turning the shanks every 45 minutes, until fork-tender, 1½ to 2 hours.

Transfer the shanks to a platter and cover with foil to keep warm. Tilt the braising pot to pool the juices at one end and skim off and discard any surface fat. Pour what remains in the pot into a medium-mesh sieve set over a bowl. Discard the bay leaves. With a rubber spatula, scrape over and press down on the garlic cloves so the pulp goes through but not the skins; be sure to scrape the pulp clinging to the bottom of the strainer into the sauce. Whisk in the lemon juice. Taste and add salt, pepper, and more lemon juice if needed. To serve, pour the sauce over the shanks and shower them with the chopped herbs and a little freshly ground pepper.

Make ahead note: The dish can be made up to three days ahead. After braising, transfer the shanks to a baking dish. Strain and season the sauce as directed in the recipe. Pour a little strained sauce over the shanks to moisten them. Refrigerate the shanks and the sauce separately, both tightly covered. Before serving, reheat the chilled sauce, pour it over the shanks in the baking dish, cover the dish with foil, and warm in a 325°F oven for about 30 minutes. Finish with the herbs and black pepper, and serve.

tip: After the long braise, the garlic cloves are tender enough to push through a sieve, creating a flavorful purée that thickens the pan sauce. Don't forget to scrape the pulp clinging to the bottom of the strainer.

drink choices

The lamb calls for a deeply flavored red wine with herbal notes. A Syrah from France's northern Rhône Valley, such as either the 2004 Cave de Chante-Perdrix St. Joseph (organic), $22, or the 2004 Jean Luc Columbo Crozes-Hermitage, $24, would be a good choice.

Chicken with Vinegar

Serving suggestion:
Steam small red or white potatoes until tender. Just before serving, sauté the potatoes in butter until browned and crispy.

& Onions
Poulet au Vinaigre

In my experience, a poultry sauté is one of the most overlooked techniques in French cooking. It's easier than pan-frying and more elegant than a stew. A sauté refers to dredging a cut-up bird (usually a small chicken) in flour before cooking it in a deep skillet with either butter or olive oil and very little, if any, added liquid. As the chicken cooks, it simmers in its own juices mingled with the fat, creating a very concentrated, rich sauce. Most cooks add some aromatics (onions, leeks, or shallots) and a bit of wine or vinegar to balance the richness.

In my version, I first sauté the onion, turning it sweet and tender before adding it to the sautéed chicken. I also love the combination of tarragon and chicken, but if you're not a tarragon fan, you can substitute another delicate herb, such as parsley, chervil, or chives. I encourage you to try it with tarragon, though, because even those who are averse to the herb have told me they love it in this dish. I find that finishing the dish with a dab of crème fraîche brings all the flavors into focus.

Chicken with Vinegar & Onions

Serves four to six.

3 Tbs. unsalted butter
2 medium-small yellow onions, thinly sliced (about 2½ cups)
Kosher salt and freshly ground black pepper
3 Tbs. Champagne vinegar (see Tasting Panel, p. 71, for recommendations)
1 4-lb. chicken, cut into 8 pieces (or 2 bone-in, skin-on breasts and 4 bone-in, skin-on thighs)
½ cup all-purpose flour
2 Tbs. extra-virgin olive oil
½ cup dry white wine, such as Sauvignon Blanc or Pinot Gris
2 tsp. chopped fresh tarragon leaves
2 Tbs. crème fraîche (or heavy cream)

In a 12-inch skillet, melt 2 Tbs. of the butter over medium heat. Add the onions, sprinkle with a couple of big pinches of salt and a few grinds of pepper, and stir to coat the onions. Cover, reduce the heat to medium low, and continue to cook, stirring occasionally, until the onions are tender and lightly browned, about 20 minutes. Scrape them into a small bowl and set the skillet over medium-high heat. Add 1 Tbs. of the vinegar and stir with a wooden spoon to dissolve any browned bits on the bottom of the pan. Pour the vinegar into the onions and set the skillet aside.

If using chicken parts, cut each breast crosswise into two equal-size portions and trim any excess fat or skin from the thighs. Rinse and pat dry.

Spread the flour in a pie plate, and season the chicken pieces with salt and pepper. Set the skillet over medium-high heat and add the olive oil and the remaining 1 Tbs. butter. While the butter melts, dredge half of the seasoned chicken pieces in the flour, shaking off the excess. Set them skin side down in the skillet. Brown, turning once, until the skin is crisp and the chicken is evenly browned, 6 to 8 minutes total. Lower the heat if the chicken or the drippings threaten to burn. Transfer the chicken pieces to a pan or platter and repeat with the remaining chicken.

When all the chicken is browned, pour off all of the fat. Return the skillet to medium-high heat, add the wine, and scrape the bottom of the pan with a wooden spoon to dissolve the drippings. Add the remaining 2 Tbs. of vinegar, the sautéed onions, and 1 tsp. of the tarragon. Return the chicken pieces, skin side up, to the skillet, arranging them in a single snug layer. Partially cover, leaving a small gap for the steam to escape, and lower the heat to maintain a low simmer. Continue to simmer gently, turning every 10 minutes, until the chicken is tender and cooked through, about 30 minutes total.

Transfer the chicken to a platter. Increase the heat to a more rapid simmer, and stir in the crème fraîche (or cream); the sauce may appear broken at first, but it will come together. Taste for salt and pepper. Add the remaining 1 tsp. tarragon and spoon over the chicken to serve.

Make ahead note: This dish can be made a day or two ahead, but don't add the last teaspoon of tarragon. Reheat gently in a covered baking dish in a 325°F oven for about 30 minutes, adding a few tablespoons of water or chicken broth if the chicken appears dry. Sprinkle with the tarragon and serve.

tip: Leave the lid of the skillet slightly ajar to let some steam escape during cooking. This concentrates the liquid for a more intense sauce, and it also ensures that the liquid doesn't boil or simmer too hard, which would overcook the chicken.

drink choices

The vinegar and crème fraîche elements in this dish call for a racy white wine with herbal elements. Sauvignon Blanc is a great choice; look for wines from the Sancerre or Pouilly-Fumé regions of France. The 2004 André Vatan Sancerre, $16, and the 2004 Henri Bourgeois Pouilly-Fumé, La Porte de l'Abbaye, $16, would be good bottles to try.

Beef Stew with Red

Serving suggestion: Mashed potatoes would be a perfect foil for the daube's rich wine sauce. For recipes, visit FineCooking.com. Or you could serve the daube with wide egg noodles tossed with butter and parsley.

Wine & Carrots
Daube de Boeuf aux Carottes

Very simply, a daube (pronounced dohb) is a red-wine-based beef or lamb stew. This type of dish has countless flavor permutations, of course, but the most famous (and my favorite) is the Provençal daube, seasoned with local herbs and a bit of orange zest. The orange was originally the bitter Seville orange, but you can make a fine daube with a few strips of navel orange (add a strip of lemon, too, if you want to sharpen the flavor). I also like to add some sort of vegetable garnish to sweeten and brighten the stew. Here I've used carrots cut into hefty chunks so they hold their shape during the long cooking, but you could also use a combination of parsnips, baby onions, and celeriac.

When buying meat for a daube, your best bet is to select a small chuck roast and cut it yourself. Most butchers and meat markets cut their stew meat way too small for my preference. In my mind, a proper daube should be a knife-and-fork affair—meaning the chunks are larger than bite size (see the photo tip at right).

Molly Stevens, an award-winning author and contributing editor to Fine Cooking, *got hooked on bistro fare while working at La Varenne cooking school in France.* ◆

Beef Stew with Red Wine & Carrots
Serves six.

- 1 3-lb. boneless beef chuck roast
- 2 Tbs. extra-virgin olive oil
- 2 slices thick-cut bacon, cut into ½-inch pieces
- Kosher salt and freshly ground black pepper
- 8 oz. shallots (8 to 10 medium), thinly sliced (about 2 cups)
- 2 Tbs. brandy, such as Cognac
- 2 Tbs. tomato paste
- 2 to 3 cloves garlic, finely chopped (2 to 3 tsp.)
- 2 tsp. herbes de Provence
- 2 cups hearty red wine, such as Côtes de Provence or Côtes du Rhône
- 1 14.5-oz. can whole, peeled tomatoes
- 4 strips orange zest (2½ inches long, removed with a vegetable peeler)
- 1 lb. slender carrots, peeled and cut into ¾- to 1-inch chunks (about 2 cups)
- ¼ cup coarsely chopped fresh flat-leaf parsley

Using your fingers and a thin knife, pull the roast apart along its natural seams. Trim off any thick layers of fat. Carve the roast into 1½- to 2-inch cubes and arrange them on a paper-towel-lined tray to dry.

Position a rack in the lower third of the oven. Heat the oven to 325°F.

Heat the oil and bacon together in a 7- or 8-qt. Dutch oven over medium heat, stirring occasionally, just until the bacon is browned but not crisp, 5 to 6 minutes. With a slotted spoon, transfer the bacon to a small plate. Season about one-third of the beef with salt and pepper, and arrange the cubes in a sparse single layer in the pot to brown. Adjust the heat so the beef sizzles and browns but does not burn. Cook until all sides are a rich brown, a total of about 10 minutes. Transfer to a large plate or tray, and season and brown the remaining beef in 2 more batches.

When all the beef chunks are browned, pour off all but about 1 Tbs. of drippings, if necessary. Set the pot over medium-high heat, add the shallots, season with a large pinch of salt and several grinds of pepper, and sauté until they just begin to soften, about 1 minute. Add the brandy and let it boil away. Add the tomato paste, garlic, and herbes de Provence, stirring to incorporate, and sauté for another 1 minute. Add the wine, stirring and scraping the bottom of the pan with a wooden spoon to dislodge the caramelized drippings, and bring to a boil. Pour in the liquid from the tomatoes, holding the tomatoes back with your hand. Then one by one, crush the tomatoes with your hand over the pot and drop them in. Add the orange zest, and return the beef (along with accumulated juices) and bacon to the pot. Finally, add the carrots, bring to a simmer, cover, and slide into the oven.

Cook the stew, stirring every 45 minutes, until the meat is fork-tender (taste a piece; all trace of toughness should be gone), 2 to 3 hours. Before serving, skim off any surface fat (if there is any), taste for salt and pepper, and stir in the parsley.

Make ahead note: This dish can be made up to three days ahead. Reserve the chopped parsley and don't bother skimming the surface fat. Instead, transfer the cooled stew to a bowl or baking dish, cover tightly, and refrigerate. Before reheating, lift off the layer of solid fat that will be on the surface. Reheat gently in a 325°F oven in a covered baking dish, stirring once, for about 30 minutes, or until hot. Taste for salt and pepper and add the parsley just before serving.

tip: Rather than buying already cut-up stew meat, buy a whole chuck roast and cut it into 1½- to 2-inch cubes. These larger chunks won't dry out during the long braise, and they make the stew more satisfying to eat. For more on chuck, see From Our Test Kitchen, p. 66.

see From Our Test Kitchen, p. 66.

drink choices

This stew needs a rich, earthy red from the Old World, such as a Grenache blend from the southern Rhône Valley. Try the 2005 Mas Grand Plagniol "Tradition," Costières de Nîmes, $10, or the 2004 Château du Trignon, Gigondas, $18.

the secrets to fluffy & flavorful

Rice Pilaf

Start with long-grain white rice and then layer on the flavors

BY RIS LACOSTE

When I make rice pilaf, I expect two things: light, fluffy texture—the individual grains of rice should be firm and separate, not mushy and stuck together—and bold, full flavors. Fortunately, it's easy to achieve both. The unique cooking process that gives pilaf its distinctive texture also provides several opportunities to incorporate flavor into the dish.

The pilaf method: toast, simmer, rest

The basic technique for making pilaf is pretty straightforward: The rice first toasts in fat, then simmers in liquid, and finally rests off the heat. I've found that at each step, there's a trick or two that will help deliver the fluffy texture I want. And there's also a chance to layer on flavor (see the sidebar on p. 42).

Toasting the rice briefly over medium-low heat in oil, butter, or another fat is key to getting dry, separate grains of rice. And the toasting process itself also gives the rice a subtle nutty flavor. During toasting, the grains shouldn't actually turn golden or brown. They will, however, lose their translucency, and the starches on the outside of each grain will firm up. As a result, the grains will absorb liquid slowly and thus maintain their shape as they cook. Toasting rice over medium-low heat also helps keep the starches from escaping from the grains, which could result in sticky rice.

Use a little less liquid than usual and simmer gently. Instead of using the standard 2:1 liquid to rice ratio, I use 1¾ cups liquid for every 1 cup of rice. This helps ensure a dry, separate texture. Once you add

the liquid, stir the pot once and no more. Then let the rice simmer undisturbed for 18 minutes (rather than the typical 20 minutes). Again, the less the rice is agitated, the less chance there will be for starches to gum things up.

Finally, let the rice sit undisturbed off the heat with the cover on for 5 minutes. This allows the starch to firm up, which means the grains will be more likely to separate rather than stick when you fluff the rice and fold in your finishing touches.

Use the right rice

The pilaf technique will take you far toward getting good results, but to guarantee perfect texture, it's also important to use the right kind of rice. The best choice is long-grain white rice. The individual grains are long and slender, and they contain a type of starch that is more apt to let the grains stay separate and fluffy as they cook. (For more rice science, see p. 44.)

I usually use Carolina brand long-grain white rice; its mild flavor makes it perfect for all sorts of seasonings. But other long-grain varieties work, too. Basmati rice, for example, is an aromatic variety that's popular in India and Pakistan. It cooks up very dry, so it's wonderful for pilaf. Another long-grain variety is Thai jasmine rice, which is aromatic and a tad stickier than basmati. I recommend using the Carolina rice for the southwestern pilaf on p. 43 and the pilaf with sage, Parmigiano, and prosciutto on p. 44. Basmati rice would work deliciously in the pilaf with onions, orange & cherry on p. 42. And you could try jasmine rice in the saffron pilaf recipe at right.

(see the sidebar on p. 42); (For more rice science, see p. 44.); on p. 43; on p. 44; on p. 42; at right

Saffron Rice Pilaf with Red Pepper & Toasted Almonds
Serves six to eight.

The flavors in this pilaf remind me a little of paella. It's a great partner for salmon, shrimp, or mussels.

2½ cups low-salt chicken broth or water
Pinch saffron (about 20 threads)
1 Tbs. extra-virgin olive oil
1 medium onion, small diced (1¼ cups)
1 red bell pepper, cored, seeded, and small diced (about 1 cup)
1½ cups long-grain white rice
1 tsp. kosher salt; more as needed
Pinch ground cayenne
¼ cup roughly chopped fresh Italian parsley
1 large clove garlic, minced (1½ tsp.)
¼ cup slivered almonds, toasted
1 Tbs. roughly chopped fresh oregano

On the stovetop or in the microwave, heat the broth until hot. Add the saffron, cover, and let sit for 15 to 20 minutes.

In a heavy-based 3-qt. saucepan with a tight lid, heat the oil over medium heat. Reduce the heat to medium low and add the diced onion and bell pepper. Cook, stirring occasionally, until soft but not browned, about 5 minutes. Add the rice, salt, and cayenne, and stir well to coat each grain with oil. Toast for a full 5 minutes, stirring regularly to keep the grains separated and to prevent them from sticking to the bottom of the pan (the rice may turn opaque before 5 minutes is up, but keep going). Reduce the heat to low if there are any signs of scorching. Stir in 2 Tbs. of the parsley and the garlic.

Add the saffron broth, stir once, and bring to a boil over medium heat. Cover, reduce the heat to low, and cook for 18 minutes. Remove from the heat, and let the pilaf sit, still covered, for 5 minutes.

Once the pilaf has rested, remove the lid and fluff the rice with a fork (see How to fluff pilaf, p. 43). Using the fork, gently fold in the almonds, the remaining 2 Tbs. parsley, and the oregano. Taste for seasoning and adjust as needed.

Rice Pilaf with Spiced Caramelized Onions, Orange, Cherry & Pistachio

Serves six to eight.

The flavors of this pilaf are wonderful with curries and with full-flavored fish like salmon.

4 Tbs. unsalted butter
3 medium onions: 2 sliced (about 3 cups); 1 small diced (about 1¼ cups)
½ tsp. ground allspice
½ tsp. ground cinnamon
Pinch ground cloves
1½ tsp. kosher salt; more as needed
Freshly ground black pepper
1 orange, zest finely grated (about 2½ tsp.) and juiced (about 6 Tbs.)
¾ cup sweetened dried tart cherries
1½ cups long-grain white rice
¾ cup shelled pistachios, toasted and roughly chopped (3.5 oz.)

In a 12-inch heavy-based skillet, melt 2 Tbs. of the butter over medium heat. Add the sliced onions, reduce the heat to medium low, and cook, stirring occasionally, until soft and lightly caramelized, 20 to 25 minutes. Add the allspice, cinnamon, and cloves, and stir well. Reduce the heat to low and cook another 5 minutes, stirring occasionally, to allow the onion to absorb the flavors of the spices and caramelize a bit more. Season with ½ tsp. of the salt and a few grinds of black pepper. Set aside.

Pour the orange juice over the cherries in a small bowl to hydrate them, if necessary adding enough water to cover completely.

In a heavy-based 3-qt. saucepan with a tight lid, melt the remaining 2 Tbs. butter over medium heat. Reduce the heat to medium low and add the diced onion. Cook, stirring occasionally, until soft but not browned, about 5 minutes. Add the rice and the remaining 1 tsp. salt and stir well to coat each grain with butter. Toast for a full 5 minutes, stirring regularly to keep the grains separated and to prevent them from sticking to the bottom of the pan (the rice may turn opaque before 5 minutes is up, but keep going). Reduce the heat to low if there are any signs of scorching.

Add 2½ cups water, stir once, and bring to a boil over medium heat. Cover, reduce the heat to low, and cook for 18 minutes. Remove from the heat, and let the pilaf sit, still covered, for 5 minutes.

Once the pilaf has rested, remove the lid and fluff the rice with a fork (see How to fluff pilaf, p. 43). Strain the cherries and discard the orange juice. Using the fork, gently fold in the cherries, caramelized onions, pistachios, and orange zest. Taste for seasoning and adjust as needed.

Building layers of flavor: 1, 2, 3

1 aromatic base

Creating a deeply flavored pilaf begins before you toast the rice. Choose a flavorful fat (for instance, olive oil, butter, or ghee), and then sauté your aromatic ingredients in it. Many delicious pilafs start with nothing more than onions and butter, but you can also add garlic, spices, herbs, and other finely chopped vegetables.

2 flavorful liquid

Building up the dish's flavor profile continues when you add the liquid. You might choose chicken broth instead of water, or use a bit of both with wine or a fruit juice. As the liquid boils down, it concentrates, infusing the pilaf with intense flavor.

3 finishing touches

Finally, when you fluff the rice before serving it, you can fold in ingredients that add textural interest as well as flavor. These final mix-ins might be uncooked ingredients, like fresh herbs, nuts, and cheeses, or precooked items like crispy bacon or caramelized onions.

How to fluff pilaf

Without a doubt, a fork is the best tool for fluffing rice pilaf. A spoon encourages clumping, but a fork's narrow tines gently separate the grains without breaking them, which helps preserve the perfect texture you've taken pains to achieve. Use a light hand, because vigorous stirring could break up the grains and encourage them to cling together.

Here's my fork-fluffing technique:
Slip the tines down into the rice alongside the edge of the pan. Gently lift and toss the rice toward the center of the pan. Continue this process as you work your way around the perimeter. Then add your finishing-touch ingredients and gently fold them in with the fork, using a similar gentle fluffing motion.

Southwestern Rice Pilaf
Serves six to eight.

This dish makes a delicious accompaniment to steak or chicken fajitas.

2 Tbs. extra-virgin olive oil
1 medium onion, medium diced (1½ cups)
1 medium poblano, stemmed, seeded, and finely diced (½ cup)
4 large cloves garlic, minced (2 Tbs.)
1½ tsp. chili powder
1 tsp. ground cumin
1½ cups long-grain white rice
1 tsp. kosher salt; more as needed
2½ cups low-salt chicken broth
1 14-oz. can diced tomatoes, drained well
1 lime
½ cup coarsely chopped fresh cilantro
1 jalapeño, stemmed, seeded, and minced

In a heavy-based 3-qt. saucepan with a tight lid, heat the oil over medium heat. Add the onion, poblano, and garlic, and reduce the heat to medium low. Cook for 3 minutes, stirring occasionally. Add the chili powder and cumin and cook, stirring frequently, until the onion is softened and the spices are very fragrant, about 3 minutes.

Add the rice and salt, and stir well to coat each grain with oil. Toast for a full 5 minutes, stirring regularly to keep the grains separated and to prevent them from sticking to the bottom of the pan (the rice may turn opaque before 5 minutes is up, but keep going). Reduce the heat to low if there are any signs of scorching.

Add the chicken broth and tomatoes, stir once, and bring to a boil over medium heat. Cover, reduce the heat to low, and cook for 18 minutes. Remove from the heat and let the pilaf sit, still covered, for 5 minutes. Meanwhile, finely grate 1 Tbs. zest from the lime, and then cut the lime into wedges.

Once the pilaf has rested, remove the lid and fluff the rice with a fork (see How to fluff pilaf, above right). Using the fork, gently fold in the cilantro, jalapeño, and lime zest. Season to taste with salt. Serve with the lime wedges for spritzing over the rice.

Rice Pilaf with Sage, Parmigiano & Prosciutto

Serves six to eight.

I love to serve this with roast chicken, along with asparagus or fava beans.

2 Tbs. extra-virgin olive oil
¼ lb. very thinly sliced prosciutto (about 5 slices), cut crosswise into 1-inch-wide strips
4 Tbs. unsalted butter
3 Tbs. chopped fresh sage
4 large cloves garlic, minced (2 Tbs.)
3 large shallots, thinly sliced (1 scant cup)
1½ cups long-grain white rice
1 tsp. kosher salt; more as needed
1 cup dry white wine
1½ cups low-salt chicken broth
2 oz. Parmigiano-Reggiano, coarsely grated on the large holes of a box grater (about ⅔ cup)

In a 3-qt. heavy-based saucepan with a tight lid, heat the olive oil over medium heat. Cook half the prosciutto in the hot oil, stirring occasionally, until browned and crispy, 1 to 2 minutes. With tongs or a slotted spoon, transfer the prosciutto to a paper towel to drain. Repeat with the remaining prosciutto.

Add 2 Tbs. of the butter to the pan and reduce the heat to low. When the butter has melted, add 2 Tbs. of the sage and cook for a few seconds, and then add the garlic and shallots. Cook, stirring occasionally, until the shallots are soft but not browned, about 5 minutes. Add the rice and salt and stir well to coat each grain with oil. Toast for a full 5 minutes, stirring regularly to keep the grains separated and to prevent them from sticking to the bottom of the pan (the rice may turn opaque before 5 minutes is up, but keep going).

Add the wine, stir well, and cook over medium heat until the wine is mostly reduced, about 3 minutes. Add the chicken broth, stir once, and bring to a boil. Cover, reduce the heat to low, and cook for 18 minutes. Remove the pan from the heat and let sit, still covered, for 5 minutes.

Once the pilaf has rested, remove the lid and fluff the rice with a fork (see How to fluff pilaf, p. 43). Cut the remaining 2 Tbs. butter into several pieces and, using the fork, gently fold it into the rice with the remaining 1 Tbs. sage, the Parmigiano, and the cooked prosciutto. Taste for seasoning and adjust as needed.

Award-winning chef Ris Lacoste was executive chef at 1789 Restaurant in Washington, D.C., for 10 years. She will be opening a restaurant of her own soon. ◆

tip: the fat adds extra flavor

In the recipe at left, I crisp prosciutto in olive oil before sautéing the aromatics and toasting the rice. The prosciutto's fat and flavor infuse the oil and everything that subsequently cooks in it.

Water is A-OK

As much as I love broth for pilafs, there's nothing wrong with cooking your rice in water. As long as you've added interesting ingredients during the sauté stage and a few flavorful finishing touches, a pilaf made with water will still be very tasty. In fact, water is my liquid of choice when I want the rice to retain its white color, as in the Rice Pilaf with Spiced Caramelized Onions, Orange & Cherry on p. 42.

food science

Why long grain?

There are many kinds of rice, but only long-grain white rice is perfect for pilaf. Why? Because of its starch content. Different rice varieties contain different kinds and amounts of starch, and starch content is what ultimately determines whether rice grains become fluffy or sticky as they cook. Long-grain rice is rich in a type of starch (called amylose) that is quite stable and doesn't get sticky during cooking, so the rice cooks up with firm, separate grains. Medium- and short-grain rice varieties, on the other hand, contain high amounts of a different type of starch (called amylopectin), which makes the rice grains become soft and sticky as they cook.

Crème Brûlée

These luxurious custards topped with crisp caramel are surprisingly simple to make

BY KIMBERLY Y. MASIBAY

Every cook needs a show-stopping, foolproof dessert in his or her arsenal. For me, that dessert is crème brûlée. It's rich, creamy, crispy, and sweet, and it's also amazingly easy to make (but that can be our secret).

The trick with crème brûlée, or any custard for that matter, is keeping the eggs in the mixture from overcooking and curdling. But honestly, it's not a big deal. My recipe, on the next page, has all the built-in safeguards, so you don't have to worry about a thing.

Temper the eggs and use a water bath

Crème brûlée is undeniably rich, but its texture should be light and silky, not thick and heavy and certainly not curdled. Achieving that silken texture is a simple matter of keeping the eggs from getting too hot at two key points in the recipe. First, when you're combining the hot (165°F) cream and the egg yolks for your custard base, you temper the egg yolks by whisking in a little bit of the cream to gently raise the yolks' temperature before stirring in the rest of the cream. And second, you bake the custards in a water bath.

A water bath insulates the custards from the direct heat of the oven and is your best insurance against overcooking and curdling. Direct heat can take a ramekin of custard from cooked to curdled in a minute, but since heat travels through water more slowly, you have a wider window of opportunity to catch the custards at the perfect degree of doneness.

A fiery finishing touch

Exquisite as the custard is, it's the caramelized sugar topping that makes crème brûlée special. Before the topping goes on, what you've got are humble-looking egg custards. But all that changes once you sprinkle on the sugar, fire up your blowtorch (see sidebar, p. 47), and melt the sugar into a thin, crisp caramel crust.

Although you can cook the custards a couple of days ahead and stash them in the fridge, it's best to wait until the last minute to give them their crowning glory or the topping will start to lose its crunch. After you caramelize the sugar, let the crème brûlée rest for a couple of minutes—just long enough for the caramel to cool and harden.

Making crème brûlée, step by step

Classic Crème Brûlée

Yields four 5-oz. custards;
serves four.

One of the greatest things about
this impressive dessert is that
you can make the custards—
minus the burnt-sugar topping—
a couple of days ahead. Of
course, you can eat them on the
day you make them, too; just be
sure to chill the custards for at
least 3 hours before topping
them with sugar.

1¾ cups heavy cream
1 vanilla bean or 1 tsp. pure
**   vanilla extract**
4 large egg yolks (ideally cool
**   or cold)**
¼ cup plus 2 to 4 tsp. granulated
**   sugar**
Pinch kosher salt

Position a rack in the center
of the oven and heat the oven
to 300°F. Fill a teakettle with
water and bring to a boil. Put
four 5- or 6-oz. ramekins
(about 3 inches in diameter
and 1¾ inches deep) in a
baking dish that's at least as
deep as the ramekins.

Use a light hand when you whisk in the vanilla
seeds so you don't whip air into the cream.

Strain the custard base into a large Pyrex
measuring cup; the spout makes it easy to
pour the custard into ramekins later.

1. Mix the custard base

Pour the cream into a small saucepan. If
using a vanilla bean, cut it in half lengthwise
with the tip of a paring knife and, with the
back of the blade, scrape out the sticky,
black seeds. Add the seeds and scraped
pod halves to the cream. Whisk briefly to
disperse the seeds (photo at left).

Bring the cream just to a simmer over
medium heat. Remove the pan from the heat,
cover, and let sit for about 10 minutes.

Meanwhile, in a medium mixing bowl
lightly whisk the egg yolks, ¼ cup of the
sugar, and a pinch of salt just to combine.
Set aside.

With an instant-read or a candy thermometer, check the temperature of the cream; it
should be no higher than 165°F. (If it is, let
cool to 165°F before proceeding.)

Lightly whisk about ½ cup of the cream
into the yolk mixture and stir for about
30 seconds; this tempers the yolks. Then
gently whisk in the remaining cream, stirring
for about 15 seconds to blend. Use a light
hand—you don't want to make the mixture
frothy or the baked custards will have a
foamy-looking surface. If using vanilla extract,
stir it in now.

Set a fine sieve over a large Pyrex measuring cup or a heatproof bowl with a spout.
Pour the custard base through the sieve to
strain out any solids (photo at left).

For variations, just infuse the cream with flavorings

Orange: Omit the vanilla
bean and after the cream
comes to a simmer, remove
from the heat and immediately
add 1 Tbs. Grand Marnier or
Triple Sec, 2 tsp. (firmly packed)
finely grated orange zest, and
½ tsp. vanilla extract. Cover
and let sit for 10 minutes.

Ginger: Omit the vanilla
bean (or extract), and instead
add ½ Tbs. (firmly packed)
finely grated fresh ginger to
the cold cream before bringing it to a simmer.

Café au lait: Omit the
vanilla bean (or extract),
and right after the cream
comes to a simmer, remove
it from the heat and whisk in
1½ tsp. instant espresso
powder (for sources, see
p. 72) until dissolved. Cover
and let sit for 10 minutes.

Earl Grey tea: Omit the
vanilla bean (or extract), and
after the cream comes to a
simmer, remove from the heat
and immediately add 5 tea
bags (you may have to prod
the bags with a spoon to
submerge them). Cover and
let sit for 10 minutes.

Photos: Scott Phillips

2. Bake the custards

Divide the custard base evenly among the four ramekins in the baking pan. There should be a little more than an inch of custard in each ramekin; it should not come all the way to the rim. Slowly pour hot water from the teakettle into the baking pan (don't get any water in the ramekins) until the water comes about two-thirds of the way up the sides of the ramekins.

Carefully transfer the baking pan to the center of the oven, taking care not to slosh hot water onto yourself or into the ramekins. Lay a sheet of aluminum foil over the pan. Bake the custards until the edges are set about 1/3 inch in from the sides of the ramekins and the center is slightly jiggly (like Jell-O), 40 to 55 minutes. To test for doneness, reach into the oven with tongs and give one of the ramekins a gentle shake or nudge. If the custard responds with a wavelike motion rather than a slight jiggle, it's not firm enough; bake for another 5 minutes and check again. (If you're not sure about the doneness, stick an instant-read thermometer into the center of a custard—don't worry about making a hole; you'll cover it with sugar later—it should register 150° to 155°F.) The custards should not brown or rise.

Carefully remove the baking pan from the oven and take the ramekins out of the water bath using rubber-band-wrapped tongs or a slotted spatula (see the tip on p. 29). Let the ramekins cool on a rack at room temperature for 30 minutes and then transfer, uncovered, to the refrigerator to cool completely. Once the custards are refrigerator-cold, wrap each ramekin with plastic wrap. Refrigerate for at least 3 hours or up to 2 days before proceeding.

3. Caramelize the topping

Just before serving, remove the ramekins from the fridge and set them on a work surface. Working with one custard at a time, sprinkle 1/2 to 1 tsp. of the remaining sugar over each one—the more sugar, the thicker the crust. You may need to tilt and tap the ramekin to even out the layer of sugar. Wipe any sugar off the rim of the ramekin. Hold the torch flame 2 to 3 inches from the top of the custard and slowly glide it back and forth over the surface until the sugar melts and turns a deep golden brown. Allow the sugar to cool and harden for a few minutes, and then serve immediately, before the sugar softens and gets sticky.

Yes, you really do need a mini blowtorch

Homemade crème brûlée is just as good as and probably better than any you've had in a restaurant. But to get great results, you need the right tool: a mini blow torch (for sources, see p. 72). It really makes the difference between professional and pitiable results. A mini blowtorch isn't expensive, and it's fun to fire it up and finish off the crème brûlée while your guests look on. I've attempted to caramelize the sugar under the broiler, and although it can be done, I find the process annoying and the results disappointing—the custard tends to get warm, and its texture changes for the worse.

Kimberly Y. Masibay is senior editor for Fine Cooking. ◆

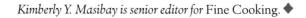

A New Take on

Bold flavors and extra-crunchy crumbs make this oven-crisped chicken the best you've ever had

BY TONY ROSENFELD

Like many of you, I love chicken breasts and cook them often, so often, in fact, that I run the risk of getting bored. So lately I've been thinking about ways to jazz up chicken breasts, and I think I've hit on something that will hold my interest for a good long time: crispy, crunchy coatings.

But don't worry: I'm not talking about fried chicken (which is great every now and then, especially when it's made in someone else's kitchen). Rather, with my method, you can bake the chicken in the oven but still enjoy all the crispness of deep-frying. And in the process, you also give the chicken breasts a great flavor boost.

Start with crisp crumbs, then slather on flavor

And now the million-dollar question: How do I get the crunchy crumb coating without frying? Here's my secret: The crumbs are crisp before the chicken even goes into the oven.

The first step in my method is making the crispy crumbs. I cook extra-coarse homemade breadcrumbs in oil in a skillet until they're browned and crunchy. Then, depending on the recipe, I'll boost the crumbs' crunch quotient by tossing them with another munchy ingredient like crumbled corn flakes or tortilla chips. And I might also mix in extra flavor with ingredients like fresh herbs, grated cheese, olives, or sun-dried tomatoes before pressing the mixture onto the chicken.

To get the crumbs to stick to the chicken, I forgo the traditional breading process: dipping the food into flour, then egg, then crumbs. Instead, I simply coat the breasts with a sticky, flavorful marinade, and then I pack on the crumbs. The marinade serves two purposes: One, it makes the chicken tasty. And two, the stickiness, which comes from ingredients like honey, yogurt, or marmalade, serves as the "glue" that binds the breadcrumbs to the chicken. If time allows, I suggest you let the chicken breasts sit or "marinate" in the sticky mixture for up to a day so the flavors really permeate the meat. But on busy weeknights, it's perfectly fine to slather on the flavor right before you coat and bake the chicken.

The result is anything but blah. And if my experience is any indication, once you start using this method, you won't have to worry about becoming bored with chicken for a long, long time.

Toasted Breadcrumbs
Yields about 2 cups.

These breadcrumbs form the base for the coating in the crispy chicken recipes on the following pages. If you want to cook up a batch in advance, see the sidebar on p. 51.

About ½ lb. fresh white bread, preferably a firm country loaf (to yield 4 cups coarse crumbs)
2 Tbs. extra-virgin olive oil or melted unsalted butter
¼ tsp. kosher salt

Tear or cut the bread into 1- to 2-inch pieces. Put a few handfuls into the bowl of a food processor (the bread shouldn't be crowded or squished), and pulse into coarse crumbs, including smaller pieces the size of oatmeal flakes and larger pieces about the size of small peas. Pour the crumbs into a large mixing bowl. Repeat until you have made 4 cups of breadcrumbs.

Toss the breadcrumbs with the olive oil or butter and the salt. Set a large (preferably 12-inch), heavy-based skillet (I use cast iron) over medium heat. Add the breadcrumbs and cook, stirring or tossing often—they should sizzle and make a steady popping noise—until they start to color and crisp, about 5 minutes. Reduce the heat to medium low and continue to cook, stirring, until the crumbs dry out and crisp and have browned nicely, about 6 minutes.

Let cool and use in one of the recipes that follow. The crumbs will continue to crisp as they cool.

Crispy Coated Chicken

A surprise twist: This crunchy coating gets a boost from lemon and capers.

Crispy Chicken Breasts with Lemon & Capers

Serves four.

You'll need to make a double batch of breadcrumbs for this recipe. You might want to use two pans so you can make the two batches at the same time.

4 small boneless, skinless chicken breast halves (6 to 7 oz. each), trimmed of excess fat
¾ cup freshly grated Parmigiano-Reggiano
5 Tbs. capers (preferably nonpareils), rinsed, patted dry, and chopped
2 Tbs. chopped fresh thyme
3 Tbs. extra-virgin olive oil
2 Tbs. Dijon mustard
1 lemon, zest finely grated, cut into wedges
½ tsp. kosher salt
½ tsp. freshly ground black pepper
3½ cups Toasted Breadcrumbs (see recipe, p. 48)

Heat the oven to 450°F. Put a flat rack on a large rimmed baking sheet lined with foil.

With a meat pounder or a heavy skillet, lightly pound the chicken between two sheets of plastic wrap to even out the thickness of the breasts.

In a large bowl, mix ¼ cup of the Parmigiano, 2½ Tbs. of the capers, 1 Tbs. of the thyme, and the oil, mustard, lemon zest, salt, and pepper. Squeeze one or two of the lemon wedges to get 1 Tbs. juice and add to the mixture, along with 2 Tbs. water. Add the chicken and toss to coat well. You can proceed directly to coating the chicken breasts with crumbs, or let them marinate in the fridge for up to 24 hours.

Put the breadcrumbs in a large shallow dish and toss with the remaining ½ cup Parmigiano, 2½ Tbs. capers, and 1 Tbs. thyme. Working with one piece at a time, transfer the chicken to the dish of crumbs, scoop some crumbs on top, and press well a couple of times so the crumbs adhere to both sides. Transfer to the rack on the baking sheet.

Bake the chicken until it's firm to the touch and registers 165°F on an instant-read thermometer, about 20 minutes. Serve immediately with the remaining lemon wedges for squeezing over the chicken.

A 4-step method for crisp chicken from the oven

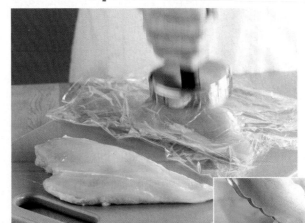

1. Pound just enough to even out the thickness so the chicken will cook evenly (don't make them too thin). If tenderloins are attached, remove, bread, and bake them with the breasts (they'll cook faster).

2. Flavor the chicken with sticky ingredients that will help the breadcrumbs adhere to the meat.

3. Coat with precooked crumbs that are already very crisp.

Pack on the crumbs

These crumbs are coarser than your average breadcrumbs, so it takes a little extra force to get the crumbs to adhere. My method is to pat a healthy amount of breadcrumbs on top of the chicken and then use the heel of my hand and a firm rotating motion to press the crumbs onto the chicken. Don't shake off the excess when transferring the breasts to the baking sheet; you want to keep as many crumbs on the chicken as possible.

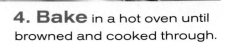

4. Bake in a hot oven until browned and cooked through.

Definitely not your mother's breaded chicken: The lively Mexican flavors in this crispy coating make it a good match for a cold beer.

Crispy Cheddar & Jalapeño Coated Chicken Breasts

Serves four.

4 small boneless, skinless chicken breast halves (6 to 7 oz. each), trimmed of excess fat
1 cup plain yogurt, preferably whole-milk
1 Tbs. chopped fresh thyme
1 Tbs. light brown sugar
2 tsp. chili powder
1 tsp. garlic powder
1 tsp. kosher salt
½ tsp. freshly ground black pepper
2 cups Toasted Breadcrumbs (see recipe, p. 48)
¼ lb. tortilla chips, crushed into coarse crumbs (about 1⅓ cups)
¼ lb. sharp Cheddar, grated (about 1 lightly packed cup)
½ to ⅔ cup sliced jarred jalapeños, chopped and patted dry
1 lime, cut into wedges

Heat the oven to 450°F. Put a flat rack on a large rimmed baking sheet lined with foil.

With a meat pounder or a heavy skillet, lightly pound the chicken between two sheets of plastic wrap to even out the thickness of the breasts.

In a large bowl, mix the yogurt with half of the thyme, the brown sugar, chili powder, garlic powder, salt, and pepper. Add the chicken and toss to coat well. You can proceed directly to coating the chicken breasts with crumbs, or let them marinate in the fridge for up to 24 hours.

Put the breadcrumbs in a large shallow dish and toss with the tortilla chips, Cheddar, jalapeños, and the remaining thyme. Working with one piece at a time, transfer the chicken to the dish of crumbs, scoop some crumbs on top, and press well so the breadcrumbs adhere to both sides. Transfer to the rack on the baking sheet.

Bake the chicken until it's firm to the touch and registers 165°F on an instant-read thermometer, about 20 minutes. Serve immediately with the lime wedges for squeezing over the chicken.

Two ways to get a head start

Make the crumbs ahead. They'll keep for up to 3 days in an airtight container at room temperature. Or if you want to whip up a few batches of crumbs, you can store them in a zip-top bag in your freezer for a couple of months.

Marinate ahead. You can pound the chicken and immerse it in the sticky flavor bath the day before you plan to cook it. The results will be excellent because the flavors will really sink into the meat.

Crispy Orange-Sesame Chicken Breasts

Serves four.

4 small boneless, skinless chicken breast halves (6 to 7 oz. each), trimmed of excess fat
1 large navel orange
½ cup sweet orange marmalade
¼ cup honey
2 Tbs. soy sauce
1 Tbs. canola or peanut oil
½ tsp. Asian sesame oil
1 tsp. Thai chile sauce (like Sriracha) or other hot sauce
½ tsp. kosher salt
2 cups Toasted Breadcrumbs (see recipe, p. 48)
½ cup sesame seeds, lightly toasted

Heat the oven to 450°F. Put a flat rack on a large rimmed baking sheet lined with foil.

With a meat pounder or a heavy skillet, lightly pound the chicken between two sheets of plastic wrap to even out the thickness of the breasts.

Using a rasp-style (Microplane) grater, grate the zest from the orange.

With a serrated knife, cut 4 very thin slices from the center of the orange (save the rest of the orange for snacking or another use).

In a large bowl, combine the zest with the marmalade, honey, soy sauce, canola or peanut oil, sesame oil, chile or hot sauce, and salt. Add the chicken and toss to coat well. You can proceed directly to coating the chicken breasts with crumbs, or let them marinate in the fridge for up to 24 hours.

In a large shallow dish, toss the breadcrumbs with the sesame seeds. Working with one piece at a time, transfer the chicken to the dish of crumbs, scoop some crumbs on top, and press well a couple of times so the breadcrumbs adhere to both sides. Transfer to the rack on the baking sheet. Dip the orange slices in the leftover marmalade mixture to coat both sides and set on the rack.

Bake the chicken until it's firm to the touch and registers 165°F on an instant-read thermometer, about 20 minutes (the orange slices should be lightly browned). Serve immediately, topped with the orange slices.

Marmalade is the tangy binder for the delicious sesame coating on these breasts.

Add a crusty baguette and a bottle of Chianti for Friday dinner with friends.

Herbed Chicken Breasts with a Crispy Black Olive & Parmigiano Crust

Serves four.

The olives, Parmigiano, and sun-dried tomatoes give this crust a wonderful savory essence and a healthy dose of salt, too. For this reason, I decrease the amount of salt in the marinade. You can also omit the salt from the breadcrumbs recipe on p. 48 if you like.

4 small boneless, skinless chicken breast halves (6 to 7 oz. each), trimmed of excess fat
2 Tbs. extra-virgin olive oil
2 Tbs. whole-grain mustard
4 tsp. chopped fresh thyme
2 tsp. chopped fresh rosemary
½ tsp. kosher salt
½ tsp. freshly ground black pepper
2 cups Toasted Breadcrumbs (see recipe, p. 48)
1 cup pitted Kalamata olives, rinsed, patted dry, and chopped
¾ cup freshly grated Parmigiano-Reggiano
3 Tbs. chopped oil-packed sun-dried tomatoes (about 3 large tomato halves; pat dry before chopping)
1 lemon, cut into wedges

Heat the oven to 450°F. Put a flat rack on a large rimmed baking sheet lined with foil.

With a meat pounder or a heavy skillet, lightly pound the chicken between two sheets of plastic wrap to even out the thickness of the breasts.

In a large bowl, mix the oil and mustard with half of the thyme, half of the rosemary, and the salt and pepper. Add the chicken and toss to coat well. You can proceed directly to coating the chicken breasts with crumbs, or let them marinate in the fridge for up to 24 hours.

Put the breadcrumbs in a large shallow dish and toss with the olives, Parmigiano, sun-dried tomatoes, and the remaining thyme and rosemary. Working with one piece at a time, transfer the chicken to the dish of crumbs, scoop some crumbs on top, and press well a couple of times so the crumbs adhere to both sides (these crumbs will be a little wet, so really press them on). Transfer to the rack on the baking sheet.

Bake the chicken until it's firm to the touch and registers 165°F on an instant-read thermometer, about 20 minutes. Serve immediately with the lemon wedges for squeezing over the chicken.

Tony Rosenfeld is a contributing editor to Fine Cooking. ◆

Getting to Know Asian Vegetables

You see them at the market, you eat them in restaurants—now here are some tempting ways to cook them

BY ANDREA REUSING

L ast year, several hours after a hurricane warning, a trip to the market revealed what people buy when confronted with the prospect of weathering several days without grocery shopping. The milk, bread, and eggs were nearly gone, as were the broccoli, carrots, and lettuces. There was even a hefty dent in the rutabagas. But the bok choys, napa cabbages, snow peas, and Japanese eggplant were nearly untouched. They lay in their neat bins, ready to endure the storm alone. And when I reached for a bunch of plump baby bok choy, I noticed a few curious looks. A couple of shoppers with dinner on their minds even asked me how I was going to prepare it.

It seems to me that while most home cooks have seen several varieties of Asian vegetables in grocery stores, they're often uncomfortable buying them because they're not sure how to cook them. But these lovely vegetables are actually very easy to cook, even with no special knowledge of Asian cuisines. It's just a matter of getting acquainted with their flavors and with the ingredients that enhance them, and finding the cooking methods that work best for each one. Generally, I prefer simple preparations that allow the vegetables' pure flavor to shine, as in the recipes that follow. Once you try them, I'm sure that you, too, will be inspired to add these often overlooked vegetables to your repertoire.

Snow peas, Japanese eggplant, napa cabbage, and bok choy are easy to cook once you know which flavorings and cooking methods best suit them.

Bok choy (and baby bok choy) has a mild, sweet cabbagy flavor and a soft crunch. It has a gentle bitterness that stands up to strong, rich flavors.

Shopping & prepping

Look for tight, unwilted heads ranging from bright green to dark green, with no signs of yellowing or drying. Wash bok choy well. You can leave baby bok choy whole or cut it in half, but cut larger bok choy into pieces for stir-frying.

Flavor partners

Bok choy harmonizes with assertive flavors like sesame, soy sauce, garlic, ginger, oyster sauce, chiles, and mushrooms.

Best cooking methods

Bok choy is excellent steamed, quick-braised, and stir-fried. Its chubby, spoon-shaped stalks capture sauces, making it a great last-minute addition to rich stews.

Ideas

My favorite way of cooking bok choy is to quickly sauté it in hot oil flavored with a little garlic or ginger and then briefly braise it in broth until just tender. I also like to add it to pork shoulder that's been slow-braised with soy sauce, a little sugar, and star anise.

Braised Bok Choy with Sherry & Prosciutto

Serves four to six as a side dish.

This is delicious with braised pork or beef short ribs, or simply with a pan-seared steak.

1 Tbs. vegetable oil
4 medium cloves garlic, thinly sliced
6 heads baby bok choy (about 7 inches long and 2 inches in diameter at their widest), cut in half lengthwise
⅛ tsp. kosher salt; more as needed
¼ cup dry sherry (or Chinese rice wine)
½ cup homemade or low-salt chicken broth
1 Tbs. soy sauce
¼ tsp. granulated sugar
1 tsp. cornstarch mixed with 1 tsp. cold water to form a slurry
4 thin slices prosciutto, sliced crosswise into ¼-inch strips (⅓ to ½ cup)

Put the oil and garlic in a small wok or a deep, heavy-based, 10-inch, straight-sided sauté pan with a lid. Set over medium-high heat and cook, stirring frequently, until the garlic begins to sizzle steadily, about 1 min-
ute. Add the bok choy (the pan will be crowded) and, using tongs, turn it in the oil and garlic, and then season it with the salt. When the tender tops begin to wilt, in about 1 minute, add the sherry (or rice wine) and toss again for about 15 seconds before adding the chicken broth, soy sauce, and sugar. Reduce the heat to medium, cover, and simmer until the bok choy tops are completely wilted and the stalks are crisp-tender, about 5 minutes. Transfer the bok choy to a plate.

Give the cornstarch slurry a stir to recombine and then whisk it into the cooking liquid. Simmer vigorously until the liquid has thickened, about 30 seconds. Remove from the heat and return the bok choy to the pan. Add the prosciutto and toss quickly to coat the bok choy with the broth and to mix in the prosciutto. Season to taste with salt and serve.

Japanese eggplant

is sweet and rich, with tender skin and a soft, creamy flesh. It's less bitter than large globe eggplant, so it doesn't need to be salted before cooking. Also, because this skinny variety is small and firm, it cooks faster and doesn't need as much oil as larger eggplants.

Shopping & prepping

Select firm, purple-black, shiny fruits with no soft or brown spots. Peeling is optional, and you can cut it almost any way you want: sliced, diced, or halved.

Flavor partners

It goes well with basil, mint, garlic, lime, chiles, miso, sesame, peanuts, red curry, vinegar, and honey.

Best cooking methods

Japanese eggplant is great roasted, grilled, steamed, or added to stews.

Ideas

Spread butter and grated Parmigiano on halved Japanese eggplant before roasting. Or drizzle steamed eggplant with a salsa verde of chopped parsley, capers, lemon juice, and olive oil.

Roasted Eggplant with Chiles, Peanuts & Mint

Serves four to six as a side dish.

I usually serve this dish as an appetizer, but you can also serve it as a side dish for roasted lamb or pork.

¼ cup unsalted peanuts
5 Tbs. plus 1 tsp. peanut oil
Kosher salt
4 skinny Japanese eggplant (about 7 inches long and 1½ inches in diameter)
¼ tsp. crushed red pepper flakes; more to taste
2 Tbs. fresh lime juice
1 tsp. honey
12 medium fresh mint leaves, coarsely torn (about 3 Tbs.)

Position a rack in the center of the oven and heat the oven to 425°F.

Scatter the peanuts in a pie plate or other small baking dish and toss them with 1 tsp. oil and a generous pinch of salt. Roast, shaking the pan once or twice, until they are golden brown, about 5 minutes. Set aside to cool, and then coarsely chop them. Reduce the oven temperature to 375°F.

Rinse the eggplant. Trim off their tops and then cut the eggplant in half lengthwise. In a large, shallow bowl, toss the eggplant with 2 Tbs. of the oil and the red pepper flakes. Put the eggplant cut side up on a rimmed baking sheet and sprinkle generously with salt. Roast until the eggplant is tender when pierced with a fork and the flesh is a light golden brown, 10 to 12 minutes.

Meanwhile, in a small dish, whisk the remaining 3 Tbs. oil with the lime juice, honey, and ¼ tsp. salt. Season to taste with more salt, if necessary.

With the eggplant still on the center rack, turn the broiler on to high and broil the eggplant until well browned on top, about 5 minutes. Transfer the eggplant to a serving platter. Drizzle with the dressing. Sprinkle with mint and peanuts and serve.

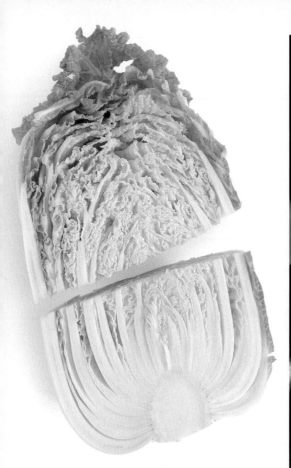

Napa cabbage has
ruffled, light-green leaves that are as tender as lettuce and crunchy white stems that are similar in texture to green cabbage.

Shopping & prepping
Look for medium-size cabbages that feel heavy for their size and have plenty of light-green leaves. You can cut napa cabbage any way you would cut green cabbage.

Flavor partners
Napa's delicate floral spiciness pairs well with garlic, chives, mushrooms, carrots, radishes, ginger, and cured meats, such as bacon, prosciutto, speck, and even prepared duck confit.

Best cooking methods
Napa cabbage is juicy and sweet when braised, sautéed, or stir-fried, but it's equally good raw in salads or slaws.

Ideas
I like to slice it thinly and put together either a slaw with sliced radishes, lime juice, and a little sugar, or a fresh salad with apples and a vinaigrette made with chives and apple-cider vinegar.

Stir-Fried Napa Cabbage with Garlic, Fresh Chile & Basil
Serves four as a side dish.

Try this with roasted chicken, sautéed chicken thighs, or pan-seared fish fillets.

1 medium-small head napa cabbage
 (about 1¾ lb.)
1 Tbs. canola oil
3 medium cloves garlic, coarsely chopped
 (about 1 Tbs.)
1 Tbs. fish sauce
1½ tsp. granulated sugar
¼ tsp. kosher salt
½ medium serrano chile, coarsely chopped
 (don't seed)
¼ cup roughly torn fresh basil leaves
2 to 3 tsp. fresh lime juice
2 medium scallions, thinly sliced on an
 extreme diagonal, for garnish

Slice the cabbage in half lengthwise. Position one half cut side up and slice it across the middle at the point where the ruffled, leafy top gives way to white stem (top left photo). Remove the core, slice the stem end lengthwise into 1½-inch-thick wedges, and cut the wedges crosswise into 1½-inch pieces (the leaves will separate). Cut the leafy half in the same way. Keep the leaves and stems separate. Repeat with the remaining half cabbage. You should have about 5 cups stems and 4 cups leaves.

Heat a wok or a 12-inch skillet over high heat for about 45 seconds and then add the oil, swirling it to coat the pan. When the oil is hot and shimmering, add the garlic and the white stems. Stir-fry until the stems brown lightly in spots and begin to release some liquid, about 2 minutes. Add the fish sauce, sugar, salt, and chile and toss. Continue to stir-fry until the stems are barely tender, about 2½ minutes.

Add the cabbage leaves, stirring quickly to move them to the bottom of the pan. As soon as the stems are just tender and the tops are barely wilted, 30 to 40 seconds more, remove from the heat and stir in the basil and 2 tsp. lime juice. Season to taste with salt, garnish with the scallions, and add more lime juice, if you like. Serve immediately.

Snow peas have more real pea flavor and are often less starchy than sugar snaps. Popular in the 1970s, snow peas should be poised for a revival because of their fresh green crunch, versatility, and fast cooking time.

Shopping & prepping

Choose dark green, dense-looking peas with no signs of drying or cracking. Trim them by breaking off the stem end and pulling the string away from the pod.

Flavor partners

Snow peas partner well with scallions, toasted sesame seeds, ginger, shellfish, and rich nut oils.

Best cooking methods

Snow peas are good eaten raw, blanched, steamed, and stir-fried.

Ideas

For a quick warm salad, briefly blanch and toss snow peas with a little vegetable oil, sea salt, and toasted sesame seeds. Or blanch them and toss them with good-quality butter and salt. I also like to quickly sauté them along with torn butter lettuce and scallions.

Stir-Fried Snow Peas with Shiitakes and Ginger

Serves four as a side dish.

I like to serve these alongside steamed fish or sautéed chicken.

2 tsp. soy sauce (preferably Kikkoman "milder")
½ tsp. Asian sesame oil
1 Tbs. plus 1 tsp. canola or other vegetable oil
6 medium shiitake mushrooms, stemmed and cut into ¼-inch slices (about 1 cup)
1 heaping Tbs. finely julienned fresh ginger (from about a 1-inch piece; see From Our Test Kitchen, p. 66)
¾ lb. snow peas (about 4 cups), trimmed (break off the stem end of each pea and pull the string away from the pod)
Kosher salt
1 tsp. sesame seeds, toasted, for garnish (optional)

In a small bowl, combine the soy sauce and sesame oil with 2 Tbs. water and set aside.

Heat a 10-inch skillet over medium-high heat for about 30 seconds and add 1 Tbs. canola oil, swirling it to coat the pan. When the oil is very hot, add the shiitakes and cook, stirring once, until they begin to brown lightly, about 1 minute. Add the ginger and stir-fry until the mushrooms are golden and the ginger has softened, 1 to 2 minutes more. Add the remaining 1 tsp. canola oil and then the snow peas and a pinch of salt. Stir-fry for 30 seconds. Add the soy sauce mixture and continue to stir-fry until the peas are crisp-tender and the liquid has reduced to a glaze, 1 to 2 minutes. Season with salt to taste and garnish with the sesame seeds, if using. Serve immediately.

Andrea Reusing is the chef and owner of Lantern restaurant in Chapel Hill, North Carolina. ◆

Quick-Braised Fish

A one-pan meal that's fast enough for weeknights and

Make a flavorful sauce with aromatics and vegetables.

Nestle the fish into the sauce, pile on some vegetables, and cook in the oven.

BY ALLISON EHRI

To many of us, the word "braising" conjures up thoughts of slow-cooked short ribs, pot roast, or chicken, but probably not fish. The moist, slow heat of a braise is ideal for melting tough cuts of meat into tender morsels, so why bother using the technique with fish, which is naturally tender? Because by braising fish, you'll get the benefits—melt-in-your-mouth texture and a full-flavored pan sauce—without the long cooking time. The recipes here are speedy enough for a weeknight yet fancy enough for company. And the chunky vegetables in the braising liquid double as a vegetable side dish, so in the end, you have a saucy, hearty, one-pan meal.

I use a simple three-step method. First, I make the sauce, which includes vegetables, aromatics, and a liquid like wine or clam juice. Next, I nestle the fish into the sauce, piling some of the vegetables on top to keep the fish moist. Then I cover the pan and finish the dish in the oven. Once it's done, I remove the fish from the sauce. Though the sauce is perfectly delicious as is, in two of the recipes (the red snapper and the salmon), I like to reduce it slightly to concentrate the flavors, especially when I'm cooking for guests. This is also the perfect opportunity to add a few finishing touches, like vinegar or fresh herbs.

A few tools are helpful to have on hand when braising fish. I use an ovenproof skillet to make these dishes, but if you don't have one, you can transfer the fish and sauce to a Pyrex dish for the oven braising (just note that cooking times may be slightly longer). Also, a fish spatula comes in handy when removing the fish from the pan (see Where to Buy It, p. 72).

Photos: Scott Phillips

Fancy enough for company

Remove the fish and finish the sauce.

TRY IT WITH OTHER FISH

Once you've mastered the quick-braising method with snapper, cod, and salmon, you can experiment with other fish, such as grouper, barramundi, black sea bass, striped bass, or halibut. Remember that cooking times may vary, depending on the thickness and texture of the fish, so be sure to sneak a peek before removing it from the sauce.

Braised Red Snapper Puttanesca

Serves four.

Black sea bass makes a good substitute for snapper in this recipe. If you buy a whole fish, see p. 69 for how to bone it.

4 5-oz. skinless red snapper fillets (about ¾ inch thick)
Kosher salt and freshly ground black pepper
3 Tbs. extra-virgin olive oil
3 medium cloves garlic, minced (about 1 Tbs.)
2 14½-oz. cans petite-diced tomatoes
2 anchovy fillets, minced
½ cup pitted Kalamata olives, halved lengthwise (about 3 oz.)
3 Tbs. coarsely chopped fresh basil leaves
1 Tbs. capers, rinsed
¼ tsp. crushed red pepper flakes
1 Tbs. coarsely chopped fresh mint
2 tsp. red-wine vinegar

Position a rack in the center of the oven and heat the oven to 325°F. Season the snapper all over with salt and pepper. Let sit at room temperature while you prepare the sauce.

Heat 2 Tbs. of the olive oil in a 12-inch ovenproof skillet over medium-low heat. Add the garlic and cook, stirring, until softened but not golden, about 1 minute. Add the tomatoes and their juice, anchovies, olives, 2 Tbs. of the basil, capers, and pepper flakes to the pan. Bring the sauce to a brisk simmer and cook, stirring occasionally, until the tomatoes are tender and the juices have reduced to a saucy consistency, about 8 minutes.

Nestle the snapper fillets into the sauce, spooning some on top to keep the fish moist. Drizzle with the remaining 1 Tbs. olive oil. Tightly cover the pan with a lid or aluminum foil and braise in the oven until the fish is almost cooked through, 10 to 15 minutes, depending on thickness (see the tip on p. 60).

With a slotted spatula, transfer the snapper to 4 shallow serving bowls. If the sauce seems too thin, simmer over medium-high heat until thickened to your liking. Stir the remaining 1 Tbs. basil and the mint and vinegar into the sauce and spoon it over the fish.

Serving suggestion: Serve with polenta or couscous.

tip: To check if your fish is done, use a paring knife to peek between two bits of flesh in the center of the fillet. The very middle should look ever-so-slightly translucent, which means it's almost cooked through. The fish will continue to cook as you finish your sauce, so it'll be perfectly done by the time you're ready to serve it.

Salmon Braised in Pinot Noir

Serves four.

4 5-oz. skinless salmon fillets (preferably 1 inch thick)
Kosher salt and freshly ground black pepper
2 Tbs. unsalted butter
6 oz. medium-small cremini or white mushrooms, quartered (about 18, 2½ to 3 cups)
1 large celery stalk, cut into small dice (about ¾ cup)
2 small carrots, cut into small dice (about ½ cup)
1 small leek, white and light green parts only, cut into medium dice (⅓ to ½ cup)
2 tsp. tomato paste
1 cup Pinot Noir
1 bay leaf
1 large sprig fresh thyme, plus 1 tsp. chopped fresh thyme leaves
1 cup homemade or low-salt chicken broth
½ cup heavy cream
1 Tbs. chopped fresh flat-leaf parsley

Position a rack in the center of the oven and heat the oven to 325°F.

Season the salmon all over with salt and pepper. Let sit at room temperature while you prepare the sauce.

Melt the butter in a 12-inch oven-proof skillet over medium-high heat. Add the mushrooms and celery and cook, stirring occasionally, until the mushrooms are browned on at least one side, 3 to 5 minutes. Add the carrots and leeks and cook, stirring occasionally, until just softened, about 4 minutes (reduce the heat to medium if the pan starts to get dark). Add the tomato paste and cook, stirring, for 1 minute. Add the Pinot Noir, bay leaf, and thyme sprig, scrape the bottom of the pan with a wooden spoon to release any browned bits, and boil until the wine is reduced by about half, 2 to 4 minutes. Add the chicken broth and cream and bring to a brisk simmer.

Nestle the salmon fillets into the vegetables and pile some of the vegetables on top of the fillets to keep the fish moist. Tightly cover the pan with a lid or aluminum foil and braise in the oven until the fish is almost cooked through, 10 to 15 minutes, depending on thickness (see the tip at left).

With a slotted spatula, transfer the salmon to 4 shallow serving bowls. Concentrate the sauce by placing the pan over medium-high heat and boiling until it's thickened to your liking. Discard the bay leaf and thyme sprig. Stir in the chopped thyme and parsley, season to taste with salt and pepper, spoon the sauce over the salmon, and serve.

Serving suggestion: Mashed potatoes or rice pilaf makes a nice accompaniment to this dish.

Braised Cod with Fennel, Potatoes & Littlenecks

Serves four.

You could use halibut in place of the cod.

4 5-oz. cod fillets (preferably 1 inch thick)
Kosher salt and freshly ground black pepper
3 Tbs. extra-virgin olive oil
1 small fennel bulb (about ¾ lb.), trimmed (leave core intact) and cut into ½-inch wedges, plus 1 Tbs. chopped fronds
2 large cloves garlic, finely chopped
1 medium-large shallot, chopped
2 8-oz. bottles clam juice
8 oz. small baby red or fingerling potatoes, scrubbed and sliced into ⅛-inch-thick coins, ends discarded (about 6 potatoes)
1 large tomato, cut into small dice (12 oz., about 1½ cups)
2 Tbs. anisette liqueur, such as Pernod or Sambuca
1 bay leaf
1 large sprig fresh thyme
¼ tsp. roughly chopped or coarsely ground fennel seed
A generous pinch of saffron, crumbled (about 25 threads)
12 littleneck clams, scrubbed
1½ Tbs. chopped fresh flat-leaf parsley leaves

Position a rack in the center of the oven and heat the oven to 325°F. Season the cod with salt and pepper. Let it sit at room temperature while you prepare the braising mixture.

Heat the olive oil in a 12-inch oven-proof skillet over medium-high heat. Add the fennel, sprinkle with a pinch of salt and pepper and brown on both sides, about 5 minutes total. Remove the pan from the heat and transfer the fennel to a plate. Put the pan over low heat and add the garlic, shallot, ½ tsp. salt, and ¼ tsp. pepper. Cook, stirring, until just softened, 1 to 2 minutes.

Add the clam juice, potatoes, tomato, liqueur, bay leaf, thyme, fennel seed, and saffron to the skillet. Raise the heat to medium and bring to a simmer. Simmer for 3 minutes to start the potatoes cooking. Nestle the cod pieces and clams into the sauce, piling the fennel on top of the fish and making sure all of the potatoes are submerged. Tightly cover the pan with a lid or aluminum foil and braise in the oven until the fish is almost cooked through, 10 to 15 minutes, depending on thickness (see the tip at far left).

With a slotted spatula, transfer the cod to 4 shallow bowls. Bring the braising liquid, clams, and vegetables to a brisk simmer on top of the stove, cover the pan, and cook until the clams are opened and the vegetables are tender, 3 to 6 minutes more. Divide the opened clams (discard any unopened ones) and vegetables among the bowls. Add the fennel fronds and parsley to the braising liquid in the pan. Bring to a simmer and pour over the fish and vegetables.

Serving suggestion: Crusty garlic bread served alongside is perfect for soaking up the flavorful sauce.

Allison Ehri is Fine Cooking's *test kitchen associate and food stylist.* ◆

tip: Fillets that are ¾ to 1 inch thick work best, but if you can find only long, thin ones, they will do. Score the fish crosswise on the bone side, being sure to cut only halfway through. Flip the fillets over and fold them in half, skin side in, and proceed as if they were thick fillets. As the fish cooks, it will firm up and hold this shape.

With a few shortcuts, these
Playful Desserts
are easy to put together

BY GALE GAND

A s the executive pastry chef of an innovative restaurant, it's my job to come up with sensational desserts that not only taste great but also prompt gushing oohs and aahs with their originality. The catch is that most of these creations require hours of prep time, not to mention years of experience. You couldn't make them at home, and truth be told, neither could I. With twin toddlers, a 10-year-old, four restaurants, and a TV show, I run on a tight schedule. But I still like to impress my family and friends with imaginative desserts that are big on flavor yet easy to make. With a few simple tricks—and a little creativity—I've found that I can pull it off. And so can you. Here's how I've done it in the three desserts on these pages.

I limit the number of ingredients. Measuring, cutting, and chopping a lot of ingredients takes time. For these desserts, I never use more than eight ingredients—often fewer. But I'm a stickler for quality. I look for the best raw materials, so I don't have to do much to them to coax out great flavor. For the pear tarts, for example, try to get your hands on some juicy pears at the peak of ripeness.

I use store-bought doughs. The secret to making these desserts without spending hours in the kitchen is to use prepared ingredients like frozen puff pastry, phyllo dough, and wonton wrappers, as well as jarred spreads, juice concentrates, and ice cream. To liven up my homemade sweets and elicit that jolt of surprise, I sometimes put a whimsical twist on a classic dessert, as in my redesigned pear tarts (the crust opens like a blossom), or a sweet spin on a savory dish, like my sweet chips and dip or fried wontons with orange dipping sauce.

A sweet take on chips 'n' dip

Phyllo Chips with Vanilla Ice Cream & Strawberry Mash "Dip"

Serves eight.

Forget about nachos and salsa—for dessert lovers like me, this is the ultimate take on chips and dip.

3 9x14-inch sheets frozen phyllo dough, thawed overnight in the refrigerator (see box at right)
2 oz. (4 Tbs.) unsalted butter, melted
6½ Tbs. granulated sugar; more as needed
1 pint strawberries, rinsed and hulled
1 pint good-quality vanilla ice cream, slightly softened

Position a rack in the center of the oven and heat the oven to 375°F. Line a 13x17-inch baking sheet with parchment. Put one sheet of phyllo on the pan and brush with some of the melted butter. Sprinkle evenly with 1½ Tbs. sugar and lay another sheet of phyllo on top. Brush with the melted butter and sprinkle with 1½ Tbs. sugar. Lay the last sheet of phyllo on top, brush with more melted butter, and sprinkle with 1½ Tbs. sugar.

With the tip of a sharp knife, cut the phyllo lengthwise into 4 even strips. Then cut each strip on the diagonal, alternating the direction of the knife to form little triangles (see photo below right). Cover with parchment and set another baking sheet on top. This will keep the phyllo from buckling during baking.

Bake until the phyllo is golden brown (lift the pan and top piece of parchment to check the color), about 15 minutes. To keep the phyllo chips extra flat, let them cool before unstacking the pans and removing the chips. They are best served the same day but will stay crisp for 2 days if stored in an airtight container.

While the chips are baking, make the strawberry mash. With a pastry cutter or a potato masher, smash the strawberries in a medium bowl with the remaining 2 Tbs. sugar until pulverized but still a bit chunky. Taste; I like it on the tart side since the phyllo chips and ice cream are quite sweet. Cover with plastic wrap and keep chilled.

Put two scoops of vanilla ice cream in eight individual dessert bowls and spoon about an eighth of the strawberry mash over each portion. Tuck some phyllo chips in the ice cream or serve the chips on the side. If the ice cream is soft enough, you can use the chips to scoop it like a dip.

ingredient

Twin-pack phyllo is best
We used phyllo from a 1-lb. twin pack to test this recipe. Twin-pack sheets are 9 by 14 inches, smaller than those from a single pack. If you can find only larger, single-pack phyllo, either cut the sheets to size or use the larger sheets as they are, sprinkling 2 Tbs. sugar instead of 1½ Tbs. between each layer. Frozen phyllo dough is available in grocery stores. For this recipe you'll need only three phyllo sheets. Thaw one entire roll and refreeze what you don't need.

tip

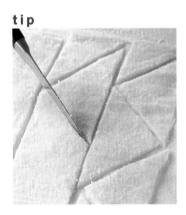

To make it easier to cut the phyllo chip triangles, slightly separate each strip before you begin.

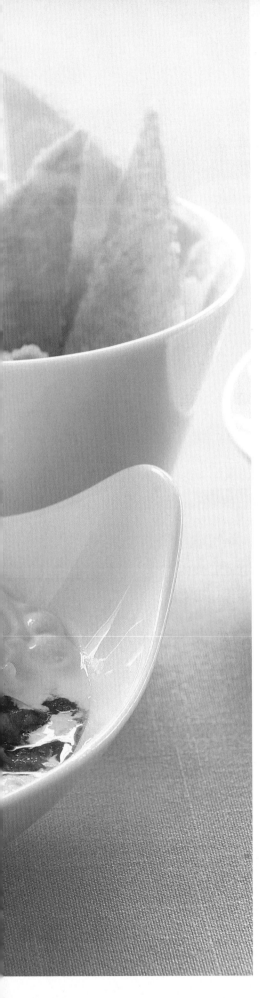

Mini tarts open like blossoms

Free-Form Pear Tarts with Almond & Cinnamon

Yields 4 tarts.

Serve topped with a quenelle of vanilla ice cream, if you like. (To learn how to make ice-cream quenelles, see From Our Test Kitchen, p. 66).

¼ cup granulated sugar
¼ tsp. ground cinnamon
1 sheet frozen puff pastry (9¾-inch square), thawed overnight in the refrigerator
Flour for dusting
2 Tbs. almond paste (from a can or tube)
4 tsp. sour cream
2 small firm-ripe pears (preferably Bartlett), peeled, cored, and cut into 12 wedges each

Position a rack in the center of the oven and heat the oven to 425°F.

Line a baking sheet with parchment. Combine the sugar and cinnamon in a small bowl. Unroll or unfold the puff pastry on a lightly floured surface. Pinch any creases together and then smooth them out with your fingertips. Cut the pastry sheet into four equal squares and transfer them to the lined baking sheet.

Roll 1½ tsp. of almond paste into a small ball, flatten it slightly with the palm of your hand, and put it in the center of one puff pastry square. Drop 1 tsp. of sour cream on top. Sprinkle about ½ Tbs. of the cinnamon sugar over the sour cream. Arrange four pear wedges in the center of the puff pastry, two leaning away from the center one way and two leaning the other way. Sprinkle with another ½ Tbs. of the cinnamon sugar. Repeat with the remaining three puff pastry squares and filling ingredients—you won't need all of the sliced pears.

Fold the corners of the puff pastry over the pears until the tips are just touching but not overlapping and press the dough against the pears. (The tarts won't look pretty now, but they'll be beautiful once they bake and puff up.) Bake until puffed and golden brown on the edges, 22 to 27 minutes. Let cool. Any juices that leak onto the baking sheet will harden to a candy-like consistency, so break off and discard these bits before serving.

ingredient

Almond paste

Made with finely ground blanched almonds and sugar, almond paste is commonly used in cake batters and pastry fillings. It's also the base ingredient in marzipan (which is made by adding hot sugar syrup and light corn syrup to almond paste). In this recipe, almond paste provides a subtle, perfumy almond flavor that marries perfectly with the sweetness of the pears. You'll find cans or tubes of almond paste in most grocery stores. For mail-order sources, see p. 72.

tip

Arrange four pear slices in the center of a puff pastry square, sprinkle with cinnamon sugar, and then bring the pastry edges together so they touch but don't overlap. This allows the puff pastry tips to "blossom" while baking.

An unexpected sweet filling for fried wontons

Nutella

Available in many supermarkets, Nutella is a brand of creamy chocolate-hazelnut spread whose flavor is similar to that of gianduja, the hazelnut-flavored chocolate from the Piedmont region of Italy. Italian children enjoy Nutella spread on a slice of crusty bread. But it's also great when you need a chocolate filling in a pinch. You can substitute other brands of chocolate-hazelnut spread. For mail-order sources, see p. 72.

tip

Use a second teaspoon to help drop a dollop of Nutella on the lower half of the wonton wrappers.

Fried Chocolate-Hazelnut Wontons with Orange Dipping Sauce

Serves six.

Look for wonton wrappers in the produce section of the supermarket. If not frying immediately, you can stuff the wontons and refrigerate them for up to 2 days. Just cover tightly with plastic wrap to prevent them from drying out. The sauce can also be made ahead and refrigerated for one day.

24 wonton wrappers, preferably square
**1 13-oz. jar Nutella (or other chocolate-
  hazelnut spread), chilled**
¾ cup heavy cream
½ cup thawed orange juice concentrate
2 tsp. Grand Marnier
¼ tsp. pure vanilla extract
3 cups vegetable oil for frying
Confectioners' sugar for serving

Set out a bowl of water and a pastry brush. If necessary, trim the wonton wrappers into squares. Lay the wrappers on a work surface, orienting them so they look diamond shaped instead of square. Working quickly, put 1 heaping tsp. of chilled Nutella in the lower half of each diamond. Brush the edges of one wonton with a little water and fold the top point of the diamond down to meet the bottom, forming a triangle. Gently press around the filling to force out any air and pinch the edges to seal. Repeat with the remaining wontons. Set the wontons on a baking sheet, cover, and keep chilled.

In a small bowl, combine the heavy cream with the orange juice concentrate, Grand Marnier, and vanilla. Refrigerate the sauce until ready to serve.

Heat the oil to 365°F in a heavy 3-qt. saucepan over medium heat. Set a baking sheet lined with a thick layer of paper towels next to the pot. Slip 6 to 8 wontons into the oil and fry, turning occasionally, until golden brown, 2 to 3 minutes. Scoop them out with a slotted spoon and drain on the paper towels while you fry the rest.

Arrange 4 wontons on individual serving plates and sprinkle with confectioners' sugar. Serve with small individual dishes (I like tea bowls or sake cups) filled with the orange sauce for dipping.

Gale Gand is the executive pastry chef and partner at four restaurants in Chicago, including Tru and Gale's Coffee Bar. ◆

Guide to hot chiles	66
How to julienne ginger	67
Best chuck for stew	67
Sizing up shallots	67
Calibrate your thermometer	68
Leftovers: Lamb "pizzas"	68
Effective hand-washing	68
Filleting fish	69
Homemade crema	70
Making quenelles	70

BY JENNIFER ARMENTROUT

FC's field guide to
fresh hot chiles

In our experience, most supermarkets do a decent job of stocking a variety of fresh hot chiles, but identifying them is another thing. They're often mislabeled, and sometimes they're just in an anonymous jumble. On this page are some of the varieties that commonly appear in markets. Fresh chiles should be smooth, firm, and glossy. Some jalapeños may have "scar cracks" at their stem ends, but other varieties should be blemish-free. For more on chiles, check out the bonus download at FineCooking.com.

Jalapeño
Medium hot. Usually sold green, but occasionally sweeter, ripe red jalapeños appear in markets. Vegetal flavor. An all-purpose hot chile often used raw in salsas and guacamole.

Thai bird
Very hot. Either red (most common), green, orange, or yellow. Peppery, nutty flavor. Use in Southeast Asian stir-fries, curries, soups, and salads.

Habanero
Very, very hot. Either orange (most common), red, yellow, or green. Incendiary, fruity flavor. Use in fruit salsas, hot sauces, and marinades.

Banana wax
Mild. Yellow-green, long, and tapered. Sweet, slightly fruity flavor. Add raw to mild salsas or roast and use in tacos or as a pizza topping.

Fresno
Mild to medium hot. Almost always sold red; often mistaken for a red jalapeño. Spicy, sweet flavor, like that of a red bell pepper but hot. Try raw in slaws and dips or cooked in soups.

Serrano
Very hot. Sold green (unripe) or red (ripe). Tangy, herbal, vegetal flavor. Use raw in hot salsa or cooked in curries and chili.

Anaheim
Mild. Usually sold green. Sweet, crisp, vegetal flavor. Typically roasted and peeled before using in sauces and salsas. Also used for chiles rellenos.

Poblano
Mild to medium hot. Dark green and large. Sweet vegetal flavor, reminiscent of green bell pepper but hot. Usually roasted for use in sauces and enchiladas, or stuffed, batter-dipped, and fried to make chiles rellenos.

Cutting ginger into fine julienne

The recipe for Stir-Fried Snow Peas with Shiitakes & Ginger on p. 57 calls for ginger cut into very fine julienne. Here's how to do it (this method works for thicker julienne, too—just make the cuts a little wider).

Peel the ginger with a paring knife or by scraping off the skin with the side of a spoon.

Slice the ginger very thinly lengthwise. Stack several of the slices and then shingle them.

Thinly slice down the row of shingles to make your julienne.

Choose chuck for the best beef stew

One of the best cuts of beef for making beef stew is chuck. Chuck comes from the well-exercised shoulder and upper foreleg of the steer, so it has lots of tough connective tissue and sinew, a quality that makes it unsuitable for dry-heat, short-cooking methods like grilling and sautéing. But slow, moist, gentle cooking (stewing or braising) transforms the toughness into delectable fork-tenderness and rich flavor.

So when you go to shop for the Beef Stew with Red Wine and Carrots recipe on p. 39, you know you want chuck. But the chuck is a big part of the steer—it accounts for more than 25% of the animal—and it consists of several different muscles, each with its own characteristics affecting texture and cooking times. At the market, you'll have a choice of cuts from the chuck, and some are better for stews than others. To avoid confusion, head to the store with the cheat sheet below. Cuts labeled with any of these terms will give you a stew with more uniform texture and great flavor.

—Molly Stevens, contributing editor

Look for these labels

* ❖ Top blade
* ❖ Blade
* ❖ Flat iron
* ❖ Shoulder
* ❖ 7-bone roast (named after the 7-shaped blade bone)
* ❖ Chuck short ribs (purchase extra since they're fattier and need heavy trimming)

Sizing up shallots

Shallots are a great way to bring a mellow oniony flavor to your cooking without the biting astringency of a regular onion. They're a big flavor element in the Beef Stew with Red Wine and Carrots on p. 39, and we also particularly like to use them raw in vinaigrettes or cooked in pan sauces.

The size of shallots is quite variable, and some shallots have more than one lobe. When we call for a medium shallot, we're referring to a ¾ to 1 ounce shallot, regardless of how many lobes it has. A medium shallot yields about 2 tablespoons finely chopped or ¼ cup thinly sliced. One lobe of a large double-lobed shallot may be equivalent to a medium shallot.

—Allison Ehri, test kitchen associate

A medium shallot (shown life-size here) is quite a bit larger than a quarter and weighs a little less than an ounce.

Calibrate your instant-read thermometer

An instant-read thermometer is a must-have tool for checking temperatures and gauging the doneness of all sorts of things. Because you rely on your thermometer for accuracy, it's a good idea to check its calibration occasionally and adjust it as need be.

To check the calibration, bring a small pan of water to a rolling boil and take the water's temperature; it should be 212°F or a few degrees less, depending on your altitude and air pressure. (For the boiling point in your location, visit www.virtualweberbullet.com/boilingpoint.html.)

If the calibration is off, you can adjust a standard (analog) thermometer by turning the hex nut under the thermometer's face with pliers (photo above). If the nut resists, use a second set of pliers to grip the sides of the face and turn the tools in opposite directions.

There are only a few models of digital thermometers that can be adjusted. Some calibrate automatically, and others need manual adjustment; follow the manufacturer's instructions for your model.

food safety

Wish your hands a happy birthday

We doubt it's news to you that hand washing is an important part of cooking, but you might be surprised to learn that to effectively remove germs, you should soap your hands for at least 20 seconds, and that's longer than you probably think it is. Next time you wash your hands, try this: Sing the "Happy Birthday" song twice as you vigorously lather your hands with soap. That takes 20 seconds—longer than you thought, right? It's not necessary to do this if you just need to wash some bread dough off your hands, but it's a good practice after handling raw meat and seafood or other potentially hazardous foods. And if "Happy Birthday" isn't in your top 10, the "ABC" song takes 20 seconds, too.

leftovers:

Braised lamb shanks become a pizza

Use the leftovers from the Braised Lamb Shanks with Garlic & Vermouth recipe on p. 35 to make a richly flavored topping for a weeknight pizza supper.

Middle Eastern Style Lamb Pita "Pizza"

Serves two to four.

- 2 Tbs. extra-virgin olive oil; more for brushing
- ½ small yellow onion, finely diced (about ½ cup)
- 1 medium clove garlic, finely chopped (about 1 tsp.)
- Kosher salt
- 1½ tsp. cumin seeds, roughly chopped and toasted
- ½ tsp. ground allspice
- ¼ tsp. crushed red pepper flakes
- ¼ tsp. freshly ground black pepper; more as needed
- ¾ cup Pomì brand chopped tomatoes with juice (or substitute canned petite-diced tomatoes)
- 2 leftover braised lamb shanks, plus 1 Tbs. sauce (from Braised Lamb Shanks with Garlic & Vermouth recipe, p. 35)
- 2 Tbs. roughly chopped fresh mint
- 2 tsp. fresh lemon juice; more as needed
- 2 regular-size (6- to 7-inch) pita pockets, split in half to form four thin rounds
- ½ cup plain whole-milk yogurt

Position two oven racks in the upper and lower thirds of the oven and heat the oven to 450°F.

Heat the olive oil in a 10-inch skillet over medium heat until just shimmering. Cook the onion and garlic in the oil with a pinch of salt, stirring occasionally, until softened, 3 to 5 minutes. Add ¾ tsp. of the toasted cumin seeds, the allspice, red pepper flakes, and black pepper and cook, stirring, until just fragrant, about 30 seconds. Add the tomatoes and cook, stirring occasionally, until all the liquid has evaporated, 5 to 8 minutes. Remove from the heat.

Meanwhile, pull the lamb meat from the bones and cut it into chunks (you should have about 1½ cups). Pulse the lamb in the food processor until it is roughly chopped, resembling the texture of very coarsely ground meat. Add the tomato sauce, lamb sauce, 1 Tbs. of the mint, the lemon juice, and ¾ tsp. salt and pulse just to combine. Adjust the salt, pepper, and lemon juice to taste.

Put the pita halves on two baking sheets and brush them generously on both sides with olive oil. Position them with the inner sides facing up and divide the lamb mixture among the pitas, spreading it evenly over the surfaces. Bake until crisp, 5 to 10 minutes. Serve the pitas drizzled with some of the yogurt and sprinkled with the remaining toasted cumin, mint, and some freshly ground black pepper. Serve with the remaining yogurt on the side.

How to fillet a whole fish

While testing the Braised Red Snapper Puttanesca recipe on p. 59, we occasionally couldn't find snapper fillets, but we could find whole snappers. No problem—filleting a snapper (or any other similar fish) is easy if you follow these steps. Just be sure to use your sharpest knife, whether it's a fillet knife or a chef's knife.

A note on fish scales

Before you fillet a whole fish, it should be scaled. Doing the job yourself isn't difficult, but it's messy, because the scales tend to fly all over and you find them in weird places around the kitchen for days after. For this reason, we always ask the fish monger to do the scaling for us. And actually, a good fish monger will also fillet the fish for you, but where's the fun in that?
—*A. E.*

1 *Rinse the fish under running water and pat dry. Position it on a cutting board with its back towards you. Using a sharp knife held behind the gills and side fin, cut straight down halfway through the fish to the backbone, being sure to include the meaty spot right behind the top of the head.*

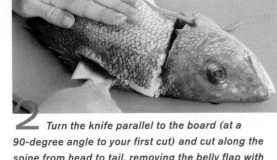

2 *Turn the knife parallel to the board (at a 90-degree angle to your first cut) and cut along the spine from head to tail, removing the belly flap with the fillet. You'll need to apply a fair amount of pressure at first to break through the rib bones. As you cut, press down firmly on top of the fish to steady it.*

3 *Finish removing the fillet by cutting all the way through the skin at the tail. Repeat steps 1 through 3 on the other side of the fish.*

4 *Remove the rib bones and belly flap by cutting under the top of the rib bones to the bottom of the fillet at a 45-degree angle. There is some meat here, but on small fish it is minimal. (On larger fish like tuna, this fatty belly is thicker and very flavorful.)*

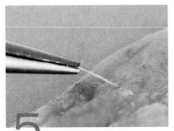

5 *Finally, check for pin bones. Some fish have little bones that run along the midline of the fillet and are nearly impossible to see. To remove them, feel along the fillet to locate each bone and then pluck it out with a pair of clean needle-nose or fish pliers. Pull the bones out in the direction they are pointing, as you would a splinter.*

Skinning is optional

Put the fillet, skin side down, on the cutting board. Starting at the tail end and holding the knife parallel to the cutting board, slice between the flesh and the skin, as close to the skin as possible, until you can grasp the tail end of the skin with a paper towel. With the knife angled ever so slightly down toward the skin, slice along the skin, using a gentle sawing motion. As you slice, simultaneously pull on the tail skin in the opposite direction to maintain pressure on the cutting edge of the knife. If you miss a spot, trim it away.

**Buy tangy
Mexican crema,
or make it yourself**

Crema is the Mexican version of French crème fraîche. Both are slightly soured and thickened cream, milder and less thick than American sour cream, with crema being the thinnest. The recipe for Lime Chicken with Poblano Sour Cream on p. 78a will have a more authentic touch if made with crema. You can buy crema in Mexican markets or even in some supermarkets, but it's easy to make it yourself, and the result has a smoother flavor than that of the commercially prepared version.

Homemade Crema (Mexican Sour Cream)

Yields about 1 cup.

Use crema as you would sour cream, dolloping or drizzling it on soups, tacos, potatoes, or anything else that needs a little tang. Start with pasteurized cream if you can find it—it makes a richer, thicker crema than ultrapasteurized cream does.

1 cup heavy cream (pasteurized or ultrapasteurized)
1 Tbs. buttermilk (with active cultures)

In a small saucepan, warm the cream over medium-low heat to about 95°F, just enough to take off the chill. If it goes over 100°F, let it cool before continuing.

Stir in the buttermilk and transfer to a clean glass jar. Set the lid loosely on top of the jar—don't tighten—and let sit in a warm spot, such as near the stove or on top of the fridge, until the cream starts to thicken, 18 to 24 hours. Stir, tighten the lid, and refrigerate until the cream is thicker and thoroughly chilled, 12 to 24 hours more. Stir well before using. The crema should have a thick but pourable consistency.

It will keep for about 2 weeks in the refrigerator, continuing to thicken as it ages.

Quenelles dress up a plate

Sometimes all that stands between home cooking and restaurant-quality food is presentation. There are lots of tricks up a chef's sleeve for stage-dressing food, and one of them is the quenelle. The term traditionally refers to a small football-shaped dumpling of poached meat or fish pâté, but these days it's generally used to describe a three-sided oval shape that makes for a classy presentation of ice cream (see the picture of the pear tarts on p. 64), goat cheese, crème fraîche, mashed potatoes, or anything soft and scoopable.

To make a quenelle, you need two spoons of the same size. The spoons' size determines the quenelle's size. —A. E. ◆

1 *Hold a spoon in each hand with the bowls facing each other. With one spoon, scoop up a heaping spoonful of ice cream (or other food). Raspberry sorbet is shown here.*

2 *Press the second spoon against the side of the ice cream and scoop the contents out of the first spoon. You should have a nice smooth side where the ice cream was in the first spoon.*

3 *Repeat to form a third side. If it's not shaped to your liking, keep scooping until you have a nice three-sided football shape.*

Champagne Vinegar

BY LAURA GIANNATEMPO

While we don't necessarily think of Champagne vinegar as a pantry staple, it's a great ingredient for livening up vinaigrettes or adding a little punch to sauces (as in the Chicken with Vinegar & Onions recipe on p. 37). To find out which is best, *Fine Cooking* staffers conducted a blind tasting of five widely available brands, all from California or Italy. The results were anything but unanimous (we all seemed to have a different favorite), and no vinegar stood out as the undisputed winner. They're ranked below with our tasting notes.

Then we held a second tasting to sample Champagne vinegars made in France. This time, the comments were unequivocal—our tasters found them full-bodied and interesting, with authentic Champagne flavor. These vinegars are harder to find (although not necessarily more expensive), but if you're looking for that little hit of *je ne sais quoi*, they're worth seeking out, which is why they're in the winner's circle at right.

Top Picks

These three French Champagne vinegars were all made from Champagne wine that's fermented slowly in oak barrels to give it richness and complexity. Our favorite was **Delouis Fils.** We liked its rich, fruity aroma and mellow flavor, layered with hints of apple and caramel. But we also liked the herbal, honey-spice aroma and bright, balanced flavor of **Reims Champagne Vinegar by Clovis**, as well as the intense, oaky flavor of **La Marne.** For sources, see Where to Buy It, p. 72.

1 BELLINO
$4.19 (16.9 fl. oz.)

This amber-colored vinegar had a mild, fruity flavor with a pleasant tartness and slight floral notes. Some tasters also detected a sharp, green-apple flavor. In the vinaigrette, it seemed to maintain its character better than did most other vinegars.

Note: prices will vary.

2 O BASICS
$10.29 (6.8 fl. oz.)

This clear, light vinegar was on the mild side, with a subtle floral aroma and notes of nuts and sherry. It had a pleasantly fruity, oaky flavor and a slightly musty aftertaste that gave it some character. This vinegar would be a good choice for brightening up any vinaigrette or sauce.

3 COLAVITA
$8.49 (16.9 fl. oz.)

This vinegar's tart, lemony aroma, which some thought reminiscent of apples, was promising. But the flavor disappointed: Some of our tasters found it too acidic and not sufficiently complex. It would make a perfectly fine substitute for most commercial white-wine vinegars.

4 KIMBERLEY
$7.48 (12.7 fl. oz.)

By far the most distinctive of the bunch, this vinegar (available at Whole Foods Markets) was a dark amber color with a markedly sweet, oaky aroma. The flavor, too, was butterscotchy with sweet undertones, which reminded some tasters of sherry. While we liked its character, we found its flavor profile a bit too cloying for a Champagne vinegar.

5 B.R. COHN
$11.49 (6.7 fl. oz.)

This vinegar had the panel divided: Most tasters thought it was bland and lacking complexity, with an off flavor. A few found it had a decent balance of acidity and fruitiness. Overall, it wasn't a favorite, and given its steep price, we'd probably opt for a different brand if we had an alternative. ◆

Crème Brûlée, p. 45

A mini blowtorch is an essential tool to make Kim Masibay's crème brûlée. Kim prefers torches with longer nozzles; her two favorites are the Bonjour Professional Chef's Torch, available at Cooking.com (800-663-8810) for $39.95, and the Messermeister Cheflamme, available at ChefTools.com (866-716-2433) for $44.95.

Kim also likes Chicago Metallic's six-piece crème brûlée set, which includes an 8-inch-square aluminized-steel baking pan, a chrome wire rack, and four 6-ounce porcelain ramekins. It's $19.99 at KitchenKapers.com (800-455-5567).

Look for Madagascar vanilla beans (three for $6.29) at Penzeys .com (800-741-7787) and for Medaglia d'Oro instant espresso powder at GourmetSleuth.com (408-354-8281).

Bistro Cooking at Home, p. 33

To cook Molly Stevens's bistro dishes, you'll need a large Dutch oven. We like Staub and Le Creuset brands, both available at ChefsResource.com (866-765-2433). Molly recommends Delouis Fils Champagne vinegar for her Chicken with Vinegar and Onions. You'll find it at Amazon.com ($6.48 for a 16.9 fl. oz. bottle; search for "white-wine vinegar from Champagne").

Asian Vegetables, p. 53

Fish sauce, soy sauce, and Asian sesame oil are available in the ethnic food sections of many supermarkets. But you can also mail-order these products, as well as Chinese rice wine, from OrientalPantry.com (978-264-4576).

Crispy Chicken, p. 48

You'll need a heavy-duty rimmed baking sheet for Tony Rosenfeld's crispy chicken. If you don't have one, try DifferentDrummersKitchen.com (800-375-2665), where Chicago Metallic baking sheets are $7.99 each.

Quick-Braised Fish, p. 58

A 12-inch ovenproof skillet is best for these fish braises. We like All-Clad's stainless steel skillet, available at Cooking.com (800-663-8810) for $134.95. You'll find fish spatulas at Cooking Enthusiast.com (800-792-6650; search for "slotted spatula"); prices start at $27.99.

Playful Desserts, p. 62

Both almond paste and Nutella are available in many supermarkets. If you can't find them, you can mail-order Nutella ($3.39 for a 13-ounce jar) at Amazon.com and almond paste ($9.25 for a 10-ounce can) at KingArthurFlour.com (800-827-6836). For baking sheets, see the source under Crispy Chicken at left.

Letters, p. 10

Dansko clogs are available in many shoe stores. To find one near you, log on to Dansko.com. You can also buy them online for about $115 at Zappos.com.

Tasting Panel, p. 71

The vinegars ranked in our tasting panel are available in most grocery stores, including Whole Foods Markets. Among the French Champagne vinegars we liked, Delouis Fils ($6.48 for a 16.9 fl. oz. bottle; search for "white wine vinegar from Champagne") and La Marne ($16 for a 25 fl. oz. bottle) are both available at Amazon.com. Reims Champagne Vinegar by Clovis is available at Igourmet.com for $6.99 for a 16.75 fl. oz. bottle.

Back cover

Most specialty stores, and some grocery stores, sell du Puy lentils. You can also find them online at Kalustyans.com (800-352-3451) for $4.99 a pound. Kalustyan's also sells several brands of walnut oil, starting at $9.99 for a 250 ml bottle. ◆

Photos: Scott Phillips

advertisershoppingguide
A directory of our advertisers' products and services

www.finecooking.com/shopping

Appliances

Art Culinaire *p. 76* Lacanche professional ranges, handcrafted in France.
www.frenchranges.com

Clarke Appliance Showroom *p. 30A* Clarke is New England's premier distributor of luxury appliances like Wolf and Sub-Zero. Our fully functioning kitchens are like playgrounds for grownups. Test out an appliance with a favorite recipe.
800-242-5707
www.clarkecorp.com

Earthstone Wood-Fire Ovens *p. 76* Wood-fired brick ovens for indoor and outdoor use. Can double as a fireplace. Great for baking, grilling, and roasting.
1-800-840-4915
www.earthstoneovens.com

Bakeware

A Cook's Wares *p. 76* We have what you need for your kitchen: The finest cookware, bakeware, cutlery, utensils and small appliances. Since 1981.
www.cookswares.com

Grill Friends *p. 7* Since 1957, Harold Import Company has been a leading supplier of kitchenware products to the specialty retail trade, offering almost 3000 items. Our products are available in thousands of stores worldwide. What can HIC offer your business?
girlsatthegrill.com

LaPrima Shops *p. 27* LaPrimaShops. com is your on-line source for the finest products from Bialetti Cookware, Espresso and Cappuccino Makers to over 90 of SiliconeZone's Bakeware and Kitchen tools.
www.laprimashops.com

The Pepper Mill *p. 76* The world's first kosher gourmet kitchenware store, with brand-name cookware and bakeware, kosher gourmet foods and baking ingredients.
1-866-871-4022
www.thepeppermillinc.com

Pillivuyt USA, Inc. *p. 11* Over 400 porcelain items for cooking and serving. Virtually nonstick with easy-to-clean impenetrable glaze. Durable, versatile, and a joy to use.
www.pillivuytus.com

Silpat by Demarle *p. 27* Makers of Silpat®, the original nonstick baking sheet, used by professional chefs and bakers around the world. Silpat: It's not just for cookies!
www.demarleusa.com

Books

Cookbook Publishers *p. 77* Custom community fundraising cookbooks. Free kit.
1-800-227-7282
www.cookbookpublishers.com

Taunton Books *p. 27* *How To Break An Egg.* This one-stop reference is packed with over 1,400 sometimes-whimsical, always-wise tips for solving kitchen dilemmas.
www.taunton.com/books

Cookware

All-Clad Metalcrafters *p. 13* All-Clad invented the technology that produces the finest professional cookware, bakeware, kitchen tools, and accessories. The unrivaled original remains the choice of professional chefs and discerning cooks.
www.allclad.com

Fagor Cookware *p. 7* Manufacturer of stainless steel pressure cookers, specialty cookware, and kitchen accessories. Sold at fine retail stores nationwide. Shop online for parts and accessories.
www.fagoramerica.com

Falk Culinair *p. 73* Fine cookware for fine cooks. Stainless lined, solid copper cookware from Belgium. No other cookware conducts heat more efficiently or evenly than Falk.
www.copperpans.com

Scanpan USA, Inc. *p. 9* Scanpan USA, Inc. is the importer and wholesaler of Scanpan cookware in the U.S. For details on products, technology, pricing, and retail sources, please visit our web site.
800-828-1005
www.scanpan.com

Swiss Diamond Cookware *p. 3* Swiss manufacturer of patented diamond reinforced non-stick cookware, up to 200,000 real diamonds per pan. Diamonds guarantees lifetime non-stick performance, oven, dishwasher, metal untensil safe.
www.swissdiamondusa.com

The Water Broiler Pan *p. 76* Drannan Cookware Inventive Stainless Water-Broiler® - WaterRoaster™ Pan surprisingly eliminates smoke, splatter, flare-ups, and scrubbing. "Works wonderfully." (Pierre Franey, NY Times). "I love it." (Retired Chef).
www.waterbroiler.com

Cutlery

Chef's Choice *p. 17* The perfect partner for all your entire cutlery for a lifetime of incredibly sharp knives!
800-342-3255
www.chefschoice.com

Ergo Chef *p. 77* Ergo Chef is revolutionizing the culinary industry with ergonomic cutlery that matches user comfort with the highest quality construction.
www.ergochef.com

J.A. Henckels *p. 2* J.A.Henckels World's Finest Cutlery since 1731. J.A. Henckels continues to define the standard of cutlery with unique innovations and designs to create superior products.
www.jahenckels.com

Japanese Chefs Knife *p. 77* Top-brand Japanese chef's knives.
www.japanesechefsknife.com

Messermeister *p. 79* Messermeister markets one of the most extensive selections of innovative cutlery and related accessories for the professional and home chef.
www.messermeister.com

Norton Professional Sharpening Solution *p. 7* Norton, the leading worldwide manufacturer of professional culinary sharpening stones for over a century, offers cutlery sharpening kits for home cooks that are easy to use and store.
800-848-7379
www.nortonstones.com

The Holley Manufacturing Co. *p. 73* Professional sharpening services for cooks. We can sharpen and restore the cutting power of even the hardest Japanese knives. Free easy shipping in our own boxes. Visit our website.
www.holleyknives.com

Wildfire Cutlery *p. 77* Carbon steel kitchen knives that are uniqely designed, with a full tang & hardwood handle. For complete catalog see us at www.wildfirecutlery.com.
www.wildfirecutlery.com

Gourmet Foods

Avocado of the Month Club *p. 76* Your online source for delicious, premium avocados delivered straight to your front door.
www.aotmc.com

Divine Delights *p. 11* Your premium source for artisan petits fours. Delightful holiday assortments of hand-decorated bite sized cakes and confections. Shipped fresh nationwide.
800-915-9788
www.divinedelights.com

La Tienda *p. 76* Quality Spanish food selected by a dedicated family.
www.tienda.com

Ladd Hill Orchards *p. 77* Premium, Oregon-grown fresh or dried chestnuts and chestnut flour. Certified organic by guaranteed organic certification agency.
www.laddhillchestnuts.com

Meyenberg Goat Milk Products *p. 3* Gourmet goat milk products include whole and low fat fresh goat milk, powdered and evaporated goat milk, and award-winning goat milk butter and cheeses.
www.meyenberg.com

Millie's Pierogi *p. 77* Handmade pierogi, made fresh and shipped fresh to your door! Cabbage, potato-cheese, cheese, prune, or blueberry fillings.
www.milliespierogi.com

Montecito Country Kitchen *p. 77* Montecito Country Kitchen offers delicious herbs, spices, olive oils and exotic salts. Those beautifully packaged products, including wonderful gift ideas, are indispensable for insightful cooks.
www.montecitocountrykitchen.com

Petaluma Coffee and Tea Co. *p. 77* Since 1989, fair-trade coffees and gourmet teas.
1-800-929-JAVA
www.petalumacoffee.com

Trenton Bridge Lobster Pound *p. 77* Your one-stop shopping for the freshest lobster, clams, and other shellfish shipped overnight to your door. Delivery Tuesday through Saturday.
www.trentonbridgelobster.com

Trois Petits Cochons, Inc. *p. 73* Artisanal charcuterie. By using all-natural, high-quality ingredients, and by crafting small, handmade batches, the excellent quality of our pates, terrines, and mousses is guaranteed.
www.3pigs.com

Upton Tea Imports *p. 77* 380+ varieties of garden-fresh tea, plus accessories.
1-800-234-8327
www.uptontea.com

Ingredients

Bulk Foods *p. 76* Offering a wide selection of spices, nuts, dried fruits, and other ingredients.
www.bulkfoods.com

Magic Seasoning Blends *p. 73* Chef Paul Prudhomme's all-natural magic seasoning blends, sauces and marinades, pepper sauce, smoked meats, cookbooks, gift packs, sweet potato pecan pie, and much more!
800-457-2857
www.chefpaul.com

Rafal Spice Co. *p. 77* Spices, herbs, teas, coffees, and food specialties.
1-800-228-4276
www.rafalspicecompany.com

San Francisco Herb Co. *p. 76* Quality spices and herbs by the pound.
1-800-227-4530
www.sfherb.com

Sugarcraft, Inc. *p. 76* Baking, cake decorating, candy, and cookie supplies.
www.sugarcraft.com

Kitchen Design & Tableware

Plum Pudding Kitchen *p. 27* Your online source for "irresistibly Italian" Vietri dinnerware, flatware, glassware, and much more. Let us help you set a special table!
888-940-7586
www.plumpuddingkitchen.com

Replacements, Ltd. *p. 76* World's largest inventory: old and new china.
1-800-REPLACE
www.replacements.com

The Bowl Mill *p. 17* One-piece hardwood bowls made on 19th-century lathes in Vermont, ranging from 8" to 20" in diameter featuring maple, yellow birch, and cherry.
1-888-472-1022
www.bowlmill.com

Totally Bamboo *p. 77* Featuring over 150 products, Totally Bamboo is the industry pioneer of bamboo cutting boards and kitchen design. Order all of our fine products directly online!
www.totallybamboo.com

Kitchen Tools & Utensils

Bella Copper *p. 77* The world's leading heat diffuser/defroster plate provides superior heat conduction for more even cooking and faster defrosting. Available in solid copper or pure silver. A gourmet kitchen essential.
1-805-215-3241
www.bellacopper.com

Grill Friends *p. 7* Since 1957, Harold Import Company has been a leading supplier of kitchenware products to the specialty retail trade, offering almost 3000 items. Our products are available in thousands of stores worldwide. What can HIC offer your business?
www.girlsatthegrill.com

House On the Hill *p. 76* Over 400 molds for springerle, speculaas, gingerbread, marzipan, fondant and cake decorating. Order now for holiday cookie baking. Catalog on request.
www.houseonthehill.net

Kerekes *p. 77* Your complete online source for professional chef tools, cookware, bakeware, and cake decorating supplies used by top chefs at the finest restaurants and kitchens.
www.bakedeco.com

Messermeister *p. 79* Messermeister markets one of the most extensive selections of innovative cutlery and related accessories for the professional and home chef.
www.messermeister.com

Mix-In-Guide *p. 77* The best way to get ingredients into your mixer bowl. Easy on. Easy off. Stainless steel ingredient chute for stand mixers.
www.mix-in-guide.com

Kitchen Tools & Utensils

J.K. Adams Company *p. 13* J.K. Adams, has been the premiere Vermont manufacturer of handcrafted, heirloom-quality, woodware for the kitchen and table since 1944.
1-800-570-CHEF
www.jkadams.com

Let's Gel *p. 11* Stand in comfort! Let's Gel was started with one simple goal, to make the time you spend standing in your kitchen more comfortable.
866-GEL-MATS
www.letsgel.com

WMF of America *p. 3* WMF is the only brand that can make cooking, dining, and drinking an event. WMF is the singular choice.
www.wmf-usa.com

Schools, Travel & Organizations

Culinary Business Academy *p. 11* Extensive and comprehensive personal chef business knowledge and training from the world's recognized leader in the personal chef industry. Nobody offers what we offer.
800-747-2433
www.culinarybusiness.com

Greenwood CVB *p. 17* Indulge at our fabulous restaurants and take a cooking class at our famous cooking school. Treat yourself at our luxurious new spa and explore quaint shops, fascinating museums and historic tours.
800-748-9064
www.greenwoodms.org

La Villa Bonita *p. 27* La Villa Bonita offers a delicious immersion in the culinary joys of Mexico, with its culinary vacation packages in a 16th-century mansion in Cuernavaca.
800-505-3084
www.lavillabonita.com

Le Cordon Bleu *p. 9* Master the culinary arts. Earn the Grand Diplome in approximately nine months. Three- to five-week intensive courses and online hospitality programs are also available.
800-457-2433
www.cordonbleu.edu

The Inst. of Culinary Education *p. 77* NYC cooking classes, tours, tastings, and parties.
1-212-847-0700
www.iceculinary.com

Product #052014

Side dishes that get *rave* reviews!

Side Dish is a must-have collection of the best side-dish recipes from *Fine Cooking*.

Here, in one handy place, find delicious, kitchen-tested recipes for brightly flavored vegetable sautés, creamy potato gratins, fluffy rice pilafs, savory stuffings, and much more, all conveniently categorized as:

- Quick
- Make Ahead
- Can Feed a Crowd

Plus eight favorite main dishes to mix and match with the sides for exciting menu options.

With *Side Dish*, you'll never again ask: what should I serve with. . . ? You'll have 101 delicious answers! Only $7.99, order yours today!

Call 800-888-8286, offer code M580073
Or go to: FineCooking.com/SideDish

This special issue is not part of any regular magazine subscription.
Available to ship 2/12/07
Plus $3.50 s&h. Payable in U.S. funds

 **The Taunton Press**
Inspiration for hands-on living®

© 2007 The Taunton Press

cook's market

For more information from our advertisers, see the Shopping Guide on pages 74-75.

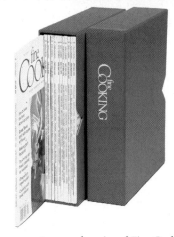

nutrition**information**

Recipe	Page	Calories		Protein	Carb	Fats (g)				Chol.	Sodium	Fiber	Notes
		total	from fat	(g)	(g)	total	sat	mono	poly	(mg)	(mg)	(g)	
In Season	18												
Roasted Parsnips w/ Cinnamon & Coriander		250	120	2	31	14	2	10	1.5	0	160	9	based on 4 servings
Winter Pastas	26a												
Baked Fettucine w/ Asparagus, Lemon & Mascarpone		1040	520	39	96	57	29	16	10	195	770	13	based on 4 servings
Baked Ziti w/ Tomato, Mozzarella & Sausage		1070	390	54	113	44	20	17	5	110	1140	8	based on 4 servings
Campanelle w/ Broccoli Raab, Sausage & Olives		550	300	21	42	33	8	20	4	30	1540	5	based on 4 servings
Cavatappi w/ Roasted Peppers, Capocollo & Ricotta		1080	520	35	106	57	32	18	3	190	780	9	based on 4 servings
Classic Macaroni & Cheese		740	400	27	58	45	31	12	2	135	1040	3	based on 8 servings
Spaghetti w/ Portabellas, Sage & Walnuts		750	400	18	72	44	18	16	7	70	670	5	based on 4 servings
Baked Rigatoni w/ Cauliflower in a Spicy Pink Sauce		530	210	21	60	24	12	9	2	65	970	6	based on 8 servings
Bistro Cooking at Home	33												
Chicken w/ Vinegar & Onions		500	280	40	9	32	11	13	5	145	400	1	based on 6 servings
Braised Lamb Shanks w/ Garlic & Vermouth		360	180	32	1	20	7	10	1.5	120	360	0	based on 6 servings
Beef Stew w/ Red Wine & Carrots		580	230	49	20	25	9	12	1.5	160	630	4	based on 6 servings
Rice Pilaf	40												
Southwestern Rice Pilaf		200	40	5	36	4.5	0.5	3	0.5	0	290	2	based on 8 servings
Rice Pilaf w/ Sage, Parmigiano & Prosciutto		300	110	9	33	12	5	4	0.5	30	550	0	based on 8 servings
Rice Pilaf w/ Onions, Orange, Cherry & Pistachio		320	100	7	49	12	4.5	4.5	2	15	210	3	based on 8 servings
Saffron Rice Pilaf w/ Red Pepper & Toasted Almonds		200	40	5	34	4	0.5	2.5	1	0	170	1	based on 8 servings
Crème Brûlée	45												
Classic Crème Brûlée		470	390	5	18	43	26	13	2	345	85	0	based on 4 servings
Crispy Chicken	48												
Toasted Breadcrumbs		110	40	2	14	4.5	0.5	2.5	0.5	0	230	1	based on ¼ cup serving
Crispy Orange-Sesame Chicken Breasts		380	140	39	21	16	3	6	6	95	330	3	based on 4 servings
Herbed Chicken Breasts w/ an Olive-Parmigiano Crust		330	150	36	6	17	3	10	2	95	710	1	based on 4 servings
Crispy Cheddar & Jalapeño Coated Chicken Breasts		300	100	38	10	11	4	3.5	2	105	320	1	based on 4 servings
Crispy Chicken Breasts w/ Lemon & Capers		290	100	37	9	11	2.5	5	1.5	95	540	1	based on 4 servings
Asian Vegetables	53												
Braised Bok Choy w/ Sherry & Prosciutto		70	30	5	4	3.5	0.5	1	1	5	530	1	based on 6 servings
Stir-Fried Napa Cabbage w/ Garlic, Fresh Chile & Basil		80	30	3	10	3.5	0	2	1	0	440	3	based on 4 servings
Stir-Fried Snow Peas w/ Shiitakes & Ginger		110	50	3	13	6	0.5	3	2	0	360	3	based on 4 servings
Roasted Eggplant w/ Chiles, Peanuts & Mint		170	130	2	8	15	2.5	7	5	0	140	3	based on 6 servings
Quick-Braised Fish	58												
Braised Red Snapper Puttanesca		320	150	31	12	17	2.5	12	2.5	50	1360	0	based on 4 servings
Salmon Braised in Pinot Noir		480	190	36	11	22	11	6	2.5	145	440	2	based on 4 servings
Braised Cod w/ Fennel, Potatoes & Littlenecks		340	110	33	21	12	1.5	8	1.5	75	530	4	based on 4 servings
Playful Desserts	62												
Free-Form Pear Tarts w/ Almond & Cinnamon		380	170	5	47	19	5	10	2	5	300	4	based on 1 tart
Phyllo "Chips" w/ Ice Cream & Strawberry "Dip"		190	90	2	26	10	6	2.5	0.5	30	60	1	based on 8 servings
Fried Chocolate-Hazelnut Wontons w/ Dipping Sauce		460	220	6	53	25	9	10	4	45	210	3	based on 6 servings
Test Kitchen	66												
Homemade Crema (Mexican Sour Cream)		50	50	0	0	6	3.5	1.5	0	20	5	0	based on 1 Tbs.
Middle-Eastern-Style Lamb Pita "Pizza"		560	260	38	24	29	9	16	3	130	850	4	based on 4 servings
Quick & Delicious	78a												
Jerk Chicken Drumsticks		330	160	35	3	18	5	7	4	125	200	0	based on 6 servings
Lime Chicken w/ Poblano Sour Cream		540	350	39	4	39	11	17	6	160	700	1	based on 4 servings
Asian-Style Beef Barbecue in Lettuce Packages		410	100	28	48	11	3.5	4	1.5	45	710	3	based on 4 servings
Lamb Chops w/ Lemon, Thyme & Mustard Butter		720	510	50	0	57	27	22	4	225	500	0	based on 4 servings
Tuna Teriyaki w/ Scallion Salad		320	90	42	15	10	2.5	3	3	65	2050	1	based on 4 servings
Colossal Shrimp w/ Watercress & Tomato Salad		290	170	21	10	19	3	13	2.5	170	480	3	based on 4 servings
Deviled Pork Chops		650	270	85	6	30	10	14	2	230	870	0	based on 4 servings
Back Cover													
Warm French Lentil Salad w/ Smoked Sausage		390	180	17	30	21	3.5	9	6	25	610	7	based on 6 servings

The nutritional analyses have been calculated by a registered dietitian at Nutritional Solutions in Melville, New York. When a recipe gives a choice of ingredients, the first choice is the one used in the calculations. Optional ingredients and those listed without a specific quantity are not included. When a range of ingredient amounts or servings is given, the smaller amount or portion is used. When the quantities of salt and pepper aren't specified, the analysis is based on ¼ teaspoon salt and ⅛ teaspoon pepper per serving for entrées, and ⅛ teaspoon salt and 1/16 teaspoon pepper per serving for side dishes.

Around the world in seven quick recipes

BY LORI LONGBOTHAM

Grab your passport, fire up your broiler, and get ready to cook your way around the world. Each of these recipes cooks under the broiler, which, like grilling, gives food great flavor lickety-split. The only hard part will be deciding which dish to make tonight. Will it be the English deviled pork chops or the French lamb chops with lemon-thyme butter? Jamaican jerk chicken drumsticks or Mexican chicken thighs? Teriyaki tuna or Asian beef barbecue? Whichever recipe you choose, don't worry about having to trot the globe to rustle up the ingredients—most are readily available at your supermarket.

Broiling tips

No preheating is necessary. Not only does the broiler cook food quickly, it heats up in just a few minutes, unlike the oven which can take 15 to 20 minutes to reach the desired temperature. So just turn it on and get ready to cook.

Be ready to move the pan around. Take a close look at your broiler and see how it releases its heat. If the heat is concentrated right down the center of the oven, arrange the food right down the center of the broiler pan. Most broilers have hot and cool spots, so be ready to move the broiler pan around to compensate.

Some pieces may cook faster than others. The pieces you're broiling won't be exactly the same size, so they won't cook in the same amount of time; remove what's done and continue to cook anything that needs more time.

Jerk Chicken Drumsticks

Serves five to six.

- **10 thin scallions, white and tender green parts, coarsely chopped**
- **1 Scotch bonnet or habanero chile, seeded and coarsely chopped**
- **2 Tbs. distilled white-wine vinegar**
- **1 Tbs. fresh thyme leaves**
- **3 medium cloves garlic, chopped**
- **1¼ tsp. ground allspice**
- **1 tsp. kosher salt; more as needed**
- **½ tsp. freshly ground black pepper**
- **10 chicken drumsticks (3½ lb.)**
- **Vegetable oil or cooking spray for the pan**

In a food processor, pulse the scallions, chiles, vinegar, thyme, garlic, allspice, salt, and pepper to a thick paste.

Transfer the paste to a large bowl, add the chicken, and toss to coat. Let stand for 10 minutes.

Position an oven rack in the center of the oven and heat the broiler to high. Line the bottom of a broiler pan with foil and replace the perforated top part of the pan. Oil the pan or coat with cooking spray. Arrange the chicken on the broiler pan. Season generously on all sides with salt.

Broil the chicken in the center of the oven, turning once after about 10 minutes, until fully cooked and nicely browned in spots, about 20 minutes total. Transfer to a platter and serve.

Tip: Scotch bonnet chiles are authentic, but they're very hot and can be hard to find; the habanero chile is a good substitute. If you want to tame the heat, use less habanero or Scotch bonnet but don't substitute a less spicy variety.

Lime Chicken with Poblano Sour Cream

Serves four.

4 large poblano chiles
1 large lime
½ cup sour cream or Mexican crema
2 Tbs. chopped fresh cilantro, plus a few sprigs for garnish (optional)
2 tsp. kosher salt; more to taste
1 Tbs. ground coriander
1 tsp. ground cumin
½ tsp. freshly ground black pepper
8 medium (5- to 6-oz.) bone-in, skin-on chicken thighs, trimmed
3 Tbs. extra-virgin olive oil

Position an oven rack 5 to 6 inches from the broiler element and heat the broiler to high. Line the bottom of a broiler pan with foil and re-place the perforated top part of the pan. Broil the poblanos, turning 3 times, until black-ened, 12 to 15 minutes total. Put the poblanos in a medium bowl, top with a dinner plate, and let stand for 5 minutes.

Meanwhile, cut the lime in half. Cut one half into wedges and squeeze the other half to get 2 tsp. juice. Measure the juice into a small bowl and stir in the sour cream or crema and the chopped cilantro.

Transfer the poblanos to a cutting board to cool a bit,

then peel away the burned skin, discard the stems and seeds, and cut into ½-inch dice. Add to the sour cream mixture and stir to combine. Season to taste with salt.

In a small bowl, combine the 2 tsp. salt with the corian-der, cumin, and pepper. Coat the chicken with the oil and season on both sides with the spice mixture. Put the chicken skin-side down on the broiler pan, and broil until well browned, 7 to 10 minutes. Turn the chicken over with tongs and continue to broil, checking frequently, until the chicken is dark brown and cooked through (an instant-read thermometer should register at least 165°F), 4 to 6 minutes more. If the chicken threatens to burn before it's cooked through, move the pan to a lower rack.

Transfer the chicken to serving plates, spoon the poblano sour cream on the side, and garnish with cilantro sprigs, if using, and the lime wedges for squeezing over the chicken. Serve hot.

Tip: Look for Mexican crema in the dairy case or near the tortillas in super-markets. To make your own, see p. 70.

Deviled Pork Chops

Serves four.

¼ cup Dijon mustard
1 Tbs. firmly packed dark brown sugar
2 tsp. fresh lemon juice
2 tsp. Worcestershire sauce
¼ tsp. ground cayenne
4 1-inch-thick, bone-in, center-cut loin pork chops (2½ to 3 lb.)
Kosher salt
1 Tbs. coarsely chopped fresh flat-leaf parsley (optional)

Stir together the mustard, brown sugar, lemon juice, Worcestershire, and cayenne in a small bowl.

Position an oven rack 3 to 4 inches from the broiler element and heat the broiler to high. Line the bottom of a broiler pan with foil and replace the perforated top part of the pan. Arrange the pork on the broiler pan and season generously on both sides with salt. Brush about half of the mustard mixture

over the top of the chops. Broil until the chops are deeply browned in spots, 6 to 8 minutes. Turn the chops over with tongs, brush with the remaining mustard mixture, and continue to broil until the pork is browned and just cooked through (an instant-read thermometer in the center of a chop should register 145°F), about 5 min-utes more. Let rest a few minutes before serving. Sprinkle the better-looking sides of the chops with the parsley, if using, and transfer to serving plates.

Lori Longbotham is a New York City-based food writer and recipe developer. ◆

Colossal Shrimp with Watercress & Tomato Salad

Serves four.

- **1 clove garlic**
- **1 tsp. kosher salt**
- **1 small red onion, finely diced (about ¾ cup)**
- **6 Tbs. extra-virgin olive oil**
- **6 Tbs. coarsely chopped fresh flat-leaf parsley**
- **3 Tbs. fresh lemon juice**
- **3 tsp. finely grated lemon zest (from 1 lemon)**
- **⅜ tsp. freshly ground black pepper**
- **8 colossal shrimp (6 to 8 count; about 1 lb.), peeled and deveined**
- **2 pints red or yellow grape or cherry tomatoes, or a combination, halved**
- **8 cups watercress sprigs, washed and dried (from about 8 oz. untrimmed watercress)**

Peel and chop the garlic clove. Sprinkle with ¼ tsp. of the salt and, using the side of a chef's knife, mash and scrape the garlic into a paste. Transfer to a medium bowl and whisk in half the onion, 2 Tbs. of the olive oil, 2 Tbs. of the parsley, 1 Tbs. of the lemon juice, 1 tsp. of the zest, and a generous ⅛ tsp. pepper. Add the shrimp and marinate, stirring occasionally, for 20 minutes.

Meanwhile, in another bowl, stir together the tomatoes, ¾ tsp. salt, the remaining onion, and the remaining ¼ cup olive oil, ¼ cup parsley, 2 Tbs. lemon juice, 2 tsp. zest, and ¼ tsp. pepper. Stir from time to time.

Position an oven rack 3 to 4 inches from the broiler element and heat the broiler to high. Line the bottom of a broiler pan with foil and replace the perforated top part of the pan. Arrange the shrimp on the broiler pan. Broil until the shrimp are beginning to turn bright pink and are firm to the touch on top, about 3 minutes. Turn the shrimp over, rotate the broiler pan from back to front, and broil until the shrimp are just opaque throughout (cut into a piece to check), 1 to 2 minutes longer.

To serve, arrange the watercress on 4 plates, top with the tomatoes and their sauce, and arrange 2 shrimp on top.

Tip: To help the shrimp cook evenly, arrange them on the broiler pan in a line that will be directly under the broiler element.

Lamb Chops with Lemon, Thyme & Mustard Butter

Serves four.

- **4 Tbs. unsalted butter, softened**
- **1 tsp. whole-grain Dijon mustard**
- **1 tsp. fresh thyme leaves, lightly chopped**
- **¾ tsp. finely grated lemon zest**
- **⅛ tsp. kosher salt; more as needed**
- **⅛ tsp. freshly ground black pepper; more as needed**
- **8 lamb loin chops (1½- to 2-inch-thick chops; about 3 lb.), trimmed**

In a small bowl, mash together the butter, mustard, thyme, zest, salt, and pepper until well combined. Refrigerate until ready to use.

Position an oven rack 5 to 6 inches from the broiler element and heat the broiler to high. Line the bottom of a broiler pan with foil and replace the perforated top part of the pan. Arrange the chops on the pan. Season both sides of the lamb generously with salt and pepper. Broil until the first side is well-browned, about 8 minutes. Turn the chops over with tongs and continue to broil until they're well browned and the center is cooked to your liking, 3 to 5 minutes longer for medium rare (cut into a chop near the bone to check).

Transfer the lamb to serving plates and top each chop with a dab of the flavored butter. Serve hot.

Serving suggestion:
Serve with sautéed haricots verts and tiny boiled potatoes.

Asian-Style Beef Barbecue in Lettuce Packages

Serves four.

¾ cup long-grain white rice
½ tsp. kosher salt; more as needed
2 medium hearts of romaine or 1 large head red or green leaf lettuce, separated into leaves
1 cup small cilantro sprigs
1 cup small mint leaves (or larger leaves torn into small pieces)
6 medium radishes, thinly sliced (about ¾ cup)
½ cup thinly sliced scallions, including tender green parts
½ cup hoisin sauce (I like Koon Chun brand)
1 lb. flank steak, 1 inch thick
¼ tsp. freshly ground black pepper
2 tsp. sesame seeds

Bring 1½ cups water to a boil in a small saucepan over high heat. Add the rice and salt, reduce the heat to low, cover, and simmer gently until the rice is tender and the water absorbed, about 20 minutes.

Meanwhile, arrange the lettuce leaves in a bowl and set the cilantro, mint, radishes, and scallions in separate piles on a plate. In a small bowl, combine ¼ cup of the hoisin with 2 Tbs. water; reserve for assembly.

Position an oven rack 5 to 6 inches from the broiler ele-

ment and heat the broiler to high. Line the bottom of a broiler pan with foil and replace the perforated top part of the pan. Season the steak with a large pinch of salt and the pepper. Broil the steak until it loses its raw appearance on top and begins to brown, about 3 minutes. Brush the steak with about 2 Tbs. the remaining hoisin, and broil until lightly browned, 2 minutes longer. Turn the steak over with tongs and broil until it begins to brown, about 3 minutes. Brush generously with the remaining hoisin, and broil 2 to 3 minutes longer for medium rare (130°F on an instant-read thermometer), or to desired doneness (don't let the hoisin burn; if necessary, move the pan to a lower rack).

Transfer the steak to a cutting board, sprinkle with the sesame seeds, and let rest for 5 minutes. Cut into thin slices across the grain at a slight angle. Arrange the steak and rice in separate bowls. Let diners assemble their own packages, filling the lettuce leaves with the rice, steak, cilantro, mint, radishes, scallions, and a drizzle of the diluted hoisin.

Tuna Teriyaki with Scallion Salad

Serves four.

6 Tbs. soy sauce
3 Tbs. firmly packed dark brown sugar
1 tsp. finely grated fresh ginger
1 medium clove garlic, finely chopped
1 tsp. Asian sesame oil
4 6-oz. tuna steaks, 1 inch thick
⅛ tsp. ground cayenne
8 slender scallions, dark green parts only, trimmed and thinly sliced diagonally (about ¾ cup)
¼ cup fresh cilantro leaves
2 Tbs. rice vinegar

Make the teriyaki sauce: Bring the soy sauce, brown sugar, ginger, and garlic to a boil over medium-high heat in a small saucepan. Boil until the mixture has thickened slightly, about 2 minutes. Stir in ½ tsp. of the sesame oil.

Broil the tuna: Position an oven rack 5 to 6 inches from the broiler element and heat the broiler to high. Line the bottom of a broiler pan with foil and replace the perforated top part of the pan. Season the tuna on both sides with the cayenne and arrange on the broiler pan. Broil the tuna for 2 minutes, brush generously with the

teriyaki sauce, and broil until the glaze sets, about 2 minutes longer.

Turn the tuna over with a spatula and broil for 2 minutes, brush generously with the teriyaki sauce, and broil until the tuna is pale pink in the center or to desired doneness (cut into a piece to check), about 2 minutes longer. Brush with any remaining teriyaki sauce.

Meanwhile, stir together the scallions, cilantro, vinegar, and the remaining ½ tsp. sesame oil. Transfer the tuna to serving plates, top with the scallion salad, and serve.

Tip: If your scallions are large and strong-flavored, slice them as thinly as you can and soak them in ice water for 10 to 15 minutes. Dry the scallions on paper towels before making the salad.

IT'S HARD TO LET GO

Messermeister blends ergonomic perfection with exacting performance. The elite edge is crafted using an exclusive 3-step hand-finishing process that allows you to slice, dice, chop, split, trim, pare, carve and julienne with precision and delight. The revolutionary bolsterless edge enables continuous cutting along the full length of the edge and the contoured handle and polished spine create a knife so comfortable, some chefs call it sensual. It's a feeling that you'll want to hold on to forever.

Messermeister
THE KNIFE FOR LIFE™
www.messermeister.com

Rustic French flavor à la minute

This classic bistro salad would make a fine first course to a warming winter dinner, but it's also good at the center of a weeknight meal. Just add a loaf of crusty bread and a tangle of lightly dressed mesclun greens for an easy but satisfying supper.

Season while hot for superior flavor

Toss the lentils with a little vinegar and salt immediately after draining, and you'll see a big boost in the flavor of the salad. Like potatoes, lentils firm up as they cool, which slows their ability to absorb seasonings.

For more bistro recipes, turn to p. 33.

Warm French Lentil Salad with Smoked Sausage

Serves four to six.

The very small, dark greenish-brown du Puy lentils (also called French lentils) are firmer than brown lentils and hold their shape better during cooking (for sources, see p. 72). In France, the sausage would be saucisson à l'ail, a semi-cooked, smoked garlic sausage. Kielbasa makes a fine substitute.

1½ cups du Puy lentils (about 10 oz.)
3 fresh thyme sprigs
2 bay leaves
3 garlic cloves, smashed
¼ tsp. black peppercorns
1 small onion, peeled
1 small carrot, peeled and split lengthwise
8 oz. smoked sausage, such as kielbasa
1 cup dry white wine or dry white vermouth
2½ Tbs. red-wine vinegar; more as needed
2 tsp. Dijon mustard
Kosher salt
3 Tbs. extra-virgin olive oil
3 Tbs. walnut oil
¼ cup chopped fresh flat-leaf parsley
¼ cup finely chopped scallions (3 to 4 scallions)
Freshly ground black pepper

Pick over and rinse the lentils, and put them in a 3- to 4-qt. saucepan. Pile the thyme, bay leaves, garlic, and peppercorns on a 5-inch square of double-layer cheesecloth. Gather up the edges and tie into a little pouch with kitchen twine. Add the pouch to the pan along with the onion and carrot. Fill the pan with cold water to cover the lentils by about 2 inches, and bring to a boil over medium-high heat. Immediately lower to a gentle simmer—boiling can break the lentils—and simmer, uncovered, until just tender, 30 to 40 minutes. (If the water level drops below the surface of the lentils as they simmer, add a little more water.)

Meanwhile, put the sausage in a small saucepan or deep skillet. Add the wine and enough water to cover by about ½ inch. Bring to a simmer. Reduce the heat as needed to cook at a bare simmer (bubbles should only occasionally break the surface), uncovered, until a metal skewer inserted into the center comes out feeling hot to the touch, 15 to 20 minutes.

While the lentils and sausage cook, make the vinaigrette: In a medium bowl, whisk 1½ Tbs. of the vinegar with the mustard and a pinch of salt. In a steady stream, whisk in the olive and walnut oils. Season to taste with salt.

Drain the lentils, discarding the herb pouch, carrot, and onion. Transfer to a large bowl and add 1 tsp. salt and the remaining 1 Tbs. vinegar, tossing to coat. Drain the sausage, and, if necessary, peel off the casing (bite into a piece first—many sausage casings are thin enough to leave on). Slice into ¼-inch rounds. Add the sausage and vinaigrette to the lentils, tossing to coat. Stir in the parsley and scallions, and season with a generous amount of black pepper, plus more salt and vinegar to taste.

Molly Stevens, a contributing editor to Fine Cooking, *is the author of the award-winning* All About Braising. ◆

Photos: Scott Phillips

fine Cooking

FOR PEOPLE WHO LOVE TO COOK

MAY 2007 NO. 85

sear & sauce for
fast shrimp sautés

e best
ecipes
r spring:

azed ham
th 3 sauces

mple carrot
de dishes

ky, buttery
scuits

rawberry-
ubarb pie

ick ginger
icken soup

w.finecooking.com

5 CAN $7.95

seared shrimp & asparagus
with a lemon-garlic sauce

05

4470 56529 1

Penthouse.
Central Park.
Sunrise.

So what's cooking in the kitchen?

fine Cooking

MAY 2007 NO. 85

FOR PEOPLE WHO LOVE TO COOK

sear & sauce for
fast shrimp sautés

e best
ecipes
r spring:

azed ham
th 3 sauces

mple carrot
de dishes

ky, buttery
scuits

awberry-
ubarb pie

ick ginger
icken soup

w.finecooking.com

5 CAN $7.95

seared shrimp & asparagus
with a lemon-garlic sauce

Above the rhythms of the Big Apple, B. Smith, restaurateur and lifestyle designer and her husband and business partner, Dan Gasby, create a pas de deux. In their sophisticated GE Monogram kitchen, a pair of dishwashers are completely in tune with this harmonious relationship.

imagination at work

Beach house.
Sag Harbor.
Sunset.

So what's cooking in the kitchen?

At water's edge, B and Dan harvest herbs and tomatoes that enliven the flavors in the *cioppino*. Their spacious GE Monogram kitchen, with both a speed oven and a multi-function oven, gives further credence to the adage: two are better than one.

GE Monogram®
Visit monogram.com

fine Cooking

APRIL/MAY 2007   ISSUE 85

38

44

RECIPE FOLDOUT

84A Quick & Delicious
**Seven dishes that
bridge the seasons**

Ginger Chicken Soup

ON THE COVER

56 Fast Shrimp Sautés

UP FRONT

6 Index

8 Menus

10 Letters

14 Links

16 Contributors

18 In Season
Artichokes

20 Enjoying Wine
Greek wine

24 Equipment
❖ **Innovative
nutcracker**
❖ **Clip-on spoon rest**
❖ **Yogurt maker**
❖ **Double-duty sinks**

30 Great Finds
Salumi

32 Artisan Foods

34 Readers' Tips

24

18

20

30

34

The Taunton Press
Inspiration for hands-on living®

visit our web site: **www.finecooking.com**

48   51   56   60

FEATURES

38   DINNER WITH FRIENDS
A Taste of Spring
**Welcome the season with a menu inspired
by the market's freshest ingredients**
by Tasha DeSerio

44   ### The Most Delicious Glazed Ham
**From the market to the kitchen, here's
how to shop for and bake the perfect ham**
by Bruce Aidells

48   ### How to Make
Flaky, Buttery Biscuits
**An unusual mixing method is the secret to the
flakiest buttermilk biscuits you've ever tasted**
by Peter Reinhart

51   ### Carrots, Pure & Simple
**This quartet of delicious recipes shows that
you don't have to fuss to highlight the essential
sweet flavor of carrots**
by Dan Barber

56   COVER STORY
Sear & Sauce for Fast Shrimp Sautés
A few key techniques guarantee great results
by Tony Rosenfeld

60   ### Rhubarb's Greatest Hits
**Brighten up your favorite desserts with
sweet-tart rhubarb**
by Karen Barker

64   TOOL PRIMER
Knife Sharpeners
**We'll help you sort through the options
to find the one that's right for you**
by Adam Ried

72

IN THE BACK

72   From Our
Test Kitchen
❖ Ramps, morels,
and fiddleheads
❖ Cornish hens
❖ Slicing onions
❖ Leftovers: ham
❖ Fresh chervil

78   Where To Buy It

84   Nutrition
Information

BACK COVER

Make It Tonight
**Bourbon-
Chocolate Mousse**

73

74

index

◆ QUICK
Under 45 minutes

◆ MAKE AHEAD
Can be completely prepared ahead but may need reheating and a garnish to serve

◆ MOSTLY MAKE AHEAD
Can be partially prepared ahead but will need a few finishing touches before serving

◆ VEGETARIAN
May contain eggs and dairy ingredients

57 *Spicy Seared Chipotle Shrimp with Zucchini & Chorizo*

recipes

Cover Recipe

◆ Hot Garlicky Shrimp with Asparagus & Lemon, 59

Appetizers

◆◆◆ Roasted Red Pepper & Walnut Dip with Pomegranate Molasses, 75

◆◆◆ Wild Mushroom Toasts, 40

Salads

◆◆ Carrot Salad with Walnut Oil & Honey, 54

◆◆◆ Garden Lettuces with Garlic Chapons, 41

Soups

◆ Ginger Chicken Soup, 84a

◆◆ Velvety Carrot Soup with Ginger, 55

Pasta & Gnocchi

◆ Pan-Fried Gnocchi with Bacon, Onions, & Peas, 84a

◆◆ Penne with Asparagus, Olives & Parmigiano Breadcrumbs, 84a

Meat & Poultry

◆ Broiled Lamb Skewers with Baby Arugula & Lemon Vinaigrette, 84a

◆ Fried Ham with Redeye Gravy, 76

Oven-Glazed Ham with Cherry-Pomegranate Glaze & Sauce, 47

Oven-Glazed Ham with Maple, Tea & Cardamom Glaze & Sauce, 47

Oven-Glazed Ham with Tangerine Marmalade Glaze & Sauce, 47

Roasted Cornish Game Hens with Wildflower Honey & Orange, 42

Seafood

◆ Hot Garlicky Shrimp with Asparagus & Lemon, 59

41 *Garden Lettuces with Garlic Chapons*

49 *Flaky Buttermilk Biscuits*

◆ Sear-Roasted Halibut with Roasted Red Pepper Purée, 84a

◆ Shrimp with Fennel, Tomato & Pernod Sauce, 58

◆ Spicy Seared Chipotle Shrimp with Zucchini & Chorizo, 57

Eggs

◆ Garlic & Herb Fried Eggs on Toasts with Prosciutto Crisps, 84a

Beans

◆◆ Smoky Black Bean & Cheddar Burrito with Baby Spinach, 84a

Side Dishes

◆◆ Carrot Salad with Walnut Oil & Honey, 54

Ham Bone Collards, 76

◆◆ Maple Pan-Roasted Baby Carrots, 53

◆◆ New Potatoes with Butter, Shallots & Chervil, 42

◆◆ Pan-Seared Artichokes with Sherry Vinegar & Thyme, 19

◆◆ Roasted Asparagus with Lemon & Olive Oil, 42

Condiments

◆◆ Baby Carrots Pickled in Champagne & Sherry Vinegars, 54

◆◆◆ Rhubarb & Dried-Cherry Chutney, 11

Biscuits & Muffins

◆ Caramelized Onion Biscuits, 50

◆◆ Cheese Biscuits, 50

◆◆ Cinnamon-Rhubarb Muffins, 63

◆◆ Flaky Buttermilk Biscuits, 49

◆◆ Fresh Herb Biscuits, 50

Desserts

◆◆◆ Bourbon-Chocolate Mousse, back cover

◆◆ Rhubarb Brown Sugar Crumble, 63

◆◆◆ Strawberry-Rhubarb Compote with Vanilla & Cardamom, 61

◆◆ Strawberry-Rhubarb Pie, 62

◆◆◆ Vanilla Ice Cream with Espresso-Caramel Sauce, 43

Photos: Scott Phillips

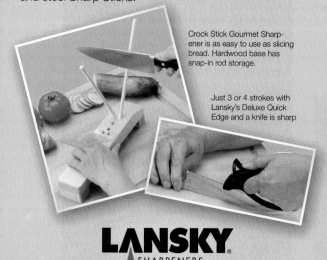
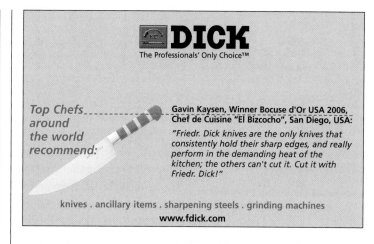

Spring to the rescue

The rich and comforting foods of winter are great for keeping us warm, but by April, we're ready for something a little lighter. Just in time, spring arrives, bringing with it beautiful, seasonal vegetables to inspire us. Here, then, are menu ideas for special occasions as well as everyday eating that get you into the swing of the season. (And don't miss the fabulous spring menu feature starting on p. 38.)

Note: Before you start cooking, be sure to check the yield of every recipe; you might have to double or halve it.

Graduation Dinner Party

Set out the carrots to nibble on before dinner.

Baby Carrots Pickled in Champagne & Sherry Vinegars, *p. 54*

Roasted Cornish Game Hens with Wildflower Honey & Orange, *p. 42*

Pan-Seared Artichokes with Sherry Vinegar & Thyme, *p. 19*

Rhubarb Brown Sugar Crumble, *p. 63*

To drink: A young, fruity Pinot Noir with bright red-berry and spice notes, like the 2005 Chateau St. Jean, Sonoma County, $20

Easter Dinner

The glazed ham needs to rest for 20 to 30 minutes after it's baked, giving you time to make the sauce and roast the asparagus and carrots.

Oven-Glazed Ham with Tangerine Marmalade Glaze & Sauce, *p. 47*

Roasted Asparagus with Lemon & Olive Oil, *p. 42*

Maple Pan-Roasted Baby Carrots, *p. 53*

Flaky Buttermilk Biscuits, *p. 49*

Strawberry-Rhubarb Pie, *p. 62*

To drink: A juicy Pinot Gris from Oregon, like the 2005 King Estate, $16

3 ideas for any night of the week

Easy entertaining

Wild Mushroom Toasts, *p. 40*

Sear-Roasted Halibut with Roasted Red Pepper Purée, *p. 84a*

Sautéed spinach with garlic

Bourbon-Chocolate Mousse, *back cover*

To drink: A crisp, dry Riesling like the 2005 Mönchhof Estate, Mosel, Germany, $15

A boldly flavored pasta supper

Penne with Asparagus, Olives & Parmigiano Breadcrumbs, *p. 84a*

Garden Lettuces with Garlic Chapons, *p. 41*

Vanilla Ice Cream with Espresso-Caramel Sauce, *p. 43*

To drink: A crisp Sauvignon Blanc with tart citrus and herb notes, like the 2005 Dry Creek Vineyards Fumé Blanc, Sonoma County, $13.50

Celebrate the season

Broiled Lamb Skewers with Baby Arugula & Lemon Vinaigrette, *p. 84a*

New Potatoes with Butter, Shallots & Chervil, *p. 42*

Strawberry-Rhubarb Compote with Vanilla & Cardamom, *p. 61, over vanilla ice cream*

To drink: A supple, spicy Shiraz blend, like the 2005 Penfolds Koonunga Hill Shiraz-Cabernet, southeastern Australia, $14

A Few Great Cooks

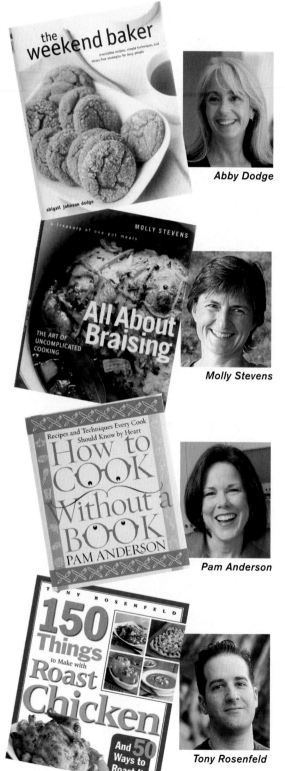

Abby Dodge

Molly Stevens

Pam Anderson

Tony Rosenfeld

It's a funny thing, but every time we run a story written by one of our contributing editors, that feature always winds up at the top of the reader survey poll we do for every issue. I guess it really isn't so odd when you think about who these people are: They're great cooks completely devoted to making food that home cooks will enjoy cooking and eating. Not only do they write for *Fine Cooking,* but they also spend their spare time mentoring other cooks, speaking about cooking, and writing cookbooks.

Most of you longtime readers are probably on a first-name basis with Abby (Dodge), Molly (Stevens), Pam (Anderson) and Tony (Rosenfeld), but if you're a newcomer to *Fine Cooking,* I can tell you a few great ways to get to know them. First, visit www.finecooking.com, where many of their recipes and techniques, from Abby's pies and Molly's braises, to Pam's sauces and Tony's sautés, are available to you. Second, check out the amazing cookbooks they've written. Abby's *The Weekend Baker,* Molly's *All About Braising,* and Pam's *How to Cook Without a Book* were classics the minute they hit the shelves. And now, we're excited to let you know that Tony has just written his first cookbook, *150 Things to Make With Roasted Chicken—and 50 Ways to Roast It.* It's being published by our very own Taunton Press this spring (and is available to order from our Web site now).

Tony has a killer knack for taking everyday food and making it really sing, so the very idea of 150 of his delicious recipes all in one place— from Roast Chicken with Caramelized Shallots and Fingerling Potatoes to Spicy New Mexican Green Chile Chicken Stew—is enough to make me grab a copy of this book for everyone I know. And now that I've read through all the valuable tips and techniques he has included (brining, grill-roasting, sear-roasting, making a pan sauce, carving a chicken, making herb butters, spice rubs, and vinaigrettes), I'm convinced that it's a downright steal at $14.95. With 50 ways to roast a chicken (and the recipes work for one or two chickens) and 150 ways to use the leftovers, you could cook from this book for a year and not get bored.

Congratulations to Tony and thanks to all of our contributing editors for keeping us endlessly supplied with tasty recipes and useful techniques.

—*Susie Middleton, editor*

P.S. If you've got any rhubarb left over after making the desserts on pp. 60–63, make my chutney, at right. It keeps for two weeks in the fridge.

Rhubarb & Dried-Cherry Chutney

Yields about 1 cup.

This is a lovely condiment for grilled pork loin or roasted chicken.

1 cup medium-diced fresh rhubarb
½ cup small-diced onion
¼ cup coarsely chopped dried cherries
¼ cup granulated sugar
¼ cup sherry vinegar
1 Tbs. honey
½ tsp. finely grated lemon zest
¼ tsp. kosher salt

Combine all the ingredients in a small saucepan. Bring to a boil over medium-high heat, cover, and simmer over medium to medium-low heat until the onions are mostly translucent and the juices are beginning to thicken, about 5 minutes. Uncover and simmer, stirring frequently with a heatproof spatula, until very thick, another 6 to 8 minutes. Let cool completely in the pan before storing in an airtight container in the refrigerator for up to 2 weeks.

Pound cake worth its weight in gold but lighter than air

Thank you, Nicole Rees. I have been after the ultimate pound cake for at least 25 years, and I finally found it in your wonderful recipe in *Fine Cooking* #84 (January 2007). I can't tell you how many pound cakes I've tried, only to throw them away. This one is simply heavenly, with a fine, light texture and the lovely vanilla and butter taste you want in a pound cake. I am so happy I decided to try it. It's a real winner.

—*Jeri Woodward, Seal Beach, California*

Prep, then put it away

Susie Middleton's "Mess in Place" editorial (*Fine Cooking* #84) rings true, especially when cooking for a crowd. I always do my "mise" (didn't know it had a name) when I bake, but I take it a step further by immediately returning the used item back to the cabinet. That way, there's no second guessing whether I've added it or not. It's especially helpful when the phone rings or your child needs your attention right away.

—*Eileen Taylor, via email*

Editors' note: "Mise" is short for "mise en place," which is the French term for having everything prepped and organized before starting to cook.

And with your chocolate tart, how about a pint of stout?

Congratulations on your terrific magazine. As an avid home cook, I find your balance of sensible instruction, luscious recipes, and menu ideas to be splendid. I do have one bone to pick, however. I notice wine suggestions at every turn, whether it be in an article or as a suggestion with a recipe or a menu. Wine is an excellent companion to food, but it seems that another flavorful and artistic choice has been overlooked by your talented staff—beer.

In the last 5 to 10 years, we've enjoyed a dramatic increase in variety, choice, and availability of quality beer.

American craft brewers and artisan brewers from around the world create interesting and versatile beers that can be the perfect finishing touch for flavorful meals.

For instance, I believe you haven't lived until you've had a smooth and rich stout alongside dessert—one as simple as homemade chocolate brownies or as decadent as tiramisù. The world of cheese pairing knows no better companion than beer. Beer is also a great ingredient for sauces, braises, and marinades. As a self-proclaimed beervangelist, I'd love to see you explore the rewarding world of beer in *Fine Cooking*.

—*Fred Bueltmann, president, Michigan Brewers Guild*

Editors' reply: Well, you must have been sending us subliminal messages, Fred, as we've had beer on the brain, too. We recently assigned two beer stories that will appear in issues later this year. Tim Gaiser, our wine writer, is working on a beer primer (with food pairings) for our August issue. And we'll also be featuring a brewery in our Artisan Foods department. Oh, yes, and we haven't forgotten to add a few beer pairing suggestions to recipes coming up this summer. ◆

Here's the place to share your thoughts on our recent articles or on your food and cooking philosophies. Send your comments to Letters, *Fine Cooking*, PO Box 5506, Newtown, CT 06470-5506, or by email to fc@taunton.com.

fine Cooking

EDITOR **Susie Middleton**

EXECUTIVE EDITOR   ART DIRECTOR
Sarah Jay   **Annie Giammattei**

SPECIAL ISSUES EDITOR
Joanne McAllister Smart

TEST KITCHEN MANAGER/RECIPE EDITOR
Jennifer Armentrout

SENIOR EDITOR **Kimberly Y. Masibay**

ASSOCIATE EDITORS
**Rebecca Freedman,
Laura Giannatempo, Lisa Waddle**

ASSOCIATE WEB EDITOR **Sarah Breckenridge**

SENIOR COPY/PRODUCTION EDITOR
Enid Johnson

ASSISTANT ART DIRECTOR **Pamela Winn**

TEST KITCHEN ASSOCIATE/FOOD STYLIST
Allison R. Ehri

EDITORIAL ASSISTANT **Kim Landi**

EDITOR AT LARGE **Maryellen Driscoll**

TEST KITCHEN INTERN **Safaya Tork**

CONTRIBUTING EDITORS
**Pam Anderson, Abigail Johnson Dodge,
Tim Gaiser, Tony Rosenfeld, Molly Stevens**

PUBLISHER **Maria Taylor**

SENIOR MARKETING MANAGER
Karen Lutjen

CIRCULATION DIRECTOR
Dennis O'Brien

SINGLE COPY SALES MANAGER
Mark Stiekman

ASSOCIATE ADVERTISING SALES MANAGER
Linda Petersell

CORPORATE ACCOUNTS MANAGER
Judy Caruso

NATIONAL ACCOUNTS MANAGERS
Patricia Coleman, Linda Delaney

ASSOCIATE ACCOUNTS MANAGER
Chris Dunham

ADVERTISING SALES ASSOCIATE **Stacy Purcell**

Fine Cooking: (ISSN: 1072-5121) is published seven times a year by The Taunton Press, Inc., Newtown, CT 06470-5506. Telephone 203-426-8171. Periodicals postage paid at Newtown, CT 06470 and at additional mailing offices. GST paid registration #123210981.

Subscription Rates: U.S. and Canada, $29.95 for one year, $49.95 for two years, $69.95 for three years (GST included, payable in U.S. funds). Outside the U.S./Canada: $36 for one year, $62 for two years, $88 for three years (payable in U.S. funds). Single copy, $6.95. Single copy outside the U.S., $7.95.

Postmaster: Send address changes to *Fine Cooking*, The Taunton Press, Inc., 63 South Main St., P.O. Box 5506, Newtown, CT 06470-5506.

Canada Post: Return undeliverable Canadian addresses to *Fine Cooking*, c/o Worldwide Mailers, Inc., 2835 Kew Drive, Windsor, ON N8T 3B7, or email to mnfa@taunton.com.

Printed in the USA.

HOW TO CONTACT US:

Fine Cooking

The Taunton Press, 63 S. Main St., P.O. Box 5506, Newtown, CT 06470-5506   203-426-8171

www.finecooking.com

Editorial:

To submit an article proposal, write to *Fine Cooking* at the address above or:

Call: **800-309-0744**
Fax: **203-426-3434**
Email: **fc@taunton.com**

Customer Service:

For subscription inquiries, you can:

▪ Visit our subscriber service section at:
   www.finecooking.com

▪ Email us: **fcservice@taunton.com**

▪ Call our customer support center:

   To report an address change, inquire about an order, or solve a problem, call:
   800-477-8727

   To subscribe, purchase back issues, books or videos, or give a gift, call:
   800-888-8286

Advertising:

To find out about advertising:

Call: **800-309-8940**
Email: **fcads@taunton.com**

Member Audit
Bureau of Circulation   The Audit Bureau

Retail:

If you'd like to carry *Fine Cooking* in your store, call the Taunton Trade Company at:
866-505-4674

Mailing List:

Occasionally we make our subscribers' names and addresses available to responsible companies whose products or services we feel may be of some interest to you. Most of our subscribers find this to be a helpful way to learn about useful resources and services. If you don't want us to share your name with other companies, please contact our Customer Service Department at:
800-477-8727

The Taunton Guarantee:

If at any time you're not completely satisfied with *Fine Cooking*, you can cancel your subscription and receive a full and immediate refund of the entire subscription price. No questions asked.

Copyright 2007 by The Taunton Press, Inc. No reproduction without permission of The Taunton Press, Inc.

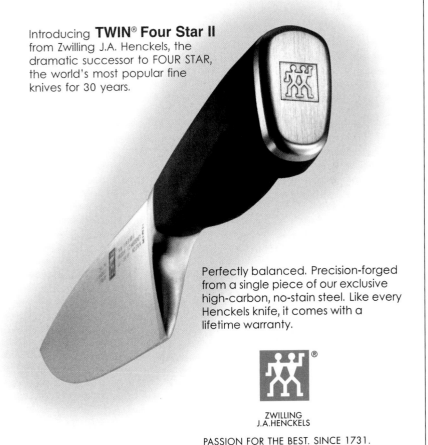

What's New at FineCooking.com

Visit our homepage often at FineCooking.com to see what's "on the front burner." This month, we have special Web collections on knives and knife skills, plus a guide for planning your Easter menu.

ON THE FRONT BURNER
Easter Menu Planner

Look no further for delicious Easter meals that celebrate spring. Our collection offers complete menus, including a make-ahead dinner starring roasted leg of lamb and a casual buffet to feed a crowd. We also have advice on buying a ham, carving a leg of lamb, and choosing wines. Or create your own menu from our seasonal recipes, such as:

Perfect Popovers

Herb-Crusted Rack of Lamb

Butter Lettuce & Artichoke Salad

Sweet & Savory Pierogis

Orange Layer Cake

…and much more

ON THE FRONT BURNER
All About Knives

Good, sharp knives can make your cooking more enjoyable and more efficient. Our special feature includes:

❖ The 3 must-have knives for your kitchen

❖ Our favorite specialty knives

❖ 11 essential knife skills, each paired with a recipe that lets you practice your technique

In addition, bonus videos demonstrating how to sharpen and hone your knives

Book Preview

Looking for ways to get fresh meals on the table every night? Food Network host Robin Miller has plenty of strategies up her sleeve, from prepping ingredients days in advance to making creative use of leftovers. Her newest book, *Quick Fix Meals,* is being published by The Taunton Press this month—get a preview at FineCooking.com.

Free email newsletter!

Subscribe at FineCooking.com to get great recipes, tips, techniques, and videos delivered directly to your inbox twice a month.

Faux _fried_ **U.S. Farm-Raised Catfish with** _homestyle_ _biscuits_.
ADJECTIVE TECHNIQUE ADJECTIVE NOUN

Always fresh, healthy, mild and flaky, U.S. Farm-Raised Catfish suits

any recipe. For some of my favorites, visit **catfishinstitute.com**

FOOD NETWORK CHEF _Cat Cora_

★ U.S. FARM-RAISED ★
Catfish™
YOU'RE GONNA LOVE IT.

Whether she's cooking for a wedding for 200 or entertaining a couple of friends at home, Tasha DeSerio ("Spring Menu," p. 38) likes to put together elegant but easy-to-prepare menus that feature local, seasonal vegetables. Formerly a cook at Chez Panisse restaurant and café, Tasha is the proprietor of Olive Green Catering in Berkeley, California. She also teaches cooking and writes about food.

Few people know meat the way Bruce Aidells ("Ham," p. 44) does. In addition to writing *Bruce Aidells's Complete Book of Pork* and *The Complete Meat Cookbook,* Bruce founded the Aidells Sausage Company and continues to help various pork producers develop fine hams and bacon for retail (see Where to Buy It, p. 78). Eager for a new challenge, Bruce will star in cooking segments this spring on his local ABC affiliate (KGO) in the San Francisco Bay Area.

Peter Reinhart ("Biscuits," p. 48) was the co-founder of Brother Juniper's Bakery in Santa Rosa, California, and is the author of seven books on bread and food, including *The Bread Baker's Apprentice,* which was named Cookbook of the Year in 2002 by both the James Beard Foundation and the International Association of Culinary Professionals. His new book, *Whole Grain Breads,* will be published in the fall. Peter is a baking instructor at Johnson & Wales University in Charlotte, North Carolina.

Dan Barber ("Carrots," p. 51) was introduced to farming as a child at Blue Hill Farm in the Berkshire Mountains of Massachusetts. Today, Dan is the chef and co-owner of two restaurants: Blue Hill, in New York City, and Blue Hill at Stone Barns, in

Pocantico Hills, New York. He also serves as the creative director of Stone Barns Center for Food & Agriculture, which supplies fresh ingredients to his restaurants.

Tony Rosenfeld ("Shrimp Sautés," p. 56) is a contributing editor to *Fine Cooking.* He's also a co-owner of b.good, a group of healthful fast-food restaurants in the Boston area for which he oversees the food. "We're opening our third store in three years, and it's pretty gratifying that we still do everything in-house, from cutting a couple of hundred pounds of potatoes each day for the baked fries to making all of the different homemade sauces."

Karen Barker ("Rhubarb," p. 60) is the pastry chef and co-owner—with husband Ben Barker—of the Magnolia Grill restaurant in Durham, North Carolina. She describes her baking as "down-home American with a modern twist." A native of Brooklyn, New York, Karen is a graduate of The Culinary Institute of America and is the author of two cookbooks, *Not Afraid of Flavor* and *Sweet Stuff: Karen Barker's American Desserts.* She won a James Beard Award for outstanding pastry chef in 2003.

Like many of us, Adam Ried ("Knife Sharpeners," p. 64) is a kitchen equipment junkie with loads of questions about the good, the bad, and the ugly of the cookware world. With 10 years of equipment-testing experience under his belt, Adam now works as a food and travel writer, as a recipe developer and tester, and as the cookware specialist on the PBS show *America's Test Kitchen.* ◆

Tasha DeSerio

Peter Reinhart

Dan Barber

The Taunton Press
Inspiration for hands-on living®

INDEPENDENT PUBLISHERS SINCE 1975

TAUNTON, INC.
Founders, **Paul and Jan Roman**

THE TAUNTON PRESS
President **Suzanne Roman**

*Executive Vice President &
Chief Financial Officer* **Timothy Rahr**

*Executive Vice President &
Publisher, Magazine Group* **Jon Miller**

Publisher, Book Group **James Childs**

Chief of Operations **Thomas Luxeder**

DIRECTORS
Creative & Editorial Director **Susan Edelman**
Human Resources Director **Carol Marotti**
Technology Services Director **Jay Hartley**
Controller **Wayne Reynolds**
Advertising Director **David Gray**
Fulfillment Director **Patricia Williamson**
Financial Analysis Director **Kathy Worth**
Circulation Director **Dennis O'Brien**

THE TAUNTON PRESS

Books: *Marketing:* Melissa A. Possick, Audrey Locorotondo. *Publicity:* Nicole Salvatore, Janel Noblin. *Editorial:* Helen Albert, Kathryn Benoit, Peter Chapman, Steve Culpepper, Pamela Hoenig, Carolyn Mandarano, Nicole Palmer, Jennifer Peters, Amy Reilly, Jennifer Russell, Erica Sanders-Foege, Kathleen Williams. *Art:* Chris Thompson, Alison Wilkes, Nancy Boudreau, Amy Griffin, Sandra Mahlstedt, Wendi Mijal, Lynne Phillips, Carol Singer. *Manufacturing:* Thomas Greco, Laura Burrone.

Business Office: Holly Smith, Gayle Hammond, Patricia Marini. *Legal:* Carolyn Kovaleski. *Magazine Print Production:* Philip Van Kirk, Nicole Anastas, Jennifer Kaczmarcyk.

Circulation: David Pond, Andrew Corson, Catherine Hansen.

Distribution: Paul Seipold, Walter Aponte, Frank Busino, David DeToto, Leanne Furlong, Deborah Greene, Frank Melbourne, Reinaldo Moreno, Raymond Passaro, Ulysses Robinson, Alice Saxton, Nelson Wade.

Finance/Accounting: *Finance:* Brett Manning. *Accounting:* Patrick Lamontagne, Lydia Krikorian, Judith O'Toole, Shannon Marrs, Elaine Yamin, Carol Diehm, Dorothy Blasko, Susan Burke, Lorraine Parsons, Larry Rice, James Tweedle, Priscilla Jennings.

Fulfillment: Diane Goulart. *Fulfillment Systems:* Jodi Klein, Kim Eads, Nancy Knorr, Thomas Kuzebski. *Customer Service:* Ellen Grassi, Kathleen Baker, Bonnie Beardsley, Deborah Ciccio, Katherine Clarke, Alfred Dreher, Monica Duhancik, Eileen McNulty, Patricia Parks, Deana Parker, Patricia Pineau, Betty Stepney. *Data Entry:* Melissa Dugan, Anne Champlin, Mary Ann Colbert, Caryne-Lynne Davis, Maureen Pekar, Debra Sennefelder, Andrea Shorrock, Marylou Thompson, Barbara Williams.

Human Resources: Linda Ballerini, Christine Lincoln, Dawn Ussery.

Information Technology Services: *Applications Development:* Heidi Waldkirch, Jun Lu, Frank Miller, Robert Nielsen, Linda Reddington, John Vaccino, Daniel

Photos, from top: Michael DeSerio, Ron Manville, Nicholas Basilion

It's Artichoke Time:
Eat your heart out

BY RUTH LIVELY

There's something deeply satisfying about eating a whole artichoke one leaf at a time, dipping each leaf in melted butter or a tangy vinaigrette. And when you're done with the leaves, the best part awaits you: the soft, fleshy bottom with its sweet, earthy flavor.

Leaf by leaf is how I ate artichokes growing up, but over the years I've become partial to cooking the hearts. To me, this is when artichokes really get interesting— even though it takes a little extra prep work (see photos opposite) to get at this treat.

An edible flower

The part of the artichoke we eat is the flower bud. If left on the plant, the bud would open and the central choke would blossom into a lovely violet-blue flower.

The peak season for artichokes runs from March through May, but they have a secondary season in the fall. If you're lucky, in spring you can also find baby artichokes. These are not younger artichokes but rather small buds that grow on side shoots off the central stem. They don't have a developed choke inside, so they're easier and quicker to prep.

Artichokes' mild, delicate flavor goes hand in hand with all kinds of fats: butter, olive oil, mayonnaise, cream, and cheeses, particularly well-aged ones. Citrus juices and vinegars help cut their sweetness a bit, while fresh herbs and spices, such as thyme, rosemary, chives, tarragon, and mint, along with coriander and fennel seeds, add a fresh, perfumy note.

Tips for buying and prepping

Buy artichokes that feel heavy for their size, with leaves closed up tightly. Avoid very browned and battered artichokes, although a little darkening on the leaves is all right. The discoloration is usually a result of a light frost, and some people argue that frost-kissed artichokes taste the best. While the cut end of the stem will probably be a little browned, pass over any that are blackened or dry—they're past their prime. Stored in the crisper drawer of the refrigerator, unwashed artichokes keep well for up to a week.

When you cut artichokes, exposure to the air, or oxidation, causes the cut sides to darken. To maintain their color, you can rub the trimmed areas with lemon or drop them in a bowl of water with a few squeezes of lemon juice. But if you're going to sauté or roast the artichokes, don't bother with the lemon. Instead, toss them with a little olive oil right after prepping them; this seems to seal the surface enough to prevent oxidation.

Boil or steam to eat whole

To prepare artichokes for cooking whole, cut off the top inch with a serrated knife. Trim the stem, leaving as much as 3 inches attached, if you like (stems are perfectly edible and delicious). With scissors, trim off the prickly tops of each remaining leaf.

At this point, you can either boil or steam them. I usually boil them in water with a little olive oil, white wine, and one or more flavorings, such as lemon juice, orange zest, peeled and sliced garlic cloves, peppercorns, coriander, or fennel seeds. Cook them until a leaf pulls out without lifting the whole head out of the water, 30 to 45 minutes.

When cool enough to handle, gently squeeze the artichokes to extract excess water, transfer them to individual plates, and serve with a dipping sauce.

DIPPING SAUCE IDEAS:

Melted butter, lemon juice, and minced fresh chervil or chives.

Mayonnaise thinned with lemon juice and spiked with grated garlic and cayenne or curry powder.

Vinaigrette with olive oil, sherry vinegar or red-wine vinegar, and some anchovy paste or black-olive paste.

Pan-Seared Artichokes with Sherry Vinegar & Thyme

Serves four to six.

These artichokes are a versatile side dish for grilled, roasted, or braised chicken, lamb, or beef—or even duck breasts or veal chops.

6 large artichokes
4 Tbs. extra-virgin olive oil
3 Tbs. sherry vinegar
3 medium cloves garlic, peeled and cut in half lengthwise
1 tsp. finely grated lemon zest (from 1 medium lemon)
½ tsp. kosher salt; more as needed
⅛ tsp. freshly ground black pepper; more as needed
1 tsp. chopped fresh thyme

Prepare the artichoke hearts following the photo-directions below.

Cut each half into two wedges and toss them with 1 Tbs. olive oil in a large bowl. Combine the vinegar with ¼ cup water in a small dish. Set aside.

Heat the remaining 3 Tbs. olive oil and garlic in a 10-inch straight-sided sauté pan over medium-high heat and cook, stirring, until the garlic just starts to turn golden, 2 to 3 minutes. Remove the garlic with a slotted spoon and discard. Add the artichokes to the pan (they may splatter at first) and arrange them with one cut side down. Cook until nicely browned, 3 to 5 minutes. Turn and cook the other cut side until nicely browned, about 3 minutes more. Turn the artichokes on their curved side. Scatter the lemon zest on the artichokes and season with the salt and pepper.

Reduce the heat to low, add the vinegar and water, cover, and simmer until the liquid has reduced to about 1 Tbs. and the artichokes are tender when pierced with a skewer, about 5 minutes. (If the artichokes are still a bit undercooked after the liquid has reduced, turn off the heat and let them sit, covered, for a few more minutes until they reach the desired doneness.)

Remove the pan from the heat, scatter the thyme on the artichokes and stir well. Season to taste with more salt and pepper. Serve immediately, or let rest, uncovered, and serve slightly warm.

How to prep artichoke hearts

1 *Snap off the dark-green outer leaves of the artichoke until only the pale, tender inner leaves remain.*

2 *Cut off all but 1 inch of the stem as well as the top third of the artichoke leaves.*

3 *Use a paring knife to peel away the tough outer layer of the stem and to remove the base of the leaves, leaving a smooth surface.*

4 *Cut the artichoke in half lengthwise; with a melon baller or small spoon, scoop out and discard the hairy choke and thorny inner leaves.*

Easy ways with artichokes

The tender innermost leaves of artichokes and their meaty bottoms are called artichoke hearts. They're wonderful sautéed, braised, or roasted. And if they're very fresh, they're tender enough to eat raw.

Depending on the size of the artichokes and the recipe, you can use trimmed hearts cut in half or further cut them into quarters, wedges, or thin slices. Here are some ideas for using them:

Sauté thinly sliced artichoke hearts in olive oil with garlic. Add a splash of white wine and cook until tender.

Make an artichoke risotto by stirring sautéed artichokes gently into the rice during the last few minutes of cooking.

Braise artichoke halves or quarters with onion, whole garlic, carrots, and thyme in vegetable broth and white wine.

Compose a refreshing salad with thin slices of raw artichoke hearts tossed with olive oil, lemon juice, salt, pepper, and shaved Parmigiano.

Roast halved or quartered artichoke hearts in olive oil with potato wedges, thick slices of lemon, and black olives.

Ruth Lively cooks, writes, and gardens in New Haven, Connecticut. ◆

Discovering the Wines of Greece

BY TIM GAISER

My biggest wine discovery of 2006 was, without a doubt, Greece. After making two trips there last year and tasting several hundred remarkable wines, I'm convinced that Greek wines are the next big thing. And I'm not alone. Much of the wine community is buzzing with excitement about Greece, comparing it to the Spain of 10 years ago. Like Spanish wines then, Greek wines don't yet have a big following outside their own country, so you can still find great values over here. The combination of talented young winemakers, perfect climate, and brilliant indigenous grape varieties all add up to some of the most delicious and unusual wines in the world, and now's the perfect time to discover them. To get you started, here's a short primer on the country's best growing regions, grapes, and wines.

Macedonia, Thessaly, Peloponnese, and Santorini are some of Greece's major wine-producing regions.

The grapes of Greece

During my travels, I found plenty of good values made from international varieties like Chardonnay and Cabernet Sauvignon, but I was most impressed with the wines made from indigenous Greek grapes. Here are six varieties to look for, along with recommended bottles that, in my opinion, rank among the best wines Greece has to offer. (For sources, see p. 78.)

Reds

Most Greek reds are light, fruity quaffers, perfect for everyday drinking, but these two outstanding indigenous grapes are capable of producing world-class wines.

Xinomavro
(ksee NOH mah vroh)

Xinomavro wines come in a range of styles, from light and fruity to intense, tannic, and age-worthy. Xinomavro combines the complex, supple fruit of Pinot Noir with the high natural acidity and tannin of Barbera.

What's it good with?

You can serve this wine with casual and formal dishes alike, anything from meatloaf, pasta with tomato sauce, and pizza to roast or grilled lamb, pork, or beef.

Recommended bottles:

2004 Alpha Estate Xinomavro, Amyndeon, $38

2004 Boutari, Xinomavro, Naoussa, $14

Agiorghitiko
(ah yor YEE tee koh)

One of the greatest of all Greek grapes and wines, Agiorghitiko is grown primarily in the Peloponnese. With its ripe, dusty fruit and earthy qualities, Agiorghitiko reminds me of a Cabernet-Sangiovese blend.

What's it good with?

This wine is a natural partner for braised, grilled, or roasted lamb or veal. Rosé wines from Agiorghitiko grapes are delicious with grilled tuna or swordfish.

Recommended bottles:

2005 Palivou Agiorgitiko Rosé, Nemea, $12

2003 Gaia Estate, Agiorgitiko, Nemea, $18

2004 Domaine Spiropoulos Agiorgitiko, "Red Stag," Peloponnese, $25

(continued on p. 22)

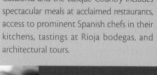
enjoying **wine**

(continued from p. 20)

Whites
Vibrantly fruity and tangy, Greek whites are perfect for spring and summer sipping.

Assyrtiko
(ah SEER tee koh)

The greatest surprise and delight of my travels, Assyrtiko combines the acidity and mineral elements of Riesling with the delectable fruit qualities of Chardonnay. Expect succulent apple-pear fruit with bright citrus notes and pronounced minerality in a bone-dry wine. The Domaine Sigalas wine listed below is possibly my very favorite Greek wine.

What's it good with?
Assyrtiko is a delicious partner for grilled fish, chicken, or pork topped with citrusy sauces, or for pasta with cream sauces.

Recommended bottles:
2005 Domaine Sigalas Assyrtiko, Santorini, $18

2005 Tsantali Ambelonas, Sauvignon Blanc-Assyrtiko, Agios Pavlos, $14

Moschofilero
(mos koh FEE le roh)

This versatile and aromatic grape hails from the Peloponnese region (see map, p. 20). It has distinctive gray skin and floral aromas, and it's used to make delicious dry still and sparkling wines as well as sweet dessert wines. With its exotic notes of flowers, spicy fruit, and crisp citrus, Moschofilero reminds me of a cross between a tangy Pinot Gris and a spicy Gewurztraminer.

What's it good with?
Enjoy Moschofilero as an aperitif with spring rolls or other Asian-inspired starters.

Recommended bottle:
2005 Tselepos Moschofilero, Mantinia, $16

Also look for:

Roditis
(roh DEE tees)

Like Pinot Grigio, Roditis has tangy lemon-lime notes and delicate floral aromas. Try the 2005 Ktima Kir Yianni "Petra," Naoussa, $14; or the 2005 Domaine Skouras white, (Roditis-Moschofilero blend), $13.

Malagousia
(mah lah gou ZYA)

Malagousia is an aromatic grape, making for full-bodied wines with appealing exotic fruit, citrus, and jasmine flavors, reminiscent of Viognier. Try the 2005 Domaine Gerovassiliou Malagousia, Epanomi, $17.

Contributing editor Tim Gaiser is a master sommelier and wine educator. ◆

THE WORLD IS YOUR KITCHEN.

When you own a Viking kitchen, you need a really good reason to leave. Introducing The Viking Life. Culinary events, private classes with renowned chefs, intimate wine tastings, exotic travel experiences, culinary cruises and more. Visit thevikinglife.com

THE **VIKING** LIFE

FOOD   TRAVEL   WINE

what's new

Get cracking

For convenience, nothing beats shelled walnuts, almonds, hazelnuts, and other nuts. But for snacking, it's fun to crack your own. Traditional pliers-style nutcrackers can be a hassle—you end up with a mess of scattered shells and a sore hand. The Chef's Planet nutcracker, on the other hand, makes the task not only easy but enjoyable. When I tried it with a bag of mixed nuts, it excelled at opening all types with minimal squeezing. The ergonomic handle and cracker fit in my palm and protected my fingers from being pinched while containing both the shells and the meat. The dishwasher-safe plastic nutcracker is $15 at ChefsPlanet.com.

Nutcracker	24
Mix-and-measure bowls	24
Clip-on spoon rest	24
New loaf pan design	26
Yogurt maker	26
Kitchen scrubber	28
Double-duty sinks	28

BY LISA WADDLE

Mix-and-measure bowls

With these bowls from Dutch by Design, you can measure your liquids and then whisk them together in the same bowl. Lines on the inside of the richly colored melamine bowls indicate milliliters and ounces, and a wide spout makes pouring a breeze. The bowls are available at DutchByDesign.com ($17.95 for the 1 liter and $27.50 for the 2.5 liter).

A clip-on spoon rest

Where do you put your wooden spoon after stirring a pot of marinara, risotto, chili, or any type of sauce? If it goes on the counter, a plate, or even a spoon rest, you just have one more thing to clean. Along comes the Trudeau Pot Clip, which attaches to the side of any pot and holds your spoon horizontally above it. The spoon (or any other utensil) stays handy, the counter is less cluttered, and drips fall back into the pot, saving one step of cleanup. These spring-loaded clips come in four bright colors and are made of stainless steel and heat-resistant silicone. They sell for $6.99 at ChefTools.com.

Photos except where noted: Scott Phillips

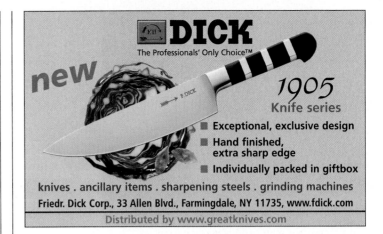

Quicker quick bread

Despite their name, quick breads can seem anything but quick while they're baking—they can sometimes take up to an hour. This longer, slimmer loaf pan from King Arthur Flour helps speed along the cooking. While traditional loaf pans measure 8½ by 4½ inches, this one is 12 by 4 inches. When I tested the two sizes side by side with pumpkin bread, the King Arthur pan shaved 25 percent (or 16 minutes) off the cooking time, and the resulting loaf yielded appealingly trim slices. The white ceramic tea loaf pan sells for $16.95 at KingArthurFlour.com.

test drive

Is this yogurt maker right for you?

I love yogurt, and making my own in reusable glass jars always seemed like a good idea, but I worried that it would be a huge project. Turns out, it's not. With a yogurt maker like the one at right from Euro Cuisine, the process is extremely easy. Just mix room-temperature milk with 6 ounces of plain yogurt or a packaged yogurt starter, pour the mixture into the jars, pop them into the machine, and turn it on. Come back 6 to 12 hours later and—voilà!—you've got yogurt.

How it performs

From the get-go, I was pleased with the results I achieved. My first batch was on the runny side, but the flavor was so much better than store-bought—clean, rich, and fresh—that I was encouraged to try again. And through trial and error, I've tweaked my yogurt's flavor and consistency—both of which depend mainly on the type of milk you begin with and the starter you use—to suit my taste.

To create the thick, creamy, mildly tangy results I desire, I use organic whole milk, a splash of heavy cream, and very thick, full-fat Fage Total Greek yogurt

as my starter and let the yogurt ferment for about 10 hours. For extra thickness, it helps to boil the milk and let it cool to room temperature before adding the starter; it also helps to stir in a little dry milk powder, because the extra protein helps the yogurt thicken. Each batch is good for about a week.

Features

This yogurt maker has a heater base, a cover, seven reusable glass jars with lids, and, of course, an instruction manual with a few recipes. As far as yogurt makers go, it's about as simple as they come, but I think a couple of extra features would make it truly user-friendly: a built-in timer, for starters, and an automatic on/off function.

I guess Euro Cuisine thought likewise, because in the time since I acquired this machine (model Y80), it has released an upgrade with a built-in timer. I suggest you look for that one. I've been able to find it only at Williams-Sonoma.com, where it sells for $39.95. While you're there, you can also buy Euro Cuisine's yogurt starter, $19.50 for 10 packets.

Pros: Easy to use. Generous three-year warranty. Yummy, pure, natural yogurt. Reusable glass jars.

Cons: Unless you buy the upgraded model, you have to keep track of the time yourself and remember when to turn off the machine. Jars need to be thoroughly rinsed before being placed in the dishwasher, or they won't come out clean.

The bottom line: If you eat a lot of yogurt (this machine makes seven 6-ounce jars) and you like the idea of creating your own, you can't go wrong. If you're a big fan of the texture of supermarket yogurts, which tend to be enhanced with pectin or gelatin, be aware that homemade yogurt won't be quite as firm.

—*Kimberly Y. Masibay, senior editor*

60% Cacao. 100% Impressive.

BAKE WITH OUR DEEP, INTENSE CHOCOLATE FOR PURE PLEASURE IN EVERY BITE.

GHIRARDELLI
CHOCOLATE

GHIRARDELLI® INDIVIDUAL CHOCOLATE LAVA CAKES

Yield - 6 servings

Center: 1/2 bar (2 oz) 60% Cacao Bittersweet Chocolate Baking Bar
1/4 cup heavy cream

Cake: Nonstick cooking spray
1 bar (4 oz) 60% Cacao Bittersweet Chocolate Baking Bar
8 Tbsp. (1 stick) unsalted butter
2 whole eggs
2 egg yolks
1/3 cup sugar
1/2 tsp. vanilla extract
1/4 cup cake flour

Raspberries and whipped cream for garnish

To make centers, melt chocolate and cream in double boiler. Whisk gently to blend. Refrigerate about 2 hours or until firm. Form into 6 balls; refrigerate until needed.

To make cake, heat oven to 400°F. Spray six 4-ounce ramekins or custard cups with cooking spray. Melt chocolate and butter in double boiler; whisk gently to blend. With an electric mixer, whisk eggs, yolks, sugar, and vanilla on high speed about 5 minutes or until thick and light. Fold melted chocolate mixture and flour into egg mixture just until combined. Spoon cake batter into ramekins. Place a chocolate ball in the middle of each ramekin.

Bake about 15 minutes or until cake is firm to the touch. Let it sit out of the oven for about 5 minutes. Run a small, sharp knife around inside of each ramekin, place a plate on top, invert and remove ramekin. Garnish with raspberries and a dollop of whipped cream.

MOMENTS OF TIMELESS PLEASURE.™

Visit your local grocery store for a complete range of delectable Ghirardelli baking chips, bars and cocoa. www.ghirardelli.com

does it work?

Better than steel wool

You'd never guess what this object is for by just looking at it. It resembles a pile of gift ribbon, but it's actually meant for cleaning. Made from thin strips of cloth treated with an abrasive (it feels like very fine-grit sandpaper), the Sandclean does an amazing job of scrubbing pots, plates, and stovetops—tea and coffee stains disappeared from my mugs with just a few swipes. Unlike steel wool, it doesn't rust or shred. It can be easy to forget the power behind the cloth, though—it scratched a plastic measuring cup and is not recommended for stainless-steel pans, crystal, bone china, or any delicate, painted surface. The Sandclean is available at Korin.com; it comes in two strengths, medium grit for $7.50 and rough grit for $8.50.

Everything *in* the kitchen sink

The kitchen sink just became a whole lot more interesting. Two manufacturers have recently introduced double-duty sinks—one of them can cook and the other washes dishes.

Boil and drain without lifting a pot

The Kohler PRO CookCenter has an integrated 8-quart cooking pot and heating element, so you can blanch green beans, simmer a soup, or boil pasta right in the sink—no more lugging heavy pots of water from sink to stove and back again. To boil pasta, just swivel the faucet over the pot, fill it with water, and turn on the heat. Instead of pouring off the water, you push a button and it drains. When you don't need the heating element, the cooking side of the sink converts to a small, regular sink. The CookCenter comes with a steamer insert and double boiler. Prices start at $3,360. For more information visit US.Kohler.com.

Dishes come clean in this sink

If you've ever fantasized about leaving dirty dishes in the sink and having them clean themselves, Kitchen-Aid's Briva In-Sink Dishwasher is your dream come true. One side of this stainless steel, double-bowl sink is a regular 8½-inch-deep sink. The other side is where the magic happens. It's a top-loading 14-inch-deep dishwasher that can hold up to five place settings. If you ever want to free up both sides of the sink, simply remove the racks, lid, and spray arm from the dishwasher, and it becomes an ordinary (though rather deep) sink. The In-Sink Dishwasher starts at $1,800; for more information go to KitchenAid.com. ◆

The Perfect Cure

Delicious Italian-style cured meats made in the USA

BY LAURA GIANNATEMPO

The centuries-old Italian art of salt-curing and air-drying meats and sausages to make *salumi* (Italian-style cold cuts) is taking the United States by storm. Chefs from coast to coast are adding house-cured salumi plates to their menus, and a growing number of artisans are making high-quality salumi—including prosciutto, mortadella, and a variety of salami—right here in the U.S. We're featuring a few great examples of these domestic salumi here. We also spoke to a young couple in San Francisco who's selling their terrific salumi at local farmers' markets (see Artisan Foods, p. 32). ◆

A soppressata like no other

Fra'Mani's soppressata, modeled after northern Italy's *soppressa vicentina,* which is larger and more delicate in flavor than most soppressatas, won us over with its moist texture, full pork flavor, and well-balanced spiciness with hints of clove. Slice it as thinly as possible for your salumi platter. Fra'Mani also offers four other kinds of dry salami—all delicious—and a selection of fresh sausages. *Fra'Mani soppressata, $210 for 9 pounds (including shipping) at FraMani.com. Fra'Mani salumi are also available sliced to order at some specialty stores.*

Smoked prosciutto, sliced & ready to eat

La Quercia, in Iowa, makes our favorite domestic prosciutto, so we were delighted to find that it also makes fantastic speck, which is smoked prosciutto. It has a mild smoky flavor that complements the prosciutto's natural sweetness. We're also partial to its tender, silky texture and nice chew. *Speck Americano, $69 for six 3-ounce packages, and Prosciutto Americano, $65 for six 3-ounce packages at LaQuercia.us. Whole Foods Markets and some specialty stores carry both.*

Sorting it all out

Salumi, Salame, Salami? No, they're not typos. There really is a difference.

Salumi is the Italian word for a variety of salt-cured, air-dried meats, usually made with pork. **Salami** are cured sausages; they're just one type of salumi. **Salame** is simply the singular of salami.

Salame with a twist

This mole salame made by Armandino Batali (Mario Batali's father) in his salumi shop in Seattle intrigued us with its unusual flavors. Spiced with typical Mexican mole ingredients, including chocolate, cinnamon, ancho, and chipotle peppers, it becomes more nuanced with each bite, finishing with a nice spicy kick. Along with regular pancetta and salami, the store offers several other untraditional salumi, including a lamb prosciutto. *Mole salame, $10.80 a pound at SalumiCuredMeats.com.*

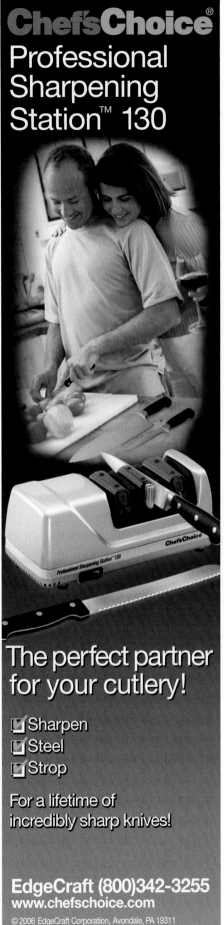

Handcrafting Salumi in San Francisco

BY LAURA GIANNATEMPO

Toponia Miller and Taylor Boetticher didn't spend their honeymoon in Paris or the Caribbean. Instead, these two young Bay Area chefs planned a six-month trip to Europe with one thing in mind: meat. Armed with a passion for French charcuterie and Italian salumi (see Great Finds, p. 30), they made it a point to visit towns and regions in France, Spain, and Italy known for their cured meats.

While in Tuscany, they met one of Italy's foremost salumi makers, Dario Cecchini, and ended up spending three months at his side learning how to turn humble cuts of pork, like legs and shoulders, into rich, flavorful salumi. That's when it became clear they were not going to open a restaurant or start a catering business back in San Francisco. Instead, they would cure their own meats.

Together with their friend and fellow chef Chuck Traugott, they started Fatted Calf, an artisanal charcuterie that handcrafts a variety of salumi—including a subtly spiced fennel salame, a mild and rustic Genoa salame, and a tender, silky bresaola (salt-cured beef)—as well as fresh sausages and French-style pâtés, confits, and terrines.

Toponia, Taylor, and Chuck make all their salumi and meats by hand and in small batches out of a rented kitchen. They use only sustainably raised, antibiotic-free meats and high-quality sea salts and seasonings, including locally grown organic garlic and herbs as well as other organic ingredients when they're available. Their pork comes from heritage breeds, mainly Berkshires and Red Waddles, but they don't always use the same breed for one kind of salame. "One batch is never exactly the same as the next; there are always subtle differences," says Toponia. Their salumi are hearty and delicious, with delicate hints of spices and seasonings that enhance the pork flavor rather than overwhelm it.

They sell their products exclusively at the Berkeley Farmers' Market and at San Francisco's Ferry Plaza Farmers' Market, but they have plans to open their own shop this fall—with an annexed kitchen and curing room—in the new Oxbow Public Market in Napa, California. *For more information, visit FattedCalf.com.* ◆

Fatted Calf's artisanal salumi include, clockwise from the top: Genoa salame, fennel salame, and pepper salame. Bottom: slices of bresaola.

To make salami, the first step is to grind the meat (usually pork). Each type of Fatted Calf salame is ground differently (some are coarser than others, and some have hand-cut fat in them as well). The ground meat is then seasoned with sea salt, spices, herbs, and sometimes wine and forced into natural hog or beef casings. Antonio Jeronimo, one of Fatted Calf's four workers, is shown cranking the handle of a "stuffer" to force the meat into a casing.

Once in their casings, the salami hang for 72 hours at room temperature to dry the meat slightly and to get the fermentation process started. This encourages the growth of the good bacteria that give salame its distinctive tangy flavor. The casings also start to develop a thin layer of mold, which helps prevent the meat from oxidizing and the fat from becoming rancid. Finally, the salami are transferred to a cold storage area. They are ready to eat after 60 to 100 days, depending on the type.

for 70 years we've been making the world's finest espresso and cappuccino.

now it's your turn.

the illy a casa℠ espresso membership program. everything you need to make the italian espresso preferred by the finest chefs, baristas and restaurateurs around the world. For coffee lovers with uncompromising taste, we offer the secret to making authentic espresso and cappuccino at home: join the illy a casa espresso membership program.

You'll receive our exclusive introductory kit featuring the Francis Francis! X5 espresso machine in a choice of nine colors, an illy artist cup collection and more.* An inspired union of Italian design and advanced technology, the X5 lets you make the highest quality espresso with illy E.S.E. pods, whole bean or ground coffee. As a member, all you have to do is purchase 4 cans of illy every month for 12 months. You'll enjoy convenient home delivery, plus the flexibility to customize your coffee order for your taste and needs.

join now and receive your introductory kit:

the francis francis! X5 espresso machine

4 rufus willis artist cups

it's yours for 3 monthly payments of $65** (a kit value of $730)

30-day risk-free trial

to enroll, call **1 877 4MY ILLY** (1-877-469-4559), or go to **illyusa.com/finecook**

use source code **PFC307** when ordering.

illy

*Offer subject to availability. Introductory kit includes an espresso machine, espresso cups, sugar sticks and machine cleaner. **Your only obligation is to make 3 monthly payments of $65 within the first 3 months + shipping and handling for the introductory kit, plus purchase a minimum of 4 cans of illy per month for 12 months (or the equivalent amount of coffee within 12 months). Coffee prices vary from $11.00 - $14.50 (8.8 ozs. per can; 18 pods per package) and are subject to change. If for any reason you are not satisfied, you may return the introductory kit within the first 30 days of purchase for a refund. **Return shipping charges are not refundable.** illy reserves the right to substitute cups of equal or greater value. Offer valid through 11/30/07. A complete description of terms and conditions are contained on our website at www.illyusa.com.

Binder clip holds thermometer in place

I love my probe-style digital thermometer but found it would fall into or out of the pot when I was making candy. Now I attach a medium-size metal binder clip onto the side of the pot and slide the probe through the handles. It keeps the probe in the pot but lets it move slightly to allow for stirring.

—*Laura Conger, Woodside, California*

A prize for the best tip

We want your best tips—we'll pay for the ones we publish—and we'll give a prize to the cleverest tip in each issue. Write to Tips, *Fine Cooking*, PO Box 5506, Newtown, CT 06470-5506 or email fctips@taunton.com.

The prize for this issue's winner: A Swissmar Wenger Grand Maître 7-piece knife block set; value, $200.

Paper plate to funnel spices

When I need to measure ground black pepper or other spices, it can be messy trying to grind directly into the teaspoon. Instead, I grind the spice onto a paper plate, then fold the plate in half, creating a funnel that neatly tips the spice into the measuring spoon.

—*Maggie DeFazio, Holbrook, New York*

Flavor sugar with citrus zest

Instead of garnishing desserts with confectioners' sugar, I sometimes like to use an orange-lemon sugar. I combine the zest of 2 oranges and 1 lemon with about 1 cup of granulated sugar in a food processor and process until it's fine but not powdery. The zest gives the sugar a wonderful fragrance and a bit of color, too. I love the sugar over lemon bars and other desserts, but it's also great for sweetening a cup of tea or sprinkling over buttered toast.

—*Kate Johnston, Sacramento, California*

TOO GOOD TO FORGET
Two avocado tips from *Fine Cooking* #9

Keeping halved avocados green

To keep cut avocados from turning brown when you want to store them, refrigerate them flesh side down in a bowl of water into which you have squeezed a little bit of lemon juice. The avocados will keep beautifully for a few days this way. The same method can also be used when preparing slices of avocado ahead of time for salads or garnishes.

—*Janet C. deCarteret, Bellevue, Washington*

Mashing avocado

For a quick and easy way to make a sublime guacamole, mash the avocado by putting the flesh through a potato ricer. The ricer gives the avocado a uniform consistency that is unequaled by any other mashing method. Be sure to mix in a few drops of lemon juice to prevent the avocado from browning.

—*Antoinne Von Rimes, Santa Barbara, California*

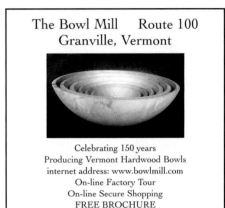

Empty paper towel tubes store silicone mats

To keep my silicone baking mats neat and easy to find, I store them rolled up in empty cardboard paper towel tubes. On the outside of the tube I write what size mat it holds.

—*Victoria DeLaney,
San Diego, California*

Containing nuts while chopping

When chopping hard ingredients like roasted nuts, I put a cutting board inside my 11x13-inch baking pan, and then use my chef's knife to chop away. Pieces may bounce and roll off the board, but they land within the confines of the pan instead of on the counter or the floor. This method works even better if your pan has tall sides—mine is 3 inches high.

—*Charles McEniry,
Stoughton, Wisconsin*

Saving leftover buttermilk

I can't always use an entire carton of buttermilk before it goes bad, so I portion it into zip-top plastic bags which I then flatten, stack, and freeze for up to two months. When I need to use it, I immerse the bag in warm water or defrost it on the counter. The thawed buttermilk won't be as creamy as it once was, so it's not ideal for sauces, but it works fine in baked goods like scones or cakes.

—*Shirley Polk, Oliver, British Columbia*

Whisk rather than stir

When baking, I find it easier to whisk together the dry ingredients in a bowl rather than stirring with a spoon. The whisk gets rid of any clumps and mixes thoroughly.

—*Kerry Sherck, Adamant, Vermont*

Baking liner keeps cupcakes from sliding

Having broken my cupcake carrier, I was in a quandary about how to transport two dozen cupcakes from my home to my grandsons'. All I had handy was my sheet-cake carrier, so I put a silicone baking mat on the bottom and filled it with cupcakes. It held them securely and safely, with no sliding around, so not a bit of frosting was smudged when I reached my destination.

—*Donna Bridger,
Olympia Fields, Illinois*

Perfect lattice strips for pies

To cut even strips of dough for a lattice-top pie, I use my rasp-style grater (without a handle) as a guide. The long sides have curved, raw edges that are perfect for cutting through the dough. I lay the grater on the rolled out dough and press down to cut a strip. Then I move the grater so that the bottom edge is in the center of the strip I just cut and press down again, creating a strip that's half as wide as the grater. I continue this pattern over the entire pie round.

—*Jean Brayman,
Fremont, Michigan*

TWO WAYS TO FREEZE FRESH HERBS:

Make herb infusions in broth

I grow a variety of fresh herbs and can make only so much herb vinegar or flavored oil. To preserve the bounty, I make an herb-infused broth I can use all year round. I put herbs and chicken broth in equal amounts in a blender, pulse until smooth, then pour into ice cube trays and freeze. I pop the cubes out and store them in plastic bags in the freezer. One cube is about 2 tablespoons, and it adds great flavor to stews, sauces, and sautés.

—*Angela Buchanan,
Longmont, Colorado*

Freeze herbs whole

I freeze extra herbs from my garden by putting them on cookie sheets in the freezer. Once they're frozen, I transfer them to a plastic bag. They retain most of their vibrant flavor, and hardier herbs like rosemary and thyme can practically be interchanged for fresh. Leafy herbs like basil and parsley suffer in the looks department, though, turning dark and mushy, so they're best used only for cooking

—*Mary Rowsell, Russell, Ontario* ◆

BY TASHA DESERIO

Some people plan dinner parties in their head or by paging through cookbooks or magazines for ideas. My approach is to let the market be my muse. And after months of hearty winter produce, the arrival of delicate spring vegetables at my local farmstand offers plenty of inspiration. It's easy to stroll through the market, eyeing a bunch of asparagus here and a basket of mushrooms there, and before I know it, I've got a plan for a simple but lovely dinner for six. That's what this menu is all about—highlighting what's fresh at the market, preparing it without too much fuss, and enjoying it with a few friends.

Even if it's still a bit cool where you live, warmer weather is just around the corner, and you'll soon see its effects at farmers' markets or in the produce section of your supermarket. Here's how I've created a menu around some of the fresher and perhaps even locally grown ingredients you'll come across.

Wild mushrooms are the happy result of plentiful spring rains. I like to sauté them with shallots and fresh thyme and add a little crème fraîche. Then I spoon them on toasts as "a little something" for guests as they arrive.

Garden lettuces are also coming into season. I'm lucky because my husband grows beautiful lettuces in our garden, but you'll see fine mesclun mixes in most markets. I like to serve these tender greens with garlic chapons, which are toasted crusts of bread that are rubbed with garlic.

Fresh asparagus and new potatoes round out a main course of roasted Cornish game hens. I cook the asparagus as simply as possible, roasting them with olive oil and tossing with lemon juice. And I treat the potatoes with a very light hand as well. I boil small ones (Yukon Golds or Yellow Finns work well) and then toss them with butter, shallots, and chopped fresh chervil, one of my favorite seasonal herbs.

I admit that my choice of dessert has no obvious link to the season. But who's going to argue with a dish of vanilla ice cream drizzled with an espresso-flavored caramel sauce? Some things are inspirational at any time of year.

A Taste of Spring

Welcome the season with a menu inspired by the market's freshest ingredients

Menu for six

Wild Mushroom Toasts

❖

**Garden Lettuces
with Garlic Chapons**

❖

**Roasted Cornish Game
Hens with Wildflower Honey
& Orange**

**New Potatoes with Butter,
Shallots & Chervil**

**Roasted Asparagus
with Lemon & Olive Oil**

❖

**Vanilla Ice Cream with
Espresso-Caramel Sauce**

Wild Mushroom Toasts
Serves six.

These toasts are best slightly warm, so hold off on toasting the bread until just before serving. You can use cremini mushrooms if you can't find the exotic varieties listed below.

1 lb. wild mushrooms, such as chanterelles, maitakes, hedgehogs, or morels
2 Tbs. unsalted butter
2 Tbs. extra-virgin olive oil; more as needed
Kosher salt
2 medium shallots, finely chopped (about ¼ cup)
2 tsp. chopped fresh thyme
½ cup crème fraîche (about 4 oz.)
1 Tbs. chopped fresh flat-leaf parsley
Freshly ground black pepper
18 slices baguette (cut ¼ to ½ inch thick)
¼ cup freshly grated Parmigiano-Reggiano

Gently clean the mushrooms with a damp cloth or a paring knife to remove any dirt or dark spots (see From Our Test Kitchen, p. 72, for tips on cleaning morels). Cut off any tough stems.

If the mushrooms appear muddy, quickly dip them into a large basin of water and drain. Leave small, bite-size mushrooms whole; quarter or halve larger mushrooms.

Melt 1 Tbs. of the butter together with 1 Tbs. of the oil in a 10-inch straight-sided sauté pan over medium-high heat. Add the mushrooms and a generous pinch of salt, and cook, stirring frequently, until any liquid has evaporated and the mushrooms are nicely browned, 5 to 8 minutes. (If the mushrooms are dry and the pan begins to scorch, add a drizzle of olive oil.) Remove the pan from the heat and transfer the mushrooms to a cutting board. Let them cool slightly and chop them coarsely.

Return the pan to the stovetop over medium heat and add the remaining 1 Tbs. butter and 1 Tbs. oil. When the butter has melted, add the shallots, thyme, and a pinch of salt. Cook, stirring, until the shallots are tender and lightly golden, about 3 minutes. Return the mushrooms to the pan, stir in the crème fraîche (if you're making this ahead, see the note at right), and cook, stirring, to coat the mushrooms with the crème fraîche. Stir in the parsley and season with several grinds of pepper. Season with more salt and pepper to taste. Remove from the heat and hold in a warm spot.

Shortly before serving, position an oven rack about 6 inches from the broiler element and heat the broiler to high. Arrange the bread slices on a baking sheet and brush them with olive oil. Broil until the bread is golden, 1 to 2 minutes. Flip and toast the other side, about 1 minute. Spread the warm mushroom mixture on the toasts, sprinkle some of the Parmigiano-Reggiano on top, and serve.

Make-ahead tip: The mushroom topping can be made several hours ahead and refrigerated, but hold back about half of the crème fraîche. When you're ready to serve, reheat the mushrooms over low heat and add the rest of the crème fraîche (don't overheat or the cream will break).

Garden Lettuces with Garlic Chapons

Serves six.

Chapons are large, rustic croutons that are made from the crust of bread rather than the crumb and then rubbed with garlic. They add a nice hint of garlic to a simple tossed green salad.

¾ lb. crusty, country-style bread
    (I like an Italian bâtard or levain)
6 Tbs. extra-virgin olive oil; more
    for brushing on the bread
Kosher salt
1 clove garlic, peeled and halved
2 medium shallots, minced
    (about ¼ cup)
3 Tbs. sherry vinegar or red-wine
    vinegar
6 large handfuls mixed baby lettuce
    (about ½ lb.), washed and spun dry
Freshly ground black pepper

Position a rack in the center of the oven and heat the oven to 400°F.

Using a serrated knife, carve the crust off the bread into rustic, curved slabs that are about ¼ inch thick. Save the rest of the bread for another use (such as making breadcrumbs). Brush the crusts on both sides with olive oil and season lightly with salt. Put the crusts on a baking sheet and bake until crisp and golden brown, 6 to 8 minutes. When cool enough to handle, rub the crusts lightly with the cut sides of the garlic clove. Snap the crusts into bite-size pieces. Discard the garlic.

In a small bowl, combine the shallots and vinegar with a pinch of salt and let sit for at least 10 minutes and up to 2 hours.

When ready to serve, put the chapons and lettuce in a large mixing bowl and season with a generous pinch of salt and a few grinds of pepper. Drizzle the lettuce with the 6 Tbs. olive oil. Scoop the shallots out of the vinegar and sprinkle them on the lettuce. Gently toss the salad, making sure that all of the lettuce is evenly dressed. Taste and adjust the seasoning with more olive oil, the remaining vinegar in the bowl (or more if necessary), salt, and pepper. Serve immediately on a chilled platter or individual plates, with the chapons tucked in among the lettuces.

Timeline for prepping

Up to a week ahead

Make the caramel sauce.

The night before

Marinate the hens.

Wash the lettuce and refrigerate, covered with a damp towel.

Clean the mushrooms and refrigerate, covered with a damp towel.

In the afternoon

Make the mushroom topping.

Make the chapons.

Cut the bread for the toasts.

Trim the asparagus.

Peel the potatoes and cover with water in a pot.

About 30 minutes before guests arrive

Mince the shallots and combine with the vinegar for the salad.

Mince the shallots and combine with the lemon for the potatoes.

Set the butter out to soften for the potatoes.

Brush the baguette slices with oil.

Put the hens on a baking sheet and leave at room temperature.

Soon after guests arrive

Put the hens in the oven.

Finish the Wild Mushroom Toasts.

Before serving each course

Toss the salad.

Make the pan jus for the hens.

Boil the potatoes.

Roast the asparagus.

New Potatoes with Butter, Shallots & Chervil

Serves six.

2¼ lb. small (2-inch) new potatoes, such as Yukon Gold or Yellow Finn, peeled and halved lengthwise (about 14 potatoes)
Kosher salt
1 large shallot, minced (about ¼ cup)
2 tsp. fresh lemon juice
6 Tbs. unsalted butter, cut into 8 pieces, softened to room temperature
2 Tbs. chopped fresh chervil or flat-leaf parsley
Freshly ground black pepper

Put the potatoes in a medium pot, add water to cover by 1 inch, and season generously with about 2 Tbs. salt (the water should taste almost as salty as sea water). Bring to a boil, reduce the heat to a simmer, and gently cook the potatoes until tender when pierced with a fork, 10 to 12 minutes. (You want them to maintain their shape, so be careful not to overcook them.)

Meanwhile, combine the shallot, lemon juice, and a pinch of salt in a small bowl, and let sit for at least 10 minutes and up to 2 hours.

Drain the potatoes and return them to the warm pot. Immediately add the shallot mixture, butter, and chervil or parsley and gently stir to combine. Season with salt and pepper to taste and serve.

Roasted Asparagus with Lemon & Olive Oil

Serves six.

These roast quickly, so just pop them in the oven when the hens come out.

2 lb. asparagus, preferably thin spears (about 2 bunches)
¼ cup extra-virgin olive oil
Kosher salt
2 to 3 tsp. fresh lemon juice; more as needed

Position a rack in the center of the oven and heat the oven to 450°F. Snap off and discard the fibrous bottom ends of the asparagus spears. Put the asparagus on a large, rimmed baking sheet and drizzle with the olive oil. Gently toss the asparagus with the oil until it's evenly coated. Distribute the asparagus so that it's in an even layer. Sprinkle generously with salt and roast until tender (bite into a spear to check), 10 to 15 minutes. Transfer the asparagus to a platter, toss with lemon juice and salt to taste, and serve.

Roasted Cornish Game Hens with Wildflower Honey & Orange

Serves six to eight.

Cornish game hens work well for entertaining. They're a nice departure from chicken, and they don't require any last-minute carving. Marinating in honey and basting with butter adds flavor and encourages the skin to brown, but sometimes they also need a flash under the broiler to finish.

3 Cornish game hens (1½ to 2 lb. each)
6 Tbs. plus ⅓ cup dry white wine, such as Sauvignon Blanc or Pinot Grigio
1½ Tbs. honey (I prefer wildflower honey)
1½ Tbs. chopped fresh thyme
2 bay leaves, preferably fresh, each torn into about 4 pieces
Pinch crushed red pepper flakes
1 medium orange
1 small yellow onion, cut crosswise into ¼-inch-thick slices
1 Tbs. kosher salt
Freshly ground black pepper
3 Tbs. unsalted butter, melted, for basting, plus 1 Tbs. butter, not melted, for the sauce
1 cup low-salt chicken broth

Vanilla Ice Cream with Espresso-Caramel Sauce

Serves six; yields about 1½ cups sauce.

You can make the caramel sauce up to a week in advance and refrigerate; it may separate, so stir to combine as you gently reheat the sauce before serving. If you don't have an espresso machine, just pick up a cup at the local café.

¾ cup heavy cream
1 cup granulated sugar
3 Tbs. brewed espresso
1 Tbs. Kahlúa (optional)
3 pints vanilla ice cream
About ½ cup chocolate-covered espresso
**   beans, roughly chopped, for sprinkling**
**   (optional; for sources, see p. 78)**

Measure the heavy cream into a liquid measuring cup. Put ½ cup water in a small, heavy saucepan with steep (at least 4-inch) sides. Add the sugar and swirl the pan to moisten it. Cover and bring to a boil over medium heat, swirling the pan occasionally, until the sugar dissolves, about 1 minute. Increase the heat to high and cook, still covered but checking frequently, until the sugar starts to turn light brown, 3 to 7 minutes. Remove the lid and continue to cook, swirling the pan occasionally, until the sugar turns dark amber, 2 to 4 minutes. Immediately remove the pan from the heat, and slowly and very carefully stir in the heavy cream; it will bubble and splatter. Continue to stir until the sauce is smooth.

Pour the caramel into a small, heatproof bowl, and let it cool slightly. Stir in the espresso and the Kahlúa, if using.

To serve: If the caramel is cold or has thickened from sitting, reheat it gently over low heat. Put a scoop or two of ice cream into six individual cups or dishes. Drizzle some caramel on top and sprinkle with a spoonful of espresso beans, if using.

Tasha DeSerio is co-owner of Olive Green Catering in Berkeley, California. ◆

Discard the giblets from the hens or reserve for another use. Using kitchen shears, cut along both sides of the backbones and remove them. Then cut each hen in half along the breastbone. Trim off the wing tips and put the hens in a large bowl.

In a small bowl, combine the 6 Tbs. wine, honey, thyme, bay leaves, and red pepper flakes, and stir to dissolve the honey (it's all right if it doesn't dissolve completely).

Using a vegetable peeler, peel the zest from the orange in large strips, letting the strips drop into the bowl with the hens. Add the honey mixture and the sliced onion to the bowl. Toss well, cover, and refrigerate for at least 4 hours or overnight, tossing the hens occasionally.

About half an hour before cooking, remove the hen halves from the marinade and gently pat them dry, trying not to disturb the thyme clinging to them. Arrange the hens on a heavy-duty rimmed baking sheet and let sit at room temperature for 30 minutes. (Discard the remaining marinade.) Position a rack in the top third of the oven and heat the oven to 450°F.

When ready to roast, season the hen halves on both sides with the salt and several grinds of pepper. Turn them skin side up. Roast the hens, basting occasionally with the melted butter and rotating the pan for even browning as needed, until an instant-read thermometer inserted into the meaty part of a thigh registers 175° to 180°F (be careful not to hit the bone), about 30 minutes.

If the skin is somewhat pale, baste the hens, turn the broiler to high, and broil, rotating the pan frequently, until the hens are nicely golden, about 2 minutes. (Watch carefully to prevent burning.) Transfer the hens to a serving platter and tent with aluminum foil.

While the rimmed baking sheet is still hot, add the remaining ⅓ cup wine and use a wooden spoon to scrape the brown bits from the bottom of the pan. Pour the wine and juices into a small saucepan and add the chicken broth. Boil the sauce over high heat until it thickens ever so slightly, 2 to 3 minutes; it should be more like a jus than a thick sauce. Off the heat, whisk in the remaining 1 Tbs. butter. Taste and add salt and pepper, if needed. Keep warm.

To serve, pour a small amount of the sauce on and around the hens and pass the remainder at the table.

The Most Delicious
Glazed Ham

From the market to the kitchen,
here's how to shop for and bake the perfect ham

BY BRUCE AIDELLS

Whether it's for Easter dinner or just a big family gathering, nothing is easier to make or pleases a crowd quite like a baked ham. Since hams are sold fully cooked, the heavy lifting has already been done for you. All you need to do is warm it up, slice, and serve. It's almost embarrassingly easy, and if that's all you did, it would be quite tasty. But there's a very simple way to make a plain baked ham even better: brush it with a sweet glaze while it's heating and then whisk together a quick, snappy sauce using the pan juices. My method and recipes that follow will show you how. Before you can start cooking, though, you need to shop. Read on for a quick course on how to choose a ham.

A city ham is brined, smoked, and cooked

What is a ham? At its most basic, it's a hind leg of pork, but that definition doesn't tell you whether the meat has been salt-cured, brine-cured, smoked, air-dried, aged, cooked, or some combination of all of those. Ham can be prepared in numerous ways, but for the recipe on the next page, you'll need one that's been cured with a brine, then smoked and fully cooked. These are called city hams, as opposed to uncooked country hams, which are cured by rubbing the meat directly with salt and sugar. Pretty much all the cooked hams you see in the supermarket are going to be city hams.

Making sense of ham grades: it's all about the water

In the past, city hams were immersed in a brine for three or four weeks before being smoked and cooked. But most producers today "brine" their hams by injecting them with a curing solution of water, salt, sugar, and usually phosphates and nitrites as well. Injecting a ham flavors and preserves it more quickly than does immersing it in a brine, and it also forces extra water into the meat. The amount of water in the ham determines its grade, which you'll find on the label.

Ham. This highest grade of ham has a clean, delicate pork flavor and a fine, lean texture that resembles that of a chop. It's considerably more expensive than other grades, though, and your local supermarket may not carry it. Ordering by mail will, of course, only add to the cost of the ham. (For sources, see p. 78.)

Ham in natural juices. This grade is somewhat confusingly named since the "natural juices" are actually added water (many hams in this grade weigh up to 10% more than their raw weight due to the extra water). These hams have a fine, meaty quality when baked, and the added water does help ensure that they stay juicy. This grade is a good value and is readily available at most supermarkets.

Ham, water added. The percentage of added water in this grade will be stated on the label (usually in fine print). A ham that says "water added—15%" means it weighs 15% more than its raw weight.

Ham and water product. Most producers of this lowest grade pump as much water as they can into the ham, which adds weight and allows them to sell it at a lower price. If the amount of water exceeds 50%, the ham must be labeled "water and ham product," since there is more water by weight than meat.

A ham from any of these four grades will work fine for the Oven-Glazed Ham recipe on the next page, but for the best flavor and texture, I recommend buying "ham" or else "ham in natural juices."

What about nitrite-free hams?

Nitrites are used in curing hams to preserve the meat's color and inhibit bacterial growth. Lately, chemical nitrites have fallen somewhat out of favor due to health concerns—studies in the 1970s showed that when exposed to high heat, nitrites could potentially become carcinogenic, specifically in bacon.

As a result, some producers now sell "nitrite-free" hams. These hams still contain nitrites, but they're from a natural source, such as celery juice (nitrates in the celery juice become nitrites during processing).

The standard supermarket ham will keep for about 10 days in the refrigerator, but if you buy a nitrite-free ham, be aware that it will have a shorter shelf life.

A half-ham can serve a crowd

The two highest grades of ham (see text at left) are sold as either whole or half hams. For up to 14 people, a half-ham is sufficient.

The butt half is the upper part of the ham. Its meat tends to be very tender and flavorful—and there's more of it—but it often contains part of the hip bone, which makes carving a little awkward.

The shank half is the lower part of the ham. It's easier to carve, but because the muscles in this region get more exercise, this cut is tougher and chewier.

Bone-in ham delivers more flavor

I prefer bone-in hams over boneless. I find that any meat cooked on the bone has better flavor, and in the case of ham, it also has better texture. When producers remove the bone from a ham, they have to then reshape the meat (in a machine called a vacuum tumbler) so it won't fall apart when sliced. This can give boneless ham a bit of a spongy texture. And there's one more reason I like bone-in hams: The leftover bone is great for flavoring soups, beans, and other dishes (see p. 76 for a collard greens recipe using a ham bone). If you can find only boneless ham, try to pick one that has the natural shape of the leg, which indicates that it was minimally tumbled.

Avoid spiral-cut hams

"Spiral-cut" hams are partially boned hams that have been sliced before packaging. I don't recommend them because they tend to dry out when baked, and they often come already coated with a commercial-tasting glaze.

Follow this simple method for a perfect glazed ham

Oven-Glazed Ham with a Pan Sauce

Serves twelve to fourteen.

A supermarket "city ham" is already fully cooked, so heating it isn't essential. But a warm ham tastes better, and baking concentrates the meat's flavor and improves its texture. It also allows you to jazz up the ham with one of my glaze and pan sauce combinations.

1 half-ham, preferably bone-in (7 to 9 lb.)
1 glaze & sauce recipe, at right

Follow the instructions below:

To carve the ham, slice it thinly, working your way around the bone as best you can. Don't worry if the slices are not an even thickness.

BAKE THE HAM:

Position a rack in the lower third of the oven and heat the oven to 325°F.

Trim away any skin and external fat to a thickness of about ¼ inch. Set the ham fat side up and score the fat ¼ inch deep with diagonal slices every 2 inches so that it forms a cross-hatched diamond pattern.

Set the ham in a sturdy roasting pan or a baking dish. It should fit fairly snugly with only a couple of inches of space on any side. Add the liquid from the glaze & sauce recipe to reach a ¼-inch depth. Bake, adding water as needed to maintain ¼ inch of liquid, until an instant-read thermometer inserted into the center of the ham registers 105° to 110°F, 1¾ to 2¼ hours (it should take about 15 minutes per pound).

BRUSH WITH THE GLAZE:

Remove the ham from the oven and raise the temperature to 425°F. Add more water to the pan so the liquid is about ½ inch deep.

Using a large spoon or pastry brush, smear the glaze (from a recipe at right) generously over the top of the ham. Return the pan to the oven (even if it hasn't reached 425°F yet) and bake until the glaze on the ham bubbles and begins to darken, 10 to 15 minutes; the ham should have an internal temperature of 120° to 125°F.

Remove the ham from the oven and transfer to a carving board or large platter. Tent loosely with foil and let rest for 20 to 30 minutes while you make the pan sauce. During this period, the ham's internal temperature should rise to 130° to 140°F.

MAKE THE SAUCE:

Pour the pan juices into a gravy separator or a 4-cup Pyrex measuring cup. Let sit for 10 to 15 minutes to allow any fat to rise and then pour or spoon off the fat and discard (some hams don't exude much fat).

Pour the pan juices into a 2-qt. saucepan, whisk in the sauce ingredients (except the cornstarch mixture) from the glaze & sauce recipe and bring to a boil. Taste the sauce, and if the flavor isn't as intense as you'd like, continue to boil to concentrate the flavors as desired.

Stir in about half the cornstarch mixture and whisk until the sauce thickens slightly, about 15 seconds. Add more of the cornstarch mixture for a thicker sauce. Set aside and keep warm while the ham rests.

Carve the ham, arrange on a platter, and serve with the sauce alongside.

Before you start, choose one of these glaze & sauce recipes

Cherry-Pomegranate Glaze & Sauce

Yields enough for 1 Oven-Glazed Ham.

1¼ cups pomegranate juice (see From Our Test Kitchen, p. 72)
½ cup cherry preserves
2 Tbs. Dijon mustard
¼ cup packed light brown sugar
¼ cup kirschwasser or other cherry liqueur
¼ cup sweetened dried tart cherries
1 Tbs. cornstarch mixed with 3 Tbs. water

For baking the ham: Pour 1 cup of the pomegranate juice into the roasting pan and add enough water to reach a ¼-inch depth, as indicated in the Oven-Glazed Ham recipe. Add more water during baking as needed.

To make the glaze: Gently warm ¼ cup of the cherry preserves in a small saucepan. Stir in the mustard and brown sugar to combine. Smear over the ham as instructed in the Oven-Glazed Ham recipe.

To make the sauce: In a small saucepan combine the kirschwasser, dried cherries, and the remaining ¼ cup pomegranate juice. Bring to a boil, cover, and simmer for 5 minutes. Add this mixture, along with the remaining ¼ cup cherry preserves, to the pan juices and boil as instructed in the Oven-Glazed Ham recipe. Add the cornstarch mixture as instructed.

Maple, Tea & Cardamom Glaze & Sauce

Yields enough for 1 Oven-Glazed Ham.

1 cup brewed tea (something basic like Lipton is fine)
1 cup apple cider
½ cup pure maple syrup
¼ cup packed light brown sugar
¼ tsp. ground cardamom
2 Tbs. cider vinegar
1 Tbs. cornstarch mixed with 3 Tbs. water

For baking the ham: In a medium bowl, combine the tea, cider, and ¼ cup of the maple syrup. Pour this mixture into the roasting pan and add enough water to reach a ¼-inch depth, as indicated in the Oven-Glazed Ham recipe. Add more water during baking as needed.

To make the glaze: In a small bowl, mix 2 Tbs. of the maple syrup with the brown sugar and cardamom to make a thick, wet paste. Smear over the ham as instructed in the Oven-Glazed Ham recipe (use a spatula or your fingers if it's easier).

To make the sauce: Add the remaining 2 Tbs. maple syrup and the vinegar to the pan juices and boil as instructed in the Oven-Glazed Ham recipe. Add the cornstarch mixture as instructed.

Tangerine Marmalade Glaze & Sauce

Yields enough for 1 Oven-Glazed Ham.

I like tangerine marmalade for this recipe, but you can use any orange, lemon, or other citrus marmalade or even apricot preserves.

1½ cups store-bought orange juice
½ cup tangerine or other citrus marmalade
¼ cup packed light brown sugar
¼ tsp. ground ginger
⅛ tsp. ground cloves
2 Tbs. fresh lemon juice, more to taste
1 Tbs. cornstarch mixed with 3 Tbs. water

For baking the ham: Pour the orange juice into the roasting pan and add enough water to reach a ¼-inch depth, as indicated in the Oven-Glazed Ham recipe. Add more water during baking as needed.

To make the glaze: Gently warm ¼ cup of the marmalade in a small saucepan set over medium-low heat. Stir in the brown sugar, ginger, and cloves to combine. Smear over the ham as instructed in the Oven-Glazed Ham recipe.

To make the sauce: Add the remaining ¼ cup marmalade and lemon juice to the pan juices and boil as instructed in the Oven-Glazed Ham recipe. Add more lemon juice to taste. Add the cornstarch mixture as instructed.

Bruce Aidells is the author of Bruce Aidells's Complete Book of Pork *and* The Complete Meat Cookbook. ◆

How to Make Flaky, Buttery Biscuits

An unusual mixing method is the secret to the flakiest buttermilk biscuits you've ever tasted

BY PETER REINHART

There are two types of people in the world: those who like tender biscuits and those who like flaky biscuits. I am without a doubt in the flaky camp. And in my quest to create a biscuit that's as flaky as the best pie dough and so delicious that it needs no added butter or jam, I've experimented with lots of recipes and techniques. The method I've settled on is somewhat unorthodox, but it's virtually foolproof, and more important, it consistently delivers the most amazing biscuits.

Usually, flaky biscuits are made by cutting cold fat—either butter, shortening, or lard—into flour, mixing in liquid, and then rolling or patting out the dough and cutting it. Sounds straightforward, but the results can be unpredictable, particularly for the novice. Several variables influence whether biscuits turn out flaky or not: the choice of fat, its temperature, how thoroughly you cut it into the flour, and how much you work the dough as you mix and shape it. And it's hard to be consistent in all these matters. My recipe eliminates most of the variability by incorporating a few clever tricks.

The only fat I use is very cold butter. Some people insist that you can't make a flaky biscuit without shortening and lard, which are pure fats, but I wholly disagree. Although it's true that butter is only 85% fat (the remaining 15%

Flaky Buttermilk Biscuits

Yields about ten 2¾-inch biscuits or eighteen 2-inch biscuits.

8 oz. (1¾ cups) unbleached all-purpose flour; more as needed for shaping the dough
1 Tbs. granulated sugar
2¼ tsp. baking powder
¾ tsp. kosher salt
¼ tsp. baking soda
4 oz. (8 Tbs.) very cold unsalted butter
¾ cup very cold buttermilk

Heat the oven to 500°F and position a rack in the middle of the oven. Line a rimmed baking sheet with parchment. Put the flour, sugar, baking powder, salt, and baking soda in a large mixing bowl and stir with a whisk to distribute the ingredients evenly.

1 Cut the butter into small bits and toss with the flour. With a sharp knife or a bench knife, cut the cold butter crosswise into ¼-inch-thick slices. Stack 3 or 4 slices and cut them into three even strips. Rotate the stack a quarter turn and cut the strips in half. You should create 6 small bits of butter per slice. Toss the butter bits into the bowl with the flour mixture. Continue cutting all the butter in the same manner and adding it to the flour mixture.

When all the butter is in the bowl with the flour, use your fingers to separate the butter bits (they tend to stick to each other), coat all the butter pieces with flour, and evenly distribute them throughout the flour mixture. Don't rub the butter too hard with your fingertips or palms, as this will melt the butter. You're just trying to break the butter pieces apart, not blend the butter into the flour.

2 Give it a little stir. When all the butter is evenly distributed, add the cold buttermilk and stir with a large spoon until all or most of the flour is absorbed by the buttermilk and the dough forms a coarse lump, about 1 minute.

3 Pat and fold the dough. Dust a work surface with flour and dump the dough onto the floured surface, cleaning out the bowl with a spatula or a plastic bowl scraper. Dust the top of the dough and your hands with flour, and press the dough into a ¾-inch-thick

rectangle. Sprinkle a small amount of additional flour on the top of the dough. If making one of the variations on p. 50, sprinkle on one-third of the cheese, onions, or herbs now. Fold the dough over on itself in three sections, as if folding a letter (also called a tri-fold). With a bench knife or metal spatula, lift the dough off the counter and dust under it with flour to prevent sticking, if necessary. Dust the top with flour and press the dough out again into a ¾-inch-thick rectangle (sprinkle on another one-third of the variation ingredient, if using) and repeat the tri-fold. Repeat this procedure one more time (three times in all).

4 Cut the biscuits and bake. After the third tri-fold, dust under and on top of the dough, if needed, and roll or press the dough into a ½-inch-thick oval. Dip a 2-inch or 2¾-inch round biscuit cutter (for sources, see p. 78) in flour and start cutting biscuits, dipping the cutter in flour between each biscuit. Press straight down to cut and lift straight up to remove; twisting the biscuit cutter will seal the sides and interfere with rising. Use a bench knife or spatula to transfer the biscuits to the baking sheet, placing them about ½ inch apart.

Gently gather any scraps of dough, pat and roll out again, and cut more biscuits from the remaining dough. You can gather and roll the scraps two times total and still get good results (the more times you roll out, the tougher the biscuits will be).

Put the baking sheet in the oven and reduce the temperature to 450°F. Bake for 8 minutes; rotate the pan 180 degrees; continue baking until both the tops and bottoms of the biscuits are a rich golden brown and the biscuits have doubled in height, revealing flaky layers on the sides, 4 to 6 minutes more. It's all right if some butter seeps from the biscuits. Remove the pan from the oven and set it on a cooling rack, leaving the biscuits on the pan. Cool the biscuits for at least 3 minutes and serve them hot or warm (they will stay warm for about 20 minutes).

is a combination of water and milk solids), nothing can match butter for flavor, and my results prove that you absolutely can use it to make a flaky biscuit.

I don't cut the butter into the flour. This step really sets my recipe apart from the pack. Instead of using a pastry cutter to blend the butter into the flour, I simply slice the butter into small, thin bits and toss them with the flour. That's it. This method ensures that the butter bits stay large, and when there are large bits of fat in the dough, there will be scrumptious flakes in the biscuits later.

I mix the dough briefly. When I add the buttermilk to the flour and butter, I stir just enough to bring the mixture together into a coarse ball of dough. Overworking the dough turns biscuits tough.

Finally, I fold the dough. For my biscuits, I borrow the folding technique that's used in croissant and puff pastry dough. It creates many layers of dough and fat, which encourages the biscuits to puff up while they bake, creating maximum flakiness.

Start cold, end hot

When making the dough, use very cold butter and buttermilk, the colder the better. For the most flakiness, the butter needs to remain in firm bits and pieces.

Bake in a super-hot oven. Heat the oven to 500°F, and then after you put the pan into the oven, reduce the heat to 450°F. The high heat sets the dough quickly, trapping the butter, which releases steam as it melts and encourages the dough to puff.

Shown clockwise from top right: Cheese Biscuits, Fresh Herb Biscuits, and Caramelized Onion Biscuits.

3 Easy Variations

Cheese Biscuits

Because of all the delicious cheese, these biscuits may spread a bit as they bake, but they're so good, it really doesn't matter how they look.

2 cups grated sharp Cheddar, Gruyère, Gouda, or provolone

Make the biscuit dough as directed in steps 1 through 3 of the recipe on p. 49.

When making the tri-folds, sprinkle one-third of the cheese on the dough surface before each fold. If some of the cheese falls off while folding the dough, simply scoop it up and add it to the next fold. It will look like a lot of cheese, but it will melt and almost disappear into the biscuits when you bake them.

Roll out, cut, and bake the biscuits as directed in step 4.

Caramelized Onion Biscuits

2 large yellow onions, halved lengthwise, trimmed, and thinly sliced lengthwise
1 Tbs. vegetable oil
2 Tbs. granulated sugar
1 Tbs. balsamic vinegar

At least a few hours and up to a day before you plan to make the biscuits, put the onions and the oil in a large skillet over medium heat and cook, stirring occasionally, until they are soft and translucent, 8 minutes. Add the sugar and balsamic vinegar, and continue cooking and stirring until the onions are very soft and caramelized, 10 to 15 min-

utes. If the onions brown too much or the bottom of the pan gets too brown before the onions are soft, add some water, about 2 Tbs. at a time. Let the onions cool at room temperature for 30 minutes, chop coarsely, transfer to a container, seal, and refrigerate until cold.

Make the biscuit dough as directed in steps 1 through 3 of the recipe on p. 49. When making the tri-folds, spread one-third of the caramelized onions on the dough surface before each fold.

Roll out, cut, and bake the biscuits as directed in step 4.

Fresh Herb Biscuits

Strong herbs like rosemary, oregano, sage, and thyme can easily overpower the biscuits; use these in moderation.

¾ cup minced fresh tender herbs such as basil, parsley, dill, chervil, cilantro, or a combination

Make the biscuit dough as directed in steps 1 through 3 of the recipe on p. 49.

When making the tri-folds, sprinkle one-third of the herbs on the dough surface before each fold. If some of the herbs fall off while folding the dough, simply scoop them up and add to the next fold.

Roll out, cut, and bake the biscuits as directed in step 4.

Peter Reinhart is the author of seven books on bread and food. He teaches classes on food and culture, as well as baking, at Johnson & Wales University. ◆

Carrots
Pure & Simple

This quartet of delicious recipes shows that you don't have to fuss to highlight the essential sweet flavor of carrots

BY DAN BARBER

Eighteen years ago, I sat in the dining room of the famed restaurant Lutèce, where André Soltner, the chef and owner, stood pointing a raw carrot at me. "I don't want to re-create the carrot," he said, shaking his head. "That's not my job. My job is to find the best carrot and respect it." He was responding to what he thought was the mindlessly, maybe even recklessly, creative new breed of young chefs. As he towered over me in his starched whites and chef's hat, both his words and his tone—one part advice, three parts threat—made a lasting impression.

These days, as chef of a restaurant attached to an 80-acre working farm just north of New York City, I've had ample opportunity to heed Chef Soltner's words. The restaurant's menu is dictated by the day's harvest, and my job consists largely of letting the ingredients speak for themselves. This is particularly true for carrots, which are naturally delicious. Whether they're slender or stout, orange or purple, Nelsons or Chantenays, or just your garden-variety supermarket carrots, there's no need to fuss when cooking them.

My recipes show off the versatility of carrots without forgetting Chef Soltner's wisdom. There's a very simple roasted carrot recipe with a touch of pure maple syrup; it's especially wonderful with winter carrots but delicious at any time of year. The carrot-walnut salad is bright and crunchy; dressed

Pickled

Pan-roasted

A soup

A salad

with orange juice, cider vinegar, honey, and walnut oil, it's a perfectly refreshing summer dish and a far cry from the predictable carrot salads we've all had at one time or another. The pickled baby carrots zing with vinegary tartness and provide yet another way to enjoy (or to preserve) the harvest. And the carrot soup gets a hint of warmth from fresh ginger, which complements the carrots' earthiness. Serve the soup garnished with raw apple for an elegant first course or sip it from a mug alongside a grilled cheese sandwich on an autumn afternoon.

A word on where to find the best carrots. If you can, I urge you to shop for your carrots at a farmers' market (to find one near you, see p. 78) or a store that carries locally grown carrots. Your reward will be remarkable flavor. And the recipes on the following pages will be all the more delicious for it.

Carrots & the seasons

Carrots are available all the time at the grocery store, and they'll always look and taste the same. But when you grow them yourself or buy them from a farmer, you'll notice that their character changes with the seasons. The young carrots at the farmers' market in late spring and early summer have a delicate flavor and juiciness that's best appreciated fresh—shave them into a salad for an afternoon lunch and you needn't do much more. But in late fall, after the first soft frosts have spoken, their flavor becomes more complex and sweet, a result of the cold temperatures converting the roots' starches to sugars. To highlight this natural sweetness, roasting is the best option—apply just enough heat to caramelize the sugars.

Carrots come in many colors and shapes, from purple to white, slender to chubby, tapered to conical, even round. While all share certain qualities, some varieties are juicier, earthier, and sweeter than others.

Photos: Scott Phillips

Maple Pan-Roasted Baby Carrots
Serves four.

For this recipe, baby carrots are ideal, but you can also use mature carrots if you cut them down to size, as shown in the photo tip below. You start cooking the carrots on the stovetop and then move them to the hot oven to roast. The direct heat of the stovetop jump-starts the caramelizing of the carrots.

1 Tbs. extra-virgin olive oil
1 lb. carrots with their tops on, preferably baby carrots, peeled and stems trimmed to about ½ inch
1 Tbs. pure maple syrup
½ tsp. kosher or sea salt; more as needed
¼ tsp. freshly ground black pepper; more as needed

Position a rack in the middle of the oven and heat the oven to 400°F.

In a large (12-inch) ovenproof skillet or sauté pan, heat the oil over high heat (the oil shouldn't smoke but should crackle when you add the carrots). Add the carrots and cook, stirring frequently, until they blister and turn golden brown in spots, 1 to 2 minutes. Add the maple syrup, salt, and pepper and toss well to coat the carrots. Remove from the heat.

Spread the carrots evenly in the skillet and transfer it to the hot oven. Roast until the carrots are tender, browned in spots, and just a little shriveled, 12 to 15 minutes. Season to taste with salt and pepper before serving.

tip: To cut a large carrot into 6 baby-carrot-size pieces, slice the carrot in half crosswise; then halve the narrower bottom end and quarter the wider stem end.

Baby Carrots Pickled in Champagne & Sherry Vinegars
Yields about 20 pickled carrots.

Serve these zesty little pickles as a starter or cocktail nibble or add them to an antipasto platter.

Kosher salt
¾ lb. baby carrots with their tops on (18 to 20 carrots, about 6 inches long and ½ inch thick at the wide end)
2 Tbs. whole coriander seeds
1 cup dry white wine
1¼ cups honey
1 cup Champagne vinegar
½ cup sherry vinegar

Bring a medium saucepan of salted water to a boil over high heat. Fill a large bowl with ice water.

Meanwhile, peel the baby carrots and remove all but about ½ inch of the green stems. Boil the carrots until barely tender, about 5 minutes. Immediately drain the carrots and then immerse them in the bowl of ice water.

In a small saucepan, toast the coriander seeds over medium heat just until they become fragrant and lightly browned, 3 to 5 minutes. Add the white wine and boil until reduced to about ¼ cup, 6 to 10 minutes.

In a medium saucepan, heat the honey over medium-high heat until it bubbles, about 3 minutes. Add the Champagne and sherry vinegars, and then the coriander and wine mixture; simmer for 5 minutes—watch carefully and reduce the heat as necessary to prevent a boil-over.

Arrange the carrots upright in a clean 1-qt. canning jar or other nonreactive container, and pour the honey mixture over the carrots. Let cool to room temperature. Cover and refrigerate for at least 4 hours but preferably 24 hours before serving the pickles. They will keep, refrigerated, for 2 to 3 weeks.

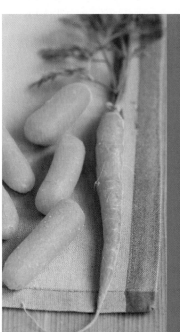

Which is the real baby carrot?

Those stubby carrot nubbins on the left in the photo may be called baby carrots, but they're actually mature carrots that have been whittled down to bite-size pieces. The true baby carrot is the immature one on the right. Real baby carrots are tender and juicy; they're usually just 4 to 5 inches long and are generally sold in bunches, with their tops on.

Carrot Salad with Walnut Oil & Honey
Serves six.

You might be surprised how well the toasty flavors of the walnuts and walnut oil complement the freshly grated carrot. This salad would be a delicious accompaniment to roast pork or chicken.

1½ lb. carrots, peeled and grated on the medium holes of a box grater
1 cup walnuts, toasted and chopped
½ cup dried currants
1 orange, juiced (about ½ cup)
3 Tbs. apple-cider vinegar
1 Tbs. honey
3 Tbs. untoasted walnut oil (for sources, see p. 78)
Kosher or sea salt
Freshly ground black pepper
2½ Tbs. finely chopped chives

Combine the grated carrots, walnuts, and currants in a medium serving bowl.

In a small bowl, whisk together the orange juice, cider vinegar, and honey. Slowly whisk in the walnut oil. Season with salt and pepper to taste.

Toss the carrot mixture with the vinaigrette and 2 Tbs. of the chives. Adjust the seasoning to taste. You can serve the salad immediately, but it will taste even better if you let it sit at room temperature for 15 to 20 minutes. Sprinkle with the remaining ½ Tbs. chives right before serving.

Velvety Carrot Soup with Ginger

Yields about 8½ cups; serves eight.

This recipe looks long, but half of the ingredients are for making a quick vegetable broth. Look for carrot juice in the produce section of your supermarket.

FOR THE BROTH:
¼ cup medium-diced peeled carrots
½ cup medium-diced dark green leek tops (from 1 to 2 leeks; rinse thoroughly after dicing; save the white and pale green parts for the soup)
½ medium onion, cut into medium dice (about ¾ cup)
¼ fennel bulb, cut into medium dice (about ½ cup)
¼ celery stalk, cut into medium dice (about 2 Tbs.)
1 small clove garlic, smashed and peeled
1 small bay leaf
1 sprig thyme
1 sprig parsley

FOR THE SOUP:
3 Tbs. extra-virgin olive oil
5 medium shallots, thinly sliced (about 1 cup)
¾ cup thinly sliced leeks, white and pale green parts only (from 1 to 2 leeks; rinse thoroughly after slicing)
2 small cloves garlic, smashed and peeled
Kosher or sea salt
3¾ cups medium-diced peeled carrots (about 1½ lb.)
2 Tbs. granulated sugar
2 cups carrot juice, either homemade or store-bought
1 Tbs. peeled finely grated fresh ginger
Freshly ground black pepper

3 to 4 tsp. fresh lemon juice
1 small Fuji apple

Make the broth: Put the carrots, leek tops, onion, fennel, celery, garlic, bay leaf, thyme, and parsley in a 4-qt. (or larger) saucepan. Add 10 cups cold water and bring to a simmer over medium-high heat. Reduce the heat to medium low and simmer for 1 hour. Strain the broth into a heatproof bowl and discard the solids. Measure out 5 cups of broth for use in the soup; save the remaining broth for another use. Rinse and dry the saucepan and return it to the stove.

Finish the soup: In the saucepan, heat the olive oil over medium-low heat. Add the shallots, leeks, garlic, and a generous pinch of salt. Cook, stirring occasionally, until the vegetables are softened but not browned, about 5 minutes. Stir in the carrots and sugar. Cover, reduce the heat to low, and cook, stirring occasionally, until the carrots are soft, 15 to 20 minutes.

Add the 5 cups broth and the carrot juice. Bring to a simmer, uncovered, over medium-high heat. Reduce the heat to low and simmer gently for 10 minutes.

Wrap the ginger in a small square of cheesecloth and use the cloth to squeeze the ginger

juice into the soup (discard the squeezed-dry ginger). Remove the pan from the heat.

Working in batches, purée the soup in a blender until smooth. Pour each batch of the puréed soup into a medium-mesh sieve set over a clean heatproof container. Use a rubber spatula to help the soup pass through, but don't press on the solids yet. Once the last batch has drained through the sieve, press lightly on the solids (but don't mash them through the sieve) to extract the remaining liquid. Discard the solids. Season to taste with salt, pepper, and 1 to 2 tsp. of the lemon juice.

When ready to serve, peel and core the apple and cut it into medium dice. In a small bowl, toss the apple with 2 tsp. of the remaining lemon juice. Reheat the soup, if necessary, and ladle it into individual serving bowls or cups. Serve immediately, garnishing each bowl with a small spoonful of the diced apple.

Dan Barber is the chef and co-owner of two restaurants: Blue Hill in New York City and Blue Hill at Stone Barns in Pocantico Hills, New York. ◆

Sear & Sauce for

A few key techniques guarantee great results time and again

BY TONY ROSENFELD

Drying the shrimp well helps ensure a good sear.

A single layer of shrimp in a very hot pan promotes the best browning.

Tossing the shrimp in a sauce finishes the cooking and layers on the flavor.

One of the things I love most about shrimp—and the reason I make it often on weeknights—is that it cooks so quickly. But if that is shrimp's best attribute, it can also be its fatal flaw. It cooks *so* fast that it's easy to overcook, and the sad result can be tough, dry shrimp whose sweet goodness has all but vanished. You won't have that problem in these saucy shrimp sautés, however, because my technique preserves shrimp's tender interior and boosts its delicate flavor. I start with a good sear and finish with a sauce, which guarantees moist, succulent results every time.

The first trick to a great shrimp sauté is to dry the shrimp well before cooking. Surface moisture is the enemy of browning, causing the seafood to steam instead of sear.

Next tip: Get the pan good and hot. I heat the dry pan on medium high for a minute or two before I even add the oil. Once it's hot—if you hold your hand above the surface, you'll feel the heat radiating off it—I add the oil. It will start to shimmer almost immediately, which tells you that the pan is hot enough to start sautéing. Only then do I add the shrimp.

Here are a couple more pointers: Arrange the shrimp in a single layer and don't fiddle with them once they're in the pan. It's tempting to keep tossing them around, but if you leave them alone for a couple of minutes, they'll brown better.

To turn these shrimp sautés into a more complete meal, I use the same pan to prepare an intensely flavored sauce with a vegetable or two, some broth, an acidic liquid for a little tang, and perhaps a touch of spice for excitement. Bring this to a boil and return the shrimp to the pan. It'll take just a minute or two for them to pick up the flavors of the sauce and cook to a perfect doneness.

Fast Shrimp Sautés

Spicy Seared Chipotle Shrimp with Zucchini & Chorizo

Serves three.

½ cup low-salt chicken broth
½ small chipotle, seeded and minced, plus 2 Tbs. adobo sauce (from a can of chipotles en adobo)
1 Tbs. tomato paste
1 tsp. light brown sugar
1 lb. shrimp (21 to 25 per lb.), peeled, deveined, rinsed, and patted dry
¾ tsp. kosher salt; more as needed
Freshly ground black pepper
¼ cup extra-virgin olive oil
¼ lb. chorizo, cut into ¼-inch dice (scant 1 cup)

1 medium zucchini, cut into ½-inch dice (2 cups)
1 small yellow onion, thinly sliced (1 cup)
½ small red bell pepper, sliced into strips about ¼ inch wide and 2 to 3 inches long (½ cup)
¼ cup chopped fresh cilantro
2 Tbs. fresh lime juice; more as needed

In a measuring cup, whisk together the chicken broth, chipotle, adobo sauce, tomato paste, and brown sugar.

Sprinkle the shrimp with a scant ¼ tsp. salt and a few generous grinds of black pep-per. Put a 12-inch skillet (not nonstick) over medium-high heat for 1½ minutes. Add 2 Tbs. of the oil and once it's shimmering hot, add the shrimp in a single layer. Cook undisturbed until the shrimp browns nicely, about 2 minutes. Flip and brown the second side, about 1½ minutes. Transfer to a large plate. The shrimp should still be a little undercooked.

Add the remaining 2 Tbs. oil and the chorizo to the pan and cook, tossing, until it starts to brown, about 1 minute. Add the zucchini, onion, and pepper,

sprinkle with ½ tsp. salt, and cook, tossing often, until the zucchini browns in places and is just tender, about 4 minutes.

Add the broth mixture to the skillet and bring to a boil. Reduce the heat to medium low. Stir in the shrimp, about half of the cilantro, and the lime juice. Cook, stirring often, until the zucchini is tender and the shrimp are opaque throughout (cut one in half to check), 2 to 3 minutes. Season to taste with salt, pepper, and more lime juice. Serve immediately, sprinkled with the remaining cilantro.

For the best sautés, look for shrimp that are:

Frozen.
There's very little truly "fresh" shrimp to be had in the United States. Most supermarkets simply defrost frozen shrimp and put them on ice at the fish counter. There's no telling how long they've sat around, so buying shrimp that's still frozen is a better way to ensure freshness. Until a few years ago, this meant buying a solid block of frozen shrimp in ice. Now you can buy individually quick frozen, or IQF, shrimp in 1- or 2-pound plastic bags and defrost as many as you need quickly (it takes only 15 or 20 minutes) when you're ready to use them.

Big.
I prefer larger shrimp because they offer more of a buffer against overcooking. Bigger shrimp are more expensive, but they're also easier to peel and clean. Look for 21 to 25 count, which refers to the number of shrimp per pound, rather than size designations like "jumbo" or "large," which are not standardized.

Not treated with STP.
Many shrimp these days are soaked in a saltwater solution called STP (sodium tripolyphosphate), which helps shrimp maintain its moisture during processing and cooking. This may not sound like such a bad thing, but this solution can give shrimp a saltier flavor and a bit of a spongy texture. To avoid shrimp that contains STP, check the ingredient list on bags of frozen shrimp. If you're buying from a fish counter, ask if it's been treated. If you can find only STP-treated shrimp, be sure to reduce the salt in the recipe.

Wild.
I think wild shrimp tend to have a sweeter, more pronounced flavor and a firmer texture than the farmed variety. If you're lucky enough to find some wild-caught shrimp (frozen shrimp will be labeled wild or farmed), grab them, as only about 20% of shrimp sold in the United States is wild-caught.

Shrimp with Fennel, Tomato & Pernod Sauce
Serves three.

1 lb. shrimp (21 to 25 per lb.), peeled, deveined, rinsed, and patted dry
¾ tsp. kosher salt; more as needed
Freshly ground black pepper
¼ cup extra-virgin olive oil
3 cups very thinly sliced fennel (1 small to medium bulb, trimmed and cored first)
3 cloves garlic, smashed
¼ cup Pernod (French anise-flavor liqueur)
1 14½-oz. can petite-diced tomatoes
1 tsp. chopped fresh thyme
¼ cup chopped fresh flat-leaf parsley

Sprinkle the shrimp with a scant ¼ tsp. salt and a few generous grinds of black pepper. Put a 12-inch skillet (not nonstick) over medium-high heat for 1½ minutes. Add 2 Tbs. of the oil and once it's shimmering hot, add the shrimp in a single layer. Cook undisturbed until the shrimp browns nicely, about 2 minutes. Flip the shrimp and brown the second side, about 1½ minutes. Transfer to a large plate. The shrimp should still be a little undercooked.

Reduce the heat to medium. Add the remaining 2 Tbs. oil and the fennel and garlic. Sprinkle with ½ tsp. salt and cook, tossing often, until the fennel is very soft and golden brown in places, 6 to 8 minutes.

Carefully add the Pernod (it may flame up) and cook, stirring, until any flames die out and the Pernod has almost evaporated, about 1 minute. Add the tomatoes and their juice, the thyme, and about half the parsley. Bring to a boil and then reduce the heat to a gentle simmer and cook for 3 minutes to meld the flavors. Add the shrimp, and cook, tossing, until it's opaque throughout (cut one in half to check), 1 to 2 minutes. Season to taste with salt and pepper. Serve immediately, sprinkled with the remaining parsley.

Perfect doneness

In these recipes, it's hard to tell when the shrimp are done by just looking at them. So here's what to do: Cut a shrimp in half at the thickest part. It should look creamy white and opaque throughout, and the texture should be firm and springy but still moist. If it's a little translucent, cook a minute longer.

Hot Garlicky Shrimp with Asparagus & Lemon

Serves three.

1 lb. shrimp (21 to 25 per lb.), peeled, deveined, rinsed, and patted dry
¾ tsp. kosher salt; more as needed
Freshly ground black pepper
1 lemon
6 Tbs. extra-virgin olive oil
4 medium cloves garlic, thinly sliced
¾ lb. asparagus, bottoms snapped off, halved lengthwise if thick, and cut into 2-inch lengths (2 cups)
⅛ to ¼ tsp. crushed red pepper flakes
⅔ cup low-salt chicken broth
½ tsp. cornstarch

Sprinkle the shrimp with a scant ¼ tsp. salt and a few generous grinds of black pepper. Using a peeler, gently shave the zest in strips from the lemon, taking care not to get any of the bitter white pith. Squeeze the lemon to get 1 Tbs. juice.

Put a 12-inch skillet (not nonstick) over medium-high heat for 1½ minutes. Add 2 Tbs. of the oil and once it's shimmering hot, add the shrimp in a single layer. Cook undisturbed until the shrimp browns nicely, about 2 minutes. Flip the shrimp and brown the second side, about 1½ minutes. Transfer to a large plate. The shrimp should be a little undercooked.

Reduce the heat to medium, add the remaining 4 Tbs. oil and the garlic and cook, tossing, until the garlic starts to sizzle steadily, about 30 seconds. Add the asparagus, lemon zest, and red pepper flakes, sprinkle with ½ tsp. salt and cook, tossing often, until the garlic is golden brown and the asparagus looks blistery in places, 2 to 3 minutes. Add the chicken broth, cover, with the lid ajar, and cook until the asparagus is just tender, 1 to 2 minutes.

In a small dish, whisk together the cornstarch with 1 Tbs. water, stir into the asparagus mixture, and bring to a boil. Stir in the shrimp, reduce the heat to low, and cook, tossing, until the shrimp is opaque throughout (cut one in half to check), 1 to 2 minutes. Stir in the 1 Tbs. lemon juice and then add salt, pepper, and additional lemon juice to taste. Serve immediately.

Tony Rosenfeld is a contributing editor to Fine Cooking. ◆

Rhubarb's

Brighten up your favorite desserts with sweet-tart rhubarb

BY KAREN BARKER

Rhubarb can stir up some pretty strong feelings. Just ask around and you'll see what I mean. Some people love it, others swear they'll never eat it. My suspicion is that at least some of those reluctant to try rhubarb either aren't entirely familiar with it or haven't discovered its full potential. Rosy-red in color with a unique sweet-tart flavor, rhubarb can give a wonderful seasonal spark to just about any dessert; it's just a matter of knowing how much sugar to add to balance its tartness and choosing flavor partners that enhance its elusive sweet edge. When the very first stalks of rhubarb show up at the market in early spring, I like to use it in classic desserts that everyone loves, from pies to crumbles, muffins, and compotes.

Botanically, it's a vegetable

Although it's usually treated as a fruit and used mainly in desserts, rhubarb is technically a vegetable. The edible parts are the fleshy celery-like stalks. If you grow your own, be aware that the green leaves are poisonous if eaten and need to be removed.

When shopping for rhubarb, look for firm, crisp, unblemished stalks with a bright, intense color. I prefer thinner stalks, as larger ones tend to be overly stringy and tough. Wrap the stalks tightly in plastic and refrigerate them. They should stay crisp for up to five days.

You can also freeze sliced or diced rhubarb in plastic bags for up to six months. Frozen rhubarb tends to release more liquid and doesn't hold its shape as well as fresh rhubarb, so use it where texture is not essential, as in the muffins on p. 63.

To prep rhubarb for cooking, trim off the ends and any leaves still attached. Peel the fibrous exterior only if it's very tough. Cut rhubarb as you would celery, into slices or small dice, depending on the recipe.

In the kitchen, it's more like a fruit

The simplest way to cook rhubarb is to simmer it in a little liquid with sugar and other flavorings, as I do in the compote at right. You can also bake with rhubarb by adding it to cake or muffin batters, just as you would blueberries and other fruits.

In sweet preparations, rhubarb needs a good amount of sugar to balance its tartness. Cooking helps offset its natural astringency but also causes it to release a surprising amount of liquid. In compotes or sauces, where a juicy consistency is desirable, this is a boon. But if you're making a filling for a pie or crumble, you need to add a thickener, such as cornstarch or tapioca, to prevent it from being too loose.

My favorite rhubarb desserts are simple and revolve around everyday pantry ingredients. I make a Strawberry-Rhubarb Pie that's as easy as pie gets and all comfort. Sour cream adds richness to my Cinnamon Rhubarb Muffins, but it's the juice released by the rhubarb that makes them so tender and moist that you can still serve them the next day. A generous amount of oatmeal streusel tops my Rhubarb Brown Sugar Crumble, providing a crunchy contrast to the tart, juicy filling. And my Strawberry-Rhubarb Compote comes together in a heartbeat and is extremely versatile. I spoon it over buttermilk cheesecake, ice cream, or a silky panna cotta. To tell you the truth, it even makes a delicious spread for a cold pork loin sandwich.

Grow your own

To have your own supply of rhubarb, plant roots in early spring (for sources, see p. 78); seeds take much longer to become established. It's best to wait until the second year after planting to harvest, as the stalks usually aren't thick and robust enough the first year. Rhubarb is a forgiving plant that can withstand a considerable amount of neglect. In fact, you might want to plant it in a spot where you won't mind seeing it every year, as it will come back again and again.

Greatest Hits

A juicy pie

A tender muffin

A zesty crumble

A zippy compote

Strawberry-Rhubarb Compote with Vanilla & Cardamom
Yields about 4½ cups.

Cardamom gives this compote an alluring flavor. It's excellent spooned over ice cream, cheesecake, or panna cotta, and even as a spread for a pork sandwich. It will keep, covered and refrigerated, for up to 4 days.

4 cups ½-inch-thick sliced rhubarb (about 1¼ lb.)
½ cup granulated sugar; more to taste
6 Tbs. fresh orange juice; more to taste
3 Tbs. honey
¼ tsp. plus ⅛ tsp. ground cardamom
¼ tsp. kosher salt
1 small vanilla bean
3 cups hulled and thickly sliced strawberries (about 2 pints)

Combine the rhubarb, sugar, orange juice, honey, all the cardamom, and salt in a heavy-bottomed stainless steel 3-qt. saucepan. With a paring knife, slit open the vanilla bean lengthwise, scrape out the seeds with the back of the knife, and add the seeds and the scraped pod to the saucepan.

Bring to a simmer over medium-low heat, stirring often. Simmer until the rhubarb releases its juice and becomes tender but still retains its shape, 5 to 6 minutes. Add the strawberries and simmer until they start to soften and the rhubarb breaks down slightly, 1 to 3 minutes.

Pour the mixture into a bowl. Make an ice bath by filling a larger bowl with ice and water. Chill the compote over the ice bath at room temperature, stirring occasionally, until completely cool, 10 to 15 minutes. Discard the vanilla pod. Taste the compote and add more sugar and orange juice, if needed.

Strawberry-Rhubarb Pie

Serves eight.

Don't worry if the crust cracks slightly during baking; it only adds to the homemade look of the pie.

FOR THE CRUST:

12 oz. (2⅔ cups) unbleached all-purpose flour; more for rolling

2½ tsp. granulated sugar

¾ tsp. kosher salt

4 oz. (8 Tbs.) cold unsalted butter, cut into small pieces

4 oz. (½ cup plus 1 Tbs.) cold vegetable shortening, cut into small pieces

FOR THE FILLING:

4 cups ½-inch-thick sliced rhubarb (about 1¼ lb.)

1 lb. strawberries, hulled and sliced ½ inch thick (about 2½ cups)

1½ cups plus 2 Tbs. granulated sugar

¼ cup plus 1½ Tbs. quick-cooking tapioca

2 Tbs. fresh orange juice

1 tsp. finely grated orange zest

½ tsp. ground cinnamon

¼ tsp. ground clove

¼ tsp. ground allspice

¼ tsp. kosher salt

2 Tbs. cold butter, cut into small pieces

FOR THE GLAZE:

1 large egg yolk

Make the crust: In a food processor, combine the flour, sugar, and salt, and pulse to combine. Add the butter and shortening and pulse until the mixture resembles coarse meal, about 1 minute. Transfer the mixture to a large bowl.

Fill a measuring cup with ½ cup very cold water. While tossing and stirring the flour mixture with a fork, add the water 1 Tbs. at a time until the dough just begins to come together in small clumps and holds together when you pinch a little between your fingers (you may need only ¼ cup of water).

Transfer the dough to a clean work surface and gather it together with your hands. Lightly knead the dough once or twice, divide it in half, and shape the halves into disks. Wrap the disks separately in plastic and refrigerate for at least 1 hour or up to 2 days.

Prepare the filling: Position a rack in the center of the oven and heat the oven to 375°F. In a large mixing bowl, combine the rhubarb, strawberries, sugar, all the tapioca, orange juice, zest, cinnamon, clove, allspice, and salt. Toss gently to mix well, and then let sit for at least 10 minutes and up to 30 minutes (while you roll out the bottom crust).

Assemble the pie: If the dough was refrigerated for several hours or overnight, let it sit at room temperature until pliable, about 20 minutes. On a lightly floured surface, roll out one of the dough disks into a ⅛-inch-thick circle, 12 to 13 inches in diameter, and transfer it to a 9-inch Pyrex pie plate. Pour the filling into the pie shell and dot the top with the cold butter. In a small bowl, beat the egg yolk with 1 tsp. water. Brush the edges of the pie shell with some of the egg glaze.

Roll out the second dough disk as above and set it over the fruit filling to form a top crust. Press the edges of the dough together to seal the crust, trim the overhang to ½ inch, and fold it under. Flute or crimp the dough all around. Brush the top crust with the remaining egg glaze (you won't need all of it). Cut four 1- to 1½-inch-long steam vents in the top crust.

Set the pie on a foil-lined rimmed baking sheet and bake until the pastry is golden brown and the fruit juices bubble thickly out of the pie, 70 to 80 minutes. Transfer to a rack and let cool completely before serving, about 4 hours.

What pairs well with rhubarb?

Spring strawberries and rhubarb are a classic combination, but other sweet fruits such as peaches, apples, and pears make wonderful partners, too. Accent flavors like vanilla, caramel, cinnamon, ginger, orange juice, and orange zest as well as brown sugar make a nice complement, showing off rhubarb's bright personality. Nuts provide great textural contrast.

Cinnamon-Rhubarb Muffins

Yields 12 medium muffins.

These muffins are best when freshly baked, but they're still good the second day. Just reheat them in a 350°F oven for 3 to 4 minutes to refresh them.

FOR THE MUFFINS:
- **9 oz. (2 cups) all-purpose flour**
- **¾ cup granulated sugar**
- **2½ tsp. baking powder**
- **1 tsp. ground cinnamon**
- **½ tsp. baking soda**
- **½ tsp. kosher salt**
- **1 cup sour cream**
- **4 oz. (8 Tbs.) unsalted butter, melted and cooled slightly**
- **2 large eggs**
- **1 tsp. pure vanilla extract**
- **1½ cups ¼-inch-diced rhubarb (7¼ oz.)**

FOR THE TOPPING:
- **3 Tbs. granulated sugar**
- **½ tsp. ground cinnamon**

Position a rack in the center of the oven and heat the oven to 400°F. Line a 12-cup muffin tin with paper or foil baking cups.

Make the muffin batter: In a large mixing bowl, combine the flour, sugar, baking powder, cinnamon, baking soda, and salt and whisk to blend.

In a medium bowl, whisk together the sour cream, melted butter, eggs, and vanilla until smooth. Lightly stir the sour cream mixture into the dry ingredients with a spatula until the batter just comes together; do not overmix. Gently stir in the diced rhubarb. The batter will be thick.

Divide the batter among the muffin cups, using the back of a spoon or a small spatula to settle the batter into the cups. The batter should mound a bit higher than the tops of the cups.

Make the topping: In a small bowl, combine the sugar and cinnamon and mix well. Sprinkle a generous ½ tsp. of the cinnamon-sugar mixture over each muffin.

Bake the muffins until they're golden brown, spring back most of the way when gently pressed, and a pick inserted in the center comes out clean, 18 to 22 minutes. Transfer to a rack and let the muffins cool in the pan for

5 to 10 minutes. Carefully lift the muffins out of the pan—if necessary, loosen them with the tip of a paring knife—and let them cool somewhat. Serve warm.

Rhubarb Brown Sugar Crumble

Serves six to eight.

Vanilla ice cream is a natural with this homey favorite.

- **1 Tbs. unsalted butter, softened at room temperature**

FOR THE TOPPING:
- **4½ oz. (1 cup) all-purpose flour**
- **1 cup lightly packed light brown sugar**
- **½ cup old-fashioned oats**
- **½ tsp. ground cinnamon**
- **¼ tsp. kosher salt**
- **4 oz. (8 Tbs.) cold unsalted butter, cut into small pieces**

FOR THE FILLING:
- **7 cups ⅓-inch-thick sliced rhubarb (about 2 lb.)**
- **1 cup lightly packed light brown sugar**
- **¼ cup cornstarch**
- **1 Tbs. fresh lemon juice**
- **2 tsp. finely grated lemon zest (from 1 medium lemon, using a rasp-style grater)**
- **¼ tsp. kosher salt**

Position a rack in the center of the oven and heat the oven to 350°F. Grease an 8x8-inch Pyrex baking dish with the softened butter.

Make the topping: In a food processor, combine the flour, brown sugar, oats, cinnamon, and salt and pulse several times to combine. Add the cold butter and pulse until the mixture has the texture of coarse meal and clumps together when squeezed lightly, about 1 minute.

Make the filling: Combine the rhubarb, brown sugar, cornstarch, lemon juice, lemon zest, and salt in a large bowl and stir with a spatula until evenly mixed. Transfer the rhubarb mixture to the baking pan, and sprinkle the topping evenly over the fruit; the pan will be very full, but the crumble will settle as it bakes.

Bake until the topping is lightly browned, the rhubarb is tender (probe in the center with a skewer to check), and the juices are bubbling thickly around the edges, 45 to 60 minutes. Transfer to a rack to cool to warm or room temperature and to allow the juices to thicken, at least 1 hour.

Karen Barker is the pastry chef and co-owner of the award-winning Magnolia Grill restaurant in Durham, North Carolina. ◆

Knife Sharpeners
Find the One That's Right for You

BY ADAM RIED

When it comes to sharpeners, choices abound. We'll help you sort through the options—from simple stones to high-tech electric machines—to find your best match.

As a cook, I like to think my kitchen ducks are in a row. Recipe reviewed? Check. Ingredients prepped? Always. Work space organized and tidy? Of course. Knives sharp? Um... well... OK, I'll confess: Knife sharpening usually falls by the wayside. But I'm not alone. When I was preparing for this article, I borrowed dozens of knives from fellow cooks, and judging from the condition of those blades, it seems that lots of other cooks are lax about sharpening their knives, too.

That's a pity, because the merits of a sharp knife become apparent the moment you swipe through an onion with one. It's pure pleasure. A sharp knife cuts easily and precisely, requiring little more pressure than the knife's own weight to do the job.

By the end of this project, I was used to working with truly sharp knives. From now on, that's how I'll be keeping mine, and I hope to help you put aside your qualms and make knife sharpening part of your routine, too. Of course, that means you'll need a knife sharpener—the question is, which one?

Different sharpeners for different people

Making sense of every available model (there are scores on the market) and explaining all the technicalities about each one would require volumes. But introducing you to many of the types of sharpeners so you know what your options are—well, that much this article can do. From there, you can ask yourself some questions: How much time are you willing to invest in learning to use the tool? And how much time are you willing to spend sharpening? How much money can you spend? Then you can shop around, talk to experts at cutlery or kitchenwares shops, and ultimately find a specific model you like.

Photos: Scott Phillips; illustrations, Steve Hunter

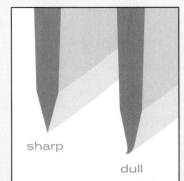

To get the lay of the land, I picked the brains of several experts on the subject of knife sharpeners. And then the *Fine Cooking* staff and I spent some time using 14 sharpeners in five general categories.

Our lineup included sharpening stones, a variety of manually operated sharpeners in several designs, and electric machines. Some of the devices were costly; others, cheap. Some were surprisingly easy to use; others had a steeper learning curve, requiring dexterity, coordination, or patience. But overall, we were pleasantly surprised to find most of the sharpeners fairly easy to use and effective. By the end of our research, we felt confident that transforming a blade from dull to sharp is much easier than we had imagined.

So rest assured, somewhere among these choices, you'll find a sharpener that's well suited to you. But before you start to explore your options, it's worthwhile to learn a thing or two about knife edges and how sharpeners in general work.

Understanding edges and angles

To form a knife's cutting edge, the metal on one or both sides of the blade is ground at an angle, called a bevel. Some blades have two bevels at slightly different angles; these are called double beveled.

Many popular American and European kitchen knives have roughly 20-degree bevels on both sides of the blade (see illustration at right). Some traditional Asian knives, however, have a different edge design, with a bevel on just one side of the blade, or bevels of a narrower angle, closer to 15 degrees than 20. A knowledgeable retailer should be able to explain the edge geometry of your knife

The blunt truth about dulling. The cutting edge of a blade is very fine, thin, straight, and therefore, sharp. Contact with hard surfaces, such as bone, or alas, your cutting board, causes that thin edge to roll over, as shown above. This makes a knife feel dull.

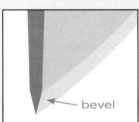

What's a bevel? The cutting edge of a knife is ground at an angle, or beveled. On most kitchen knives, the angle is about 20 degrees. This is the angle you want to maintain when you're sharpening.

A steel is not a sharpener

Knife experts may debate the technicalities of sharpening, but there's accord on one point: Regular maintenance of the edge can slow down, though not prevent, dulling. The tool that professionals and home cooks alike use to maintain the edges of their knives is often called, in a confusing misnomer, a "sharpening steel." But a sharpening steel doesn't technically sharpen; rather, it hones, straightening microscopic serrations along the cutting edge of the blade. True sharpening removes metal from the blade to re-create that fine, thin edge. Most steels won't remove much, if any, metal.

The surface of a steel may be smooth, finely grooved, or covered with super-fine diamond abrasive, but regardless of the finish, steels are meant to do one thing—hone. A steel can also help straighten microscopic curls in the cutting edge, provided they are not too severe. If you have a good sharp knife, steeling it once or twice a week will extend the length of time it stays sharp, but if your knife is already dull, don't expect a steel to sharpen it.

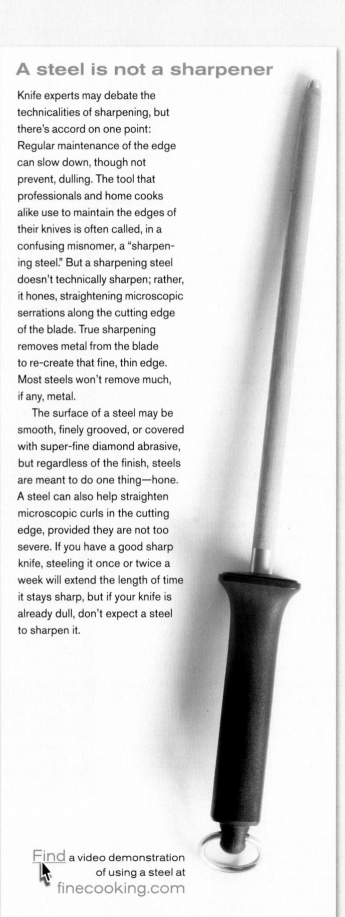

Find a video demonstration of using a steel at finecooking.com

and how to tailor the sharpening process to accommodate it.

How a sharpener restores an edge

Knife sharpeners work by stripping away metal to form new bevels, ideally at an angle that closely matches the original. But you don't need to obsess over getting the angle exactly right. For most kitchen knives, consistency trumps precision, says David Marks, a professional knife sharpener and owner of Stoddard's, a Boston cutlery store and sharpening service: "As long as you keep the same angle throughout the process, it doesn't matter if you're off by a couple of degrees from the original angle." Since consistency is key, many knife sharpeners incorporate some means of setting the angle for you.

To renew a dull edge, sharpeners use abrasives. By running the knife against the abrasive, you can strip away metal and restore the edge. Different sharpeners use different abrasives: diamond, ceramic, tungsten carbide, natural stone, and manufactured stone, to name a few. These abrasives can range from coarse to fine: 220 grit, for example, is coarse, while 1,000 grit is fine. (The higher the grit number, the finer the abrasive.) Coarse abrasives efficiently strip away metal but rough up the cutting edge. To smooth the edge, many sharpeners also include a fine abrasive.

Let's take a look at your options

Our observations about the types of sharpeners on the following pages are based heavily on our experience using them. Why? Because if a sharpener is a pain to use, then it's going to stay in the drawer where it will be of minimal benefit to our knives. We tried the sharpeners with a variety of knives—all stainless steel—including paring, slicing, boning, utility, and chef's knives of various lengths; most were tragically dull when we started. We didn't try serrated, ceramic, or other specialty knives.

For sources for the sharpeners shown here, see Where to Buy It, p. 78.

Is it sharp?

If your knife effortlessly glides into a tomato with no pressure or pushing, you know it's sharp.

How often should you hone and sharpen?

Many professional chefs hone or "steel" their knives before every cooking session. In an ideal world, you would do the same. In reality, though, steeling daily or even weekly can help. So hone whenever it crosses your mind—even the casual use of a steel will extend the life of an edge.

Actually sharpening the knife is another story. How often to sharpen depends on how you care for and use your knives. If you cook a lot, steel less often than you should, and really enjoy a sharp knife, you will probably need to sharpen two or three times a year. You'll know it's time to sharpen when honing doesn't restore the edge as it once did. Keep in mind that while you can hone as often as you'd like, you shouldn't sharpen too often. Eventually, sharpening begins to wear away the blade. As you remove metal, you move up the blade toward the spine, and the blade becomes thicker, making it more difficult to get a good edge.

Option #1

Sharpening stones

The stone is arguably the oldest, most venerated sharpening tool. There's a variety to choose among: natural, manufactured, ceramic, and diamond (see sidebar, opposite). And stones come in different grits (often in kits with two or three grits, or as a single reversible stone with different grits on each side); you generally have to use at least two, coarse and then fine, to sharpen properly. Prices depend on size, material, and number of grits in the kit and range from $5 to more than $100.

We tried large (8-inch) and small (5-inch) stones, including a ceramic stone used with water, and two diamond stones, one used with water and the other used dry. And we followed the manufacturer's directions for the recommended motion (pushing, pulling, circular stroke, start from the tip, start from the heel). Generally, the directions were easy to follow.

What the experts say David Marks, the expert knife sharpener at Stoddard's, applauds anyone who wants to learn to use a stone. "There's something nice about the ritual," he says, "and you can really customize your edge." Marks also points out that nothing you do with a stone is irreversible. If you're worried that you've done something wrong, just get some help and try again to correct any minor mistakes you may have made.

Chef Deepak Kaul, at the restaurant Rendezvous in Central Square in Cambridge, Massachusetts, says that sharpening on a stone reinforces the "intimate connection" between him and his knives.

Our experience A stone requires patience, concentration, and time. At first, we found stones challenging, but with practice we started getting good results. The hardest part is judging and maintaining the angle. (We worked without angle guides, but some stones come with them, or you can purchase guides separately.) Some of our testers also found it difficult to switch the blade from side to side and to sharpen evenly along the length of the blade. Most of us found larger stones easier to use than smaller ones.

That said, if you stick with the process, you may eventually find yourself in the "stone zone"—when the motion feels natural and your hands almost effortlessly set the blade at an acceptable angle.

Pros You can get precise control over the sharpening angle; appeals to the artisan in us; shape and size allow for easy storage.

Cons Requires practice to do well; initially challenging to set and maintain angle (though you can buy angle guides); time consuming; water and especially oil stones can be messy.

Is it right for you?

If you're hurried or harried, this probably isn't the choice for you. But if you're a knife enthusiast or have a bit of the artisan in your soul, using a stone can be a satisfying tactile and mental experience.

Stone materials

There are numerous specific types of sharpening stones, but most fall under two broad categories: natural or manufactured. **Natural stones** are usually quarried and can be quite expensive. **Manufactured stones** are constructed from a variety of materials. Some common options are India stones, ceramic stones, and diamond stones.

Whether natural or manufactured, all stones come in various grades, densities, and grits, and they therefore remove metal at different rates. A knowledgeable retailer can help you choose one that's right for you.

Wet or dry?

Sharpening stones can be used wet or dry. When you sharpen a knife, it sheds particles of metal. The advantage of wetting a stone with oil or water during use is that the lubricant will remove the particles, which otherwise might clog the stone's surface and reduce its effectiveness and longevity. The disadvantage is that it's messier than using the stone dry.

Find a video demonstration of using a sharpening stone at finecooking.com

Pull-over sharpeners

These inexpensive, basic sharpeners have a tungsten-carbide abrasive set into a plastic handgrip. To use, hold the knife steady on a work surface with the blade facing up and, holding the sharpener in your other hand, run it along the length of the blade. Easy.

What the experts say These are easy to use, but Bob Kufahl, of Lansky Sharpeners, says tungsten carbide is an aggressive abrasive that can leave the cutting edge more "ragged" than he likes; to smooth the edge, he recommends following up with a fine-grit sharpener.

Our experience We looked at several models with very similar designs and tried the $9 unit shown below. It got the job done, but some of us worried that we might slip and cut ourselves on the upward-facing blade. That said, no one got hurt, so perhaps we worried needlessly.

Pros The sharpening angle is set so you don't have to worry about it when you sharpen; very quick; very simple; very cheap; pretty effective.

Cons Feels dangerous to some; doesn't create a polished edge.

Is it right for you?

If you're looking for a super-simple, super-quick sharpening option, and you don't mind the finish being a bit rough, this could be the ticket. You can't beat the price.

Pull-through sharpeners

Most sharpeners in this category have guides to set the sharpening angle. To use them, you hold the sharpener steady on a work surface while you draw the blade through the slots.

Some are single-stage sharpeners, with one kind of abrasive; others have multiple stages so you can aggressively sharpen and then refine the edge. The types of abrasives vary widely, as do the prices, from about $10 to $90. We tried five models, priced in the low to middle range.

What the experts say In terms of design, these sharpeners vary wildly, so most experts were reluctant to discuss them as a general category. One knife retailer did mention, however, that he finds these devices better suited to maintaining a reasonably sharp edge than to restoring a very dull one, since they are generally less aggressive than an electric sharpener and don't let you adjust the angle the way a stone does.

Our experience "Is that all there is to it?" was the common sentiment; however, many testers did say that they needed to concentrate on the pressure and position of the blade in the angle guides. With some exceptions, testers were more impressed with the ease of use than with the results.

Pros Fast and easy to use; small and easy to store; some models include a fine-grit stage to "finish" the edge, which can also be used for edge maintenance in place of a steel.

Cons Some testers found the blades' motion through the slots to be rough and unpleasant; effectiveness varied widely among models.

Is it right for you?

If you want a quick sharpening solution or maintenance device, consider a pull-through sharpener. Design and effectiveness vary widely, so consult a trusted retailer for advice.

V-stick sharpeners

You can find several models of these sharpeners on the market, with varying angles, number of sticks, abrasives, and prices (from about $10 to $50). To use, set the sticks into the base at the desired angles, hold the blade perpendicular to the work surface, and draw the blade down the length of the stick while pulling from the heel to the tip. Alternate sticks to cover both sides of the blade. We tried a $12 version with ceramic rods (above), as well as a $30 version with diamond-coated rods (shown on p. 64).

What the experts say Howard Korn, cutlery expert and owner of KnifeCenter .com, likes these systems because they're compact, simple to use, and the clever design lets you vary the sharpening angle.

Our experience We were impressed by how effectively these sharpened. And one tester was very enthusiastic, exclaiming, "I would use this all the time." Some testers noted that it took concentration to control the knife movement.

Pros Compact and easy to store; low tech; very effective; design helps you set your knife at the correct angle yet leaves you in control.

Cons Requires concentration to maintain correct knife position through the entire stroke.

Is it right for you?

If you'd like to get involved in the sharpening process but don't want to devote the time that stones require, here's your sharpener. As one user put it, "There's a Zen quality to the motion and the sound. I like that."

Option #5

Electric sharpeners

Electric sharpeners are similar to some pull-throughs—you pull the knife through several stages of abrasives, ranging from coarse to fine—but they add a motor to the equation for more aggressive metal removal. The angle is set for you, and in each stage there are two slots, one for sharpening each side of the cutting edge. The abrasives are generally diamond or ceramic. Prices range from about $40 to $400. We worked with a mid-priced, three-stage model with diamond abrasives that cost about $130.

What the experts say Electric sharpeners have their fans and their detractors. Everyone we consulted said that the machines are simple to use and effective—KnifeCenter.com's Howard Korn describes them as "easy and straightforward"—yet nearly every expert shared a couple of concerns:

• The coarser stages can be aggressive, so you run the risk of wearing down your knives prematurely if you overuse the coarse stage, apply too much pressure, or use too many strokes. The machines can be fine when used carefully, but their high-speed motors can remove a lot of steel. So be careful with timing as you draw the knife through the slot to make sure all areas of the blade get even contact.

• The machines can present a problem for knives with bolsters (the wider portion of the blade just before the handle) that are too thick to fit through the slots. After repeated use, a notch can develop near the heel of the blade, where grinding stops because the bolster won't fit.

Our experience Our testers' reactions ran the gamut from "fantastic!" to "easy to use, but the grinding sound really freaks me out." Everyone agreed that the machine noticeably improved even the dullest blades. Because the machine seemed so self-explanatory, some testers dove right in without consulting the directions, and therefore timed their strokes incorrectly or used the most aggressive stage needlessly; both can cause the edge to wear down unevenly over time.

Pros Fast; clean; very simple; effective when used carefully; removes all the angle guesswork by setting and maintaining it for you; let's you hone blades (by using the fine-grit stage) or truly sharpen them (by using the coarse stage).

Cons Loud, high-pitched grinding noise during use; could be too aggressive if used without reading the directions; with extended use, might damage knives with thick bolsters; expensive.

Is it right for you?

If you want very sharp knives at all times and don't want to work too hard at getting them that way, an electric sharpener is your tool, indisputably quicker and easier than stones and many manual systems, and more convenient than sending knives off to a professional sharpening service. If you choose an electric sharpener, don't just dive in—invest time up front and learn how to use the machine properly.

Professional sharpening services

Consult the yellow pages or the Internet to find a professional sharpening service in your area. You might also inquire at cookware and cutlery shops or at good hardware stores. Or if you're willing to pack up your knives, you can send them off to be sharpened. Many professional services charge about $1 per inch of blade, while others may have set prices, such as $3 for paring knives, or $8 for 8- to 10-inch chef's knives; serrated blades or very badly damaged knives may cost extra.

What the experts say Before you entrust a sharpener with your knives, ask questions and start developing a relationship. Look for a reputable, experienced knife sharpener who will inform you about his equipment and methods (see "Finding a pro," at right).

Our experience What's not to love? Once you know and trust your sharpener, simply drop off a dull knife, wait a couple of days, and pick up a sharp one. The most exertion you'll experience is pulling out your wallet.

Pros As easy and fully hands-off a sharpening method as you can come by; minimizes the chances of premature blade wear if done properly.

Cons You have to spend a couple of days without your knives while they are out being sharpened; can be costly over time.

Knife care 101

When it comes to knife use, care, and storage, a modicum of TLC can help prevent damage and preserve sharpness.

1 Avoid outright abuse such as hacking through bones or frozen foods.

2 Choose a relatively soft cutting board, like wood—preferably end-grain butcher block—or polyethylene plastic.

3 Store knives on a magnetic strip or in a block. Avoid knocking the cutting edge against other surfaces.

4 Use a bench scraper, not your knife, to scoop up chopped foods from the cutting board.

5 Wash knives by hand.

Is it right for you?

If you're a hands-off type who would rather call a professional than attempt a project yourself, wrap up those knives and send them out.

Finding a pro

It's not a good idea to turn over your knives to just anyone who offers sharpening services. Ask around for recommendations: your friends, a cook at your favorite restaurant, or a local cutlery retailer. Or post an inquiry for "reputable knife sharpener" on your favorite cooking-related blog, Web site, or e-group.

When you find a likely candidate, ask a few questions:

1) Do they use stones or machines to sharpen? The use of a stone suggests the person might be a real knife enthusiast.

2) If they use a machine, is it fully automated, or does it require a human attendant? The latter may be preferable, because knives can easily be oversharpened on a sharpening wheel.

3) Do they sharpen all knives the same way, or can they adjust their methods for different blades?

4) Can they duplicate the factory edge? Sharpen serrated or specialty knives? Correct damaged blades without removing too much metal?

5) Will they show you a knife they have sharpened? If so, take a careful look. Does the edge appear to be evenly sharp from the heel to the tip? For knives with bolsters, the cutting edge and the bottom edge of the bolster should be flush. There should be no evidence of a notch near the bolster.

Last, take a look around. You'll be better off at a store that sells quality cutlery than at a place that sharpens lawnmower blades.

Adam Ried is a freelance food writer with 10 years of equipment-testing experience under his belt and the proud owner of a collection of newly sharp knives (which he intends to keep that way). ◆

Edible signs of spring

People who live in wintry climates look forward to spring for obvious reasons, but for food-lovers, there's an added bonus: fresh ramps, morels, and fiddleheads. These spring treats are at their prime for only a few weeks a year, and they can be difficult to find because they're not grown commercially, at least not extensively. Instead, they're usually gathered in the wild by foragers.

You may have some of these delicacies growing in your own neck of the woods, but before you forage, be sure you know exactly what you're looking for—there are inedible look-alikes out there, and some are poisonous. To be on the safe side, bring along a seasoned forager to help with identification, or forget foraging altogether and just buy them from a reputable source. If you can't find them locally, see Where to Buy It on p. 78 for a mail-order source.

—Allison Ehri, test kitchen associate

Morels

These conical honeycombed mushrooms are treasured for their rich, intense flavor and are delicious when simply sautéed in butter. Enjoy them on their own, or top roasted or grilled meats and poultry with them.

Store fresh morels in a brown paper bag in the fridge and use them within a few days. They're often home to little critters, so before cooking, cut them in half and examine their chambers, flicking out any unwanted guests. Unless they're extremely dirty, don't wash morels; just brush them off with a damp towel.

Fiddlehead ferns

Fiddlehead fern fronds emerge from the soil coiled into tight pinwheels and are edible only before they begin to unfurl into their mature form. They have a grassy-earthy flavor that's tasty in a mushroom ragoût or a mixed vegetable sauté.

Store fiddleheads in the refrigerator in a zip-top plastic bag lined with moist paper towels for three to five days. To clean them, rub off the brown chaff from the outside (some stores may have done this for you) and wash them thoroughly in cold water. Before cooking, trim the ends and then tame their slight bitterness by blanching briefly in salted boiling water before sautéing or grilling them.

Ramps

Part of the onion family, ramps taste like a cross between spring onions and scallions, with an earthy-garlicky undertone. Also known as wild leeks, they're good in everything from scrambled eggs to stir-fries. Try baking fish on a bed of ramp leaves, and sauté the ramp stems and bulbs to pile on top.

Store freshly picked, uncleaned ramps at room temperature with the bulbs submerged in water, like a bouquet. Use before the leaves start to wilt, in about three days.

To clean ramps, rinse, remove the roots, and peel off the paper-thin coating over the bulb. Once you've done this, the entire ramp is edible. To store cleaned ramps, wrap them loosely in moist paper towels, seal in a zip-top bag, and store in the refrigerator; they'll keep for about five days.

Spring delicacies	72
Slicing onions	73
Fresh chervil	73
Cornish game hens	73
Pomegranate products	74
Leftovers: 2 ways with glazed ham	76

BY JENNIFER ARMENTROUT

Slicing onions
Direction makes a difference

Lengthwise

When you slice lengthwise, you're cutting with the grain of the onion. These slices hold up better during cooking, so they're a good choice for dishes like pot roast or French onion soup, where you want to see pretty strips of onion after a long cooking time.

Crosswise

When you cut the onion crosswise (across the grain), you get slices that cook down and lose their shape quickly. This cut is ideal if you want melt-in-your-mouth onions for a marmalade or for topping a steak sandwich

—A. E.

Getting to know fresh chervil

Chervil is one of the herb choices for flavoring the New Potatoes with Butter, Shallots & Chervil on p. 42. This delicate herb has a very mild flavor that hints of anise, pepper, and parsley. It's frequently used in French cooking, most notably as part of the fresh herb blend known as fines herbes (equal parts chervil, chive, tarragon, and parsley). Fines herbes are used in many egg dishes and to finish sauces. Fresh chervil's flavor is fleeting, so add it at the very end of cooking. If your market doesn't stock fresh chervil, request it. Dried chervil is no substitute, as it tends to have little flavor.

What are Cornish game hens?

You might be surprised to learn that the tasty little birds known as Rock Cornish game hens (or just Cornish game hens) aren't actually game birds. Marketers added the word "game" to the name to make them sound more exotic. In reality, they're 5- to 6-week-old farm-raised chickens, and since they can be either male or female, they may not always be hens, either.

A cross between a Cornish chicken and a White Plymouth Rock chicken, Rock Cornish game hens range in size from 1½ to 2 pounds, and they have a milder flavor than that of mature chickens.

Roasting, grilling, and broiling are the best cooking methods for Cornish hens. You can roast them whole or cut them into halves for grilling, broiling, and speedier roasting, as in the recipe for Roasted Cornish Game Hens with Wildflower Honey & Orange on p. 42. —A. E.

Add a splash of
pomegranate to your cooking

Judging by the number of prepared foods flavored with pomegranate these days—salad dressings, vodka, ice cream, even chewing gum and lollipops—this once exotic fruit has become a hot ingredient. Here are a few products you can use to add the sweet-tart flavor of pomegranates to your own cooking. (For mail-order sources for the harder-to-find products, see Where to Buy It, p. 78.)

grenadine
(pomegranate syrup)

Primarily used in drinks like Shirley Temples, tequila sunrises, and pink lemonade, true grenadine is pomegranate juice sweetened with sugar syrup. It's also good in sorbets and ice creams. The name comes from the French word for pomegranate: *grenade*. When purchasing grenadine, check the label to make sure you're getting the real deal; some brands are artificially flavored or contain fruits other than pomegranate.

Pomegranate
molasses

Also known as pomegranate paste, concentrate, or essence, this boiled-down pomegranate juice is a key ingredient in many Middle Eastern cuisines. The name "molasses" reflects its thick, syrupy texture and not its flavor, which is nothing like sugarcane molasses. Its intensely sour yet sweet flavor can be a revelation. It especially complements walnuts, as in the dip recipe at right. It partners well with poultry and lamb, too—try adding a touch to your favorite chicken or meat marinade. Or just drizzle it over vanilla ice cream.

Unless you live near a Middle Eastern market, you'll probably have to mail order pomegranate molasses (see p. 78). It's well worth seeking out, though, and once opened, it lasts almost indefinitely in the refrigerator.

Pomegranate
vinegar

There are several vinegars flavored with pomegranate, and some are better than others. We like to use Cuisine Perel's pomegranate balsamic vinegar in marinades for red meat, and O's pomegranate Champagne vinegar is lovely in vinaigrettes.

Pomegranate
juice

Introduced in the United States in 2002 by California grower POM Wonderful, pomegranate juice gets the credit for starting the pomegranate craze. Look for it in the produce section, where you'll see other brands as well. We especially like the fruity tang it adds to pan sauces, as in the recipe for Lamb Chops with Pomegranate Red-Wine Sauce in *Fine Cooking* #76 (visit www.finecooking.com for the recipe). And on p. 44 of this issue, author Bruce Aidells pairs pomegranate juice with cherry preserves to make a glaze for baked ham.

Roasted Red Pepper & Walnut Dip with Pomegranate Molasses

Yields about 1¼ cups; may be doubled.

Variations of this dip, called *muhammara*, are made throughout the eastern Mediterranean region. Walnuts and pomegranate molasses are constants, but the types and numbers of chiles can vary. Some versions are fiery, but this one, based on a recipe by Paula Wolfert, is not very spicy at all, and it always gets rave reviews. Serve it with pita chips.

¾ cup walnuts, lightly toasted
2 large red bell peppers (about 1¼ lb.), roasted, peeled, and seeded
2 small mildly hot red chiles (such as Fresno or red jalapeño), roasted, peeled, and seeded
¼ cup crumbled stone-ground wheat crackers, such as Nabisco Wheatsworth
1 Tbs. fresh lemon juice; more as needed
1 Tbs. pomegranate molasses; more as needed
½ tsp. ground cumin (preferably from freshly toasted and ground cumin seed); more for garnish
½ tsp. kosher salt; more as needed
½ tsp. granulated sugar
1 Tbs. extra-virgin olive oil; more for garnish
1 Tbs. pine nuts, toasted (optional)

Finely chop the walnuts in a food processor. Blot the peppers and chiles dry with paper towels. Add the peppers, chiles, crackers, lemon juice, pomegranate molasses, cumin, salt, and sugar to the food processor. Process until mostly smooth. With the machine on, slowly pour the oil down the feed tube. Taste and add more lemon juice, pomegranate molasses, or salt, as needed.

You can serve the dip right away, but it's better if allowed to mellow in the refrigerator overnight. (The dip keeps for about 1 week.) Return to room temperature before serving, garnished with a drizzle of oil, a generous pinch of cumin, and the pine nuts, if using.

leftovers:

Two ways to use up a baked ham, deliciously

If you make one of the glazed baked hams on pp. 44 to 47, you're probably going to have leftovers. Fortunately, there are tons of things you can do with ham beyond a ham sandwich. Here are a couple of southern-inspired ideas, one for ham and one for the ham bone.

Ham Bone Collards

Serves six.

A ham bone is the perfect flavoring for a big pot of collards, known in the South as a "mess of greens." If you don't have a ham bone, a smoked ham hock can stand in.

2 Tbs. vegetable oil
1 medium yellow onion, halved and thinly sliced lengthwise
½ tsp. cayenne
2½ cups homemade or low-salt chicken broth
1 meaty ham bone (from a baked ham, recipe p. 46)
1½ to 2 lb. collard greens (1 large or 2 medium bunches), stemmed, roughly cut into 3-inch pieces, and rinsed (8 packed cups)
2½ tsp. malt vinegar; more as needed
Kosher salt and freshly ground black pepper
Hot sauce to taste

In an 8-qt. pot, heat the oil over medium heat. Add the onion and cook, stirring frequently, until it begins to brown, 5 to 7 minutes. Reduce the heat to medium low and continue to cook until it's softened and golden brown, 3 to 5 minutes more. Stir in the cayenne and cook for about 30 seconds.

Add the broth, the ham bone, and ½ cup water. Pile on the collards, cover with the lid ajar, and bring to a simmer over medium-high heat. Reduce the heat to medium low and simmer, stirring occasionally, for 30 minutes. Remove the lid and continue to simmer until the greens are very tender, about 15 minutes more.

Take the pot off the heat. Put the ham bone on a cutting board, and cover the pot to keep the greens hot. When the ham bone is cool enough to handle, pull off and shred or dice any meat clinging to the bone. Stir the meat into the greens, along with the vinegar. Season with salt, pepper, and more vinegar to taste. Pass the hot sauce at the table so diners can spice up the greens to their own tastes.

Fried Ham with Redeye Gravy

Serves four.

To make this southern classic, you simply fry slices of ham and then deglaze the pan with coffee to make the redeye gravy. Usually it's made with fatty country ham, but the glazed baked hams from this issue tend to be leaner than country ham, so we've tweaked the recipe to make up for the missing fat. It may not be traditional, but it still makes a tasty and quick breakfast or weeknight supper.

2 Tbs. unsalted butter, softened
2 tsp. all-purpose flour
4 large or 8 small ¼-inch-thick slices leftover baked ham (from recipe, p. 46), glazed edges trimmed off
1 cup brewed coffee
1 tsp. light brown sugar
1 large sprig thyme (optional)

In a small bowl, combine 1 Tbs. of the butter with the flour. Stir with a spoon or knead with your fingertips until blended.

Heat the remaining 1 Tbs. butter in a large (preferably cast-iron) skillet over medium heat until melted and hot. Add as much of the ham as will fit without crowding and fry gently until hot and browned in spots, 1 to 2 minutes per side. Move to a platter and repeat with the remaining ham, moving it to the platter as well.

Pour the coffee into the skillet and scrape the bottom of the pan with a wooden spoon to release the drippings. Add ⅓ cup water and the sugar and thyme, if using. Simmer vigorously for about 1 minute. Whisk in the butter and flour mixture until melted, and then continue to simmer until the sauce has thickened to a light gravy consistency and the raw flour flavor has cooked off, 3 to 5 minutes. Serve alongside the ham. ◆

where to buy it

Spring Menu, *p. 38*

If you can't find wild mushrooms, you can order them online at Earthy.com (800-367-4709). To top her Vanilla Ice Cream with Espresso-Caramel Sauce, Tasha DeSerio recommends chocolate-covered espresso beans from Peets Coffee. An 8-ounce pack sells for $6 at Peets.com (800-999-2132).

Enjoying Wine, *p. 20*

To find Greek wines, Tim Gaiser recommends using the search engine Wine-searcher.com, which can locate practically any wine and provide you with retailer contact information as well as pricing.

Glazed Ham, *p. 44*

The highest grade of ham (labeled simply "ham") is available at Whole Foods Markets. Vande Rose Farms' bone-in half-ham (which Bruce Aidells helped develop) is produced without antibiotics or hormones from the Duroc heritage pork breed; it's $85 for a 7- to 8-pound ham at PreferredMeats.com (800-397-6328). Jones Dairy Farm's old-fashioned bone-in hickory-smoked half-ham is available at JonesDairyFarm.com (800-563-1004) for $90 for a 10- to 14-pound ham (average 12 pounds). Harrington's of Vermont (www.harringtonham.com; 802-434-4444) makes traditional bone-in hams by smoking them over corncobs and maple; a 6½-pound half-ham starts at $54.95.

Flaky Biscuits, *p. 48*

You'll need 2- or 2¾-inch biscuit cutters to make Peter Reinhart's flaky biscuits. You can buy a set of four round biscuit cutters, ranging in size from 1½ to 2¾ inches, at The Baker's Catalogue (KingArthurFlour .com; 800-827-6836); the price is $10.95.

Carrots, *p. 51*

Dan Barber encourages buying carrots at a local farmers' market. To find one near you, visit LocalHarvest.org or www.ams .usda.gov/farmersmarkets. If you can't find baby carrots locally, you can mail order them from Melissas .com (800-588-0151). French virgin untoasted walnut oil is available at Lepicerie .com (866-350-7575), where an 8½-ounce bottle sells for $14.75.

Shrimp Sautés, *p. 56*

Good-quality Spanish chorizo is available at specialty food stores or online at Tienda .com (800-710-4304) and Zingermans.com (888-636-8162). Canned chipotles en adobo are available in the Mexican food section of many supermarkets or online at MexGrocer.com (877-463-9476), where a 7-ounce can is $2.25.

Rhubarb, *p. 60*

To make Karen Barker's muffins you'll need a 12-cup muffin pan and paper or foil baking cups. Both are available at KingArthurFlour.com (800-827-6836), where a Chicago Metallic muffin pan is $18.95, and a pack of 120 paper muffin cups is $4.95. Madagascar vanilla beans (3 for $6.29) are available at Penzeys.com (800-741-7787). And if you'd like to grow your own rhubarb, you can find rhubarb roots at most garden centers; or you can order them online from seed catalogs like JohnnySeeds .com (877-564-6697).

From Our Test Kitchen, *p. 72*

Look for pomegranate molasses, pomegranate syrup, and pomegranate Champagne vinegar in specialty stores or buy them online at Kalustyans.com (800-352-3451). Pomegranate molasses starts at $6.99, pomegranate syrup is $12.99 for a 750ml bottle, and O Basics pomegranate Champagne vinegar is $12.99 for a 200ml bottle. You'll find 6½-ounce bottles of Cuisine Perel pomegranate balsamic vinegar at GourmetCountry.com for $9.25. Morels, fiddleheads, and ramps are available in well-stocked grocery stores, when in season. If you can't find them, you can mail order them at Earthy.com (800-367-4709).

(continued on p. 80)

Photos: Scott Phillips

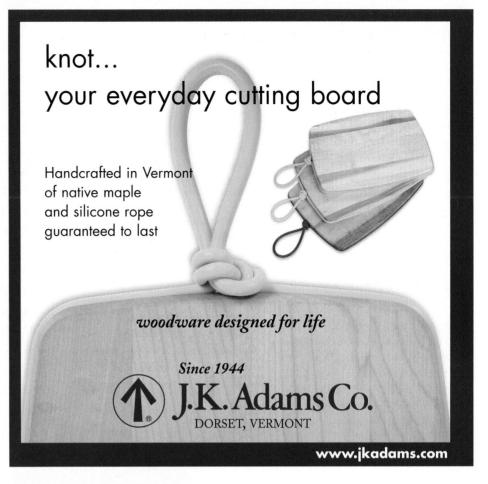
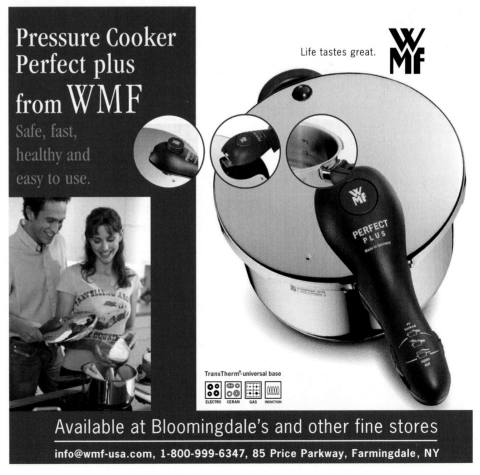

Knife Sharpeners, *p.64*

Here's where to find the knife sharpeners pictured in this article.

Page 64: The Diamond Vee knife sharpener by DMT is available at KnifeCenter.com (800-338-6799) for $28.95.

Page 67: The Norton IM200 Professional Sharpening System is $77.95 at SharpeningSupplies .com (800-351-8234).

Page 68: The Deluxe Easy Grip tungsten carbide knife sharpener by Lansky Sharpeners is $6.71 at KnifePro.com.

Page 69: Left, from top: The Knife-Life two-stage knife sharpener by Wüsthof is available at KitchenKapers.com (800-455-5567) for $19.99.; the Ozitech Diamond Fingers knife sharpener by Furi is also available at

KitchenKapers.com (800-455-5567) for $29.99; the Twinsharp Select knife sharpener by Zwilling J.A. Henckels is $39.95 at Amazon.com. Right: the Standard Turn-Box Crock Stick sharpener by Lansky Sharpeners is $13.93 at PremiumKnives .com (877-541-4076).

Page 70: The EdgeSelect 120 by Chef's Choice is $139.99 at ChefsCatalog.com (800-884-2433).

There are several professional knife sharpening services available by mail. We tried The Holley Manufacturing Company and were happy with the results. For information, visit HolleyKnives.com.

Knife sharpener manufacturers

Some of the major manufacturers of knife sharpeners are listed below; visit their Web sites to learn about specific products:

Anolon.com

AccuSharp.com

BokerUSA.com

ChefsChoice.com

ChicagoCutlery.com

DMTSharp.com

EdgeProInc.com

ErgoChef.com

Farberware.com

FDick.com

Fiskars.com

FuriTechnics.com

GlobalKnives.US

KershawKnives.com

LamsonSharp.com

Lansky.com

MasterGradeKnife Sharpener.com

Messermeister.com

NortonStones.com

RazorEdgeSystems.com

www.RussellHobbs.com

SmithAbrasives.com

Spyderco.com

WaringProducts.com

www.Wusthof.com

Zwilling.com
(for Zwilling J.A. Henckels) ◆

cook's market

Ingredients

Bulk Foods *p.80* Offering a wide selection of spices, nuts, dried fruits, and other ingredients.
www.bulkfoods.com

The Catfish Institute *p.15* Always fresh, healthy, mild and flaky, U.S. Farm-Raised Catfish suits any recipe.
www.catfishinstitute.com

Citadelle-Shady Maple Farm *p.21* Founded in 1925, Citadelle is a farmer's cooperative boasting over 2000 members that believe in producing unique, premium maple products to serve consumers who are passionate about quality brands and packaging. Citadelle brands include: Shady Maple Farm, Maple Gold and Camp.

Colavita USA *p.37* Extra-virgin olive oil unmatched for flavor and freshness, vinegars, pastas, and sauces. Colavita's authentic Italian products are available at food stores everywhere. Visit our website.
www.colavita.com

Magic Seasoning Blends *p.35* Chef Paul Prudhomme's all-natural magic seasoning blends, sauces and marinades, pepper sauce, smoked meats, cookbooks, gift packs, sweet potato pecan pie, and much more!
800-457-2857
www.chefpaul.com

Rafal Spice Co. *p.81* All the spices, herbs, teas, coffees, and food specialties you'll need for all your special and every-day recipes! Order now and be prepared.
800-228-4276
www.rafalspicecompany.com

San Francisco Herb Co. *p.81* We are an importer offering a complete line of quality spices and culinary herbs sold by the pound. Buy direct and save. Since 1973.
800-227-4530
www.sfherb.com

Sugarcraft, Inc. *p.81* Sugarcraft Inc., Hamilton, Ohio. We carry baking, cake decorating, candy, and cookie supplies, etc. We import specialty items!
www.sugarcraft.com

Kitchen Design & Tableware

The Bowl Mill *p.35* One-piece hardwood bowls made on 19th-century lathes in Vermont, ranging from 8" to 20" in diameter featuring maple, yellow birch, and cherry.
800-828-1005
www.bowlmill.com

Plum Pudding Kitchen *p.25* Your online source for "irresistibly Italian" Vietri dinnerware, flatware, glassware, and much more. Let us help you set a special table!
888-940-7586
www.plumpuddingkitchen.com

Rangecraft Manufacturing, Co. *p.77* Specializing in the manufacture of a wide selection of high-quality metal range hoods, including copper, brass, and stainless steel. Quality finishes include matte, brushed, antique, mirror, or hammered.
877-RCHOODS
www.rangecraft.com

Replacements, Ltd. *p.80* World's largest inventory: old and new china, crystal, sterling, silver-plate, and stainless. All manufacturers, fine and casual. 10 million pieces, 200,000 patterns. Buy and sell.
800-REPLACE
www.replacements.com

Totally Bamboo *p.81* Featuring over 150 products, Totally Bamboo is the industry pioneer of bamboo cutting boards and kitchen design. Order all of our fine products directly online!
www.totallybamboo.com

Zak Designs *p.7* Zak Designs is the source for your kitchen. Incorporating great designs with color and function, Zak creates modern and innovative tabletop and kitchen prep collections.
www.laprimashops.com

Kitchen Tools & Utensils

Bella Copper *p.81* The world's leading heat diffuser/defroster plate provides superior heat conduction for more even cooking and faster defrosting. Available in solid copper or pure silver. A gourmet kitchen essential.
805-215-3241
www.bellacopper.com

Component Design Northwest *p.25* CDN offers more than 60 different cooking thermometers and timers for the casual or gourmet chef. Find CDN products at gourmet specialty stores or online.
800-338-5594
www.cdn-timeandtemp.com

Diamond Machining Technology *p.13* For professional knife sharpening results, rely on DMT®, your premiere source for diamond and unbreakable ceramic sharpeners. Made in the USA for over thirty years.
www.dmtsharp.com

Gel Pro *p.25* STAND IN COMFORT! Let's Gel was started with one simple goal, to make the time you spend standing in your kitchen more comfortable.
866-GEL-MATS
www.letsgel.com

Grill Friends *p.7* Since 1957, Harold Import Company has been a leading supplier of kitchenware products to the specialty retail trade, offering almost 3000 items. Our products are available in thousands of stores worldwide. What can HIC offer your business?
www.girlsatthegrill.com

J.K. Adams Company *p.79* J.K. Adams, has been the premiere Vermont manufacturer of handcrafted, heirloom-quality, woodware for the kitchen and table since 1944.
www.jkadams.com

Kerekes *p.80* Your complete online source for professional chef's tools, cookware, bakeware, and cake decorating supplies used by top chefs at the finest restaurants and kitchens.
www.bakedeco.com

Mix-In-Guide *p.81* The best way to get ingredients into your mixer bowl. Easy on. Easy off. Stainless steel ingredient chute for stand mixers.
www.mix-in-guide.com

WMF of America *p.79* WMF is the only brand that can make cooking, dining, and drinking an event. WMF is the singular choice.
www.wmf-usa.com

Schools, Travel & Organizations

Cook Street *p.11* Cook Street is a contemporary culinary and wine center dedicated to professional and recreational education with a focus on French and Italian regional cuisine.
www.cookstreet.com

Culinary Business Academy *p.77* Extensive and comprehensive personal chef business knowledge and training from the world's recognized leader in the personal chef industry. Nobody offers what we offer.
800-747-2433
www.culinarybusiness.com

Greenwood CVB *p.7* Indulge at our fabulous restaurants and take a cooking class at our famous cooking school. Treat yourself at our luxurious new spa and explore quaint shops, fascinating museums and historic tours.
800-748-9064
www.greenwoodms.org

L'Academie de Cuisine *p.21* L'Academie de Cuisine has been the premier culinary school outside Washington, DC, for the last 28 years. It offers full-time programs of study in the culinary and pastry arts.
800-664-2433
www.lacademie.com

La Villa Bonita *p.25* La Villa Bonita offers a delicious immersion in the culinary joys of Mexico, with its culinary vacation packages in a 16th-century mansion in Cuernavaca.
800-505-3084
www.lavillabonita.com

Le Cordon Bleu *p.35* Master the culinary arts. Earn the Grand Diplome in approximately nine months. Three- to five-week intensive courses and online hospitality programs are also available.
800-457-2433
www.cordonbleu.edu

Luxury Destinations, Ltd. *p.11* Luxury culinary vacations for the gourmet traveller at out fabulous villas in France, Italy and Morocco. Memorable food, wine and culture in beautiful surroundings.
www.rhodeschoolofcuisine.com

Mediterranean Kitchens *p.11* Culture Through Cuisine. Hands on cooking classes in Sicily, Morocco & Israel. Visits to market, artisanal food producers and wineries. Guided historical and cultural walking tours.
www.mediterranean-kitchens.com

The Sagamore *p.11* Situated on a 72-acre island in Lake George, NY, The Sagamore offers elegant accommodations, dining, golf and a spa getaway.
www.thesagamore.com

To Grandmother's House We Go *p.11* Culinary and cultural tours to Sicily, Italy and Oaxaca, Mexico. Small groups. Sign up now for October 7-15, 2007 Sicily tour.
www.tograndmothershousewego.com

Zingerman's Bakehouse *p.11* Long known for their full flavored, traditionally-made breads, and pastries, Zingerman's Bakehouse now offers BAKE!; a hands-on teaching bakery in Ann Arbor.
www.zingermansbakehouse.com

nutrition**information**

Recipe	Page	Calories		Protein	Carb	Fats (g)				Chol.	Sodium	Fiber	Notes
		total	from fat	(g)	(g)	total	sat	mono	poly	(mg)	(mg)	(g)	
Letters	10												
Rhubarb & Dried-Cherry Chutney		60	0	0	14	0	0	0	0	0	35	1	based on 2 Tbs.
In Season	18												
Pan-Seared Artichokes w/ Sherry Vinegar & Thyme		160	80	5	18	9	1.5	7	1	0	250	9	based on 6 servings
Spring Menu	38												
Wild Mushroom Toasts		610	140	17	102	16	8	6	1	30	1300	4	based on 6 servings
Garden Lettuces w/ Garlic Chapons		210	130	3	17	15	2	10	2	0	320	2	based on 6 servings
Roasted Cornish Game Hens w/ Honey & Orange		330	210	22	4	23	9	9	3.5	140	490	0	based on 8 servings
New Potatoes w/ Butter, Shallots & Chervil		250	100	3	34	12	7	3	0.5	30	480	3	based on 6 servings
Roasted Asparagus w/ Lemon & Olive Oil		100	80	2	3	9	1.5	7	1	0	150	1	based on 6 servings
Vanilla Ice Cream w/ Espresso-Caramel Sauce		590	270	6	77	30	19	7	1	100	120	1	based on 6 servings
Glazed Ham	44												
Glazed Ham w/ Cherry-Pomegranate Glaze & Sauce		320	100	34	18	11	4	5	1	110	135	0	based on 14 servings
Glazed Ham w/ Tangerine Marmalade Glaze & Sauce		300	100	34	15	11	4	5	1	110	85	0	based on 14 servings
Glazed Ham w/ Maple, Tea & Cardamom Glaze & Sauce		300	100	34	14	11	4	5	1	110	80	0	based on 14 servings
Biscuits	48												
Flaky Buttermilk Biscuits		100	45	2	10	5	3.5	1.5	0	15	125	0	based on 18 biscuits
Caramelized Onion Biscuits		110	50	2	14	6	3.5	1.5	0.5	15	125	1	based on 18 biscuits
Cheese Biscuits		150	80	5	10	9	6	2.5	0	25	200	0	based on 18 biscuits
Fresh Herb Biscuits		100	45	2	10	5	3.5	1.5	0	15	125	0	based on 18 biscuits
Carrots	51												
Maple Pan-Roasted Baby Carrots		80	30	1	13	3.5	0.5	2.5	0	0	210	3	based on 4 servings
Carrot Salad w/ Walnut Oil & Honey		290	180	5	27	20	2	3.5	14	0	210	5	based on 6 servings
Velvety Carrot Soup w/ Ginger		130	45	2	19	5	0.5	3.5	0.5	0	200	3	based on 8 servings
Baby Carrots Pickled in Champagne & Sherry Vinegars		10	0	0	2	0	0	0	0	0	15	0	based on 1 carrot
Shrimp Sautés	56												
Hot Garlicky Shrimp w/ Asparagus & Lemon		380	250	27	6	29	4	20	3.5	225	560	1	based on 3 servings
Shrimp w/ Fennel, Tomato & Pernod Sauce		400	170	27	22	20	3	13	2.5	225	960	3	based on 3 servings
Spicy Seared Chipotle Shrimp w/ Zucchini & Chorizo		500	310	36	12	34	8	20	4	255	1240	2	based on 3 servings
Rhubarb	60												
Cinnamon-Rhubarb Muffins		250	110	4	32	12	7	2.5	0	70	200	1	based on 12 muffins
Rhubarb Brown Sugar Crumble		430	120	3	77	14	8	3.5	0.5	35	100	3	based on 8 servings
Strawberry-Rhubarb Compote w/ Vanilla & Cardamom		50	0	1	13	0	0	0	0	0	15	1	based on ¼ cup
Strawberry-Rhubarb Pie		630	260	6	87	29	13	9	4.5	50	150	4	based on 8 servings
Test Kitchen	72												
Roasted Red Pepper Dip w/ Pomegranate Molasses		60	40	1	5	4.5	0.5	1	2.5	0	60	1	based on 1 Tbs.
Ham Bone Collards		170	80	15	10	9	2	4	2.5	30	210	4	based on 6 servings
Fried Ham w/ Redeye Gravy		300	150	34	2	16	7	7	1	120	75	0	based on 4 servings
Quick & Delicious	84a												
Broiled Lamb Skewers w/ Arugula & Lemon Vinaigrette		650	490	32	8	55	15	32	4.5	115	760	1	based on 2 servings
Penne w/ Asparagus, Olives & Parmigiano Breadcrumbs		470	210	11	53	24	3.5	16	3	0	790	4	based on 4 servings
Pan-Fried Gnocchi w/ Bacon, Onions & Peas		470	290	9	35	33	10	18	3	40	880	3	based on 3 servings
Garlic & Herb Fried Eggs on Toasts w/ Prosciutto Crisps		410	210	15	35	23	4.5	14	2.5	220	880	2	based on 3 servings
Ginger Chicken Soup		160	80	16	4	10	2	4	3	45	700	0	based on 4 servings
Sear-Roasted Halibut w/ Roasted Red Pepper Purée		550	410	27	5	46	7	30	4.5	85	610	0	based on 4 servings
Smoky Black Bean & Cheddar Burrito w/ Baby Spinach		510	190	19	63	21	6	10	4	15	1020	9	based on 4 servings
Back Cover													
Bourbon-Chocolate Mousse		300	210	6	21	23	13	3	0	40	140	2	based on 4 servings

The nutritional analyses have been calculated by a registered dietitian at Nutritional Solutions in Melville, New York. When a recipe gives a choice of ingredients, the first choice is the one used in the calculations. Optional ingredients and those listed without a specific quantity are not included. When a range of ingredient amounts or servings is given, the smaller amount or portion is used. When the quantities of salt and pepper aren't specified, the analysis is based on ¼ teaspoon salt and ⅛ teaspoon pepper per serving for entrées, and ⅛ teaspoon salt and 1⁄16 teaspoon pepper per serving for side dishes.

BY MARYELLEN DRISCOLL

Bridging the seasons

Spring can sometimes feel as if it's in the throes of an identity crisis. It's that in-between-winter-and-summer thing: warm one day, chilly the next. For a cook, this is actually good. Tender peas, scallions, spinach, and arugula begin to flourish, yet comfort foods still have their place. The recipes in this collection are all inspired by winter's hearty fare, but they're lighter, brighter renditions, freshened up with spring ingredients: Chicken soup gets pep from an infusion of ginger and an aromatic cilantro-scallion purée. Rustic penne pasta with olives, Parmigiano, and breadcrumbs gets tossed with crisp-tender sautéed asparagus. Fresh baby spinach and a burst of tangy lime find their way into a smoky black-bean burrito. All these dishes are easy to prepare on week-nights, and their combinations of flavors are perfectly suited to this season.

Sear-Roasted Halibut with Roasted Red Pepper Purée

Serves four.

2½ oz. roasted red pepper (about ½ large jarred roasted pepper)
2 Tbs. sherry vinegar
½ tsp. honey
1 medium clove garlic, peeled
¼ cup plus 2 Tbs. extra-virgin olive oil
Kosher salt and freshly ground black pepper
4 6- to 7-oz. center cut, skin-on halibut fillets
1 Tbs. thinly sliced fresh chives or chopped marjoram

Position a rack in the center of the oven and heat the oven to 375°F.

In a blender, combine the red pepper, vinegar, and honey. Turn the blender on, let it run for a few seconds, and then drop the garlic through the feed hole. With the blender still running, slowly pour in the ¼ cup oil and process until the mixture is smooth, about 1 minute, stopping to scrape down the lid and sides of the blender jar as necessary. Season with salt and pepper to taste.

Set the fish skin side down on a plate and season with salt and pepper. Heat the remaining 2 Tbs. oil in a large ovenproof skillet (preferably cast iron) over medium-high heat until shimmering. Put the fish skin side up in the skillet, and cook until well browned, 3 to 5 minutes. Flip the fish, turn off the heat, and transfer the pan to the oven. Roast until the fish is flaky, moist, and cooked through (use the tip of a paring knife to check), 5 to 7 minutes.

Transfer the fish to dinner plates, spoon about 1 Tbs. purée onto or around each piece, sprinkle with the chives or marjoram, and serve immediately with the remaining purée on the side.

Tip: Any leftover purée will keep, refrigerated, for up to 5 days. You can serve it with chicken or pork, or thin the purée with additional olive oil to make a dressing for steamed, sautéed, or roasted asparagus or a salad of romaine hearts, red onion, and hard-boiled egg.

Garlic & Herb Fried Eggs on Toasts with Prosciutto Crisps

Serves three.

- 3 ¾-inch-thick slices rustic bread, such as sourdough boule or peasant bread
- 2 thin slices prosciutto, cut lengthwise into ½-inch-wide strips
- 3 Tbs. plus 1 tsp. extra-virgin olive oil
- 1½ tsp. minced fresh oregano
- 1 medium clove garlic, minced
- 3 large eggs
- Kosher salt and freshly ground black pepper
- Parmigiano-Reggiano, for shaving

Position a rack in the center of the oven and heat the broiler to high. Lay the bread slices and prosciutto strips on a foil-lined rimmed baking sheet and brush the bread on both sides with 2 Tbs. of the olive oil. Broil until the bread is golden brown on both sides and the prosciutto is lightly crisp, 2 to 4 minutes per side. Put the prosciutto strips in a small bowl (they'll continue to crisp as they cool), and set the bread slices on three plates.

Put the oregano in a small bowl. Heat 1 Tbs. of the oil in a 10-inch nonstick skillet over medium-low heat. Add the garlic to the pan and cook, stirring occasionally, until it's sizzling and fragrant but not browned, about 30 seconds. Scrape the garlic and oil into the bowl of oregano, stir to combine, and set aside.

Add the remaining 1 tsp. oil to the pan, swirling to evenly coat. Add the eggs and distribute the garlic-herb mixture evenly on top. Season with salt and pepper, cover, and cook until the yolks' edges have just begun to set, 2 to 3 minutes. (The eggs should cook gently, so lower the heat if needed.) Separate the eggs with the edge of the spatula, if necessary, and slide each egg onto a slice of the bread. Drizzle any remaining oil in the pan over the toasts, top with the prosciutto crisps, and use a vegetable peeler to shave a few strips of Parmigiano over the toasts.

Pan-Fried Gnocchi with Bacon, Onions, & Peas

Serves three.

- Kosher salt
- 1 lb. frozen gnocchi
- 3 oz. thick-cut bacon (about 3 slices), cut into ½-inch-wide pieces
- 4 Tbs. extra-virgin olive oil
- 2 medium-small yellow onions, thinly sliced (about 2 cups)
- ½ cup frozen peas
- 1 tsp. minced fresh thyme
- Freshly ground black pepper
- 2 Tbs. grated Parmigiano-Reggiano; more for serving

Bring a large saucepan of salted water to a boil. Cook the gnocchi according to package directions. Reserve ½ cup of the cooking water, and drain.

Meanwhile, in a large (preferably 12-inch) nonstick skillet, cook the bacon over medium heat until crispy on both sides, about 5 minutes. Transfer to a plate lined with paper towels and set aside. Pour off any fat from the skillet.

In the same skillet, heat 2 Tbs. of the oil over medium-high heat. Add the onions and cook until they begin to brown, 3 to 5 minutes.

Reduce the heat to medium and continue to cook, stirring occasionally, until the onions are limp and golden brown, 10 minutes more. Stir in the peas and thyme, season with salt and pepper to taste, and transfer to a small bowl.

Wipe the skillet clean with a paper towel, and heat the remaining 2 Tbs. oil over medium-high heat. Add the gnocchi and cook, tossing occasionally, until they're lightly brown, about 5 minutes. Gently stir in the onion mixture, bacon, and Parmigiano, along with enough of the reserved cooking water to moisten and coat the gnocchi, about 4 Tbs. Serve immediately, sprinkled with additional Parmigiano.

Tip: Gnocchi are Italian dumplings made of potatoes or flour (or both) and eggs. Look for them in the frozen foods section of the supermarket.

Maryellen Driscoll is Fine Cooking's *editor at large.* ◆

Penne with Asparagus, Olives & Parmigiano Breadcrumbs

Serves four.

Kosher salt
5 Tbs. extra-virgin olive oil; more for drizzling
1 cup coarse fresh white breadcrumbs (from about 4 slices of bread, crusts removed)
¼ cup finely grated Parmigiano-Reggiano
½ lb. penne rigate
1 lb. medium asparagus, woody ends snapped off, cut diagonally into 2-inch pieces
1 medium clove garlic, minced
½ cup coarsely chopped pitted Kalamata olives (about 20)
Finely grated zest of 1 medium lemon (about 1½ Tbs. loosely packed)
Freshly ground black pepper

Bring a large pot of well-salted water to a boil.

In a 12-inch skillet, heat 3 Tbs. of the oil over medium heat. Add the breadcrumbs and cook, stirring occasionally, until they're crispy and golden brown, about 5 minutes. Transfer to a medium bowl and stir in the Parmigiano and a pinch of salt. Wipe the skillet clean with a paper towel.

Cook the pasta in the boiling water until al dente.

Reserve a few tablespoons of the cooking water and drain the pasta.

Heat 1 Tbs. of the oil over medium-high heat in the skillet. Add the asparagus and cook, stirring frequently, until crisp-tender, about 4 minutes. Lower the heat to medium low and push the asparagus to the side. Add the remaining 1 Tbs. oil and the garlic and cook, gently mashing with the tip of a wooden spoon or spatula until fragrant, about 30 seconds. Toss the garlic with the asparagus. Remove from the heat.

Stir in the olives and lemon zest, and season with salt and pepper to taste. Add the pasta to the skillet, stirring to blend. Add enough reserved cooking water to slightly moisten, as needed, and drizzle with olive oil to enrich. Serve garnished with the breadcrumbs.

Tip: To save time, make the breadcrumbs ahead and store in a sealed container. Also, you can just snap rather than cut the asparagus into 2-inch pieces.

Smoky Black Bean & Cheddar Burrito with Baby Spinach

Serves four.

4 burrito-size (9- to 10-inch) flour tortillas
15 grape tomatoes, quartered lengthwise (from 1 pint)
2 Tbs. fresh lime juice; more as needed
¼ cup chopped fresh cilantro
Kosher salt
2 Tbs. extra-virgin olive oil
¼ cup raw pepitas (optional)
1 tsp. seeded and minced chipotle plus 1 tsp. adobo sauce (from a can of chipotles en adobo)
¾ tsp. ground cumin
1 19-oz. can black beans, drained and rinsed
½ cup grated sharp Cheddar
1½ oz. baby spinach (about 1½ cups)
¼ to ½ cup sour cream (optional)

Heat the oven to 250°F. Wrap the tortillas in aluminum foil and warm in the oven.

Meanwhile, in a small bowl toss the tomatoes with 1 Tbs. of the lime juice, about 1½ Tbs. of the cilantro, and a generous pinch of salt. Set aside.

If using the pepitas, heat 1 Tbs. of the olive oil and the pepitas in a 12-inch skillet over medium heat. Cook, stirring frequently, until they are puffed and some are golden brown,

1 to 2 minutes. Using a slotted spoon, transfer the pepitas to a plate lined with a paper towel. Sprinkle with a generous pinch of salt and toss.

Return the pan to medium heat. Add the remaining 1 Tbs. olive oil. (Or if not using pepitas, heat the 2 Tbs. oil over medium heat.) Add the chipotle, adobo sauce, and cumin. Stir to blend into the oil, and then add the beans and 2 Tbs. water to the pan, stirring to blend. Simmer until warmed through, about 2 minutes. Reduce heat to low. Mash about half of the beans with a fork. Stir in the cheddar and the remaining 2½ Tbs. cilantro and 1 Tbs. lime juice. Season to taste with salt. If the beans seem too thick, add a tablespoon or two of water to thin to a soft, spreadable consistency.

Working with one tortilla at a time, spread about ¼ of the beans along the bottom third of a tortilla. Top with ¼ of the spinach, and sprinkle with about ¼ of the tomatoes and pepitas (if using). If you like, add a little lime juice and sour cream on top. Fold the bottom edge over the filling, fold in the sides, and roll up the burrito.

Ginger Chicken Soup

Serves four as a light main course.

- **1 1-inch piece fresh ginger**
- **2 medium cloves garlic, unpeeled**
- **10 to 12 oz. boneless, skinless chicken thighs, trimmed of excess fat (about 3 medium)**
- **2 cups low-salt chicken broth**
- **1 Tbs. soy sauce**
- **2 tsp. fresh lemon juice**
- **¼ tsp. Asian chile paste, like sambal oelek or Sriracha**
- **¼ cup packed fresh cilantro**
- **2 Tbs. thinly sliced scallion (green tops only)**
- **Kosher salt**
- **1 Tbs. mild vegetable oil, like canola or safflower oil**
- **1 cup packed baby spinach (about 2 oz.)**

Peel the ginger and slice it into four ¼-inch coins. Using the flat side of a chef's knife or a meat pounder, smash the coins. Smash the garlic and remove the skin.

In a medium saucepan, combine the ginger, garlic, chicken, broth, soy sauce, lemon juice, chile paste, and 1 cup water. Bring to a boil over medium-high heat. Reduce the heat to low and gently simmer until the chicken is cooked through, about 10 minutes. Using a pair of tongs, transfer the chicken to a plate. Use a slotted spoon to remove the ginger and garlic and discard. Keep the broth warm.

Finely chop the cilantro and scallion. Put them in a mortar, add a pinch of salt and 2 tsp. of the oil, and pound and mash with the pestle (see tip). Once the mixture begins to blend, add the remaining teaspoon of oil. Continue to grind the pestle into the cilantro mixture until it is aromatic and has the consistency of a paste.

Once the chicken is cool, slice it thinly and portion it into four soup bowls. Return the broth to a simmer and season with salt to taste. Add the spinach to the broth and continue to simmer until it's wilted, 1 to 2 minutes more. Ladle the broth and spinach evenly over each portion of chicken and then top each with a dollop of the cilantro paste.

Tip: If you don't have a mortar and pestle, mince the scallions and cilantro, transfer to a small bowl to combine with the oil, and scrape the mixture back onto a cutting board. Position the blade of a chef's knife at a 30-degree angle to the board and repeatedly drag the blade over the cilantro mixture using a bit of pressure to mash it.

Broiled Lamb Skewers with Baby Arugula & Lemon Vinaigrette

Serves two.

- **2 Tbs. fresh lemon juice**
- **2 tsp. sour cream**
- **1 small clove garlic, minced**
- **Kosher salt**
- **¼ cup plus 1 Tbs. extra-virgin olive oil**
- **¾ lb. boneless lamb shoulder chops or lamb leg steaks, trimmed of extra fat and cut into 1-inch cubes (1½ cups)**
- **Coarsely ground black pepper**
- **4 oz. baby arugula (about 4 cups)**
- **½ cup very thinly sliced red onion (½ small)**
- **¼ cup crumbled feta or blue cheese (1 oz.)**

Position an oven rack 4 inches from the broiler element and heat the broiler to high. In a small bowl, combine the lemon juice, sour cream, garlic, and a pinch of salt. Slowly whisk in the ¼ cup olive oil.

In a medium bowl, combine the lamb with the 1 Tbs. olive oil, ½ tsp. salt, and ¼ tsp. pepper. Toss to coat evenly. Thread the lamb onto four small (8-inch) bamboo or metal skewers.

Put the skewers on a broiler pan and broil the lamb, flipping once, until browned on the outside but still pink inside (medium doneness), 2 to 4 minutes per side. Transfer the skewers to a small, shallow baking dish. Whisk the vinaigrette to recombine and pour 3 Tbs. over the skewers, turning to coat.

In a medium bowl, toss the arugula and onion with enough of the remaining vinaigrette to lightly coat (you may not need it all). Season with salt and pepper to taste. Pile the greens on two plates, top each salad with two lamb skewers, sprinkle with the cheese, and serve immediately.

Tip: If using bamboo skewers, soak them in water for 30 minutes before threading them.

A shortcut to sweetness & light

Chocolate mousse can turn any meal into a special occasion, and this simple version—made by folding whipped egg whites into a ganache—comes together so quickly that it can elevate even a weeknight dinner.

Bourbon-Chocolate Mousse
Yields 3 cups; serves four.

½ cup heavy cream
3 Tbs. confectioners' sugar
2 Tbs. bourbon
1 tsp. pure vanilla extract
4 oz. bittersweet chocolate, finely chopped (¾ cup)
4 large egg whites*, preferably at room temperature
Pinch table salt

Put 4 small (at least ¾ cup) individual serving bowls in the refrigerator.

Bring the heavy cream and sugar to a boil in a small saucepan and remove the pan from the heat (don't just turn off the burner). Stir in the bourbon and vanilla. Add the chocolate and let it sit for 5 minutes without stirring. Whisk the chocolate and cream until smooth and then transfer the ganache to a large bowl. Don't refrigerate.

In a medium bowl, beat the egg whites and the salt with a hand mixer on high speed just until they form stiff peaks when you lift the beaters.

With a rubber spatula, fold about one-quarter of the beaten whites into the ganache to lighten it. Then gently fold in the remaining whites, taking care not to deflate them. Divide the mousse among the chilled bowls and refrigerate for at least 30 minutes but preferably 1 hour and up to 24 hours.

Serving suggestion: Top the mousse with a dollop of whipped cream or crème fraîche and sprinkle with cocoa powder, if desired. Garnish with fresh raspberries or strawberries.

*The egg whites in this recipe are not cooked, but we don't recommend using pasteurized egg whites, because they tend to separate after they're folded into the ganache.

Allison Ehri is Fine Cooking's *test kitchen associate and food stylist.* ◆

Keep an eye on the whites

Egg whites can go from perfectly stiff to lumpy in a matter of seconds, so as you get close, stop the mixer frequently to check on them. They're ready when the peaks stand up straight but still have visible air bubbles.

onus grilling guide: 10 crowd-pleasing recipes you'll use all summer

fine
Cooking

JULY 2007 NO. 86

FOR PEOPLE WHO LOVE TO COOK

ow to make
the best fruit cobblers

everything
n the grill:

picy chicken

flank steak
for twelve

shrimp
skewers

mini pizzas
bruschetta

plus:
beautiful
reen salads

outdoor
itchen ideas

w.finecooking.com

5 CAN $7.95

07

4470 56529 1

Retreat | **Your complete Viking outdoor kitchen.**

1-888-845-4641 or vikingrange.com

fine Cooking

JUNE/JULY 2007   ISSUE 86

36   40

RECIPE FOLDOUT

26a **Grilling for a Crowd**
Mix and match main courses, starters, and sides to feed up to 12

ON THE COVER

60 **Fruit Cobbler**

UP FRONT

6   Index

8   Menus

10   Letters

14   Contributors

16   Links

18   Q&A

20   In Season
   Poblanos

22   Enjoying Wine
   **Buying a
   mixed case**

24   Great Finds
   Pasta, updated

26   Equipment
   ❖ **Silicone steamer**
   ❖ **Digital timer**
   ❖ **Glass-door
      refrigerator**
   ❖ **Saucepan review**

32   Artisan Foods
   Wheat beers

34   Readers' Tips

22

24

26

20

34

The Taunton Press
Inspiration for hands-on living®

visit our web site: **www.finecooking.com**

43 46 52 54

FEATURES

36 Appetizers, Hot Off the Grill
Mini burgers, pizzettas, and skewers—choose one for a starter or make them all for a party
by Allison Ehri

40 Delicious Finishes for Grilled Fish
Follow these tips for perfectly grilled fish steaks, and serve them with one of four lively toppings
by Maria Helm Sinskey

43 Quick Pastas with a Kick
A little heat punches up the flavor of pastas made with summer favorites: corn, tomatoes, and zucchini
by Scott Conant

46 The Art of Making Green Salads
Focus on the greens and don't weigh them down
by Annie Wayte

52 Lemon Cheesecake, To Go
Bring these tart and creamy treats to your next picnic—they pack well, and everyone will love them
by Meg Suzuki

54 A Kitchen That Goes All Out
An outdoor kitchen in Vermont keeps everything within arm's reach—and the elements out
by Lisa Waddle

58 RESTAURANT FAVORITE
Chinese Chicken Salad
The best version of this popular salad has lots of crunchy texture and a boldly flavored dressing
by Barbara Lauterbach

60 COOKING WITHOUT RECIPES
Make a Memorable Fruit Cobbler
For this summertime favorite, all you need is a simple method and your choice of ripe fruit
by Abigail Johnson Dodge

RECIPE FOLDOUT

78a
Quick &
Delicious
Summer with a twist

64

IN THE BACK

64 From Our
Test Kitchen
❖ White balsamic
❖ Gravlax
❖ Storing salad greens
❖ Cookout leftovers
❖ Cleaning the grill

70 Food Science
Produce safety

72 Tasting Panel
Cannellini beans

73 Where To Buy It

78 Nutrition
Information

BACK COVER

Make It Tonight
Balsamic-Macerated Strawberries with Basil

70

72

index

◆ QUICK
　Under 45 minutes

◆ MAKE AHEAD
　Can be completely
　prepared ahead but
　may need reheating
　and a garnish to serve

◆ MOSTLY MAKE AHEAD
　Can be partially
　prepared ahead but will
　need a few finishing
　touches before serving

◆ VEGETARIAN
　May contain eggs
　and dairy ingredients

21 *Quesadillas with Roasted Poblanos & Onions*

58 *Chinese Chicken Salad*

recipes

Cover Recipe

◆◆ Raspberry-peach cobbler with cornmeal biscuits, 61

Appetizers

◆◆ Bacon-Wrapped Stuffed Apricots, 39

◆◆◆ Farmers' Market Crudités with Buttermilk Herb Dip, 26a

◆ Gravlax, 66

◆ Grilled Bruschetta with Rosemary-White Bean Purée & Heirloom Tomatoes, 26a

◆◆ Mini Tuna Burgers with Mint-Caper Aïoli on Pita Triangles, 38

◆◆ Pancetta & Pineapple Skewers, 38

◆◆ Prosciutto-Wrapped Melon with Mint & White Balsamic Vinegar, 64

◆ Shrimp Skewers, 37

◆◆◆ Tomato & Olive Pizzettas with Fennel Seeds & Aged Goat Cheese, 39

Salads

◆◆◆ Arugula & Fennel Salad with Orange & Fennel Seed Dressing & Toasted Hazelnuts, 50

◆◆◆ Butter Lettuce with Poppy Seed & Tarragon Crème Fraîche Dressing, 48

◆ Chinese Chicken Salad, 58

◆◆ Chopped Tomato & Cucumber Salad with Mint & Feta, 26a

◆◆ Egg Salad with Smoked Salmon, Capers & Dill, 78a

◆ Grilled Southwestern Potato Salad, 26a

◆◆◆ Mâche with Spicy Melon & Pink-Peppercorn Dressing, 51

◆◆◆ Mixed Green Salad with Red-Wine & Dijon Vinaigrette, 47

◆◆◆ Orzo & Grilled Vegetable Salad with Feta, Olives & Oregano, 78a

◆ Warm Pasta Salad with Grilled Tomatoes, Zucchini & Pecorino, 26a

Soups

◆ Tomatillo Gazpacho, 78a

Pasta

◆◆ Orecchiette with Caramelized Onions, Green Beans, Fresh Corn & Jalapeño, 45

◆◆◆ Orzo & Grilled Vegetable Salad with Feta, Olives & Oregano, 78a

◆ Rigatoni with Summer Squash, Spicy Sausage & Goat Cheese, 44

◆ Spaghetti with Spicy Shrimp, Cherry Tomatoes & Herbed Breadcrumbs, 44

◆ Warm Pasta Salad with Grilled Tomatoes, Zucchini & Pecorino, 26a

Chicken

◆ Chinese Chicken Salad, 58

◆ Grilled Thai Chicken Breasts with Herb-Lemongrass Crust, 26a

◆ Spicy Fried Chicken, 78a

Beef, Lamb & Pork

◆ Argentine Spice-Rubbed Flank Steak with Salsa Criolla, 26a

◆ Grilled Asian Pork Tenderloin with Peanut Sauce, 78a

　Grilled Herb-Crusted Leg of Lamb with Fresh Mint Sauce, 26a

◆ Steak & Eggs Rancheros, 68

Seafood

◆ Gravlax, 66

◆ Grilled Fish Steaks, 41

◆ Grilled Salmon Bundles with Saffron, Tomatoes & Olives, 78a

◆◆ Mini Tuna Burgers with Mint-Caper Aïoli on Pita Triangles, 38

◆ Shrimp Skewers, 37

Eggs

◆◆ Egg Salad with Smoked Salmon, Capers & Dill, 78a

◆ Steak & Eggs Rancheros, 68

Sandwiches & Quesadillas

◆◆ Grilled Portabella Sandwiches with Tomatoes, Mozzarella & Basil, 78a

◆◆ Quesadillas with Roasted Poblanos & Onions (*Rajas*), 21

Side Dishes

◆◆ Chopped Tomato & Cucumber Salad with Mint & Feta, 26a

◆◆◆ Grilled Asparagus & Onions with Balsamic Vinegar & Blue Cheese, 26a

◆◆ Grilled Corn on the Cob with Thyme & Roasted Red Pepper Butter, 26a

◆ Grilled Southwestern Potato Salad, 26a

◆◆◆ Orzo & Grilled Vegetable Salad with Feta, Olives & Oregano, 78a

◆ Warm Pasta Salad with Grilled Tomatoes, Zucchini & Pecorino, 26a

Condiments & Sauces

◆◆◆ Lemon, Dill & Cucumber Sauce, 42

◆◆◆ Pimentón Vinaigrette, 37

◆◆◆ Sea Salt, Chile & Lime Butter, 42

◆◆◆ Sun-Dried Tomato, Olive & Caper Relish, 42

◆◆◆ Tarragon-Scented Mayonnaise with Cornichons & Capers, 42

Desserts

◆◆◆ Balsamic-Macerated Strawberries with Basil, back cover

◆◆ Lemon Cheesecake Squares, 53

◆◆◆ Lemon Curd, 53

◆◆ Plum cobbler with almonds, lemon zest & ginger, 61

◆◆ Raspberry-peach cobbler with cornmeal biscuits, 61

◆◆ Triple berry cobbler with pecans & cinnamon, 61

Photos: Scott Phillips

Take It All Outside

If you're like us, once warmer weather hits, you're out the screen door, determined to spend as much time in the open air as the season allows. Squeezing the most out of longer days and sultry nights is infinitely easier thanks to the grill, which encourages outdoor cooking and eating. But easy doesn't have to mean boring. In this issue you'll find some uncomplicated ideas to help you break out of your barbecuing rut, whether by grilling some appetizers (p. 36) or making a vibrant topping for grilled fish (p. 40). And with the Fourth of July and other family gatherings coming up, take a look at our special pullout designed to make cooking for a crowd easier. Just be sure to check recipe yields: You may need to double or halve recipes, depending on your needs.

Summer Supper for Vegetable Lovers

You won't miss the meat in this satisfying meal, most of which can be made ahead.

Tomatillo Gazpacho, *p. 78a*

Grilled Portabella Sandwiches with Tomatoes, Mozzarella & Basil, *p. 78a*

Arugula & Fennel Salad with Orange & Fennel Dressing & Toasted Hazelnuts, *p. 50*

Triple Berry Cobbler with Pecans & Cinnamon, *p. 61*

To drink: A supple, fruity Pinot Noir that can be served slightly chilled, like the 2005 Meridian Pinot Noir, California, $12

Make-Ahead Picnic

All of these dishes pack well, and they can be made the day before.

Spicy Fried Chicken, *p. 78a*

Orzo & Grilled Vegetable Salad with Feta, Olives & Oregano, *p. 78a*

Lemon Cheesecake Squares, *p. 53*

To drink: A fruity Chenin Blanc like the 2005 Bogle Chenin Blanc, California, $10

Alfresco Dinner Party

You can make the dessert, the salad dressing, and the cucumber sauce earlier in the day. Fire up the grill for the pizzettas appetizer and then grill the fish.

Tomato & Olive Pizzettas with Fennel Seeds and Aged Goat Cheese, *p. 39*

Grilled Halibut with Lemon, Dill & Cucumber Sauce, *p. 42*

Mixed Green Salad with Red-Wine & Dijon Vinaigrette, *p. 47*

Plum Cobbler with Almonds, Lemon Zest & Ginger, *p. 61*

To drink: A zesty, citrusy Sauvignon Blanc like the 2006 Babich, Marlborough, $12

Quick Friday Night Dinner for Friends

The pork needs to marinate for only 10 minutes and then grills in less than 10. The rest of this dinner comes together quickly, too.

Grilled Asian Pork Tenderloin with Peanut Sauce, *p. 78a*

Mâche with Spicy Melon & Pink-Peppercorn Dressing, *p. 51*

Balsamic-Macerated Strawberries with Basil, *back cover*

To drink: A rich Shiraz blend like the Penfolds Bin 138 Grenache-Shiraz-Mourvèdre, Barossa Valley, $19

The Italian Original.

Inside Out

Last summer, we got into the habit of leaving the sliding door in our kitchen wide open all the time. It started out of laziness, as the slider is the preferred entrance and exit of our two large Labs, Gus and Scout, who always seem to be on the wrong side of it. Instead of ordering ourselves those cute doorman uniforms, we decided to give in and leave the door open. Our house sits high on a hill above a cove, so a nice breeze usually takes care of any flying critters that might wander in, at least before sunset.

This same door opens onto a small deck that connects to our terrace, or I should say, our summer living room. And we quickly discovered that leaving that door open was more than just convenient; it

brought about some good karma, creating a friendly flow of indoor-outdoor activity that lasted all season. Most evenings around 6, for example, my father-in-law would wander up from his house next door, walk inside, pour himself a drink, and then head back out to the terrace to sit under the shade of the umbrella. On Saturday mornings, our friend Neal would bicycle up the driveway, head inside to pour himself a cup of coffee, then join us (surrounded by newspapers) in an Adirondack chair. And when the summer invasion of cousins arrived, the shell-collectors could patter in, hands full, and wash off their treasures in the kitchen sink.

On nights when we were grilling for 20, I could tote my supplies and ingredients

in and out much more easily through that open door. More often than not we ate dinner outside, too, with folks vying for a spot on the terrace wall, sitting on a stone step, moving a plant aside to grab a stool, or just standing up, eating in shorts and flip-flops.

For us, keeping a door open helped enhance that relaxed feeling you get from cooking, eating, and living outdoors. I'm sure you have your own "open door," whether it's a special place, like a camp or a beach cottage that you visit every year, or a deck or screened porch you've added on or always loved. Maybe it's a ritual, like a regular Friday night front-porch gathering with your neighbors or even a little time spent every evening on the roof of your apartment building, as one of our Brooklyn-dwelling editors does.

Whatever you do, we hope that this issue of *Fine Cooking* will help you enjoy doing it. Since we know you love to cook, we've dedicated nearly this entire issue to outdoor cooking and living. We're especially excited about our "Grilling for a Crowd" pullout on p. 26a. All of the recipes serve 10 to 12 people, so all you need to do is pick and choose among them and you've got the makings for your next cookout. We also have a close-up look at a cook's outdoor dream kitchen (p. 54)—in Vermont, not California. And, of course, a lot of outdoor-friendly recipes, from grilled appetizers (p. 36), to fried chicken for a picnic (p. 78a).

Enjoy the summer, and don't forget to leave the door open once in a while.

—*Susie Middleton, editor*

Instead of ordering ourselves those cute doorman uniforms, we decided to give in and leave the door open for Gus and Scout, who always seem to be on the wrong side of it.

U.S. Farm-Raised Catfish _lettuce_ _tacos_ **with** _tomato_ _salad_.

VEGETABLE   NOUN   ADJECTIVE   NOUN

Always fresh, healthy, mild and flaky, U.S. Farm-Raised Catfish suits

any recipe. For some of my favorites, visit **catfishinstitute.com**

FOOD NETWORK CHEF _Cat Cora_

U.S. FARM-RAISED
Catfish™
YOU'RE GONNA LOVE IT.

So simple, even an adult can do it

We loved the article on crème brûlée in the February/March 2007 issue (*Fine Cooking* #84). My 10-year-old daughter watched a popular movie where one of the basketball players "confessed" that he makes it. So we set her and a friend loose. We wound up doubling the recipe, which took 12 eggs (counting the four that fell on the floor).

You're probably wondering if I really set my daughter free with a blow torch. Well, instead we used our broiler and kept the ramekins in for four minutes. The results were fantastic. Love your magazine.

—*Samuel J. Tobin, via email*

For people who cook, whether they like it or not

I have to laugh when I read the tagline under your *Fine Cooking* logo: For People Who Love to Cook. I *hate* cooking. I am a terrible cook. However, I love your magazine because you make me look good. I learn and understand the "hows" and "whys" of cooking from you. I hate wasting my time and money on other magazines, cookbooks, and food just to have a recipe turn out badly. I know, with complete confidence, that I can trust any recipe in your magazine to be excellent. Thanks!

—*Julie Bickler, via email*

Love those lamb shanks

Good as is, better doubled

Molly Stevens's recipe for Braised Lamb Shanks with Garlic & Vermouth (*Fine Cooking* #84) was phenomenal. Following the suggestion of braising a day or two ahead of serving them, I prepared three lamb shanks using the amount of sauce in the recipe and decided that while it was adequate, the next time I will at least double the amount of sauce. Garlic- and chive-mashed red-skinned potatoes and tender asparagus accompanied the lamb, for a meal I would be proud to serve to anyone.

—*Robert C. Oster, Hastings, Michigan*

Humming a little bistro tune

I got your February/March 2007 (*Fine Cooking* #84) issue in the middle of a cooking mania. I had just gotten a new Le Creuset 5.5-quart Dutch oven, and I dove into the bistro recipes (viewing them as British classics more than French ones) and the bok choy recipe (Braised Bok Choy with Sherry & Prosciutto). My poor husband had been working extra-long hours, but he got to come home to these dishes, and he is still humming over the lamb shanks.

He agreed that the bok choy is "companyable"—a classification I put in my recipe database. One thing on that recipe: It calls for kosher salt, but since it also calls for adding soy sauce, rice wine, and prosciutto, I couldn't imagine also adding salt. I'm really glad I didn't. It was superb, and the kosher salt would have sent it over the edge.

Also, for your recipes that call for honey, try using maple syrup. It's a wonderful substitute and keeps better than honey, which always seems to crystallize before I can use it up.

—*Meg Wilson, Austin, Texas* ◆

Here's the place to share your thoughts on our recent articles or on your food and cooking philosophies. Send your comments to Letters, *Fine Cooking,* PO Box 5506, Newtown, CT 06470-5506, or by email to fc@taunton.com.

fine

Cooking

EDITOR
Susie Middleton

ART DIRECTOR
Annie Giammattei

SPECIAL ISSUES EDITOR
Joanne McAllister Smart

TEST KITCHEN MANAGER/RECIPE EDITOR
Jennifer Armentrout

SENIOR EDITOR **Kimberly Y. Masibay**

ASSOCIATE EDITORS
**Rebecca Freedman,
Laura Giannatempo, Lisa Waddle**

ASSOCIATE WEB EDITOR **Sarah Breckenridge**

SENIOR COPY/PRODUCTION EDITOR
Enid Johnson

ASSISTANT ART DIRECTOR **Pamela Winn**

TEST KITCHEN ASSOCIATE/FOOD STYLIST
Allison R. Ehri

EDITORIAL ASSISTANT **Kim Landi**

EDITOR AT LARGE **Maryellen Driscoll**

TEST KITCHEN INTERN **Safaya Tork**

CONTRIBUTING EDITORS
**Pam Anderson, Abigail Johnson Dodge,
Tim Gaiser, Sarah Jay, Tony Rosenfeld,
Molly Stevens**

PUBLISHER **Maria Taylor**

SENIOR MARKETING MANAGER
Karen Lutjen

CIRCULATION DIRECTOR
Dennis O'Brien

SENIOR SINGLE COPY SALES MANAGER
Jay Annis

CORPORATE ACCOUNTS MANAGER
Judy Caruso

NATIONAL ACCOUNTS MANAGERS
**Patricia Coleman
Linda Delaney**

ADVERTISING SALES ASSOCIATE
Stacy Purcell

Fine Cooking: (ISSN: 1072-5121) is published seven times a year by The Taunton Press, Inc., Newtown, CT 06470-5506. Telephone 203-426-8171. Periodicals postage paid at Newtown, CT 06470 and at additional mailing offices. GST paid registration #123210981.

Subscription Rates: U.S. and Canada, $29.95 for one year, $49.95 for two years, $69.95 for three years (GST included, payable in U.S. funds). Outside the U.S./Canada: $36 for one year, $62 for two years, $88 for three years (payable in U.S. funds). Single copy, $6.95. Single copy outside the U.S., $7.95.

Postmaster: Send address changes to *Fine Cooking,* The Taunton Press, Inc., 63 South Main St., P.O. Box 5506, Newtown, CT 06470-5506.

Canada Post: Return undeliverable Canadian addresses to *Fine Cooking, c/o* Worldwide Mailers, Inc., 2835 Kew Drive, Windsor, ON N8T 3B7, or email to mnfa@taunton.com.

Printed in the USA.

HOW TO CONTACT US:

Fine Cooking
The Taunton Press, 63 S. Main St., P.O. Box 5506,
Newtown, CT 06470-5506   203-426-8171
www.finecooking.com

Editorial:
To submit an article proposal, write to *Fine Cooking* at the address above or:

Call:	**800-309-0744**
Fax:	**203-426-3434**
Email:	**fc@taunton.com**

Customer Service:
For subscription inquiries, you can:

- Visit our subscriber service section at:
  www.finecooking.com
- Email us: **fcservice@taunton.com**
- Call our customer support center:

  To report an address change, inquire about an order, or solve a problem, call:
  800-477-8727

  To subscribe, purchase back issues, books or videos, or give a gift, call:
  800-888-8286

Advertising:
To find out about advertising:

Call:	**800-309-8940**
Email:	**fcads@taunton.com**

Member Audit
Bureau of Circulation The Audit Bureau

Retail:
If you'd like to carry *Fine Cooking* in your store, call the Taunton Trade Company at:
866-505-4674

Mailing List:
Occasionally we make our subscribers' names and addresses available to responsible companies whose products or services we feel may be of some interest to you. Most of our subscribers find this to be a helpful way to learn about useful resources and services. If you don't want us to share your name with other companies, please contact our Customer Service Department at:
800-477-8727

The Taunton Guarantee:
If at any time you're not completely satisfied with *Fine Cooking*, you can cancel your subscription and receive a full and immediate refund of the entire subscription price. No questions asked.

Allison Ehri ("Grilled Appetizers," p. 36), *Fine Cooking*'s test kitchen associate and food stylist, admits that every time she grills up a round of her tasty appetizers she has to reserve a secret stash for herself. They're so good, her guests grab every single morsel, leaving her empty handed. A graduate of the French Culinary Institute in New York City, Allison worked as a freelance recipe tester, developer, and writer for several national food magazines before joining the staff of *Fine Cooking*.

Maria Helm Sinskey

("Grilled Fish Toppings," p. 40) is the culinary director and executive chef at Robert Sinskey Vineyards and the author of *The Vineyard Kitchen: Menus Inspired by the Seasons*. Maria is currently studying for a masters of wine degree and is at work on her second cookbook, which will focus on wines from around the world. She lives in Napa, California, with her husband and two daughters.

Maria Helm Sinskey

Before opening the award-winning L'Impero in New York City in 2002, chef Scott Conant ("Quick Summer Pastas," p. 43) spent years learning the ins and outs of regional Italian cooking, both in Italy and in some of New York's finest Italian restaurants. After L'Impero, he went on to open Alto restaurant in 2005. Scott is also the author of two cookbooks: *Scott Conant's New Italian Cooking* and *Bold Italian,* due out this fall.

Scott Conant

Annie Wayte ("Green Salads," p. 46) began her culinary career in London, eventually becoming the chef at fashion designer Nicole Farhi's restaurant, Nicole's. The restaurant was replicated in 1999 in New York and housed in Farhi's flagship store. In 2002,

Annie Wayte

Annie opened Farhi's third dining venture, the Notting Hill Café 202, which she brought to New York in 2005 as simply 202. Annie's cooking style, which blends English, Mediterranean, and Middle Eastern cuisines, emphasizes seasonality and high-quality ingredients. Her first cookbook, *Keep It Seasonal: Soups, Salads, and Sandwiches,* was published last year.

Cooking instructor and freelance writer Meg Suzuki had no trouble finding tasters for her Lemon Cheesecake Squares (p. 52). When she's not in the kitchen, you'll find her playing traditional Japanese drums with San Jose Taiko, and her hungry colleagues are always looking for snacks. Before heading out west, Meg was assistant test kitchen director for *Cook's Illustrated* magazine.

Barbara Lauterbach

("Chinese Chicken Salad," p. 58) could write the book on chicken salad. In fact she has. In *Chicken Salad: 50 Favorite Recipes,* Barbara collected versions of the luncheon standby from family and friends and added her own innovative takes. She attended cooking schools in London, Paris, Florence, and Bologna, and now teaches at King Arthur Flour Baking Education Center in Norwich, Vermont, and at La Combe, in southwest France.

Abigail Johnson Dodge

("Fruit Cobbler," p. 60) was the founding director of *Fine Cooking*'s test kitchen. She is now a contributing editor and the author of several cookbooks, including *Great Fruit Desserts* and, most recently, *The Weekend Baker*. When not writing and developing recipes, Abby travels and teaches cooking classes nationwide. ◆

The Taunton Press
Inspiration for hands-on living®

INDEPENDENT PUBLISHERS SINCE 1975

TAUNTON, INC.
Founders, **Paul and Jan Roman**

THE TAUNTON PRESS
President **Suzanne Roman**

*Executive Vice President &
Chief Financial Officer* **Timothy Rahr**

*Executive Vice President &
Publisher, Magazine Group* **Jon Miller**

Publisher, Book Group **James Childs**

Chief of Operations **Thomas Luxeder**

DIRECTORS
Creative & Editorial Director **Susan Edelman**
Human Resources Director **Carol Marotti**
Technology Services Director **Jay Hartley**
Controller **Wayne Reynolds**
Advertising Director **David Gray**
Fulfillment Director **Patricia Williamson**
Financial Analysis Director **Kathy Worth**
Circulation Director **Dennis O'Brien**

THE TAUNTON PRESS

Books: *Marketing:* Melissa A. Possick, Audrey Locorotondo. *Publicity:* Nicole Salvatore, Janel Noblin. *Editorial:* Helen Albert, Kathryn Benoit, Peter Chapman, Steve Culpepper, Pamela Hoenig, Carolyn Mandarano, Nicole Palmer, Amy Reilly, Jennifer Russell, Erica Sanders-Foege, Kathleen Williams. *Art:* Chris Thompson, Alison Wilkes, Nancy Boudreau, Amy Griffin, Sandra Mahlstedt, Wendi Mijal, Lynne Phillips, Carol Singer. *Manufacturing:* Thomas Greco, Laura Burrone.

Business Office: Holly Smith, Gayle Hammond, Patricia Marini. *Legal:* Carolyn Kovaleski. *Magazine Print Production:* Philip Van Kirk, Nicole Anastas, Jennifer Kaczmarcyk.

Circulation: David Pond, Andrew Corson, Catherine Hansen.

Distribution: Paul Seipold, Walter Aponte, Frank Busino, David DeToto, Leanne Furlong, Deborah Greene, Frank Melbourne, Reinaldo Moreno, Raymond Passaro, Ulysses Robinson, Alice Saxton.

Finance/Accounting: *Finance:* Brett Manning. *Accounting:* Patrick Lamontagne, Lydia Krikorian, Judith O'Toole, Elaine Yamin, Carol Diehm, Dorothy Blasko, Susan Burke, Lorraine Parsons, Larry Rice, James Tweedle, Priscilla Jennings.

Fulfillment: Diane Goulart. *Fulfillment Systems:* Jodi Klein, Kim Eads, Nancy Knorr, Thomas Kuzebski. *Customer Service:* Ellen Grassi, Kathleen Baker, Bonnie Beardsley, Deborah Ciccio, Katherine Clarke, Alfred Dreher, Monica Duhancik, Paula Ferreri, Eileen McNulty, Patricia Parks, Deana Parker, Patricia Pineau, Betty Stepney. *Data Entry:* Melissa Youngberg, Anne Champlin, Mary Ann Colbert, Caryne-Lynne Davis, Maureen Pekar, Debra Sennefelder, Andrea Shorrock, Marylou Thompson, Barbara Williams.

Human Resources: Linda Ballerini, Christine Lincoln, Dawn Ussery.

Photos, from top: Ben Fink, Melanie Dunea, Scott Phillips

TAUNTON MAGAZINES

Fine Woodworking • Fine Homebuilding
Threads • Fine Gardening • Fine Cooking

Our magazines are for people who are passionate about their pursuits. Written by practicing experts in the field, Taunton Press magazines provide authentic, reliable information supported by instructive and inspiring visuals.

TAUNTON BOOKS

Our books are filled with in-depth information and creative ideas from the finest authors in their fields. Whether you're practicing a craft or engaged in the creation of your home, Taunton books will inspire you to discover new levels of accomplishment.

WWW.TAUNTON.COM

Our website is a place where you can discover more about the interests you enjoy, converse with fellow enthusiasts, shop at our convenient on-line store or contact customer service.

EMPLOYMENT INFORMATION

To inquire about career opportunities, please e-mail us at tauntonjobs@taunton.com or visit our website www.taunton.com. You may also write to The Taunton Press, Human Resources, 63 S. Main St., Box 5506, Newtown, CT 06470.

CUSTOMER SERVICE

We are here to answer any questions you might have and to help you order our magazines, books and videos. Just call us toll-free at 800-477-8727.

The Taunton Press, Inc., Taunton Direct, Inc., Taunton Trade, Inc., and Taunton Interactive, Inc., are all subsidiaries of Taunton, Inc.

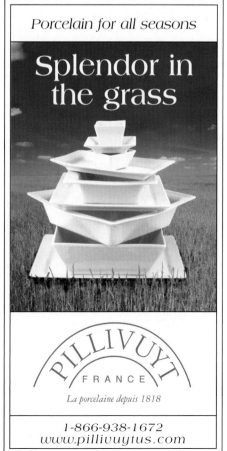

What's New at FineCooking.com

Visit our homepage often at FineCooking.com to see what's "on the front burner." This month, we have special Web collections on internationally inspired grilling and easier weeknight cooking using planned leftovers.

ON THE FRONT BURNER
Cooking for Today and Tomorrow

The concept of planned leftovers is a busy cook's best friend. These innovative recipes and ideas may make leftover night your favorite dinner of the week.

RECIPES

Seared rib-eye steak becomes a spicy Vietnamese soup

Five pasta dinners from one versatile sauce

Three fresh takes on chicken salad

Creamy risotto is transformed into crisp croquettes

ON THE FRONT BURNER
Global Grilling

Virtually every world cuisine has some tradition of cooking over an open fire, and we've gathered together recipes, ingredients, and tools from those traditions. What better time than summer to try these far-flung ideas?

MENUS AND RECIPES

A backyard Tuscan feast

A variety of international skewers: lamb kebabs, chicken yakitori, and satay

Latin-style flank steak with chipotle butter

GREAT FINDS

A Greek cheese perfect for grilling

A Japanese-inspired charcoal oven

TIPS & TOOLS

Getting the most from leftover chicken

Smart storage containers

Book Preview

Explore the great diversity of America's own melting-pot grill culture in The Taunton Press's newest cookbook, *Barbecue Nation* by Fred Thompson, with home-grown grilling recipes from all over the country. Get a preview at FineCooking.com.

Free email newsletter!

Subscribe at FineCooking.com to get great recipes, tips, techniques, and videos delivered directly to your inbox twice a month.

almond-crusted chicken tender salad

for a delicious side or a filling entrée, enjoy a baby greens salad topped with almond-crusted chicken tenders and a sweet orange-teriyaki-honey dressing.

dressing ingredients

1/4 cup	Kikkoman Teriyaki Marinade & Sauce
1/4 cup	olive oil
2 tbsp	honey
2 tbsp	vinegar
1 tsp	freshly grated orange peel

salad ingredients

1 lb	chicken breast tenders
	freshly ground black pepper
1	egg
1 tbsp	Kikkoman Teriyaki Marinade & Sauce
1/2 cup	all-purpose flour
1/2 cup	Kikkoman Panko Bread Crumbs
1/2 cup	smoked almonds, finely chopped
2-3 tbsp	vegetable oil
6 cups	mixed baby salad greens
2	oranges, peeled and cut into segments

orange-teriyaki-honey dressing

Whisk together teriyaki sauce, olive oil, honey, vinegar and orange peel.

chicken salad

1. Season chicken tenders with pepper. Beat egg with teriyaki sauce in shallow bowl until well blended.
2. Place flour in shallow dish. Combine bread crumbs and almonds in another shallow dish.
3. Dust both sides of chicken with flour, then dip into egg mixture and finally coat with almond mixture.
4. In 12-inch skillet, heat 2 tbsp vegetable oil over medium-high heat. Add chicken and cook 6 to 7 minutes, or until no longer pink in center, turning over once and adding more oil as needed.
5. Divide salad greens among 4 dinner plates. Arrange chicken and orange segments on greens. Serve with Orange-Teriyaki-Honey Dressing.

Serves 4

Discover more unique recipes.

yourteriyaki.com

I've been looking everywhere for micro-greens. Where can I buy them? Will they soon be as available as mâche and frisée?

—Deb Cerami, Westfield, New Jersey

Lee Jones responds: As their name implies, micro-greens are the very small leaves of plants such as arugula, broccoli, radish, and mustard. They are harvested as 7- to 14-day-old seedlings, compared with baby greens, which grow about 45 days, and mature greens, which grow for 65 to 80 days. Many chefs have become fans of microgreens for their intense flavor and color. Because they are so delicate and so labor-intensive to harvest, microgreens are much more expensive than mature greens ($40 a pound for microgreens versus $4 a pound for baby lettuces), so you'll most likely see them used sparingly to garnish plates or add extra punch to sandwiches and pizza.

Microgreens dehydrate quickly and don't have much of a shelf life, so you can find them in only a few high-end markets or sold directly by the growers. Growing your own may be a more affordable option. Some seed companies—Johnny's Selected Seeds (JohnnySeeds.com), for instance—offer a mix of seeds that can be harvested at the micro stage. As more people experience microgreens in restaurants and want to use them at home, you'll most likely start to see them in farmers' markets.

Lee Jones is part owner of The Chef's Garden (Chefs-Garden.com) in Huron, Ohio, which grows more than 75 varieties of microgreens and 40 varieties of microherbs. They supply 400 chefs worldwide.

Have a question of general interest about cooking? Send it to Q&A, *Fine Cooking*, PO Box 5506, Newtown, CT 06470-5506, or by email to fcqa@taunton .com, and we'll find a cooking professional with the answer.

For a recent party, I chilled a bottle of white wine but then didn't open it. Is it best to leave it in the fridge or should I return it to my wine rack?

—S. Blasco, New York City

Tim Gaiser responds: While it's fine to keep a bottle of wine chilled for a week or even two, the air inside a refrigerator is too dry to be a good long-term place to store wine. After about six weeks, the cork will dry out, shrink, and allow air into the bottle, oxidizing the wine. (The exception: If the bottle has a synthetic cork or screw cap, it won't have this shrinkage problem.)

So rather than letting the bottle of wine languish in the refrigerator, why not find a reason to drink up? If you don't think you'll have an opportunity to open it within two weeks, you should remove the bottle from the refrigerator to enjoy at a future time. The temporary chill will have little effect on a wine unless it's a Champagne or white wine that's older than about three years.

Master sommelier Tim Gaiser is a contributing editor to Fine Cooking.

What is seven-spice pepper? Is it related to five-spice powder?

—Carrie Herting, Bayport, New York

Patty Erd responds: These two Asian spice mixtures share one common ingredient: Sichuan pepper. Seven-spice pepper is a Japanese seasoning also called *shichimi togarashi*. The blend usually includes Sichuan peppercorns, cayenne, black or white sesame seed (sometimes both), poppy seed, dried orange peel, nori (a type of seaweed), and hemp seed. Fragrant, with a pungent flavor, it is used as a condiment for soba noodles or soups and is sprinkled on grilled meats and fish to counterbalance fatty flavors. You can buy it at most Asian markets and some well-stocked grocery stores, or by mail order.

Five-spice powder, often called Chinese five-spice powder, contains Sichuan pepper as well as cinnamon, star anise, fennel, and cloves. Found in Asian markets and most supermarkets, it's used in Cantonese barbecue marinades, in braised dishes, and on roasted meats.

Until two years ago it was illegal to import Sichuan peppercorns into the United States, so many versions of both spice blends substituted ginger or regular black pepper. Check the label of your spice mix to make sure you're buying what you want.

Patty Erd is co-owner of The Spice House, a seasoning store with four retail locations in the Midwest and online at TheSpiceHouse.com. ◆

RIZO

DESIGN TOSHIYUKI KITA

Single Touch. Multi-function.

RIZO. Cooking Made Easy.

RIZO is user-friendly, allowing even beginners to cook rice easily with just the touch of a button. It also offers a healthy alternative to home cooking with the steam cook feature and steaming plate accessory that prepares vegetables and other foods without added oil. RIZO is the new Zojirushi Micom Rice Cooker & Warmer that provides the best in style, technology and simplicity. RIZO, designed by the internationally celebrated designer Toshiyuki Kita, seamlessly integrates itself with virtually any kitchen top.

ZOJIRUSHI

Zojirushi America Corporation

Contact us at: (800)733-6270   www.zojirushi.com

RIZO™ Micom Rice Cooker & Warmer   NS-XAC05 / NS-XBC05

Capacity: 3 cups / 0.5 liter **Color:** RIZO Stainless (XR) / RIZO White (WR) / RIZO Yellow (YR)
Accessories: Steaming Plate, Measuring Cup, Nonstick Rice Spatula, Spatula Stand

Poblanos
These beauties taste best roasted

BY RUTH LIVELY

If you asked me to name one chile pepper I couldn't do without, I'd have to say it's the poblano. I like cooking with all kinds of chiles, but the rich, sweet flavor of poblanos and the complexity they add to a dish make them a favorite in my kitchen.

About the size of small bell peppers, poblanos have glossy dark-green skins and wide shoulders that taper sharply to a point. Although they do turn red when mature, at the market you'll find them only in their green stage. Poblanos are typically mild with just a bit of zing, but their heat level varies depending on growing conditions (warmer climates and more sunlight can increase the heat), so you'll occasionally come across spicy ones.

When buying poblanos, look for firm peppers with shiny skins. Avoid any with wrinkled skins, soft flesh, or shriveled stems. Stored in the crisper drawer in a loosely closed plastic bag, they'll last for about a week.

Bring out the best flavor and texture by cooking

Poblanos are most commonly roasted and peeled before being added to a dish. (For how to roast poblanos, see the sidebar opposite.) When raw, they have a thin but tough skin and a pungent, grassy flavor with a trace of bitterness that disappears during cooking. Roasted poblanos, on the other hand, have a deep, sumptuous flavor and a pleasant, velvety texture.

Roasted poblanos are fantastic with cheese, especially ones that melt, like Cheddar, Monterey Jack, and Gruyère—think quesadillas and grilled cheese sandwiches—but they complement soft or crumbly cheeses like ricotta, queso fresco, and goat cheese, too. They make a great side dish with grilled pork, chicken, and beef, as well as shrimp, crab, and eggs. And they're especially good tossed with corn, summer squash, and starchy foods like potatoes, rice, and beans. Lime, garlic, and cilantro are also classic flavor partners, but don't stop there: basil, chives, oregano, thyme, cumin, coriander, and paprika are good with poblanos, too.

Strips of roasted poblanos, usually combined with sautéed white onion (and sometimes chopped garlic), are called *rajas,* which means strips in Spanish. You can serve *rajas* as a side dish or in fillings for quesadillas (see the recipe at right), tacos, burritos, and even omelets. The poblano also stars in most renditions of chiles rellenos, the classic Mexican stuffed and fried peppers.

Did you know?

Ancho chiles (or just anchos) are dried ripe poblanos. They have a deep, rich, peppery flavor with a slight chocolate undertone.

Photos: Scott Phillips

Quesadillas with Roasted Poblanos & Onions (*Rajas*)

Serves four as a main course, six to eight as an appetizer.

2 small fresh poblanos
1 Tbs. plus 2 tsp. vegetable oil
½ large white onion, thinly sliced lengthwise (about 1½ cups)
Kosher salt and freshly ground black pepper
Four 8-inch flour tortillas
2 cups grated Monterey Jack cheese (about 8 oz.)
½ cup loosely packed fresh cilantro
½ cup sour cream

Roast and peel the poblanos following the directions in the sidebar at top right. Slice them into ¼-inch-wide strips and put them in a small bowl.

Put a baking sheet in the oven and heat the oven to 150°F (or its lowest setting).

Make the rajas: Heat 1 Tbs. of the oil in a 10- or 12-inch nonstick skillet over medium-high heat. Add the onion and cook, stirring frequently, until soft and lightly browned, 3 to 5 minutes. Add the poblano strips, season with a generous pinch of salt and a few grinds of pepper, and cook, stirring occasionally, until the peppers are heated through, 1 to 2 minutes more. Transfer to a plate and wipe the skillet clean.

Make the quesadillas: Heat ½ tsp. of the oil in the skillet over medium-high heat until hot. Add one tortilla and scatter over it a quarter of the cheese, a quarter of the poblano mixture, and a quarter of the cilantro. When the tortilla smells toasty and the bottom is browned in spots, in 1 or 2 minutes, fold it in half, pressing it with a spatula to flatten it. Transfer to the baking sheet in the oven to keep warm. Repeat with the remaining ingredients to make three more quesadillas. Cut each quesadilla into wedges and serve with the sour cream on the side.

> Roasted poblanos will last about a week, covered, in the refrigerator.

How to roast poblanos

You can roast poblanos on a gas burner, a hot grill, or under a broiler. Whatever method you choose, your goal is to blister and char the skin all over.

Blacken the peppers. Turn a burner to high and char the poblanos directly over the flame, turning them with tongs as soon as each side becomes fully blackened. It will take 6 to 8 minutes per pepper.

If you don't have a gas stove, you can char poblanos similarly over a hot grill fire or lay them on a foil-lined baking sheet and char them under a hot broiler, turning them with tongs.

Steam and peel. Immediately after roasting, put the poblanos in a bowl, cover, and set aside to steam and loosen the skins. When cool enough to handle, peel the charred skin off with your hands or a small paring knife. Pull out and discard the stems and seed clusters.

More ways with roasted poblanos

Punch up scrambled eggs by stirring in *rajas* (recipe at left) or thin strips of roasted poblanos and chopped cilantro.

Toss together a refreshing salad of diced roasted poblanos, grilled corn, and diced red onion dressed with an olive oil and lime juice vinaigrette and garnished with plenty of chopped cilantro.

Whip up a southwestern-style grilled cheese sandwich with large pieces of roasted poblano, Cheddar, thick slices of grilled red onion, and some arugula. Spread the bread with mayonnaise spiked with a garlic-cilantro-ancho purée.

Make a green rice pilaf by sautéing chopped onion and garlic and then adding rice, followed by a purée of roasted poblanos and cilantro thinned with chicken broth.

Ruth Lively cooks, writes, and gardens in New Haven, Connecticut. ◆

How much wine do I need?

Plan on two 5-ounce glasses per person, or about a bottle for every two people. You'll also want to purchase a bottle or two more than you think you'll need, because you don't want to run short on wine in the middle of the meal.

Finding inexpensive wines

Your local wine retailer is a good place to start when looking for the best wine values. He or she will be able to steer you to the best bargains and new releases. It also pays to explore wines and grapes you haven't encountered before. Many of the up-and-coming wine regions around the world produce excellent wines at affordable prices, because they have yet to be discovered by mass markets.

Buying a Mixed Case (or Two) for Your Summer Cookout

BY TIM GAISER

In the summer, I try to simplify my life as much as possible. And when it comes to outdoor entertaining, there's one small thing that really helps: buying a mixed case or two of wine. That way, I can relax, knowing that I won't have to make a rushed trip to the wine shop and that I have a nice assortment that will please a large crowd.

The challenge is to find good-quality wines that will make everyone happy without breaking the bank. You also need to look for wines that feel right for drinking outdoors; they should be light, refreshing, and cool—even the reds.

Here are a few guidelines that will make your search for great outdoor-dining wines as easy as summer itself.

What makes a good summer wine
Wines for a cookout should be easy to sip, easy to pair with a variety of foods (from cold salads to hearty fare from the grill), and easy to serve to a crowd. They should be easy on the wallet, too. Stick with wines that are $12 or less, as you can rack up a pretty hefty bill if you fill your case with pricey bottles.

I'm always on the lookout for whites that offer vibrant, youthful fruit and crisp acidity with little or no oak. Sauvignon Blanc, Pinot Grigio, and Albariño are especially good. Generally, I find Chardonnay too rich for summer sipping. But if I can find a lightly oaked or unoaked bottle, I'll add it to the mix. My vote also goes to dry, crisp rosés from southern France or Spain.

These wines are generally made from the Grenache grape, which produces some of the tastiest pink wines.

My favorite summer reds are those with lots of fruit and moderate spice and oak notes. Pinot Noir is a personal favorite, not only because it's delicious slightly chilled but also because it goes well with outdoor cuisine. Lighter Côtes du Rhône wines made from a blend of Grenache and other grapes are also easy-drinking and versatile. Zinfandel and Syrah (or Shiraz) are a bit heartier but perfect with anything from the grill. Whatever your choice, try to avoid wines that are overly alcoholic (anything over 15% alcohol), tannic, or oaky. All three of these elements make for robust wines that tend to overwhelm most summer fare.

Customize your case to the menu
Consider what you'll be serving and choose two or three types of wines that match the food but are different enough to please a variety of palates. If it's chicken or seafood on the grill, for example, fill your case with bottles of Sauvignon Blanc, a lightly oaked Chardonnay, and maybe a light Côtes du Rhône. If you're cooking burgers, steaks, or other red meats, look mainly for Rhône blends, Zinfandels, or Shiraz, with maybe a sturdy white Viognier in the mix. It's always nice to include a couple of bottles of a good sparkler to serve as an aperitif, as well as a bottle or two of a dry rosé, which pairs well with almost anything.

Great picks for a mixed case

Here are some of my current favorites for summer entertaining. (Retail prices are approximate.)

A sparkler

NV Rotari Brut Arte Italiana, Italy, $11

Sparkling wine is a great way to start any alfresco dinner, and this is one of the best sparkling values around.

Whites

2006 Geyser Peak Sauvignon Blanc, California, $10

This is a quintessential Sauvignon Blanc, bursting with vibrant tropical and citrus fruit. Try it with composed salads with goat cheese or cold poached salmon with fresh dill.

2005 Burgans Albariño, Rias Baixas, Spain, $12

Albariño is the most popular Spanish white today, thanks to its orange and peach fruit and mineral notes. The Burgans is delicious as an aperitif and also great with shellfish, smoked fish, or light pasta salads.

2005 Pepperwood Grove Viognier, California, $9

This is a true find: a good, inexpensive Viognier with lush apricot and melon fruit and spice and lime zest notes. Try it with grilled chicken or spice-rubbed grilled turkey cutlets.

2006 Penfolds Koonunga Hill Chardonnay, Australia, $10

This the ultimate crowd-pleasing Chardonnay, with ripe apple and tropical fruit and just the right amount of oak. Pair it with cold shrimp and pasta salads or just about anything except red meat.

A rosé

2005 Bodegas Muga Rosado, Rioja, Spain, $11

Tempranillo-based rosados from Spain are some of the best summer wines around, with their tart red-berry flavors and mineral notes. They're also great picnic wines and perfect with everything from cold pasta salads to pizza and sandwiches.

Reds

2005 Beringer Founders' Estate Pinot Noir, California, $12

Supple, velvety, and spicy, this is one of the great values in Pinot Noir. Enjoy a glass with friends before dinner, then try it with grilled swordfish or salmon.

2005 Three Thieves Zinfandel, California, $11

I can't think of a better summer red than this Zinfandel, with a screw cap for easy cookout pouring. It's perfect with anything from the grill, including burgers, ribs, and sausages.

2005 Chapoutier Côtes du Rhône "Belleruche," France, $11

This spicy, rich Grenache blend is a classic summer red. Try it with grilled chicken or Italian sausages.

2005 Woop Woop Shiraz, South Eastern Australia, $11

With jammy blackberry, strawberry, and spice flavors and a touch of oak, this Shiraz is a natural with grilled beef, lamb, or spice-rubbed pork loin.

Contributing editor Tim Gaiser is a master sommelier. ◆

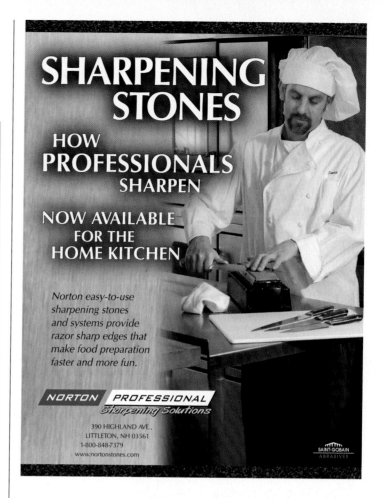

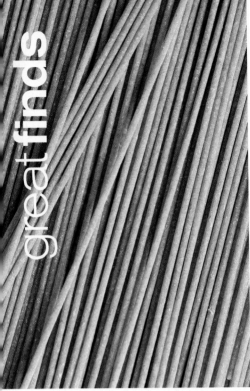

A different whole grain

Made with 100% whole farro, a grain similar to spelt, this spaghetti is amazingly sweet, rich, and nutty. And what's best, it lacks the assertive flavor of whole-wheat pasta. Think great nutritional benefits sans the strong wheatiness. Toss it with any sauce you would pair with regular pasta. *Rustichella d'Abruzzo farro spaghetti, $5 for an 8.8-oz. pack at MarketHall Foods.com (888-952-4005).*

Just like homemade tortellini

We love tortellini, but making it at home is a serious project. And until recently, we couldn't find a brand of packaged ones we really liked. Then we discovered Bertagni's porcini mushroom tortelloni, which is just a tad larger than tortellini, and we fell in love. Made with real eggs, the pasta is silky and ultra-thin, with a rich, eggy flavor. The filling is earthy and intensely mushroomy yet surprisingly delicate and light. *Bertagni tortelloni, about $5 for an 8.8-oz. pack, is available at some Whole Foods Markets and at specialty food stores.*

Update Your Pasta Pantry
Intriguing pastas and nifty pasta tools

BY LAURA GIANNATEMPO

Distinctively shaped

This short, twisty, dumpling-like pasta hailing from the northwestern coast of Italy is handmade with just durum wheat flour and water and then slowly air-dried. When cooked, it becomes pleasantly soft and plump while maintaining a nice, satisfying chew. It's fantastic paired with a vibrant, summery pesto sauce. *La Bella Angiolina trofie, $9.25 for a 1-pound bag at ChefsTools.com (866-716-2433).*

A sleek measuring tool for spaghetti

We like the cool design and convenience of this one- to four-portion stainless-steel spaghetti measure. Its two slim measuring components are joined in the middle and rotate flat, making it easy to stash in a drawer. *Typhoon Italian Job spaghetti measure, $10 at Typhoonus.com (877-897-4872).* ◆

Scoop pasta right out of the water

Carrying a heavy pot to the sink to drain pasta can be a hassle. That's why we like this handy colander: You can scoop pasta out of the water directly into a nearby saucepan or bowl. (Plus, all the water stays in the pot, so you never have to worry about reserving pasta water.) We find it particularly useful for gnocchi and filled pastas, which are too delicate to drain in a traditional colander and are easy to scoop out because they float when cooked. *Oxo Good Grips scoop colander, large ($19.99) and small ($14.99) at Oxo.com (800-545-4411).*

what's new

A clean cut

These new carbon-steel paring knives boast a coat of bright color, even on the blade, which makes them easy to spot on a counter or in a crowded knife drawer. The nonstick finish on the 4-inch blade helps it glide easily through cheeses and other sticky foods. I particularly like the colorful protective sheath, which helps keep the edge sharp and makes this knife a natural for a picnic. You can find these Kuhn Rikon knives in red, green, orange, blue, pink, and yellow at Amazon.com for $8.

Memory aid

Keeping track of when you opened that carton of chicken broth (and when it's time to toss it) is easier with this compact digital timer. Outfitted with a magnet or suction cup, it attaches to plastic storage containers or jar lids. With the reset of a button, it counts hours and days. I found it convenient for fridge and pantry staples like soy milk, bacon, and vinaigrettes, taking the guesswork out of how long ago they were opened or made. The timers display up to 99 days and run on a replaceable battery that lasts about 18 months. Sold two to a pack for $10, the timers are available at HowManyDaysAgo.com.

Colorful paring knives	26
Silicone steamer	26
Digital timer	26
Large spatulas	27
Tongs that illuminate	27
Cedar grilling paper	27
Cleaning mitt	28
Glass-door refrigerator	28
Silicone & metal muffin pans	28
Large saucepans reviewed	30

BY LISA WADDLE

Steamer folds for easy storage

Silicone versions of kitchen staples have flooded the housewares stores lately, but here's an update worth considering. Unlike folding metal steamers, this silicone version won't scratch nonstick cookware, and it's flexible enough to fit in pans from 4½ inches to 8½ inches in diameter. There's no center post—just three silicone legs—on this dishwasher-safe steamer, which is heat-resistant up to 650°F. Best of all, you can fold it or stuff it in a drawer for storage. For a list of stores carrying the Chef'n SleekStor VeggiSteam, which has a suggested retail price of $10, go to Chefn.com.

fine Cooking©

Grilling for a Crowd

Create a custom menu for 10 to 12 guests with these recipes

BY TONY ROSENFELD

Summer party menu

Once warmer weather hits, so does the urge to entertain. With this pullout, we've made it easy to assemble a winning meal: Just mix and match from the following crowd-friendly main dishes, starters, and sides. When planning, keep in mind that the main dishes should be marinated several hours or a day in advance. All of these recipes serve 10 to 12 people.

Mains: Choose 1

Grilled Herb-Crusted Leg of Lamb with Fresh Mint Sauce

Grilled Thai Chicken Breasts with Herb-Lemongrass Crust

Argentine Spice-Rubbed Flank Steak with Salsa Criolla

Starters: Choose 1

Farmers' Market Crudités with Buttermilk Herb Dip

Grilled Bruschetta with Rosemary-White Bean Purée & Heirloom Tomatoes

Sides: Choose 2

Chopped Tomato & Cucumber Salad with Mint & Feta

Grilled Southwestern Potato Salad

Warm Pasta Salad with Grilled Tomatoes, Zucchini & Pecorino

Grilled Asparagus & Onions with Balsamic Vinegar & Blue Cheese

Grilled Corn on the Cob with Thyme & Roasted Red Pepper Butter

sides

Grilled Corn on the Cob with Thyme & Roasted Red Pepper Butter

Serves eight.

The butter in this dish is at once sweet and tangy, a bright addition to plain old grilled corn on the cob.

4 oz. (½ cup) unsalted butter, softened to room temperature
2 jarred roasted red peppers, drained well, patted dry, and finely chopped (½ to ⅔ cup)
1 large shallot, minced (¼ cup)
1½ Tbs. sherry vinegar
1 Tbs. chopped fresh thyme
2 tsp. kosher salt
½ tsp. freshly ground black pepper; more as needed
8 ears corn, shucked
2 Tbs. olive oil

Put the butter, red peppers, shallot, vinegar, 2 tsp. of the thyme, 1 tsp. of the salt, and the black pepper in a food processor and pulse until blended (it's fine if it's still slightly chunky and looks a little separated). Transfer to a large piece of plastic wrap and roll tightly, twisting the ends so the bundle acquires a sausage shape. (Store in the refrigerator for up to 1 week.) When ready to grill the corn, slice the butter into ⅓-inch-thick rounds.

Heat a gas grill to medium or prepare a low charcoal fire. If desired, cut each ear of corn in half. Toss the corn with the oil, the remaining 1 tsp. salt, and a few grinds of black pepper. Put the ears on the grill and if using gas, reduce the heat to medium low. Cover and grill the corn, turning every couple of minutes, until browned all over and tender, about 15 minutes. Transfer to a large platter, top with about half of the butter and the remaining 1 tsp. thyme. Serve, passing the remaining butter on the side.

How hot is your grill fire?

On both gas and charcoal grills, the length of time you can hold your outstretched palm an inch or two above the grill grate indicates the temperature range. If you can stand the heat for less than 1 second, the grill is very hot, over 600°F. If you can hold your hand in place for 1 to 2 seconds, the grill is considered hot, or between 400° and 500°F. If you can withstand 3 to 4 seconds, the grill is medium, or 350° to 375°F. If you can hold your hand in place for 5 to 7 seconds, the grill is medium low, or 325° to 350°F.

Chopped Tomato & Cucumber Salad with Mint & Feta

Serves ten to twelve.

This bright salad is a great addition to a large, summer buffet, though it also makes a fine lunch or light dinner accompanied by some warm pita. If serving as a main course, toss in some diced grilled chicken breasts for more substance, if you like.

2 pints ripe grape or cherry tomatoes, halved lengthwise
½ cup lightly chopped fresh mint
1 Tbs. chopped fresh thyme
2 tsp. kosher salt
1 tsp. freshly ground black pepper; more as needed
½ lb. feta cheese, coarsely crumbled (2 cups)
1 lemon, zest finely grated (1 Tbs.) and juiced (¼ cup)
1 English (seedless) cucumber, cut into ½-inch dice (4 cups)
4 scallions (both white and green parts), trimmed and thinly sliced (½ cup)
2 cups pitted Kalamata or Gaeta olives, halved
⅓ cup extra-virgin olive oil

In a medium bowl, toss the tomatoes with ¼ cup of the mint, ½ Tbs. of the thyme, the salt, and ½ tsp. of the pepper. In another medium bowl, toss the feta with the lemon zest, the remaining ½ tsp. pepper, ¼ cup mint, and ½ Tbs. thyme. Let both sit for at least 15 minutes and up to 1 hour at room temperature.

In a large bowl, toss the cucumber, scallions, and olives with the tomatoes and feta. Combine up to 1 hour ahead; let sit at room temperature. Just before serving, add the olive oil and half of the lemon juice and toss well. Season with pepper and more lemon juice if needed, and serve.

Grilled Southwestern Potato Salad

Serves ten to twelve.

This potato salad is filled with favorite flavorings of the Southwest—corn, chiles, red onions, peppers, and some crisp bacon.

2 large red onions, cut into ½-inch disks and threaded onto metal skewers
4 red bell peppers, halved, cored, and seeded
¾ cup extra-virgin olive oil
2 tsp. plus 2 Tbs. kosher salt; more as needed
1 tsp. freshly ground black pepper; more as needed
1½ cups cooked fresh corn kernels (from 2 ears)
½ lb. bacon (8 to 9 slices), cooked until crisp, drained, and crumbled
¾ cup chopped fresh cilantro
1 tsp. chili powder
3 lb. red potatoes, cut into 1½-inch pieces
3 Tbs. cider vinegar; more as needed

Heat a gas grill to medium or prepare a charcoal fire with medium- and low-heat areas. Put the onions and peppers on a rimmed baking sheet and sprinkle with 2 Tbs. of the oil, 2 tsp. of the salt, and the pepper. Turn and rub the vegetables to coat all over with the oil and seasonings.

Grill the vegetables, covered, until they have good grill marks, about 5 minutes. Flip, cover, and continue to grill until the peppers are softened and nicely browned, about 5 more minutes. As they finish cooking, transfer the peppers to the baking sheet. Reduce the heat on the gas grill to medium low or transfer the onions to the cooler part of the fire and continue cooking until they are just tender and browned (it's fine if they're charred in places), about 8 more minutes. Move to a cutting board and let cool. Scrape the skins off the peppers if you like. Coarsely chop the peppers and onions and toss in a large serving bowl along with the corn, bacon, cilantro, and chili powder.

Put the potatoes in a large pot, cover with cold water by a couple of inches, stir in the remaining 2 Tbs. of salt, and bring to a boil. Reduce to a simmer, cover, and cook until the potatoes are just tender, 12 to 15 minutes. Drain and toss with the grilled vegetables, the remaining ½ cup plus 2 Tbs. oil, and the vinegar. Season with salt, pepper, and more vinegar to taste. Let sit at least 30 minutes and up to 2 hours at room temperature before serving.

Make it pretty

Put some thought into serving and garnishing your dishes. The color of the serving plate or platter should complement the color of the food. Keep garnishes simple, using just an herb or ingredient from the recipe to clue people into the flavor of the dish.

Warm Pasta Salad with Grilled Tomatoes, Zucchini & Pecorino

Serves ten to twelve as a side dish or six as a main course.

1½ lb. ripe plum tomatoes (about 8), cored and halved lengthwise
1¼ lb. small zucchini (about 4), trimmed and halved lengthwise
5 Tbs. extra-virgin olive oil
4 tsp. chopped fresh thyme
2 tsp. kosher salt; more as needed
1 tsp. freshly ground black pepper; more as needed
6 oz. Pecorino Romano, shaved with a vegetable peeler (about 2 cups)
1 lb. dried penne
¼ cup thinly sliced fresh chives
2 tsp. balsamic vinegar

Prepare a medium fire on a gas grill or a medium-hot charcoal fire. In a large bowl, toss the tomatoes and zucchini with 2 Tbs. of the oil, 2 tsp. of the thyme, and the salt and pepper.

Set the vegetables cut side down on the grill and cook without moving them until they have good grill marks, 5 to 7 minutes. Flip and cook until browned and tender, 6 to 8 more minutes. Transfer to a cutting board and let cool for a couple of minutes. Coarsely chop, return them to the same large bowl along with 1½ cups of the pecorino, and toss. Let sit for up to a couple of hours at room temperature.

Bring a large pot of well-salted water to a boil over high heat. Add the pasta and cook, stirring often, until just al dente, about 11 minutes. Drain well and toss with the tomato mixture, 3 Tbs. of the chives, the remaining 3 Tbs. olive oil and the balsamic vinegar. Season generously with salt and pepper to taste and transfer to a serving bowl. Sprinkle with the remaining 1 Tbs. chives, 2 tsp. thyme, and ½ cup pecorino, and serve.

Make ahead: You can grill the tomatoes and zucchini a couple of hours before serving. Hold them in a large bowl at room temperature. Cook the pasta just before guests arrive and toss it with the vegetables.

Grilled Thai Chicken Breasts with Herb-Lemongrass Crust

Serves twelve.

Before chopping the lemongrass, be sure to cut off the spiky green top and enough of the bottom to eliminate the woody core. Peel off a few of the outer layers until you're left with just the tender heart of the stalk.

1½ cups chopped fresh cilantro (leaves and tender stems)
¾ cup coconut milk
¼ cup finely chopped lemongrass (from about 2 stalks)
12 fresh basil leaves
3 Thai bird chiles, 2 jalapeños, or 2 medium serranos, stemmed, seeded, and finely chopped
3 cloves garlic, minced
1½ Tbs. kosher salt
2 tsp. packed light brown sugar
1½ tsp. freshly ground black pepper
¾ tsp. ground coriander

12 boneless, skinless chicken breast halves (5 to 5½ lb.), trimmed (remove tenderloins if still attached)
2 limes, cut into wedges for serving

Combine 1¼ cups of the cilantro with the coconut milk, lemongrass, basil, chiles, garlic, salt, brown sugar, pepper, and coriander in a food processor or blender and purée until smooth. Arrange the chicken breasts in a nonreactive baking dish or other vessel large enough to accommodate them in a snug single layer. Pour the marinade over the breasts and turn to coat them well. Cover and refrigerate for at least 2 hours and up to 1 day.

Heat a gas grill to medium high or prepare a medium-hot charcoal fire. Grill the chicken (covered on a gas grill) until it has good grill marks on the first side, 4 to 5 minutes. Flip the chicken (cover a gas grill) and continue to cook until firm to the touch and completely cooked through (check by making a slice into one of the thicker breasts), 5 to 6 more minutes. Transfer to a platter and let rest for 5 minutes. Sprinkle with the remaining ¼ cup cilantro and serve with the lime wedges.

Serving suggestion: Though these breasts are great served hot off the grill, they're also fine served cold in the coming days, either plain or sliced atop a salad.

Wine pairing: A fruity Chenin Blanc like the 2005 Pine Ridge Chenin Blanc-Viognier, California, $13.50.

Grilled Herb-Crusted Leg of Lamb with Fresh Mint Sauce

Serves ten to twelve.

Boneless leg of lamb is the perfect cut for feeding a crowd. It's large, wonderfully flavorful, easy to prepare, and cooks to varied doneness. I like butterflying (or further flattening out) this cut and gently pounding it to make it more uniform for cooking.

FOR THE LAMB:
1 large or 2 small boneless legs of lamb (about 5½ lb.)
2 Tbs. kosher salt
2 tsp. freshly ground black pepper
¼ cup Dijon mustard
4 large cloves garlic, finely chopped (about 2 Tbs.)
2 Tbs. chopped fresh thyme
2 Tbs. chopped fresh rosemary

FOR THE SAUCE:
2 Tbs. granulated sugar; more as needed
1 tsp. kosher salt; more as needed
½ tsp. freshly ground black pepper; more as needed
1 cup chopped fresh mint (about 1 bunch)
¼ cup white-wine vinegar; more as needed
2 Tbs. olive oil

At least 1 day ahead, marinate the lamb: Set the lamb flat on a large cutting board. Trim any excess fat and then make deep horizontal slices into the thicker parts and open like a book to make an even thickness all around. Lay a piece of plastic wrap on top of the lamb and using a meat mallet or the bottom of a heavy skillet, pound to flatten slightly and make the thickness more uniform. Cut the meat into 2 or 3 more-manageable pieces. Sprinkle all over with 1 Tbs. of the salt and 1 tsp. of the pepper.

In a small bowl, mix the mustard, garlic, thyme, rosemary, and the remaining 1 Tbs.

salt and 1 tsp. pepper. Spread all over the lamb, transfer to a large nonreactive dish, cover, and refrigerate for at least 24 hours and up to 2 days.

Just before grilling, make the sauce: In a medium bowl, whisk ¼ cup water with the sugar, salt, and pepper—they don't have to dissolve completely. Stir in the mint, vinegar, and oil. Let sit while the lamb grills. Taste and season with more sugar, salt, and pepper if needed. (The sauce should have a sharp, acidic tang to complement the rich lamb.)

Grill the lamb: Heat a gas grill to medium high or prepare a charcoal fire with hot and medium-hot areas. Put the lamb on the grill (on the hotter part if using a charcoal fire) and cook (covered on a gas grill) without disturbing it until it's nicely browned, 6 to 8 minutes. Flip, reduce the heat on the gas grill to medium (or move to the cooler part of the charcoal fire), and cook until an instant-read thermometer inserted into a thicker part of the lamb registers 130°F for medium rare, 5 to 8 more minutes.

Transfer the lamb to a cutting board, tent with foil, and let rest for 10 minutes. Slice thinly across the grain. and serve with the mint sauce.

Wine pairing: Look for a spicy Shiraz blend such as the 2004 Peter Lehmann "Clancy's," Barossa Valley, $16.

mains

Argentine Spice-Rubbed Flank Steak with Salsa Criolla

Serves twelve.

Chimichurri is the star salsa of the Argentine grill, but the lesser known salsa criolla was my favorite when I visited that country. Full of onions, red peppers, and herbs, the mixture is a light but intensely flavorful condiment for grilled steak.

3 cloves garlic, minced and mashed to a paste with a pinch of salt
2 Tbs. chopped fresh thyme
1 Tbs. freshly ground black pepper
1 Tbs. chili powder
2 tsp. brown sugar
1½ Tbs. plus 2 tsp. kosher salt
4½ lb. flank steak (about 3 medium steaks), trimmed of excess fat
1 large ripe tomato, cored, seeded, and finely diced (about 1¼ cup)
1 medium yellow onion, minced (about 1⅓ cups)
½ red bell pepper, cored, seeded, and minced (about ½ cup)
½ cup extra-virgin olive oil
⅓ cup white-wine vinegar

In a small bowl, mix about two-thirds of the garlic paste with 1 Tbs. of the thyme, 2 tsp. of the black pepper, the chili powder, brown sugar, and 1½ Tbs. of the salt. Arrange the steaks on a rimmed baking sheet and pat the spice rub all over them. Cover and let sit for at least 4 hours and up to 1 day in the refrigerator.

In a 1-qt. sealable container, combine the tomato, onion, red pepper, oil, and vinegar with ¼ cup water, and the remaining garlic paste, 1 Tbs. thyme, 2 tsp. salt, and 1 tsp. black pepper. Shake well. Refrigerate for up to 1 day before serving.

Heat a gas grill to medium high or prepare a hot charcoal fire. Grill the steak (covered on a gas grill) until it has good grill marks on the first side, 4 to 5 minutes. Flip the steak; if using a gas grill, reduce the heat to medium and cover the grill. Continue to cook until done to your liking (make a slit in the steak to take a peek), 4 to 5 minutes more for medium rare; 6 to 7 minutes more for medium.

Let the steak rest on a cutting board for 5 minutes and then slice thinly across the grain. Stir or shake the salsa criolla and serve with the steak.

Wine pairing: A supple, fruity Merlot like the 2003 Black Box, California, $25 (3 liters).

Strategies for feeding a crowd

With a little planning and prepping, your cookout will go smoothly and you'll be able to spend more time with your guests. Here are some tips for entertaining a crowd:

Clean out the refrigerator or prepare a large cooler to accommodate all the meats, side dishes, and drinks.

Make sure you have more than enough plates, napkins, glasses, and utensils. In a crowd, people tend to lose track of their glasses, and someone is bound to drop a fork.

Lay in an extra supply of charcoal or gas for the grill.

Create a cooking timeline so that everything will be ready when you need it. Work backwards from serving time, recognizing that some dishes, like the vegetable side dishes here, can be grilled before guests arrive, as they hold fine for an hour or two.

Marinate the meats and make the complementary sauces or dips the day before.

Complete the more labor-intensive tasks like chopping vegetables, herbs, and other flavorings a couple of hours ahead of time.

Grilled Asparagus & Onions with Balsamic Vinegar & Blue Cheese

Serves ten to twelve as a side dish.

This warm salad with its rich ingredients is just the thing for a cool early- or late-summer get-together. The tanginess of the balsamic adds some bounce to the blue cheese and complements the sweetness of the grilled vegetables and figs.

2½ lb. asparagus (about 2 large bunches), trimmed
8 Tbs. extra-virgin olive oil
1 tsp. kosher salt
Freshly ground black pepper
1 large sweet onion (such as Vidalia), cut into ½-inch disks and threaded onto metal skewers
2 Tbs. balsamic vinegar
2 tsp. chopped fresh thyme
3 oz. good-quality blue cheese, crumbled (¾ cup)
⅓ cup thinly sliced dried Black Mission figs (preferably small ones)
¼ cup pine nuts, toasted

Heat a gas grill to medium or prepare a medium charcoal fire.

Put the asparagus on a rimmed baking sheet, drizzle with 2 Tbs. of the oil, and season with ½ tsp. of the salt and a few generous grinds of black pepper. Turn to coat. Grill the asparagus (covered on a gas grill) until they have nice grill marks, about 4 minutes. Turn and continue cooking until tender and browned, about 4 more minutes; transfer to a large platter. Reduce the heat on the gas grill to medium low or let the charcoal burn down a bit.

On a rimmed baking sheet, coat the onions with 2 Tbs. of the oil, the remaining ½ tsp. salt, and several grinds of pepper. Grill, covered, until tender and browned, 8 to 10 minutes per side. Return the onions to the baking sheet.

In a small bowl, whisk together the remaining ¼ cup olive oil, the vinegar, and thyme. Toss the asparagus with about half the vinaigrette and then arrange neatly on the platter. Scatter the onions over the asparagus and drizzle with the remaining vinaigrette. Sprinkle with the blue cheese, figs, and pine nuts, and serve; this can sit for up to 1 hour at room temperature.

Grilling checklist

Essential equipment to assemble before firing up the grill:

Long-handled, spring-loaded tongs to handle everything. Never use that giant fork that comes with a barbecue tools set; it just pokes holes in meat and lets precious juices escape.

Large spatula or two. These come in handy when turning large pieces of meat or handling delicate vegetables.

Hot pads or dishtowels. Mitts can be too bulky, but folded dishtowels work as well as potholders. Have an extra towel on hand for cleanup.

Metal skewers. You'll need these for grilling the onions for the Grilled Asparagus & Onions with Balsamic Vinegar & Blue Cheese, or the Grilled Southwestern Potato Salad.

Wire-bristled brush. Use to clean the grill grate (which is easiest while it's still warm).

Table or other launching and landing surface. If your grill doesn't have an adjacent shelf, you'll need a small table or some other place to stage food for the grill and stack a few clean plates and platters for food coming off the grill.

Instant-read thermometer. Take the guess-work out of when your meats are done.

Tony Rosenfeld is a contributing editor at Fine Cooking. ◆

starters

Farmers' Market Crudités with Buttermilk Herb Dip

Serves twelve as an appetizer; yields 3 cups dip.

Though I have listed my own favorite vegetables for these crudités, feel free to go with whatever looks good at the market.

FOR THE DIP:
- 1 cup plain whole-milk yogurt
- 1 cup sour cream
- 1 cup freshly grated Parmigiano-Reggiano
- ⅓ cup buttermilk
- 1 cup thinly sliced fresh chives
- 2 Tbs. chopped fresh dill
- 2 Tbs. chopped fresh thyme
- 1 small clove garlic, minced and mashed to a paste with a pinch of salt
- 1 Tbs. cider vinegar
- ¼ tsp. Tabasco; more to taste
- 1½ tsp. kosher salt
- 1½ tsp. coarsely ground black pepper

FOR THE CRUDITES:
- 1 lb. pickling cucumbers (I like using small French or Armenian types), cut into spears 3 to 4 inches long and ½ inch thick
- 1 lb. sugar snap peas, strings and stem ends trimmed
- 1 lb. small, slender carrots, peeled and cut into 3- to 4-inch lengths (halve or quarter them lengthwise if they're thick)
- 1 pint grape or cherry tomatoes

In a large bowl, whisk all of the ingredients for the dip. Season with more Tabasco, salt, and pepper, to taste. Let sit for 15 minutes.

Arrange the vegetables on a large platter, with the dip in the center, or put each vegetable in its own bowl and arrange with the dip on a tray. Let guests help themselves.

Make ahead: The dip can be made up to 1 day ahead.

Wine pairing: A crisp Pinot Grigio like the 2005 Zenato Delle Venezie, $17 (magnum).

Grilled Bruschetta with Rosemary-White Bean Purée & Heirloom Tomatoes

Serves ten to twelve.

- ¾ cup extra-virgin olive oil; more as needed
- 4 cloves garlic, smashed and peeled
- Two 3- to 4-inch sprigs plus 1 tsp. chopped fresh rosemary
- 2 large ripe heirloom tomatoes (about 1¼ lb.), cut into ½-inch dice (about 3 cups)
- 2 Tbs. chopped fresh mint
- 1½ tsp. kosher salt; more as needed
- One 15-oz. can cannellini beans, rinsed well and drained
- ⅓ cup freshly grated Parmigiano-Reggiano
- 1 to 2 Tbs. fresh lemon juice
- ½ tsp. freshly ground black pepper; more as needed
- 1 lb. baguette, cut into ½-inch-thick slices

Heat the oil, garlic, and rosemary sprigs in a small saucepan over medium heat until they start to sizzle steadily and become fragrant, 2 to 3 minutes. Let the oil cool to room temperature. Strain the oil into a measuring cup. (If making ahead, store in the refrigerator and use within 3 days.)

Put the tomatoes in a medium bowl and toss with 3 Tbs. of the garlic oil, the mint, and 1 tsp. of the salt.

Put the beans in a food processor and add about 6 Tbs. of the garlic oil, the Parmigiano, 1 Tbs. of the lemon juice, the chopped rosemary, remaining ½ tsp. salt, and the black pepper and purée until smooth. Season to taste with more salt, pepper, and lemon juice.

Heat a gas grill to medium high or prepare a medium-hot charcoal fire. Brush both sides of the bread with the remaining garlic oil. (If you run out, use plain olive oil to finish.) Sprinkle lightly with salt. Grill the bread until crisp, with nice grill marks on both sides, 1 to 2 minutes per side.

Spread the grilled bread with the bean purée, top with a generous spoonful of the tomatoes and their juices, sprinkle lightly with pepper, and set out on a large platter so your guests can help themselves.

Wine pairing: Try a crisp, herbal Sauvignon Blanc from New Zealand like the 2006 Kim Crawford, Marlborough, $14.

The Rebirth of a Legend.

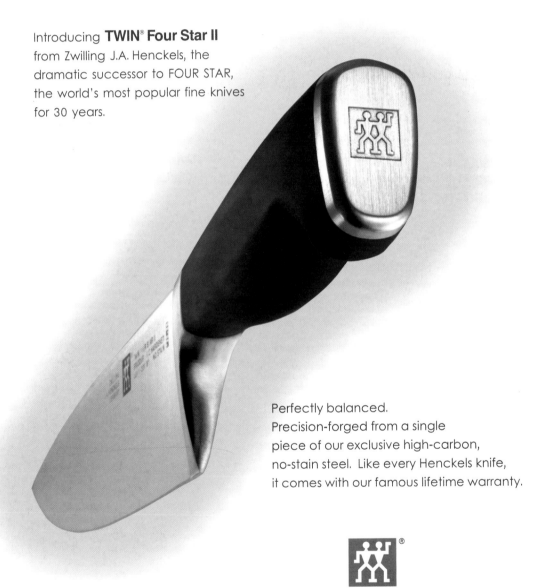

Introducing **TWIN® Four Star II** from Zwilling J.A. Henckels, the dramatic successor to FOUR STAR, the world's most popular fine knives for 30 years.

Perfectly balanced. Precision-forged from a single piece of our exclusive high-carbon, no-stain steel. Like every Henckels knife, it comes with our famous lifetime warranty.

ZWILLING
J.A.HENCKELS

PASSION FOR THE BEST. SINCE 1731.

jahenckels.com

The leading independent product testing organization ranks Henckels TWIN knives #1 and #2 among all brands.

Paper planks

Grilling on aromatic wood planks gives meats and fish a subtle smoky flavor. These paper-thin, disposable slices of cedar wood are a nice alternative to investing in a whole piece of wood, or if you don't want to deal with cleaning and storing the wood. You soak the papers in water or wine for 10 minutes to make them pliable and prevent them from catching fire. Then you wrap them around fish, vegetables, chicken, or beef. The bundles go directly on grill grates or on a baking sheet in the oven. Salmon fillets picked up a delicate, woody flavor when wrapped in the papers, even baked in the oven. From Fire & Flavor Grilling Company, the papers are sold at Whole Foods Markets and come in two sizes: 6x6 inches, eight for $10 (good for shrimp and tofu) and 6x9½ inches, four for $10 (for larger pieces of meat and fish). You can also buy them at FireAndFlavor.com.

Point & shine

Grilling in the dark is never a good idea—you end up burning the food or yourself. The Lumatong lets you shine some light on the subject with an LED flashlight attached to 20-inch, heavy-duty grilling tongs. Developed by Steven Raichlen, author of *The Barbecue Bible*, the tongs shoot a small but bright beam of blue-tinged light at the press of a button. With wide scalloped ends and Bakelite handles that keep their cool, the tongs work well, despite a locking mechanism that was a bit uncomfortable on the pair I tried. The light snaps off for easy cleaning and can be used on other similar-size tongs. The Lumatong sells for $20 at Store .Grilling4all.com.

5 things to do with an
oversize spatula

If you haven't already added an oversize spatula to your collection, consider that its usefulness extends beyond the cookie sheet. Here are some suggestions:

1 Moving a cake layer from the rack to a decorating pedestal or serving plate.

2 Lifting a whole fish from a baking pan or the grill.

3 Transferring pie dough from the counter to a pie or tart pan.

4 Flipping large pancakes.

5 Moving pizzas in and out of the oven, as a stand-in for a pizza peel.

King Arthur Flour sells one called a cookie shovel for $16 at KingArthurFlour.com.

Cleaning mitt for stainless steel

Creating the look of a professional kitchen is easy with stainless-steel appliances. Keeping those surfaces shiny is another matter. I find cleaning sprays for stainless steel drying to my skin, so I was eager to try this chemical-free solution from Simplehuman. It's a hand mitt made of microfiber that uses only water. You dampen one side of the mitt, wipe down the appliance, and then turn the mitt over and use the dry side to polish the surface. Little elbow grease is required to get a mirror finish. To clean, toss the mitt in the washing machine. The Simplehuman mitt is $5, and you can buy it at Simplehuman.com.

Seeing clearly

Nothing gives a kitchen a cutting-edge look like a glass-door refrigerator. But for those times when your leftovers aren't quite ready for their close-up, the new Sub-Zero 601RG features a switch to dim or turn off the interior light. The see-through door goes a long way toward ending open-door fridge loitering, as does the alarm, which beeps if the door is left ajar for more than 30 seconds. The 20.1-cubic-foot capacity all-refrigerator sells for $4,100 and comes in stainless steel or overlay to let you match your cabinets. Go to Sub Zero.com to find a dealer.

If your leftovers aren't up to general viewing, you can dim or turn off this refrigerator's interior light.

Muffin pan marries metal with silicone

This bakeware update is nice for small batches of muffins or cupcakes, because you don't have to fill the unused cups with water; just pop them out. It's also convenient to cool and transport the muffins in their own silicone jackets, which peel off easily and don't require any greasing. KitchenAid plans to offer a replacement set of silicone cups in the near future, in case you want to bake successive batches, or to replace those that have wandered off in school lunches. Available at Amazon.com for $35.

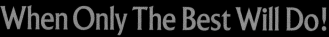

review
Large Saucepans

BY MARYELLEN DRISCOLL

A good-quality saucepan is a critical piece of any cookware ensemble. Most home cooks have one or two that are in the 1- to 3-quart range. Not so many of us, however, own a really large saucepan—at least 3 ½ quarts in capacity. It's not quite a stockpot, but it's roomy enough to boil potatoes or pasta, simmer a marinara, steam vegetables, or make polenta. It's good for making a large batch of oatmeal or rice or even a small batch of stew or a soup. In short, it's a pan you could use almost every day.

We focused this review on 3½- to 4½-quart saucepans with a helper handle. We consider this loop-shaped handle an essential with this size saucepan; it's a real asset when you have to carry a pan filled with boiling water and potatoes from the stove to the sink and then drain it into a colander. We also limited our focus to pans with a traditional stainless-steel cooking surface (not nonstick or anodized aluminum).

After putting six saucepans that met our criteria through their paces, we discovered that they all performed well overall. In every pan, onions sautéed evenly, rice didn't burn, water came to a boil at a similar rate, and the long handles stayed cool, though the helper handles did not. These results weren't all that surprising. All of the pans have an aluminum core, which is a superior heat conductor. And even large saucepans have a relatively small cooking surface (about 8 inches), making it easier for heat to be distributed evenly. Finally, since saucepans are most often used for moist-heat cooking like boiling, steaming, and simmering, and since water is a terrific transporter of heat, this would minimize any minor differences among the pans.

There was one pan that we gravitated to more than the others, the Cuisinox, and we've listed that as our favorite. But every other pan had something going for it, whether in shape, weight, or handle design. So instead of ranking them, as we usually do, we've grouped them as equals. All the pans here are dishwasher safe.

Overall Favorite
Cuisinox Elite

3.8 quarts
$102, KnifeMerchant.com

This was the pan we wanted to keep using. It strikes a nice balance in size and weight, and it's one of the better values of the bunch, too.

Highlights:
Measurement markings in liters and quarts on the pan's inside wall.

Rim gracefully rolled for smooth pouring.

Softly rounded interior bottom edge (where the base of the pan meets the wall), making it easy to scrape and stir with a wooden spoon or spatula.

Tempered-glass lid available for purchase at Cuisinox.com. (The pan comes with a traditional stainless steel lid.)

Induction-friendly pans

Several of the pans shown here work on induction cooktops, which are becoming a popular alternative to electric and gas (they're very responsive, safe, and energy efficient). To be compatible with induction, a pan must have a magnetic layer in the base (stainless steel, aluminum, and copper alone are not magnetic). One way to know is to put a magnet on the bottom of the pan. If it sticks well, the pan is induction friendly.

the good cook

Elegant affairs start here

PAULA DEEN
It Ain't All About the Cookin'
0992 $25 $1

barefoot contessa at home
ina garten
0455 $35 $1

Giada De Laurentiis
EVERY DAY PASTA
0612 $32.50 $1

Photo from *Barefoot Contessa At Home*

ryday italian
DE LAURENTIIS
1 $30 $1

giada's
4564 $32.50 $1

INA GARTEN BAREFOOT CONTESSA FAMILY STYLE
1461 $35 $1

MOLTO ITALIANO
MARIO BATALI
2931 $34.95 $1

The BON APPÉTIT COOKBOOK
0331 $34.95 $1

joy OF COOKING
0026 $30 $1

choose

4 *cookbooks for*

$1 *each*

with membership

DIA'S ITALY
MATTICCHIO BASTIANICH
5 $35 $1

RACHAEL RAY 2,4,6,8 GREAT MEALS FOR COUPLES OR CROWDS
A 30-MINUTE MEAL COOKBOOK
†0380 $19.95 $1

PAULA DEEN CELEBRATES
PAULA DEEN
0141 $26 $1

The Deen Bros. Cookbook
Recipes from the Road
0943 $24.95 $1

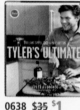
TYLER'S ULTIMATE
0638 $35 $1

MARTHA STEWART'S BAKING HANDBOOK
2998 $40 $1

† Softcover; *Counts as two choices; • Softcover Spiralbound; ◆ Hardcover Spiralbound. All prices listed are for publishers' editions.

aking
Greenpan
5 $40 $1

BOOT CAMP
0679 $29.95 $1

rfect Recipes
r Having People Over
Pam Anderson
20 $35 $1

Welcome to the Table
0620 $24.95 $1

Save up to $156 off publishers' edition prices!

the good cook

NOTE: To select a book that counts as 2, write the book number in one row of boxes and 9999 in the next row.

Please write 4-digit book numbers here:

For faster ordering, join online at JoinTheGoodCook.com

☐ **Yes!** Please enroll me in *The Good Cook* according to the risk-free membership plan described on page 2. Send me the 4 BOOKS I have indicated at right. Bill me $4, plus shipping and handling. I agree to buy just 2 more books in the next year.

Do you have a phone?
☐ Yes   ☐ No
Have you ever bought anything by mail?
☐ Yes   ☐ No
How have you paid?
☐ Cash ☐ Credit Card
☐ Check
☐ Money Order   #604

Sign Here:_____
Must be 18 & over or parent must sign.

Mr./Mrs.
Miss/Ms._____

Address_____

_____

City_____ State_____ ZIP_____

Choose

4 cookbooks for

$1 each
with membership

Save More Now! Send me this book at 50% off publisher's edition price, plus shipping and handling, and reduce my commitment to 1 book in one year. Books that count as 2 choices are not eligible.

▼ Hear about our great online-only sales! Please supply us with your e-mail address. ▼

THE WORLD AT YOUR TABLE
ourmet
Better Homes
COOK BOOK
7 $40 $1
◆0158 $29.95 $1

5KRZ90   ← Go Online and enter this Code
1•09•7•25•1•Z90•07•A(−)•604

Members accepted in USA and Canada only. Canadian members serviced from Canada, where offer is slightly different. Sales tax added where applicable. Membership subject to approval.

▼ Write book number here:

TGC0704PT-03   4/29/07

Any of these pans would make a fine choice

All-Clad Stainless

4 quarts
$195, ChefsResource.com

Highlights:

Relatively deep (5 inches), which is useful for cooking potatoes or beans or anything that tends to foam up precariously, like caramel or soba noodles.

Lid fits snugly so that minimum steam escapes.

Compatible with induction cooktops.

Same size pan exists without a helper handle for $10 less. (Go for the helper handle.)

Demeyere Apollo Silvinox

4.2 quarts
$135, CooksWares.com

Highlights:

Base is wider than most (8¾-inch diameter), but the pot isn't so deep (4¼ inches), so it's ideal for sautéing larger quantities of onions and vegetables (say, for a soup) or browning meat for a ragù or chili.

Slightly rounded and extended rim prevents drips and dribbles.

Rounded handle is comfortable and not too long, which is a plus for storage.

Compatible with induction cooktops.

KitchenAid Gourmet Excellence

4 quarts
$140, CutleryAndMore.com

Highlights:

Relatively deep (5 inches), which is useful for cooking potatoes or beans or anything that tends to foam up precariously, like caramel or soba noodles.

Slightly curved rim prevents drips while pouring.

Handle's arch provides good leverage when lifting this bottom-heavy pan, but its defined edges can feel uncomfortable as you roll the pan to empty its contents.

ScanPan Fusion 5

4 quarts
$100, ScanPanCookware.com

Highlights:

Measurement markings in liters and quarts on the pan's inside wall.

Rounded bottom edge inside the pan for easier stirring.

Rolled rim for smoother pouring.

Relatively short handle makes it easier to store.

Compatible with induction cooktops.

Viking

4½ quarts
$205, DifferentDrummersKitchen.com

Highlights:

Extra-large capacity with a wide base (8¾-inch diameter) and comparatively low sides (4¼ inches) make it well suited for sauces, soups, or stews that require an initial browning of ingredients.

At 4½ pounds (without the lid), it's the heftiest of the bunch.

Compatible with induction cooktops.

Dishwasher safe, but hand-washing is recommended.

Cleaning tip

Stainless-steel saucepans can sometimes develop white, cloudy spots on the surface. These are mineral deposits left after boiling water, particularly hard tap water. Clean the pan with a little vinegar and warm water and the spots will easily wash away.

Maryellen Driscoll is Fine Cooking's editor at large. ◆

Rich & Creamy
German-Style Wheat Beers
from an American Microbrewery

BY LAURA GIANNATEMPO

Greg crafts his Ramstein wheat beers—Blonde, Classic, and Winter—with the same meticulous care he witnessed in Germany.

Greg Zaccardi studied to be a chemist but somehow ended up brewing beer. "There's actually a lot of chemistry involved in beer making," he says by way of explanation. "You have to know how certain enzymes and molecules work and how to control each step to get the flavor and body you want."

Greg is the founder and driving force behind the High Point Brewing Company in Butler, New Jersey, the first wheat-only microbrewery in the United States—at least when he started it in 1996. Now he also brews a couple of lagers and a pale ale.

When asked why wheat beer, Greg credits his German girlfriend (now his wife), who took him on his first trip to southern Germany. There he tasted some amazing wheat beers, called *hefeweizen*. It was the desire to recreate those sweet, rich flavors and creamy texture that led him to apprentice at a small German wheat brewery and then to fly straight home and start making his own brews.

Greg crafts his Ramstein wheat beers—Blonde, Classic, and Winter—with the same meticulous care he witnessed in Germany: He tailors the ratio of wheat to barley and of light- to dark-roast grains to each type of beer and determines the quantity of hops needed to achieve the flavor balance he's after.

"My goal is to produce an elegant beer rooted in the European tradition but with a personality of its own, a beer that showcases

To make wheat beer, Greg Zaccardi uses 50% malted wheat and 50% malted barley, which he pours into a hopper.

the great ingredients we use," says Greg. His grains and hops come from Germany, and he uses a proprietary yeast from a small brewery in Bavaria. "Yeast is critical," he says. And this one gives his unfiltered weizens their distinctive overtones of banana, apple, and clove. Ramstein beers are available in New Jersey, New York, and Pennsylvania. *For information, visit RamsteinBeer.com or call 973-838-7400.*

2 *A mill cracks the grain, creating the "mash," which is mixed with water in a large tank. Greg raises the water temperature incrementally, activating enzymes that convert starches into sugar.*

3 *Once the conversion is completed, three-quarters of the mash is pumped into a vessel called a lauter tank, while the remaining quarter is boiled, or "decocted," to deepen its flavor and color (boiling time varies with the type of beer). The decocted mash is transferred back to the lauter tank to combine with the rest of the batch. The lauter tank acts like a coffee filter, slowly separating the solids from the sweet liquid.*

4 *Head brewer Paul Scarmazzo pours hops into the liquid to add bitterness. Hops boil with the liquid for about two hours, before the wort (liquid with hops) is pumped into fermentation tanks.*

5 *Fermentation begins when Greg or Paul adds yeast, which consumes the sugars and produces carbon dioxide (hence natural carbonation), alcohol, and flavor. Greg (at left) samples the liquid to monitor sugar concentration and clarity. The beer is ready when the sugar level has decreased by about 75%. He doesn't filter his wheat beers before bottling.* ◆

Winning tip

Ice cream sandwiches at the ready

My family loves ice cream sandwiches, so when I make homemade ice cream, I transfer it into zip-top freezer bags and lay them flat in the freezer. Once the ice cream freezes, I peel off the bag and use a biscuit cutter to cut out rounds of ice cream to sandwich between two cookies. You can do this with store-bought ice cream, too

—Coreen Franke,
Saskatoon, Saskatchewan

A prize for the best tip

We want your best tips—we'll pay for the ones we publish—and we'll give a prize to the cleverest tip in each issue. Write to Tips, *Fine Cooking*, PO Box 5506, Newtown, CT 06470-5506 or email fctips@taunton.com.

The prize for this issue's winner: A 6½-quart Perfect Plus Pressure Cooker from WMF with insert, trivet, and instructional DVD; value, about $220.

A great way to clean hands after handling chiles

I've found an easy way to clean my hands thoroughly after chopping hot peppers: I rub a small amount of vegetable or olive oil on my fingers for a minute and then wash them with a little dish soap. The oil removes the capsaicin, which is what irritates the skin and can so easily be transferred to your eyes or mouth.

—Sarah Kingston,
Provo, Utah

Hot packs keep picnic items warm

I went to a potluck last summer and needed to keep corn on the cob hot until dinnertime. I heated a hot pack in the microwave (make sure yours is the microwavable kind) and put it in the bottom of a small insulated cooler. Then I wrapped each cob of corn in aluminum foil, piled them on the hot pack, and set a platter on top. It was more than two hours before we ate, and the corn was still hot.

This idea would also work with casserole dishes right from the oven. Wrapping the dish in foil offers an extra layer of insulation.

—Valarie Pelissero,
Portland, Oregon

TOO GOOD TO FORGET
From *Fine Cooking* #10

Easier eggplant

When preparing eggplant—especially for grilling—I like to leave the skin on for flavor and because it helps keep the tender flesh from falling apart. But sometimes the skin can become a chewy mess. I compromise by scoring the entire eggplant from top to bottom with a dinner fork. The fork's closely spaced tines leave fine "stripes" on the eggplant's skin, not unlike the way cucumbers are often left with stripes of peel. When cooked, the skin is much more manageable.

—Michael Wodjenski,
New Milford, Connecticut

Keeping corn on the cob warm

Whenever I cook corn on the cob for a dinner party, I take the corn out of the boiling water with tongs, put the cobs in a colander, then set the colander over the cooking pot of water while I assemble the rest of the dinner. Even with the burner off, the steam from the boiled water keeps the corn moist and hot until it gets to the table.

—Nadia Collins, via email

Yogurt substitutes for buttermilk

I love the taste of buttermilk in baked goods, but somehow I never seem to have it on hand. However, I always have yogurt in the fridge and find it makes a good substitute when combined with milk. If the recipe calls for 1 cup of buttermilk, I use ½ cup milk combined with ½ cup yogurt. (Because buttermilk is low fat or nonfat, the yogurt and milk should be low fat or nonfat as well.)

—Catherine Subick,
Philadelphia

Store nut butter jars upside down

I've found it's better to store my jars of natural nut butters upside down. This way the solids collect at the top of the jar and the oil separates to the bottom. Stirring to reincorporate the oil is easier if you don't have to scrape stiff solids from the bottom of the jar.

—Anne Huber,
West Lafayette, Indiana

Grapefruit knife carves bread easily

I used to have a hard time cutting neat lids out of loaves of bread to create bread bowls for soups and dips. Because a grapefruit knife is serrated on both sides, it quickly cuts through the top of a loaf and gives me a perfect lid every time.

—Tina Petok,
Davidson, North Carolina

Microwave long-cooking vegetables before grilling

We love to grill zucchini, carrots, and potatoes, but too often we find that the carrots and potatoes burn on the outside before fully cooking through. Now, before grilling, I par-cook potatoes, carrots, and other hard vegetables for a couple of minutes in the microwave on high to give them a head start.

—Geoff Mayo, Toronto

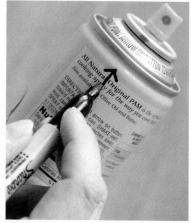

Protect yourself from cooking spray

Occasionally, when wrestling with a stubborn cap on a can of cooking spray, the cap will finally pop off, causing the nozzle to spray—usually all over my clothes. To avoid this, I use a sticker or marker to indicate on the side of the can which way the nozzle is facing. I always turn the nozzle away from me when removing the cap, and this way, my clothes don't suffer.

—Siobhan Crosby,
Portland, Oregon

TWO TIPS FOR CORN COB HOLDERS:

Use Styrofoam to organize corn holders

I grew tired of searching for my corn cob holders and getting pricked by their sharp ends, so I made a holder for them. I cut a piece of Styrofoam to fit in my utensil drawer and stuck the holders in the Styrofoam. Now they're easy to find.

—Lisa Spraggins, Dallas

Stick corn holders in a cork

After pricking my fingers too many times searching for corn cob holders in my drawer, I now store each pair in a wine cork. One goes on each end of the cork, and they're easy to spot in my drawer.

—Cindy Johnston,
Lakewood, Washington ◆

Mini burgers, pizzettas, and skewers—choose one for a starter or make them all for a party

BY ALLISON EHRI

Come summertime, most of us turn to the grill to do the heavy lifting, whether it's for hamburgers, hot dogs, or baby back ribs. But as someone who loves to both cook *and* be outdoors as much as possible, I use the grill for just about anything. My latest discovery is how great the grill is for making all kinds of nifty appetizers, from shrimp skewers to tiny tuna burgers and pizzas. You can grill up one or two as predinner noshes, or you can make a

Appetizers, Hot

whole bunch and stagger them throughout a party, as I do (see my prep strategy on p. 38). These tasty little nibbles are small enough that they disappear in one or two bites—no plates or forks required (just napkins)—and they're guaranteed crowd-pleasers.

Another reason these cute bites are perfect for an outdoor party is that they're super quick to prepare and take only minutes to cook—in fact, you can do most of the work ahead, so you have time to socialize with your guests. The trick is to keep things simple. That's not to say you can't throw in a twist or two to make these bites feel a little special.

Both skewers, for example, benefit from the subtle smokiness of a pimentón (smoked paprika) vinaigrette used as a marinade. I add mint to give fresh nuance to the aïoli that accompanies the mini tuna burgers. And a splash of Pernod or sambuca (both anise-flavored liqueurs) really boosts the fennel-seed flavor of the mini pizzas topped with fresh tomato, olives, and aged goat cheese. I also love to play with contrasting flavors and textures: The pancetta and pineapple skewers are both sweet and salty, and the almond and cheese inside the stuffed apricots provide a nice crunchy-melty contrast.

Off the Grill

Shrimp Skewers
Serves six; yields 12 skewers.

36 shrimp (21 to 25 per lb.; about 1½ lb. total), peeled (tail segment left on) and deveined
Twelve 8-inch bamboo skewers, soaked in water
1 recipe Pimentón Vinaigrette (see below)

Thread three shrimp onto each skewer. Lay the skewers in a large Pyrex baking dish (or other large nonreactive container) and pour the pimentón vinaigrette over the skewers, turning them to coat completely. Marinate for at least 30 minutes in the refrigerator.

Heat a gas grill to medium high or prepare a medium-hot charcoal fire. Grill the skewers (covered on a gas grill, uncovered on a charcoal grill), flipping once, until the shrimp are just cooked through, about 4 minutes total.

Make ahead: The shrimp can be skewered up to 1 day ahead and marinated up to 4 hours ahead and refrigerated.

Pimentón Vinaigrette
Yields about ½ cup.

Pimentón is smoked Spanish paprika. You can find it in specialty food stores or online (see Where To Buy It, p. 73).

1 large clove garlic
Generous ½ tsp. kosher salt
¼ cup extra-virgin olive oil
1½ Tbs. fresh lemon juice
1 Tbs. sherry vinegar
1 tsp. sweet (dulce) pimentón
½ tsp. freshly ground black pepper

Chop the garlic, sprinkle it with the salt, and mash it into a paste with the side of a chef's knife (or use a mortar and pestle). In a medium bowl, mix the garlic paste, oil, lemon juice, vinegar, pimentón, and pepper.

Make ahead: This can be made up to 2 days ahead and refrigerated.

Pancetta & Pineapple Skewers

Serves six; yields 12 skewers.

**4 oz. pancetta, cut into twenty-four
½- to ¾-inch cubes**
**6 oz. pineapple (about ½ small pineapple),
peeled and cut into twenty-four
½- to ¾-inch cubes**
**Twelve 8-inch bamboo skewers, soaked
in water**
1 recipe Pimentón Vinaigrette (p. 37)

Put the pancetta in a small pot, cover it with cold water, and bring to a boil. As soon as the water boils, drain the pancetta in a colander and let it cool slightly.

Heat a gas grill to medium high or prepare a medium-hot charcoal fire. Thread two pancetta cubes and two pineapple cubes onto each skewer, alternating the pancetta and the pineapple. Put the skewers in a large Pyrex baking dish (or other large nonreactive container) and pour the Pimentón Vinaigrette over the skewers, turning to coat them completely. Grill the skewers (covered on a gas grill, uncovered on a charcoal grill), checking for flare-ups and turning and flipping the skewers as necessary to cook on all sides until the pancetta is crisp, about 6 minutes total.

Make ahead: The skewers can be assembled up to 1 day ahead and marinated up to 4 hours ahead and refrigerated.

Make it a party

Here's a strategy for doing it all.

Up to 2 days ahead

Make a double batch of Pimentón Vinaigrette.

Soak the skewers and toothpicks.

Up to 1 day ahead

Assemble all the skewers and the apricots.

Prep everything for the pizzettas but the dough.

Up to 4 hours ahead

Marinate the shrimp skewers.

Coat the pineapple skewers in the vinaigrette.

Cut the pitas.

Pick the mint leaves.

Up to 2 hours ahead

Make the aïoli and refrigerate.

Shape the tuna burgers and refrigerate.

Set up a work surface near the grill.

Up to 1 hour ahead

Roll and cut the pizza dough and refrigerate.

Season the apricots.

Mini Tuna Burgers with Mint-Caper Aïoli on Pita Triangles

Serves six to eight; yields about 18.

You can make the aïoli with a pasteurized egg if raw eggs are an issue.

1 large egg, separated
2 Tbs. capers, rinsed
1 large clove garlic, coarsely chopped
1 Tbs. fresh lemon juice
¼ tsp. kosher salt; more as needed
**⅛ tsp. freshly ground black pepper; more
as needed**
**½ cup extra-virgin olive oil; more for
brushing**
**2 Tbs. chopped fresh mint, plus 18 large
leaves for garnish**
1 lb. tuna steak, cut into 1-inch chunks
3 regular pitas, each cut into 6 triangles

Put the egg yolk, capers, garlic, lemon juice, salt, and pepper in a food processor and purée until smooth. With the motor running, slowly drizzle the oil through the feed tube to form an emulsion. Stop the motor, add the 2 Tbs. chopped mint, and pulse to combine. Spoon ¼ cup of the aïoli into a small bowl.

Add the tuna and egg white to the food processor bowl and pulse until just chopped. Line a baking sheet with waxed paper or parchment. Drop 18 rounds of the tuna mixture by heaping tablespoons onto the baking sheet. Use your hands to shape the mounds into mini burgers about ⅓ inch thick.

Heat a gas grill to high or prepare a hot charcoal fire.

Brush one side of the tuna burgers with oil and season with salt and pepper. Gently flip the burgers and oil and season the other side. Put the pita triangles on another baking sheet, brush both sides with oil and sprinkle both sides with a little salt and pepper. Grill the

pitas on both sides until lightly browned and a little crisp but still pliable, 1 to 2 minutes total. Transfer to a serving platter.

Grill the burgers (covered on a gas grill, uncovered on a charcoal grill) on one side until they have nice grill marks, about 2 minutes. Flip the burgers, loosening them with a metal spatula if necessary, and grill the other side until marked and just cooked through, about 2 minutes more.

While the burgers are cooking, spread a little of the reserved aïoli inside each pita. As the burgers come off the grill, tuck one into each pita along with a mint leaf and serve immediately.

Make ahead: The burgers can be shaped up to 2 hours ahead and refrigerated.

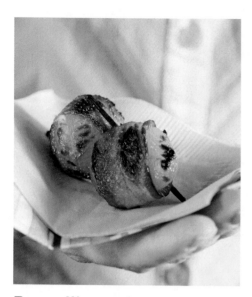

Bacon-Wrapped Stuffed Apricots

Serves six to eight; yields 24.

Apricot sizes can vary; if yours are on the smaller side, just trim the cheese a bit and squish it in.

24 dried apricots (about 7 oz.)
3 oz. plain Havarti, cut into ½- to ¾-inch squares ¼ inch thick
24 almonds (about 1 oz.)
12 strips bacon (about 12 oz.), cut in half crosswise
24 toothpicks, soaked in water
Freshly ground black pepper

Heat a gas grill to high or prepare a hot charcoal fire.

Pry open the apricots and put a piece of cheese and an almond into each one. Wrap a piece of bacon around each apricot, trimming as necessary so it overlaps by ½ inch, and secure it with a toothpick. Season the apricots all over with pepper.

Reduce the grill heat to medium (scatter the coals a bit or raise the grate if using charcoal). Use tongs to grill the apricots on all sides with the grill open, propping them between the bars to hold them up on the narrow sides. Move the apricots around often to avoid flare-ups. Cook until the bacon is crisp all over, about 6 minutes total. Serve immediately and remind guests to remove the toothpicks.

Make ahead: The apricots can be assembled up to 1 day ahead and refrigerated.

Tomato & Olive Pizzettas with Fennel Seeds & Aged Goat Cheese

Serves six to eight; yields 18 mini pizzas.

You can find pizza dough in the grocery store, or try your favorite pizzeria—most will sell their dough. Sambuca or Pernod makes a nice sweet contrast with the salty cheese, and it brings out the flavor of the fennel.

Flour for the work surface
1 lb. pizza dough
Extra-virgin olive oil for brushing
Kosher salt and freshly ground black pepper
2 tsp. fennel seeds, coarsely chopped
One 1-inch-thick slice Bûcheron (about 6 oz.), cut into 36 thin wedges (if the cheese crumbles, let it warm to room temperature) or a log of fresh goat cheese, cut into thin rounds
14 pitted Kalamata olives, quartered
18 cherry or grape tomatoes, sliced into ¼-inch rounds, ends discarded
Crushed red pepper flakes
1½ tsp. sambuca or Pernod

Heat a gas grill to medium high or prepare a medium-hot charcoal fire with the coals banked to one side to provide a cooler area on the grill.

On a well-floured surface roll out the pizza dough with a rolling pin until it's ⅛ inch thick. If the dough is very elastic and resists rolling, cover it with plastic and let it rest for about 5 minutes. You may have to repeat this step a few times until the dough is relaxed and willing to roll. Using a 3-inch ring cutter, cut the dough into 18 rounds. Discard the excess dough. Brush the top of the dough rounds with oil and sprinkle with salt,

pepper, and fennel seeds, pressing gently to make sure they adhere. Transfer the rounds to a baking sheet, fennel side up.

Working with half of the pizzettas at a time, grill them fennel side down (covered on a gas grill, uncovered on a charcoal grill) for 1 minute. Check the pizzettas: If they have puffed up, flatten them with a metal spatula. Brush the floured sides (which are facing up) with oil. Grill until the bottom is nicely browned and crisp, about 1 more minute. Loosen with a metal spatula, if necessary, and return the pizzettas, grilled side up, to the baking sheet. (If using a gas grill, turn the heat down to medium.)

Working quickly, top each with 2 wedges of Bûcheron, 3 olive pieces, 3 tomato slices, and a pinch of red pepper flakes. Use a small spoon to sprinkle each pizzetta with a few drops of sambuca or Pernod.

Return the pizzettas to the medium-heat gas grill or to the cooler side of a charcoal grill. Continue grilling, covered, until the pizzettas are crisp and the cheese is melted, about 2 minutes. Transfer to a platter and serve while you repeat with the remaining dough rounds.

Make ahead: The pizzetta toppings can be prepared up to 1 day ahead and refrigerated. The dough can be rolled and cut up to 1 hour ahead and refrigerated, covered.

Allison Ehri is Fine Cooking's *test kitchen associate and food stylist.* ◆

Sea Salt, Chile & Lime Butter

Lemon, Dill & Cucumber Sauce

Delicious Finishes

Follow these tips for perfectly grilled fish steaks, and serve them with your choice of four lively toppings

BY MARIA HELM SINSKEY

I eat more fish in the summer, and most often it's grilled; I love the nice caramelization and smoky flavor that the fire provides. Plus, the easy elegance of grilled fish makes it perfect for practically effortless entertaining, especially when jazzed up with full-flavored accompaniments like the ones featured here. Though all four toppings have very different flavor profiles and are made using different methods, they all make great mates for fish.

If the mention of "grill" and "fish" in the same sentence makes you nervous, maybe you've had the experience of having fish cling tenaciously to the grate, only to be torn when flipped. But a few important hints can prevent your fish from sticking and falling apart and ensure moist, beautiful results.

Instead of fillets, go for fish steaks. Fillets can work on the grill, but they can also be dicey. Fillets are trickier to grill because

they're cut parallel to the bone, which makes them more delicate and flaky. Fish steaks, on the other hand, are cross-cut, which makes them sturdier, firmer, and less prone to flaking (see From Our Test Kitchen, p. 64, for more on fish steaks and fillets). Tuna, salmon, swordfish, and halibut are all in season during the summer. If you find wild salmon, grab it— it has more flavor and a better texture than farmed.

The thickness of the fish matters. A fish steak should be no less than 1 inch thick and ideally about 1¼ inches. This size cooks more slowly and evenly, so the fish stays nice and moist. If you don't see such steaks at the fish counter, ask your fishmonger to cut them for you. (If you can't find thick steaks, shorten the cooking time for the fish.)

Consider the fish's personality as you pair it with a topping. The topping recipes on p. 42 may be used with your choice of fish, which means you can pick what's freshest at the fish counter. However, I do have a

favorite pairing for each one. Rich and tangy, the caper-studded tarragon mayonnaise perks up lean, mild halibut, while the briny intensity of the olive relish cuts through the fattiness of grilled tuna. As the chile-lime butter melts over grilled salmon, it infuses the oily, meaty flesh with a spicy brightness. Finally, the delicate, fresh mix of lemon and dill in the cucumber sauce livens up grilled swordfish, which, though well loved, can use a flavor boost.

The next day, make a salad with the leftovers. Any tarragon mayonnaise, olive relish, or cucumber sauce you have left can be mixed with cold, leftover grilled fish for a salad or sandwich the next day. Flake the fish the way you might canned tuna and mix it with the sauce. If you didn't use all the lime butter, spread it on grilled bread or melt it and toss it with croutons to add to a salad.

Sun-Dried Tomato, Olive & Caper Relish

Tarragon-Scented Mayonnaise with Cornichons & Capers

for Grilled Fish

Grilled Fish Steaks

Serves four to six.

I like salmon and tuna cooked medium rare, which means that salmon will be translucent in the center, and tuna will have a red band. Halibut and swordfish are best cooked through—firm to the touch and opaque throughout. Be sure to make your topping before starting to grill.

1½ Tbs. olive oil; more for brushing the grill
Four to six 1¼-inch-thick fish steaks (6 to 8 oz. each), such as tuna, salmon, swordfish, or halibut
1 tsp. kosher salt
1 topping of your choice (recipes on p. 42)

Clean and oil the grates on a gas grill following the instruc- tions on p. 69 and heat the grill to medium high, or prepare a medium-hot charcoal fire.

Meanwhile, generously coat both sides of the fish with the oil and season both sides with salt. Let the fish sit at room temperature for 15 minutes (while the grill heats). Grill the fish steaks directly over the heat source (covered on a gas grill, uncovered on a charcoal grill), without touching, until they have good grill marks, 2 to 4 minutes. Flip the steaks and grill until the second sides have good grill marks and the fish is done to your liking, another 2 to 4 minutes. (Check for doneness by slicing into one of the thicker pieces.) Serve immediately with the topping of your choice.

Tips for grilling fish

Grilled fish steaks are a wonderful choice for entertaining because you can grill them to your guests' individual preferences. Follow the tips below, and the steaks will look gorgeous, too.

Begin with a clean, well-oiled grill, and let it heat up. A major culprit behind sticking fish is the debris left on the grates. Clean and oil the grill as described on p. 67 for best results. Hot grates keep fish from sticking by causing the proteins in the fish to contract and release, so be sure your grates are thoroughly heated before you start to grill.

Don't move the steaks for the first few minutes of cooking. You need to give the side that's facing down time to cook (and contract) before turning the fish.

Use tongs and a spatula to move the fish steaks. Tongs work really well for turning sturdy fish steaks, but sometimes a little unseen debris on the grill rack will cause the fish to stick. If this happens, slide a thin spatula under- neath the stubborn spot to release it.

Cut into the fish to check for doneness. Once you've grilled a lot of fish steaks, you'll know by feel when they're done to your liking. If you're not there yet, cut into the side of the fish with a paring knife to see what's going on inside. (Poke it with your finger, too, so you learn what different done- nesses feel like—the harder the flesh, the more done it is.)

Four ways to add flavor to fish

Tarragon-Scented Mayonnaise with Cornichons & Capers

Yields 1²/₃ cups, enough for six to eight servings.

This tangy tarragon-infused sauce complements mildly flavored fish like halibut or even tuna. Most mayonnaise is made with an egg yolk, but this recipe uses a whole egg, which gives the mayonnaise a looser consistency.

1 large egg
4 tsp. fresh lemon juice
¾ tsp. kosher salt; more as needed
Freshly ground black pepper
½ cup extra-virgin olive oil
½ cup canola or vegetable oil
¼ cup finely chopped cornichons (or gherkins)
2 Tbs. chopped capers
1 Tbs. minced shallot
1 Tbs. finely chopped fresh flat-leaf parsley
1 Tbs. chopped fresh tarragon
½ tsp. sweet paprika

Whisk the egg, lemon juice, salt, and a few grinds of black pepper in a bowl until well combined. Combine the oils and drizzle them into the egg mixture, whisking constantly. Once all the oil is added, the sauce should be shiny and thick. Fold in the remaining ingredients and season with salt and pepper to taste. Refrigerate for up to 1 day before using.

Note: You can make the sauce with a pasteurized egg if raw eggs are an issue or with store-bought mayonnaise (use about 1 heaping cup in place of the egg and oils).

Sun-Dried Tomato, Olive & Caper Relish

Yields a generous 1 cup, enough for four to six servings.

This Mediterranean-inspired relish pairs nicely with most grilled fish. For a shortcut, pulse the tomatoes and olives a few times in a food processor and then add the remaining ingredients and pulse to combine.

½ cup finely chopped oil-packed sun-dried tomatoes, drained
¼ cup finely chopped oil-cured olives
5 Tbs. extra-virgin olive oil
2½ Tbs. fresh lemon juice
1 Tbs. chopped capers
1 Tbs. minced fresh flat-leaf parsley
1 Tbs. minced shallot
2 tsp. minced fresh oregano
½ tsp. finely grated orange zest
Kosher salt and freshly ground black pepper

Combine all the ingredients, seasoning with salt and pepper to taste. You can make the relish up to 2 days ahead, which will allow the flavors to marry.

Note: The saltiness of the ingredients in this relish will vary, so make sure to adjust the seasonings to taste.

Lemon, Dill & Cucumber Sauce

Yields 2 cups, enough for six servings.

Delicate and light, this sauce, which has a loose texture that's somewhere between a vinaigrette and a salad, complements almost any grilled fish.

1 medium English cucumber, peeled and finely diced to yield 2 cups

2 Tbs. fresh lemon juice
½ tsp. granulated sugar
Kosher salt and freshly ground black pepper
¼ cup extra-virgin olive oil
2 Tbs. minced fresh dill
1 Tbs. minced shallot
2 tsp. minced fresh mint

Put the cucumber in a medium bowl. Add the lemon juice and the sugar, toss to combine, and season with salt and pepper to taste. Stir in the olive oil, dill, shallot, and mint, and add more salt and pepper if necessary. Let sit for 30 minutes to allow the flavors to marry. Taste for seasoning again just before serving and adjust if necessary.

Sea Salt, Chile & Lime Butter

Yields about ¹/₂ cup, enough for four to six servings.

The subtle spiciness of French Basque piment d'Espelette chile powder (see Where to Buy It, p. 73) is perfect for this butter, though crushed red pepper flakes make a fine substitute. Try the butter on salmon or halibut.

¼ lb. (8 Tbs.) unsalted butter, softened to room temperature
3 Tbs. finely chopped fresh cilantro

2 tsp. fresh lime juice
1 tsp. coriander seeds, lightly toasted and coarsely ground
¾ tsp. freshly grated lime zest
½ tsp. coarse sea salt, like fleur de sel or sel gris
½ tsp. piment d'Espelette chile powder or crushed red pepper flakes
¼ tsp. minced garlic

Beat the butter in a small bowl with a spoon to loosen it. Mix in the remaining ingredients until they're evenly distributed. Scrape the butter onto a sheet of parchment or plastic wrap and roll it into a neat log, using the parchment or plastic as a guide. Twist the ends and refrigerate the butter until firm, about 1 hour. Keep the butter chilled until ready to use.

How to use: Slice thin rounds from the butter log and top the fish with a couple of them the second it comes off the grill.

Maria Helm Sinskey is the author of The Vineyard Kitchen: Menus Inspired by the Seasons. ◆

Quick Pastas with a Kick

A little heat punches up the flavor of pastas made with summer favorites: corn, tomatoes, and zucchini

BY SCOTT CONANT

People often ask me what I cook at home, and I never know what to tell them. I think they're expecting to hear all about fancy, complicated dishes. But the truth is that with two busy restaurants, I don't spend much time at the stove when I'm home. What you'll most likely find me making when I get some time off is a simple, satisfying pasta, preferably one that's quick to make but still packed with flavor—just like the ones here.

To get great flavor quickly, I sauté summer vegetables like corn, tomatoes, and zucchini and boost their flavor with bold ingredients like caramelized onions, goat cheese, and grated pecorino. I also like to add a little heat to give my pastas an extra kick. This can come in the form of spicy sausage paired with summer squash, a pinch of cayenne in a marinade for shrimp, or even a little jalapeño added to a sauté of corn, green beans, and caramelized sweet onions. But don't worry: While these pastas are spicy, they're not fiery hot.

Finally, to bind the ingredients and create a well-balanced pasta with a saucy consistency, I always reserve some of the cooking water before I drain the pasta and add a little back when I toss the pasta with the other ingredients (see p. 45 for details).

Spaghetti with Spicy Shrimp, Cherry Tomatoes & Herbed Breadcrumbs

Serves four.

Fresh mint adds a bright, unexpected twist to this light, summery pasta.

⅓ cup plus 4 Tbs. extra-virgin olive oil
1 Tbs. plus 2 tsp. chopped fresh flat-leaf parsley
2 tsp. chopped fresh chives
Heaping ¼ tsp. crushed red pepper flakes
Pinch cayenne
½ tsp. kosher salt; more as needed
1 lb. raw shrimp (21 to 25 per lb.), peeled, deveined, and cut crosswise into quarters
¼ cup coarse fresh breadcrumbs (made from a baguette or other artisan bread)
1 Tbs. chopped fresh mint
Freshly ground black pepper
2 medium shallots, finely chopped
1 lb. dried thin spaghetti
4 cups cherry or grape tomatoes (2 pints), halved

In a large bowl, combine 2 Tbs. of the olive oil, 2 tsp. of the parsley, the chives, red pepper flakes, cayenne, and salt. Add the shrimp and stir to coat evenly. Cover the bowl with plastic and marinate in the refrigerator for about 20 minutes.

Bring a large pot of well-salted water to a boil over high heat.

In a small sauté pan, heat 2 Tbs. of the olive oil over medium heat. Add the breadcrumbs and cook, stirring frequently, until lightly browned, 1 to 3 minutes. Transfer to a small bowl and let cool. Mix the remaining 1 Tbs. parsley, the mint, a grinding of pepper, and a pinch of salt into the breadcrumbs.

Heat the remaining ⅓ cup olive oil in a 12-inch skillet over medium heat. When the oil is hot, add the shallots and cook, stirring occasionally, until lightly browned, 2 to 4 minutes.

Put the spaghetti in the boiling water and cook until just shy of al dente, about 5 minutes.

While the spaghetti cooks, add the shrimp and halved tomatoes to the skillet. Season with salt and pepper and cook, stirring frequently, until the tomatoes start to soften and the shrimp is nearly cooked through, about 5 minutes.

Reserve ½ cup of the pasta-cooking water and drain the spaghetti. Return the pasta and 2 Tbs. of the reserved water to the pot. Add the shrimp mixture and toss over medium heat until the shrimp is cooked through and the spaghetti is perfectly al dente, 1 to 2 minutes more. Add more of the pasta water as necessary to keep the dish moist. Season to taste with salt and pepper, transfer to warm shallow bowls, and top each serving with the breadcrumbs.

Rigatoni with Summer Squash, Spicy Sausage & Goat Cheese

Serves four to six.

Goat cheese brings the flavors of this pasta together while adding its own rich nuance.

Kosher salt
1 lb. dried rigatoni
3 Tbs. extra-virgin olive oil
¾ lb. bulk hot Italian sausage (or links, casings removed)
⅓ cup finely chopped shallots (about 3 medium)
2 cups ¾-inch-diced yellow and green summer squash
3 oz. fresh goat cheese, crumbled (about ¾ cup)
2 tsp. finely chopped fresh flat-leaf parsley
Freshly ground black pepper
¼ cup grated Parmigiano-Reggiano (optional)

Bring a large pot of well-salted water to a boil over high heat. Put the rigatoni in the boiling water and cook until just shy of al dente, about 10 minutes.

While the pasta cooks, heat ½ Tbs. of the oil in a 12-inch skillet over medium-high heat. Add the sausage and cook, breaking it into pieces with a spatula or spoon, until it's almost cooked through, 3 to 5 minutes. Using a slotted spoon, transfer the sausage to a bowl. Pour the fat out of the skillet but do not wipe it clean. Heat the remaining 2½ Tbs. oil in the skillet over medium heat and cook the shallots until they begin to soften, about 1 minute. Raise the heat to medium high and add the squash. Cook, stirring frequently, until the squash is barely tender, 3 to 5 minutes.

Reserve ½ cup of the pasta-cooking water and drain the rigatoni. Return the rigatoni to its cooking pot and add the sausage, the squash mixture, and 2 Tbs. of the reserved pasta water. Toss over medium heat until the sausage is cooked through and the rigatoni is perfectly al dente, about 3 minutes. Add more of the pasta water as necessary to keep the dish moist.

Remove from the heat, add the goat cheese and parsley, and toss until the cheese melts and coats the pasta. Season to taste with salt and pepper, transfer to warm shallow bowls, and top each serving with some of the grated Parmigiano, if using.

Orecchiette with Caramelized Onions, Green Beans, Fresh Corn & Jalapeño

Serves four.

The flavors in this pasta build with each bite. Try it once, and it will become a summertime staple. If you can't find orecchiette, you can use farfalle instead.

Kosher salt
⅓ cup extra-virgin olive oil
2 cups thinly sliced sweet onion (from 1 large onion)
1 lb. dried orecchiette
½ lb. fresh green beans, washed, trimmed, and sliced on the diagonal into 1-inch lengths
1 cup fresh corn kernels (from about 2 ears)
1 jalapeño, stemmed, halved lengthwise, seeded, and thinly sliced crosswise
Freshly ground black pepper
¼ cup grated Pecorino Romano
1 Tbs. chopped fresh flat-leaf parsley

Bring a large pot of well-salted water to a boil over high heat.

Heat the olive oil in a 12-inch skillet over medium-high heat. When the oil is hot, add the onion and a large pinch of salt and cook, stirring frequently, until the onion is beginning to soften and brown, about 5 minutes. Lower the heat to medium and continue cooking, stirring frequently, until the onion is very soft and a light golden brown, about 15 more minutes (if the onion begins to look like it's burning, add 2 Tbs. warm water and lower the heat).

Put the orecchiette in the boiling water and cook until just shy of al dente, about 9 minutes. Add the green beans to the pasta water in the last minute of cooking.

While the pasta cooks, add the corn, jalapeño, and a pinch of salt to the onions and cook, stirring occasionally, until the corn kernels begin to soften, 3 to 5 minutes. Remove from the heat.

Reserve ½ cup of the pasta and green bean cooking water and drain the pasta and green beans together in a colander.

Return the orecchiette, green beans, and 2 Tbs. of the reserved water to the pot. Add the onion mixture and toss over medium heat until the green beans are crisp-tender and the orecchiette is perfectly al dente, 1 to 2 minutes. Add more of the pasta water as necessary to keep the dish moist. Season to taste with salt and pepper, transfer to warm shallow bowls, and top each serving with the pecorino and parsley.

Scott Conant is the chef and owner of L'Impero and Alto restaurants in New York City. ◆

Pasta water: the secret ingredient

To moisten the dish and help the flavors come together, follow these steps:

Reserve about ½ cup of the pasta-cooking water. The water contains starches released by the pasta, which will help enrich the overall dish and create a more saucy consistency.

Drain the pasta when it's just shy of al dente. You'll briefly cook the pasta with the rest of the ingredients and the pasta water; if the pasta is slightly underdone when everything is combined, it won't overcook.

Add the reserved pasta water to the pasta and sauce and toss. The starches in the water help the sauce cling to the pasta, which in turn acts like a sponge, absorbing the flavors.

The Art of Making Green Salads

Focus on the greens and don't weigh them down

BY ANNIE WAYTE

New York is a tough place to spend the summer if you're a chef; there's no relief from the triple-digit heat of the kitchen. So it's not a surprise that when the long, hot days are upon us, I want little more than a refreshing green salad for supper. No tomatoes, no cucumbers, no cheese; just beautiful leaves—whether tender butter lettuce or peppery arugula—tossed in a light dressing with only a couple of additions, be it a scattering of fresh herbs or ethereally thin slices of raw vegetables.

Though it's not difficult to make, there is an art to assembling a good green salad. What it requires is a little care in choosing and handling the greens and a lot of restraint with both the dressing and any additional ingredients, so the unique personality of each green can really shine.

Select the freshest greens and handle with care

The key to making beautiful, brightly flavored green salads is to start with the best greens you can find. Buy whole heads of lettuce or loose leafy greens at a grocery store with lots of turnover, or preferably at a farmers' market. Not only is the flavor of these greens better and their texture crisper than that of most bagged lettuce, but you can also see clearly what you're getting.

Greens should feel firm and perky. Avoid buying leaves that are discolored or turning brown on the edges. When choosing a whole head of lettuce, look for tightly packed leaves. At home, remove any leaves that are limp or damaged before washing the rest.

Wash greens well. It's important to wash your greens thoroughly, as even a little grit or sand can ruin a carefully prepared salad. (For how to wash greens, see p. 49.) To me, dirt and sand coming off the leaves is a good sign: It means that those greens came out of the soil without all the handling the prewashed bagged greens see. Just as important as washing is drying the leaves well; otherwise, your dressing won't cling to them.

(continued on. p. 48)

"Skip the bagged lettuce," says chef Annie Wayte, who prefers buying whole heads for salad.

Mixed Green Salad with Red-Wine & Dijon Vinaigrette

Serves six to eight.

Consider this a guide to building a mixed green salad and use whichever leaves are available at the grocery store or farmers' market. I love to add fresh herbs and celery leaves for an extra flavor boost.

1 Tbs. red-wine vinegar
¾ tsp. Dijon mustard
¼ tsp. minced garlic
3 Tbs. extra-virgin olive oil
Kosher salt and freshly ground black pepper

1 head red or green romaine (¾ to 1 lb.), trimmed, washed, dried, and torn into bite-size pieces (about 5 cups)
1 cup mâche, trimmed, washed, and dried (1 to 2 oz.)
1 cup oak leaf lettuce, trimmed, washed, and dried (1 to 2 oz.)
1 cup mizuna or baby spinach leaves, trimmed, washed, and dried (1 to 2 oz.)
Leaves from 1 head celery
½ cup basil leaves (green or purple), torn into small pieces
½ cup chervil sprigs
¼ cup chopped chives

Combine the vinegar with the mustard and garlic in a small bowl and whisk in the olive oil. Season with salt and pepper to taste.

Just before serving, toss the romaine, mâche, oak leaf lettuce, mizuna or spinach, celery leaves, and herbs in a large bowl with just enough of the vinaigrette to lightly coat them (you may not need all of the vinaigrette). Season with salt and pepper to taste and serve.

Rip greens with your hands. When you're ready to assemble your salad, gently rip washed and dried greens by hand into manageable pieces, discarding any thick ribs. Using your hands prevents the leaves from bruising and keeps them fresh and beautiful.

Use a light hand with the dressing and toppings

Where many people go wrong with green salads is in dressing them. A dressing should not dominate the salad. Its role is to marry the ingredients and to enhance and breathe life into the greens, not drown them. So begin with a modest amount of dressing—you can always add more. (See p. 51 for more tips on dressing green salads.)

The flavor of the dressing, too, should not overwhelm. Usually, a ratio of one part acid to three parts oil provides a good balance. But always taste your dressing and adjust it as needed, adding more oil if it's too sharp or more vinegar if it needs punch. For extra flavor, I also add a smidgen of mustard and chopped garlic or shallot.

Even a basic vinaigrette will boost the flavor of your green salads more than most bottled dressings will. But every now and then, I like to play with my vinaigrettes, adding little hits of additional flavor, such as a splash of citrus juice or walnut or hazelnut oil. Sometimes I add a pinch of lemon, orange, or lime zest or some chopped ginger for zing, or a spoonful of puréed melon or apricot for mellow sweetness.

Finally, while I like to keep my green salads green, I find that adding just a few flavorful toppings can give them a bit more personality when I want it. But at the risk of sounding like a broken record, I always use a light touch. If I add any vegetables, for example, I slice them paper thin, so they don't weigh down the greens. Fresh herbs also contribute a bright note without weighing things down, and even toasted nuts, if used judiciously, add just the right amount of crunch to a green salad.

Butter Lettuce with Poppy Seed & Tarragon Crème Fraîche Dressing
Serves six.

Crème fraîche gives this salad a mild tanginess that marries beautifully with butter lettuce's delicate flavor.

1 Tbs. poppy seeds
¼ cup crème fraîche
2 Tbs. plain yogurt
2 Tbs. coarsely chopped fresh tarragon plus 2 Tbs. whole tarragon leaves
2 tsp. fresh lemon juice
¼ tsp. minced garlic
Pinch cayenne
Kosher salt
2 or 3 heads butter lettuce (about 12 oz. total), trimmed, washed, dried, and torn by hand into bite-size pieces (about 10 cups)
Freshly ground black pepper

Toast the poppy seeds lightly in a small skillet over medium heat for 1 to 2 minutes. Transfer to a cool plate.

In a small bowl, combine the crème fraîche, yogurt, chopped tarragon, lemon juice, garlic, and poppy seeds. Stir in 1 or 2 Tbs. water to thin the mixture to a creamy salad-dressing consistency. Season with cayenne and salt to taste.

Just before serving, toss the butter lettuce in a large bowl with just enough of the dressing to lightly coat the leaves. Season with salt and pepper to taste. Arrange the salad on individual serving plates, scatter the whole tarragon leaves on the top, and serve.

Get to know your greens

In summertime, grocery stores and farmers' markets abound with a variety of salad greens, ranging from sweet to spicy to bitter, with textures that can be silky, crunchy, or even bristly. Here are some of my favorites.

Watercress

has a spicy kick and is very versatile. It's often used in sandwiches and soups, but I like to make it the star of a salad. Trim the base of the stalks and keep the bouquet of leaves intact.

Arugula

packs a bold, peppery flavor that's great for salads, soups, and sauces. It mixes well with milder greens, but it's also great by itself. If you find mature arugula too strong, choose baby leaves. Keep the leaves whole, unless they're very large.

Mâche

is also known as lamb's lettuce. It has dainty, velvety-textured leaves with a mild yet tangy flavor. It's usually sold in small rosettes with the root attached. Use it alone or tossed into a mixed green salad.

Mizuna

looks pretty and has a mild, earthy flavor, which makes it a great salad green on its own, although it also blends well with other leaves. Keep the leaves whole.

Red & green leaf lettuces

(such as the frilly Lollo Rossa and the smooth Red Oak Leaf) have leaves that grow from a single stalk in a loose bunch rather than forming a tight head. They have a sweet, delicate flavor that's delicious both on its own and mixed with other greens.

How to wash salad greens

To minimize bruising, I like to wash greens in a large bowl of cold water rather than under running water. I gently swirl the leaves in the water to encourage the soil and grit to disperse. Then I lift the leaves out, drain the water in the bowl, and repeat until the leaves are thoroughly clean. Finally, I spin the leaves in small batches in a salad spinner until thoroughly dry. The salad spinner should be only half full. If you overload it, the greens won't dry well. (For another method for washing salad greens, see Food Science, p. 70. For how to store washed greens, see From Our Test Kitchen, p. 64.)

Butter lettuce

(including bibb and Boston) has a subtle, buttery flavor that marries well with citrus and dairy-based vinaigrettes. The silken leaves require very gentle handling.

Romaine

has a sweet, gentle flavor and a crisp bite, and it's versatile: It partners well with most greens and a variety of dressings. For milder flavor and softer texture, remove the outer leaves or buy hearts of romaine.

Arugula & Fennel Salad with Orange & Fennel Seed Dressing & Toasted Hazelnuts
Serves four.

Orange and fennel seeds add a lovely aromatic note to peppery arugula, while thin slices of fennel and chopped hazelnuts provide a nice crunch.

½ tsp. fennel seeds
¼ cup fresh orange juice
1 Tbs. fresh lemon juice
1 Tbs. minced shallot
2 tsp. finely grated orange zest
Scant ¼ tsp. minced garlic
¼ tsp. Dijon mustard
1½ Tbs. extra-virgin olive oil
1½ Tbs. hazelnut oil
Kosher salt and freshly ground black pepper
1 small fennel bulb
5 oz. arugula, trimmed, washed, and dried (about 5 cups)
¼ cup hazelnuts, toasted and coarsely chopped

Toast the fennel seeds lightly in a small skillet over medium heat for about 2 minutes.

Transfer to a cutting board and let the seeds cool. Chop them coarsely.

Combine the orange juice, lemon juice, shallot, orange zest, and garlic in a small bowl. Let sit for 20 minutes and then stir in the fennel seeds and Dijon mustard. Whisk in the olive oil and hazelnut oil and season to taste with salt and pepper.

Cut off the top and bottom of the fennel bulb. Cut it in half lengthwise. Lay one half flat on its cut surface and slice crosswise as thinly as possible. Stop slicing when you hit the core (a little core is all right, but you don't want wide areas of core in your slices). Repeat with the second half. You should have about 1½ cups sliced fennel.

Put the sliced fennel in a large bowl with the arugula and toasted hazelnuts. Toss with enough of the dressing to lightly coat the leaves (you may not need all of the dressing). Season with salt and pepper to taste and serve.

Mâche with Spicy Melon & Pink-Peppercorn Dressing
Serves four.

Puréed melon adds a hint of sweetness to the dressing, while pink peppercorns impart a perfumy note to this pretty salad.

1 tsp. pink peppercorns
3 Tbs. unsalted sunflower seeds
1 medium ripe melon (cantaloupe, Crenshaw, Charentais, or Galia), peeled, cut into thirds, and seeded
1 Tbs. white balsamic vinegar; more to taste (see p. 64 for more information)
2 tsp. fresh lime juice; more to taste
¼ tsp. chopped fresh hot chile (such as Serrano, jalapeño, or Thai bird's eye)
¼ tsp. minced garlic
1 Tbs. extra-virgin olive oil
1 tsp. coarsely chopped mint leaves, plus 12 large mint leaves, torn into small pieces
Kosher salt
3 oz. mâche, trimmed, washed, and dried (about 3½ cups)

Toast the pink peppercorns lightly in a small skillet over medium heat for 1 to 2 minutes. Lightly crush them with a mortar and pestle or on a cutting board with the bottom of another small skillet. Set aside. In the same skillet you used to toast the peppercorns, lightly toast the sunflower seeds over medium heat for 1 to 2 minutes. Remove from the pan and set aside.

Coarsely chop approximately one-third of the melon and purée it in a blender until smooth, about 45 seconds. You should have 1 scant cup melon purée. Pour it into a medium bowl and add the vinegar, lime juice, chile, garlic, and half the crushed peppercorns. Slowly whisk in the olive oil. Stir in the chopped mint leaves and salt to taste. If the dressing is too sweet add a little more vinegar or lime juice.

Just before serving, cut the remaining melon lengthwise into 8 long, elegant slices, each about 1 inch thick. In a large bowl, toss the mâche and torn mint leaves with just enough dressing to lightly coat the leaves. Season with salt to taste. Arrange the mâche on serving plates with two slices of melon per plate. Scatter the toasted sunflower seeds and remaining pink peppercorns on the top. Serve the remaining melon dressing on the side.

Five tips for a perfectly dressed salad

Thoroughly dry the leaves before adding the dressing. Droplets of water will dilute your dressing and prevent it from clinging to the leaves.

Dress your salad just before you serve it. Tossing the greens with the dressing any earlier will cause them to become limp and soggy.

Use just enough dressing to lightly coat the greens. Pick up and taste a leaf as a test. If it needs a little more moisture, add a few additional drops of dressing. But keep checking the leaves to make sure they don't become too wet.

Toss with your hands. Tossing a salad with clean hands rather than utensils is easier on the leaves. You can also get a feel for whether the leaves have enough dressing.

Scatter a few toppings on the salad for excitement—just be sure to use a light hand. Chopped or whole fresh herbs such as basil, mint, parsley, chives, cilantro, chervil, tarragon, dill, and celery leaves contribute a bright, aromatic note. Thinly sliced raw vegetables like fennel, zucchini, radishes, and mushrooms add flavor and texture. Toasted whole sunflower, poppy, or sesame seeds are good for crunch. And toasted and chopped nuts add both crunch and richness.

Annie Wayte is the chef at New York City's Nicole's and 202. She's also the author of Keep It Seasonal: Soups, Salads, and Sandwiches. ◆

Lemon Cheesecake to Go

Bring these tart and creamy treats to your next picnic—they pack well, and everyone will love them

BY MEG SUZUKI

When I pull these sunny cheesecake squares out of my cooler, whether at a concert in the park or at a lakeside barbecue, they disappear in seconds. My friends just love the contrast of the silky, puckery-tart lemon curd and the sweet (but not too sweet) cheesecake layer below.

Though the recipe for them may look long, they're not at all difficult to make. Summer is, after all, vacation time, and this recipe lets you take a vacation from all the worry that usually accompanies cheesecake making: There's no water bath to set up, no leaking springform pan to worry about, and no adjusting the oven temperature halfway through to avoid cracking. In fact, because the cheesecake gets completely covered with lemon curd, there's no need to worry about cracking at all.

Want more? The graham cracker crust is made with just two ingredients and requires no blind baking. The custard for the cheesecake comes together in the food processor in less than a minute, and no eggs need to be separated. Once chilled, the cheesecake easily cuts into 16 even pieces, which makes serving them a breeze. We've even included a handy tip on packing them (see the box at right).

Cooking the lemon curd does require an extra step, but you can—and should—do it while the cheesecake bakes. You'll love the silken texture it adds as you bite through it to the creamy cheesecake layer below. Consisting of just four ingredients, the lemon curd is bright, acidic, and tastes only of fresh lemons.

Picnic tips

These lemon cheesecake squares are a perfect addition to a picnic menu. To make packing and serving easier, flatten a paper muffin liner, set a cheesecake square in the center, and fold the sides up. Repeat for the remaining squares, and then pack them in a box or a plastic container. The cheesecake squares need to be kept cool, so remember to include freezer packs in your picnic basket.

Lemon Cheesecake Squares
Yields sixteen 2-inch squares.

These squares need to set up in the refrigerator, so allow at least 5 hours of chilling time before you serve (or pack) them. You can substitute lower-fat cream cheese for regular, if you like. The cheesecake itself will be slightly less creamy but still fabulous.

9 graham crackers (about 5 oz.)
2 oz. (4 Tbs.) unsalted butter, melted
1 lb. cream cheese or Neufchâtel (⅓-less-fat cream cheese), at room temperature and cut into approximately 1-inch pieces
¾ cup granulated sugar
3 Tbs. fresh lemon juice (from 1 or 2 lemons)
1 Tbs. finely grated lemon zest (from 1 or 2 lemons, preferably using a rasp-style grater)
2 large eggs
1 recipe Lemon Curd (at right), warm or at room temperature

For the crust: Cut two 8x16-inch pieces of parchment. Put the strips in an 8x8 baking pan (preferably straight-sided) so that they cross each other and the excess hangs over the pan's sides. Push the parchment into the bottom and corners of the pan.

Position a rack in the center of the oven and heat the oven to 325°F.

Break the graham crackers into a food processor and process until finely ground. Add the melted butter and pulse until the mixture resembles damp sand. Transfer the crumbs to the lined pan and press them firmly and evenly into the pan. Set aside.

For the cheesecake: Rinse, dry, and reassemble the food processor. In the cleaned bowl, combine the cream cheese, sugar, lemon juice, and lemon zest. Process until smooth, about 30 seconds, stopping halfway to scrape the sides of the bowl. Add the eggs and process until the mixture is perfectly smooth and blended, stopping to scrape the sides of the bowl as necessary, about another 20 seconds.

Pour the cheesecake mixture into the prepared pan. Bake until the sides are slightly puffed and the center is dry to the touch, about 40 minutes.

To finish: When the cheesecake comes out of the oven, pour all of the curd onto the cheesecake and use an offset spatula to spread it evenly. Let cool to room temperature and refrigerate for at least 5 hours, preferably overnight. You can refrigerate it uncovered, as no detectable skin forms on the curd.

When the cheesecake is thoroughly chilled, carefully lift it out of the pan using the parchment "handles" and onto a cutting board. Slide the parchment out and discard it. Using a large, sharp knife, cut the cheesecake into quarters, and then cut each quarter into four equal squares. To make clean cuts, wipe the knife blade with a damp paper towel between each slice.

The lemon curd is cooked properly when it begins to steam and has thickened considerably.

Lemon Curd
Yields enough to cover the cheesecake, about 1 cup.

Make the lemon curd while the cheesecake bakes; it pours and spreads best while still warm. When cooking the curd, don't let it come to a boil, or the eggs will overcook.

½ cup fresh lemon juice (from 2 or 3 lemons)
½ cup granulated sugar
2 large eggs
1 oz. (2 Tbs.) unsalted butter, cut into pieces

Set a fine strainer over a medium bowl. In another medium bowl, whisk the lemon juice, sugar, and eggs until thoroughly combined and most of the sugar has dissolved.

Pour the lemon mixture into a small, nonreactive saucepan. Cook over medium heat, stirring frequently with a wooden spoon or heatproof spatula, until the curd is steaming (but not boiling) and thickened and registers about 175°F on an instant-read thermometer, 3 to 7 minutes.

Take the curd off the heat, add the butter, and stir until the butter has melted. Pour the curd through the strainer to get rid of any lumps. Set aside but use to top the cheesecake while still warm.

Meg Suzuki is a cooking instructor and writer based in San Jose, California. ◆

A Kitchen That Goes All Out

An outdoor kitchen in Vermont keeps everything within arm's reach—and the elements out

BY LISA WADDLE

Outdoor kitchens may be popular in California and Florida, but you don't have to live in a sunny climate to enjoy cooking in your back yard. Just take a look at Deborah Krasner's outdoor kitchen in Vermont, a state more known for snowfall than cookouts.

Krasner, author of *The New Outdoor Kitchen*, just published by The Taunton Press, was inspired to start building out back after finding herself wheeling the Weber kettle grill onto her snow-covered patio every January to indulge her love of grilling.

Naturally, in designing her all-weather kitchen, Krasner started with the idea of a covered space. Her kitchen's cedar-shake roof provides shelter from the elements, and a louvered, copper-roofed cupola acts as a vent for smoke and grease.

Although a second, exterior kitchen might seem a luxury, Krasner's compact design demonstrates that you don't need a lot of space to feed your craving for food cooked alfresco. At only 10 feet by 10 feet, Krasner's kitchen is compact yet complete enough to include four sources of grilling heat—a wood-fired masonry oven, a gas grill

Bird's-eye view

Located conveniently close to the house, Deborah Krasner's 10x10-foot outdoor kitchen (shown without roof) is small but has everything she needs, including four sources of grilling heat, a refrigerator, and a sink.

Photos: Eric Roth; illustration, Martha Garstang Hill

Cooking alfresco. *Deborah Krasner extends the outdoor cooking season in Vermont with her all-weather kitchen. Patio dining as well as counter seating make entertaining a crowd easy.*

Inspired?
Next steps to take

To get started planning your own outdoor kitchen, Deborah Krasner suggests:

Start an idea file. Clip magazine and catalog photos of layouts, equipment, lighting, and outdoor furniture. Collect manufacturer brochures of equipment you're considering, price lists, and names of landscape designers and contractors.

Create a budget. How long you plan to stay at your current location will determine whether you spend the bulk of your money in the setting (patio, water lines) or equipment (which can move with you).

Audition a spot. Use a portable grill, table, and chairs to create a temporary outdoor space. Figure out where guests will sit so the grill doesn't smoke them out and experience how close your site is to neighbors' lights or noise.

Design a layout. Photograph your outdoor space at different hours of the day to see sun and shade patterns. Then draw a site map and sketch in appliances, utilities, storage, and seating.

Consider building in stages. Budget constraints might make building over several years a good option. Year one could involve burying electrical, natural gas, and/or water lines and laying stone or decking, while you use a portable grill. Year two could feature installation of a sink and counters. Year three could involve upgrading equipment and constructing a roof or adding landscaping.

with two side burners, an electric smoker, and a charcoal smoker.

"Part of our motivation for building an outdoor kitchen was that we've become more ambitious in our cooking over time and wanted to explore more outdoor cooking methods," Krasner says. "Our initial design requirements were a place for a permanent masonry oven, a roof overhead, and a location not far from the house."

Thanks to the availability of all-weather equipment and smart design, Krasner packed much more than that into her out-

side space. Among her favorite features are a large apron-front sink ("for washing vegetables straight from the garden or rinsing big birds for the wood-fired oven") and an eating bar with stools ringing the outside of the kitchen to accommodate guests.

Of course, building outside, especially in a back yard that experiences all four seasons, means special consideration in selecting materials. Krasner chose soapstone counters and stainless-steel cabinets because they can withstand the forces of nature and are easy to maintain. The kitchen's floor is made

of concrete paving stones, which look natural and don't hold heat in the summer.

Taking the time to make your outdoor kitchen as efficient, comfortable, and complete as possible will entice you outside to cook and entertain more often, Krasner says.

"It has changed our outdoor life as well as what we cook and eat," she adds. "We grill or smoke on the coldest of winter days, thanks to the roof."

Six details that make this kitchen work

Small in scope, Deborah Krasner's outdoor kitchen is packed with efficient design details.

1 An outdoor masonry oven was the impetus for building the outdoor kitchen, so it naturally became the focal point for the design.

2 Side burners on the gas grill are great for finishing sauces, boiling water for corn on the cob or lobsters, or even just heating up a kettle for tea when grilling in colder weather.

3 A cool zone away from the stove is vital so that there is counter space for food before and after cooking.

4 An undercounter refrigerator may seem a luxury until you keep running back inside for sauces, condiments, and vegetables. This one has to be disconnected in the winter, as does the sink.

5 Storage space for glasses, dishes, and table linens saves trips back to the house. Besides open shelves, Krasner included closed, all-weather drawers and cabinets for year-round storage.

6 More than one entrance. The one thing Krasner would change if she were doing this again would be to build another entrance to the kitchen. She says people are constantly coming in to poke at what's on the grill or grab themselves a soda. With only one entrance, there's often a bottleneck, and guests get trapped inside.

Looking back toward the patio dining space from inside the kitchen, above, shows the proximity of the outdoor cooking space to the main house.

Weather-resistant stainless-steel drawers, right, are large enough to hold serving bowls and table linens, so there's no need for overhead storage cabinets that would block the view.

For more ideas

The New Outdoor Kitchen: Cooking Up a Kitchen for the Way You Live and Play by Deborah Krasner showcases more than a dozen outdoor kitchens that vary in size, price, ambition, and creativity. You can order it from The Taunton Press at www.taunton.com.

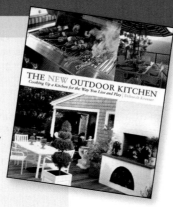

Lisa Waddle is an associate editor at Fine Cooking. ◆

Chinese Chicken Salad

The best version of this popular salad has lots of crunchy texture and a boldly flavored dressing

BY BARBARA LAUTERBACH

In all my travels through Asia, I never came across anything quite like the Chinese chicken salad I see in casual restaurants all over the United States. Built from layers of shredded chicken, chopped cabbage, Asian vegetables, crunchy toppings, and tangy ginger-chile dressing, this main-dish salad was probably born on the West Coast in the 1980s. No matter where it came from, there's no doubt it's taken on a life of its own.

Forget the canned mandarin oranges and keep the crunchy toppings. Now that so many restaurants seem to have their own interpretations of this popular salad on the menu, it's no surprise that there are some pretty mediocre versions. In fact, quite a few cookbooks have fallen prey to this trend. If you see the words "mandarin oranges" (think mushy) or "chow mein noodles" (think dry), run. Instead, think crisp (napa cabbage and snow peas) and crunchy (toasted almonds, baked wonton strips, and sesame seeds). My recipe takes advantage of these textures (see the photos at right) to create a main-dish salad that's both refreshing and satisfying.

A great Chinese chicken salad needs a bold dressing; don't be tempted to substitute something from a bottle. My bright dressing gets its sweet and hot flavors from two types of Asian chile sauces, tamari (or soy sauce), garlic, and fresh ginger. These are balanced by the cool acidity of rice vinegar. It might be tempting to skip using one or two of these ingredients, but I think you'll be disappointed. A vibrant dressing makes the kind of salad that has everyone asking for more (and asking for the recipe).

Chinese Chicken Salad

Serves four as a main course.

Most supermarkets carry sweet and hot chile sauces, but if you have trouble finding them, try an Asian market.

FOR THE SALAD:

2 bone-in, skin-on split chicken breasts (about 2¼ lb.)
Kosher salt and freshly ground black pepper
8 square wonton wrappers
Vegetable oil cooking spray
⅔ cup sliced almonds
2 oz. snow peas, trimmed and cut on the diagonal into thirds (½ cup)
1 Tbs. white sesame seeds
½ small head napa cabbage, trimmed and cut crosswise into ½-inch-wide strips (3 to 3½ cups)
½ romaine heart, cut crosswise into ½-inch-wide strips (1½ to 2 cups)
3 large scallions (white and green parts), thinly sliced on the diagonal (½ cup)

FOR THE DRESSING:

¼ cup rice vinegar
1½ Tbs. tamari or soy sauce
1 Tbs. sweet Asian chile sauce
2 medium cloves garlic, finely chopped (2 tsp.)
2 tsp. minced fresh ginger
½ tsp. kosher salt
½ tsp. hot Asian chile sauce
¼ tsp. freshly ground black pepper
¼ cup peanut oil
1 Tbs. Asian sesame oil

Prepare the salad ingredients: Heat the oven to 425°F. Season the chicken breasts with salt and pepper. Roast on a rack set in a rimmed baking sheet or roasting pan until an instant-read thermometer inserted in the thickest part of a breast registers 165°F, 40 to 45 minutes. Let cool. Remove and discard the skin and then shred the meat. Reduce the oven temperature to 375°F.

Stack the wonton wrappers on a cutting board and cut them into ½-inch-wide strips. Line a baking sheet with foil and spray lightly with cooking spray. Separate the strips, lay them on the baking sheet, and mist them lightly with the cooking spray. Sprinkle lightly with salt. Scrunch each strip to give it a wavy shape, if you like. Bake at 375°F until golden, 7 to 9 minutes. Reduce the oven heat to 350°F.

Spread the sliced almonds on a baking sheet and toast in the oven until golden, 6 to 8 minutes.

Bring a medium saucepan of salted water to a boil. Have a bowl of ice water ready. Boil the snow peas just until bright green but still crisp, about 20 seconds. Drain and transfer to the ice water to stop the cooking. Drain.

Put the sesame seeds in a dry skillet and shake or stir over medium heat until light golden brown, 3 to 4 minutes. Remove them from the hot pan to prevent overcooking.

Make the dressing and assemble the salad: In a medium bowl, combine the vinegar, tamari, sweet chile sauce, garlic, ginger, salt, hot chile sauce, and pepper. Gradually whisk in the peanut and sesame oils.

In a large bowl, toss the cabbage, romaine, and snow peas. In another bowl, toss the chicken and scallions with ¼ cup of the dressing. Add the chicken to the greens, and then add the sesame seeds and almonds. Toss with enough of the remaining dressing to coat well. Garnish each serving with the baked wonton strips.

Barbara Lauterbach is a cooking instructor and cookbook author. ◆

Three ways to add crunch

Blanch the snow peas to set their color and retain their crispness.

Cut the napa cabbage and romaine crosswise for juicy strips.

Bake—don't fry—the wonton wrapper strips and scrunch them for maximum crunch and eye appeal.

How to Make a Memorable

For this summertime favorite, all you need is a simple method and your choice of ripe fruit

BY ABIGAIL JOHNSON DODGE

As a cookbook author, I spend my days crafting recipes with precise equations of ingredients, measurements, and times. But when I'm off the clock, I can relax and take a more freewheeling approach to my baking. In summer, that means cobbler. This deep-dish fruit dessert, topped with a buttery biscuit crust, is endlessly versatile. And once you get the hang of making one—I'll walk you through the five basic steps on the next two pages—it's easy to whip one up with whatever fruit, spices, and flavorings you happen to crave at the moment.

Because cobblers are so much about the fruit, starting with the ripest, most fragrant fruit possible is key. That's where the flexibility of this method is such a plus. Even if I set out with a blueberry cobbler in mind, I can change course if I find peaches that are outstanding. I'm also a fan of combining summer fruits, so if there aren't enough ripe, sweet plums or nectarines, I can round out my filling with up to three kinds of fruit. To help the fruits bake evenly, I generally leave berries whole, with the exception of strawberries, which I halve, or quarter if they're large. I slice peaches, nectarines, and plums into 1-inch-thick wedges. Because not every fruit (nor every eater) requires the same level of sweetness, I'm always ready to adjust the amount of sugar in the filling or topping accordingly.

Cobbler dough is much more laid back than pie or tart dough. There's no chilling, rolling, or anxiety required. I use a food processor to cut the butter into the dry ingredients and then mix in the sour cream by hand until the dough clumps together. I then divide the dough by hand and drop the pieces onto the fruit filling to bake; the resulting biscuits' texture is appealingly rustic, with lots of crunchy peaks.

Cobblers are something I usually make on the spur of the moment, but when I do have the luxury of time and can plan ahead, I'll prepare the topping and the fruit (rinsed, drained, and cut but not tossed with the other ingredients) up to 8 hours ahead and pop them in the fridge until it's time to assemble and bake the dessert.

Raspberry-peach cobbler with cornmeal biscuits

Fruit Cobbler

Five easy steps to a delicious fruit cobbler

Yields one 9x13-inch cobbler; serves eight to ten.

1 Get ready

Read the method from start to finish and gather your ingredients before you begin baking. Position a rack in the center of the oven and heat the oven to 350°F. Have ready a 9x13-inch Pyrex dish or similar.

What you'll need:

One recipe Sour Cream Cobbler Dough (at right)
8 cups fruit, prepared as directed in Step 3
½ to ¾ cup granulated sugar
1 to 2 Tbs. all-purpose flour, for tossing
Pinch table salt
1 or 2 filling flavorings
1½ Tbs. granulated, turbinado, or demerara sugar (optional)

2 Make the dough

Sour Cream Cobbler Dough

Yields enough topping for one cobbler.

7½ oz. (1⅔ cups) all-purpose flour
⅓ cup granulated sugar or packed light brown sugar
1 Tbs. baking powder
¼ tsp. table salt
3 oz. (6 Tbs.) cold unsalted butter, cut into 10 pieces
Up to two dough flavorings (optional)
¾ cup sour cream, chilled

In a food processor, combine the flour, sugar, baking powder, and salt. Pulse briefly to blend the ingredients, about 10 seconds. Add the butter pieces and pulse until they are the size of small peas, 5 to 7 one-second pulses.

Dump the mixture into a large mixing bowl. Add any dough flavorings (see the box below right), if using, and stir until evenly dispersed. Add the sour cream. Using a rubber spatula, gently smear the ingredients together until the flour is evenly moistened and the dough begins to form large, soft, moist clumps. Bring the dough together into an 8-inch-long log. Divide the log into 10 roughly equal round pieces. Refrigerate the pieces in the bowl while preparing the fruit.

do ahead:
You can prepare the dough up to 8 hours ahead; simply cover the bowl with plastic wrap and store it in the refrigerator until you're ready to proceed with the recipe.

Dough flavorings

Choose 1 or 2 (optional)

Finely grated lemon zest: ½ tsp.

Finely grated orange zest: ¾ tsp.

Finely ground cornmeal: ¼ cup (1¼ oz.)

Ground cinnamon: ¾ tsp.

Toasted almonds, pecans, walnuts, pistachios, or hazelnuts: ½ cup, chopped

3 Prepare the fruit filling

Put the fruit in a large bowl. Toss with ½ to ¾ cup granulated sugar (use less for very ripe, sweet fruit and more for fruit that's not perfectly ripe and sweet), 1 Tbs. all-purpose flour (if your cobbler has any berries in it, use 2 Tbs. flour), and a pinch of table salt.

If you want to add optional filling flavorings, choose 1 or 2 from the list in the box below and gently toss them into the fruit now, making sure to mix them in evenly.

Fruit

Choose up to 3, for a total of 8 cups. All fruit should be ripe, well rinsed, and drained.

Apricots: cut into 1-inch-thick wedges

Blackberries

Blueberries

Peaches or nectarines: cut into 1-inch-thick wedges

Plums or pluots: cut into 1-inch-thick wedges

Raspberries

Strawberries, hulled: if small, leave whole; if medium, cut in half; if large, cut in quarters

Filling flavorings

Choose 1 or 2 (optional)

Finely grated lemon zest: 1¼ tsp.

Finely grated orange zest: 1 tsp.

Ground cinnamon: ½ tsp.

Ground nutmeg: ¼ tsp.

Minced fresh ginger: 2 tsp.

Pure almond extract: ¼ tsp.

Pure vanilla extract: 1 tsp.

4 Assemble the cobbler

Pile the fruit into the baking dish, scraping in any remaining juices or sugar from the bowl, and spread evenly. Remove the pieces of dough from the refrigerator and arrange them randomly on top of the filling, leaving spaces between the pieces. Don't be tempted to flatten the dough—the large pieces are important for proper and even baking of the filling and topping. If desired, sprinkle a little sugar evenly over the cobbler (see the list below).

Sugar sprinkle

Choose 1 and use 1½ Tbs. (optional)

Demerara sugar
Granulated sugar
Turbinado sugar

5 Bake the cobbler

Bake until the filling is bubbling and the topping is browned, 50 to 60 minutes. Let sit about 20 minutes to allow the juices to settle. You can serve this cobbler hot or warm (it will stay warm at room temperature for 1 to 1½ hours). Serve with lightly sweetened whipped cream or vanilla ice cream, if you like.

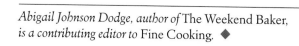

Abigail Johnson Dodge, author of The Weekend Baker, *is a contributing editor to* Fine Cooking. ◆

Look & listen for
the ripest

At first glance, that mound of melons at the market all look the same. But we all know they don't taste the same. To find a ripe one:

Lift it. A melon should feel heavy for its size; compare a few.

Look at it. It's mainly what you *don't* see that counts: No blemishes, bruises, soft spots, wrinkles, or bumps.

Smell it.

A fragrant aroma, especially near the stem end, is a good sign.

Thump it. Hold the melon to your ear and give it a few knocks. It should sound more cavernous and hollow than muffled.

The skin beneath the raised netting on a cantaloupe should be golden, not green.

Choosing a ripe melon	64
White balsamic vinegar	64
Fish steaks vs. fillets	65
Salmon medallions	65
Cured and smoked salmon	66
Gravlax	66
Best way to store salad greens	67
Leftovers: After the cookout	68
How to clean grill grates	69
Removing portabella gills	69

BY JENNIFER ARMENTROUT

A paler shade of balsamic

Though it lacks the long Italian pedigree of traditional balsamic, white balsamic vinegar is worth keeping in the pantry as a sweeter alternative to white wine or champagne vinegar. Fruity and floral in flavor, it has the sweet-and-sour balance of regular balsamic without the dark color or caramel undertones.

The methods used to make white balsamic vary from one producer to the next. The most straightforward production methods include bleaching regular balsamic vinegar and sweetening white wine vinegar with grape must (pressed grapes), preferably of the Trebbiano variety used to make regular balsamic.

Despite their ambiguous origins, the handful of white balsamics we tasted were equally delightful. They're best used as a condiment or in light vinaigrettes. Add a splash to sautéed fennel, carrots, or parsnips. Or try the recipe for mâche with melon and pink peppercorn dressing on p. 51 and the prosciutto-wrapped cantaloupe, below.

—*Allison Ehri, test kitchen associate*

Prosciutto-Wrapped Melon with Mint & White Balsamic Vinegar
Serves eight as an appetizer.

This riff on a classic Italian hors d'oeuvre is a great way to start a summer gathering. You can assemble it up to two hours ahead, if you like, but the mint will darken a bit.

1 ripe cantaloupe
2 Tbs. very thinly sliced fresh mint leaves
½ tsp. freshly ground black pepper
2 to 3 tsp. white balsamic vinegar
6 oz. very thinly sliced prosciutto, preferably imported

With a sharp knife, trim the peel from the melon. Cut it in half lengthwise and scoop out the seeds. Slice one of the halves lengthwise into slender wedges, and then cut the wedges in half crosswise. (Wrap and save the other melon half for another use.)

Put the melon wedges in a medium bowl and toss them with the mint, pepper, and vinegar to taste—the sweeter the melon, the more vinegar you can use. Tear the prosciutto lengthwise into 1- to 2-inch-wide strips and wrap a strip or two around each piece of melon. Arrange the wrapped melon on a serving platter. If making ahead, cover with plastic and refrigerate until ready to serve.

Fish steaks vs. fillets

When you're at the fish counter, not only do you have to choose what kind of fish you want, but sometimes you also have to decide whether you want it cut as a fillet or a steak.

A fish fillet (bottom) is one whole, boneless side of a fish. It may be skin-on or skinless. Fillets from large fish like salmon are frequently cut into individual portions, which are also called fillets.

A fish steak (top) usually refers to a cross-cut portion of a large fish like salmon or halibut. It comes bone-in and skin-on. It can be confusing, but fillets from big, meaty fish like tuna and swordfish are often referred to

as steaks as well, even though they're technically fillets.

For most cooking, fillets and steaks are essentially interchangeable, and the choice between the two usually comes down to aesthetics and whether or not you feel like dealing with fish bones. On the grill, however, steaks behave better than fillets because the skin and bones help hold the fish together. (And though they're really fillets, meaty fish "steaks" grill well because they're firm to begin with.) For instructions on how to grill fish steaks and accompaniments to serve with them, see "Delicious Finishes for Grilled Fish" on p. 40.

knife skills

How to turn a salmon steak into a medallion

S almon on the grill can be a little tricky because it likes to stick to the grill grates, even grates that are perfectly cleaned and oiled (see p. 69). A salmon steak is less likely than a fillet to stick, but with all the bones, it's not as neat and easy to eat as a fillet.

A salmon medallion, which is a salmon steak that's been boned and tied into a tidy little round, gives you the best of both worlds. Some fish counters sell the medallions ready to go, but if all you can find is a salmon steak, here's how to turn it into a medallion.

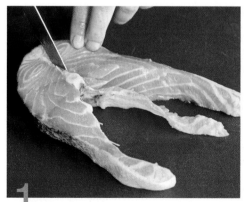

1 *Trim the lining and bones from the belly flaps and divide the steak in half along the backbone. Discard the backbone and belly trimmings.*

2 *Run a fingertip over the salmon flesh on both sides to feel for pin bones; use needlenose pliers or fish tweezers to remove them. Reverse the direction of one side and nestle the two sides together, yin-yang style.*

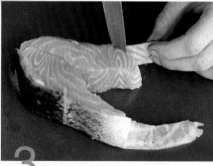

3 *Make an incision between the skin and flesh of the thicker end of each salmon piece (shown at knife point above), and then trim just enough skin off the belly flaps (shown at bottom of photo) that the flaps can wrap around and tuck in under the skin of the thicker ends (shown at center left). Tie a piece of butcher's twine around the medallion to hold it together.*

Gravlax Cold-smoked Hot-smoked

Cured & smoked salmon

Before modern transportation and refrigeration, salmon was dried and smoked—often to a crisp—to preserve it. These days, salmon is still cured and smoked, but the goal is enhanced flavor and texture, not preservation. Different methods produce different results, all of them delicious (and all of them needing refrigeration). Here's a description of what's most widely available, plus a recipe for our favorite—gravlax.

Gravlax
is salmon fillet that's been cured in a mixture of salt and sugar with herbs, spices, citrus, and alcohol (see the recipe below). In addition to adding flavor, the cure draws moisture from the salmon. Moisture allows bacteria to grow, so reducing the moisture preserves the salmon; the drier it is, the longer it will last. Without the need for preservation, today's gravlax is fairly moist, and because it's not cooked, it has a lovely silky texture and delicate flavor. Thinly sliced gravlax is delicious served on buttered toasts and topped with a little crème fraîche and chives. Avoid using it in cooked dishes where heat might destroy its texture.

Cold-smoked
salmon begins with a salt cure, usually a flavored brine. The cured salmon is then air-dried in a cool place until the surface develops a shiny layer, called the pellicle, which helps the smoke penetrate. Next, the salmon is put in a special smoker, which keeps the heat low enough that the fish doesn't cook as it's flavored by the smoke. The smoking time ranges from a few hours to a few days, depending on the desired flavor and the smoker. Like gravlax, cold-smoked salmon should not be heated. Its smoky flavor is great with capers, red onion, caviar, and boiled eggs. Try the egg salad with smoked salmon recipe on p. 78a.

Hot-smoked
salmon may be cured and air-dried like cold-smoked salmon, or it may not be cured at all. But the real difference is that hot-smoked salmon slowly cooks in the smoker, giving it a texture and appearance similar to that of regular cooked salmon. Delicious hot or cold, it makes a wonderful addition to scrambled eggs, pastas, and potato dishes.

—*Allison Ehri*

Gravlax
Serves eight to twelve as an appetizer.

Discover how satisfying and easy it is to make gravlax, and you'll want to do it again and again. This rendition is flavored with the traditional lemon and dill, but you can get as inventive as you want with the flavorings so long as you keep the salt amount the same. You can even use more sugar, if you like.

1 to 1¼ lb. skin-on salmon fillet, preferably center-cut and very fresh
4 tsp. fresh lemon juice
2 tsp. vodka (optional)
½ cup kosher salt
¼ cup coarsely chopped fresh dill

3 Tbs. granulated sugar
2 tsp. freshly cracked black pepper

Set a small perforated pan, a flat-bottomed colander or strainer basket, or even a cooling rack or a broiler pan in a baking dish or similar container to catch drippings. Line the perforated pan with a large piece of cheesecloth, allowing the edges to drape over the sides of the pan.

Remove the pin bones from the salmon and put it skin side down in the center of the cheesecloth. Brush the lemon juice and vodka (if using) evenly over the salmon. In a small bowl, mix the salt, dill, sugar, and pepper. Pack this cure mix-

ture on top of the salmon in a thick, even layer. Wrap the edges of the cheesecloth around the salmon to loosely bundle it up.

Choose another pan that's roughly the same size as the salmon—a loaf pan, for example—and put it on top of the salmon. Add about 2 lb. of weight to the pan—two 15-oz. food cans work well—to press the salmon and help it exude moisture. Refrigerate for 3 days. Gently brush off and discard the cure.

To serve, slice very thinly at a sharp angle to make wide slices. Well-wrapped gravlax will keep in the refrigerator for about 5 days.

The best way to
store salad
greens

The way in which you store delicate salad greens makes a big difference in how long they stay fresh. We've kept greens fresh for as long as two weeks using this method from food scientist Shirley Corriher.

Discard any leaves that have brown spots. Soak the greens in very cold water for 15 to 30 minutes to replenish water lost since harvesting, and then spin them dry. Wrap them loosely in dry paper towels, and put them in a zip-top plastic bag. The towels absorb excess moisture, so the greens stay moist enough that they don't wilt but not so moist that they get soggy and rot.

Partially seal the bag, gently squeeze out as much air as possible without crushing the greens, and then finish sealing the bag. This step limits the greens' exposure to air and slows down their breathing—that's right, they breathe—which in turn slows deterioration. Store the greens in your refrigerator's produce bin.

leftovers

After the cookout

In case your guests leave you with leftovers from our "Grilling for a Crowd" pullout on p. 26a, we have some ideas for using them up.

Leftover Thyme & Roasted Red Pepper Butter
Toss grilled shrimp with leftover Thyme & Roasted Red Pepper Butter and a squeeze of fresh lime juice.

Leftover Buttermilk Herb Dip
Use leftover Buttermilk Herb Dip as a spread for sandwiches or as salad dressing.

Leftover Grilled Herb-Crusted Leg of Lamb and Chopped Tomato & Cucumber Salad
Stuff a pita with leftover lamb and tomato-cucumber salad.

Leftover Argentine Spice-Rubbed Flank Steak
See the recipe below to make steak for breakfast, shown in the photo at right.

Steak & Eggs Rancheros
Serves two.

This beefed-up version of the Mexican breakfast dish huevos rancheros (ranch-style eggs) is great for lunch or dinner, too.

1 tiny clove garlic
Kosher salt
1 small tomato, cut into small dice
½ avocado, cut into small dice
¼ cup leftover Salsa Criolla (recipe, p. 26a), drained
¼ jalapeño, minced
2 Tbs. chopped fresh cilantro
Freshly ground pepper
1 Tbs. vegetable oil
Two 6-inch corn tortillas
2 large eggs
4 to 5 oz. sliced Argentine Spice-Rubbed Flank Steak (recipe, p. 26a; about four ½-inch-thick slices), warmed in the microwave or in a skillet
¼ cup crumbled feta

Peel and chop the garlic. Sprinkle the garlic with a generous pinch of kosher salt and mash it into a paste with the side of a

chef's knife. In a small bowl, combine the garlic with the tomato, avocado, leftover salsa, jalapeño, and 1 Tbs. of the cilantro. Season to taste with salt and pepper.

Have two dinner plates and a stack of paper towels ready. Heat the oil in a 10-inch nonstick skillet over medium-high heat. Using tongs, fry the tortillas one at a time until just golden and slightly crisp, about 30 seconds per side, and transfer to the paper towels. Reduce the heat to medium low and let the skillet cool down a bit. Meanwhile, blot the excess oil from the tortillas with the paper towels. Sprinkle each tortilla with a pinch of salt. Put one tortilla on each plate.

Crack the eggs into the skillet. Season with salt and pepper, cover, and cook until the yolks' edges have just begun to set, 2 to 3 minutes. (The eggs should cook gently, so lower the heat if needed.)

While the eggs are cooking, divide half the salsa between the tortillas. Divide the steak between the tortillas and top with the remaining salsa. Separate the eggs with the edge of a spatula, if needed. Slide one egg onto each tortilla. Sprinkle with the remaining 1 Tbs. cilantro and the feta. Serve immediately.

—Allison Ehri

A clean grill means less sticking

It's always a good idea to start with thoroughly cleaned and oiled grill grates. That way, there's no flavor transfer from the last thing you grilled, and foods are less likely to stick to the grates.

To clean the grates, heat them first to soften the stuck-on gunk and then scrub them with a stiff wire grill brush. Next, fold a paper towel into a little pad, grasp it with long-handled tongs, and dip it in some cooking oil. Quickly swab the grates with the towel, cleaning and oiling them at the same time. Repeat this step until the grates seem clean, and then cover the grill briefly to let it heat up again. If you're grilling something that tends to stick, like fish, give the grates another swipe of oil just before the food goes on.

Remove bitter portabella gills before cooking

A big, meaty grilled portabella mushroom makes a perfect topping for a hamburger because its size and shape are so burger-like, but it's also hearty enough to stand in for the burger itself, as in the Grilled Portabella Sandwiches with Tomatoes, Mozzarella & Basil recipe on p. 78a. Whether you plan to grill a portabella or cook it any other way, there's an important but often overlooked prep step you should take: Remove the gills on the underside of the cap. They have a bitter taste, and they exude an unattractive black liquid when they're cooked. To get rid of them, just scrape them off with a table knife or the side of a spoon. ◆

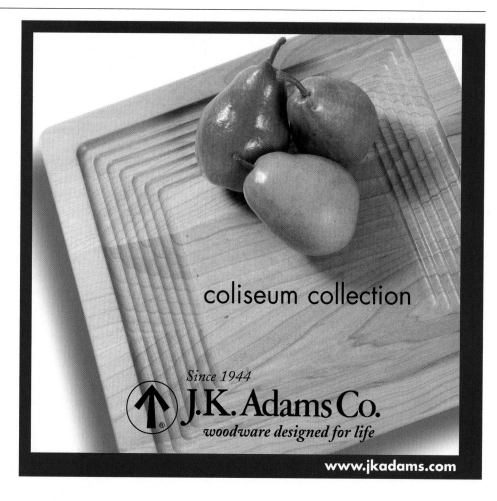

A simple guide to
Handling fruits and vegetables safely

Sometimes bad things come from good food, but there are easy ways to minimize your risk

BY LINDA J. HARRIS

For a long time, if we worried at all about getting sick from food, we focused on things like undercooked hamburger or tainted oysters. Today, in light of recent outbreaks of illness from contaminated spinach and scallions, it's hard not to think about fresh produce, too. But there's no need to swear off fresh fruits and vegetables. For one thing, the chances of getting sick are very small—contaminated produce is the exception, not the rule. And second, you can reduce your risk by following a few guidelines when you're buying and washing your fresh fruits and vegetables.

The pathogens that are often responsible for illness linked to fresh produce are the *Salmonella* and *E. coli* O157:H7 bacteria, which are the same pathogens we associate with meat and poultry. Fruit and vegetables can become contaminated at many points in the food chain, from the open fields where they're grown through distribution and retail stores all the way through to preparation in your kitchen. When the contamination occurs in the kitchen, it's usually due to contact with raw meat or poultry. (So let me emphasize that the old food safety rules still apply—designate separate cutting boards for raw meat and fresh vegetables, wash hands and surfaces thoroughly after working with raw meat and before working with fruits and vegetables.)

Identifying the sources of contamination that occur in the field has been very difficult, but irrigation water, improperly composted manure, and workers (from poor hygiene) are all considered possible origins. Some of the problems surrounding this issue are that produce is grown outdoors; the pathogens survive pretty well in water, manure, and soil; and really small numbers are capable of making you sick.

You may not have the power to prevent contamination from occurring in the field, but in your kitchen, there's one certain way to ensure the safety of your fruit and vegetables, and that's simply to cook them. As long as the temperature hits 160°F, pathogens will be killed. But we don't always want to cook these foods, especially at this time of year, so here's what you need to know to minimize your risks.

Shopping with safety in mind

When you're choosing fruits and vegetables at the store, you're probably thinking more about quality than about food safety. There's nothing wrong with that, but here are a few pointers that have produce safety in mind.

Shop in clean markets. Cleanliness is a good indication that the market takes its role in food safety seriously. The display cases should be cleaned regularly to prevent cross contamination, and damaged and decayed fruit or vegetables (which may carry more pathogens) should be removed on a regular basis.

If you're buying any cut-up fruits or vegetables or packaged greens, be sure they've been kept cold, either in a refrigerated display case or surrounded by ice. When a fruit or vegetable is cut, the cells

Washing can reduce contamination if it's there, but it can't eliminate it. Bacteria can be sticky, so rinsing them off isn't as easy as wiping dust off a table.

are ruptured, releasing the moisture and nutrients bacteria thrive on. Keeping things cold holds the pathogens in check (and it also helps protect against spoilage). The packaging on cut produce should be cold to the touch. Don't buy it if it isn't. And be sure to store the food in the fridge once you get it home. The temperature inside your refrigerator should be 40°F.

Always bag your produce. Those rolls of plastic bags in the produce section aren't just for weighing vegetables; they're also important for sanitary reasons. Even if you're buying only one avocado, it's worth putting it in a bag. Grocery carts are rarely cleaned and conveyer belts at the check-out aren't cleaned often enough, so a bag provides another barrier to germs. Also, to avoid cross-contamination, keep your fruits and vegetables separate from raw meats, poultry, and seafood, both in your grocery cart and in the checkout bags.

How to wash depends on what you're washing

You might think that simply rinsing your fruits and vegetables with water would wash off any potential pathogens, but unfortunately, it's not that easy. Washing can reduce contamination if it's there, but it can't completely eliminate it. One reason for this is that bacteria can be sticky. Rinsing them off isn't as easy as wiping dust off a table; it's more like removing grease or garden dirt from your hands. And like your hands, the surface of fruits and vegetables isn't perfectly smooth. Even fruit like apples and tomatoes aren't as smooth as they look. When you're the size of bacteria, the surface of an apple has lots of nooks and crannies to wedge into. And the more craggy the surface, the more places there are to hide, making it more difficult to eliminate pathogens.

For firm fruit and vegetables, such as apples, melons, and tomatoes, rub well while rinsing under water. For these foods, rinsing and rubbing is quite effective at removing tiny pathogens. Just use your hand or a vegetable brush under running water. (If you use a brush, be sure to replace or wash it

For leafy greens, rinsing is more effective than soaking

When cooks talk about the best way to store and wash fruits and vegetables, they're usually most concerned with flavor and aesthetic matters: preserving freshness or eliminating grit, for example. But as a food safety expert, I'm also looking for the most effective way to remove or minimize numbers of bacteria. Usually, the same method can satisfy both cooks and food safety folks. But when it comes to lettuce, spinach, or other leafy greens, we part ways.

Cooks like to wash their greens by soaking them in a big bowl of water (see p. 49). This is a very good way to remove sand and grit, but it can actually increase the risk of moving contamination around—from one leaf to everything in the bowl. A much more effective way to remove potential pathogens is to discard the outer leaves, which is where most contamination would be, and wash each individual leaf under running water.

So as a home cook, you have a choice. You can focus on grit removal and soak in a bowl of water. Or you can decide to make the very low risk of contamination even lower by rinsing under water. If you want to combine both methods, it would be best to soak the leaves first and rinse them afterwards.

regularly.) Don't worry so much about the length of time—5 seconds is about as effective as 20 seconds—but rather focus on rubbing the whole surface, which will take longer for a cantaloupe than for an apple.

For produce with softer or complex texture, such as berries, broccoli, and spinach, a simple rinse is sometimes the only option. For this type of produce, rubbing individual pieces is more difficult. It's tricky to quantify the effectiveness of various washing techniques since there are many variables at play, but we do know that merely rinsing can help, even if only a little. Cooking vegetables results in better than a 100,000-fold reduction in pathogens (if the bacteria are present in the first place). When you rinse, rub, and dry an apple, you might achieve a 1,000-fold reduction in bacteria. For soft fruits and vegetables that you can only rinse, you might get a 10-fold decrease. But that translates into a 90% reduction, so even though a simple rinse doesn't produce the kind of numbers that get microbiologists excited, it does still have an impact.

Wash fruits and vegetables even if you're going to peel them. If there are bacteria on the rind, they're easily transferred to the inner surfaces during peeling or cutting. And once you've peeled or cut up a vegetable, it's virtually impossible to wash off any contamination. Cut surfaces provide more places for a microbe to hide, and they also tend to be difficult to rub.

Drying fruits and vegetables with a paper towel or in a clean salad spinner provides another measure of safety. This is because bacteria become suspended in water droplets after washing, so by removing the water, you're increasing the efficiency of the wash.

Linda J. Harris is a faculty member at the University of California, Davis, where she is the associate director for research at the Western Institute for Food Safety and Security and a specialist in cooperative extension in the Department of Food Science and Technology. Her research focuses on microbial food safety with an emphasis on fruits, vegetables, and tree nuts. ◆

Cannellini Beans

These plump creamy-white beans, which sometimes go by the name of white kidney beans, lend a mellow, earthy flavor to anything from soups and stews to salads, dips, and purées. Dried cannellini beans give excellent results, but we don't always have the time or inclination to soak and simmer them, especially on a hot summer day. That's when we turn to canned cannellini—give them a rinse, toss with a few aromatics, and a refreshing salad is ready in minutes. To find out which brand of cannellini is worth stashing in your pantry, we held a blind tasting of six widely available brands. While differences in flavor and texture weren't dramatic, top honors went to the beans with a creamier texture and a cleaner bean flavor.

BY LAURA GIANNATEMPO

Top Pick
BUSH'S
79¢ (15 oz.)

These rose-tinged beans were soft and creamy, with a clean bean flavor, a good salt level, and a pleasant hint of sweetness. While we singled them out mainly for their well-balanced flavor, their good looks won us over. Nice and plump, they were uniform in size and largely intact, making them a top choice for dishes where appearance matters, such as bean salads.

Runners-up
Beans numbered in order of preference; prices will vary.

1 PASTENE
99¢ (15 oz.)

These handsome beans almost tied for first place with Bush's. Tasters loved their mild, earthy flavor and well-balanced saltiness and praised their smooth, "peachy white," almost intact skins. But their texture didn't please everyone: A few thought their skins were a bit tough and their interior faintly chalky. Overall, they were tasty and attractive enough to use in any kind of bean dish.

2 PROGRESSO
$1.27 (19 oz.)

These cream-colored beans were large and uniform in shape, with a nutty flavor and just enough salt to bring out their earthiness. A couple of tasters, though, detected a slightly metallic flavor and a "tinny" aftertaste. While they had thin, tender skins and a smooth flesh ("like a perfect purée"), their texture was a bit uneven, with some beans seeming tougher than others.

3 RIENZI
79¢ (15 oz.)

Quite firm and a bit dry, these beans seemed a little undercooked. They'd be a good choice for recipes where further cooking is needed—in soups, for example. While they had very few split skins and held their shape pretty well, their flavor wasn't stellar: A bit bland and bitter, they tasted a little "processed," reminding some tasters of canned tuna.

4 GOYA
$1.29 (1 lb. 13 oz.)

These beans had a full, "beany" flavor (some tasters noticed a "fruity" aftertaste) and a decent creamy texture, but it was appearance that brought down their overall score. They were grayish, broken, and mushy, with lots of skins slipping off—by far the worst looking of the bunch. A good choice for dips and purées, where shabby looks isn't a flaw.

5 EDEN ORGANICS
$1.69 (15 oz.)
No salt added

We really missed the salt in these beans, so much so that it seemed as if "all the flavor was sucked out of them." Their texture was relatively smooth and buttery, if a bit too soft, and they didn't look bad either, but it was hard to get past their bland, watery flavor. ◆

where to buy it

Grilled Appetizers, *p. 36*

You can find sherry vinegar in specialty stores and some supermarkets, but you can also order it online at Tienda.com (800-710-4304); prices start at $12.95. IGourmet.com (877-446-8763) sells pimentón for $2.99 for a 2.7-ounce container. If your local grocery store doesn't carry Bûcheron cheese, you can find it at MurraysCheese.com for $11.99 a pound.

Lemon Cheesecake Squares, *p. 52*

Parchment paper for lining baking pans is available at BakersCatalogue.com (800-827-6836); a package of 100 half-sheets sells for $18.95.

Chinese Chicken Salad, *p. 58*

Both sweet and hot Asian chile sauces are available in Asian groceries and some supermarkets, as well as from online stores like EthnicGrocer.com and TempleOfThai.com.

Outdoor Kitchen, *p. 54*

Deborah Krasner hosts five-day culinary vacations at her Vermont home in the summer and fall. Visit CulinaryVermont.com for details.

Fruit Cobbler, *p. 60*

BulkFoods.com (419-537-1713) is a good mail-order source for turbinado and demerara sugars. Prices start at $3.51 and $4.25 per pound, respectively.

In Season, *p. 20*

Poblano seedlings are available at many garden centers. TheChileWoman.com sells a variety of organically grown chile seedlings, including poblanos.

Toppings for Grilled Fish, *p. 40*

To help lift fish from the grill, both tongs and a fish spatula are invaluable. Visit Oxo.com (800-545-4411) for locking tongs in various sizes (from $8.99). Fish spatulas are available in many kitchenwares stores, or visit PCD.com (800-792-6650), where prices start at $34.99.

Look for Espelette chile powder (piment d'Espelette) at ChefShop.com (800-596-0885), where a 1.4-ounce jar sells for $10.99.

Cooking for a Crowd, *p. 26a*

The basic tools you'll need for grilling are available in most kitchenwares stores, including online stores. You can also try visiting a Web site that specializes in them, like BBQproshop.com or Barbecue-Store.com.

For the grilled Thai chicken breast recipe, look to your local Asian market or visit TempleOfThai.com (877-811-8773) for Thai bird chiles (2 ounces for $3.99) and lemongrass (3 pieces for $4.99). ◆

The Catfish Institute *p. 11* Always fresh, healthy, mild and flaky, U.S. Farm-Raised Catfish suits any recipe.
www.catfishinstitute.com

Kitchen Design & Tableware

Ironwood Gourmet *p. 77* Professional-grade culinary tools for your kitchen. Beautiful, functional wooden kitchenware and tableware.
www.ironwoodgourmet.com

Plum Pudding Kitchen *p. 25* Your online source for "irresistibly Italian" Vietri dinnerware, flatware, glassware, and much more. Let us help you set a special table!
888-940-7586
www.plumpuddingkitchen.com

Poggi Bonsi *p. 29* Direct importers of artisan Italian ceramics, olive wood utensils and cutting boards, and Umbrian kitchen towels.
www.poggibonsigifts.com

Replacements, Ltd. *p. 76* World's largest inventory: old and new china, crystal, sterling, silver-plate, and stainless. All manufacturers, fine and casual. 10 million pieces, 200,000 patterns. Buy and sell.
800-REPLACE
www.replacements.com

The Bowl Mill *p. 15* One-piece hardwood bowls made on 19th-century lathes in Vermont, ranging from 8" to 20" in diameter featuring maple, yellow birch, and cherry.
800-828-1005
www.bowlmill.com

Totally Bamboo *p. 76* Featuring over 150 products, Totally Bamboo is the industry pioneer of bamboo cutting boards and kitchen design. Order all of our fine products directly online!
www.totallybamboo.com

Kitchen Tools & Utensils

Bella Copper *p. 77* The world's leading heat diffuser/defroster plate provides superior heat conduction for more even cooking and faster defrosting. Available in solid copper or pure silver. A gourmet kitchen essential.
805-215-3241
www.bellacopper.com

Component Design Northwest *p. 73* CDN offers more than 60 different cooking thermometers and timers for the casual or gourmet chef. Find CDN products at gourmet specialty stores or online.
800-338-5594
www.cdn-timeandtemp.com

Grill Friends *p. 7* Since 1957, Harold Import Company has been a leading supplier of kitchenware products to the specialty retail trade, offering almost 3000 items. Our products are available in thousands of stores worldwide. What can HIC offer your business?
www.girlsatthegrill.com

Gel Pro *p. 23* Stand In Comfort! Let's Gel was started with one simple goal, to make the time you spend standing in your kitchen more comfortable.
866-GEL-MATS
www.letsgel.com

J.K. Adams Company *p. 69* J.K. Adams, has been the premiere Vermont manufacturer of handcrafted, heirloom-quality, woodware for the kitchen and table since 1944.
www.jkadams.com

Kerekes *p. 77* Your complete online source for professional chef's tools, cookware, bakeware, and cake decorating supplies used by top chefs at the finest restaurants and kitchens.
www.bakedeco.com

Mix-In-Guide *p. 76* The best way to get ingredients into your mixer bowl. Easy on. Easy off. Stainless steel ingredient chute for stand mixers.
www.mix-in-guide.com

WMF of America *p. 13* WMF is the only brand that can make cooking, dining, and drinking an event. WMF is the singular choice.
www.wmf-usa.com

Schools, Travel & Organizations

Culinary Business Academy *p. 25* Extensive and comprehensive personal chef business knowledge and training from the world's recognized leader in the personal chef industry. Nobody offers what we offer.
800-747-2433
www.hireachef.com

La Villa Bonita *p. 29* La Villa Bonita offers a delicious immersion in the culinary joys of Mexico, with its culinary vacation packages in a 16th-century mansion in Cuernavaca.
800-505-3084
www.lavillabonita.com

Le Cordon Bleu *p. 7* Master the culinary arts. Earn the Grand Diplome in approximately nine months. Three- to five-week intensive courses and online hospitality programs are also available.
800-457-2433
www.cordonbleu.edu

Wines, Beverages & Accessories

Covington Cellars *p. 77* Award winning boutique Washington winery offers wine samples of our limited production wines that sell out fast! An excellent addition to any cellar!
253-347-9463
www.covingtoncellars.com

Woodbridge Wines *p. 79* For 25 years, we have aged our wines in small oak barrels and handcrafted each vintage. Woodbridge: Taste our small winery tradition™.
www.woodbridgewines.com

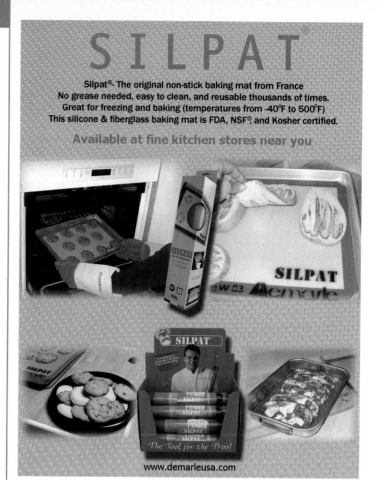
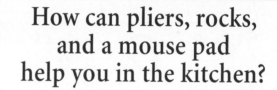

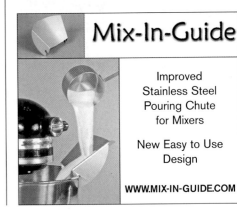

EAT 5 TO 9 SERVINGS OF FRUITS AND VEGETABLES A DAY FOR BETTER HEALTH
Department of Health and Human Services
National Institutes of Health
National Cancer Institute

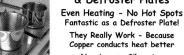

Recipe	Page	Calories		Protein	Carb	Fats (g)				Chol.	Sodium	Fiber	Notes
		total	from fat	(g)	(g)	total	sat	mono	poly	(mg)	(mg)	(g)	
In Season	20												
Quesadillas w/ Roasted Poblanos & Onions		240	140	10	15	16	8	4.5	2	35	450	1	based on 8 servings
Grilling for a Crowd	26a												
Farmers' Market Crudités w/ Buttermilk Herb Dip		110	45	5	13	5	3.5	0	0	20	250	3	based on 12 servings
Grilled Bruschetta w/ White Bean Purée & Tomatoes		260	120	5	28	14	2	10	1.5	0	430	2	based on 12 servings
Grilled Herb-Crusted Leg of Lamb w/ Fresh Mint Sauce		290	100	40	4	12	3.5	6	1	120	870	0	based on 12 servings
Grilled Thai Chicken Breasts w/ Herb-Lemongrass Crust		240	70	39	3	7	4	1.5	1	105	510	0	based on 12 servings
Argentine Spice-Rubbed Flank Steak w/ Salsa Criolla		320	160	35	3	18	6	5	1	65	615	0	based on 12 servings
Chopped Tomato & Cucumber Salad w/ Mint & Feta		190	150	4	7	17	4.5	11	1.5	15	830	1	based on 12 servings
Grilled Southwestern Potato Salad		270	150	6	27	17	3	11	2	5	610	4	based on 12 servings
Warm Pasta Salad w/ Tomatoes, Zucchini & Pecorino		260	90	9	32	11	4	4	1	15	480	2	based on 12 servings
Grilled Asparagus & Onions w/ Balsamic & Blue Cheese		150	120	3	8	13	2.5	8	2	5	200	2	based on 12 servings
Grilled Corn on the Cob w/ Thyme & Red Pepper Butter		210	140	3	18	16	8	6	1.5	30	300	3	based on 8 servings
Grilled Appetizers	36												
Shrimp Skewers		170	90	18	1	10	1.5	7	1.5	170	290	0	based on 6 servings
Pancetta & Pineapple Skewers		160	130	3	5	15	3.5	9	1.5	15	450	1	based on 6 servings
Mini Tuna Burgers w/ Mint-Caper Aioli on Pita Triangles		280	160	16	14	18	3	11	2.5	50	260	2	based on 8 servings
Bacon-Wrapped Stuffed Apricots		180	90	7	16	10	4	3	1	20	280	2	based on 8 servings
Tomato & Olive Pizzettas w/ Fennel Seeds & Goat Cheese		280	130	9	26	15	4.5	6	1	15	670	1	based on 8 servings
Grilled Fish & Toppings	40												
Grilled Fish w/ Sun-Dried Tomato, Olive & Caper Relish		420	230	40	4	26	4.5	16	4.5	65	570	1	based on 6 servings
Grilled Fish w/ Lemon, Dill & Cucumber Sauce		360	180	40	2	21	4	12	3.5	65	390	0	based on 6 servings
Grilled Fish w/ Sea Salt, Chile & Lime Butter		410	240	40	1	27	12	9	3.5	105	450	0	based on 6 servings
Grilled Fish w/ Tarragon-Scented Mayonnaise		440	260	40	2	29	4.5	17	6	80	400	0	w/ 2 Tbs. mayonnaise
Summer Pasta	43												
Spaghetti w/ Spicy Shrimp & Cherry Tomatoes		830	310	35	93	35	5	23	4.5	170	460	6	based on 4 servings
Rigatoni w/ Squash, Spicy Sausage & Goat Cheese		500	170	19	61	19	6	9	2	25	760	3	based on 6 servings
Orecchiette w/ Caramelized Onions & Green Beans		680	190	19	104	22	4	13	2.5	5	570	8	based on 4 servings
Green Salads	46												
Mixed Green Salad w/ Red-Wine & Dijon Vinaigrette		60	45	1	2	5	0.5	3.5	0.5	0	170	1	based on 8 servings
Butter Lettuce w/ Poppy Seed & Tarragon Crème Fraîche		60	40	2	3	4.5	2.5	1	0.5	10	150	1	based on 6 servings
Mâche w/ Spicy Melon & Pink-Peppercorn Dressing		120	60	3	15	7	1	3	3	0	180	3	based on 4 servings
Arugula & Fennel Salad w/ Orange & Fennel Seed Dressing		160	120	3	9	14	1.5	10	1.5	0	170	3	based on 4 servings
Lemon Cheesecake Squares	52												
Lemon Cheesecake Squares		260	150	4	24	16	9	4.5	1	95	160	0	based on 16 servings
Chinese Chicken Salad	58												
Chinese Chicken Salad		540	270	45	20	31	5	15	9	105	1060	4	based on 4 servings
Fruit Cobblers	60												
Plum Cobbler w/ Almonds, Lemon Zest & Ginger		350	120	5	52	14	7	4.5	1	30	190	3	based on 10 servings
Triple Berry Cobbler w/ Pecans & Cinnamon		340	130	5	48	15	7	4.5	2	30	190	5	based on 10 servings
Raspberry-Peach Cobbler w/ Cornmeal Biscuits		310	90	4	50	10	7	2	0.5	30	190	5	based on 10 servings
Test Kitchen	64												
Gravlax		80	35	8	2	4	1	1.5	1.5	20	1230	0	based on 12 servings
Steak & Eggs Rancheros		460	270	27	22	30	9	15	4	255	910	6	based on 2 servings
Prosciutto-Wrapped Melon w/ Mint & White Balsamic		70	20	7	7	2.5	1	0	0	15	580	1	based on 8 servings
Quick & Delicious	78a												
Egg Salad w/ Smoked Salmon, Capers & Dill		340	260	18	3	30	6	19	3.5	325	1580	1	based on 4 servings
Orzo & Grilled Vegetable Salad w/ Feta & Olives		380	210	8	36	23	4.5	15	2.5	10	450	4	based on 6 servings
Grilled Salmon Bundles w/ Saffron, Tomatoes & Olives		430	250	39	3	28	4	16	7	105	390	1	based on 4 servings
Grilled Portabella Sandwiches w/ Tomatoes & Mozzarella		540	300	18	43	34	8	12	3	20	850	5	based on 4 servings
Tomatillo Gazpacho		190	140	4	12	15	2.5	10	2	0	170	6	based on 6 servings
Spicy Fried Chicken		150	45	18	8	5	1.5	2	1	55	210	1	based on 6 servings
Grilled Asian Pork Tenderloin w/ Peanut Sauce		300	110	39	7	12	3.5	2.5	0.5	100	490	1	based on 5 servings
Back Cover													
Balsamic-Macerated Strawberries w/ Basil		40	5	1	10	0	0	0	0	0	0	2	based on 8 servings

The nutritional analyses have been calculated by a registered dietitian at Nutritional Solutions in Melville, New York. When a recipe gives a choice of ingredients, the first choice is the one used. Optional ingredients with measured amounts are included; ingredients without specific quantities are not. When a range of ingredient amounts or servings is given, the smaller amount or portion is used. When the quantities of salt and pepper aren't specified, the analysis is based on ¼ teaspoon salt and ⅛ teaspoon pepper per serving for entrées, and ⅛ teaspoon salt and ⅟₁₆ teaspoon pepper per serving for side dishes.

Grilled Asian Pork Tenderloin with Peanut Sauce

Serves four to five.

1 cup light coconut milk
½ cup smooth peanut butter, preferably a natural variety
¼ cup soy sauce
3 Tbs. fresh lime juice
3 Tbs. dark brown sugar
2 large cloves garlic, minced (2½ tsp.)
2 tsp. ground coriander
2 small pork tenderloins (about 2 lb. total)
Vegetable oil for the grill

In a large bowl, whisk the coconut milk, peanut butter, soy sauce, lime juice, brown sugar, garlic, and coriander to make a smooth sauce.

Trim the pork of excess fat and silverskin. Butterfly the tenderloins by splitting each one lengthwise almost but not quite all the way through, so the halves remain attached.

Open each tenderloin like a book, cover with plastic wrap, and pound to an even ½-inch thickness with a meat mallet or the bottom of a small skillet. Put the pork tenderloins in the bowl with the marinade and turn to coat. Let marinate for 10 to 20 minutes (or up to several hours in the refrigerator).

While the pork marinates, heat a gas grill with all burners on high. Clean and oil the grate as described in From Our Test Kitchen, p. 64. Remove the tenderloins from the marinade, letting excess marinade drip back into the bowl (don't discard the marinade). Grill the tenderloins, covered, turning once, until just cooked through, 5 to 7 minutes total (cut into one to check). Transfer to a carving board and let rest for 5 minutes.

Meanwhile, pour the marinade into a small saucepan and add 2 Tbs. water; bring to a boil, reduce the heat, and simmer for 3 minutes. Remove from the heat. If the sauce seems too thick, thin it with 1 or 2 tsp. water. Slice the pork and serve with the sauce on the side.

Serving suggestion:
Serve with steamed jasmine or short-grain rice and stir-fried spinach or snow peas.

Tomatillo Gazpacho

Yields about 5 cups; serves four to six as a first course.

One 14-oz. can low-salt chicken broth
1 lb. tomatillos (8 to 12 medium), husked, rinsed, and cut into medium dice (3 cups)
1 medium clove garlic, minced
2 Tbs. extra-virgin olive oil
2 medium avocados, cut into small dice (1½ cups)
½ seedless English cucumber, cut into small dice (2 cups)
½ large red bell pepper, cut into small dice (½ cup)
¼ small red onion, finely diced (¼ cup)
2 Tbs. chopped fresh cilantro
1 Tbs. fresh lime juice; more as needed
Kosher salt and freshly ground black pepper

Heat the broth in a 3-qt. saucepan over medium-high heat. Add the tomatillos and garlic, bring to a boil, reduce the heat, and let simmer until the tomatillos are cooked through but still hold their shape, about 1 minute. Let cool slightly, about 5 minutes, and then carefully purée the mixture in a blender along with the olive oil. Pour the purée into a nonreactive 9x13-inch pan and refrigerate to cool quickly.

When the purée has cooled, remove the pan from the refrigerator and stir in the avocado, cucumber, bell pepper, onion, cilantro, and lime juice. Season to taste with salt and pepper. Refrigerate for at least 1 hour and up to 4 hours. Before serving, taste and adjust the seasoning with more lime juice, salt, and pepper, as needed. Spoon the gazpacho into individual serving bowls or mugs.

Serving suggestion:
Serve with tortilla chips.

Note: This recipe is quick to prepare but needs to chill for at least an hour for the flavors to develop.

Photos: Scott Phillips

Grilled Portabella Sandwiches with Tomatoes, Mozzarella & Basil

Serves four.

Vegetable oil for the grill
¼ cup mayonnaise
¼ cup freshly grated Parmigiano-Reggiano (½ oz.)
1 Tbs. minced garlic (3 to 4 medium cloves)
4 good-quality sandwich rolls, cut in half
¼ cup extra-virgin olive oil
2 Tbs. balsamic vinegar
4 large portabella mushrooms, stems and gills removed and discarded and caps wiped clean (see From Our Test Kitchen for more, p. 64)
Kosher salt and freshly ground black pepper
4 to 8 thin slices fresh mozzarella or sharp provolone
½ cup lightly packed fresh basil leaves (about ½ oz.)
2 medium ripe tomatoes, sliced (about 9 oz.)

Heat a gas grill with all burners on high. Clean and oil the grate as described in From Our Test Kitchen, p. 64.

In a small bowl, mix the mayonnaise, Parmigiano, and 1 tsp. of the garlic; spread the mixture over the cut sides of each roll.

In another small bowl, whisk the olive oil, vinegar, and the remaining 2 tsp. garlic. Brush the oil mixture over both sides of each mushroom cap and sprinkle generously with salt and pepper. Grill the mushrooms, gill side down, until grill-marked, about 3 minutes. Flip and continue to grill until cooked through, about 3 minutes more. Reduce the heat to low, flip the mushrooms again, and top each with a portion of cheese. Put the rolls, cut sides up, on the grill along with the mushrooms. Cover the grill and cook until the rolls are crisp and warm and the cheese melts, 2 to 3 minutes.

Put the rolls and mushrooms on a platter. Arrange a few basil leaves on the bottom half of each roll. Sprinkle the tomatoes lightly with salt. Put the tomatoes and then the mushrooms on the basil leaves. Cap the sandwiches with the tops of the rolls and serve.

Orzo & Grilled Vegetable Salad with Feta, Olives & Oregano

Serves four to six as a side dish or two to three as a vegetarian main dish.

1 Tbs. kosher salt; more as needed
8 oz. orzo (1¼ cups)
Vegetable oil for the grill
2 small Italian eggplants (about ¾ lb. total), sliced into ½-inch-thick rounds
1 medium red bell pepper, quartered, stemmed, and seeded
⅓ cup plus 2 Tbs. extra-virgin olive oil
2 Tbs. red-wine vinegar
1 Tbs. Dijon mustard
½ small red onion, cut into small dice (about ⅔ cup)
½ cup crumbled feta (2½ oz.)
½ cup pitted, coarsely chopped Kalamata olives
3 Tbs. chopped fresh oregano

In a 4-qt. saucepan, bring about 2 qt. water and the salt to a boil over high heat. Add the orzo and cook, stirring occasionally, until just tender, about 8 minutes (or according to package directions). Drain but don't rinse the pasta and pour it onto a rimmed baking sheet to cool evenly and quickly.

Heat a gas grill with all burners on high. Clean and oil the grate as described in From Our Test Kitchen, p. 64. Toss the eggplant and bell pepper with 2 Tbs. of the olive oil and a generous sprinkling of salt. Lay the vegetables on the grill and cook, with the grill covered, turning once, until cooked through and grill-marked, 2 to 3 minutes per side. Transfer to a cutting board. Allow the vegetables to cool slightly and then cut them into small dice.

In a liquid measuring cup, whisk the vinegar with the mustard and a generous pinch of salt. Slowly whisk in the remaining ⅓ cup olive oil.

When ready to serve, combine the orzo, grilled vegetables, onion, feta, olives, and oregano in a medium bowl. Pour on the dressing, toss well, and serve.

Serving suggestion:
This salad would be delicious with grilled lamb chops or lamb burgers.

Spicy Fried Chicken

Serves four to six.

**9 oz. (2 cups) all-purpose
flour**
½ cup plain low-fat yogurt
2 Tbs. chili powder
**2½ tsp. kosher salt; more
as needed**
2 tsp. Bell's Poultry Seasoning
2 tsp. onion powder
**2 tsp. freshly ground black
pepper**
½ tsp. celery seed
½ to ¾ tsp. cayenne
2½ cups vegetable oil
**8 chicken drumsticks, skin
removed**

Put the flour in a large, sturdy
brown paper bag and the
yogurt in a medium bowl. To
the flour, add 1 Tbs. of the
chili powder, 2 tsp. of the
salt, 1 tsp. each of the poultry
seasoning, onion powder,
and pepper, and ¼ tsp. each
of the celery seed and cayenne. Roll the top of the bag
closed and shake to combine.

To the yogurt, add the
remaining 1 Tbs. chili powder,
the remaining 1 tsp. each
poultry seasoning, onion
powder, and pepper, ½ tsp.
of the salt, the remaining
¼ tsp. celery seed, and ¼ to
½ tsp. cayenne. Mix well.

In an 11- or 12-inch straight-
sided sauté pan or cast-iron
skillet, heat the vegetable oil
over medium heat.

Add the drumsticks to the
yogurt mixture and stir and
toss (with your hands or
tongs) to coat completely.
Put 4 of the drumsticks in
the bag with the flour mixture,
close the bag, and shake
vigorously (over the sink in
case any flour escapes) to
coat well. Shake off excess
flour, put the drumsticks on
a plate, and repeat with the
remaining chicken.

Put the drumsticks in the
hot oil, cover, and fry until
they're golden brown on
the bottom, 5 to 7 minutes.
Turn each drumstick and
continue to fry, uncovered,
turning occasionally as
needed to brown evenly, until
golden brown and cooked
through, 5 to 10 minutes
longer (cut into a piece to
check). Put the drumsticks
on a wire rack set over paper
towels to drain and sprinkle
all over with salt while still
hot. Serve hot, warm, or at
room temperature.

Tip: If you use a
large sauté pan (ideally
12 inches), you'll be able to
fry all your chicken in one
batch—a real time saver.

Grilled Salmon Bundles
with Saffron, Tomatoes & Olives

Serves four.

**2 medium plum tomatoes,
cored and cut into medium
dice (about 1 cup)**
**¼ cup pitted and coarsely
chopped black oil-cured
olives (20 to 25 olives)**
¼ cup extra-virgin olive oil
**1 Tbs. minced fresh garlic
(3 to 4 medium cloves)**
½ tsp. chopped fresh thyme
**½ tsp. kosher salt; more as
needed**
Pinch saffron (15 to 20 threads)
Freshly ground black pepper
**Four 6-oz. center-cut, skin-on
salmon fillets**

Heat a gas grill with all burners on high.

In a medium bowl, com-
bine the tomatoes, olives,
olive oil, garlic, thyme, salt,
saffron, and pepper to taste.

Set one piece of salmon,
skin-side down, on a 12x18-
inch piece of heavy-duty foil;
sprinkle lightly with salt and
pepper. Spoon a quarter of
the tomato mixture over the
fish and seal tightly. Repeat
to make four packets.

Set the foil packets on the
hot grate and cook, with the
grill covered, until the fish is
opaque throughout, about
8 minutes (open a packet
and cut into the fish to check).
Let the salmon rest for a few
minutes before serving.

Tip: You can serve the
salmon packets warm
or at room temperature,
but don't let them sit
out for more than about
45 minutes.

Pam Anderson is a contributing editor to Fine Cooking *and
the author of* Perfect Recipes for Having People Over. ◆

BY PAM ANDERSON

Summer with a twist

Just as we love to eat fireside during the chilly months, we can't wait to fire up the grill or spread a picnic blanket as soon as the weather turns warm. As you start taking your meals outdoors, these recipes for summery classics with flavor twists will help you keep things interesting. Feel like burgers? Skip the meat aisle and instead head for the produce department and pick up a package of portabella mushrooms for grilling. For a change, perk up ordinary egg salad with smoked salmon, capers, and dill; add zing to fried chicken with a spicy yogurt marinade; or make your next batch of gazpacho with tomatillos rather than tomatoes. And next time salmon's on the menu, why not try a new cooking technique? Simply seal the fillets in foil with saffron, olives, tomatoes, and orange zest and pop the packets on the grill— it's foolproof.

Gas is fast

I cook on a gas grill when I'm in a hurry because it gets hot much faster than charcoal does. You can certainly use charcoal for any of the grilling recipes here; just factor in some extra time for the grill to heat up. See From Our Test Kitchen, p. 64, for pointers on cleaning and oiling your gas grill grate.

Egg Salad with Smoked Salmon, Capers & Dill

Serves four as a main course.

6 large eggs
6 oz. cold-smoked salmon, cut into small dice (1 scant cup) (for more on smoked salmon, see From Our Test Kitchen, p. 64)
6 Tbs. extra-virgin olive oil
½ small red onion, cut into small dice (about ⅔ cup)
⅓ cup capers, drained
2 Tbs. minced fresh dill
1 Tbs. fresh lemon juice
1 tsp. finely grated lemon zest
Kosher salt and freshly ground black pepper

Put the eggs in a medium saucepan with enough water to cover. Cover the pan and bring the water to a boil over medium-high heat. As soon as the water boils, remove the pan from the heat and let stand, covered, until the eggs are hard-cooked, 10 minutes. Put the eggs in ice water to cool.

Peel the eggs, chop finely, and put them in a medium bowl. Add the salmon, oil, onion, capers, dill, and lemon juice and zest. Season with salt and pepper to taste. Toss gently but well and serve.

Serving suggestion:

Serve this salad on a bed of lettuce or on toasted sandwich bread as a main course; spoon it onto toasted pita triangles for an hors d'oeuvre.

6 ribeyes

A bag of hickory charcoal

45 minutes until sunset

1 bottle of

WOODBRIDGE
BY ROBERT MONDAVI
2005

CABERNET SAUVIGNON
California

MAKE EVERY DAY A LITTLE LESS EVERYDAY | WOODBRIDGE
BY ROBERT MONDAVI

Bringing out the best in berries

This quick dessert pairs two icons of the season—strawberries and basil—in an unexpected way. The sweet and sour balsamic vinegar helps amplify the flavor of the berries, even if they're less than ripe.

Balsamic-Macerated Strawberries with Basil

Serves four as a dessert;
six to eight as a filling or topping.

For this recipe, there's no need for an expensive, artisanal balsamic vinegar—a grocery-store vinegar is perfectly well suited.

2 lb. fresh strawberries, rinsed,
**   hulled, and sliced ⅛ to ¼ inch**
**   thick (about 4 cups)**
1 Tbs. granulated sugar
2 tsp. balsamic vinegar
8 to 10 medium fresh basil leaves

In a large bowl, gently toss the strawberries with the sugar and vinegar. Let sit at room temperature until the strawberries have released their juices but are not yet mushy, about 30 minutes. (Don't let the berries sit for more than 90 minutes, or they'll start to collapse.)

Just before serving, stack the basil leaves on a cutting board and roll them vertically into a loose cigar shape. Using a sharp chef's knife, very thinly slice across the roll to make a fine chiffonade of basil.

Portion the strawberries and their juices among four small bowls and scatter with the basil to garnish, or choose one of the serving suggestions at right.

Sarah Breckenridge, associate
Web editor ◆

Sweet ways to serve

❖ Serve the strawberries over grilled or toasted pound cake (photo above).

❖ Put the berries on split biscuits for short-cakes; top with whipped cream and scatter with the basil.

❖ Layer the berries with ice cream or yogurt for a parfait. Garnish with the basil.

❖ Spoon the strawberries over a poached or roasted peach half.

❖ Use the berries as a filling for crêpes or a topping for waffles.

❖ Mash the berries slightly and fold into whipped cream for a quick fool. Garnish with the basil.

Hull berries carefully

To maintain a strawberry's beautiful shape, use a paring knife to remove the cap with an angled cut.

Bonus section: Quick dinners inspired by the farmers' market

fine
Cooking

SEPTEMBER 2007   NO. 87

FOR PEOPLE WHO LOVE TO COOK

how to grill
the juiciest chicken

no-cook
tomato sauces

a Mexican
take on steak

perfecting
grilled bread

new ideas for
corn off the cob

3 easy peach
desserts

dressing up
grilled eggplant

w.finecooking.com

95 CAN $7.95

Grilled Rosemary Chicken
Thighs with Sweet & Sour
Orange Dipping Sauce

09

7 1486 03446 9

To really appreciate fine Italian art,
all you have to do is turn on your stove.

The finest Italian Cappuccino at home.

L'Arte del Cappuccino

fine Cooking

AUGUST/SEPTEMBER 2007 ISSUE 87

34 38

RECIPE FOLDOUT

78A Quick & Delicious
Summertime, and
the cooking is easy

Farmers' Market Quesadillas

ON THE COVER

30 **Chicken Thighs
on the Grill**

*Grilled Rosemary Chicken Thighs with
Sweet & Sour Orange Dipping Sauce*

UP FRONT

6 Index

8 Menus

10 Letters

14 Contributors

16 Q&A

17 Links

18 In Season
Cucumbers

20 Enjoying Beer
Beer 101

22 Equipment
❖ Lifting oven
❖ Crinkle cutter
❖ Food vacuum-
    sealers
❖ Ice maker
❖ Ice cream scoop
    review

28 Readers' Tips

22

18

20

28

The Taunton Press
Inspiration for hands-on living®

visit our web site: **www.finecooking.com**

40   44   48   58

FEATURES

30   COVER: WEEKNIGHT COOKING
**Chicken Thighs
Take a Turn on the Grill**
More flavorful than chicken breasts, boneless
thighs cook quickly and stay juicy
by Pam Anderson

34   **Endless Summer Corn Sautés**
For a versatile side dish, take the corn off the cob
and layer on the flavors
by Susie Middleton

38   **No-Cook Tomato Sauces**
Great tomatoes don't need cooking to become
a great sauce
by Evan Kleiman

40   **Grilled Bread—for Satisfying Sides,
Starters, and Mains**
by Elizabeth Karmel

44   **Steaks, Mexican Style**
If fajitas are the first thing that comes to mind,
think again
by Jim Peyton

48   **Dressing Up Grilled Eggplant**
Bold vinaigrettes and sauces make a
simple summer favorite something special
by Tasha DeSerio

52   **Scallions: More Than a Garnish**
These little green onions can be a side dish on their
own or a starring ingredient in soups and stir-fries
by Tony Rosenfeld

56   EXPLORING CUISINES: THAI
Fresh from the Sea, a Thai Classic
Bright, tangy flavors and perfectly cooked seafood
come together in this refreshing, summery salad
by Nancie McDermott

58   **Peaches & Cream**
Ripe, juicy peaches and honey-sweetened
whipped cream are all you need to create these
quick summer desserts
by Carole Bloom

70

66

IN THE BACK

62   From Our
      Test Kitchen
      ❖ Buying corn
      ❖ Canning pickles
      ❖ Malted milk shakes
      ❖ Aged Gouda
      ❖ Leftovers: Eggplant
        & Pasta Salad

68   Food Science
      Grilling, Demystified

70   Tasting Panel
      Chocolate ice cream

72   Where To Buy It

78   Nutrition
      Information

BACK COVER

Make It Tonight
Corn Sauté with
Canadian Bacon,
Potatoes & Peppers

63

62

index

◆ **QUICK**
Under 45 minutes

◆ **MAKE AHEAD**
Can be completely prepared ahead but may need reheating and a garnish to serve

◆ **MOSTLY MAKE AHEAD**
Can be partially prepared ahead but will need a few finishing touches before serving

◆ **VEGETARIAN**
May contain eggs and dairy ingredients

53 *Grilled Flank Steak with Sesame Sauce & Grilled Scallions*

33 *Grilled Tandoori-Style Chicken Thighs*

57 *Thai Seafood Salad*

recipes

Cover Recipe
◆ Grilled Rosemary Chicken Thighs with Sweet & Sour Orange Dipping Sauce, 32

Appetizers
◆ Grilled Goat Cheese Crostini with a Tangle of Marinated Roasted Peppers, 42
◆ Thai Seafood Salad, 57

Salads
◆ Arugula Salad with Pears, Prosciutto & Aged Gouda, 78a
◆◆◆ Create-Your-Own Pasta Salad with Grilled Eggplant, 67
◆◆ Feta & Dill Galette with Lemony Spinach Salad, 78a
  Grilled Corn, Shrimp & Chorizo Salad, 43
◆ Thai Seafood Salad, 57

Soups
◆◆ Green Gazpacho, 19
◆◆ Summer Bouillabaisse with Smoky Rouille, 78a
◆ Summer Corn Chowder with Scallions, Bacon & Potatoes, 55

Breads, Biscuits & Quesadillas
◆◆ Cream Shortcake Biscuits, 61
◆◆ Farmers' Market Quesadillas, 78a
  Grilled Corn, Shrimp & Chorizo Salad, 43
◆◆ Grilled Garlic Bread, 41
◆ Grilled Goat Cheese Crostini with a Tangle of Marinated Roasted Peppers, 42

Pasta & Pasta Sauces
◆ Angel Hair Pasta with Sautéed Cherry Tomatoes, Lemon & Tuna, 78a
◆◆◆ Create-Your-Own Pasta Salad with Grilled Eggplant, 67
◆◆◆ No-Cook Tomato Sauce, 39
◆◆◆ No-Cook Tomato Sauce with Basil Pesto, 39
◆◆◆ No-Cook Tomato Sauce with Cheese, 39
◆◆ No-Cook Tomato Sauce with Tapenade, 39
  Pork Lo Mein with Seared Scallions & Shiitakes, 54

Light Main Dishes
◆ Corn Sauté with Canadian Bacon, Potatoes & Peppers, back cover
◆◆ Farmers' Market Quesadillas, 78a
◆◆ Feta & Dill Galette with Lemony Spinach Salad, 78a
◆ Thai Seafood Salad, 57

Chicken
◆ Grilled Five-Spice Chicken Thighs with Soy-Vinegar Sauce & Cilantro, 31
◆ Grilled Rosemary Chicken Thighs with Sweet & Sour Orange Dipping Sauce, 32
◆ Grilled Tandoori-Style Chicken Thighs, 33
  Indonesian Grilled Chicken Thighs with Mango-Peanut Salsa, 33
◆ Roasted Chicken Thighs with Late-Summer Vegetables & Pan Sauce, 78a

Beef & Pork
◆ Chili-Rubbed Rib-Eye Steak with Corn & Green Chile Ragoût, 78a
  Grilled Flank Steak with Sesame Sauce & Grilled Scallions, 53
  Pork Lo Mein with Seared Scallions & Shiitakes, 54
◆ Steak Adobo, 46
◆ Steak with Red Onion, Wine & Port Sauce, 45
  Steak with Three-Chile Sauce, 47

Seafood
◆ Angel Hair Pasta with Sautéed Cherry Tomatoes, Lemon & Tuna, 78a
  Grilled Corn, Shrimp & Chorizo Salad, 43
◆◆ Summer Bouillabaisse with Smoky Rouille, 78a
◆ Thai Seafood Salad, 57

Side Dishes
◆ Corn & Mushroom Sauté with Leeks & Pancetta, 37
◆ Corn Sauté with Canadian Bacon, Potatoes & Peppers, back cover
◆◆ Corn Sauté with Ginger, Garlic & Fresh Cilantro, 37
◆◆ Corn, Sweet Onion & Zucchini Sauté with Fresh Mint, 36
◆◆◆ Create-Your-Own Pasta Salad with Grilled Eggplant, 67
◆◆◆ Grilled Eggplant, 49
◆◆ Grilled Eggplant with Garlic-Cumin Vinaigrette with Feta & Herbs, 51
◆ Grilled Eggplant with Olive, Orange & Anchovy Vinaigrette, 50
◆◆ Grilled Eggplant with Roasted Red Pepper Relish with Pine Nuts, Currants & Marjoram, 51
◆ Grilled Eggplant with Toasted-Breadcrumb Salsa Verde, 50

Vinaigrettes, Condiments & Sauces
◆◆◆ Basic Vinaigrette, 67
◆◆ Garlic-Cumin Vinaigrette with Feta & Herbs, 51
◆ Olive, Orange & Anchovy Vinaigrette, 50
◆◆ Pickled Cauliflower with Carrots & Red Bell Pepper, 64
◆◆ Roasted Red Pepper Relish with Pine Nuts, Currants & Marjoram, 51
◆◆ Spiced Pickled Beets, 65
◆ Toasted-Breadcrumb Salsa Verde, 50

Desserts
◆◆ Cream Shortcake Biscuits, 61
◆◆ Honey Whipped Cream, 59
◆◆ Marinated Peaches, 59
◆◆ Peaches & Cream Dessert, 59
◆◆ Peaches & Cream Parfait, 60
◆◆ Peaches & Cream Shortcakes, 61

Beverages
◆◆ Double-Chocolate Malted Milk Shake, 66

Photos: Scott Phillips

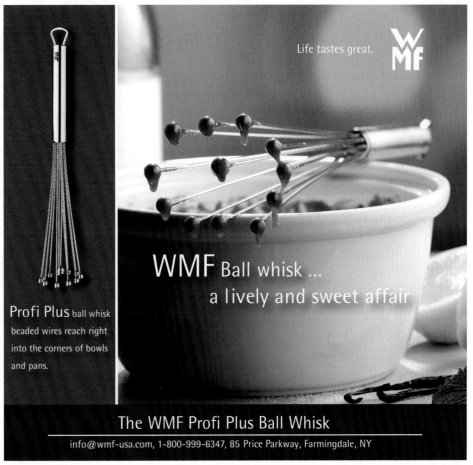

Simple meals
for late summer's harvest

This is the time of year when a cook's job becomes infinitely easier. The arrival of fabulous fruits and vegetables in gardens and markets provides plenty of inspiration for meals that showcase the season's harvest. In this issue, we offer an abundance of recipes to help you make the most of the tomatoes, eggplant, corn, peaches, and other fresh ingredients reaching their peak. The menu ideas here also recognize that as summer winds down, most of us still want to eat lightly and squeeze in as many outdoor meals as possible. As a result, you won't find many dishes requiring stewing or braising. Now is the time for quick stovetop cooking and outdoor grilling, so you can get out of the kitchen and enjoy the last of the warm weather. Remember to check the yield on each recipe, as you may need to double or halve it to suit your needs.

Easy Ways with Asian Flavors

Asian flavors liven up chicken and vegetables in this light, easy meal.

Grilled Five-Spice Chicken Thighs with Soy-Vinegar Sauce & Cilantro, *p. 31*

Corn Sauté with Ginger, Garlic & Cilantro, *p. 37*

To drink: A crisp, slightly sweet Riesling like the 2005 Mönchhof Estate Riesling, Mosel, $14

Three ideas for a weekend lunch on the deck

Pair a hearty soup with a fresh starter or salad for a satisfying midday meal.

Grilled Goat Cheese Crostini with Marinated Roasted Peppers, *p. 42*

Summer Bouillabaisse with Smoky Rouille, *p. 78a*

To drink: A light fruity red that can be served slightly chilled, like the 2005 Beringer Founders' Estate Pinot Noir, California, $12

Feta & Dill Galette with Lemony Spinach Salad, *p. 78a*

Summer Corn Chowder with Scallions, Bacon & Potatoes, *p. 55*

To drink: A citrusy Sauvignon Blanc like the 2006 Souverain, Alexander Valley, $15

Green Gazpacho, *p. 19*

Grilled Corn, Shrimp & Chorizo Salad, *p. 43*

To drink: A vibrant Italian Pinot Grigio like the 2005 Alois Lageder, Delle Venezie, $16

Cool foods for a hot night

Leave the stove off for this make-ahead meal.

No-Cook Tomato Sauce with Basil Pesto over pasta of your choice, *p. 39*

Arugula Salad with Pears, Prosciutto & Aged Gouda, *p. 78a*

Peaches & Cream Parfait, *p. 60*

To drink: An herbal crisp white like the 2006 Allan Scott Marlborough Sauvignon Blanc, New Zealand, $16

Put it on the grill

This no-fuss meal lets you stay outside with guests. Be sure to marinate the flank steak at least four hours ahead.

Grilled Garlic Bread, *p. 41*

Grilled Flank Steak with Sesame Sauce & Grilled Scallions, *p. 53*

Grilled Eggplant with Toasted-Breadcrumb Salsa Verde, *p. 50*

Peaches & Cream Dessert, *p. 59*

To drink: A young fruit-forward red like the 2005 Rosemount Estate Shiraz Cabernet, Southeastern Australia, $10

Casual summer suppers

Both the chicken and the eggplant in these two meals can be grilled ahead of time and served at room temperature.

Corn, Sweet Onion & Zucchini Sauté with Fresh Mint, *p. 36*

Grilled Rosemary Chicken Thighs with Sweet & Sour Dipping Sauce, *p. 32*

To drink: A youthful red like the 2005 Red Guitar Tempranillo Garnacha, Navarra, Spain, $14

Grilled Eggplant with Garlic-Cumin Vinaigrette, Feta & Herbs, *p. 51*

Angel Hair Pasta with Sautéed Cherry Tomatoes, Lemon & Tuna, *p. 78a*

To drink: A zesty rosé like the 2005 Falesco Vitiano Rosé, Italy, $12

from the editor

The Thrill of the Shoot

The life of a magazine editor is oh-so-glamorous, especially when it comes to photo shoots. You have only to look at me turned upside down scrubbing a patio table (top left) to see how true this is. Cover shoots are particularly exciting. We spend a lot of time in hurry-up-and-wait mode. People get tired, cranky, and hungry (we can't eat the prop food, and we often forget to order lunch). Our photographer, Scott (top right), is constantly reminding us that we're "burning daylight," and we drive our food stylist, Allison (at the grill), absolutely nuts asking her to fluff up a piece of frisée one more time. Our art director, Annie (in pink), always finds that there's one key prop (the one she picked out to add just the right shot of color to the cover) that didn't make it from the office to our location. And everybody gets annoyed at the editor (me), because I never seem to like the props, the light, the food—or something. (That's why they try to distract me by asking folks back at the office to call me during the shoot.)

All kidding aside, every cover shoot has its challenges, but we always feel good at the end of the day when we get something beautiful. We were particularly happy with the grilled chicken kebab shot we did for this cover. It just looks iconically delicious.

The photos shown here were taken that day; the location was my house, where we often shoot covers because of the abundance of natural light. (Plus, we have the added companionship of Gus and Scout, who like to wiggle their way into photos.)

We took these behind-the-scenes shots because I thought it would be fun to write about a shoot on our new editors' blog, The Kitchen Sink, which you can find at FineCooking.com. (If you go to the site, a link to the blog is on the home page.)

I'm excited about the blog because we'll get a chance to show you a little bit of what goes into making the magazine (including reports from the test kitchen). We'll also get to share with you new restaurants, favorite markets, new recipes, and great foodie destinations. We'll post our favorite new equipment and ingredient finds, and we'll review a book or two. And we'll probably let you know what we're cooking at home from time to time. The best part is that you can log on and comment on any of these blogs, so it will help us get to know you a little better, too. Let us know what's cooking at your house; we hope it's chicken thighs, grilled bread, peach desserts, or something else yummy from this issue.

—Susie Middleton, editor

Photos: Scott Phillips and Susie Middleton

CHOCOLATE FONDANT
White Chocolate Crème Anglaise

Serves 8

Chocolat fondant:
Butter, softened
Flour
8oz dark chocolate fondette
8oz butter
5 eggs
5 egg yolks
2.8oz sugar
3.5oz sifted all-purpose flour

White chocolate crème anglaise:
1/2 cup milk
1/2 cup double cream
6 egg yolks
2.8oz sugar
2oz white chocolate, chopped or grated

Raspberries for garnish

Preheat oven to 170°C.

Chocolate fondant:

Butter the insides of 8 ramekins or dariole moulds, and sprinkle with a little flour.

Melt the dark chocolate in a bain marie, then fold in the butter.

Beat together the eggs, egg yolks and sugar until pale. Combine with the melted chocolate, then fold in the sifted flour. Divide the mixture equally between the moulds. Set aside.

White chocolate crème anglaise:

Warm the milk and cream in a saucepan. In a separate bowl, beat together the egg yolks and sugar until smooth and pale.

Gradually add the milk and cream to the eggs, stirring constantly. Pour the custard back into the saucepan and stir over a low heat until it thickens.

Place the white chocolate in a bowl, and add the custard, stirring until the chocolate melts. Strain and cool.

Place the ramekins in the oven and bake for 7-10 minutes, until the outside is set, but the inside is still liquid.

To serve: Turn the chocolate fondants out onto plates, and decorate with the white chocolate crème anglaise and raspberries.

A sharp alternative

I found the article on knife sharpeners in the April/May 2007 issue (*Fine Cooking* #85) very interesting. I wanted to let you know of another option I recently discovered and like. It's the Gatco knife-sharpening kit. (Gatco is an American company based in Getzville, New York, whose full name is Great American Tool Company.) The regular version, which I have, comes with three stones—coarse, medium, and fine—together with a clamping device that holds the knife and stones, and a bottle of honing oil. The clamping device makes it possible to sharpen angles from 11 to 29 degrees. It sounds complicated, but I have found it easy to use. There is also a version that includes a very coarse stone and a honing stone for serrated knives. I found my kit at a Canadian store that specializes in fine tools.

— *Charles B. Chapman, London, Ontario*

Of cookouts, cats, and convenience

I'm writing with three comments. First, the Grilled Asparagus & Onions with Balsamic Vinegar & Blue Cheese recipe in the pullout "Grilling for a Crowd" in *Fine Cooking* #86 (June/July 2007) was devoured with great reviews at a potluck cookout last night. I knew the minute I saw the recipe that it was going to be wonderful. I used fat asparagus and found they handled the grilling much better than the thinner ones I usually buy. They can afford to lose moisture on the grill, and their flavor intensifies.

I also loved reading the editor's letter, "Inside Out," about how her dogs are always on the wrong side of the door. It reminded me of how well our cats have trained us. We don't have an ocean breeze to keep the bugs away, but we do like to keep the sliding door open, with only the screen door closed. Our impatient kitties would scratch a hole in the lower corner of the screen in their constant desire to be in or out. We found ourselves repeatedly replacing the screen. Finally we saw the wisdom of our cats and cut an L-shaped slit in the corner of the screen, creating a flap that allowed the felines to come and go at will. It's far less unsightly than a mangled screen and does a surprisingly good job at keeping the winged bugs out.

Finally, I really wish you offered your recipes online. I tend to shop based on what looks good when I'm in the grocery store, thus I like to copy my favorite recipes into my Palm so that the ingredient list is always available for shopping. If you offered the recipes to subscribers, I would definitely subscribe to the magazine. Not only that, I would be willing to pay extra to download recipes.

—*Cynthia Kammann, Baltimore, Maryland*

Editors' reply: We do, in fact, already have part of our recipe archive available online at FineCooking.com. Since last year, we've been steadily adding to that archive, and we recently introduced a feature that lets you save your favorite recipes to a personal file. And this fall, we'll be launching a subscription-based site that will offer complete access to our recipe archives, along with several other interactive features. So please stay tuned.

A cook is born

I'm a senior at Fairfield University in Connecticut. Recently, after a morning and afternoon of watching the Food Network, I got inspired to take a trip to the grocery store and cook up something delicious for dinner. I headed for the magazine section and came across the April/May 2007 issue of *Fine Cooking* (#85). I thumbed through and saw recipes that made my mouth water. I also noticed that the ingredients were familiar, and I knew I could use the same things for a bunch of recipes.

I came home and cooked the New Potatoes with Butter, Shallots & Chervil; the Roasted Asparagus with Lemon & Olive Oil; and the Maple Pan-Roasted Baby Carrots. The recipes were easy to follow, and I have to tell you, this was one of the best meals I have had in my 22 years. I was so proud and happy after making it, and the great thing is, I have enough leftover ingredients to prepare the same dishes or try some new recipes.

The suggestions for wine were extremely helpful as well, especially since I'm unsure of what would best be paired with specific flavors. I'm so happy that I found the magazine, and I will definitely keep the recipes for future dishes. Thank you so much. It made me want to experiment with cooking more.

—*Ioanna Psaroudakis, via email* ◆

fine Cooking

EDITOR
Susie Middleton

ART DIRECTOR
Annie Giammattei

SPECIAL ISSUES EDITOR
Joanne McAllister Smart

SENIOR FOOD EDITOR/TEST KITCHEN MANAGER
Jennifer Armentrout

SENIOR EDITOR **Rebecca Freedman**

ASSOCIATE EDITORS
Laura Giannatempo, Lisa Waddle

MANAGING WEB EDITOR **Sarah Breckenridge**

SENIOR COPY/PRODUCTION EDITOR
Enid Johnson

ASSOCIATE ART DIRECTOR **Pamela Winn**

TEST KITCHEN ASSOCIATE/FOOD STYLIST
Allison R. Ehri

EDITORIAL ASSISTANT **Kim Landi**

EDITORS AT LARGE
Maryellen Driscoll, Kimberly Y. Masibay

TEST KITCHEN INTERN **Will Moyer**

CONTRIBUTING EDITORS
**Pam Anderson, Abigail Johnson Dodge,
Tim Gaiser, Sarah Jay, Tony Rosenfeld,
Molly Stevens**

PUBLISHER **Maria Taylor**

ASSISTANT PUBLISHER
Karen Lutjen

CIRCULATION DIRECTOR
Dennis O'Brien

SENIOR SINGLE COPY SALES MANAGER
Jay Annis

CORPORATE ACCOUNTS MANAGER
Judy Caruso

NATIONAL ACCOUNTS MANAGER
Linda Delaney

ADVERTISING SALES ASSOCIATE
Stacy Purcell

Fine Cooking: (ISSN: 1072-5121) is published seven times a year by The Taunton Press, Inc., Newtown, CT 06470-5506. Telephone 203-426-8171. Periodicals postage paid at Newtown, CT 06470 and at additional mailing offices. GST paid registration #123210981.

Subscription Rates: U.S. and Canada, $29.95 for one year, $49.95 for two years, $69.95 for three years (GST included, payable in U.S. funds). Outside the U.S./Canada: $36 for one year, $62 for two years, $88 for three years (payable in U.S. funds). Single copy, $6.95. Single copy outside the U.S., $7.95.

Postmaster: Send address changes to *Fine Cooking,* The Taunton Press, Inc., 63 South Main St., P.O. Box 5506, Newtown, CT 06470-5506.

Canada Post: Return undeliverable Canadian addresses to *Fine Cooking, c/o* Worldwide Mailers, Inc., 2835 Kew Drive, Windsor, ON N8T 3B7, or email to mnfa@taunton.com.

Printed in the USA.

contributors

Contributing editor Pam Anderson ("Chicken Thighs," p. 30) is the author of *Perfect Recipes for Having People Over*. Her newest book, *The Perfect Recipe for Losing Weight and Eating Great—Change Your Life for Good*, will be published next spring. She teaches cooking classes nationally and is the food columnist for *USA Weekend* magazine.

While Susie Middleton ("Corn Sautés," p. 34) has never met a vegetable she didn't like, she does have a few favorites, and in-season corn is one of them. As editor of *Fine Cooking*, Susie oversees the magazine, its Web site, and special issues. Still, she's not above tackling less cerebral tasks when necessary, as you can see in one of the photos on p. 10.

Evan Kleiman ("No-Cook Tomato Sauce," p. 38) fell in love with Italy's cuisine during her many trips to that country when she was a student of Italian literature and film. Now owner of Angeli Caffè in Los Angeles, she is also the author of six cookbooks, including *Cucina Fresca* and *Pasta Fresca,* and the host of Good Food, a weekly radio show on KCRW, Santa Monica's NPR station.

The author of *Taming the Flame,* Elizabeth Karmel ("Grilled Bread," p. 40) teaches across the country and runs her company, Girls at the Grill. She is also the executive chef at Hill Country, a new Texas barbecue restaurant in New York City, and the head counselor for Camp BBQ, a barbecue camp for adults.

Jim Peyton ("Steak, Mexican Style," p. 44) has studied Mexican cuisine for more than 30 years and has written three books on the

subject, including *Jim Peyton's New Cooking from Old Mexico*. He also runs the Web site LoMexicano.com, which features recipes, cooking information, and Mexican cooking ingredients.

When it comes to eggplant, Tasha DeSerio ("Grilled Eggplant," p. 48) believes that simple preparations help this hearty vegetable shine. "I wanted to replace the associations most people have of eggplant being heavy or greasy," she says. Now a caterer and cooking teacher, Tasha cooked for five years at Chez Panisse in Berkeley, California.

Contributing editor Tony Rosenfeld ("Scallions," p. 52) co-owns a growing empire of healthful fast-food restaurants in the Boston area called b.good and is about to open Dinner Trends, a menu-assembly kitchen where customers put together meals to take home from pre-prepped ingredients. Tony's first cookbook, *150 Things to Make with Roast Chicken*, was published last spring.

Nancie McDermott ("Thai Seafood Salad," p. 56) became interested in Asian cuisine as a Peace Corps volunteer in Thailand. She is the author of *Real Thai, Real Vegetarian Thai*, and *Quick & Easy Thai*. Her most recent books, *300 Best Stir-Fry Recipes* and *Southern Cakes,* were published this year.

Carole Bloom ("Peaches & Cream," p. 58) has been teaching the pastry arts nationwide for more than 25 years and has written eight books and numerous articles about baking. Her latest book is *The Essential Baker: The Comprehensive Guide to Baking with Chocolate, Fruit, Nuts, Spices, and Other Ingredients.* ◆

Elizabeth Karmel

Tashia DeSerio

Nancie McDermott

The Taunton Press
Inspiration for hands-on living®

INDEPENDENT PUBLISHERS SINCE 1975

TAUNTON, INC.
Founders, **Paul and Jan Roman**

THE TAUNTON PRESS

President **Suzanne Roman**

Executive Vice President & Chief Financial Officer **Timothy Rahr**

Executive Vice President & Publisher, Magazine Group **Jon Miller**

Chief of Operations **Thomas Luxeder**

Group Publisher, Home **Paul Spring**

DIRECTORS

Creative & Editorial Director **Susan Edelman**

Human Resources Director **Carol Marotti**

Technology Services Director **Jay Hartley**

Controller **Wayne Reynolds**

Advertising Director **David Gray**

Fulfillment Director **Patricia Williamson**

Financial Analysis Director **Kathy Worth**

Circulation Director **Dennis O'Brien**

THE TAUNTON PRESS

Books: *Marketing:* Melissa A. Possick, Audrey Locorotondo. *Publicity:* Nicole Salvatore, Janel Noblin. *Editorial:* Helen Albert, Kathryn Benoit, Peter Chapman, Steve Culpepper, Pamela Hoenig, Courtney Jordan, Carolyn Mandarano, Nicole Palmer, Jennifer Russell, Erica Sanders-Foege, Kathleen Williams. *Art:* Alison Wilkes, Nancy Boudreau, Amy Griffin, Sandra Mahlstedt, Wendi Mijal, Lynne Phillips, Carol Singer. *Manufacturing:* Thomas Greco, Laura Burrone.

Business Office: Holly Smith, Gayle Hammond, Patricia Marini. *Legal:* Carolyn Kovaleski. *Magazine Print Production:* Philip Van Kirk, Nicole Anastas, Jennifer Kaczmarcyk.

Circulation: David Pond, Andrew Corson, Catherine Hansen.

Distribution: Paul Seipold, Walter Aponte, Frank Busino, David DeToto, Leanne Furlong, Deborah Greene, Frank Melbourne, Reinaldo Moreno, Raymond Passaro, Michael Savage, Alice Saxton.

Finance/Accounting: *Finance:* Brett Manning. *Accounting:* Patrick Lamontagne, Lydia Krikorian, Michelle Mendonca, Judith O'Toole, Elaine Yamin, Carol Diehm, Dorothy Blasko, Susan Burke, Lorraine Parsons, Larry Rice, James Tweedle, Priscilla Jennings.

Fulfillment: Diane Goulart. *Fulfillment Systems:* Jodi Klein, Kim Eads, Nancy Knorr, Thomas Kuzebski. *Customer Service:* Kathleen Baker, Bonnie Beardsley, Deborah Ciccio, Katherine Clarke, Alfred Dreher, Paula Ferreri, Eileen McNulty, Patricia Parks, Deana Parker, Patricia Pineau, Betty Stepney. *Data Entry:* Melissa Youngberg, Anne Champlin, Mary Ann Colbert, Caryne-Lynne Davis, Maureen Pekar, Debra Sennefelder, Andrea Shorrock, Marylou Thompson, Barbara Williams.

Human Resources: Linda Ballerini, Christine Lincoln, Dawn Ussery.

Photos: from top, Scott Phillips, Michael DeSerio, Sylvia Ramer

IMAGINE YOUR LIFE IN A VIKING KITCHEN.

VIKING

VIKING

Information Technology Services: *Applications Development:* Heidi Waldkirch, Jun Lu, Frank Miller, Robert Nielsen, Linda Reddington, John Vaccino, Daniel Woodhouse. *Desktop and Network Support:* Kenneth Jones, Petre Cotofana, Paul DelPadre, Gabriel Dunn, Michael Lewis, Jay Ligouri.

Operations: Joseph Morits, Roberta Calabrese, Kevin DeGroate, Leah Flynn, John Gedney, Marc Imbimbo, Jennifer Licursi, Susan Nerich, Jeannette Pascal, Amy Reilly. *T Room:* Michael Louchen, Geraldine Benno, Anna Pendergast, Anne Scheurer, Norma-Jean Taylor. *Maintenance:* Lincoln Peters.

Promotion: Jane Weber, *Promotion Creative:* Jennifer Wheeler Conlon, Kristen Coons, Michele Mayernik, Sandra Motyka, Nicole Pallatto, William Sims. *Promotion Operations:* Diane Flanagan, John Cavallaro, Sandra Hannan, Kate Krentsa.

Taunton Creative: Michael Amaditz, Sarah Opdahl. *Video:* Gary Junken, Michael Dobsevage.

Publishing Services: Deborah Cooper. *Publishing Technologies:* Mark Merritt, Tracy Goodpaster. *Photography:* Scott Phillips. *Prepress:* Richard Booth, William Bivona, David Blasko, Richard Correale, William Godfrey, Brian Leavitt, Chansam Thammavongsa. *Advertising Production:* Laura Bergeron, Lisa DeFeo, Steven Molnar, Patricia Petro, Kathryn Simonds, Martha Stammer.

TAUNTON DIRECT

Donna Capalbo, Keri DeGross, Michele Ladyko, Kathleen McGreevy, Michael Valanzola.

TAUNTON INTERACTIVE

Jodie Delohery, Robert Harlow, David Hall, Bill Tine, Christopher Casey, Mark Coleman, Trish Dardine, Ruth Dobsevage, Lisa Durand, Erika Foreman, Geoff Krajeski, Steve Lombardi, Victoria North, Michael Stoltz, Dawn Viglione.

TAUNTON TRADE

Kevin Hamric, Director; John Bacigalupi, Brett DeMello, Allison Hollett, Elizabeth Quintiliano, Rebecca Shafton. *Single Copy Sales:* Jay Annis, Mark Stiekman, Valerie Droukas.

TAUNTON MAGAZINES

Fine Woodworking • Fine Homebuilding Threads • Fine Gardening • Fine Cooking

Our magazines are for people who are passionate about their pursuits. Written by practicing experts in the field, Taunton Press magazines provide authentic, reliable information supported by instructive and inspiring visuals.

TAUNTON BOOKS

Our books are filled with in-depth information and creative ideas from the finest authors in their fields. Whether you're practicing a craft or engaged in the creation of your home, Taunton books will inspire you to discover new levels of accomplishment.

WWW.TAUNTON.COM

Our website is a place where you can discover more about the interests you enjoy, converse with fellow enthusiasts, shop at our convenient on-line store or contact customer service.

EMPLOYMENT INFORMATION

To inquire about career opportunities, please visit our website at careers.taunton.com. You may also write to The Taunton Press, Human Resources, 63 S. Main St., Box 5506, Newtown, CT 06470.

CUSTOMER SERVICE

We are here to answer any questions you might have and to help you order our magazines, books and videos. Just call us toll-free at 800-477-8727.

The Taunton Press, Inc., Taunton Direct, Inc., Taunton Trade, Inc., and Taunton Interactive, Inc., are all subsidiaries of Taunton, Inc.

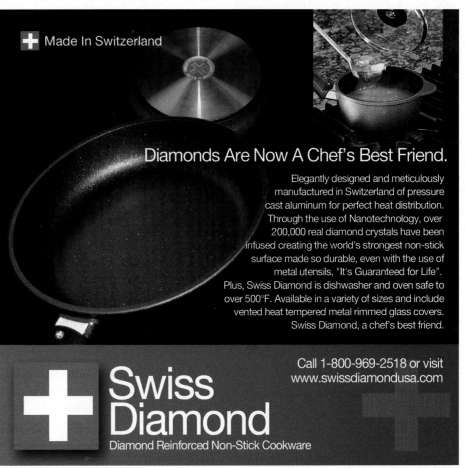

When I barbecue chicken, what's the best way to keep the sauce from burning?

—*Selmin Cicek, Stamford, Connecticut*

Elizabeth Karmel responds: That's the No. 1 question I hear about grilling chicken. Most barbecue sauces contain a lot of sugar, and sugar burns quickly. But there are two steps you can take to keep your sauce from burning. First, grill the chicken over indirect heat (meaning no heat directly underneath the chicken). Indirect heat is the best way to get chicken that is both golden brown and caramelized on the outside and completely cooked inside. Generally, the only chicken you grill over direct heat is boneless chicken breasts, due to their quick cooking time.

The second step is to brush your chicken with barbecue sauce only during the final 10 minutes of the cooking time. It's worth noting that this practice of waiting to the end to brush on the sauce applies not just to chicken but to any meat you are grilling.

Elizabeth Karmel is the author of Taming the Flame: Secrets for Hot-and-Quick Grilling and Low-and-Slow BBQ.

Have a question of general interest about cooking? Send it to Q&A, Fine Cooking, PO Box 5506, Newtown, CT 06470-5506, or by email to fcqa@taunton .com, and we'll find a cooking professional with the answer.

How long is it safe to let cooked meat stay in the refrigerator? Are there any reliable measures besides smell and taste?

—*Stephanie Rosenfeld, via email*

Michael Doyle responds: Packages of raw meat and poultry are stamped with a "use by" date, which refers to the product's peak of quality, and you should either cook or freeze it by that date. After cooking, ground meat or poultry should be eaten or thrown away within two days; whole cuts of meat or poultry can be kept three to five days once cooked. If you freeze raw meat to extend its shelf life, remember that it should be cooked as soon as it thaws.

Time is only one factor in the safety of raw meat, though—the others are temperature and handling. If meat is kept at unsafe temperatures or mishandled, foodborne bacteria can grow on it before the "use by" date on the package. The proper temperature for storing raw and cooked meat is 40°F or below, which will prevent bacteria from growing, though not kill any that already exists. Potential mishandling includes cooked meat that has been left out at room temperature for more than two hours, products that have been defrosted at room temperature for more than two hours, and cross contamination from other raw meats.

But how can you tell if meat has gone bad? Off odors and flavors are obvious indicators. Color, however, isn't because some meat packers use packaging systems that preserve color. So the most reliable indicator of freshness is still the "sell by" or "use by" date.

Dr. Michael Doyle is director for food safety at the University of Georgia.

Can you suggest a vegetarian alternative to gelatin?

—*Samantha Pembroke, St. Louis, Missouri*

Eric Tucker responds: Gelatin is a protein made from animal bones, skins, and cartilage. Of the vegetarian alternatives available, the one I like best is agar-agar, which is derived from red sea algae. I use it in all kinds of custards, icings, and cheesecakes, as well as in a decadent vegetarian pâté. Flavorless and colorless, agar-agar comes in powder, flake, or stick form and can be found at health-food stores or Asian markets. The most widely available and consistent brand I've found is Eden Foods.

Agar-agar and gelatin behave differently in a couple of ways. Agar-agar, which usually sets up stiffer than gelatin, will set up and remain solid at room temperature. Gelatin, on the other hand, needs refrigeration to set up and will eventually melt at room temperature.

The two are similar in that you have to melt agar in a hot liquid (above 140°F), as you do with gelatin. And agar's gelling properties, like gelatin's, are sensitive to acids (vinegar and citrus), so depending on the concentration of acids you may need more dried agar-agar.

Eric Tucker is the executive chef at the vegetarian Millennium restaurant in San Francisco and co-author of the cookbook The Artful Vegan. ◆

What's New at FineCooking.com

This summer, we're rolling out new features, a new editors' blog, and—as always—special seasonal collections "on the front burner."

on the front burner

Vacation cooking

Simple, fresh recipes that don't require a lot of shopping

Tips on sniffing out local specialties

Bonus download
The traveling cook's survival guide

Bread Salad with Corn, Cherry Tomatoes & Basil

Exploring Spanish Food

Learn the iconic dishes of Spain, like paella and tortilla, or just incorporate Iberian flavors into your everyday cooking.

menus

A Casual Dinner from Northeast Spain

A Festive Tapas Party

Feature Articles
Master Class: Paella

Stocking Your Spanish Pantry

Recipes
Gazpacho

Tortilla Española

Cod Stew with Chorizo, Leeks & Potatoes

Cod Stew with Chorizo, Leeks & Potatoes

free email newsletter

Subscribe at FineCooking.com to get great recipes, tips, techniques, and videos delivered directly to your inbox twice a month.

new features

★ my favorites

Save your favorite *Fine Cooking* recipes, menus, and articles to a personal favorites file.

quick and delicious tonight

Find a quick, simple recipe for each weeknight, updated daily.

Penne with Artichokes & Feta

readers' tips

Submit your own tip or vote for the best tips for each issue of the magazine.

new blogs

Visit **the kitchen sink** to get to know the *Fine Cooking* editors—where they're eating out and what they're cooking at home—plus a peek behind the scenes at the magazine.

Follow or join the **cooks talk project**, where readers focus on a cookbook for the whole year and blog about their experiences.

Cool off with refreshing
Cucumbers

BY RUTH LIVELY

Cool, crisp, and juicy, cucumbers are always a welcome addition to my summer kitchen. When the temperature soars above 80°F, I find few things as refreshing as a snack of raw cukes with a tangy, savory dip. They're also ideal for chilled soups (see my Green Gazpacho at far right), and they add a bright, fresh note to any number of salads.

Cucumbers' mild, sweet flavor makes them a good match for almost anything. I like to pair them with onions, tomatoes, peppers, and any summery herb, as well as with fish and shellfish, chicken, pork, and lamb. Creamy dairy products like yogurt, cream cheese, sour cream, feta, and goat cheese give them richness and a welcome tang, while aromatics like capers, olives, garlic, lemon, and lime add a little punch.

Firmness is your best clue to freshness when shopping for cucumbers. Avoid limp or shriveled ones. I also look for fruits that seem slender for their size. This means they're younger, so chances are they'll have either undeveloped or fewer seeds. Store cucumbers in the crisper drawer, loose or in an open plastic bag, and use them within three or four days of buying. Kept longer, they'll get slimy on the outside and mushy inside.

Peeling and seeding are not always necessary. When prepping cucumbers, some cooks remove the seeds as a matter of course. But if they're tiny and cling tight to the flesh, you can leave them. It's only when they're fully developed that they become intrusive and unpleasant to eat and should be removed. To do this, cut the cucumber in half lengthwise and scoop out the seeds with a spoon or a melon baller. Whether to peel cucumbers or not depends on how you intend to cut them. Most cucumbers have thick, tough skins, so if you're cutting them in big chunks, it's best to peel them. If you're slicing them thinly, the skins are more palatable—and prettier—so you can leave them on. Cucumbers with naturally thin, tender skins, like the English variety (see sidebar at right), don't need peeling.

A world of cucumbers

There are dozens of cucumber varieties, all of which can be used pretty much interchangeably. Here are some of the most common types available:

1. Picklers

Picklers are short and blocky, with blunt ends and bumpy skins. Their firm texture makes them perfect for pickling, but you can use them raw as well.

2. Slicers

Slicers are your basic, all-purpose cucumbers. They're about 8 inches long with round ends and smooth to slightly knobby dark-green skin. The ones you buy at the supermarket are often waxed to protect them during shipping and to extend their shelf life. Scrub them well or peel before using.

3. English

Also known as greenhouse, European, or seedless cucumbers, English cucumbers are 10 to 12 inches long and slender and are usually sold in plastic sleeves. With their thin skins, undeveloped seeds, and uniform shape, they are ideal for slicing into salads and garnishing appetizers.

Quick ideas for raw cukes

I don't usually cook cucumbers. To me, it's the crunchy texture and fresh flavor of raw cucumbers that's most appealing. Here are some of my favorite ways to use them:

Whip up a zippy garnish for grilled meats. Stir thinly sliced cucumbers and chopped shallots with plain Greek yogurt and lots of chopped herbs.

Make a bread salad. Combine chopped cucumbers, tomatoes, sweet pepper, and onion with cubes of day-old artisan bread or pieces of lightly toasted pita. Add aromatics like olives, capers, or chopped preserved lemon and douse with a zesty vinaigrette.

Update tea-time cucumber sandwiches. Spread whole-grain bread squares or pita triangles with cream cheese mixed with feta, finely chopped herbs, finely minced shallot or grated garlic, and lemon zest. Top with thin cucumber slices and watercress.

Toss together a cool Asian noodle salad. Stir cooked rice or soba noodles with diced cucumbers and sweet pepper, chopped cilantro and basil, and a creamy peanut dressing with minced jalapeño. Garnish with chopped toasted peanuts.

Make a simple salad. Sliced cucumbers take to an impressive variety of dressings:

Drizzle with olive oil and a little lemon juice and sprinkle with salt and chopped fresh oregano.

Toss in a creamy buttermilk dressing with lots of chopped fresh dill.

Go Asian with a mix of rice vinegar, soy sauce, sesame oil, grated fresh ginger, and a squirt of lime juice.

Grow your own: It's easy

Cucumbers are among the easiest crops to grow. Plant the seeds directly in the ground in spring, after the soil has warmed. They sprout within days and grow quickly into vines with tendrils that wrap around whatever they touch. Although you can grow cucumbers on the ground, you'll harvest prettier, cleaner, and straighter fruits if you let them climb up some sort of trellis. Once cucumbers start bearing (usually about six weeks after planting), pick them regularly to keep production going.

Green Gazpacho

Yields a scant 6 cups; serves six.

To dress up this cold soup, serve it with lumps of cooked lobster, crab, or shrimp.

1½ lb. cucumbers (4 to 5 picklers or 2½ large slicers), peeled, seeded, and cut into 1-inch pieces (to yield 3 cups)
1 Tbs. kosher salt; more to taste
1 large yellow pepper
1 medium ripe avocado
1 medium sweet onion, cut into 1-inch pieces (2 cups)
¼ tsp. freshly ground black pepper; more to taste
3 oz. fresh crustless Italian country-style bread, cut into 1-inch cubes (2 cups)
1 tsp. chopped garlic
¼ cup coarsely chopped fresh flat-leaf parsley
3 Tbs. coarsely chopped fresh cilantro
1 Tbs. coarsely chopped fresh basil or mint
⅔ cup extra-virgin olive oil; more for garnish
2 Tbs. red-wine vinegar

Put the cucumbers in a colander over a bowl or in the sink and toss with 1½ tsp. of the salt. Let them sit for 30 minutes to draw out the juices and remove any trace of bitterness. Meanwhile, core and seed the pepper and cut three-quarters of it into 1-inch pieces. Wrap the remaining quarter and refrigerate; you'll need it later. Cut the avocado in half, peel one half, and cut it into 1-inch chunks. Lightly coat the cut surface of the remaining half with oil, wrap it in plastic, and refrigerate for later.

Rinse and drain the cucumber. Put the cucumber, pepper, avocado, onion, the remaining 1½ tsp. salt, and the pepper in a food processor and purée. Transfer the purée to a large bowl and reassemble the processor. Process the bread, garlic, and herbs until the bread is reduced to crumbs and the herbs are fully chopped. Add the oil and vinegar to the mixture and process briefly to thoroughly combine. Add the bread mixture and 1 cup water to the cucumber purée and stir until well blended. Cover and refrigerate at least 2 hours or overnight. Let come to a cool room temperature before serving.

When ready to serve, peel the reserved avocado half and cut it into ½-inch dice. Cut the reserved pepper into ¼-inch dice. Stir the soup and assess its consistency. If it seems too thick, add water until it's thinned to your liking. Season to taste with salt and pepper. Divide the soup among shallow bowls and garnish with the avocado and pepper. Drizzle about 1 tsp. of olive oil over each bowl and serve.

Ruth Lively cooks, writes, and gardens in New Haven, Connecticut. ◆

Beer 101

In the dog days of summer, cold beer can be the perfect match for food—here's an overview of your options

BY TIM GAISER

While just a few years ago it would have been unthinkable to see beer pairings on the menu of a nice restaurant, these days more than a few chefs and sommeliers believe that beer works just as well as wine with food—and sometimes better. I'm not talking about the mass-produced lagers favored by armchair quarterbacks but about high-quality and intriguing craft beers. Some are produced only in small quantities, while others are widely available, but many are exceptionally food-friendly—particularly in summer when we want something cool and refreshing to go with our meals. But as with wine, there are so many different styles of beer that choosing the right one can be daunting. This article will help you sort through your options and find the right beer for what's on your menu.

What's the ideal temperature for serving beer?

As with wine, be careful not to serve beer too cold. An overly chilled beer will have little aroma and flavor. Instead, serve lighter lagers between 48° and 52°F, lighter ales at 54° to 58°F, and richer ales and lagers at 57° to 65°F.

How do you store beer?

Although few beers get better with aging, it's still important to store them properly, keeping them away from excessive heat, temperature fluctuations, and light. Good storage conditions would provide a constant temperature of between 55° and 60°F without light or vibration (itself a source of heat).

Types of beer

Most beers fall into one of two categories—ales and lagers—based on the kind of yeast used for fermentation.

Ales

Ales are made with top-fermenting yeasts, strains of yeast that rise to the surface during fermentation, creating a thick yeast head. Ales have a distinctive fruitiness, which is offset by the addition of bitter hops, and are produced in a wide range of colors and styles. Here are some of the most common:

Pale Ales and India Pale Ales (or IPA)

Made with lightly roasted malt, these beers are golden to copper in color and relatively mild, with a distinctive bitter finish. India pale ales have a higher alcohol content and more hops, giving them a pronounced bitterness.

What to pair them with: The crisp, citrusy notes of pale ales and IPAs pair well with a range of foods, from pizza, buffalo wings, and hamburgers to spicy Thai cuisine and Indian curries.

Brown Ales

Deep amber to brown in color, brown ales display flavors of chocolate and caramel due to the deeply roasted malts from which they're made.

What to pair them with: Try them with hearty stews and braises as well as with aged cheeses.

Porters

Made with well-roasted malt, porter ales are deeply colored, full bodied, and richly flavored beers with bold, chocolatey notes.

What to pair them with: Porters' deep flavor and full body are best suited to the rich flavors of stews and other hearty fare rather than to the light, bright flavors of summer.

Stouts

Exceptionally rich and creamy, these extra-dark, almost black ales are made with long-roasted malt, which gives them a caramel-like flavor.

What to pair them with: Stouts pair well with braised meats and rich, meat-based soups or stews.

Lagers

The term lager denotes any beer made with bottom-fermenting yeasts, strains of yeast that ferment at cooler temperatures and settle to the bottom during fermentation. Lagers tend to be yellow-gold or amber in color, although there are deeper-colored versions, too. The most widespread types of lagers include:

Pilsners

Pilsners are excellent all-purpose beers with a light body, a clean, crisp flavor, and prominent hoppiness, or bitterness.

What to pair them with: Pilsners are perfect served as an aperitif or paired with shellfish, grilled fish, or grilled or roasted chicken. They're also a great match for spicy Asian, Indian, and Middle-Eastern food.

American-style lagers and amber lagers

Pale, crisp American lagers are the most well-known and marketed beers in the United States. These clean, zesty brews have a light body and a mild flavor with just a touch of hoppy bitterness. Amber lagers are reddish brown in color with a medium body and a caramelly malt flavor.

What to pair them with: Both are versatile beers that pair with a range of foods, from hearty barbecue to spicy Mexican.

Bocks

Traditionally brewed in fall or early spring to coincide with festivities like Christmas and Easter, bock beers (now brewed year-round) are strong, wonderfully rich dark amber lagers.

What to pair them with: Bocks are natural partners for hearty grill fare, such as sausages and marinated meats.

Find a guide to specialty beers, including wheat beers & lambics, at finecooking.com

A six-pack of favorites

Six great beer picks for the summer and beyond.
Retail prices, per six-pack (except where noted), are approximate.

Anchor Liberty Ale (pale ale), USA, $8.99

Samuel Smith's Nut Brown Ale, U.K., $3.99 per 1-pint bottle

Guinness Extra Stout, Ireland, $3.49 per 1-pint bottle

Pilsner Urquell, Czech Republic, $7.99

Samuel Adams Boston Lager (amber lager), USA, $6.99

Dos Equis Amber (amber lager), Mexico, $7.99

Is beer better straight from the bottle or poured into a glass?

Although there's nothing wrong with having a cold one right from the bottle, beer is always better when served in a glass. Pouring beer into a glass releases all the aromatics, just as with wine. If you're interested, you can experiment with a variety of beer-glass shapes, which can affect the tasting experience.

What's the correct pouring technique?

Hold the glass at a 45-degree angle and pour the beer slowly and evenly, gradually tilting the glass upright. You should end up with about an inch of foam as you finish pouring.

Contributing editor Tim Gaiser is a master sommelier and wine educator. ◆

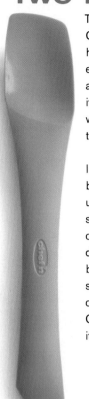
what's new

Two-in-one tool

This silicone spoon/spatula from Chef'n is my new go-to tool. It has a steel core, so it's sturdy enough for mixing thick batters and soups, and the silicone means it's heat-resistant, so there are no worries when scraping rice from the bottom of a nonstick pan.

It's part of Chef'n's Switchit line of utensils, which means both ends are angled for optimum use. The narrow end works for scraping tomato paste out of the can, while the shallow spoon delivers a quick taste. And because it's silicone, it doesn't stain, is dishwasher safe, and comes in five vibrant colors. Cost is $11, and you can buy it at ChefTools.com.

Cherry pitter contains the mess

Pitting cherries or olives can be tedious but no longer has to be as messy: OXO's new pitter has a removable splatter shield to protect your counter and clothing. It also has the soft, nonslip handles featured on all OXO Good Grips utensils. The pitter accommodates extra-large Bing cherries but also has a recessed cup to hold smaller varieties in place. The simple design works like a hole puncher, not a garlic press, so it doesn't squash the fruit. The pitter costs $12 at Oxo.com.

Lifting oven	22
Spoon/spatula	22
Cherry pitter	22
Food vacuum-sealers	23
Crinkle cutter	24
Stylish canning jars	24
Plastic freezer jars	24
Ice maker	25
Review: Ice cream scoops	26

BY LISA WADDLE

An oven that does the heavy lifting

Anyone who has struggled to lift a heavy roast out of the oven or gotten burned leaning over an oven door to baste a turkey will appreciate the Lift Oven from Gaggenau. The 24-inch oven mounts on a wall, and the floor of the oven is actually the door—it lowers toward the counter and returns up with the touch of a button.

You can put breads or pizzas directly on the glass ceramic surface without a baking sheet or use a rack hooked to the rear to hold pans. Because heat rises, there's little energy loss when the oven floor is opened. The oven has 11 cooking modes, including roasting, broiling, and convection pastry.

Although smaller than most standard 27- to 30-inch ovens, the Lift Oven offers real benefits for anyone with back or arm troubles. You can order it through kitchen suppliers for about $3,300. Go to Gaggenau-usa.com for more information.

Keeping foods fresh longer

Food vacuum-sealers are one of the bigger-ticket kitchen appliances that raise the question, Are they worth it? I gave two of the more popular versions a test run and was impressed at how easy they make it to preserve fresh vegetables, fruit, and meat. They also reduce waste from spoiled food and make buying in bulk worthwhile.

How they work: Oxygen is the reason most foods spoil or go stale, and these machines work by simply removing the excess air from heavy-duty bags or plastic containers. Both of the models I tested excelled at extending the life of refrigerated and frozen fresh fruits and vegetables. They also prevented freezer burn on raw meat and

poultry and kept cereals and cookies from going stale. I found them particularly useful at keeping refrigerator staples like hummus, lemon curd, and broth from spoiling before I could use them. Both systems also offer plastic lids that fit Mason jars, which you can then vacuum-seal. The major difference between the two is the way they operate.

FoodSaver

OPERATION: The FoodSaver is a long, heavy appliance with a flip-up lid. You raise the lid, insert the opening of a bag into the slot, and then clamp down the lid. Then you push a button for the FoodSaver to vacuum out excess air and automatically seal the bag shut by heating a strip along the opening. To vacuum-seal FoodSaver canisters, you insert a plastic tube onto the front of the appliance, hook the other end into the canister, and press a button to vacuum out the air. A light tells you when vacuuming is complete.

VacuWare

OPERATION: Both bags and canisters are sealed by the use of a wand that attaches to the appliance. You fit the wand onto the green port on the VacuWare containers or bags, push a button, and the vacuum starts. A light goes on when all the air has been removed, and you push the button again to turn off the vacuum.

Pros:

It can be used to seal cereal bags, potato chip bags, and plastic bags.

Available rolls of bag material let you custom-size a bag to fit oversize foods, such as big cuts of meat.

Bags can be reused, although each time you open one you must cut off the top, leaving you with a smaller and smaller bag.

Cons:

Sealing the canisters requires the extra step of attaching a plastic tube to the appliance.

The FoodSaver canisters are not freezer-safe so can be used only for leftovers in the fridge or for pantry staples.

Several designs are available, but they all eat up quite a bit of counter space.

What's included: FoodSaver appliance, 2 canisters, 10 bags, two 10-foot rolls of bag material. Jar lid is an extra $9.

Price: $140 plus $19 shipping and handling from FoodSaver.com.

Pros:

Sealing freezer-safe canisters is simple and fast.

The appliance's small footprint takes up little counter space.

It comes with a small manual travel pump, which can be used at the office, in the car, or anywhere you don't have access to electricity.

Cons:

The appliance can be used only with VacuWare bags and canisters.

Sealing the bags is a two-step process that requires some practice.

Bags can't be reused.

What's included: FreshStation appliance, travel-size pump, 3 containers, 2 jar lids, 12 pouches.

Price: $160, plus $20 shipping and handling from VacuWare.com.

Bottom line

Both models performed fast and sealed well; both are also pretty loud. You'll use these more if they're in plain view, so pick a design that works with your counter space. The FoodSaver operates particularly well with bags, so choose this one if freezer storage is your goal. For keeping canisters and jars of vegetables and leftovers in the refrigerator or freezer, the VacuWare is a good choice.

Preserving the harvest

Next-generation canning jars

These marquise-shaped glass jars are a stylish update to the traditional Mason jar used for canning or pickling. Beyond looks, the new shape functions well, too: They fit together better than the traditional round jars, saving space in your canning pot and on your shelves. Made by Leifheit, the wide-mouthed jars are sold six to a package in three sizes: ½ liter ($19), ¾ liter ($22), and 1 liter ($25). Safe for freezer, dishwasher, and microwave, the jars are available from SurLaTable.com.

A crinkle cut for pickles

Improving the appearance of home-made pickles is easy with the right tool. This simple Crinkle Cutter from Norpro gives cucumbers and other fruits and vegetables a scalloped edge with no more effort than cutting them with a knife. At only $3, it's a worthy investment that you'll keep finding uses for: crudités, French fries, garnishes. You can buy it at TheKitchenStore.com.

Plastic freezing jars

Here's a new option for freezer jam fans: plastic containers from Ball. The reusable jars are made of heavy-duty plastic and are stain resistant, making them a good choice for tomato sauces, salsas, and soups. The translucent jars come with screw-on lids that lock onto the bottoms of other jars, making them easy to stack. Five 8-ounce jars come in a package for $3 (which includes a packet of freezer jam pectin). While dishwasher safe, they are not heatproof, so you can't use them for regular canning. You can buy them at CanningPantry.com.

Ice on demand

Nothing stops a party short—especially in summer—like running out of ice. To avoid having to run out to the store, a portable ice maker, though pricey, may be just the solution. This model from Haier doesn't require any plumbing or hard-wiring, so you can plug it in nearly anywhere, even outside on the patio. It's pretty bulky—it has a footprint of 16 by 14 inches and weighs almost 50 pounds—but it makes producing and storing ice cubes in three sizes practically effortless. You fill the water tank with up to 1 gallon of water and push a button to start making cubes immediately, or program a delayed start time of up to 12 hours. In 7 to 9 minutes you have your first batch of ice. The machine stores up to 2½ pounds of ice at a time, so you and your guests can keep your cool. It costs $192, and you can buy it at Shop.com.

review
Ice Cream Scoops

BY MARYELLEN DRISCOLL

Ice cream scoops are simple tools with a simple purpose, but for some reason, they don't do a very good job. Most scoops can't do better than to scrape shavings out of a pint of firmly frozen premium ice cream. Let it sit and soften and you might get a decently shaped ball of ice cream, but then it tends to stick to the scoop. Manufacturers are aware of these little nuisances, and the market is now flooded with dozens of scoops designed to address them.

**We tested scoops that
fell into four general styles**

Trigger-release scoops feature a blade set flush against a half-sphere bowl; when you squeeze the trigger, the blade scrapes under the scooped ice cream to free it. None of the six scoops we tested in this category readily served up attractive balls of ice cream. Even more problematic, ice cream tended to freeze under the blade, limiting its movement. Softened ice cream tended to stick, no matter what. Overall, these scoops didn't impress us.

Newer to the market but similar in concept are **scoops with catapult-like levers** meant to push the ice cream straight out of the bowl. We tested four of these, plus two others made of flexible silicone that are designed to eject the ice cream when you press on the bowl itself. Like the trigger-release scoops, none of these scooped well, and often they didn't release well either, especially when the ice cream was on the soft side.

In the third category are **scoops with points**. These look as if part of the bowl has been cut away, creating two pointed corners. The points are intended to dig in and scoop ice cream with greater ease. For the most part, the four models we tried did scoop successfully, but the Cuisipro (far right) dug in much more easily than the others. The Cuisipro also made nice, dense balls of ice cream, and the ice cream pretty much fell out of the scoop (the nonstick surface no doubt helped).

Last, we tested **scoops that, in essence, thaw the ice cream** as you scoop. Three of the models had defrosting fluid sealed inside the bowl and handle, and one required pouring warm water into the handle. We were surprised by how well these worked, sliding slowly but smoothly into the ice cream. They warmed the ice cream just enough to ease scooping but not enough to compromise the quality of the ice cream. Of all the models, Zeroll's carved out the best scoop, making it our first choice.

The Winners

All three of these scoops are so effective that you don't even need to soften your ice cream before you dig in.

Zeroll
ice cream scoops

**$16.90 for aluminum scoop
$21.90 for nonstick scoop
at CooksWares.com**

A popular choice with professionals, these scoops transfer heat from your hand to defrosting fluid sealed inside the handle and bowl. The ice cream gently yields to the scoop, much as it does after running a scoop under hot water. The effect, however, is more consistent, and there's no hassle of repeated dipping in water. The result is beautifully rounded balls of ice cream that readily slip out of the scoop. The nonstick model has a sleeker feel, but the less-expensive aluminum model performs just as well. These scoops must be washed by hand and cannot be put in water over 140°F.

Festive foods for every occasion!

Entertain in style with 75 proven recipes for delicious starters and hors d'oeuvres, plus the tips and techniques that ensure great results.

Family and friends will rave about savory stuffed mushrooms, homemade country pâté, crispy spring rolls, pancetta-wrapped shrimp, crab-filled quesadillas, and tempting one-bite desserts!

These extras make party planning easy:

- menus, timelines, and shopping lists
- choosing and serving cheeses
- ideas for "instant" hors d'oeuvres
- make-ahead dishes, and more.

Only $7.99, order yours now!

THE BEST OF Fine Cooking
appetizers

75 great recipes

tiny tarts & turnovers

quick dips & nibbles

festive starters

party tips & menus

Product #052017

This special issue is not part of any regular magazine subscription; mails 9/20/07 *Free standard shipping only. Payable in U.S. funds.

Barbecue Nation
Fred Thomson
Product #070863

Great gift book!

- 350 hot-off-the-grill recipes
- the best regional classics
- international barbecue dishes
- all backyard-tested!

~~$18.95~~ **Now only $17.06**

Save 10% when you order now!

Cuisipro
ice cream scoop

$13.95 at CutleryAndMore.com

The uniquely shaped bowl on this scoop allows it to dive into even the hardest ice cream (if it's rock hard, it'll take some effort, but it's manageable). Made of zinc alloy with a nonstick coating, the bowl sculpts perfect globes of ice cream and easily maneuvers around the tight corners of a pint container. The thick handle provides a comfortable grip, and the scoop is dishwasher safe. This scoop is a bit hefty, so if that's not to your liking, the lighter Zeroll might be a better fit.

How we tested

To find out how successful these "problem-solving" scoops are, we tested 22 of them under a variety of ice cream conditions—rock hard, perfectly softened, and a bit melty. Our goal was to find the scoops that could carve round, compact balls of ice cream without a struggle and release them just as easily. We scooped from rectangular half-gallon cartons and cylindrical pints.

Scooping tips

How to scoop. The more continuous and smooth the movement of the scoop, the easier it is to form an evenly shaped ball. It helps to drag the scoop around the edge of the carton rather than back and forth.

Easier entertaining. To save yourself time and trouble when serving ice cream to a crowd, scoop it ahead and store in the freezer on a chilled baking sheet or in individual bowls. Cover the ice cream well with plastic wrap.

Storing ice cream. To keep the flavor fresh and to prevent ice crystals from forming on the surface, smooth a piece of plastic wrap or waxed paper directly on the ice cream before replacing the lid. A rubber band cinched around the lid's edge will also help keep air out.

In addition to our favorite scoops shown above, we tested the following 19 scoops (listed alphabetically by category): Trigger-release scoops by Amco Housewares, Fox Run, Hamilton Beach, Oxo Good Grips, RSVP Endurance, and Zeroll; press-release scoops by Amco Housewares, Kitchen Collection, Orka/Mastrad, Oxo Good Grips, Oxo Steel, and Zack Futuro; scoops with points by KitchenAid, Oxo Good Grips, and Zyliss; and self-defrosting scoops by Fox Run and Norpro. We also tested Good Cook's twister scoop and Oxo Good Grips beak-shaped scoop.

Maryellen Driscoll is an editor at large for Fine Cooking. ◆

Winning tip

A cool way to use cast-iron pots in summer

I have a large collection of beautiful enameled cast-iron pots that I hate to put away in the summer, even though I rarely make soups or braises in hot weather. Now I've found another use for them. Cast iron retains cold as well as it does heat, so a chilled cast-iron pot turns out to a be a great way to keep summer dishes cool. My homemade ice cream easily travels across town when stored and served from one of my smaller enameled cast-iron pans, and I've used the larger ones for salads and cold fruit soups. They also work well for backyard picnics. Just chill the pot in the fridge for several hours before filling.

—*Rebecca Peterson, Atlanta, Georgia*

A prize for the best tip

We want your best tips. We'll pay for the ones we publish, and we'll give a prize for the cleverest tip in each issue. Write to Tips, *Fine Cooking*, PO Box 5506, Newtown, CT 06470-5506 or email fctips@taunton.com.

The prize for this issue's winner: Viking 5-quart stand mixer in bright red; value, $440.

Vote Help us pick the winning reader's tip for upcoming issues; go to
finecooking.com/vote

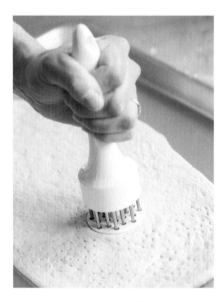

Try a meat tenderizer for docking

I was making flatbread yesterday, and the recipe called for pricking the raw dough. I don't have a pastry docker and usually just use a fork, but then I remembered a meat tenderizer hiding in a drawer. It was a huge success and worked better than a fork. I plan to use it for docking pie shells and pastry.

—*Ruth Fischer, Swarthmore, Pennsylvania*

Make anchovy paste in a garlic press

I've discovered that anchovy paste is easy to make at home. I just put a few whole anchovies in my garlic press and out comes anchovy paste, which can be mixed with a little extra-virgin olive oil for a smooth consistency.

—*Louise E. Oates, Salinas, California*

Car care aisle yields deep-frying help

When I deep fry, I like to reuse the oil at least once. To strain it before storing, I use a funnel designed for car oil. (It's made of HDPE plastic, which is known not to leach chemicals and is used in many food-storage containers.) Available in the automotive section of department and hardware stores, these funnels are larger than most kitchen funnels and have built-in strainers. Some even have a handy on/off spout, which helps prevent overflow. Look for a funnel with the finest wire-mesh strainer, clean it thoroughly before use, and use it only for food.

—*Matthew Clemente, Kingston, Ontario*

Reuse grape bags for washed greens

I buy grapes at the supermarket in perforated zip-top bags, which I've found to be perfect for storing washed greens. Because the bags allow air to circulate, the greens hold up in the refrigerator without moisture condensing in the bag.

—*Judy Wong, Oakland, California*

Hard cheese cleans your food processor

Whenever I shred carrots in my food processor, I'm left with an orange tinge on the plastic bowl that won't wash out easily. Pulsing a few small pieces of hard cheese like Parmigiano instantly removes the orange hue. And you have freshly chopped cheese for your salad.

—*Ana Weerts, Brookfield, Wisconsin*

A plastic knife for muffin removal

I use a plastic knife to remove delicate baked goods from muffin or tart tins. Plastic knives are thin and flexible, and they don't scratch the finish on my bakeware.

—*Pattie Mitchell,*
Nanaimo, British Columbia

A Popsicle stick measures batter level

Whenever I make anything that requires filling ramekins, I use a Popsicle stick marked off to the depth I need. For example, if I need 2 inches of filling, I use a ruler to mark 2 inches on the stick and then insert it into each ramekin while I fill it. This way, I have the same amount in each ramekin and don't have to worry about some being done before others.

—*Patty Nixon, Delphos, Ohio*

Easy Parmigiano matchsticks

Most people are familiar with the technique of using a vegetable peeler to make shards of Parmigiano-Reggiano to top a dish. But if you use a julienne peeler, you get cool little matchsticks of cheese, which make a nice garnish.

—*Susie Middleton, editor*

Mash bananas in the peel

When making banana bread or any other recipe calling for mashed bananas, I've found a way to save a bowl. I keep the fruit in the peel and smack the banana against the counter a couple of times. Then I roll it back and forth on a flat surface, pressing down until the skin splits. Finally, I open the peel where it split, and inside is a mashed banana ready to be mixed with the other ingredients.

—*Eva Reed, Castine, Maine* ◆

Freeze bacon to have on hand

I can rarely use a pound of bacon before its expiration date. Yet I love to cook with it, and I find that I often need a slice or two for a soup or sauce recipe. The solution? Frozen bacon, which you can quickly and easily defrost. Start with a pound of bacon. Put two or three strips on a narrow sheet of plastic wrap. Fold the wrap over to seal, and then roll into a ball. Put several of these bacon packets in a plastic freezer container for safe, fresh storage. When your recipe calls for bacon, just defrost the amount you need.

—*Linda Cornwell, Wyncote, Pennsylvania*

Chicken Thighs Take a Turn On the Grill

BY PAM ANDERSON

More flavorful than chicken breasts, boneless thighs cook quickly and stay juicy

Since they started showing up in the meat case a number of years ago, boneless, skinless chicken thighs have quickly moved to the top of my favorites-to-grill list. They offer all the benefits of boneless, skinless chicken breasts—convenience and fast cooking—without the tendency to turn tasteless and dry, thanks to their slightly higher fat content. The hearty flavor of thighs and their ability to stay juicy on the grill is sure to win over anyone who claims to be dark-meat averse.

Before grilling boneless, skinless chicken thighs, you might need a quick handling tutorial. Like any chicken part, thighs come in different sizes. Thighs from mass-produced chickens tend to be larger than those from their free-range kin, so be sure to check the weight on the package.

To prepare thighs for the grill, you'll need to remove any large pockets of fat, which could cause flare-ups. Don't worry about getting every bit, as it's the fat that will help keep the thigh moist during grilling.

Chicken thighs are multimuscular, unlike breasts, which are a single muscle. When the thigh bone is removed, those muscles become more loosely connected, which explains why boneless thighs often look a bit lumpy when unfurled on the grill. The upside is that this unevenness creates little depressions that hold onto sauces and rubs.

(continued on p. 32)

Lay the chicken flat. Unfold the boneless chicken thighs, remove any large pockets of fat, and spread the pieces flat on the grill.

Go for the grill marks. Pam puts the chicken on a hot grill and doesn't turn it for 4 to 6 minutes, so that the pieces will develop nice grill marks.

Check for doneness. Look for the chicken thighs to shrink and plump up a bit when they're ready to take off the grill.

Grilled Five-Spice Chicken Thighs with Soy-Vinegar Sauce & Cilantro

Serves four to six.

2 Tbs. Chinese five-spice powder
1 Tbs. plus 1 tsp. dark brown sugar
1 tsp. garlic powder
¾ tsp. kosher salt
2 Tbs. soy sauce
2 tsp. rice vinegar
1 tsp. Asian sesame oil
¼ tsp. crushed red pepper flakes
2½ lb. boneless, skinless chicken thighs (about 8 large, 10 medium, or 12 small), trimmed of excess fat
2 Tbs. vegetable oil; more for the grill
3 Tbs. chopped cilantro

Mix the five-spice powder, the 1 Tbs. sugar, the garlic powder, and the salt in a small bowl. In another bowl, mix the soy sauce, vinegar, sesame oil, red pepper flakes, and remaining 1 tsp. sugar.

Put the chicken in a shallow pan, drizzle with the vegetable oil, and toss to coat evenly. Sprinkle the spice mixture over the chicken; toss and rub to coat thoroughly.

Prepare a hot charcoal fire or heat a gas grill with all burners on medium high for 10 minutes. Clean the hot grate with a wire brush and then lubricate it with an oil-soaked paper towel. Put the chicken on the grate and grill (covered on a gas grill or uncovered over a charcoal fire) until one side has dark grill marks, 5 to 6 minutes for large thighs or 4 to 5 minutes for medium and small thighs. Turn and continue to grill until well marked on the other sides and cooked through, 5 to 6 minutes longer for large thighs or 4 to 5 minutes for medium and small thighs.

Move the thighs to a serving dish. Drizzle with about half of the soy mixture, sprinkle with the cilantro, and toss to coat. Let rest 4 to 5 minutes, tossing once or twice. Serve hot, warm, or at room temperature, with the remaining soy mixture passed at the table.

Doneness tests are different for chicken thighs than for breasts. For a chicken breast, you look for the meat to change color from pink to white. The dark meat of chicken thighs, though, looks pinkish brown even when they're thoroughly cooked. Food safety experts recommend that boneless thighs be cooked to an internal temperature of 165°F, but it can be pretty tough to use a meat thermometer on such a small, irregular cut, especially on the grill.

The cooking times given here (10 minutes for small thighs and 12 minutes for large ones) will pretty much guarantee a fully cooked thigh. You'll notice that when the thighs are done, they'll shrink and plump up a bit (see bottom photo, p. 31). The good thing is that you can relax when you're cooking thighs, knowing that even if you overcook them slightly, they won't dry out.

The robust flavor of chicken thighs makes them a natural for all kinds of bold spice and herb rubs. Included here are four of my favorite recipes, to give you an idea of how versatile thighs are.

Next time you reach for that package of boneless, skinless chicken breasts, stop, and pick up thighs instead. They just may become your new favorite.

Grilled Rosemary Chicken Thighs with Sweet & Sour Orange Dipping Sauce
Serves four to six.

1 Tbs. plus 1 tsp. minced fresh rosemary
2 tsp. dark brown sugar
2 tsp. kosher salt
1 tsp. freshly ground black pepper
1 tsp. crushed red pepper flakes
2 Tbs. vegetable oil; more for the grill
2½ lb. boneless, skinless chicken thighs (about 8 large, 10 medium, or 12 small), trimmed of excess fat
1 cup orange marmalade
¼ cup rice vinegar

In a small bowl, mix the 1 Tbs. rosemary with the brown sugar, salt, pepper, and red pepper flakes. In a shallow pan, drizzle the oil over the chicken and toss to coat. Sprinkle the chicken evenly with the rosemary mixture.

Warm the marmalade, vinegar, and remaining 1 tsp. rosemary in a small saucepan over low heat until just warm; set aside in a warm spot.

Prepare a hot charcoal fire or heat a gas grill with all burners on medium high for 10 minutes. Clean the hot grate with a wire brush and then lubricate it with an oil-soaked paper towel. Put the chicken on the grate and grill (covered on a gas grill or uncovered over a charcoal fire) until one side has dark grill marks, 5 to 6 minutes for large thighs or 4 to 5 minutes for medium and small thighs. Turn and continue to grill until well marked on the other sides and cooked through, 5 to 6 minutes longer for large thighs or 4 to 5 minutes for medium and small thighs.

Move the thighs to a platter and let rest 4 to 5 minutes. Serve hot, warm, or at room temperature with individual bowls of warm marmalade dipping sauce.

Skewer up some kebabs

Chicken thighs lend themselves to kebabs, which make a nice change of pace on the grill. Any of these recipes can be cooked on skewers in roughly the same amount of time.

To make kebabs, trim the thighs and then slice them lengthwise into 1½- to 2-inch-wide strips. Toss with the flavoring of choice; then thread the chicken onto six 8- or 12-inch skewers (soak wood skewers in water for at least 20 minutes first), folding each strip in half as you skewer it. If some strips are very thick, cut them in half crosswise rather than folding them so that all the pieces of chicken are roughly the same size. Grill the kebabs, turning them every 4 to 5 minutes as dark grill marks form, until cooked through, 12 to 15 minutes total.

Grilled Tandoori-Style Chicken Thighs

Serves four to six.

1½ Tbs. ground cumin
1½ tsp. curry powder
1½ tsp. kosher salt
1 tsp. garlic powder
½ tsp. ground ginger
¼ tsp. cayenne
2 Tbs. vegetable oil; more for the grill
3 Tbs. red-wine vinegar
½ cup regular or nonfat plain yogurt
2½ lb. boneless, skinless chicken thighs (about 8 large, 10 medium, or 12 small), trimmed of excess fat
3 Tbs. chopped cilantro

Mix the cumin, curry powder, salt, garlic powder, ginger, and cayenne in a medium bowl. Heat the oil in an 8-inch skillet over low heat. Stir the spices into the oil and heat until they bubble and become fragrant, 30 to 60 seconds. Return the spice blend to the bowl and stir in the vinegar and then the yogurt.

Add the chicken thighs and toss to coat evenly. Let sit 10 minutes or cover and marinate in the refrigerator for up to 12 hours.

When ready to cook, prepare a hot charcoal fire or heat a gas grill with all burners on medium high for 10 minutes. Clean the hot grate with a wire brush and then lubricate it with an oil-soaked paper towel. Put the chicken on the grate and grill (covered on a gas grill or uncovered over a charcoal fire) until one side has dark grill marks, 5 to 6 minutes for large thighs or 4 to 5 minutes for medium and small thighs. Turn and continue to grill until well marked on the other sides and cooked through, 5 to 6 minutes longer for large thighs or 4 to 5 minutes for medium and small thighs. Move the thighs to a platter and let rest 4 to 5 minutes. Sprinkle with chopped cilantro before serving.

Indonesian Grilled Chicken Thighs with Mango-Peanut Salsa

Serves four to six.

1 Tbs. ground ginger
1 Tbs. ground coriander
1½ tsp. turmeric
1½ tsp. garlic powder
3 Tbs. vegetable oil; more for the grill
1 Tbs. Asian chile paste (like sambal oelek)
1 Tbs. dark brown sugar
2 tsp. kosher salt
2½ lb. boneless, skinless chicken thighs (about 8 large, 10 medium, or 12 small), trimmed of excess fat
2 cups small-diced fresh mango (from 2 large mangos)
½ cup small-diced red bell pepper (from 1 small pepper)
½ cup salted peanuts, coarsely chopped
⅓ cup thinly sliced scallions (white and green parts of 4 to 5 scallions)
3 Tbs. chopped fresh cilantro or mint or a combination
1 Tbs. seeded, minced jalapeño
2 to 3 Tbs. fresh lime juice

Mix the ginger, coriander, turmeric, and garlic powder in a medium bowl. Heat 2 Tbs. of the oil in an 8-inch skillet over low heat. Add the spices to the hot oil and heat until they bubble and become fragrant, 30 to 60 seconds. Return

the spice blend to the bowl; stir in the chile paste, brown sugar, and salt. The mixture will be thick and pasty. Add the chicken and toss to coat evenly.

In a medium bowl, mix the mango, bell pepper, peanuts, scallions, cilantro or mint, jalapeño, and the remaining 1 Tbs. oil. Add the lime juice to taste. Set aside. (You can season the chicken and make the salsa up to 2 hours ahead and refrigerate.)

Prepare a hot charcoal fire or heat a gas grill with all burners on medium high for 10 minutes. Clean the hot grate with a wire brush and then lubricate it with an oil-soaked paper towel. Put the chicken on the grate and grill (covered on a gas grill or uncovered over a charcoal fire) until one side has dark grill marks, 5 to 6 minutes for large thighs or 4 to 5 minutes for medium and small thighs. Turn and continue to grill until well marked on the other sides and cooked through, 5 to 6 minutes longer for large thighs or 4 to 5 minutes for medium and small thighs.

Move the thighs to a platter, let rest 4 to 5 minutes, and serve hot, warm, or at room temperature with the salsa alongside.

Pam Anderson is a Fine Cooking *contributing editor.* ◆

Endless Summer Corn Sautés

For a versatile side dish, take the corn off the cob and layer on the flavors

Heat butter & olive oil + Add scallions, onions, or leeks + Add vegetables (optional) + Toss in fresh corn kernels +

Stir in ginger, garlic, or spices + Fold in fresh herbs + Squeeze on lemon or lime + Season with salt & pepper =

BY SUSIE MIDDLETON

n the Delaware summers of my childhood, there were some things as certain as death and taxes. My uncles fished for flounder and drank Budweiser. We kids picked crabs, snapped green beans, and shucked corn almost daily. And in August, we all battled the horseflies for beach plums to make into jelly and turned ripe, drippingly juicy Delaware peaches into the best hand-cranked homemade ice cream you'd ever taste.

The not-so-secret ingredient in that ice cream was the rich heavy cream (43% fat) from our local Lewes Dairy. We poured that cream on everything, including Kellogg's Special K. But our favorite destination for that cream was my grandmother Honey's succotash—a simple dish made from my father's pole beans, our local Silver Queen corn, a bit of cream and butter, and a lot of freshly ground pepper.

There was never a call to do anything different with all that fresh corn we were blessed with. (Before the rise of housing developments and the popularity of retirement, Delaware was like one big cornfield conveniently laced with brackish streams for the blue crabs to live in.) Corn was either served on the cob or off in that succotash.

All these years later, I still love good, sweet fresh corn, simply prepared. But I also like variety, which is why I had so much fun coming up with these corn side dishes. Once you grasp the simple technique of sautéing the ingredients and adding flavor in stages (see left), you can vary the character of these dishes by adding different aromatics, other vegetables, fresh herbs, and even (gasp!) a little heavy cream.

Use these sautés for more than just side dishes. Aside from being able to tailor the flavors of these dishes, you can also choose how you'd like to serve them. For instance, I like to serve my Corn, Sweet Onion & Zucchini Sauté as a bed for grilled fish. The Corn & Mushroom Sauté with Leeks & Pancetta is a great topping for a grilled steak. Or you could use any variation as a taco or quesadilla filling, a base for a frittata, or of course, a simple side dish on its own. It's your choice; the only thing that's certain is this: If you get tired of plain old corn on the cob, you can cut the kernels off and turn them into something exciting.

Clockwise from above:

Corn, Sweet Onion & Zucchini Sauté with Fresh Mint

Corn & Mushroom Sauté with Leeks & Pancetta

Corn Sauté with Ginger, Garlic & Fresh Cilantro

Corn, Sweet Onion & Zucchini Sauté with Fresh Mint

Serves four as a side dish.

2 Tbs. unsalted butter
1 Tbs. extra-virgin olive oil
1½ cups small-diced sweet onion, such as a
   Vidalia (about 7 oz. or half a large onion)
1 tsp. kosher salt; more to taste
1¼ cups small-diced zucchini (about 6 oz.
   or 1 medium-small zucchini)
2 slightly heaping cups fresh corn kernels
   (from 4 medium ears)
2 tsp. minced garlic
Scant ½ tsp. ground cumin
Scant ½ tsp. ground coriander
2 to 3 Tbs. chopped fresh mint
One-quarter lemon
Freshly ground black pepper

Melt 1 Tbs. of the butter with the olive oil in a
10-inch straight-sided sauté pan or Dutch oven
over medium-low heat. Add the onions and ½ tsp.
of the salt, cover and cook, stirring occasionally,
until the onions are soft and translucent, about
5 minutes. Uncover, raise the heat to medium, and
cook, stirring frequently, until the onions are light
golden and shrunken, another 3 to 4 minutes.

Add the remaining 1 Tbs. butter and the zucchini. Cook, stirring occasionally, until the zucchini
is slightly shrunken and almost tender, about
3 minutes. Add the corn, garlic, and the remaining
½ tsp. salt. Cook, stirring frequently and scraping
the bottom of the pan with a wooden spoon, until
the corn is tender but still slightly toothy to the
bite, 3 to 4 minutes. (It will begin to intensify in
color, glisten, and be somewhat shrunken in size,
and the bottom of the pan may be slightly brown.)
Add the cumin and coriander and cook, stirring,
until very fragrant, about 30 seconds.

Remove the pan from the heat, add all but
about ½ Tbs. of the mint, a good squeeze of
lemon, and a few generous grinds of pepper.
Stir, let sit 2 minutes, and stir again, scraping up
the brown bits from the bottom of the pan (moisture released from the vegetables as they sit will
loosen the bits). Season to taste with more salt,
pepper, or lemon. Serve warm, sprinkled with
the remaining mint.

A tidy way to cut corn

To prepare corn for sautéing, first
shuck the ears and remove all the
silks by running your hands up
and down the ear. Then break the
ears in half cleanly. (I find using
my hands to do this is easiest and
safest, but you can cut them in
half with a sharp chef's knife, too.)
Stand each half cut side down on
a large clean dish towel placed
over a cutting board. Cut the
kernels off the cob with a sharp
chef's knife and a downward sawing motion, cutting around the ear
to remove all the kernels. Discard
the cobs or save for a soup stock.
Gather the towel up and dump
the kernels into a bowl.

Corn Sauté with Ginger, Garlic & Fresh Cilantro

Serves four as a side dish.

2 Tbs. unsalted butter
1 Tbs. extra-virgin olive oil
¾ cup thinly sliced scallions (white and light-green parts, from 1 large bunch)
1 tsp. kosher salt; more to taste
2 slightly heaping cups fresh corn kernels (from 4 medium ears)
2 Tbs. minced fresh ginger
2 to 3 tsp. minced garlic
Scant 1 tsp. minced serrano chile (include the ribs and seeds for a spicier dish)
2 Tbs. chopped fresh cilantro
One-half lime
Freshly ground black pepper

Melt 1 Tbs. of the butter with the olive oil in a 10-inch straight-sided sauté pan or Dutch oven over medium heat. Add the scallions and ½ tsp. of the salt and cook, stirring occasionally, until the scallions are soft and lightly browned, about 3 minutes.

Add the remaining 1 Tbs. butter and the corn, ginger, garlic, serrano, and the remaining ½ tsp. salt. Cook, stirring frequently and scraping the bottom of the pan with a wooden spoon, until the corn is tender but still slightly toothy to the bite, 3 to 4 minutes. (It will begin to intensify in color, glisten, and be somewhat shrunken in size, and the bottom of the pan may be slightly brown.)

Remove the pan from the heat, add all but about ½ Tbs. of the cilantro, a good squeeze of the lime, and a few generous grinds of pepper. Stir, let sit 2 minutes, and stir again, scraping up the brown bits from the bottom of the pan (moisture released from the vegetables as they sit will loosen the bits). Season to taste with more salt, pepper, or lime. Serve warm, sprinkled with the remaining cilantro.

Corn & Mushroom Sauté with Leeks & Pancetta

Serves four as a side dish.

2 Tbs. extra-virgin olive oil
1½ oz. thinly sliced pancetta (4 to 5 slices)
3 Tbs. unsalted butter
1 cup small-diced leeks (white and light-green parts only, from 1 large leek)
1 tsp. kosher salt; more to taste
2 generous cups medium-diced cremini mushrooms (about 6 oz.)
2 slightly heaping cups fresh corn kernels (from 4 medium ears)
2 Tbs. chopped fresh flat-leaf parsley
1 to 2 tsp. coarsely chopped fresh thyme or oregano
Freshly ground black pepper
One-quarter lemon
3 Tbs. heavy cream

Heat 1 Tbs. of the olive oil in a 10-inch straight-sided sauté pan or Dutch oven over medium-low heat. Add the pancetta and cook, turning occasionally with tongs, until light golden and crisp, 5 to 7 minutes. Transfer the pancetta to a plate lined with paper towels, leaving the fat in the pan.

Increase the heat to medium and carefully add 1 Tbs. of the butter to the fat. When melted, add the leeks and ½ tsp. of the salt. Cover and cook, stirring occasionally and scraping up any browned bits from the pancetta, until the leeks are softened and slightly shrunken, 3 to 5 minutes. Uncover and cook, stirring frequently, until lightly browned, 1 to 2 minutes.

Add another 1 Tbs. of the butter, the remaining 1 Tbs. olive oil, the mushrooms, and the remaining ½ tsp. salt. Cover and cook, stirring occasionally, until the mushrooms are softened and a little shrunken (they will have given off a good bit of liquid), 3 to 4 minutes. Uncover and cook, stirring frequently, until the liquid evaporates and the mushrooms are lightly browned, 2 to 3 minutes (the bottom of the pan will be quite brown).

Add the remaining 1 Tbs. butter and the corn. Cook, stirring frequently and scraping the bottom of the pan with a wooden spoon, until the corn is tender but still slightly toothy to the bite, 3 to 4 minutes. (It will begin to intensify in color, glisten, and be somewhat shrunken in size, and the bottom of the pan will be brown.)

Remove the pan from the heat, add the fresh herbs, a few generous grinds of pepper, and a good squeeze of the lemon. Stir in the heavy cream. Let sit a minute or two and stir again, scraping up the brown bits from the bottom of the pan (moisture released from the vegetables as they sit will loosen the bits). Season to taste with more salt, pepper, or lemon. Crumble the reserved pancetta over top and serve warm.

Susie Middleton is editor of Fine Cooking. ◆

Great Tomatoes
Don't Need Cooking to Become a
Great Sauce

BY EVAN KLEIMAN

I've traveled to Italy for more than thirty years, and I've never seen anyone make—or eat—what we call pasta salads. But I can't tell you how often I've seen a gifted home cook make a *salsa cruda*—a beautiful sauce of chopped raw tomatoes, fresh herbs, a bit of garlic, and a healthy dose of extra-virgin olive oil—and toss it with hot pasta. Ripe tomatoes need to marinate only half an hour for their sweet juices to be coaxed into a delicious sauce, so this vibrantly flavored pasta dish comes together easily in the time it takes for the water to boil and the pasta to cook.

Start with great tomatoes and the right cut. You'll get the best results if you buy ripe tomatoes at a farmstand or farmers' market or get them from your own garden. They'll be the tastiest and juiciest, since they've been picked at their ripest. How you cut the tomatoes is important, too. A half-inch dice is the perfect size, because it will give you a juicy sauce while maintaining the integrity of the tomatoes.

Add a good amount of olive oil. The oil serves a double purpose here. First, it combines with the juices drawn by the salt to make the sauce. No oil means no sauce, just tomato juice. Second, a good fruity extra-virgin olive oil will lend its rich flavor to the dish, giving it lots of body and depth.

Toss the sauce with hot pasta. This is key: The heat of just-cooked pasta helps release the flavors in the tomatoes and creates a better integrated dish than if you mixed the sauce with cold pasta.

Heirloom tomatoes like these make a delicious no-cook tomato sauce, but any kind—or any shape—of farmstand tomato will do, as long as it's ripe.

No-Cook Tomato Sauce
(*Salsa Cruda*)
Serves four to six.

This sauce and its variations at right are for 1 lb. of imported Italian dried pasta. You can pair the sauce with any pasta shape, though it clings best to short, ridged types like penne rigate and rigatoni.

2 lb. ripe tomatoes (about 3 large or 4 medium), cored and cut into ½-inch dice (about 4 cups)
½ cup good-quality extra-virgin olive oil
⅓ cup roughly chopped fresh flat-leaf parsley or basil or both
1 Tbs. coarsely chopped fresh thyme
1 tsp. minced garlic (1 medium clove)
1 tsp. kosher salt; more to taste
¼ tsp. freshly ground black pepper; more to taste
Pinch crushed red pepper flakes (optional)

Combine all of the ingredients in a nonreactive bowl large enough to hold the tomatoes and the cooked pasta; mix well. Let the sauce sit at room temperature for at least 30 minutes and up to 3 hours.

Toss the sauce with just-cooked pasta. Adjust the seasoning to taste with salt and pepper and serve immediately.

Try an add-in for a new personality

While salsa cruda is delicious on its own, you can choose one of these tasty additions for a little variety.

Cheese

Stir the cheese (see choices below) into the No-Cook Tomato Sauce after it has sat at room temperature and just before adding the pasta. In addition to the 1 cup Parmigiano, choose ¼ to ½ lb. of another cheese, depending on how strong or sharp it is.

1 cup grated Parmigiano-Reggiano
¼ to ½ lb. of one cheese:
  Feta, crumbled
  Asiago, grated
  Maytag blue, chopped
  Gorgonzola, chopped
  Fresh mozzarella, diced
  Fresh goat cheese, crumbled

Tapenade
Yields about ¾ cup.

Mix half the tapenade into the No-Cook Tomato Sauce before it sits at room temperature. Garnish each serving of pasta with some of the remaining tapenade.

½ cup pitted Kalamata olives
¼ cup pitted green olives
¼ cup pitted oil-cured black olives
3 Tbs. extra-virgin olive oil
1 tsp. finely grated lemon zest
1 tsp. minced fresh rosemary (from 1 medium sprig)

Put all of the ingredients in a food processor and pulse until very roughly chopped, about 13 pulses.

Basil Pesto
Yields about 1¼ cups.

Stir the basil pesto into the No-Cook Tomato Sauce after it has sat at room temperature and just before adding the pasta.

2 cups firmly packed fresh basil (preferably Italian Genovese)
1 large clove garlic
1 tsp. kosher salt
Freshly ground black pepper
½ cup extra-virgin olive oil
½ cup freshly grated Parmigiano-Reggiano
½ cup pine nuts or walnuts

Put the basil, garlic, salt, and 2 or 3 grinds of pepper in a food processor and process until the basil and garlic are finely chopped, about 15 seconds. With the machine running, pour ¼ cup of the olive oil down the feed tube in a slow, steady stream. Turn off the processor and add the Parmigiano. Process until the cheese is incorporated, about 20 seconds. With the machine running, slowly add the remaining ¼ cup oil. Add the nuts and pulse until they're coarsely chopped.

Evan Kleiman is the owner and chef of Angeli Caffè in Los Angeles. She is also the author of numerous cookbooks, including Pasta Fresca. ◆

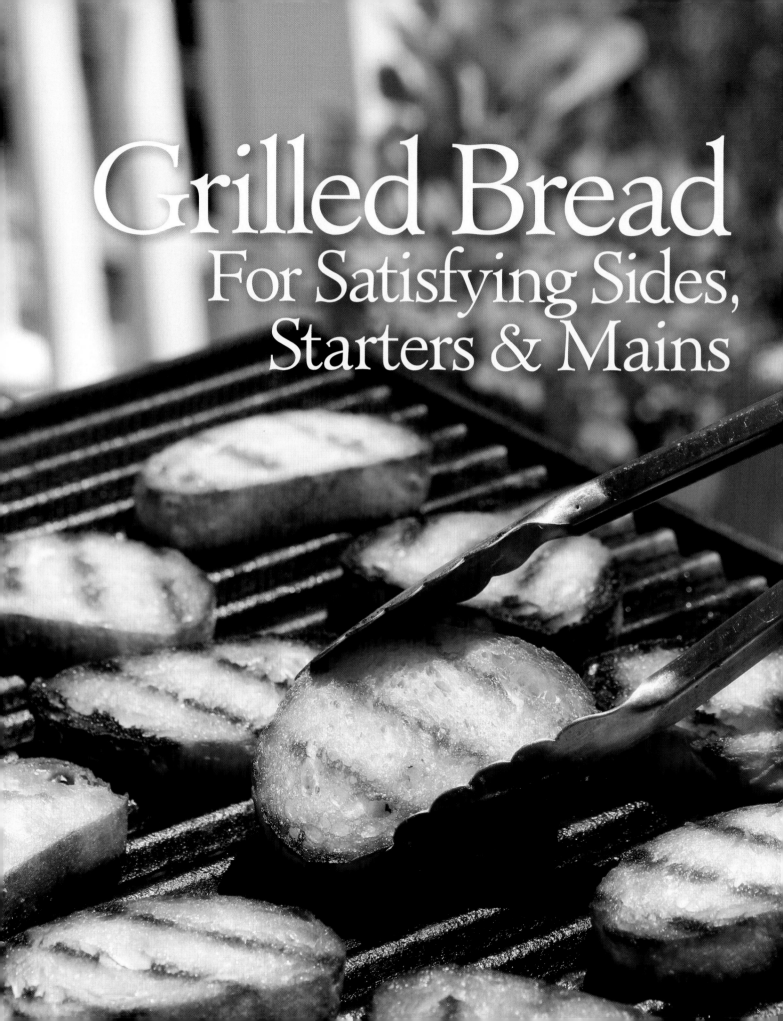

Grilled Bread
For Satisfying Sides, Starters & Mains

side dish

Grilled Garlic Bread
Serves eight.

Eight ¾- to 1-inch-thick slices crusty, artisan-style bread, like ciabatta
¼ cup extra-virgin olive oil for brushing
1 to 2 large cloves garlic, peeled and halved
Sea salt or kosher salt

Prepare a medium-low charcoal or gas grill fire. Brush both sides of the bread with the oil and grill, covered, turning once, until golden and marked on both sides, 1 to 3 minutes per side. Off the heat but while the bread is still hot, lightly rub one side of each bread slice with the cut sides of the garlic—heat and friction from the bread will cause the garlic to "melt" into the bread. Sprinkle with salt and serve.

BY ELIZABETH KARMEL

When you think of grilling, bread probably isn't the first thing that comes to mind. But to me, there is no food that better captures the flavor of the grill. Think about it: Bread dipped in olive oil is good, but how about crunchy, smoky, *grilled* bread dipped in olive oil? It's almost a meal in itself.

While grilled bread is delicious on its own, its real beauty lies in its versatility—it makes an excellent foundation for appetizers, sandwiches, and even salads. I first realized this when I started grilling bread to round out some of my favorite grilled-vegetable salads. The bread not only absorbed the vegetables' flavorful juices, which otherwise would have pooled in the bottom of the bowl, but it also gave the salads a surprising crunch and delicious, smoky flavor notes. Once I made this discovery, I started grilling bread to use in many kinds of dishes.

At its simplest, grilled bread makes a perfect accompaniment to any summer meal. The Grilled Garlic Bread featured here is a more sophisticated version of the butter-soaked garlic bread that many of us grew up with, but it's easier to make and tastier, too. If you add a topping, like the goat cheese and marinated roasted peppers in the recipe on p. 42, you have a wonderful starter. The peppers can be prepared in advance, making the crostini easy to assemble at the last minute.

And finally, for a more substantial dish, try using grilled bread as a component of a main-course salad, like the Grilled Corn, Shrimp & Chorizo Salad on. p. 43. Just before serving, pile this colorful salad onto grilled bread, which adds a great texture to the salad and makes it heartier, too.

Getting grilled bread just right

Choose artisan or rustic country breads; ciabatta is my favorite, but you can also try sourdough or a French boule.

Slice the bread ¾ to 1 inch thick.

Make sure the cooking grates are clean and heated.

Grill bread, covered, over direct medium-low heat.

Have a pair of tongs handy to turn the bread and remove it from the grill.

Patience is the key to great grilled bread. Don't be tempted to use higher heat, or the bread will burn.

Grilled Goat Cheese Crostini with a Tangle of Marinated Roasted Peppers

Serves eight as an appetizer.

Goat cheese speckled with fresh thyme is the perfect creamy counterpoint to the sweet, tangy roasted peppers in this recipe. Serve these crostini as an appetizer or paired with a simple green salad for a light lunch.

3 medium bell peppers (1 red, 1 orange, and 1 yellow)
3 Tbs. balsamic vinegar
2 Tbs. extra-virgin olive oil
1½ tsp. fresh thyme
¼ tsp. kosher salt
Freshly ground black pepper
1 recipe Grilled Garlic Bread, p. 41
One 4½- to 5½-oz. container of soft, spreadable goat cheese (such as Chavrie), at room temperature

Prepare a medium-high grill fire. Grill the bell peppers, turning occasionally, until the skin chars all over, 15 to 20 minutes. Put the charred peppers in a heatproof bowl, cover with plastic wrap, and let sit until cool enough to handle, about 30 minutes.

Meanwhile, in a large bowl, combine the balsamic vinegar, olive oil, ½ tsp. of the thyme, salt, and about 5 grinds of pepper. Mix well.

Remove the pepper skins and seeds and cut the peppers into thin strips. Add the peppers to the vinegar mixture and let them marinate for at least 1 hour and up to 3 days. (Refrigerate if making more than a few hours ahead and return to room temperature before assembling the crostini.)

Spread each slice of the grilled garlic bread with a generous layer of goat cheese, sprinkle with some of the remaining thyme, and top with a tangle of the peppers and a small grind of black pepper. Serve immediately.

starter

Good things start with grilled bread

Slather grilled bread with tapenade, top with grilled asparagus and Asiago cheese, and serve as an open-face sandwich.

Top grilled bread with roughly mashed avocado, chopped shallots, and a slice of smoked salmon.

Make a grilled-bread BLT with lots of mayonnaise, applewood-smoked bacon, tomatoes, and Boston lettuce.

Spread pesto on grilled bread and layer on thin slices of tomato and fresh mozzarella.

Toss frisée with pancetta, apples, and a blue-cheese vinaigrette, and serve over slices of grilled bread.

Top grilled bread with sliced grilled Italian sausage, grilled onions, and sliced red cabbage tossed with warm vinegar and fennel-seed dressing.

reader review

A *Fine Cooking* reader gave the Grilled Goat Cheese Crostini with a Tangle of Marinated Roasted Peppers a real-world test. Here are the results:

The goat cheese crostini made an impressive starter. They looked a lot more complicated to make than they really were. I loved how nicely the flavors blended; in fact, I was surprised that so many strong flavors could complement one another so well. I will definitely make this quick and easy recipe again.

—Maureen Gazzola,
Mill Valley, California

Photos: Scott Phillips

main dish

Grilled Corn, Shrimp & Chorizo Salad

Serves eight.

This one-dish meal marries the best flavors from summer shore dinners—seafood and corn—with the smokiness of Spanish paprika and chorizo.

FOR THE VINAIGRETTE:
²/₃ cup extra-virgin olive oil; more for drizzling
4 to 5 large cloves garlic, peeled and grated on the small holes of a box grater to yield about 2 Tbs.
Kosher salt
1 tsp. sweet smoked paprika (Spanish pimentón)
⅓ cup sherry vinegar
Freshly ground black pepper

FOR THE SALAD:
8 large ears fresh corn, husked
Extra-virgin olive oil
Kosher salt
1 cup thinly sliced scallions, both white and green parts (about 1 large bunch)

24 easy-peel shrimp in the shell (16 to 20 per lb.)
4 Spanish chorizo sausages (about 14 oz. total), split lengthwise
1 pint cherry or grape tomatoes, cut in half
Freshly ground black pepper
1 recipe Grilled Garlic Bread, p. 41

Make the vinaigrette: Combine the olive oil and the grated garlic in a small saucepan. Cook over low heat until the garlic begins to brown slightly, about 10 minutes. Add a pinch of salt and stir to dissolve. Remove from the heat and let sit until the oil cools a bit, about 3 minutes. Add the paprika and let it infuse the oil for about 12 minutes more. Strain the oil through a fine sieve and discard the garlic. (If making in advance, store in the refrigerator for up to 2 days.)

Put the vinegar in a small bowl. Add a pinch of salt and a couple of grinds of black pepper and whisk to combine. Slowly drizzle in the garlic-paprika oil, whisking constantly until well incorporated. Taste and adjust the seasonings if necessary.

Make the salad: Prepare a medium-high charcoal or gas grill fire. Brush the corn all over with olive oil and season with salt. Grill, covered, turning occasionally until all sides are charred and deeply blistered in places, 6 to 10 minutes. Remove from the grill, cut the kernels off the cobs while still warm, and put the kernels in a large bowl. Add half the vinaigrette and toss to coat the kernels. Stir in the scallions and set aside.

Reduce the grill temperature to medium, or if using charcoal, let the coals die down a bit. Grill the shrimp and the sausage, turning once halfway through the cooking time, until the shrimp are pink, curled, and cooked through,

4 to 6 minutes, and the sausages are plump and well browned, 5 to 8 minutes. Transfer the shrimp and sausages to separate platters and cover with foil to keep warm.

While still warm, peel the shrimp and gently fold into the salad, along with the rest of the vinaigrette. Slice the sausages into ⅓-inch-thick half-moon-shaped pieces and mix into the salad. Add the tomatoes and mix gently. Taste and season with pepper and more salt if necessary. Serve the salad warm or at room temperature spooned over slices of grilled garlic bread.

Elizabeth Karmel is the author of Taming the Flame: Secrets for Hot-and-Quick Grilling and Low-and-Slow BBQ. ◆

Steaks

Mexican Style

Say "Mexican steaks" and probably the first thing you think of is fajitas made with sizzling skirt steak. As good as fajitas are, it might surprise you to discover that traditional Mexican steak dishes are often more sophisticated. They feature juicy, tender steaks like rib-eyes, T-bones, and New York strips and get punched up with rich, bold spices or sauces.

I've enjoyed many steak dishes in Mexico that deliver big, meaty flavor but that also have south-of-the-border additions, such as chiles and Mexican cheeses. Often more elegant in taste and presentation than the rustic Mexican dishes most of us are familiar with, these steaks are easy to recreate at home and offer an intriguing twist to the traditional American steakhouse meal.

Size matters—thinner's better
The most obvious difference in steak dishes down south is that the steaks are generally cut thinner than those served in American restaurants—often no more than ½ inch thick. As a result, portion sizes are smaller—generally 6 to 8 ounces, compared to the 12- to 14-ounce portions seen on American plates. This is not to say that all steaks served in Mexico are thin—I have had thick T-bones in Chihuahua, smothered with chiles nearly as mild and sweet as bell peppers; and in Sonora I was served a 1-pound steak cut from the center of the tenderloin. But the custom of serving thinner cuts like those in these recipes leaves room for side

If fajitas are the first thing that comes to mind, think again

BY JIM PEYTON

3 ways to add chile flavor

A wide range of chile varieties is readily available in the United States nowadays, and each offers a different flavor and heat level. Adding further possibilities are the different forms in which you can find chiles: fresh, canned, dried, and powdered. By using a combination of chile types and forms, you can go beyond just adding heat to a dish to create a surprisingly mild, balanced, and interesting flavor.

Chile powders
are made from dried chiles. They differ from the spice jars labeled "chili powder" in that they are ground solely from a specific type of chile. Chili powder is a mix of ground chiles with the addition of spices like garlic powder and cumin. Pure chile powders allow you to add the most nuanced hit of flavor and heat to a dish. I call for ancho chile powder in the Steak Adobo recipe because of its mild, fruity flavor. It has a moderate heat level and is also good in black beans dishes and mole sauce.

Dried chiles offer
concentrated flavors that often differ so much from the fresh versions that they are given new names. For example, a dried poblano chile is called an ancho (above right). The ancho remains mild but takes on an entirely different, fruity, raisin-like flavor. Pasilla chiles (above left) are dried chilacas. Dried chiles are often rehydrated before use and then blended with a little liquid to form a paste.

dishes yet still fills the plate and the craving for red meat without breaking the bank or the diet.

Thinner cuts cook faster as well, making some of these dishes easy to serve on a weeknight. Whether prepared with a simple spice rub or a more elaborate sauce, all of these steaks take less than five minutes to pan-sear, grill, or broil.

Adding depth of flavor

What sets these steaks apart from their American counterparts is the earthy flavors and spice that comes

Canned chiles

are often easier to find than fresh ones, although the available varieties are limited. I call for canned rather than fresh chipotle chiles because they store well and are easier to work with. Chipotles are jalapeños which are smoke-dried and then packed with a tangy tomato sauce that absorbs their flavor and heat. They come out of the can soft and ready to use, and the seeds and veins are much easier to remove than they are in their dried form.

Steak with Red Onion, Wine & Port Sauce
Serves four.

The easy sauce reduction elevates this steak into a sophisticated dinner. The sauce can be made ahead and kept refrigerated for several days.

FOR THE SAUCE:
1½ cups dry red wine
½ cup ruby port
3 cups thinly sliced red onion (1 large)
4 medium white or cremini mushrooms, chopped (about ¾ cup)
3 cloves garlic, coarsely chopped
1 large chipotle chile (from a can of chipotles en adobo), seeds removed
1 Tbs. chopped fresh flat-leaf parsley
1 tsp. dried thyme
2 cups low-salt beef broth
3 Tbs. cold unsalted butter, cut into ½-inch pieces
Kosher salt

FOR THE STEAKS:
Four ½-inch-thick boneless rib-eye, New York strip, or T-bone steaks (6 to 8 oz. each)
Kosher salt and freshly ground black pepper

Combine the wine and port with the onions, mushrooms, garlic, chile, parsley, and thyme in a 3- or 4-qt. saucepan. Bring to a boil and then simmer very briskly until the liquid is reduced by half, about 10 minutes. Add the broth and reduce by half again, about 13 minutes. Strain the liquid and discard the solids. Clean the saucepan and return the strained liquid to the pan. Reduce until there is just over ⅓ cup liquid remaining, about 5 minutes. The sauce may be prepared to this point up to 2 days ahead. Refrigerate if working more than a few hours ahead.

Grill or broil the steaks: Prepare a medium-high gas or charcoal fire or heat the broiler on high. Season the steaks with salt and pepper and grill or broil until they are cooked to your liking. Medium rare takes about 1½ minutes per side; medium, 2 minutes per side. Let rest while you finish the sauce.

Bring the wine reduction to a simmer. Remove from the heat and whisk in the butter. Season to taste with salt. Spoon a tablespoon or so of sauce over each steak.

from adding Mexican ingredients. In all of these, that means some form of chile—but that doesn't mean all these dishes are hot. Depending on the variety and form (see sidebar, p. 44), chiles offer a broad range of flavors, from fruity to smoky. As you'll see in the Steak with Three-Chile Sauce recipe, incorporating more than one type of chile in a dish is a way to achieve a rounded flavor, with many notes.

A sauce reduction, as in the Steak with Red Onion, Wine & Port Sauce recipe, is another example of the depth of flavor attainable in Mexican cooking. This dish comes from the upscale *neuva cocina Mexicana* tradition—Mexico's answer to modern fusion cooking. It results in an elegant entrée that you might serve at a party, showing that Mexican food is far more than simple bean- and tortilla-based dishes.

Sauces are not the only flavor addition to steaks in Mexico. The Steak Adobo is a good example of simple grilled red meat punched up with a spice rub. By first brushing the meat with lime juice, you can add a bright, subtle flavor to the steak. Don't apply the lime juice more than 15 minutes before the meat hits the heat, though, as even a little lime juice can begin to chemically "cook" the meat, which will change the texture and make it more difficult to brown.

Also on the plate

The Mexican style of serving one or more side dishes with steaks is easy to adopt in American kitchens. One traditional accompaniment is *rajas*, or sautéed onions and roasted and peeled poblano chiles. Enchiladas, quesadillas, rice, or beans would also lend a Mexican flair to a steak dinner. All of these steak dishes would be nice with a simple bibb and avocado salad (for side dish recipe ideas, visit FineCooking.com).

Steak Adobo
Serves four.

Some cooks mix the lime juice into the powdered spices to create a paste, but I find it easier to brush the juice onto the meat and then dust it with the spices.

2 tsp. ancho chile powder
½ tsp. finely ground black pepper
⅛ tsp. ground cinnamon
⅛ tsp. ground allspice
1 Tbs. fresh lime juice
Four ½-inch-thick boneless rib-eye, New York strip, or T-bone steaks (6 to 8 oz. each)
Kosher salt
1 Tbs. olive oil

In a small bowl, mix together the chile powder, pepper, cinnamon, and allspice. Brush a liberal coating of lime juice over one side of each steak, season generously with salt, and then sprinkle on a thin coating of the spices. This can be done up to 15 minutes before cooking; any longer and the lime juice may begin to affect the texture of the meat.

Heat the oil in a heavy 10-inch skillet over medium to medium-high heat. (It shouldn't be too hot or the spices can scorch.) When the oil is hot and shimmering, lay two of the steaks in the pan, seasoned side down. Allow them to cook 1 to 1½ minutes; flip and continue cooking until they are done as you like them, about 1 minute longer for medium rare. Repeat with the remaining steaks.

Whether prepared with a simple spice rub or a more elaborate sauce, all of these steaks take less than five minutes to pan-sear, grill, or broil.

Steak with Three-Chile Sauce
Serves four.

For this dish, the earthy combination of three of Mexico's most distinctive chiles creates a nuanced result that is not nearly as hot as you might expect. Much of the spiciness is cut by the cheeses, leaving only the subtle heat that real chile aficionados love.

FOR THE SAUCE:
1 ancho chile
1 pasilla chile
1 chipotle chile (from a can of chipotles en adobo)
3 Tbs. extra-virgin olive oil
1⅓ cups medium-chopped white onion (1 medium-small onion)
2 cloves garlic, chopped
¼ cup loosely packed fresh cilantro
1 Tbs. brandy
¾ cup low-salt beef broth
¾ tsp. dark brown sugar
Heaping ¼ tsp. kosher salt; more to taste

FOR THE STEAKS:
Four ½-inch-thick boneless rib-eye, New York strip, or T-bone steaks (6 to 8 oz. each)
Juice from 1 large lime (about ¼ cup)
Kosher salt and freshly ground black pepper
1 Tbs. extra-virgin olive oil
½ cup (2 oz.) grated Oaxaca cheese (or mozzarella)
⅓ cup (1½ oz.) grated cotija, anejo, or anejo enchilado cheese (or crumbled feta)

Make the sauce: Set a dry 10-inch skillet over medium heat for 2 minutes. Toast the ancho and pasilla chiles in the skillet for about 20 seconds on each side; don't let them scorch. Remove the stems, seeds, and ribs from the chiles. Soak the chiles in a bowl of hot water for about 20 minutes; drain them and put them in a blender. Add the chipotle.

Heat 1 Tbs. of the oil in the 10-inch skillet over medium heat. Add the onions and cook, stirring frequently, until soft and golden brown, lowering the heat as necessary to prevent scorching, about 10 minutes. Add the garlic and cook for 1 minute. Put the onions and garlic in the blender, along with the cilantro, brandy, and ¼ cup water. Blend to a smooth paste, adding additional water as necessary, 1 Tbs. at a time, to purée the ingredients. Transfer the chile paste to a small bowl.

Heat the remaining 2 Tbs. olive oil in a small saucepan over medium-high heat. When the oil is just beginning to smoke, add the chile paste. Cook, stirring constantly to incorporate it into the oil, until it's very thick, 2 to 4 minutes; reduce the heat if necessary to prevent burning. Reduce the heat to medium and gradually stir in the broth. Add the brown sugar and salt. Simmer until the mixture is the consistency of a medium-thick sauce, 1 to 2 minutes. Season to taste with salt.

Cook the steaks: Position a rack 4 inches from the broiler element and heat the broiler on high. Drizzle both sides of the steaks with the lime juice and season all over with salt and pepper. Heat an 11- or 12-inch skillet, preferably cast iron, over medium-high heat, add the olive oil, and sear two of the steaks on one side, about 2 minutes. Turn the steaks and sear them on the other side, and then continue cooking, lowering the heat as needed, until they're done to your liking, about 2 minutes on the second side for medium rare. Transfer the steaks to a rimmed baking sheet and repeat with the remaining two steaks.

When all the steaks are cooked, turn the heat to medium, pour the chile sauce into the skillet, and stir to incorporate any browned bits and juices from the meat. Sprinkle some of the Oaxaca (or mozzarella) cheese on each steak, spoon some sauce over them, and then top them with some of the cotija or anejo (or feta) cheese. Put the baking sheet under the broiler to melt the cheese, about 1 minute, and serve immediately.

James Peyton is an author of Mexican cookbooks and a restaurant consultant from San Antonio. ◆

Mexican cheeses

Oaxaca cheese (above left) is a soft cow's milk variety that melts easily. It's widely available in supermarkets in the Southwest but is increasingly found across the country. It is delicious on pizzas, over nachos, or in grilled cheese sandwiches. Mozzarella makes the best substitute.

Cotija (above front) and **anejo** (above rear) cheeses are aged, crumbly, slightly salty cheeses traditionally made from cow's milk. Anejo enchilado is coated with a mild chile powder. These cheeses are excellent in pasta and salads and make a tasty garnish for tacos, quesadillas, and refried beans. Feta is the best substitute.

Dressing Up Grilled Eggplant

Bold vinaigrettes and sauces make a
simple summer favorite something special

BY TASHA DeSERIO

It's one of those happy coincidences of nature that the best eggplant hits the market during peak grilling season. I love the subtle, sweet flavor of eggplant, and grilling really brings it out. As for texture, the intense heat of the grill crisps and browns the outsides of the slices nicely, while it cooks the insides to a luscious creaminess.

When it's just my family, I tend to serve grilled eggplant simply brushed with olive oil and sprinkled with salt, so its flavor shines. But for entertaining, I like to pair it with a bold topping. Either way, it's a hearty side dish that elevates any meal.

By grilling, you get that great meaty texture and flavor of eggplant without all the oil from frying or sautéing. One of eggplant's greatest strengths—its ability to absorb other flavors—is also its greatest weakness when it comes to absorbing fats and oils. That's why I prefer grilling eggplant, a method that requires little oil and produces lighter results. The grill also imparts a delicate, smoky flavor and a crisp surface that contrasts beautifully with eggplant's soft interior.

To avoid bitterness, select and store eggplant carefully—but don't bother salting. There's plenty of disagreement among cooks about whether or not to salt eggplant before cooking. Some claim salting is essential to remove bitter juices; others believe it improves texture. I find that ripe, carefully selected eggplant is not bitter and has a delightful texture, even without salting.

In my experience, you can avoid the bitterness problem by buying eggplant when it's in season. The best eggplant arrives in the market around midsummer. The earliest crops have fewer seeds and consequently better flavor and texture. Look for ones that are evenly firm and deep in color, with shiny, unwrinkled skin. When you press gently on the flesh, it should bounce back. If it leaves a dent, the eggplant is old. Try to shop at farmers' markets, where you have a better chance of getting recently harvested vegetables.

The biggest difficulty in storing eggplant is that it does best at about 50°F. Most refrigerators are set at 41°F or lower, which is too cold for this tropical vegetable. If you can, buy eggplant the day you plan to cook it. If this isn't possible, find a cool spot in the kitchen to store it.

High heat and just the right size slices are the secret to perfect grilling. Eggplant needs to be set on a hot grill—you should hear the

A simple side dish...

master recipe

Grilled Eggplant
Serves four to six as a side dish.

1 large globe eggplant (about 1 lb.), trimmed and cut into ½-inch-thick rounds
3 Tbs. extra-virgin olive oil; more as needed
Kosher salt

Prepare a medium-high charcoal or gas grill fire. Brush both sides of the eggplant slices with olive oil and season with salt. Grill (covered on a gas grill; uncovered on a charcoal grill) until golden-brown grill marks form, 3 to 4 minutes. Turn the eggplant and grill until tender and well marked on the second sides, 3 to 4 minutes more. The interior should be grayish and soft rather than white and hard. Serve warm or at room temperature, by itself or with one of the toppings on the next two pages.

oiled slice sizzle gently. If the grill isn't hot enough, the eggplant will dry out rather than develop a nice grilled surface. To get good grill marks, resist moving the eggplant around.

Eggplant contains a lot of water and shrinks considerably when grilled, so it's important to cut it into slices of the right thickness. If you slice the eggplant too thick, the outside will char while the inside remains hard and uncooked; too thin, and it will overcook by the time it has grill marks. I've found that ½-inch-thick slices work best to produce a nicely charred outside and a tender inside. Cut into a piece of eggplant if you're not sure it's tender all the way through—the cooked flesh will be grayish and soft rather than white and hard.

Another appealing thing about eggplant is that it can be grilled several hours in advance and served at room temperature. The toppings I've included here can also be prepared ahead, but hold off on adding ingredients like garlic and toasted pine nuts until the day you plan to serve. For the Toasted-Breadcrumb Salsa Verde, wait until just before serving to combine the ingredients so the breadcrumbs don't lose their crunch.

The key to perfection is cutting eggplant slices an even ½ inch thick. With slices this size, the insides will cook through and become soft in the time it takes to char the outsides.

...goes fancy with bright toppings

Olive, Orange & Anchovy Vinaigrette

Yields enough topping for one recipe of Grilled Eggplant.

This classic combination is delicious over eggplant or lamb—or both. If you're not a fan of anchovies, don't let that discourage you. The flavor mellows considerably when combined with the other ingredients.

2 anchovy fillets (preferably salt packed), rinsed
1 small clove garlic
Kosher salt
¼ cup black olives, such as Niçoise or Kalamata, rinsed well, pitted, and chopped finely
¼ cup extra-virgin olive oil
1 Tbs. fresh orange juice
2 Tbs. red-wine vinegar; more to taste
½ tsp. finely chopped orange zest (see p. 63)
Freshly ground black pepper

With a mortar and pestle, pound the anchovy, garlic, and a pinch of salt to a paste, or mince the anchovy and garlic, sprinkle with salt, and mash into a paste with the side of a chef's knife. Unless you're using a large mortar, transfer the mixture to a medium bowl. Whisk in the olives, olive oil, orange juice, vinegar, and orange zest. Season to taste with salt, pepper, and more red wine vinegar, if necessary.

Just before serving, whisk the vinaigrette again and spoon it over grilled eggplant—you may not need it all—or serve on the side.

Toasted-Breadcrumb Salsa Verde

Yields enough topping for one recipe of Grilled Eggplant.

The toasted breadcrumbs in this topping add a nice bit of texture to grilled eggplant, but the topping is also delicious on grilled meat or fish.

½ cup fine fresh breadcrumbs, preferably from a rustic French or Italian loaf
¼ cup plus ½ Tbs. extra-virgin olive oil; more as needed
1 small shallot, very finely diced
2½ tsp. red-wine vinegar; more to taste
Kosher salt
¼ cup chopped fresh flat-leaf parsley
1 Tbs. chopped fresh basil
1 Tbs. chopped fresh mint
½ Tbs. chopped fresh marjoram or oregano
½ Tbs. capers, rinsed well and coarsely chopped
1 anchovy fillet (preferably salt-packed), rinsed and finely chopped

Heat the oven to 375°F. Put the breadcrumbs in a pie plate or on a small rimmed baking sheet, drizzle ½ Tbs. of the olive oil on top, and mix well to evenly coat the crumbs. Spread the crumbs and toast in the oven, stirring occasionally, until very crisp and golden brown, about 12 minutes. Let cool.

Combine the shallot, vinegar, and a pinch of salt in a small bowl. Let sit for at least 10 minutes and up to 2 hours.

Combine the remaining ¼ cup oil with the herbs, capers, and anchovy in a medium bowl. Set aside until ready to serve.

Just before serving, combine the shallot mixture and the toasted breadcrumbs with the herb mixture. If the salsa seems too dry, add a bit more olive oil. Season to taste with more salt or vinegar, if necessary—it should have a nice acidic kick. Spoon the salsa verde on top of grilled eggplant slices or serve on the side.

Garlic-Cumin Vinaigrette with Feta & Herbs

Yields enough topping for one recipe of Grilled Eggplant.

This dish looks especially nice served on a platter, with the feta and herbs scattered over the eggplant.

1 small clove garlic
Kosher salt
1½ Tbs. fresh lemon juice
1 small shallot, very finely diced
3 Tbs. extra-virgin olive oil
½ tsp. cumin seed, lightly toasted and pounded in a mortar or ground in a spice grinder
Pinch cayenne; more to taste
¼ cup crumbled feta
2 Tbs. coarsely chopped fresh mint
2 Tbs. coarsely chopped fresh cilantro

With a mortar and pestle, pound the garlic and a pinch of salt to a paste, or mince the garlic, sprinkle with salt, and mash into a paste with the side of a chef's knife.

Combine the garlic paste and 1 Tbs. of the lemon juice in a small bowl and let sit for 10 minutes. Combine the shallot with the remaining ½ Tbs. lemon juice and a pinch of salt in another small bowl and let sit for 10 minutes. Whisk the olive oil, cumin, and cayenne into the garlic mixture. Season to taste with salt or cayenne, if necessary.

Top grilled eggplant slices with the shallots, feta, and herbs. Whisk the vinaigrette and drizzle it on top. Serve immediately.

Roasted Red Pepper Relish with Pine Nuts, Currants & Marjoram

Yields enough topping for one recipe of Grilled Eggplant.

In the summertime, my catering company often serves this relish on bruschetta with fresh ricotta cheese, but it's also delicious with grilled eggplant. Spoon any leftovers into a sandwich.

1 Tbs. dried currants
½ Tbs. red-wine vinegar
½ Tbs. balsamic vinegar
1 small clove garlic
Kosher salt
1 large red bell pepper
2 Tbs. pine nuts, lightly toasted and coarsely chopped
1½ Tbs. extra-virgin olive oil
1 Tbs. chopped fresh marjoram
Pinch cayenne; more to taste
3 Tbs. chopped fresh flat-leaf parsley (optional)

Combine the currants and both vinegars in a small bowl.

With a mortar and pestle, pound the garlic and a pinch of salt to a paste, or mince the garlic, sprinkle with salt, and mash into a paste with the side of a chef's knife.

Roast the pepper: Set the pepper directly on a gas burner, under a hot broiler, or on a hot charcoal or gas grill. Keep rotating the pepper until it's evenly charred all over. Transfer to a small bowl, cover tightly with plastic, and let cool.

When cool enough to handle, peel the pepper over the same bowl to catch any juice; discard the skin. Don't rinse the pepper—it's fine if a few charred bits remain. (It's helpful to rinse your fingers occasionally.) Still working over the bowl, split the pepper and remove the stem and as many of the seeds as possible. Set the juice aside. Cut the pepper into very small dice and put in a medium bowl. Strain the pepper juice over the pepper. Add the currants and vinegar, garlic paste, pine nuts, olive oil, marjoram, and cayenne and stir. Season to taste with salt and cayenne.

When ready to serve, stir the relish again and spoon it over grilled eggplant, or serve it on the side. Garnish with parsley, if using.

Tasha DeSerio, a frequent contributor to Fine Cooking, *is co-owner of Olive Green Catering in Berkeley, California.* ◆

Scallions: More Than a Garnish

These little green onions can be a side dish on their own or a starring ingredient in soups and stir-fries

BY TONY ROSENFELD

Full disclosure: I'm not on any scallion board, nor have I ever received an all-expense-paid trip to some sunny scallion paradise. I just happen to love all things scallion. Almost every time I go to the market, no matter what I'm making for dinner, I'll pick up a bunch or two. For one thing, they're cheap and always seem to be in good shape, regardless of the season. But best of all, I love their sweet, mild flavor and their amazing versatility. Sure, you can sprinkle thin scallion slices on soups, salads, or pastas just before serving for an extra hit of flavor and color, but there are so many more things you can do with these dainty green alliums.

You can slowly cook thinly sliced scallions alone or with other aromatics like onions and garlic to form a rich flavor base for all kinds of soups, stews, and braises. Or you can cut them into slightly bigger pieces (2 inches is perfect) and toss them over high heat with meat and other vegetables for an Asian stir-fry or a quick pasta sauce. And who says you can't serve whole scallions as a vegetable side dish? In fact, they're delicious grilled, roasted, and even braised. Whether on the grill or in the oven, they take less than 10 minutes to cook and make a fine counterpoint to grilled steak, roasted or braised chicken, and seared or braised fish fillets. Whichever method you choose, you'll see that scallions are so quick and easy to cook and so adaptable that you'll soon find yourself joining me as a member of the unofficial fan club.

Grill, roast, or braise whole as a side dish

Choose thick scallions that have more body if you plan to cook them whole.

More ideas: Serve grilled scallions with grilled chicken thighs rubbed with Mexican spices. Or roast scallions with some olive oil, salt, and pepper and serve alongside roasted chicken, roasted leg of lamb, or a pot roast. I also like to brown a bunch of trimmed scallions gently in a little butter before braising them in chicken broth and finishing them with grated Parmigiano, fresh thyme, and black pepper.

Grilled Flank Steak with Sesame Sauce & Grilled Scallions

Serves four.

1½ lb. flank steak
1½ tsp. kosher salt
½ tsp. freshly ground black pepper
¼ cup plus 1 Tbs. soy sauce
¼ cup canola oil; more for the grill
¼ cup minced fresh ginger
1½ Tbs. minced garlic
3 Tbs. rice vinegar
2 Tbs. Asian sesame oil
1½ Tbs. light or dark brown sugar
2 tsp. cornstarch
20 scallions (preferably thick ones),
    roots trimmed
1 Tbs. sesame seeds, toasted

Season the flank steak with 1 tsp. of the salt and the pepper. Mix 1 Tbs. of the soy sauce, 1 Tbs. of the canola oil, 2 Tbs. of the ginger, and 1 Tbs. of the garlic in a large zip-top plastic bag. Add the steak and turn and massage it in the bag to cover it with the marinade. Refrigerate for at least 4 hours or as long as overnight.

Heat 1½ Tbs. of the canola oil and the remaining 2 Tbs. ginger and ½ Tbs. garlic in a small saucepan over medium heat until the ginger and garlic sizzle steadily and just begin to brown around the edges, about 3 minutes. Add ⅓ cup water, the remaining ¼ cup soy sauce, and the rice vinegar, sesame oil, and brown sugar. Bring to a boil over medium-high heat. In a small bowl, whisk the cornstarch with 2 tsp. of water and stir it into the soy mixture. Cook until it returns to a boil and thickens slightly, about 1 minute. Remove from the heat and set aside.

Heat a gas grill to medium high or prepare a fire on a charcoal grill with a medium-hot and a low zone. Rinse the scallions but do not dry them. Toss the scallions with the remaining 1½ Tbs. canola oil and ½ tsp. salt.

Clean and oil the grill grates. Grill the steak (over the hotter zone if using charcoal), covered, until it has good grill marks, 5 to 6 minutes. Flip and reduce the heat to medium if using a gas grill or transfer the steak to the cooler part of the charcoal fire. Cook, covered, until the steak is done to your liking, 4 to 5 minutes for medium rare (cut into the steak to check). Transfer to a large cutting board, brush with about a third of the sesame sauce, and let rest for 5 to 10 minutes.

While the steak rests, clean and oil the grill grates, set the scallions on the grill (over the cooler zone if using charcoal), and cook until they have good grill marks, 2 to 4 minutes. Flip and cook until they're tender, 2 to 4 minutes. Transfer to a large platter and drizzle with a couple of table-spoons of the sesame sauce.

Slice the steak thinly and serve with the scallions, a drizzle of the remaining sesame sauce, and a sprinkling of sesame seeds.

Scallion basics

Buying: Choose scallions with full white bulbs and firm green tops. Avoid scallions with soggy or browned green parts—they're past their prime.

Trimming: Remove a couple of inches from the green tops, which often have a scraggly texture. Rinse scallions under cold running water and pull off any bruised or slimy green leaves. Cut off and discard the root end, or trim it if using whole scallions.

Storing: Wrap whole, trimmed scallions in a paper towel and put them in a zip-top bag in the refrigerator. They will keep for up to a week.

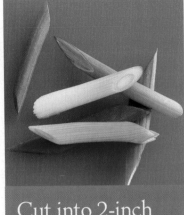

Cut into 2-inch pieces and stir-fry or sauté

For quick stir-frying and sautéing, you can use both white and green parts.

More ideas: Make a simple pasta sauce by sautéing scallions and mixing them with cream, Parmigiano, and plenty of black pepper. Or try a vegetarian stir-fry with scallions, thinly sliced zucchini, Japanese eggplant, and mushrooms. I also sear strips of skirt steak with green peppers, scallions, and a splash of Worcestershire sauce and stuff it all into a bulky roll along with some Swiss cheese.

Pork Lo Mein with Seared Scallions & Shiitakes

Serves three to four.

You can usually find Chinese noodles in the produce section of the supermarket.

¾ lb. boneless pork country-style ribs, cut into ¼-inch-wide strips
2½ Tbs. soy sauce; more to taste
2 Tbs. dry sherry
1 tsp. cornstarch
2 Tbs. plus 1 tsp. kosher salt
9 oz. fresh Chinese noodles
5 Tbs. canola or peanut oil
6 oz. scallions (14 to 16 medium), trimmed and cut into 2-inch pieces
3½ to 4 oz. shiitake mushrooms, stemmed, caps thinly sliced (2 cups)
1 Tbs. minced fresh ginger
2 medium cloves garlic, minced
¼ tsp. crushed red pepper flakes
3 cups thinly sliced napa cabbage (about 6 oz.)
2 cups mung bean sprouts, rinsed
2 tsp. Asian sesame oil

In a medium bowl, toss the pork with 1 Tbs. of the soy sauce, 1 Tbs. of the sherry, the cornstarch, and ¼ tsp. of the salt. Refrigerate for at least 15 minutes and up to 1 hour.

Bring 2 quarts of water to a boil in a large pot. Add 2 Tbs. of the salt and cook the noodles, stirring occasionally, until just tender, about 3 minutes. Drain in a colander and run under cold water until the noodles cool to about room temperature. Turn the noodles out onto a baking sheet lined with paper towels to dry.

Heat 1½ Tbs. of the oil in a 12-inch nonstick skillet over medium heat. Add the noodles and cook, tossing occasionally, until golden and slightly crisp, about 6 minutes. Meanwhile, replace the damp paper towels on the baking sheet with dry ones. When golden, transfer the noodles to the dry towels.

Heat 1½ Tbs. of the oil in the nonstick skillet over medium-high heat until shimmering hot. Add the pork and cook, tossing often, until browned and just cooked through, 2 to 3 minutes. Transfer to a plate or bowl. Pour the remaining 2 Tbs. oil into the skillet and then add the scallions, mushrooms, and ¼ tsp. of the salt. Cook, stirring occasionally, until browned, 3 to 4 minutes. Add the ginger, garlic, and pepper flakes and cook, stirring, until fragrant, 30 to 60 seconds. Add the cabbage, bean sprouts, and the remaining ½ tsp. salt. Cook, stirring often, until the cabbage just starts to soften, 1 to 2 minutes.

Add the noodles and pork to the pan and cook, stirring, until heated through, 1 to 2 minutes. Add the remaining 1½ Tbs. soy sauce, the remaining 1 Tbs. sherry, and the sesame oil and cook, tossing the ingredients, for 1 minute more. Serve immediately. Add more soy sauce to taste or pass the soy sauce at the table.

White or green: What's the difference?

Scallions' dark-green ends have a delicate sharpness reminiscent of chives and a light, crisp texture, but they wilt and discolor when cooked too long. The white parts have an oniony punch, and because their texture is more substantial, they withstand longer cooking times. In general, scallions cook pretty quickly when sautéed, grilled, roasted, or even braised, so you can use both the white and green parts. But when cooking them for a longer time (as an aromatic base for soups or stews, for example) it's best to use only the white and light-green parts.

Summer Corn Chowder with Scallions, Bacon & Potatoes

Yields about 5½ cups; serves six as a first course.

5 ears fresh corn
7 oz. scallions (about 20 medium)
3 slices bacon, cut into ½-inch pieces
1 Tbs. unsalted butter
1 jalapeño, cored, seeded, and finely diced
1 tsp. kosher salt; more to taste
Freshly ground black pepper
3½ cups low-salt chicken broth
1 large Yukon Gold potato (8 to 9 oz.), peeled and cut into ½-inch dice (about 1½ cups)
1½ tsp. chopped fresh thyme
2 Tbs. heavy cream

Husk the corn and cut off the kernels. Reserve two of the corn cobs and discard the others. Trim and thinly slice the scallions, keeping the dark-green parts separate from the white and light-green parts.

Cook the bacon in a 3- or 4-qt. saucepan over medium heat until browned and crisp, about 5 minutes. With a slotted spoon, transfer the bacon to a paper-towel-lined plate. Pour off and discard all but about 1 Tbs. of the bacon fat. Return the pan to medium heat and add the butter. When the butter is melted, add the white and light-green scallions and the jalapeño, salt, and a few grinds of black pepper. Cook, stirring, until the scallions are very soft, about 3 minutes.

Add the broth, corn, corn cobs, potatoes, and thyme and bring to a boil over medium-high heat. Reduce the heat to medium low and simmer until the potatoes are completely tender, about 15 minutes. Discard the corn cobs.

Transfer 1 cup of the broth and vegetables to a blender and purée. Return the purée to the pot and stir in the cream and all but ⅓ cup of the scallion greens. Simmer, stirring occasionally, for a couple of minutes to wilt the scallions and blend the flavors. Season to taste with salt and pepper and serve sprinkled with the bacon and reserved scallions.

Tony Rosenfeld is a contributing editor to Fine Cooking. ◆

Fresh from the Sea, A Thai Classic

Bright, tangy flavors and perfectly cooked seafood come together in this refreshing, summery salad

BY NANCIE MCDERMOTT

When I make the Thai seafood salad *yum talay,* I'm always amazed at how simple it is to gather Thailand's bright, inviting flavors into one gorgeous dish. For me, it's a quick virtual excursion to the seaside town of Hua Hin, where I first tasted this brilliant dish. I love its playful mix of flavors: the natural sweetness of fresh seafood, the breezy notes of cilantro and mint, and the sharp accent of lime juice against a little sizzle of chile heat.

In Thai cuisine, a *yum* is a hearty dish consisting mostly of meat, fish, or seafood, tossed just before serving with a simple mixture of fish sauce, fresh or dried chiles, lime juice, and herbs and often served atop a bed of salad greens. Unlike Thai curries, soups, chile sauces, and stir-fries, which are meant to be flavorful components of a rice-centered meal, a *yum* is a stand-alone dish, perfect for a light main course or even an appetizer. The word *yum* refers to the action of combining

an array of hot and tangy ingredients, and *talay* is the Thai word for ocean; thus, the mixed seafood version is called *yum talay*.

For this dish, the classic preparation is to cook the seafood just before dressing it, so that the salad is at room temperature when it's served. But if you want to cook the seafood ahead, you can chill it and take it out of the refrigerator 20 to 30 minutes before serving. Then dress the salad and sprinkle it with a handful of fresh cilantro and mint.

Thai Seafood Salad (*Yum Talay*)

Serves four as a light main course
or six as an appetizer.

This dish is easy to pull together, but it does require a little organization and prep. First cook the seafood, then make the dressing, and finally *yum* (or mix) the dressing and seafood right before serving—this is the key to keeping the vibrant flavors of this signature Thai dish distinct.

6 Tbs. fresh lime juice (from 2 limes)
4½ Tbs. fish sauce
1½ Tbs. granulated sugar
2 tsp. finely chopped unseeded fresh hot green chiles (like serrano or jalapeño)
2 tsp. finely chopped garlic (2 medium cloves)
3 Tbs. thinly sliced shallot (1 large)
⅓ cup thinly sliced scallions (4 to 5, white and green parts)
¼ cup coarsely chopped fresh cilantro
¼ cup coarsely chopped fresh mint
2 cups bite-size pieces of Boston lettuce, rinsed and spun dry (1 large head)
4 cups cooked seafood (see instructions at right)
½ cup sliced English cucumber (halve cucumber lengthwise and slice into ¼-inch-thick half-moons)
½ cup halved cherry or grape tomatoes

Make the dressing: In a medium-large bowl, combine the lime juice, fish sauce, sugar, chiles, and garlic. Stir to dissolve the sugar and combine everything well. Set aside, along with the shallots, scallions, cilantro, and mint for mixing just before serving.

Assemble the salad: Arrange the lettuce on a large serving platter or on individual serving plates as a bed for the seafood.

Transfer the cooked seafood to the bowl containing the lime-juice dressing. Add the shallots and use your hands or a wooden spoon to gently toss everything well. Add the scallions, cilantro, and mint and mix well again. Scoop the seafood onto the platter or serving plates with a slotted spoon. Toss the cucumber and tomato in the dressing remaining in the bowl and scatter around the seafood. Drizzle any remaining dressing from the bowl over the salad, especially over any lettuce not covered by the seafood. Serve immediately.

Wine Suggestion: Try a light, crisp, off-dry Riesling like the 2005 Mönchhof Estate Riesling, Mosel-Saar-Ruwer, $14, or the 2005 Selbach-Oster Riesling Kabinett, Mosel-Saar-Ruwer, $14.

whole mint

whole cilantro

coarsely chopped herbs

In some Thai dishes, like soups and curries, herb sprigs and leaves are often left whole. But for a yum, *the herbs are chopped coarsely at the last minute, so their flavor won't have time to fade.*

Cooked Seafood for Thai Salad

Yields about 4 cups.

You can find frozen cleaned squid in 1-lb. packages in the freezer section. Some markets have thawed cleaned squid on ice at the seafood counter.

24 small mussels
1 Tbs. table salt
¾ lb. medium (51 to 60 per lb.) fresh shrimp, peeled and deveined
½ lb. cleaned squid, bodies sliced crosswise into ¼-inch rings and tentacles cut in half if large
½ lb. sea scallops or bay scallops
¼ lb. fresh or pasteurized jumbo lump crabmeat

Scrub the mussels well under running water and pull off any "beards." Discard any mussels that don't close tightly when tapped on the counter. Put closed mussels in a medium saucepan. Add about ½ cup water, just enough to cover the bottom of the pan by about ¼ inch. Cover and set over high heat. Bring to a rolling boil and cook until the shells have opened, 1 to 2 minutes. Remove from the heat, transfer to a plate, and let stand until cool enough to handle. Discard any unopened ones. Remove the cooked mussels from their shells and put in a medium bowl; discard the shells and cooking liquid.

To cook the remaining seafood, bring a 3-qt. saucepan of water to a rolling boil over high heat. Add the salt and let the water return to a boil.

Pour the shrimp into the boiling water and cook until the largest one is pink on the outside, opaque on the inside, and just cooked through, about 2 minutes. The water may not return to the boil before they are done. Scoop them out with a slotted spoon and drop into the bowl with the mussels.

After the water returns to a rolling boil, add the squid and cook just until they become firm and the rings turn bright white, about 1 minute. Scoop them out and drop them into the bowl along with the shrimp and mussels.

When the water returns to a rolling boil, cook the scallops until just cooked through and no longer translucent inside, 1 to 2 minutes for bay scallops, 2 to 3 minutes for sea scallops. Scoop them out and drop into the bowl as well (if using sea scallops, you may want to halve or quarter them first).

Add the lump crabmeat chunks to the bowl of seafood. Set the seafood aside on the counter while you prepare the dressing and other ingredients for the salad. Or, if making more than 30 minutes ahead, cover and refrigerate for up to 4 hours. Let sit at room temperature for 20 to 30 minutes before dressing.

A former Peace Corps volunteer in Thailand, Nancie McDermott is a cooking teacher and cookbook author specializing in the cuisines of Southeast Asia. ◆

Peaches &Cream

BY CAROLE BLOOM

Ripe, juicy peaches and honey-sweetened whipped cream are all you need to create three quick summer desserts

When peaches are at their peak, it's hard to argue with fresh peach desserts. Oh, I love pies, cobblers, and crisps, but there's something about ripe, juicy peaches that calls for a simple preparation—and it doesn't get much simpler than peaches and cream. With a couple of twists, you can transform these two components into three delightful desserts.

First, focus on flavor. Instead of serving the peaches plain, I like to marinate them briefly in a flavorful syrup made of brown sugar and amaretto. The syrup boosts the peaches' flavor and juiciness without masking their inherent charms. And instead of sweetening the whipped cream with plain old sugar, try honey; it's a minor substitution that always makes a big impact, not only

because it's surprising but also because the floral notes of honey harmonize wonderfully with the flavor of the peaches.

Then think about presentation. Once you've got marinated peaches and honey whipped cream on hand, there are several ways to serve them. The most straight-forward option is to spoon peach slices into a dish and top them with a dollop of fluffy

Photos: Scott Phillips

Peaches & Cream Dessert
Serves four.

This simple dessert is the perfect ending to a backyard summer meal.

1 recipe Marinated Peaches (at far right)
½ recipe Honey Whipped Cream (at right)

Reserve four peach slices and divide the rest among four small serving bowls or custard cups. Top each with a large spoonful (about ⅓ cup) of the honey whipped cream. Garnish each with a reserved peach slice and serve immediately.

whipped cream—always delicious, and there's nothing to it. But when the occasion calls for something a little more elaborate, you can sandwich the peaches and cream between tender shortcake biscuits (I've provided a recipe on p. 61) or layer them with cookie crumbs in a pretty glass to make a parfait. Neither option is difficult, and the results are that much more impressive.

Honey Whipped Cream
Yields about 3 cups.

I prefer a delicately flavored honey, such as orange blossom or clover, for this recipe because I don't want the whipped cream to outshine the peaches. If making a half recipe, use a hand-held mixer.

1½ cups cold heavy cream
5 Tbs. honey

Pour the heavy cream into the chilled bowl of an electric stand mixer or into a large chilled mixing bowl. Use the wire whisk attachment on the stand mixer or a hand-held mixer to whip the cream on medium speed until it begins to thicken slightly.

Turn the mixer off and add the honey. If necessary, scrape down the sides of the mixing bowl to push the honey into the cream. Whip the cream on medium-high speed until it holds soft peaks. Use right away.

Marinated Peaches
Yields about 2 cups.

The deep flavor of brown sugar in this syrup is the perfect complement to fresh peaches. You can make the syrup a couple of weeks ahead and refrigerate it, tightly covered. Don't add the peaches too far ahead, though, as they will turn brown after a couple of hours in the marinade.

½ cup firmly packed light brown sugar
1 Tbs. amaretto
4 large ripe peaches (about 1½ lb.)

Combine the sugar and ¼ cup water in a small heavy-based saucepan and bring to a boil over medium-high heat. Remove from the heat and let the sugar syrup cool. Stir in the amaretto.

Bring a large saucepan of water to a boil. Fill a large bowl with ice water. Using a small, sharp knife, cut a small X in the pointed end of each peach. Plunge the peaches into the boiling water for 1 minute. With a slotted spoon, remove the peaches from the water and put them into the bowl of ice water to stop the cooking. When the peaches are cool enough to handle, use a small sharp knife to gently peel the skin off the peaches, starting at the X. If the skins don't peel off easily, return the peaches to the boiling water for another 30 to 60 seconds.

Halve the peaches lengthwise and remove the pits. Slice each half lengthwise into ½-inch-thick slices and put them in a medium bowl. Pour the amaretto sugar syrup over the peaches and stir gently to coat completely. Cover the bowl tightly with plastic wrap and let the peaches marinate in the refrigerator for at least 30 minutes and up to 2 hours before using.

EASY FLAVOR VARIATIONS:
Instead of the amaretto, stir peach schnapps, Grand Marnier, Cointreau, or a dessert wine, such as Muscat (Moscato), Muscat Canelli, or Sauternes into the brown-sugar syrup.

For deeper flavor, replace the light brown sugar with dark brown.

For lighter flavor, replace the light brown sugar with granulated.

Peaches & Cream Parfait

Serves four.

This dessert looks pretty served in stemmed goblets, tall water glasses, or martini glasses that hold 1¼ to 1⅓ cups.

1 recipe Honey Whipped Cream (p. 59)

1 almond biscotti or 2 amaretti cookies, crushed in a food processor or by hand

1 recipe Marinated Peaches (p. 59)

Use a large spoon or a pastry bag fitted with a large open tip to fill each goblet or glass about a quarter full with the honey whipped cream. Sprinkle a little of the biscotti or amaretti crumbs evenly over the whipped cream. Top with a scant ¼ cup of the marinated peaches. Repeat. Garnish with a dollop of cream and a sprinkle of any remaining crumbs. Serve immediately.

Peaches & Cream Shortcakes

Serves eight.

1 recipe Cream Shortcake Biscuits (at right)
1 recipe Marinated Peaches (p. 59)
1 recipe Honey Whipped Cream (p. 59)

Using a serrated knife, slice each biscuit in half horizontally. Set the bottom half on an individual serving plate and spoon about one-eighth of the marinated peaches, a scant ¼ cup, over the biscuit. Cover the peaches with a generous spoonful of whipped cream. Put the top of the biscuit on the cream. Drop a small dollop of whipped cream on the biscuit top, if you wish. Repeat with the remaining biscuits. If you have any peach slices left, arrange them around the plates. Serve immediately.

Cream Shortcake Biscuits

Yields eight 2¾-inch round biscuits.

These buttery biscuits are the perfect platform for peaches and cream. Sprinkling the tops of the shortcake biscuits with demerara sugar before baking gives them a nice crunchy texture.

9 oz. (2 cups) unbleached all-purpose flour; more for rolling and cutting the biscuits
2 Tbs. light brown sugar
2½ tsp. baking powder
¼ tsp. table salt
¼ tsp. ground nutmeg, preferably freshly grated
3 oz. (6 Tbs.) unsalted butter, chilled in the freezer for 15 minutes
1 cup plus 1 tsp. heavy whipping cream
1 Tbs. demerara sugar

Position a rack in the center of the oven and heat the oven to 400°F. Line a baking sheet with parchment or a nonstick liner.

Put the flour, brown sugar, baking powder, salt, and nutmeg in a food processor fitted with a steel blade. Pulse briefly to blend.

Cut the butter into small pieces and add to the food processor. Pulse until the butter is cut into pieces the size of large breadcrumbs, 6 to 8 pulses.

With the food processor running, immediately pour 1 cup of the cream through the feed tube and process just until the ingredients are moistened.

Turn the mixture out onto a lightly floured work surface and knead a few times just until smooth. Pat the dough into a ¾-inch-thick circle or rectangle. Dip a 2¾-inch round plain-edge biscuit cutter in flour and then cut straight down through the dough to form the biscuits. (Dip the cutter in flour before cutting each biscuit and don't twist the cutter, because it will seal the edges and keep the shortcakes from rising as they bake.)

Transfer the shortcakes to the lined baking sheet, leaving at least an inch between them. Gather the scraps together, knead briefly to smooth the dough, and shape into a ¾-inch-thick circle or rectangle. Cut out more shortcakes. Repeat as often as necessary to use most of the dough (there will be a little left over).

With a pastry brush, lightly coat the tops of the biscuits with the remaining 1 tsp. cream and then lightly sprinkle them with demerara sugar.

Bake until the bottoms are slightly golden, 14 to 16 minutes. Remove the baking sheet from the oven and let the biscuits cool completely on a rack before serving.

Cookbook author Carole Bloom's latest book is The Essential Baker: The Comprehensive Guide to Baking with Chocolate, Fruit, Nuts, Spices, and Other Ingredients. ◆

Choose fragrant peaches and use them fast

My motto when choosing peaches is simple: If they smell good, they'll taste good. I like to buy peaches at my local farmers' market, but you can find good ones in many grocery stores as well. Look for unblemished peaches that aren't too soft. When you have perfectly ripe peaches, enjoy them within a couple of days. Don't wash them until you're ready to use them or they're likely to develop mold.

Occasionally, imperfect peaches may be all that's available. If they're underripe, you can ripen them by simply leaving them out on the counter and turning them daily so they're evenly exposed to light and air. And if they're not quite as fragrant and juicy as you'd like, they'll still be fine to use for these desserts because the marinade will enhance their flavor.

Coarsely vs. finely chopped herbs

When it comes to chopped herbs, one size doesn't fit all

Coarsely chopped herbs are good for garnishing and mixing into salsas and cold salads. The leaves are chopped just enough to break them into smaller pieces and release their flavor but still large enough that some pieces have intact edges, so they're identifiable by sight rather than being anonymous chopped green bits.

Finely chopped herbs are usually best for mixing into dishes in which the flavor of the herb is more important than its appearance. Though by no means a firm rule, fresh herbs are generally added near the end of cooking, giving them enough time to infuse a dish but not so long as to overcook and muddy their flavor nuances.

Chopped herbs	62
Buying fresh corn	62
Citrus zest: julienned & chopped	63
Aged Gouda	63
Canadian bacon	63
Canning pickles	64
Malted milk	66
Leftovers: eggplant & pasta	67
Using up pickled peppers	67

BY JENNIFER ARMENTROUT

Tips for chopping herbs

Choose your sharpest knife. This is crucial. A dull knife mashes and bruises; a sharp knife cuts cleanly.

Use a rocking-chopping motion by adding wrist action as you chop, rocking the knife back and forth in a slight slicing motion each time the knife comes down on the board. This motion cuts the herbs more cleanly, so the flavor stays in the herbs rather than leaking out onto the board (which happens with a dull knife and a straight up-and-down chopping motion).

Chop herbs just before using for the freshest flavor—if possible, that is. Sometimes you have to work ahead, and in these cases, chopped herbs (covered and stored in the fridge) will stay reasonably fresh tasting for several hours. Just try to avoid chopping them any sooner than necessary.

Don't husk corn until it's time to cook it

When I see people at a farmstand or grocery store husking corn before they buy it, I always have to butt in and ask if they know that what they're doing is akin to peeling bananas before buying them. The husks protect the ears of corn within, keeping them fresh and moist. Most people tell me they're husking the corn to make sure it's worm-free and fully developed, but there are ways to find good ears without husking:

Choose ears that are snugly wrapped in their husks, which should appear fresh, green, and moist. It's all right if the tassel seems a little dry at its end, but it should feel fresh around the tip of the ear.

Run your fingers along the ear, feeling the formation of the kernels through the husks. They should feel plump and densely packed in even rows. You can feel if the kernels are immature.

Look for worm holes. If you see one, move on to another ear. If you find a worm after husking the corn, it's not a big deal. Just cut it out.

Eat the corn ASAP. As sweet corn ages, its sugar turns to starch—hence the adage to have the pot of water boiling before you pick the corn. Today's varieties have been bred to slow down the sugar-to-starch conversion, but still, the sooner you eat it, the better it'll taste. Refrigeration delays the conversion, so if you must store corn, wrap unhusked ears in damp paper towels and keep them in a plastic bag in your fridge's produce bin for two to three days.

How to julienne or chop citrus zest

Most of the time, our recipes call for finely grated citrus zest, and the tool of choice for that is the ever-handy rasp-style grater, like the Microplane. But occasionally, we want the zest to be in slightly larger pieces, usually either chopped—as in the Olive, Orange & Anchovy Vinaigrette on p. 50—or in julienne strips. In either case, the tools you'll need are a vegetable peeler, a paring knife, and a chef's knife.

1 *Using light pressure, remove the zest in long strips, leaving behind as much of the bitter white pith as possible.*

2 *If there are any patches of pith on the zest, shave them off with a paring knife.*

3 *Stack or shingle two or three strips of zest and thinly slice them lengthwise with a sharp chef's knife to make julienne strips. If chopped zest is your goal, thinly slice the julienne strips crosswise.*

A more mature Gouda

A sampling of aged Goudas:
1. *Old Amsterdam (1 year)*
2. *Prima Donna Extra Aged (14 months)*
3. *Beemster Classic (2 years)*
4. *Roomano (4 years)*
5. *Roomano (5 years)*

You're probably familiar with Dutch Gouda cheese. Usually encased in red or yellow wax and aged for one to six months, young Gouda is mellow, slightly creamy, and often not very interesting. But with one to six years of aging, this mild-mannered juvenile matures into a sophisticated and complex cheese that's worth seeking out.

One- to two-year-old Gouda is somewhat firm and light honey in color. It has a slightly creamy texture that's often accented with a charming little crunch from small white amino acid clusters, and its tangy flavor has nutty caramel notes. Brands to look for are Old Amsterdam, Prima Donna, and Beemster. These cheeses are wonderful with nuts and autumn fruits, as in the recipe for Arugula Salad with Pears, Prosciutto & Aged Gouda on p. 78a.

With a few more years, Gouda becomes firm and flaky, with a dark caramel color. It has intense toffee, butterscotch, and sherry undertones with a more pronounced crunch. Look for Roomano brand (sometimes called Pradera). A little of this cheese goes a long way; enjoy a few bites with your favorite robust red or crisp fruity white wine.

Happily, we've noticed aged Goudas appearing much more frequently in supermarket cheese cases, but if there's none yet to be found in your area, see p. 72 for mail-order sources.

—Allison Ehri, test kitchen associate

What is Canadian bacon?

If you've ever eaten eggs Benedict or an Egg McMuffin, then you've had Canadian bacon. More like ham than bacon, Canadian bacon is a cured, lightly smoked pork loin. It's much leaner than regular bacon, so it's a good option for adding a slightly smoky, meaty flavor to dishes like the corn sauté on our back cover without adding a lot of extra fat. Look for it in the grocery store meat section near other smoked pork products like ham hocks and sausages. It's often sold sliced and shingled out in a vacuum-sealed package. Because it's cured and smoked, it can be eaten without further cooking, but it's better if it's heated first by sautéing, grilling, or baking.

Pack a pint (or three) of pickles

Whether you're a home gardener or a farmers' market regular, 'tis the season for pickling and canning. For the impatient pickle fan, the two recipes here can be made as quick (refrigerator) pickles, or they may be canned for longer shelf storage. The quick pickles will be crisper, but their flavor won't be as intense.

Pickled Cauliflower with Carrots & Red Bell Pepper

Yields about 3 pints.

Serve these pickles as part of an appetizer spread with fresh tomatoes, olives, flatbread, and hummus or baba ghanoush. They're also tasty alongside grilled meats.

1 tsp. coriander seeds
1 tsp. black or brown mustard seeds (or substitute yellow)
½ tsp. cumin seeds
2 cups cider vinegar
5 medium cloves garlic, lightly crushed and peeled
Three ¼-inch-thick slices peeled fresh ginger
One-half small yellow onion, thinly sliced lengthwise
½ cup sugar
2 Tbs. kosher salt
1 tsp. black peppercorns
½ tsp. ground turmeric
¼ tsp. crushed red pepper flakes
One-half head cauliflower, cut into 1½- to 2-inch florets (about 4 cups)
5 medium carrots, peeled and sliced ½ inch thick on the diagonal (about 2 cups)
One-half red bell pepper, cut into large dice (about 1 cup)

Put the coriander, mustard, and cumin seeds in a small saucepan. Toast the spices over medium heat, swirling the pan occasionally, until fragrant and slightly darkened, about 2 minutes. Add the vinegar, garlic, ginger, onion, sugar, salt, peppercorns, turmeric, red pepper flakes, and 1 cup water to the toasted spices. Bring to a boil.

If quick pickling, pack the cauliflower, carrots, and bell pepper in a 2-qt. heat-resistant glass bowl or measuring cup. Pour the hot brine over the vegetables. Let cool to room temperature and then cover and refrigerate for at least 2 and up to 14 days.

If canning, pack the vegetables into clean, hot pint jars. Pour the hot brine over the vegetables, leaving ½-inch headspace. If you have extra brine, strain it and distribute the solids among the jars. Process for 10 minutes as described below. Store the pickles for at least 2 but preferably 7 days (or longer) before opening. Refrigerate after opening.

—Allison Ehri

Canning basics—keep the jars hot & pack them tight

Whether you're using our pickle recipes or one of your own favorites, follow these guidelines for safe canning.

1. Wash the jars and screw bands with hot, soapy water and rinse them well. Follow the manufacturer's directions for preparing the lids. The jars must be hot when you pack them; otherwise, the hot brine may cause them to shatter.

2. Pack the jars tightly, and then pour in the hot brine to cover the vegetables, allowing the specified amount of headspace (the space between the rim of the jar and its contents).

3. Remove air bubbles by slowly raising and lowering a chopstick or a plastic blade around the inside of the jars. This is crucial: A trapped air bubble may shatter a jar as it heats. Add more brine to cover the vegetables, if necessary.

4. Wipe the jars' rims with a damp cloth before putting on the lids. Secure the lids with screw bands tightened by hand into place.

5. Set the jars on a rack in a canner or pot that's half-filled with very hot water

(but not boiling, which may cause the jars to break). Add more hot water, if necessary, to cover the jars with 2 inches of water. Cover the pot, turn the heat on high, and bring the water to a boil. When it starts to boil (you'll have to peek), begin timing—see your recipe for processing time.

6. Remove the jars immediately when the time is up. Let them cool undisturbed for at least 12 hours. Never tighten the bands after the jars have been processed, as this could break the seal.

7. Test the seals. After the jars have cooled, gently remove the screw bands and test the seals by lifting the jar by its lid. (Do this over a towel to catch the jar if it hasn't sealed properly.)

8. Store sealed jars in a cool, dry place. Unsealed jars should be stored in the refrigerator and used quickly.

—Adapted from "Pickles by the Pint" by Andrea Chesman, originally published in Fine Cooking #16

Spiced Pickled Beets

Yields about 3 pints.

Believe it or not, sliced pickled beets are great on a hamburger. In fact, in Australia pickled beets and even a fried egg are often served atop a burger. But if a beet burger isn't your thing, they're also nice in salads or sautéed in butter as a side dish.

8 to 9 medium-small beets, trimmed and scrubbed (about 2¼ lb.)
2 Tbs. olive or canola oil
1½ cups red-wine vinegar
One-half small red onion, thinly sliced lengthwise
⅓ cup light brown sugar
2 Tbs. kosher salt
1 tsp. yellow mustard seeds
1 tsp. fennel seeds
1 tsp. black peppercorns
½ tsp. whole allspice

Heat the oven to 400°F. Put the beets in a glass baking dish (8x8-inch works well). Drizzle them with the oil and 2 Tbs. water. Seal the pan tightly with aluminum foil and roast the beets until just soft enough to pierce with a fork, 50 to 55 minutes. Transfer the beets to a cutting board. When cool enough to touch, rub off their skins with paper towels and quarter them lengthwise (or cut them into sixths if they seem large).

Put the remaining ingredients and ¾ cup water in a small saucepan. Bring to a boil.

If quick pickling, pack the beets in a 2-qt. heat-resistant glass bowl or measuring cup. Pour the hot brine over the beets. Let cool to room temperature and then cover and refrigerate for at least 2 and up to 14 days.

If canning, pack the beets into clean, hot pint jars. Pour the hot brine over the beets, leaving ½-inch headspace. If you have extra brine, strain it and distribute the solids among the jars. Process for 10 minutes as described at left. Store the pickles for at least 2 but preferably 7 days (or longer) before opening. Refrigerate after opening.

—Allison Ehri

Make it a malted

If you grew up in the days of the soda fountain, then you already know about malteds. For the uninitiated, a malted (or a malt) is a milk shake flavored with malted milk powder —a blend of dried milk, wheat flour, and barley malt (and sometimes sugar and other flavors depending on the brand). Barley malt, which is best known as a baking and beer brewing ingredient, is made from barley that's been germinated and roasted, causing a number of chemical and physical changes that create a distinctive sweet, "malty" flavor.

To turn a milk shake into a malted, simply add malted milk powder once the shake is nearly blended—1 tablespoon per shake is a good starting point, but you can use any amount you like. Not only does malted milk lend its unique flavor to the shake, but it also enriches and amplifies the shake's base flavor.

You can also sprinkle malted milk directly onto ice cream. The texture will be a little gritty, but it'll still taste delicious. In fact, some ice cream shops top sundaes with lots of malted milk powder and give them great names like Dusty Road or Sawdust Sundae.

Look for malted milk powder in the grocery store near the cocoa and other flavored milk mixes, or see Where to Buy It, p. 72, for a mail-order source.

Double-Chocolate Malted Milk Shake

Serves one or two.

When our chocolate ice cream Tasting Panel (p. 70) left with us with a freezer full of ice cream, we knew just what to do: make malteds. For the thickest shakes, use a dense, premium brand of ice cream, like Ben & Jerry's (our Tasting Panel winner). And if you'd rather have just a chocolate milk shake, skip the malt powder at the end.

⅓ to ½ cup very cold whole milk; more as needed

3 scoops chocolate ice cream (about 2 oz. each), slightly softened; more as needed

1 Tbs. chocolate syrup, such as Hershey's Special Dark

1 Tbs. plain malted milk powder; more to taste

Pour the milk into the mixing cup of a milk shake mixer or hand blender or into the jar of a regular blender. Add the ice cream and chocolate syrup. Blend on high speed until smooth. The blending time depends on the machine and the temperature of the ingredients. If necessary, add more milk or ice cream to adjust to your preferred consistency. When the shake is just about smooth, briefly blend in the malted milk powder. Serve immediately in a chilled glass.

Do you need a milk shake mixer?

There's a downside to milk shakes made in a regular blender: They're usually thin and lumpy, and heat from the blender's motor can build up and melt the shake if you blend too long. Milk shake mixers address both these issues. A blending disk (or disks) at the end of a long shaft both mixes and aerates, so the shake becomes thick and smooth. And the motor is far from the blending cup, so heat isn't a problem.

We took a few milk shake mixer models for a test drive. All performed well enough, but we liked the 100-watt, 2-speed Oster Classic milk shake mixer for its modern design, relatively quiet motor, double blending disk, and safety sensor, which stops the machine if the cup is removed.

So do you need one? If milk shakes are only an occasional treat in your house, then stick with a regular blender or better yet, an immersion (hand) blender. But if you dream of whipping up luscious, thick shakes at home, then yes, you need one. The Oster costs about $50. See Where to Buy It, p. 72, for a mail-order source.

Grilled eggplant & pasta are made for each other

Grilled eggplant is extremely versatile, especially in a pasta salad. If you have some eggplant leftover from the "Dressing Up Grilled Eggplant" article on p. 48, try making a custom pasta salad with it and your choice of ingredients (see below). Follow our quantity guidelines for a nicely balanced salad.

Create-Your-Own Pasta Salad with Grilled Eggplant

Serves four to six as a side dish.

If you have leftover Garlic-Cumin Vinaigrette (p. 51) or Olive, Orange & Anchovy Vinaigrette (p. 50), you can use that instead of the Basic Vinaigrette.

½ lb. penne, cellentani, or rotini pasta, cooked al dente
1½ cups diced leftover Grilled Eggplant (from p. 49)
1 recipe Basic Vinaigrette (at far right)
Additional flavorings (at right)

Combine the pasta and eggplant in a large bowl. Add the vinaigrette and your choices from the additional flavor groups at right and toss. Adjust the salt, pepper, and lemon or vinegar to taste. Serve warm or at room temperature.

Additional flavor choices:

Vegetables:
½ to ¾ cup small-diced or chopped raw vegetables
Bell pepper (any color)
Tomato
Sweet onion

1 or 2 powerful flavors:
1 to 3 anchovy filets, finely chopped
1 to 2 Tbs. capers, rinsed
⅓ cup pitted black or green olives (such as Kalamata or Manzanilla), quartered lengthwise
1 to 2 Tbs. seeded and chopped jarred pepperoncini or hot cherry peppers

Mild herbs:
¼ cup chopped
Basil   **Parsley**
Mint   **Chives**

Potent herbs:
2 tsp. finely chopped
Marjoram   **Rosemary**
Thyme   **Oregano**

Cheese:
½ cup
Finely grated Parmigiano-Reggiano or Romano
Crumbled feta
Crumbled fresh or aged goat cheese
Diced fresh mozzarella

—*Allison Ehri*

Basic Vinaigrette
Yields 5 to 6 Tbs.

¼ cup extra-virgin olive oil
2 Tbs. minced shallot or 1 small clove garlic, mashed to a paste with a pinch of kosher salt
1 Tbs. fresh lemon juice, balsamic vinegar, or red-wine vinegar; more to taste
Pinch kosher salt; more to taste
Pinch freshly ground black pepper or crushed red pepper flakes; more to taste

Whisk all the ingredients together in small bowl.

Tasty ways to use up pickled peppers

If you have a jar of pickled peppers lurking in the back of your fridge—leftover perhaps from a recipe that called for using just one or two peppers—it's time to dig it out and use it up. Here are some mix-and-match ideas for adding pizzazz to your cooking with pickled peppers.

Jalapeños are great with beans and Mexican flavors—toss them in a bean salad or stir them into chili. The acid also adds a nice balance to mango salsa.

Stuff **sweet or hot cherry peppers** with little prosciutto-wrapped fresh mozzarella balls (bocconcini) for an hors d'oeuvre.

Pepperoncini go well with sweet vegetables like carrots, corn, roasted red bell peppers, and tomatoes. Add them to sautés and salads made with these ingredients, or try the Angel Hair Pasta with Sautéed Cherry Tomatoes, Lemon & Tuna on p. 78a.

Banana peppers are a nice mild alternative to pepperoncini. We like to use them on sandwiches in place of pickles.

Mixed together, sliced pickled peppers make a beautiful and zesty topping for nachos and pizza. Seed and chop them to spice up mayo for a sandwich, especially tuna salad. Chopped peppers are also great sprinkled over grilled or smoked fatty fish like bluefish or mackerel. Sautéed greens love their spicy, acidic kick, too. Or mix them into the grilled eggplant pasta salad above. —*Allison Ehri* ◆

The Art of Grilling, Demystified

BY SARAH JAY

Die-hard grilling fanatics like to say we have an inborn need to cook over fire, that it connects us to our ancestral past. But if the act of grilling is so instinctive, why does it raise so many questions? Lid up or down? Charcoal or gas? Direct or indirect heat? Not to worry. Here we explain the science of grilling—what's really going on when you light the coals or turn on the gas—so we can all become natural-born grillers.

When & why should you use direct or indirect heat?

To some degree, your success as a griller hinges on your ability to use direct and indirect heat appropriately. Direct grilling means the food is set right over the fire. Indirect grilling means the food is set to the side of the fire, not directly over it.

To understand when and why you should use each method, it helps to think about the different types of heat transfer occurring in a grill. First, there's the very intense radiant heat emanating from the coals or gas flames. Second, the hot grill grates deliver heat by conduction. And finally, there's convection, which is the hot air circulating around the food when the lid is down.

Direct grilling uses intense radiant heat

When your food is right above the fire, the strong heat energy radiating off the coals or burners is doing most of the cooking. This type of heat is very effective at searing a steak, charring red peppers, and producing all the delicious caramelized flavors that come from high-heat cooking. Conduction also plays a role, as the blazing hot grates are what form those nice grill marks.

The trouble with direct grilling is that it's all too easy to burn the outside of your food before the inside is fully cooked. (If you've ever tried to grill, say, a large roast or even large pieces of bone-in chicken directly over a hot fire, you've experienced this.) Think of direct grilling in the same context as broiling or even sautéing: The proximity to the heat is perfect for browning meat, and it's also ideal for cooking thin, tender items like shrimp or boneless chicken breasts. Or follow the advice of Jamie Purviance, the author of *Weber's Real Grilling:* Use direct heat for anything that will cook through in less than 20 minutes: hamburgers, thinner chops, pork tenderloin, and most vegetables.

Indirect grilling relies on convection

There are a few ways to set up a grill for indirect cooking, but in all cases, your food goes over an area of the grate without fire beneath it. When you close the lid and open the vents, cool air is sucked into the grill, forcing the hot air inside to circulate. This movement of hot air cooks the food more quickly and evenly. In effect, you've turned your grill into a convection oven, with the air vents acting as the fan.

Indirect grilling is the way to go for large, tough, or fatty meats like whole chicken, spare ribs, pork shoulder, or anything that would likely burn before it cooked through over direct heat. Fattier meats have fewer flare-ups when grilled indirectly; since the fat isn't dripping onto flames, it won't ignite.

Of course, you can combine both methods for the best of both worlds. For example, you could start a very thick pork chop over the fire to develop grill marks and a nicely browned crust and then slide it over an area with no heat to finish grilling indirectly, taking advantage of the milder, more even heat of convection.

Why do foods stick to the grill?

You can blame the proteins in meat or fish for your troubles with sticking. When proteins are heated, they first unfold into long strands and then they start to coil up again into new, tighter forms (a process called coagulation). Initially, these unfolded strands of proteins will bond with the metal grates. But as they continue to coagulate, the proteins interact and bond more with themselves than with the grill grate. That's the moment you're waiting for, because at that point, they'll more or less naturally release from the grill. So the bottom line is that beef, chicken, pork, and fish will always be prone to some sticking, but if you can resist the urge to flip or move them too soon, you'll get a cleaner release.

Also, be sure the grates are hot and clean, and don't be shy about oiling the food. Hot grates are key because the heat seals up microscopic pores in the metal, where proteins would otherwise have a chance to bond. Cleaning the grates with a brush removes any cooked-on protein residue, which can also exacerbate sticking. And coating the food with oil inhibits sticking because oil acts as a lubricant (you can oil the grates if you want, but it's more efficient to coat the food).

Sugary sauces can also cause sticking due to the sugars caramelizing and bonding to the metal grates. If you're basting with a sweet sauce, try brushing it on toward the end of cooking to minimize the problem.

Is there a flavor difference between charcoal & gas?

A provocative question, and one that elicits passionate responses from both sides of the grill patio. You might assume that charcoal infuses food with lots of wood-smoke flavor—after all, charcoal is manufactured from wood. But it's not exactly true. Charcoal does produce a good deal of smoke when it's igniting, but by the time the coals have reached grilling temperatures, the smoke has subsided considerably, if not completely. So perhaps you'll get a hint of woodsy flavor in your food, but unless you toss in some wood chips (which you can also do on a gas grill), it's not likely to be dramatic.

Also, both the degree and quality of smoke can vary widely among types and brands of charcoal. For example, lump hardwood charcoal (made solely from charred wood) and compressed charcoal briquettes (which consist of wood powder, coal, and starch) produce different types of smoky flavors.

So what's actually producing that quintessential flavor that most of us associate with grilled food? It isn't wood smoke. In large part, it's the result of fats and juices dripping onto coals or metal bars, which transforms them into tiny particles that waft back up and coat the food. And you can get that delicious flavor from both charcoal and gas.

> For a little more smoky flavor from your charcoal grill, spread the coals in an even layer but light them only on one side. The fire will spread as you're cooking, igniting new coals and continually producing smoke.

Should you grill with the lid up or down?

When you're using indirect heat, the grill must be covered to create the convective atmosphere, as explained at far left.

When direct grilling, you can have the lid open or closed, but grilling pros seem to prefer to keep it closed. The main advantage is that food cooks more quickly and evenly since it's receiving both radiant and convective heat. "The more you lift the lid, the longer it takes to cook," says Elizabeth Karmel, a grilling guru and author of *Taming the Flame*. More reasons to keep the lid on: You'll get fewer flare-ups since there is less air available to fuel them, you'll trap more smoke (if you're using wood chips), and you might even get deeper grill marks since the grates will be a bit hotter.

Sarah Jay, the former executive editor of Fine Cooking, is a contributing editor. ◆

Chocolate Ice Cream

BY LAURA GIANNATEMPO

We've sipped vinegar from the bottle, sampled mayos straight from the jar, and chowed down sauceless whole-wheat pastas. So for this issue's Tasting Panel, we decided to reward ourselves with something sweet—chocolate ice cream. It's summer after all, and chocolate ice cream is a great thing to have in the freezer to make milk shakes (see the recipe in From Our Test Kitchen, p. 62) or ice cream sandwiches, or just to savor on its own.

But with all the brands available, which are worth stashing? To find out, we asked 12 *Fine Cooking* staffers to participate in a blind tasting of five widely available brands of chocolate ice cream. While flavors varied, when it came to texture, the ice creams clearly fell into two categories: creamy and dense or light and airy, depending on how much air was pumped into them during churning (more air makes fluffier ice cream). What was less clear was which style our tasters preferred. Some were partial to the denser ice creams, while others liked the airier ones better. That's why both are in the top three. Read on for a rundown of the results.

Top Pick
BEN & JERRY'S
$4.19 (16 oz.)

This ice cream got high scores for its perfectly smooth, dense, creamy texture ("reminds me of gelato," wrote one taster) and its intensely rich, well-balanced bitter-sweet chocolate flavor.

Runners-up
Ice creams are numbered in order of preference; prices will vary.

1 CIAO BELLA
$4.99 (16 oz.)

"Now we're talking," said one panelist about this dark and creamy ice cream. (It's called gelato, but its ingredients are similar to those in the other ice creams we sampled. See the sidebar opposite.) Tasters liked its smooth, rich mouth-feel as well as its bittersweet flavor with hints of nuts, although a few noticed a slightly acidic note.

2 EDY'S GRAND
$5.79 (1.79 qt.)

While definitely in the light and airy category, this ice cream (called Edy's on the East Coast and Dreyer's west of the Rockies) was not overly puffed up. Most tasters praised its deep chocolate flavor with cinnamon undertones and lingering bittersweet notes. A few thought it was a little too sweet and slightly sticky.

3 BREYERS
$5.99 (1.75 qt.)

This soft, airy ice cream had a decent chocolate flavor, but several panelists found it wanting in richness. Its slightly grainy and unappealingly icy texture also disappointed many.

4 HÄAGEN-DAZS
$3.89 (16 oz.)

This creamy, pleasantly dense ice cream ("it was the slowest to melt," noted one taster) disappointed big time in the flavor department. The chocolate was too bland and had a slightly earthy aftertaste.

You say gelato, I say ice cream

We were curious about the difference between gelato and ice cream, so we posed the question to Il Laboratorio del Gelato owner Jon Snyder. It turns out there is no clear-cut difference. "The way I see it," he says, "gelato is the Italian word for ice cream." There isn't one way to make gelato, just as there isn't one way to make ice cream. In the South of Italy, for example, gelato tends to be icier, while in the North it's creamier, with a lot more egg yolks.

That said, a couple of general rules apply. Gelato tends to have less cream and more milk than ice cream, so it has a denser texture because less air is whipped into it (cream incorporates more air than milk). Also, gelato is churned more slowly and served at slightly higher temperatures than ice cream, making it particularly smooth and creamy. Egg yolks can be used in both gelato and ice cream.

splurge

In a league of its own

Our panel's top ice creams (at left) are fine everyday treats, and they'd make tasty milk shakes, too, but if you're looking for something truly special, you'll want Il Laboratorio del Gelato's dark chocolate ice cream in your freezer. To say that it's smooth and creamy is almost an understatement. This ice cream is luxuriously rich and silky—oh, so silky—like the deepest, richest chocolate mousse with an intense, perfectly bittersweet chocolate flavor that will knock your socks off.

Il Laboratorio del Gelato ice creams are available in select stores in New York City or by mail order at LaboratorioDelGelato.com ($60 for four 18-ounce containers, plus shipping).

Go, organic!

Green & Black's organic dark chocolate is a favorite here at *Fine Cooking*. So when we found out the company had plans to launch Green & Black's organic chocolate ice cream, we couldn't wait to taste it. This is a dense, rich, satisfying ice cream with a powerful dark-chocolate flavor and a big bittersweet finish, just like its 70% chocolate bars. Green & Black's organic chocolate ice cream is available at Whole Foods Markets and other specialty food stores for $4.49 a pint.

From Our Test Kitchen, p. 62

Though aged Goudas seem to be appearing in more supermarket cheese sections, they may not be in your market yet. Good mail-order sources for aged Gouda include Artisanal Cheese.com (877-797-1200), MurraysCheese.com (888-692-4339), and Formaggio Kitchen.com (888-212-3224).

To purchase the Oster Classic chrome milk shake mixer (model 6627), visit Amazon.com, where it sells for about $50.

For malted milk powder, visit CtlColfax.com (800-962-5227), where a 1-pound canister sells for $15.50, including shipping and handling.

In Season, p. 18

Seeds for pickling and slicing cucumbers are widely available on seed racks and from seed catalogs. You may have to order English cucumber seeds. A couple of good sources are CooksGarden.com (800-457-9703) and SuperSeeds .com (207-926-3400).

Grilled Chicken Thighs, p. 30

Look to your local Asian market or go to OrientalPantry.com (978-264-4576) for sambal oelek, an Asian chile paste (8 ounces for $2.09), and five-spice powder (4 ounces for $1.49).

No-Cook Tomato Sauce, p. 38

If you're interested in growing your own tomatoes, you can find seeds at garden centers or at TomatoGrowers .com (888-478-7333). Genovese basil is available at many farmers' markets, or you can buy seeds at Richters.com (800-668-4372).

Grilled Bread, p. 40

To turn bread on the grill, Elizabeth Karmel recommends using a pair of locking tongs. They're available at kitchenwares stores, or visit OXO .com (800-545-4411), which sells them in various sizes and at prices ranging from $8.99 to $12.99.

Mexican-Style Steaks, p. 44

You can find Oaxaca, cotija, and anejo cheeses as well as ancho chile powder, chipotles en adobo, and dried ancho and pasilla chiles in many well-stocked supermarkets and in hispanic markets. Igourmet.com (877-446-8763) carries varieties of these Mexican cheeses, which range from about $8 to $11 a pound.

For all of the chiles, visit TheCmc Company.com (800-262-2780); ancho chile powder sells for $6.75 for 4 ounces, chipotles en adobo are $5.25 for 7 ounces, dried ancho chiles are $9.50 for 6 ounces, and pasilla chiles are $12.75 for 6 ounces.

Peaches & Cream, p. 58

The Cream Shortcake Biscuits get a sprinkling of demerara sugar just before baking. It's available in well-stocked supermarkets, or try mail-ordering it at Igourmet.com (877-446-8763), where a 1-pound bag sells for $3.99.

Quick & Delicious, p. 78a

Chipotles are dried, smoked jalapeños, and in any form they add an intriguing depth to dishes. McCormick packages ground chipotle, which is available in supermarkets, and SpiceHunter.com (800-444-3061) sells crushed chipotle ($7.88 per 1.85-ounce jar), which would be a fine substitute in the Farmers' Market Quesadillas if you add just a bit more than you would of the ground chipotle. ◆

Plum Pudding Kitchen *p.15* Your online source for "irresistibly Italian" Vietri dinnerware, flatware, glassware, and much more. Let us help you set a special table!
888-940-7586
www.plumpuddingkitchen.com

Poggi Bonsi *p.73* Direct importers of artisan Italian ceramics, olive wood utensils and cutting boards, and Umbrian kitchen towels.
www.poggibonsigifts.com

Replacements, Ltd. *p.76* World's largest inventory: old and new china, crystal, sterling, silver-plate, and stainless. All manufacturers, fine and casual. 10 million pieces, 200,000 patterns. Buy and sell.
800-REPLACE
www.replacements.com

Totally Bamboo *p.77* Featuring over 150 products, Totally Bamboo is the industry pioneer of bamboo cutting boards and kitchen design. Order all of our fine products directly online!
www.totallybamboo.com

Kitchen Tools & Utensils

Bella Copper *p.77* The world's leading heat diffuser/defroster plate provides superior heat conduction for more even cooking and faster defrosting. Available in solid copper or pure silver. A gourmet kitchen essential.
805-215-3241
www.bellacopper.com

Gel Pro *p.73* STAND IN COMFORT! Let's Gel was started with one simple goal, to make the time you spend standing in your kitchen more comfortable.
866-GEL-MATS
www.letsgel.com

Helen's Asian Kitchen *p.7* Since 1957, Harold Import Company has been a leading supplier of kitchenware products to the specialty retail trade, offering almost 3000 items. Our products are available in thousands of stores worldwide. What can HIC offer your business?
www.helensasiankitchen.com

J.K. Adams Company *p.11* J.K. Adams, has been the premiere Vermont manufacturer of handcrafted, heirloom-quality, woodware for the kitchen and table since 1944.
www.jkadams.com

Kerekes *p.77* Your complete online source for professional chef's tools, cookware, bakeware, and cake decorating supplies used by top chefs at the finest restaurants and kitchens.
www.bakedeco.com

WMF of America *p.7* WMF is the only brand that can make cooking, dining, and drinking an event. WMF is the singular choice.
www.wmf-usa.com

Schools, Travel & Organizations

Culinary Business Academy *p.15* Extensive and comprehensive personal chef business knowledge and training from the world's recognized leader in the personal chef industry. Nobody offers what we offer.
800-747-2433
www.culinarybusiness.com

La Villa Bonita *p.9* La Villa Bonita offers a delicious immersion in the culinary joys of Mexico, with its culinary vacation packages in a 16th-century mansion in Cuernavaca.
800-505-3084
www.lavillabonita.com

Le Cordon Bleu *p.11* Master the culinary arts. Earn the Grand Diplome in approximately nine months. Three- to five-week intensive courses and online hospitality programs are also available.
800-457-2433
www.cordonbleu.edu

The Rich Moms.com, Inc. *p.65* We co-create six figure income earners from home, marketing the fastest growing health, nutrition, cleansing and weight loss program in North America.
www.therichmoms.com

Wines, Beverages & Accessories

Covington Cellars *p.76* Award winning boutique Washington winery offers wine samples of our limited production wines that sell out fast! An excellent addition to any cellar!
www.covingtoncellars.com

Woodbridge Winery *p.3* For 25 years, we have aged our wines in small oak barrels and handcrafted each vintage. Woodbridge: Taste our small winery tradition™.
www.woodbridgewines.com

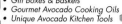

FROM THE BEST-SELLING IDEA BOOK SERIES

Get the kitchen you always wanted.

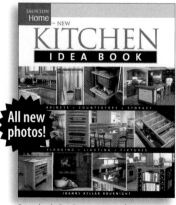

All new photos!

Paperback, Product #070773, $19.95

Find hundreds of the latest design options and styles in our *New Kitchen Idea Book.* Exciting plans and over 300 colorful photos lend practical advice on choosing:

- cabinetry & countertops
- floors, walls & ceilings
- appliances & sinks
- windows & lighting
- space-saving features
- innovative storage
- functional layouts

Plan the kitchen that works for you!
Order the *New Kitchen Idea Book* today.

Call **800-888-8286** or visit
www.taunton.com/ideabooks

© 2004 The Taunton Press

 The Taunton Press

Recipe	Page	Calories		Protein	Carb	Fats (g)				Chol.	Sodium	Fiber	Notes
		total	from fat	(g)	(g)	total	sat	mono	poly	(mg)	(mg)	(g)	
In Season	18												
Green Gazpacho		380	300	3	17	34	4.5	24	3.5	0	640	4	based on 6 servings
Chicken Thighs on the Grill	30												
Grilled Tandoori-Style Chicken Thighs		300	150	34	2	16	4	6	4	125	240	5	based on 6 servings
Grilled Five-Spice Chicken Thighs w/ Soy-Vinegar Sauce		340	180	35	6	20	4.5	8	6	125	690	0	based on 6 servings
Indonesian Grilled Chicken Thighs w/ Mango-Peanut Salsa		470	250	38	18	28	6	11	8	125	600	3	based on 6 servings
Grilled Rosemary Chicken Thighs w/ Dipping Sauce		380	170	34	19	19	4.5	7	5	125	500	0	w/ 2 Tbs. sauce/serving
Corn Sautés	34												
Corn, Sweet Onion & Zucchini Sauté w/ Fresh Mint		180	90	4	24	10	4	4	1	15	290	4	based on 4 servings
Corn & Mushroom Sauté w/ Leeks & Pancetta		300	210	5	21	23	10	10	2	45	490	3	based on 4 servings
Corn Sauté w/ Ginger, Garlic & Fresh Cilantro		160	90	3	19	10	4	4	1	15	290	3	based on 4 servings
No-Cook Tomato Sauce	38												
No-Cook Tomato Sauce (*Salsa Cruda*)		480	180	12	62	20	3	13	2.5	0	440	5	w/ pasta
No-Cook Tomato Sauce w/ Cheese		540	230	17	63	25	7	14	2.5	20	680	5	w/ pasta
No-Cook Tomato Sauce w/ Basil Pesto		730	410	15	65	47	6	29	8	0	640	6	w/ pasta
No-Cook Tomato Sauce w/ Tapenade		600	290	12	64	33	4.5	23	4	0	840	6	w/ pasta
Grilled Bread	40												
Grilled Garlic Bread		190	60	5	26	7	1	5	0.5	0	440	1	based on 8 servings
Grilled Goat Cheese Crostini w/ Roasted Peppers		280	120	8	30	14	3.5	8	1	5	540	2	based on 8 servings
Grilled Corn, Shrimp & Chorizo Salad		700	400	21	57	45	9	29	5	60	1010	6	based on 8 servings
Mexican-Style Steaks	44												
Steak Adobo		440	300	32	1	33	12	15	1.5	105	380	1	based on 4 servings
Steak w/ Three-Chile Sauce		650	450	39	9	50	18	24	2.5	130	720	1	based on 4 servings
Steak w/ Red Onion, Wine & Port Sauce		620	350	35	7	39	18	15	1.5	130	550	0	based on 4 servings
Grilled Eggplant	48												
Grilled Eggplant		80	60	1	4	7	1	5	1	0	140	3	based on 6 servings
Garlic-Cumin Vinaigrette w/ Feta & Herbs		160	130	2	6	15	3	10	1.5	5	260	3	w/ Grilled Eggplant
Toasted-Breadcrumb Salsa Verde		180	150	1	7	17	2.5	12	2	0	260	3	w/ Grilled Eggplant
Roasted Red Pepper Relish w/ Pine Nuts & Currants		140	110	2	8	12	1.5	8	2	0	190	4	w/ Grilled Eggplant
Olive, Orange & Anchovy Vinaigrette		180	160	1	6	18	2.5	13	2	0	340	3	w/ Grilled Eggplant
Scallions	52												
Summer Corn Chowder w/ Scallions, Bacon & Potatoes		180	60	8	25	7	3	2.5	1	15	320	3	based on 6 servings
Grilled Flank Steak w/ Sesame Sauce & Grilled Scallions		520	300	39	17	34	7	16	8	65	2150	2	based on 4 servings
Pork Lo Mein w/ Seared Scallions & Shiitakes		680	310	29	61	35	7	17	8	55	1360	6	based on 4 servings
Thai Seafood Salad	56												
Thai Seafood Salad (*Yum Talay*)		200	20	31	12	2.5	0.5	0	1	205	1700	1	based on 6 servings
Peaches & Cream	58												
Peaches & Cream Dessert		350	140	2	54	15	9	4.5	0.5	55	25	2	based on 4 servings
Peaches & Cream Parfait		600	310	4	72	35	21	10	1.5	130	55	3	based on 4 servings
Peaches & Cream Shortcakes		600	330	6	63	37	23	10	1.5	125	230	2	based on 8 servings
Cream Shortcake Biscuits		280	160	4	27	18	11	5	0.5	60	190	1	based on 8 servings
Test Kitchen	62												
Pickled Cauliflower w/ Carrots & Red Bell Pepper		50	0	2	12	0	0	0	0	0	220	3	based on 4 oz. serving
Spiced Pickled Beets		60	0	2	14	0	0	0	0	0	300	2	based on 4 oz. serving
Double-Chocolate Malted Milk Shake		280	110	6	39	12	7	3.5	0.5	35	130	2	based on 2 servings
Create-Your-Own Pasta Salad w/ Grilled Eggplant		260	100	9	31	11	2	7	1.5	10	500	3	based on 6 servings
Quick & Delicious	78a												
Angel Hair Pasta w/ Cherry Tomatoes, Lemon & Tuna		400	110	22	49	13	2.5	7	2.5	10	880	5	based on 4 servings
Arugula Salad w/ Pears, Prosciutto & Aged Gouda		330	230	12	16	26	7	12	5	35	650	4	based on 4 servings
Feta & Dill Galette w/ Lemony Spinach Salad		350	270	10	9	31	13	14	2	155	690	1	based on 4 servings
Chili-Rubbed Rib-Eye w/ Corn & Green Chile Ragoût		690	420	47	22	47	22	18	3.5	185	700	4	based on 2 servings
Farmers' Market Quesadillas		660	370	22	51	42	15	16	9	60	1090	5	based on 4 servings
Summer Bouillabaisse w/ Smoky Rouille		490	230	30	29	25	3.5	9	2.5	40	480	5	based on 4 servings
Roasted Chicken Thighs w/ Late-Summer Vegetables		460	280	26	12	31	7	17	5	90	690	3	based on 4 servings
Back Cover													
Corn Sauté w/ Canadian Bacon, Potatoes & Peppers		250	130	7	27	14	5	7	1.5	25	500	4	based on 4 servings

The nutritional analyses have been calculated by a registered dietitian at Nutritional Solutions in Melville, New York. When a recipe gives a choice of ingredients, the first choice is the one used. Optional ingredients with measured amounts are included; ingredients without specific quantities are not. When a range of ingredient amounts or servings is given, the smaller amount or portion is used. When the quantities of salt and pepper aren't specified, the analysis is based on ¼ teaspoon salt and ⅛ teaspoon pepper per serving for entrées, and ⅛ teaspoon salt and ⅟₁₆ teaspoon pepper per serving for side dishes.

Summer Bouillabaisse with Smoky Rouille

Serves four.

3 Tbs. extra-virgin olive oil;
  more for the sauce
1½ Tbs. chopped garlic,
  plus ½ tsp. finely grated
  or minced garlic
2 lb. ripe tomatoes, cored
  and large diced (about
  4½ cups)
1 cup dry white wine
1 tsp. sweet smoked paprika
  (Spanish pimentón)
¼ cup mayonnaise
Kosher salt
One 14-oz. can low-salt
  chicken broth (1¾ cups)
1 large pinch saffron
1 lb. halibut, cod, or other
  firm white fish, cut into
  1-inch chunks
2 cups fresh corn kernels
  (from 4 medium ears)
Freshly ground black pepper
1 to 2 Tbs. chopped fresh
  flat-leaf parsley, for
  garnish (optional)

In a 5- to 6-qt. soup pot or Dutch oven, heat the oil over medium heat. Add the 1½ Tbs. chopped garlic and cook until fragrant, about 30 seconds. Add the tomatoes and wine, increase the heat to medium high (if necessary), and simmer vigorously until the tomatoes are broken down and the mixture is slightly soupy, about 15 minutes.

While the tomatoes are cooking, whisk the ½ tsp. grated garlic, paprika, and mayonnaise in a small bowl. Whisk in a little olive oil and enough cool water to make a creamy, pourable sauce. Taste and add salt if you like.

Add the broth and saffron to the tomato mixture and simmer to slightly reduce the broth and concentrate the flavors, 5 minutes. Add the fish and simmer until it's opaque throughout, 3 to 5 minutes more. Stir in the corn. Season to taste with salt and black pepper. Serve in large bowls with a big drizzle of the sauce on top and a generous sprinkle of parsley, if using.

Variation: To dress this up for entertaining, add ½ lb. peeled medium or large shrimp and ½ lb. Manila clams or mussels. Wash the shellfish well before adding and use only the tightly closed shells. Simmer until the shells open.

Tip: You can make this soup ahead except for adding the fish, which you should do at the last minute.

Feta & Dill Galette with Lemony Spinach Salad

Serves four.

2 large eggs
⅓ cup crème fraîche or
  heavy cream
2 Tbs. chopped fresh dill,
  plus ½ cup loosely packed
  dill sprigs for the salad
  (optional)
1 tsp. lightly packed, finely
  grated lemon zest
½ tsp. kosher salt; more for
  the salad
Freshly ground black pepper
1 sheet frozen puff pastry,
  thawed
1 cup crumbled feta (about
  4 oz.); I like Valbreso and
  Mt. Vikos brands
4 small handfuls baby
  spinach (about 3 oz.),
  washed and dried, large
  stems removed
3 Tbs. extra-virgin olive oil
1 Tbs. fresh lemon juice;
  more to taste

Position a rack in the center of the oven and heat the oven to 450°F. In a medium bowl, whisk the eggs, crème fraîche or cream, chopped dill, lemon zest, salt, and about 10 grinds of pepper.

On a lightly floured surface, gently roll out the puff pastry until it measures about 11 by 13 inches. Line a rimmed baking sheet with parchment or a silicone baking mat. Lay the pastry on the baking sheet, wet the edges with water, and

fold over a ¾-inch border, mitering the corners for neatness. Distribute the feta evenly within the border, and then carefully pour the egg mixture over the cheese, taking care that it doesn't slosh onto the border. Carefully transfer the baking sheet to the oven and bake until the pastry is puffed and brown on the border and the underside, and the filling is golden brown, 18 to 20 minutes.

Slide the galette off the pan and onto a rack to cool until still warm but not hot. Move the galette to a cutting board and cut into four rectangles, so that each piece gets some border. Put the four pieces on plates.

In a large bowl, toss the spinach and dill sprigs (if using) with the olive oil and lemon juice until evenly coated. Sprinkle with salt, pepper, and more lemon juice to taste. Arrange a handful of salad on each piece of galette and serve immediately.

Note: Thaw puff pastry in the refrigerator overnight or all day while you're at work. Or thaw at room temperature for at least 45 minutes (less if your kitchen is quite warm).

Roasted Chicken Thighs with Late-Summer Vegetables & Pan Sauce

Serves three to four.

- **6 skin-on, bone-in chicken thighs (2½ to 3 lb.)**
- **Kosher salt and freshly ground black pepper**
- **3 Tbs. extra-virgin olive oil**
- **½ lb. green beans, stem ends trimmed (2 cups)**
- **10 oz. cherry or grape tomatoes (2 cups)**
- **One-half large sweet onion (like Vidalia or Walla Walla) or red onion, cut into ½-inch-thick slices**
- **½ cup pitted Niçoise or Kalamata olives**
- **2 large cloves garlic, sliced about ⅛ inch thick**
- **¾ cup dry white wine**
- **1 tsp. unsalted butter (optional)**
- **½ cup loosely packed fresh basil leaves, sliced into ½-inch strips**

Position two racks near the center of the oven and heat the oven to 425°F. Heat a 10- to 11-inch heavy, ovenproof skillet over medium-high heat. Generously season the chicken on both sides with salt and pepper. Pour 1 Tbs. of the oil into the hot skillet and swirl to coat. Arrange the chicken thighs skin side down in the pan and cook until the skin is golden brown, about 7 minutes. Turn the chicken over. If a lot of fat has accumulated, carefully spoon it off and discard.

While the chicken browns, toss the beans, tomatoes, onion, olives, and garlic in a large bowl with the remaining 2 Tbs. oil. Season with ¾ tsp. salt and several grinds of pepper and spread the vegetables on a rimmed baking sheet.

Put the skillet of chicken and the baking sheet with the vegetables in the oven, with the chicken on the higher rack. Roast the chicken until a thermometer inserted in the center of a thigh registers 170°F, 18 to 20 minutes. Continue to roast the vegetables until very soft and beginning to brown, 8 to 12 minutes more.

Meanwhile, remove the skillet from the oven and transfer the chicken to a plate. Spoon off and discard as much fat as possible from the chicken juices, add the wine, set over high heat, and boil until reduced to about ¼ cup sauce, 4 to 6 minutes; it should be syrupy and concentrated in flavor. Swirl in the butter, if using.

Remove the vegetables from the oven and toss them with the basil. Divide the vegetables among four plates. Arrange one or two chicken thighs on the vegetables and drizzle with the pan sauce. Serve immediately.

Arugula Salad with Pears, Prosciutto & Aged Gouda

Serves four.

- **2 Tbs. white-wine vinegar**
- **½ tsp. Dijon mustard**
- **¼ tsp. kosher salt**
- **⅛ tsp. freshly ground black pepper**
- **¼ cup extra-virgin olive oil**
- **5 to 6 oz. arugula, any large stems removed, leaves washed and dried (6 loosely packed cups)**
- **2 medium ripe pears, peeled if you like, cored, and cut into 1-inch chunks**
- **4 thin slices prosciutto, cut crosswise into ½-inch-wide ribbons**
- **3 oz. aged Gouda, cut into 2-inch-long sticks (1 cup)**
- **1 oz. walnuts, toasted and coarsely chopped (¼ cup)**

In a small bowl, whisk the vinegar, mustard, salt, and pepper. Slowly whisk in the oil.

In a large salad or mixing bowl, toss the arugula and the pears with half of the dressing. Divide among four plates, scatter the prosciutto and cheese on top of each salad, and drizzle with a little of the remaining dressing. Sprinkle on the nuts and serve immediately.

Tip: Gouda that's been aged a couple of years takes on a rich, almost toffee-like character; the older it is, the drier and more intense the flavor becomes. (Don't worry if it falls apart when you cut it.) I like Old Amsterdam brand. For more on aged Gouda, see From Our Test Kitchen, p. 62. You could also use a good Comté, Gruyère, or Parmigiano-Reggiano.

Chili-Rubbed Rib-Eye Steak with Corn & Green Chile Ragoût

Serves two.

- **1 tsp. chili powder**
- **1 tsp. ground coriander**
- **1 tsp. kosher salt; more to taste**
- **Two 8-oz. boneless beef rib-eye steaks (about ¾ inch thick)**
- **2 tsp. canola or other vegetable oil**
- **1 small poblano or other mildly hot fresh chile (Anaheim or Italian frying pepper), seeded and cut into ¼-inch dice (about ½ cup)**
- **Freshly ground black pepper**
- **1 generous cup fresh corn kernels (from 2 medium ears)**
- **½ cup heavy cream**
- **1 Tbs. minced oil-packed sun-dried tomatoes (from 2 medium tomato halves)**
- **1 Tbs. fresh lime juice**

In a small bowl, mix the chili powder, coriander, and salt. Rub the mixture on the steaks.

Heat the oil in a 10- to 11-inch cast-iron or other heavy skillet over high heat until very hot. Add the steaks, reduce the heat to medium high, and cook until they are well browned and done to your liking, about 3 minutes per side for medium rare. Transfer to a plate and cover loosely to keep warm.

Add the chile to the pan, season with salt and pepper, and cook over medium-high heat, stirring frequently, until softened and starting to brown, about 2 minutes. Add the corn and continue to cook until it's slightly browned, 1 to 2 minutes more. Add the cream and boil until it has reduced and the mixture is thick, 1 to 2 minutes.

Remove from the heat, stir in the sun-dried tomato, lime juice, and the accumulated juices from the steak. Taste and add more salt and black pepper, if you like. Serve the rib-eyes whole or slice them and arrange on plates. Serve immediately, with the corn ragoût on top or alongside.

Variation: Rib-eye steaks are tender, juicy, and cook well in a frying pan, but you could also use New York strip or skirt steaks.

Tip: Poblanos vary a lot in spiciness, so taste yours before you add it to the pan and hold back a bit if it's too hot. If you want more heat, add a minced jalapeño along with the poblano.

Angel Hair Pasta with Sautéed Cherry Tomatoes, Lemon & Tuna

Serves three to four.

- **Kosher salt**
- **2 Tbs. extra-virgin olive oil**
- **4 cups cherry or grape tomatoes (about 1½ lb.; a mix of colors, if possible)**
- **1 large clove garlic, minced**
- **One 6-oz. can light tuna in oil, drained and separated into chunks**
- **2 Tbs. minced jarred pepperoncini (about 4 medium peppers, stemmed and seeded)**
- **1 Tbs. lightly chopped capers**
- **1 tsp. fresh lemon juice**
- **1 tsp. cold unsalted butter**
- **½ tsp. packed, finely grated lemon zest**
- **8 oz. dried angel hair pasta**
- **3 Tbs. coarsely chopped fresh flat-leaf parsley**

Bring a large pot of generously salted water to a boil over high heat. Meanwhile, in an 11- to 12-inch skillet, heat the oil over medium-high heat until very hot. Add the tomatoes (be careful because the oil and juice can spatter) and cook until they begin to collapse and their juices run and start to thicken, 6 to 10 minutes. (If you have big, stubborn tomatoes, you may need to crush them a bit with a spatula or pierce them with a knife.) Add the garlic and cook for 30 seconds.

Remove the pan from the heat and stir in the tuna, pepperoncini, capers, lemon juice, butter, and lemon zest. Season the sauce to taste with salt and keep it warm while you cook the pasta.

Cook the pasta in the boiling water according to package directions. Drain well, arrange in individual pasta bowls, and top with the sauce and the parsley.

Tip: For a real treat, try one of the imported Spanish tunas (Ortiz brand, in particular), which are fairly expensive but very delicious.

Martha Holmberg, the former publisher and editor in chief of Fine Cooking, *is the food editor of* The Oregonian *newspaper in Portland.* ◆

Summertime, and the cooking is easy

BY MARTHA HOLMBERG

Ripe, gorgeous summer vegetables are a treat for anyone who loves to cook; the only challenge is finding the time to cook them all. These recipes will help you with that, as they're built around the season's luscious offerings yet designed for speed, too.

Be sure to stock your pantry with high-quality partners for your vegetables: lovely extra-virgin olive oil; a good block of nutty, true Parmigiano-Reggiano; fresh, firm garlic; and fragrant spices. Also, be flexible when selecting your produce. If the recipe specifies zucchini but pattypan squash is calling you, heed the call and go with what looks best. All the recipes here can handle some improvisation. Even the Chili-Rubbed Rib-Eye Steak with Corn & Green Chile Ragoût can be made with pork chops or chicken breasts if steak isn't your thing.

Farmers' Market Quesadillas

Yields 4 quesadillas.

5 Tbs. vegetable oil
1 cup small-diced fresh, mild chiles, such as Anaheim or poblano (from about 2 large chiles)
1½ cups small-diced summer squash (from about 2 small zucchini, yellow squash, or yellow crookneck)
Kosher salt and freshly ground black pepper
1 cup fresh corn kernels (from 2 medium ears)
⅛ tsp. chipotle chile powder
1 cup diced tomato (from 2 small tomatoes)
¼ cup chopped fresh cilantro
1 Tbs. fresh lime juice
Four 9-inch flour tortillas
2 cups grated sharp cheddar (8 oz.)
Sour cream for serving (optional)

Heat the oven to 200°F. Fit a cooling rack over a baking sheet and put in the oven.

Heat 1 Tbs. of the oil in a 12-inch skillet over medium-high heat until hot. Add the chiles and cook, stirring, until soft, 3 to 4 minutes. Add the squash, season with salt and pepper, and cook, stirring, until the squash softens and starts to brown, 3 to 4 minutes. Stir in the corn and chipotle powder and cook 2 minutes more. Spoon into a bowl, let cool for a few minutes, and then fold in the tomato, cilantro, and lime juice. Season to taste with salt and pepper. Set aside ¾ cup of the mixture.

Lay several layers of paper towel on a work surface. Wipe out the skillet, put it over medium-high heat, and add 1 Tbs. of the oil. When it's hot, put one tortilla in the pan. Quickly distribute ½ cup of the cheese evenly over the tortilla and about a quarter of the remaining vegetable mixture over half the tortilla. When the underside of the tortilla is browned, use tongs to fold the cheese-only side over the vegetable side. Lay the quesadilla on the paper towels, blot for a few seconds, and then move it to the rack in the oven to keep warm while you repeat with the remaining oil and tortillas. Cut the quesadillas into wedges and serve immediately with the reserved vegetable mixture and sour cream.

Note: Chipotles are dried smoked jalapeños, and in any form they add an intriguing depth to dishes. McCormick makes ground chipotle, and The Spice Hunter sells a crushed chipotle, which would be a fine substitute in this recipe; just add a bit more than you would of the ground.

<u>Faux</u> <u>fried</u> **U.S. Farm-Raised Catfish with** <u>homestyle</u> <u>biscuits</u>.
ADJECTIVE TECHNIQUE ADJECTIVE NOUN

Always fresh, healthy, mild and flaky, U.S. Farm-Raised Catfish suits
any recipe. For some of my favorites, visit **catfishinstitute.com**

FOOD NETWORK CHEF *Cat Cora*

A Sauté for Supper

Canadian bacon and potatoes make this corn sauté hearty enough to stand alone as a light main course, but it also makes a wonderful side dish or a zesty bed for grilled or roasted meat or fish.

Ingredient tip:

Made with jalapeños instead of red hot peppers, Tabasco green pepper sauce provides a milder kick than the classic sauce and a vegetal flavor reminiscent of green bell peppers. It's available in most well-stocked supermarkets.

For more corn sautés, turn to p. 34.

Corn Sauté with Canadian Bacon, Potatoes & Peppers

Serves four as a side dish or two as a main course.

2 Tbs. unsalted butter
2 Tbs. extra-virgin olive oil
½ cup small-diced Canadian bacon (3 oz.)
1 cup small-diced red onion (from about a 6-oz. onion)
1 cup small-diced red potato (from about a 5-oz. potato)
½ cup small-diced green bell pepper (from three-quarters of a 3-oz. pepper)
1 tsp. kosher salt; more to taste
2 slightly heaping cups fresh corn kernels (from about 4 medium ears)
2 tsp. minced garlic (2 medium cloves)
2 Tbs. chopped fresh flat-leaf parsley
2 Tbs. thinly sliced fresh chives
½ tsp. green Tabasco; more to taste
Freshly ground black pepper
One-half lemon

Melt 1 Tbs. of the butter and 1 Tbs. of the olive oil in a 10-inch straight-sided sauté pan or Dutch oven over medium heat. Add the Canadian bacon and cook, stirring occasionally, until the bacon is brown around the edges, about 4 minutes. Transfer to a plate lined with paper towels.

Add the remaining 1 Tbs. butter and 1 Tbs. olive oil to the pan. Add the onion, potato, bell pepper, and ½ tsp. of the salt. Reduce the heat to medium low, cover, and cook, stirring frequently, until the onions and peppers are well softened and the potatoes are barely tender and starting to brown, 5 to 7 minutes.

Uncover, increase the heat to medium, and add the corn, garlic, and the remaining ½ tsp. salt. Sauté, stirring frequently and scraping the bottom of the pan with a wooden spoon, until the corn is tender but still slightly toothy to the bite, 3 to 5 minutes. (The corn should be glistening, brighter in color, and somewhat shrunken in size, and the bottom of the pan will be slightly brown.)

Remove the pan from the heat, add the parsley, chives, Tabasco, a few generous grinds of pepper, and a small squeeze of lemon. Stir, let sit 2 minutes, and stir again, scraping up the brown bits from the bottom of the pan. (Moisture released from the vegetables as they sit will loosen the bits.) Fold the Canadian bacon into the dish, season to taste with more salt, pepper, or lemon juice. Serve warm.

Susie Middleton, editor of Fine Cooking ◆

fine Cooking

NOVEMBER 2007 NO. 88

FOR PEOPLE WHO LOVE TO COOK

a make-ahead Thanksgiving

secrets to
juicy turkey

ps for perfect
iecrust

ow to: hearty
ean soups

new wave
f spinach
alads

he fastest
innamon
olls

w.finecooking.com

5 CAN $7.95

Chocolate Espresso Pecan Pie

7 4470 56529 1

11

IT'S HARD TO LET GO

Messermeister blends ergonomic perfection with exacting performance. The elite edge is crafted using an exclusive 3-step hand-finishing process that allows you to slice, dice, chop, split, trim, pare, carve and julienne with precision and delight. The revolutionary bolsterless edge enables continuous cutting along the full length of the edge and the contoured handle and polished spine create a knife so comfortable, some chefs call it sensual. It's a feeling that you'll want to hold on to forever.

Messermeister
THE KNIFE FOR LIFE™

fine Cooking

OCTOBER/NOVEMBER 2007 ISSUE 88

44   53

RECIPE FOLDOUT

98A **Quick & Delicious**
Speedy stir-fries

Orange Chicken with Scallions

ON THE COVER

58 **A new take on a Thanksgiving favorite**

Chocolate Espresso Pecan Pie

28

20

18

UP FRONT

6   Index

8   Menus

10 Letters

14 Contributors

16 Links

18 Artisan Foods
    Raw-milk cheese

20 Great Finds
    Dessert embellishments

22 Q&A

24 In Season
    Sage

28 Equipment
    ❖ **Insulated pot**
    ❖ **Portable burners**
    ❖ **Potato ricer vs. masher**
    ❖ **Mortar & pestle review**

36 Enjoying Wine
    All-American wines

42 Readers' Tips

42

The Taunton Press
Inspiration for hands-on living®

visit our web site: **www.finecooking.com**

Cover photo and photos on these pages: Scott Phillips

64   68   70   73

FEATURES

44   COVER: HOLIDAY MENU
      Plan Ahead for a
      Delicious Thanksgiving
      **Pulling together an impressive dinner is
      a breeze when you've got a great menu
      and a solid plan**
      by Ris Lacoste

53   An Essential Guide
      to Roasting Vegetables
      **A reliable technique and great tips—plus exciting
      flavoring ideas for your favorite vegetables**
      by Jennifer Armentrout

58   Go Nuts: Add Pecans
      to More Than Just Pie
      **Try them in pineapple upside-down cake,
      apple crisp, and bourbon-glazed poundcake**
      by Karen Barker

64   A New Wave of Spinach Salads
      **Reinvent this classic with bold flavors and
      crunchy textures from around the world**
      by Joanne Weir

68   TRUE CLASSIC
      Linguine with Clam Sauce
      **Fresh clams and perfectly firm pasta are
      the keys to this simple Italian dish**
      by Perla Meyers

70   Cinnamon Buns
      in Less Than an Hour
      **A biscuit dough is the shortcut secret
      to this sweet breakfast treat**
      by Kathy Kingsley

73   COOKING WITHOUT RECIPES
      How to Make Hearty
      Bean and Vegetable Soups
      **Learn the best method for making deeply flavored
      winter soups with your choice of ingredients**
      by Molly Stevens

78

82

78

90

IN THE BACK

78   From Our
      Test Kitchen
      ❖ Pineapple rings
      ❖ Nutmeg
      ❖ Rolling out piecrust
      ❖ Buttermilk
      ❖ Pappadams
      ❖ Breakfast smoothie
      ❖ Leftovers:
        Turkey hash

88   Food Science
      Thanksgiving solutions

90   Tasting Panel
      Cottage cheese

92   Where To Buy It

98   Nutrition
      Information

84

98a *Curried Coconut Shrimp*

54 *Roasted Broccoli*

62 *Bourbon-Glazed Brown Sugar Pecan Poundcake*

recipes

◆ QUICK
 Under 45 minutes

◆ MAKE AHEAD
 Can be completely prepared ahead but may need reheating and a garnish to serve

◆ MOSTLY MAKE AHEAD
 Can be partially prepared ahead but will need a few finishing touches before serving

◆ VEGETARIAN
 May contain eggs and dairy ingredients

Cover Recipe
◆◆ Chocolate Espresso Pecan Pie, 62

Soups & Broths
◆ Cabbage and White Bean Soup, 74
◆ French Farmers' Soup, 74
◆ Mexican Black Bean Soup, 74
◆◆ Middle-Eastern Chickpea Soup, 74
◆ Minestrone, 74
◆ Turkey Broth, 47

Main Dish Salads
◆◆ Garlic Crostini with Spinach, Mushroom & Parmigiano Salad, 66
◆◆ Spinach Salad with Apples, Dried Apricots & Pappadam Croutons, 66
 Spinach Salad with Chicken, Cashews, Ginger & Fried Wontons, 65
◆ Warm Spinach Salad with Eggs, Bacon & Croutons, 67

Pasta & Noodles
◆ Linguine with Clam Sauce, 69
◆ Stir-Fried Noodles with Beef & Vegetables, 98a

Tofu
◆ Seared Baby Bok Choy with Tofu & Shiitakes, 98a

Turkey & Chicken
 Herb-Butter Roasted Turkey with Pinot Noir Gravy, 48
◆ Orange Chicken with Scallions, 98a
◆ Sesame Chicken with Ginger & Snow Peas, 98a
 Spinach Salad with Chicken, Cashews, Ginger & Fried Wontons, 65
◆ Turkey & Sweet Potato Hash, 86

Beef & Pork
◆ Hoisin Pork with Napa Cabbage, 98a
◆ Pork Tenderloin with Sage & Marsala Sauce, 26
◆ Spicy Beef with Peanuts & Chiles, 98a
◆ Stir-Fried Noodles with Beef & Vegetables, 98a

Seafood
◆ Curried Coconut Shrimp, 98a
◆ Linguine with Clam Sauce, 69

Side Dishes
◆◆ Basic Roasted Vegetables, 54
◆◆ Broccoli with Eggs & Lemony Parmesan Breadcrumbs, 51
◆◆ Classic Mashed Potatoes, 52
◆ Sausage-Maple Bread Stuffing, 50
◆◆ Sweet Potato Gratin with Caramelized Onions, 50

Condiments & Sauces
◆◆◆ Caramelized Shallot Butter, 57
◆◆◆ Cranberry Sauce with Vanilla, Maple Syrup & Cassis, 52
◆◆◆ Ginger-Lemon-Soy Splash, 57
◆◆◆ Moroccan-Style Spice Rub, 56
◆◆◆ Rosemary-Thyme-Lemon Oil, 56
◆◆◆ Sesame Salt, 57
◆◆ Three-Herb Butter, 47
◆◆◆ Toasted Garlic & Coriander Oil, 57

Desserts
◆◆ Apple Crisp with Pecans & Orange, 61
◆◆ Bourbon-Glazed Brown Sugar Pecan Poundcake, 62
◆◆ Chocolate Espresso Pecan Pie, 62
◆◆ Pecan Pineapple Upside-Down Cake, 60

Breakfast
◆ Apple-Butter Cinnamon Buns, 72
◆ Fastest Cinnamon Buns, 72
◆◆ Strawberry-Orange-Vanilla Breakfast Smoothie, 84

Beverages
◆◆ Strawberry-Orange-Vanilla Breakfast Smoothie, 84

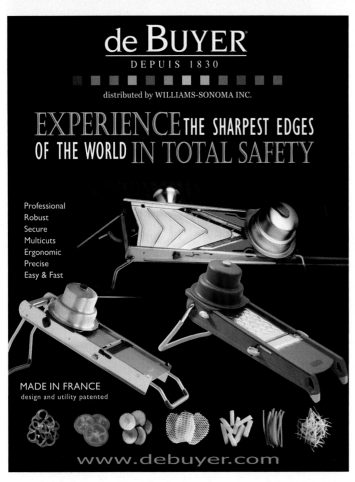

A Cook's Season

S ometimes it seems as if it's all about the turkey at this time of year. It's true, Thanksgiving does occupy a lot of our cooking brain space. But we can't forget what a great season this is for all kinds of cooking. The farmers' markets are still going strong, and days are cool and crisp, perfect for making hearty bean soups (p. 73), roasting all kinds of vegetables (p. 53), or spending a little time baking (you'll definitely want to try the Pecan Pineapple Upside-Down Cake on p. 60).

To put all these delicious recipes together for friends and family, check out our menu ideas below. Just remember to check the yield on each recipe, as you may need to double or halve it to suit your needs. Oh, and when it comes time to think turkey, turn to our great make-ahead menu from chef Ris Lacoste on p. 44. Her turkey is so juicy that it's worth cooking any time of year.

Two weeknight entertaining ideas

Each of these vibrantly flavored meals is built around a fast-cooking stir-fry, which you can prep while roasting the side vegetables in the oven.

Spicy Beef with Peanuts & Chiles, *p. 98a*

Roasted Green Beans with Sesame Salt, *p. 57*

To drink: A deeply flavored red like the 2004 Peter Lehmann Barossa Shiraz, Australia, $17

Orange Chicken with Scallions, *p. 98a*

Roasted Broccoli Crowns with Ginger-Lemon Soy Splash, *p. 57*

To drink: A crisp Riesling like the 2005 Gunderloch Kabinett Jean Baptiste, Germany, $16

For dessert: If you like, bake the Apple Crisp with Pecans & Orange on p. 61, but if you're pressed for time, why not serve vanilla ice cream with chocolate sauce and chopped, toasted pecans?

Elegant & easy fall dinner

Pork tenderloin makes a sophisticated main dish, especially when paired with seasonal vegetables, simply roasted and seasoned. The poundcake can be made up to two days ahead.

Pork Tenderloin with Sage & Marsala Sauce, *p. 26*

Roasted Butternut Squash with Moroccan-Style Spice Rub, *p. 56*

Roasted Mushrooms with Toasted Garlic & Coriander Oil, *p. 57*

Bourbon-Glazed Brown Sugar Pecan Poundcake, *p. 62*

To drink: A spicy Zinfandel like the 2005 Dry Creek Vineyard Heritage, California, $19

Three hearty soup & salad pairings

Pair one of Molly Stevens's bean and vegetable soups with a salad for a comforting midday or evening meal.

French Farmers' Soup, *p. 74*

Spinach Salad with Apples, Dried Apricots & Pappadam Croutons, *p. 66*

Minestrone, *p. 74*

Spinach Salad with Chicken, Cashews, Ginger & Fried Wontons, *p. 65*

Cabbage & White Bean Soup, *p. 74*

Warm Spinach Salad with Eggs, Bacon & Croutons, *p. 67*

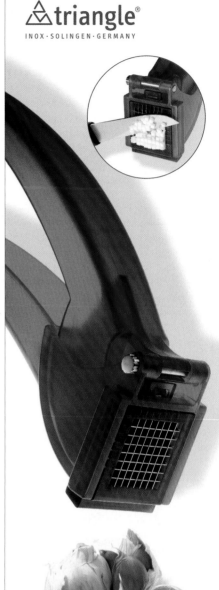

from the editor

Building Flavor From the Bottom Up

One day a soup wandered into my office. It showed up, unannounced, in a little paper cup on my desk. It was still hot, and I rummaged through my cabinets to find a spoon. I took a sip and stopped. Ahhh. There was that magic thing, that alchemy that happens in a broth that's been infused with layers of flavor—earthy beans, smoky bacon, sweet onions, piny rosemary.

Not long after, an editor followed the soup into my office, and I found out what the recipe was. It was the first test from Molly Stevens's "Cooking Without Recipes" article on hearty bean soups (see p. 73). I wasn't surprised it tasted so good, knowing that Molly had incorporated no less than seven places to boost flavor in her technique for making these soups. Starting with a rich base of sautéed aromatics and finishing with a flourish of fresh herbs, grated cheese, and crisp croutons, these soups didn't stand a chance at being dull.

Knowing how to build flavor is one of the secrets to becoming a great home cook. It's that thing that makes your friends ask why your recipes always turn out better than theirs. It's what makes the difference between so-so and sensational. It's what we try to teach you in every issue of *Fine Cooking*. Like this one.

Take chef Ris Lacoste's Thanksgiving turkey. While the rest of us might try brining or an herb butter under the skin to keep our turkeys juicy, she does both. And then she roasts the turkey under foil for the first half of cooking. Because of all three of those steps, that turkey has the juiciest, tastiest breast meat I've ever had. And that's even without the last layer of flavor: the rich Pinot Noir gravy she makes from the pan drippings.

And if you want a quick lesson in flavor boosting, check out our test kitchen manager Jennifer Armentrout's "Essential Guide to Roasting Vegetables," on p. 53. Jennifer doesn't stop at oil, salt, and pepper. She's got six ways, from spice rubs and infused oils to drizzling sauces and compound butters, to add flavor both before and after roasting her vegetables.

Admittedly, talking about great flavor in every issue can get a little frustrating for editors, since there are only so many ways to say delicious. Every once in a while, we run to check the thesaurus to see if another "flavor" word has come along. There are a few, but they tend to sound a little silly. So I hope you'll forgive me when I say, "Have a tasty Thanksgiving."

—*Susie Middleton, editor*

from our readers

Delicious, to say the least

Your July issue (*Fine Cooking* #86) is a home run. I have tried nearly every recipe in this issue, and the results have been amazing. The recipes from the "Grilling for a Crowd" special section are delicious, to say the least. And those lemon cheesecake squares—wow! They're great made with the lemon flavor, but my family and friends are split between which they like better—lemon or lime (lime needs a few drops of green food coloring). I could go on and on about the cobblers (p. 60), the Grilled Asian Pork Tenderloin with Peanut Sauce (p. 78a), the Quesadillas with Roasted Poblanos & Onions (p. 21), the grilled swordfish, (p. 40), etc. Thanks for putting together a great magazine.

—*Gina Vackaro, via email*

A finishing touch for a simple sauce

I have been an avid reader and subscriber to *Fine Cooking* for many years, and I love the magazine. This is the first time I have felt compelled to send in a letter to the editor. When I lived in Italy, I learned to love salsa cruda ("No-Cook Tomato Sauces," *Fine Cooking* #87, p. 38), and I make it whenever there are perfect tomatoes available.

I just wanted to let you know that you have left out the finishing touch that makes this sauce so wonderful. This is a step I learned in southern Italy: After portioning out individual servings of the pasta and sauce, top each with about 2 tablespoons of fresh, soft breadcrumbs that have been browned in olive oil. It's the perfect final touch.

—*Sharon Furman, via email*

How about barbecuing alternatives?

I really enjoy your publication, with its bright, easy-to-read pages and excellent photography. I look forward to receiving each issue and would only wish that it were published more often.

Now about the August/September issue (*Fine Cooking* #87): I loved the No-Cook Tomato Sauce. And Pam Anderson's "Chicken Thighs Take a Turn on the Grill" (p. 30) exemplified, as usual, her clear, concise information and directions. We don't barbecue, however, and I suspect a lot of other people don't either. People living in apartments or condos, for example, may have no place to barbecue or it may be prohibited. It would be helpful if all barbecue articles offered an alternative cooking method—oven roasting, baking, or broiling. Just a thought. Keep up the good work.

—*Joan Nazif, Vancouver, Canada*

Editors' reply: Thanks for the suggestion, Joan. In the meantime, if you would like to cook Pam's chicken thighs inside, try broiling them. Set an oiled rack about 6 inches from the broiler element and heat the broiler. Spread the thighs out on a rack set inside a foil-covered rimmed baking sheet or on the insert of a broiler pan. Broil until the thighs have plumped up and are browned in places, 5 to 6 minutes per side.

Keeping the flavor, losing the fat

First, let me tell you I have been a subscriber to *Fine Cooking* since issue # 22 (Aug./Sept. 1997), and I look forward to receiving every issue. Recently, my husband and I both had some health issues we needed to deal with, so we have been on the South Beach Diet for almost a year, with great success. We were not willing to sacrifice flavor and great food for our diet, though, so I have looked for ways to adapt many of your recipes to a good-carb, good-fat diet.

One really tasty and easy way to adapt many of the main courses and reduce fat from sautéing is to grill meats instead of cooking them on the stove. Our gas grill works well for that. I miss having the great brown stuff on the bottom of the pan, but I love the lean, grilled flavor. I do this regularly for your wonderful Arroz con Pollo (*Fine Cooking* #37, p. 82), and last night did the same with the Spicy Thai Beef Curry (*Fine Cooking* #81, p. 98c).

For the Arroz con Pollo, I cook the chicken parts and sausage on the grill while I sauté the vegetables. Since I now use brown rice, I add that with some additional broth, cook it about half way, and then combine the chicken and sausage to finish cooking. For the Spicy Thai Beef Curry, I just adapted the cooking time, putting the thinly sliced steak into the sauce in the last few minutes to heat. It worked great.

—*Anne Gomes, via email* ◆

EDITOR
Susie Middleton

ART DIRECTOR
Annie Giammattei

SPECIAL ISSUES EDITOR
Joanne McAllister Smart

SENIOR FOOD EDITOR/TEST KITCHEN MANAGER
Jennifer Armentrout

SENIOR EDITOR **Rebecca Freedman**

ASSOCIATE EDITORS
Laura Giannatempo, Lisa Waddle

MANAGING WEB EDITOR **Sarah Breckenridge**

SENIOR COPY/PRODUCTION EDITOR
Enid Johnson

ASSOCIATE ART DIRECTOR **Pamela Winn**

TEST KITCHEN ASSOCIATE/FOOD STYLIST
Allison Ehri Kreitler

EDITORIAL ASSISTANT **Kim Landi**

EDITORS AT LARGE
Maryellen Driscoll, Kimberly Y. Masibay

TEST KITCHEN INTERN **Will Moyer**

EDITORIAL INTERN **Sharon Anderson**

CONTRIBUTING EDITORS
Pam Anderson, Abigail Johnson Dodge, Tim Gaiser, Sarah Jay, Tony Rosenfeld, Molly Stevens

PUBLISHER **Maria Taylor**

ASSISTANT PUBLISHER **Karen Lutjen**

CIRCULATION DIRECTOR
Dennis O'Brien

SENIOR SINGLE COPY SALES MANAGER
Jay Annis

CORPORATE ACCOUNTS MANAGER
Judy Caruso

NATIONAL ACCOUNTS MANAGER
Linda Delaney

ADVERTISING SALES ASSOCIATE
Stacy Purcell

Fine Cooking: (ISSN: 1072-5121) is published seven times a year by The Taunton Press, Inc., Newtown, CT 06470-5506. Telephone 203-426-8171. Periodicals postage paid at Newtown, CT 06470 and at additional mailing offices. GST paid registration #123210981.

Subscription Rates: U.S. and Canada, $29.95 for one year, $49.95 for two years, $69.95 for three years (GST included, payable in U.S. funds). Outside the U.S./Canada: $36 for one year, $62 for two years, $88 for three years (payable in U.S. funds). Single copy, $6.95. Single copy outside the U.S., $7.95.

Postmaster: Send address changes to *Fine Cooking*, The Taunton Press, Inc., 63 South Main St., P.O. Box 5506, Newtown, CT 06470-5506.

Canada Post: Return undeliverable Canadian addresses to *Fine Cooking*, c/o Worldwide Mailers, Inc., 2835 Kew Drive, Windsor, ON N8T 3B7, or email to mnfa@taunton.com.

Printed in the USA.

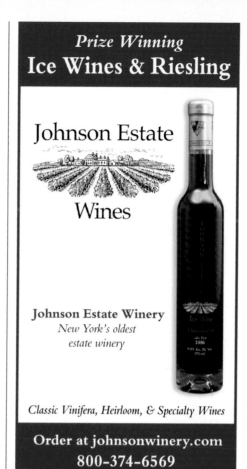

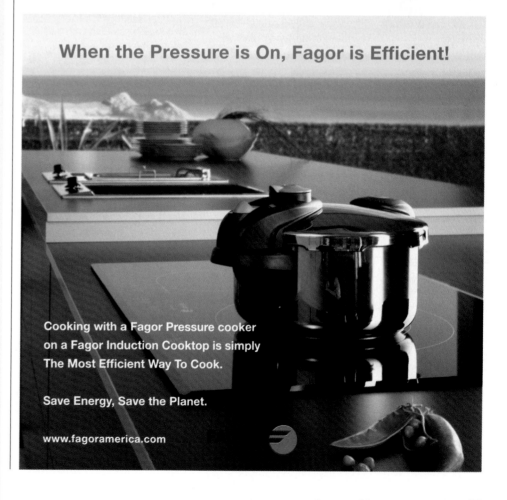

contributors

Ris Lacoste ("Thanksgiving," p. 44) has cooked many spectacular Thanksgiving dinners during her 10-year tenure as executive chef of 1789 Restaurant in Washington, DC. But the ones she cherishes most are the simple, comforting Thanksgiving meals her mother cooks every year for family and friends. Ris plans to open her own bistro-style restaurant in DC next spring.

Jennifer Armentrout

("Roasting Vegetables," p. 53) is *Fine Cooking's* senior food editor and test kitchen manager. During her vegetarian days in college, when her roommates got behind on washing their dishes, and baking sheets were the only things left, Jennifer discovered the beauty of roasting vegetables: quick, easy, and delicious. She's been at it ever since and is always happy to share her tips for getting a perfect crisp-on-the-outside, tender-on-the-inside texture.

Jennifer Armentrout

A New Yorker transplanted to North Carolina, **Karen Barker** ("Pecan Desserts," p. 58) feels drawn to her adopted region's most beloved ingredients—and that includes pecans. In this issue, she's channeled her love of these nuts into four fabulous desserts. Karen is the pastry chef and co-owner with husband Ben Barker of the Magnolia Grill restaurant in Durham. She's a graduate of The Culinary Institute of America and the author of two cookbooks, *Not Afraid of Flavor* and *Sweet Stuff: Karen Barker's American Desserts.* In 2003, she won a James Beard award for outstanding pastry chef.

Karen Barker

Joanne Weir ("Spinach Salads," p. 64) is all about "shaking things up in the kitchen" and giving new twists to classic

Ris Lacoste

dishes. She is a culinary instructor and the author of several cookbooks, including *From Tapas to Meze* and *Weir Cooking in the City,* which won a James Beard award. Joanne began her culinary career at Chez Panisse, in Berkeley, California, where she worked for five years before spending a year studying with master cooking instructor Madeleine Kamman.

Perla Meyers ("Linguine with Clam Sauce," p. 68) studied at Le Cordon Bleu in Paris. She is the author of eight cookbooks and conducts cooking workshops around the country and at her home in Washington Depot, Connecticut.

After running Great Cakes Bakery in Westport, Connecticut, for five years, **Kathy Kingsley** ("Fast Cinnamon Buns," p. 70) knows the restorative powers of sweets. She studied with master chocolatiers in Switzerland to develop the recipes for her latest cookbook, *Chocolate Therapy,* which focuses on ways chocolate can lift your spirits.

Fine Cooking contributing editor **Molly Stevens** ("Bean and Vegetable Soups," p. 73) is an expert on all things slow-cooked, whether it's braises, stews, or soups. She is, after all, the author of *All About Braising,* winner of both a James Beard award and an International Association of Culinary Professionals award. Besides being a prolific food writer, cookbook author, and editor, Molly is an accomplished cooking teacher who gives classes all over the country. In 2006, she was named the IACP cooking teacher of the year. ◆

The Taunton Press
Inspiration for hands-on living®

INDEPENDENT PUBLISHERS SINCE 1975

TAUNTON, INC.
Founders, **Paul and Jan Roman**

THE TAUNTON PRESS
President **Suzanne Roman**

Executive Vice President &
Chief Financial Officer **Timothy Rahr**

Executive Vice President &
Publisher, Magazine Group **Jon Miller**

Chief of Operations **Thomas Luxeder**

Group Publisher, Home **Paul Spring**

DIRECTORS
Creative & Editorial Director **Susan Edelman**
Human Resources Director **Carol Marotti**
Technology Services Director **Jay Hartley**
Controller **Wayne Reynolds**
Fulfillment Director **Patricia Williamson**
Financial Analysis Director **Kathy Worth**
Circulation Director **Dennis O'Brien**

THE TAUNTON PRESS

Books: *Marketing:* Melissa A. Possick, Audrey Locorotondo. *Publicity:* Nicole Salvatore, Janel Noblin. *Editorial:* Helen Albert, Kathryn Benoit, Peter Chapman, Steve Culpepper, Pamela Hoenig, Courtney Jordan, Carolyn Mandarano, Nicole Palmer, Jennifer Russell, Erica Sanders-Foege, Kathleen Williams. *Art:* Alison Wilkes, Nancy Boudreau, Amy Griffin, Sandra Mahlstedt, Wendi Mijal, Lynne Phillips, Carol Singer. *Manufacturing:* Thomas Greco, Laura Burrone.

Business Office: Holly Smith, Gayle Hammond, Patricia Marini. *Legal:* Carolyn Kovaleski. *Magazine Print Production:* Philip Van Kirk, Nicole Chappuis, Jennifer Kaczmarcyk.

Circulation: David Pond, Andrew Corson, Catherine Hansen.

Distribution: Paul Seipold, Walter Aponte, Frank Busino, David DeToto, Leanne Furlong, Deborah Greene, Frank Melbourne, Reinaldo Moreno, Raymond Passaro, Darian Pettway, Michael Savage, Alice Saxton.

Finance/Accounting: *Finance:* Brett Manning. *Accounting:* Patrick Lamontagne, Lydia Krikorian, Michelle Mendonca, Judith O'Toole, Elaine Yamin, Carol Diehm, Dorothy Blasko, Susan Burke, Lorraine Parsons, Larry Rice, James Tweedle, Priscilla Jennings.

Fulfillment: Diane Goulart. *Fulfillment Systems:* Jodi Klein, Kim Eads, Nancy Knorr, Thomas Kuzebski. *Customer Service:* Kathleen Baker, Bonnie Beardsley, Deborah Ciccio, Katherine Clarke, Alfred Dreher, Paula Ferreri, Eileen McNulty, Patricia Parks, Deana Parker, Patricia Pineau, Betty Stepney. *Data Entry:* Melissa Youngberg, Anne Champlin, Mary Ann Colbert, Caryne-Lynne Davis, Maureen Pekar, Debra Sennefelder, Andrea Shorrock, Marylou Thompson, Barbara Williams.

Human Resources: Linda Ballerini, Christine Lincoln, Dawn Ussery.

Photos, from top: Scott Phillips, Amy Albert, Stacy Zarin-Goldberg

on the web
What's new at **FineCooking.com**

This fall we're rolling out new Web-only features, new videos, and access to our complete recipe archive.

on the front burner

Ultimate Thanksgiving Survival Guide

Everything you need to know about cooking the turkey, plus more than 50 recipes for sides, stuffing, gravy, and desserts.

Features

▶ **Exclusive Web-only feature:** Secret-ingredient pumpkin pies

How-to videos

▶ **Stuffing and trussing a turkey**

▶ **Rubbing butter under the skin**

▶ **Making gravy from pan drippings**

Book excerpt

▶ **Download an excerpt** from *Fine Cooking*'s newest book, *How to Cook a Turkey and all the Other Trimmings*

HOW TO COOK A *Turkey*
AND ALL THE OTHER TRIMMINGS
From the Editors and Contributors of **Fine Cooking**

▶ **Create your own bread stuffing:** Build a customized recipe with your favorite add-ins

▶ **Equipment review:** The best roasting pans

▶ **Three ideas** for a small crowd

▶ **Expert answers** to your Thanksgiving menu dilemmas

Become a FineCooking.com Member

Fine Cooking's **complete recipe archive now online**

▶ **Browse and search** recipes by ingredient, course, cuisine, and more

▶ **Rate and review recipes**

▶ **Save and organize** your favorite *Fine Cooking* recipes, menus, and articles

And many more features to come

on the front burner

Tomato-Fest

Make the most of the early-fall harvest of juicy, ripe tomatoes with our recipes and how-to features.

Bonus download

▶ **Top 10 tomato recipes**

Recipes & Features

▶ **Fresh-tomato pasta sauces**

▶ **Rustic beefsteak tomato tart**

▶ **Creamy tomato soups**

▶ **How to use green tomatoes**

Juicy, ripe cherry tomatoes are the key to quick sauces for pasta, polenta, and more.

free email newsletter

Sign up at FineCooking.com to get great recipes, tips, techniques, and videos delivered directly to your inbox twice a month.

---

cooks talk Advice from our online forum

Visit Cooks Talk, our online discussion group, for a lively exchange of ideas, recipes, and advice. You'll find Cooks Talk on our Web site at FineCooking.com. Here are some recent highlights.

Peanut butter question

CREATED BY HEATHER: I have noticed that almost all baking recipes that use peanut butter specify that results will be better with regular, not "natural," peanut butter. Is the partially hydrogenated oil necessary for good results? Trader Joe's peanut butter is organic and contains only peanuts and salt, but it doesn't separate. Will it work as well as Skippy?

Posted by CookiMonster: I often see that warning, too, but I have yet to encounter a recipe where the natural peanut butter didn't work just fine.

Posted by Meg: I've used natural peanut butter in a very simple cookie recipe, and there was a difference. The recipe calls for an egg, peanut butter, baking soda, sugar, and maybe something else. When I've made this with "regular" peanut butter, it behaved quite well. The last time I used natural peanut butter, the recipe seemed stiffer and more crumbly. It took more effort to devise a ball shape, and I had to be more careful about how hard I pressed down with the fork to make the usual surface decoration. But they tasted just fine, and once baked, most peanut butter cookies crumble, anyway. I don't know if I'd bother purchasing "regular" peanut butter just to make cookies.

Feedback on Potato, Thyme & Olive Oil Gratin, FC #74

CREATED BY JEAN: Sliced potatoes coated with olive oil, s&p, sprinkled with fresh thyme, and baked in chicken broth at 375°F, covered for ½ hour and then uncovered until browned and done. Easy and tasty.

I used my little Emile Henry dish that fits so nicely in my toaster oven. Easy and about as healthy as you can make a potato. Served with ham, green beans, and applesauce. I'm sure I'll do this again, probably using ham broth.

Posted by SallyBR1: Excellent! I love potato gratin but refrain from making it that often because of all the fat. This sounds like a great option; plus, I could make it in individual gratin dishes.

Posted by RisottoGirl: I really prefer the style of gratin made with stock rather than cream. It is tasty and much lighter, without trying to be light. I think it works well with a wider variety of mains, too.

I make it using a fresh bay laurel leaf when I can get it. I love potatoes with bay laurel. ◆

Clockwise from the top: Cumberland, Galloway, Appalachian Spring, La Mancha

Raw-Milk Cheese
from Tennessee

BY LAURA GIANNATEMPO

"I've always been fascinated by milk," says Tim Clark, a Baptist minister and co-owner of Locust Grove Farm in Knoxville, Tennessee. "It's a living thing." That's why when he decided to convert his 25 acres of sheep pasture into a dairy three years ago, he knew he would make only raw-milk cheeses. "Pasteurization changes milk, including its flavor," he says, referring to the process of heating milk to kill certain bacteria. As a result, Locust Grove Farm is the only licensed raw-milk dairy in the state.

Tim has raised sheep for more than 20 years and has always been intrigued by the process of turning milk into cheese. But when he started farming, no one was making cheese in the Southeast, so he turned to articles and books for cheesemaking information. Then he got a hands-on crash course working on a dairy farm in Scotland with master cheesemaker Allan Brown. When he returned home, he had everything he needed to start out on his own.

With the help of business partner Sheri Palko and his wife, Brenda, Tim makes four distinctive sheep's milk cheeses: Galloway, a mild, nutty semi-hard farmhouse cheddar made by a process he learned in Scotland; Appalachian Spring, a delightfully tangy Gouda-style cheese with a faintly sweet finish; the subtly sharp, creamy La Mancha, Locust Grove's interpretation of Spain's manchego; and Cumberland, a semi-hard cheese spiced with green peppercorns, red chiles, onion, garlic, and ginger.

All the cheeses are made by hand with the farm's own sheep's milk and nothing else but cultures, vegetable rennet, and salt. Tim and Sheri are firm believers in old-time, sustainable farming practices: Their free-range sheep are on grass year-round and are never given any processed feeds, hormones, or antibiotics. *For more information, visit LocustGroveFarm.net; to order, call 865-567-5213.* ◆

To make his Galloway cheese, Tim Clark puts the milk in a large vat and slowly raises the temperature to about 87°F. Then he adds natural bacterial cultures along with rennet, which causes the curds to separate from the whey. He cuts the curds using a custom-made knife (right).

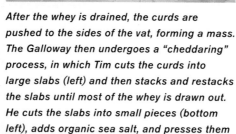

After the whey is drained, the curds are pushed to the sides of the vat, forming a mass. The Galloway then undergoes a "cheddaring" process, in which Tim cuts the curds into large slabs (left) and then stacks and restacks the slabs until most of the whey is drawn out. He cuts the slabs into small pieces (bottom left), adds organic sea salt, and presses them into molds by hand (bottom right). Then, using a manual press, he squeezes out all the liquid.

The cheese is moved to a temperature- and humidity-controlled ripening room, where it ages for a minimum of 60 days (required by law for all raw-milk cheeses).

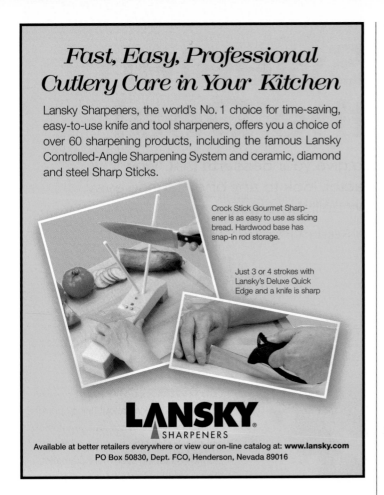

Sweeten the Deal

To give your desserts that "wow" factor, look to any one of these easy embellishments

BY REBECCA FREEDMAN

An effortless chocolate finale

We fell for these Swiss chocolate cups the minute we saw them, because they make a hassle-free base for the easiest impressive dessert ever. Just fill the cups with ice cream, mousse, or fresh berries, top with crème fraîche, and voilà—dessert is served. *Chocolate cups, $50.76 for a box of 36 at AuiSwissCatalogue .com (800-231-8154). Search for product code 004336.*

Baubles add a little drama

If you were thinking about using sprinkles or dragées to decorate your next home-made dessert, stop right there. We've found something even more dramatic: These shiny and colorful chocolate "pearls" (about a quarter-inch in diameter) are perfect for cake decorating. They're also available in white chocolate, coated in red. *Michel Cluizel chocolate pearls, $15 per tube; to order, call 212-477-7335.*

Dessert strikes gold (silver, too)

If you've ever admired fancy restaurant desserts adorned with touches of shiny gold, you'll know why we're excited to use this edible gold and silver in our own kitchens. Get creative: Try sprinkling some of the "petals" on hot chocolate or chocolate-covered strawberries. Use the powder to rim champagne or martini glasses or to dust chocolate truffles. And if you really have the Midas touch, experiment with the gold and silver leaves, which let you gild just about any food. *Edible gold and silver powder, petals, and leaves, $21 to $100, at SurLaTable.com (800-243-0852). For information and a list of other retailers, visit EasyLeafProducts.com.*

Go floral

We think candied rose, lilac, and violet petals make a cute—and tasty—addition to individual cakes or cupcakes. Try pairing them with some candied mint leaves for a little extra flavor and decoration. *Candied flower petals and mint leaves, $8 per 2-ounce package, MarketHallFoods.com (888-952-4005).* ◆

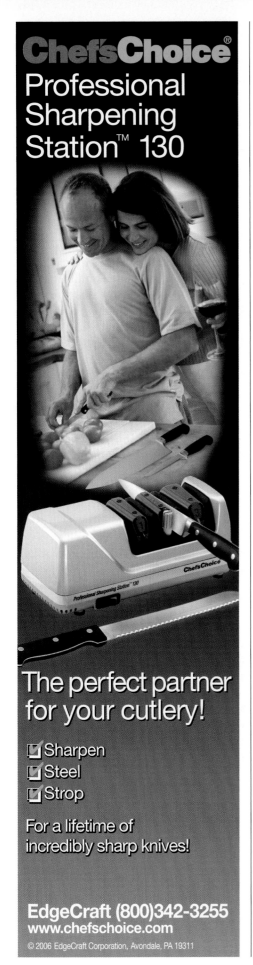

Q&A

Is there a secret to keeping my pumpkin pie filling from separating from the crust?

—Gloria Betz, via email

Carole Walter responds: A custard pie filling separates from the crust because of shrinkage, which is a normal part of the cooling process. The fact is, all baked goods shrink as they cool due to the evaporation of moisture during baking; with a pie, the filling and crust are shrinking in opposite directions, which often results in separation. There are ways to reduce the chance of this happening, though. One is to avoid extreme changes in temperature; choose a spot to cool your pie that is free of drafts, and do not put the pie in the refrigerator until it has cooled completely. I prefer serving a pie the day it is made so that it doesn't need to go into the fridge. Also, I always prebake the pastry crust for pumpkin and other custard pies to give the crust a chance to shrink before the filling is added. Even though the filling will still shrink upon cooling, separation will be minimized.

If you must bake a pumpkin pie a day ahead, your best bet may be to disguise any separation. I like to sprinkle chopped toasted pecans or almonds around the edge of the filling before serving. I've also used crushed gingersnaps or biscotti. If you like, you could pipe whipped cream decoratively around the edge. Realize that the separation may be unavoidable, and that one bite of a homemade pumpkin pie will take everyone's mind off how it looks.

Carole Walter is a baking instructor and the author of several cookbooks, including Great Pies & Tarts.

Have a question of general interest about cooking? Send it to Q&A, Fine Cooking, PO Box 5506, Newtown, CT 06470-5506, or by email to fcqa@taunton.com, and we'll find a cooking professional with the answer.

When baking bread and other pastries, some recipes call for an egg wash, others for brushing the top with milk. Are they interchangeable?

—April Finnegan, New York, New York

Nicole Rees responds: Brushing with an egg wash gives a different effect than using milk, so they are not interchangeable. Pastry chefs use an egg wash primarily for shine, though the egg yolk will contribute a golden color to the finished baked product. For a clear shine, an egg white alone can be used. Milk, on the other hand, is used to encourage browning. For example, scones and biscuits will be pale on top (even though the bottom side is brown) if not brushed with milk or cream before baking.

Dairy products contain both amino acids and certain types of sugars that react with one another in the high heat of the oven and undergo what is called the Maillard, or browning, reaction. This process creates the appetizing golden color we see, but more important, it develops the savory flavor of browned foods.

Nicole Rees is a food scientist who co-wrote the revised edition of Understanding Baking *and its companion recipe book,* The Baker's Manual.

What is the difference between cultured and old-fashioned buttermilk?

—Maria Presley, Durham, Connecticut

Cary Frye responds: What we call old-fashioned, or churned, buttermilk is very different from cultured buttermilk. It is the thin, slightly acidic liquid left over after churning butter from full-cream milk. It is drunk or used in soups and sauces in northern Europe and South Asia but is not available commercially in the United States.

The buttermilk sold in supermarkets here is cultured, created by fermenting pasteurized low-fat or nonfat milk so the milk sugars turn into lactic acid. It is thick and tart, a result of its increased acidity, which keeps the milk protein casein from being soluble and results in clabbering or curdling. (That is why you can make a stand-in for buttermilk by adding a tablespoon of lemon juice or white vinegar to a cup of milk, increasing the acidity and curdling the milk.)

Old-fashioned and cultured buttermilk cannot be used interchangeably. Cultured buttermilk is used in pancakes, scones, biscuits, and other baked products because of the tangy flavor and tender texture it imparts.

Cary Frye is vice president for regulatory affairs for the International Dairy Foods Association. ◆

Fall for Sage

BY RUTH LIVELY

It's hard to believe there was a time when the idea of cooking with sage would never have crossed my mind. I loved it as a beautiful plant in my garden, but its strong herbal aroma kept me from using it in the kitchen. Until one day, after realizing I'd run out of rosemary and thyme, I tried adding a few fresh sage leaves to a batch of potatoes I was roasting. To my delight, they made a favorite recipe even better. Cooking, it turns out, mellows sage's potent aroma and flavor to a very appealing level. Pretty soon, my one big plant wasn't enough to keep up with my ever-growing demand for this delightfully hearty, wintry herb.

Fresh is best

Although sage is available both fresh and dried, I recommend using fresh. Dried sage has a stronger, more concentrated flavor that can sometimes be bitter. If you're flavoring a soup, a stew, or a pot of beans, or if you're making a rub, dried sage, either ground or crumbled, is a decent substitute for fresh. But if you really want the sage flavor to shine, you have to use fresh leaves. Fortunately, sage plants are tough enough to withstand light frosts, so sage is available much of the year.

When looking for things to pair with sage, think rich, starchy, and sweet. It's fabulous with pork (see my recipe on p. 26); it boosts the flavor of potatoes, beans, grains, and breads (think stuffing); and it provides a good counterpoint to the sweet starchiness of winter squash, sweet potatoes, and pumpkin. It's also delicious with apples and pears.

(continued on p. 26)

From garden to kitchen

Sage plants need lots of sunshine and do best in gritty, well-drained, not-too-fertile soil. Harvest individual leaves or sprigs several inches long. Rinse them to remove dust and gently blot them dry with a kitchen towel. Whether you grow your own or buy it at the store, keep sage as dry as possible, as moisture will cause it to deteriorate quickly. The best way to store it is in the refrigerator inside a sealed plastic bag lined with a paper towel. It'll keep for two or three days.

All the pretty sages

At the market, you'll typically find only standard culinary sage (*Salvia officinalis*), which has gray-green leaves with a pebbled, slightly fuzzy texture. But at herb nurseries (See Where to Buy It, p. 92), you'll find many more sage types to grow and cook with. They have similar flavors, but they vary in shape and color. Be aware that there are some types of sage that aren't edible; so for kitchen use, make sure you buy one that is (all *Salvia officinalis* varieties are edible). Here are some of my favorites:

Berggarten is a nonflowering sage, so the plant's energy is devoted to producing lots of aromatic leaves.

Holt's Mammoth has leaves twice the size of regular sage.

Woodcote Farm has large leaves and is resistant to powdery mildew (a problem with sage in humid climates).

Variegated sages are as beautiful as they are tasty. Golden sage (far left, center) has bright-green leaves edged in creamy yellow; purple sage (lower left) has dusky purple leaves; and tricolor sage (upper left) has leaves splashed with green, purple, and beige.

U.S. Farm-Raised Catfish <u>*lettuce*</u> <u>*tacos*</u> **with** <u>*tomato*</u> <u>*salad*</u>.
VEGETABLE   NOUN   ADJECTIVE   NOUN

Always fresh, healthy, mild and flaky, U.S. Farm-Raised Catfish suits

any recipe. For some of my favorites, visit **catfishinstitute.com**

FOOD NETWORK CHEF *Cat Cora*

Pork Tenderloin with Sage & Marsala Sauce

Serves four.

I like to serve this dish with garlic mashed potatoes, braised vegetables, or just a fresh green salad.

**1 large pork tenderloin (1¼ to
  1½ lb.), trimmed and cut in
  half crosswise**
½ tsp. kosher salt
¼ tsp. freshly ground black pepper
**2 tsp. pink peppercorns, crushed
  (optional)**
2 Tbs. unsalted butter
1 Tbs. extra-virgin olive oil
½ cup sweet Marsala
1 Tbs. chopped fresh sage leaves
**Fried sage leaves (see below),
  for garnish (optional)**

Position a rack in the center of the oven and heat the oven to 375°F.

Season the pork tenderloin with the salt and pepper and rub it evenly with the pink peppercorns, if using.

Heat 1 Tbs. of the butter and the oil in a 10-inch ovenproof skillet or straight-sided sauté pan over medium-high heat. Put the pork in the pan and sear it until golden brown on all sides, about 5 minutes total. Transfer the skillet to the oven and roast until an instant-read thermometer inserted in the center of the meat registers 140°F, 10 to 15 minutes. Move the pork to a cutting board and tent loosely with foil.

Pour off and discard most of the fat left in the skillet. Set the skillet over medium-high heat and add the Marsala. Bring to a vigorous simmer, scraping the bottom of the pan with a wooden spoon to loosen any browned bits. Simmer until reduced by half, about 2 minutes. Off the heat, add the remaining 1 Tbs. butter and the chopped sage. Swirl or stir the sauce until the butter melts.

Slice the pork into 12 pieces, arrange them on a platter, and pour the hot pan sauce over the meat. Garnish with the fried sage leaves, if using.

Fried sage: garnish or snack

Fried sage makes an unusual crisp garnish for roasted meats and poultry, mashed potatoes, and even risotto. Or it can be a treat all on its own to enjoy with other nibbles like olives, toasted nuts, and cheese. And it takes only a few minutes to cook.

Always start with clean and dry whole leaves—the bigger the better—with stems left on. Pour enough olive oil in a heavy skillet to cover the bottom by about ⅛ inch and heat over medium heat until the oil shimmers. Add sage leaves in a single layer and fry until brittle but still a bright green color with no browning, 15 to 30 seconds. Transfer to a plate lined with paper towels and sprinkle with salt.

Sage ideas

Here are more delicious ways to add sage to your everyday cooking.

Roast baby potato halves on a bed of sage in a roasting pan covered with a thin layer of olive oil.

Dress up Tuscan-style beans. Simmer cannellini beans with lots of chopped fresh sage, garlic, and pepper. Dress the cooked beans while still hot with a vinaigrette of olive oil, red-wine vinegar, chopped fresh sage, and garlic.

Whip up a quick and tasty pasta sauce. Caramelize onion slices in olive oil and add chopped sage and walnut pieces during the last 10 minutes of cooking. Season and toss with hot pasta and crumbled gorgonzola.

Make a sumptuous squash soup. Sauté cubes of acorn squash with chopped onion, sage, and garlic and then simmer in chicken or vegetable broth until tender. Purée, season, and add a little cream, if you like.

Make a rich gnocchi sauce. Toss cooked and drained gnocchi in a pan of browned butter and whole sage leaves and season well.

Cook up juicy saltimbocca. Lay a thin slice of prosciutto and a large sage leaf on a pounded veal cutlet; roll up and secure with a toothpick. Season the rolls and brown them in butter. Then make a sauce by deglazing the pan with sweet Marsala.

Ruth Lively cooks, writes, and gardens in New Haven, Connecticut. ◆

From pro kitchens to yours

H ere are two new ideas for your home, copied from restaurant kitchens. Both come from American Range, a company that has just started selling to the residential market after making commercial ranges for 30 years. The range and oven come in 10 colors, and you can find a list of distributors at AmericanRange.com.

Step up to a new range

With its back burners 5 inches higher than the front ones, this range offers easier access to sauté pans and small saucepans in the rear. The Step-Up residential range is available in 24- and 30-inch styles with four burners and 36- and 48-inch styles with six burners (shown). The gas range incorporates several professional-grade features, such as a 15,500-BTU infrared broiler burner, a 5.6-cubic-foot oven cavity that uses dual convection motors, and sealed burners. Prices range from $3,450 for the 24-inch to $6,500 for the 48-inch model.

...yle range & oven	28
...el ladle	29
...s. masher	29
	32
...ers	32
	33
...k at home	33
...ars & pestles	34
...WADDLE	

Easy-open oven

Here's a space-saving alternative to the traditional downward-opening oven door: a French-door wall oven. The two doors open dependently; that is, pulling on one handle opens them both. So instead of hovering over a hot open door and reaching in to baste a turkey or check doneness on a cake, you can step closer to your food and not strain your back. The doors extend just over 15 inches when opened, compared to more than 20 inches for traditional ovens, making these a nice solution for tiny apartments or kitchens with nearby islands or tables. At nearly 30 inches wide, the oven has a cavity of 4.7 cubic feet and sells for about $3,000.

A ladle that's got it all

For dishing up stews or soups like those in our hearty bean and vegetable soup story on p. 73, a good ladle is a big help. But ladles are not all alike.

This stainless-steel version from Fissler, a company that's been making and selling kitchen tools in Europe for more than 150 years, has just been introduced in the United States. It has a comfortable, nubbed handle and a handy hook for hanging, and at nearly 11 inches long, it can dip into a deep stock pot. The bowl itself is deep enough that it's not apt to let bulky stew ingredients slip out. Some ladles have a molded lip on the side, but these can complicate pouring, forcing you to turn your wrist awkwardly to serve. The Fissler has a rimmed edge all around that prevents most drips when pouring.

You can buy the Fissler Magic Line ladle for $24 at Amazon.com.

Potato ricer vs. masher

Mashed potatoes are as essential as turkey to most Thanksgiving tables. What's the best way to deliver that smooth texture everyone loves? To find out, I put the two most commonly used tools, a ricer and a masher, to the test:

Ricer

This extrusion tool forces cooked potato through small holes, resulting in rice-like pieces of potato (hence the name). It's constructed of a hopper into which you put a cooked (peeled or not) potato and a plunger that forces the potato through the holes. Because air is incorporated into the potato as it's pressed, this tool gives you the lightest mashed potatoes possible. A ricer guarantees no lumps, and your potatoes will be very smooth. The only downside is that it can be a bit time-consuming, especially if you're using unpeeled potatoes, as the skins must be removed from the hopper after each pressing; otherwise, they clog the holes.

Masher

Hand mashers get a bad rap for leaving lumps, but I found that they can, in fact, deliver smooth, creamy potatoes. You just have to be methodical with your mashing method, getting into every corner of the pot and using a press and twist motion with the masher, adding a little liquid at a time if you must. (Be sure your potatoes are thoroughly cooked, too.) If you like the skins in your finished dish (for nutrition and texture), a masher or metal spoon is the only way to go. Don't expect mashers to deliver light or fluffy potatoes, though.

Bottom line: Which tool you use depends on your definition of ideal mashed potatoes. If you're after a bowl of textured spuds, especially good when adding extras like herbs or cheese, a masher should be your choice. If fluffy and smooth is your idea of potato nirvana, go with a ricer. Either way, be sure to buy a durable model that feels good in your hand. When you have a pile of potatoes to work through, you don't want a flimsy tool that's going to cause a hand cramp.

Pictured: RSVP Endurance jumbo potato ricer, $30 from ChefTools.com. Danesco double-action stainless potato masher, $6 from TableTools.com.

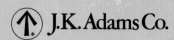

Smart Solutions for Easier Holiday Cooking

Keeping it hot

Here's a great pan for entertaining or for families who eat at different times. The Kuhn Rikon Hotpan is a stainless-steel pot with a lid that fits into a bright melamine bowl that doubles as an insulating jacket. I tried it during a dinner party and not only did it keep mashed potatoes nicely warm on the countertop for two hours, but it also freed up a burner. (And a bonus: the bowl looked good enough to serve from.) It also kept a couscous dish toasty during transport to a potluck, and the bowl served as a stay-cool shell for the pan, so I didn't need potholders or a trivet. The 18/10 stainless-steel pan has heat-resistant handles and comes in five sizes: 1 quart, 2 quart, 3 quart, 5 quart, and a 4½-quart braizer. The bowl can also be used on its own. Prices range from $100 to $200 at Amazon.com.

This stainless-steel pot nests in an insulating melamine bowl that makes it pretty enough to bring to the table while also keeping the food warm.

More room to cook

Whether you're looking to ease the stovetop crunch during Thanksgiving or need a way to keep dishes warm on a buffet, an extra burner can be a smart investment. Though the standard electric hotplate we used in college is still around, technology has advanced a bit. I put three differently fueled portable burners through their paces, assessing both their capacity to cook and to maintain steady low temperatures.

Viking portable induction cooker
Price: $500 at ChefsResource.com

This impressive induction burner with its glass-ceramic surface and stainless-steel frame allows you to adjust heat instantly and with great precision. The lowest setting is below a simmer, while "high" delivers the equivalent of 15,000 BTUs and boiled 4 cups of water in less than four minutes. Safety features include a knob that must be pushed to be turned, an automatic shut-off one minute after a pan is removed, and the fact that it won't heat up at all unless compatible cookware is used on it. It accommodates pots and pans up to 12 inches in diameter.

Deni halogen burner
Price: $150 at Deni.com

Slimmer and lighter than the Viking induction cooker, this burner is powered by quartz glass tubes filled with halogen gas, below a glass-ceramic cooktop. It plugs in and heats up instantly with the push of a button and cools down quickly. It boiled 4 cups of water in six minutes, and its lowest setting is below a simmer. Safety features include a light that blinks as long as the burner remains hot, even if the unit has been turned off. The cooking surface is 9½ inches in diameter, but it can accommodate pots and pans up to 12 inches.

Bonjour buffet tabletop burner
Price: $50 at BonjourProducts.com

Consisting of a lightweight chrome stand and a butane-powered gas burner, this is the most portable of the three burners. It also took the longest to boil water, most likely because the gas jet is rather small in diameter. The gas could easily be set low enough to hold a simmer. Once the butane tank is filled, it burns for up to three hours and unlike the other two reviewed, it does not require a plug or cord. It can accommodate pots up to 12 inches in diameter. The chrome stand does become quite hot, and the open flame is a potential safety hazard.

A lightweight stir-fry pan

In many of our stir-fry recipes (such as those in Quick & Delicious, p. 98a), we call for a 12-inch skillet or a stir-fry pan. Why not a traditional wok? Well, a classic round-bottom wok is designed to sit directly in the cooking flames. When that style is used on a western stovetop, with a ring, the result is largely unsatisfactory for stir-frying—only the very bottom of the pan gets hot enough. If your stove is one of the few with a special high-powered wok burner, then by all means use it with a traditional wok for stir-fry recipes. For the rest of us, a stir-fry pan is a better solution. Here's what to look for:

Comfortable handle— this one is made of stay-cool resin and is oven safe to 350°F

Generous flat bottom at least 6 inches across, for stability

Top diameter of 12 inches or more

Nonstick surface for easier cleaning

Sloped sides 3 to 4 inches high, for easy tossing

Instead of a heavy-gauge— and expensive—pan, look for a mid-range one that's light enough to pick up easily, even when full of food.

Pictured: The Circulon Total open stir-fry pan, $40 at Amazon.com.

Making soy milk at home

I'm a big fan of soy milk for both drinking and baking but have always balked at paying close to $3 for a quart of the commercially available brands. Making my own seemed too much of a production, until I tried the Soyabella soymilk maker by Tribest. Using it is easy: You just plug in the machine, pour soybeans (from a can or dried beans soaked overnight) into the mesh basket, screw on the top, and push a button. In 15 minutes the machine grinds the beans (rather loudly) and heats the water, producing 1 quart of hot soymilk.

I like to substitute soy milk directly for cow's milk in baking recipes such as banana bread and pancakes, but I also drink it straight, with just a pinch of salt. The Soyabella also makes raw nut or rice milk.

The goof-proof elements are part of what makes this appliance a winner: no exposed heating coil and sensors that shut the unit off if there's too much or not enough water added. It even comes with a cleaning brush and scouring pad, making it simple to keep the stainless-steel cooking chamber and mesh basket clean. And it ends up costing less than 50 cents for a quart of fresh soymilk. The Soyabella sells for $100 at EverythingKitchens.com.

review
Mortars and Pestles

BY MARYELLEN DRISCOLL

Consider material and size when shopping for one of these versatile tools

Pestle

Mortar

The mortar and pestle are ancient tools that no modern kitchen should be without. They're handy for everything from cracking peppercorns and crushing tender herbs to making pesto and guacamole. Yet, these days, electric spice grinders and food processors often take their place, and that's a pity, because after testing an assortment of mortars and pestles, we're convinced that a good set can perform as well—or even better—at many tasks.

Of the 18 mortars and pestles we tested (see "How we tested," at right), many models frustrated us or proved to be of limited use, but a few workhorses were delightfully versatile and excelled at every task we threw at them, including crushing garlic, spices, and nuts.

Our favorite

What to look for

In performing our tests, we discovered that material, shape, and size are the key characteristics to look at when shopping for a mortar and pestle.

The ideal material for a mortar and pestle is something hefty and very hard. It shouldn't be so rough as to be porous or difficult to clean, nor should it be so smooth as to be slippery.

The Thai granite model above embodied our ideal: Literally rock hard, its matte surface created friction for grinding but was smooth enough to wipe clean easily, and its heft made crushing a breeze. Several other stone models were also very effective. However, an Italian marble mortar paired with a light, relatively soft wood pestle failed to impress because the pestle required us to work harder to achieve good results, and it couldn't grind cumin seed.

In fact, all the wood mortars and pestles we tried seemed too light and soft to be

effective at all the tasks we wanted them to do. Other materials, too, had shortcomings: With porcelain, breaking was a concern (one model we tested broke on the first use). And slick surfaces like stainless steel let ingredients slip around too much.

The best mortars have a deeply rounded shape that keeps ingredients from jumping or spilling out. Wider, shallow shapes don't contain ingredients as well. A stable base is also important. When it comes to pestles, many are too narrow and rounded, so ingredients readily pop out from under them. A broader, more gently rounded base works far better.

As for size, think big rather than small. If you're looking to buy just a single mortar and pestle, a capacious mortar can mash small quantities just as well as large. But a too-small mortar is, ultimately, of limited use and lets ingredients pop out (the low-profile model at far right, however, innovatively solves this problem).

Thai granite mortar and pestle

$30.95 at ImportFood.com
7-inch diameter;
2-cup capacity

This solid, hand-carved mortar and pestle excels at the full range of tasks, from mashing delicate herbs to grinding stubborn peppercorns. The heavy, broad-based pestle needs to do little more than fall on ingredients to crush them—very little elbow grease required. And the bowl's deeply sloped shape and matte texture keep ingredients in the center, so there's no need to chase them around with the pestle. At 12 pounds, this mortar won't scoot around during use, but we suggest putting a cloth beneath it to protect your counter. Also comes in 6-, 8-, and 9-inch sizes.

Other good choices (listed in order of capacity)

Mexican molcajete y tejolote poblano

$36.95 at GourmetSleuth.com
7½- to 8-inch diameter;
3-cup capacity

Traditionally for making salsa, mole, and guacamole, good *molcajetes* (mortars) and *tejolotes* (pestles) are made from basalt (volcanic rock). *Molcajetes* vary widely in quality—some aren't even pure basalt—so purchase with care. Of the two we tried, we prefer this one's smoother surface and deeper, more rounded bowl. The cleaning brush that was included helps get the textured surface clean. We recommend putting a towel underneath for stability and to protect your counter.

Cast-iron mortar and pestle by Typhoon

$30 at Typhoonus.com
6-inch diameter;
2-cup capacity

Its hard surface, the pestle's heft, and the bowl's depth give this model many of the advantages of the Thai granite model. The pour spout is a nice feature. But it has weaknesses, too: You need to hold the mortar steady when pressing or pounding the pestle any way but straight down. Also, the cast iron will react with acidic ingredients, and to avoid rust, it needs to be washed and dried promptly after use and regularly seasoned with oil.

Pedestal-style mortar and pestle by Fox Run

$14.95 at Lehmans.com
4-inch diameter;
⅓-cup capacity

This is a common style, but we like this particular model because the pestle is wider than the others we tried. If you're strictly looking for a small model for little jobs, this is an inexpensive, effective option. Though small, the deep bowl prevents most pop-outs, but jumpy ingredients like peppercorns need to be crushed with caution.

Low-profile mortar and pestle

$16.95 at LeeValley.com
4-inch diameter

This unusual mortar and pestle is nice for crushing small amounts of hard whole spices or garlic. The pestle fits snugly into the contour of the mortar, so you don't have to chase spices around inside—or outside—the mortar. It can handle no more than a couple of tea-spoons or so of spices or a clove of garlic, and no liquids.

HOW WE TESTED We tried 18 mortars and pestles made from ceramic, porcelain, different kinds of stone, and wood. They ranged in size, capacity, and shape. To assess them, we mashed cloves of garlic, slices of ginger, pepper-corns, cumin seed, cilantro, and pine nuts, and made a curry paste.

Maryellen Driscoll is an editor at large for Fine Cooking.

All-American Wines

Many states besides California produce great-quality wines—what better time to try them than Thanksgiving?

BY TIM GAISER

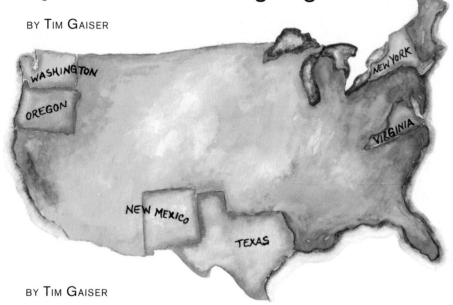

BY TIM GAISER

In the not-so-distant past, when you mentioned American wine, people automatically thought of California. But this is no longer the case. Though California wine still gets the lion's share of press and accolades, you can now find wineries in every state. The range of wines produced is incredibly diverse, and the quality keeps improving. So this Thanksgiving, look no further than our fifty states for your wine selections.

To get you started and help you sort through regions, styles, and varietals, I picked a handful of delicious and perfectly affordable wines from six American wine-producing states. With their moderate alcohol content and restrained oak and tannins, they're all great choices for the big turkey dinner. (To find sources, see p. 92).

What is an appellation?

An appellation is a defined winegrowing and winemaking region, and there are three types in the United States: state, county, and American Viticulture Areas (AVA). An AVA can be as small as Cole Valley in California, with just over 150 acres, or as large as the Ohio River Valley, which spans six states and covers more than 200,000 square miles. Unlike European appellations, which specify the grape varieties grown along with grape-growing and winemaking practices, AVAs define only the geographical boundaries of an American wine region.

Oregon

Oregon's wine industry dates back to the mid 1970s when David Lett, of the famed Eyrie Vineyards, left California in search of affordable land to start a new winery. He found a home for his Pinot Noir grapes in the Willamette Valley, south of Portland, establishing one of the state's first wineries. In time, Oregon built its reputation on world-class Pinot Noir, but its Pinot Gris is also among the best anywhere. Other wines to look for are Chardonnay, Riesling, and Pinot Blanc for whites, and Merlot, Cabernet Sauvignon, and Shiraz for reds.

Key appellations

Oregon (state)
Willamette Valley (AVA)
Umpqua Valley (AVA)
Rogue Valley (AVA)

Wines to try

White:
2006 Adelsheim Pinot Gris, Willamette Valley, $18

What it's like: Crisp and tart with luscious ripe red-apple flavor and notes of green melon and lemon.

Great with: Roasted turkey and chicken, carrots, and sweet potatoes.

Red:
2005 Chehalem "3 Vineyard" Pinot Noir, Willamette Valley, $22

What it's like: Rich and supple with tart berry flavors and a touch of toasty oak.

Great with: Mashed potatoes, rich gratins, and hearty braises.

(continued on p. 38)

To really appreciate fine Italian art,
all you have to do is turn on your stove.

The finest Italian Cappuccino at home.

L'Arte del Cappuccino

Washington

Established only in the 1980s, Washington's wine industry is even younger than Oregon's, but it has quickly come a long way. The arid plain of eastern Washington has proven to be one of the best places in the country for Cabernet Sauvignon, Merlot, and Bordeaux blends, and its Syrah and Cabernet Franc are excellent as well. Outstanding Chardonnay, Riesling, and Chenin Blanc are also made in cooler-climate areas.

Key appellations

Washington (state)
Columbia Valley (AVA)
Yakima Valley (AVA)
Walla Walla Valley (AVA)
Red Mountain (AVA)
Wahluke Slope (AVA)

Wines to try

White:
2006 Bookwalter Riesling, Columbia Valley, $16.50

What it's like: Crisp white peach and lemon-lime with floral notes.

Great with: Turkey and cranberry sauce as well as spicy dishes and bright ones like seared fish fillets with herb butter.

Red:
2004 Columbia Crest Merlot Grand Estates, Columbia Valley, $12

What it's like: Supple black cherry and plum fruit with notes of green herb.

Great with: All the elements of the traditional Thanksgiving dinner as well as braised veal and pork.

New York

Some of the country's oldest wineries are in the Finger Lakes region, including Dr. Konstantin Frank's, the first in the U.S. to successfully grow high-quality wine grapes in a cold climate. In the last 20 years, Long Island, whose climate is reminiscent of that of France's Bordeaux region, has also become a thriving wine region. Both areas are home to boutique wineries that make everything from Sauvignon Blanc, Chardonnay, Riesling, and Viognier for whites, to Cabernet Franc, Merlot, and Cabernet Sauvignon for reds.

Key appellations

New York (state)
Finger Lakes (AVA)
Long Island (AVA)
North Fork of Long Island (AVA)
Hamptons Long Island (AVA)

Wines to try

White:
2006 Dr. Konstantin Frank Dry Riesling, Finger Lakes, $18

What it's like: Ripe apricot and nectarine fruit with hints of lime zest.

Great with: Roasted chicken or turkey with cranberry sauce but also tandoori chicken with ginger and lime and other Indian dishes.

Red:
2004 Palmer Vineyards Cabernet Franc Proprietor's Reserve, North Fork of Long Island, $19

What it's like: Tart cherry and red raspberry flavor with green herb and tobacco notes.

Great with: All the elements of the traditional Thanksgiving dinner, plus pasta with lamb-sausage ragù or mustard-crusted roasted chicken.

Virginia

Virginia's warm, humid climate has traditionally made it challenging to grow grapes for high-quality wines. But outstanding wines are now being made throughout the state, thanks to technology in the form of better rot prevention and control and different clones and rootstocks that are more suited to the climate. There are now more than 100 wineries in Virginia producing a variety of wines, from Pinot Grigio, Viognier, and Chardonnay to Cabernet Franc, Merlot, and even Nebbiolo.

Key appellations

Virginia (state)
Monticello (AVA)
Shenandoah Valley (AVA)
Eastern Shore (AVA)

Wines to try

White:
2005 Blenheim Farm Viognier, Virginia, $20

What it's like: Bright peach and nectarine notes with a spicy, tart finish.

Great with: Roasted turkey and chicken or seared fish.

Red:
2003 Barboursville Nebbiolo Reserve, Virginia, $32

What it's like: Dried cherry notes with floral, truffle, and spice finishes.

Great with: All the elements of the Thanksgiving dinner as well as slow-roasted meats and hearty braises.

(continued on p. 40)

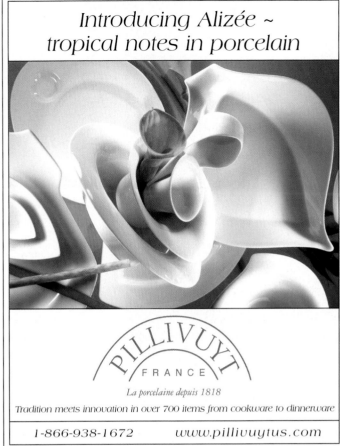

enjoying**wine**

Texas

As with Virginia, early efforts to establish vineyards in Texas were unsuccessful due to the hot, humid climate. But with new technology, growers in this state now produce an impressive range of wines from grapes as popular as Chardonnay and Merlot or as unusual as Viognier and Muscat. Reds include Cabernet Sauvignon, Merlot, and Cabernet Franc.

Key appellations

Texas (state)
Texas High (AVA)
Texas Hill Country (AVA)
Fredericksburg in the
    Texas Hill Country (AVA)

Wines to try

White:
2005 Flat Creek Estate Moscato Blanco, Texas Hill Country, $18

What it's like: Moderately sweet with strawberry and peach flavors and spice and floral notes.

Great with: Apple and pumpkin pies.

Red:
2003 Texas Hills Vineyard Cabernet Sauvignon, Newsome Vineyard, High Plains, $19

What it's like: Black cherry and cassis with green herb, bittersweet chocolate, and oak notes.

Great with: The richer dishes of the holiday meal, but also pork and beef roasts.

New Mexico

The warm summer days and cool nights along the Rio Grande Valley provide the right climatic conditions for a large number of grapes, from Sauvignon Blanc, Chardonnay, Riesling, and Muscat to Cabernet Sauvignon, Cabernet Franc, and Zinfandel. New Mexico also produces outstanding sparkling wines that are widely distributed.

Key appellations

New Mexico (state)
Rio Grande Valley (AVA)
Middle Rio Grande Valley (AVA)

Wines to try

White (sparkling):
NV Gruet Brut, New Mexico, $13.50

What it's like: Bright citrus with apple notes.

Great with: Oysters and shellfish or on its own as an aperitif.

Red:
2004 Casa Rondeña Winery Cabernet Franc, New Mexico, $20

What it's like: Ripe black fruit with notes of baking spices and herbs.

Great with: Anything hearty and rich, from turkey, stuffing, and gravy to roasted rack of lamb.

Contributing editor Tim Gaiser is a master sommelier and wine educator. ◆

THE WORLD IS YOUR KITCHEN.

When you own a Viking kitchen, you need a really good reason to leave. The Viking Life opens the door to a world of authentic flavors with classes, exclusive events, and culinary trips. From Bangkok's aromatic markets to the kitchens of Basque country and Tuscan vineyards, we'll explore the tastes and techniques of the world's most exciting cuisines. Online articles, recipes, and cooking videos provide expert food and wine insight at your fingertips. Start your journey at thevikinglife.com.

THE VIKING® LIFE

FOOD   TRAVEL   WINE

Prevent soggy tart shells

It isn't always possible to fill fruit tarts just before serving, and I used to be disappointed at how soggy the tart shell would get. I discovered that a thin layer of chocolate between the shell and the filling solves the problem. After baking and cooling the tart shell, I use a pastry brush to paint the inside of the shell with dark, milk, or white chocolate. Once the chocolate hardens, I add the pastry cream or other filling and then decorate it with the fruit. The chocolate acts as a barrier, preventing the cream from penetrating the crust, and adds a chocolate flavor.

—*Mary Bendayan, North Woodmere, New York*

No-mess butter pats

Rubbing butter under the skin of a chicken or turkey used to leave me with slick, greasy hands, and I'd get butter everywhere. A better way is to work with frozen butter, and here's how I do it: I slice the butter with an egg slicer to get even pieces, then separate the slices and put them in a plastic bag in the freezer. The frozen pats slip easily under the poultry skin.

—*K.L. Wyrill,*
San Diego, California

Preventing rust in baking pans

A source of frustration for me is finding spots of rust in my baking pans, even after carefully washing and drying them. I have found a good way to prevent this. Right after I remove baked goods from the pans, I wash the pans and dry them with a dishtowel. Then I put them in the oven, which has been turned off. The residual heat is just enough to thoroughly dry the pans and remove any moisture left behind in hard-to-reach spots. This is especially effective for muffin tins, air-insulated pans, and any baking sheets or pans with rolled edges or rims. A few minutes in the still-warm oven does the trick.

—*Maria Olaguera,*
Overland Park, Kansas

A better blender utensil: celery

When making pesto, chimichurri, or other savory sauces in my blender, I was always nicking rubber spatulas while attempting to push all the herbs and other ingredients down into the blades. One day, I stumbled on the idea of using a stalk of celery, which lets me safely push everything toward the blades (when the blender is not running) without scratching my utensil.

—*J.D. McDonald,*
Berkeley, California

Keeping gravy warm

I used to get frustrated that the gravy on my Thanksgiving table would get cold quickly in gravy boats. So now I pour the gravy into the teapot that matches my china pattern and put it on a salad plate to catch the drips. The gravy stays hot for the whole meal.

—*Marian A. Altman,*
Silver Spring, Maryland

TOO GOOD TO FORGET
From *Fine Cooking* #12

Easy-squeeze lemon wedges

Here's how to slice lemon wedges that won't squirt in your eye when you squeeze them: Cut a lemon wedge and make three or four small vertical slits across the wedge's edge. These cuts prevent the juice from squirting out forcefully. When you squeeze the lemon wedge, the juice will run out gently.

—*Cynthia A. Jaworski,*
Chicago, Illinois

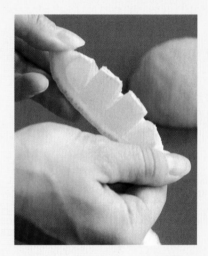

Jazzing up sugar syrup

When making simple syrups to sweeten tea or cocktails, try adding citrus zest or ginger root to the sugar and water syrup when boiling. Lime-scented syrup is great with mojitos, and ginger syrup adds interest to any tropical cocktail. The zest even lends a little color and makes for pretty drinks.

—*Christina George,*
Davis, California

New life for leftover stuffing

I like to press leftover stuffing into patties that can go with any meal, not just turkey. I dust the patties with flour and fry them in oil until golden brown. If the stuffing is very dry, I add an egg lightly beaten with a fork or a drizzle of turkey broth to make the stuffing moist enough to hold together. I drain the patties on paper towels and keep them warm in the oven until needed.

—*Emmy Fox,*
Barnard, Vermont

Easy blind baking

When prebaking a pie shell, instead of filling the unbaked pie with pie weights, beans, or rice (which can often make a mess), I just line the unbaked shell with aluminum foil and then nest another pie plate of the same size inside and bake for the desired time. I get perfect pie shells every time.

—*Carol Webb,*
Kelowna, British Columbia

STAFF CORNER

Better technique for scrubbing pans

I just got a new pan and am trying to ward off any burned-on stains. In my experience, applying a damp sponge to a cleanser like Bon Ami or Bar Keepers Friend doesn't work well. I've found that making a paste with the cleanser and scrubbing it on the pan with my finger is a more effective method. I think sponges absorb too much of the cleanser and don't create enough friction.

—*Maryellen Driscoll, editor at large*

Pyrex pan is see-through protection for cookbooks

I have a thick muffin cookbook that refuses to stay open at the selected page. Searching for something to hold down the pages, I took out my large Pyrex baking dish. It's perfect, as it keeps the book open and protects the pages, yet I can easily read through it.

—*G. Jaskiewicz,*
Stoney Creek, Ontario ◆

Plan Ahead
for a Delicious
Thanksgiving

menu

**Herb-Butter
Roasted Turkey with
Pinot Noir Gravy**

❖

**Sausage-Maple
Bread Stuffing**

❖

**Broccoli with Eggs &
Lemony Parmesan
Breadcrumbs**

❖

**Cranberry Sauce
with Vanilla, Maple Syrup
& Cassis**

❖

**Sweet Potato Gratin
with Caramelized Onions**

❖

**Classic
Mashed Potatoes**

Pulling together
an impressive
dinner is a
breeze when
you've got a
great menu
and a solid plan

BY RIS LACOSTE

My mother makes the best
Thanksgiving dinner in
the world, and last year, I
was finally able to enjoy it for
the first time in ages. As usual,
my mom turned out a delicious
meal for a crowd of twenty all
by herself in a tiny kitchen,
equipped with just a cutting
board and a paring knife.
And not a single dish was cold
when it reached the table. In
the past, I haven't been able to

join my family because I've been cooking dinner for a slightly bigger crowd—600 people—at 1789 Restaurant in Washington, DC, where I was the chef for many years. I used a few more tools, but for both of us, the key to a great meal has always been in the planning. With a good make-ahead strategy, preparing an impressive Thanksgiving spread without a lot of last-minute stress is easier than you think.

This menu, which takes inspiration from dishes I made at the restaurant as well as from some of my mother's favorite recipes, is designed to be prepared in steps. If you follow the timeline below, you'll have a stunning dinner ready by the time your guests gather around the table—and you'll be able to enjoy it, too.

The star of the menu is, of course, the turkey. Mine is slathered with a delicious herb butter that makes it incredibly flavorful and succulent. But to make sure that it's as moist and juicy as possible (especially the breast meat, which tends to dry out in the oven), I find that brining it for several hours in water, salt, and lots of aromatics works wonders. Not only do the aromatics infuse the turkey with flavor, but brining also helps the meat absorb moisture before cooking, so it ends up juicier once it's roasted. (See p. 48 for more tips on how to roast a moist turkey.)

When it comes to side dishes and gravy, I like to keep things straightforward, so I opt for tradition over experimentation. That's not to say I don't throw in an unexpected ingredient here and there. My cranberry sauce is a case in point. I add vanilla to mellow the cranberries' tartness, and I stir in a bit of crème de cassis (a black-currant-flavored liqueur) to enhance their fruitiness. And while my gravy is uncomplicated, I reduce a little Pinot Noir in the roasting pan before I add the broth and drippings to give it an elegance reminiscent of French sauces.

I also take a dish like broccoli polonaise a step further. It's traditionally topped with chopped hard-boiled eggs, bread-crumbs, and parsley, but I enrich the bread-crumbs with lemon zest for brightness and Parmigiano for extra flavor. And because no Thanksgiving menu should be without sweet potatoes (that's my opinion, anyway), I bake a sumptuous sweet potato gratin spiked with cayenne and perfumed with orange zest. My mashed potatoes, on the other hand, are as traditional—and rich—as they can be; nothing but potatoes and lots of butter and heavy cream. And my sausage-maple stuffing is homey and comforting, with a crunchy top and a soft, moist interior.

I know what you're thinking now: This is a lot to manage. But trust me, it's all doable. Just read through my prep strategy below and start getting organized. And don't forget to have some fun in the process.

Here's a plan to make it happen

One month ahead

Make the decision: Yes, I am cooking Thanksgiving dinner.

Plan the guest list.

Assess refrigerator space and equipment needs (remember, the outdoors can be a great fridge if the temperature is below 40°F).

Decide on your turkey: fresh or frozen? If you opt for an organic or heritage turkey, you may need to order it early.

The week ahead

Make your shopping list and divide it between Saturday and Tuesday shopping. You might want to add store-bought dinner rolls to your list.

Saturday:

Buy the turkey, if frozen.

Buy bread for the stuffing and ingredients for Sunday's prep.

Sunday:

Make the cranberry sauce.

Make the turkey broth.

Make the herb butter.

Cut up and dry the bread for the stuffing.

Tuesday:

Buy the remaining ingredients.

Make the brine.

Make the stuffing (but don't bake it).

Wednesday:

Prep the broccoli: Trim, cut, and parcook the broccoli; cook the eggs; chop the parsley and combine with the eggs; make, toast, and season the breadcrumbs; grate the Parmigiano and combine with breadcrumbs; zest and juice the lemon and combine.

Make the caramelized onions for the gratin.

Brine the turkey.

Chill the white wines.

Set the table.

Make-aheads for your turkey & gravy

Three-Herb Butter
Yields about 1 1/4 cups.

½ lb. (1 cup) unsalted butter, at room
  temperature
½ cup finely chopped shallots (about 3 oz.)
½ cup dry white wine
¼ cup chopped fresh flat-leaf parsley
  (from about 1 oz. parsley sprigs)
¼ cup chopped fresh thyme leaves
  (from about ¾ oz. thyme sprigs)
¼ cup chopped fresh sage leaves
  (from about ½ oz. sage sprigs)

In a 10-inch skillet, melt 1 Tbs. of the butter
over medium heat until it begins to foam.
Add the shallots and cook until soft and
fragrant, stirring occasionally, about 3 minutes. Add the wine and boil until it's completely evaporated, 5 to 8 minutes. Stir in
the parsley, thyme, and sage and cook until
fragrant, 2 minutes more. Transfer to a
medium bowl and refrigerate. When well
chilled, put the remaining butter in the bowl
of a mixer fitted with the paddle attachment.
Add the herb mixture and beat on medium
speed until blended, about 1 minute.

On a large piece of plastic wrap, shape
the herb butter into a log. Wrap in the plastic and refrigerate.

Make ahead
The butter can be made up to
1 week ahead and refrigerated or
up to 2 months ahead and frozen.
If frozen, take the butter out of the
freezer and store in the refrigerator
a day before you plan to use it.

Turkey Broth
Yields 6 to 7 cups.

1½ to 2 lb. turkey parts, such as backs,
  wings, or legs
1 large onion (about 12 oz.), coarsely
  chopped
4 large stalks celery (about 9 oz.), coarsely
  chopped
2 small carrots (about 4 oz.), coarsely
  chopped
2 cups dry white wine
6 cups low-salt chicken broth
Half a small bunch fresh flat-leaf parsley
  (about 1 oz.)
Half a small bunch fresh sage (about ½ oz.)
Half a small bunch fresh thyme (about ⅓ oz.)
3 bay leaves
1 Tbs. whole black peppercorns

Position a rack in the center of the oven
and heat the oven to 350°F. Put the turkey
parts in a small roasting pan (approximately
9x13 inches) along with the onion, celery,
and carrots and roast until the meat is well
browned, 1 to 1¼ hours. Transfer the turkey
parts and vegetables to a 4-qt. saucepan.

Add the wine to the roasting pan and
scrape any browned bits with a wooden
spoon to release them into the wine. Pour the
wine into the saucepan and add the chicken
broth, herbs, bay leaves, and peppercorns.
Bring to a boil over medium-high heat,
reduce the heat to medium low or low, and
simmer gently until the meat is falling off the
bone, 30 to 40 minutes, skimming occasionally to remove the fat and foam that rise to
the top. Strain the broth through a fine sieve,
cover, and refrigerate until ready to use.
Remove any solidified fat before using.

Make ahead
The turkey broth can be made up
to 4 days ahead and refrigerated
or up to 2 months ahead and frozen.

Thanksgiving Day

In the morning:
Pull the herb butter from refrigerator.

**Make and bake the sweet potato
gratin.**

**Transfer the stuffing to the baking
dish.**

**Peel and cut the potatoes; cover
with cold water.**

Four hours before serving:
Prep the turkey: pull from the brine,
rinse, butter, and season.

Roast the turkey.

Make roux for the gravy.

One hour before serving:
**Take the stuffing and gratin out
of the fridge.**

**Assemble the broccoli dish and let
it sit at room temperature.**

**Make the mashed potatoes and
keep warm.**

**Plate butter for the dinner rolls,
if serving.**

**Put the cranberry sauce in a
serving dish.**

Half-hour before serving:
Allow the turkey to rest.

**Raise the oven temp to 375°F and
heat the stuffing, broccoli, and
potato gratin.**

Heat dinner rolls, if serving.

Make the gravy.

Three secrets for a juicy turkey

Herb-Butter Roasted Turkey with Pinot Noir Gravy

Serves twelve, with leftovers.

To brine the turkey you need space for a 5-gallon pot in your refrigerator. If you have neither the room nor the pot, you can cook the brine in a smaller pan and proceed with one of the alternative methods described in From Our Test Kitchen, p. 78.

FOR THE BRINE:
2½ gallons water
2½ cups kosher salt
1 cup maple syrup
24 bay leaves
24 cloves garlic, peeled
⅓ cup whole black peppercorns
2 small bunches fresh flat-leaf parsley (about 4 oz.)
1 small bunch fresh sage (about 1 oz.)
1 small bunch fresh thyme (about ⅔ oz.)
6 medium sprigs fresh rosemary
Zest and juice of 4 large lemons (remove the zest in long strips with a vegetable peeler)

FOR THE TURKEY:
14- to 16-lb. natural turkey (preferably fresh)
1 recipe Three-Herb Butter (p. 47), slightly softened
2 Tbs. kosher salt
2 Tbs. freshly ground black pepper
2 oz. (4 Tbs.) unsalted butter, melted

FOR THE GRAVY:
2½ oz. (5 Tbs.) unsalted butter
2½ oz. (½ cup) all-purpose flour
4 cups turkey broth (recipe, p. 47) or low-salt chicken broth
1½ cups Pinot Noir
Kosher salt
Freshly ground black pepper

Two days ahead, prepare the brine:
Put all of the brine ingredients in a 5-gallon stockpot with a lid. Cover and bring to a boil over high heat. Reduce the heat to medium low and simmer for 5 minutes. Remove from the heat, cool to room temperature, cover the pot, and refrigerate the brine until cold, preferably overnight.

One day ahead, brine the turkey:
If already loose, trim the tail from the turkey. Otherwise, leave it attached. Remove and discard the giblets. Keep the neck and tail in the refrigerator. Rinse the turkey and put it in the pot with the brine. Refrigerate for 8 to 24 hours before roasting the turkey.

1 Brine *the turkey in water, salt, and aromatics. The meat absorbs moisture (and flavor), so it doesn't dry out while roasting.*

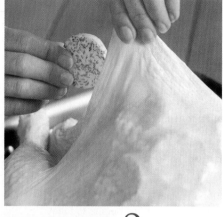

2 Rub *herb butter between the skin and meat. When the butter melts, it infuses the turkey with flavor and creates rich drippings for basting.*

3 Cover with foil *during the first two hours of roasting to further help the meat stay tender and juicy.*

Prepare and roast the turkey:
Position a rack in the bottom of the oven and heat the oven to 350°F. Remove the turkey from the brine and discard the brine. Rinse the turkey well, pat it dry, and set it in a large flameproof roasting pan. Gently slide your hand between the breast meat and skin to separate the skin so you can apply the herb butter. Slice the herb butter into ¼-inch-thick rounds and distribute them evenly between the skin and breast meat, completely covering the breast. Maneuver a few pieces between the skin and legs, too. Next, with your hands on the outside of the turkey, massage the butter under the skin to distribute it evenly and break up the round pieces so the turkey won't look polka-dotted when it's done.

Sprinkle 1 Tbs. of the salt and 1 Tbs. of the pepper in the cavity of the turkey. Tie the legs together. Fold the wings back and tuck the tips under the neck area. Flip the turkey onto its breast, pat the back dry, and brush with some of the melted butter. Sprinkle with some of the remaining salt and pepper. Flip the turkey over, pat dry again, brush all over with the remaining butter, and sprinkle with the remaining salt and pepper.

Put the reserved neck and tail in the pan with the turkey. Cover the pan very tightly with foil and put in the oven, legs pointing to the back of the oven, if possible (the legs can handle the higher heat in the back better than the breast can). Roast undisturbed for 2 hours and then uncover carefully (watch out for escaping steam). Continue to roast, basting every 15 minutes with the drippings that have collected in the pan, until an instant-read thermometer inserted in the thickest part of both thighs reads 170° to 175°F and the juices run clear when the thermometer is removed, 45 minutes to 1 hour more for a 15-lb. turkey.

Remove the turkey from the oven. With a wad of paper towels in each hand, move the turkey to a serving platter, cover with foil to keep warm, and set aside. Discard the neck and tail; reserve the drippings in the roasting pan. Let the turkey rest for 30 minutes while you make the gravy and heat the side dishes.

An easy wine gravy in three steps

2 Pour wine *into the roasting pan and reduce it to add flavor and character to the gravy. Then pour in the broth and the drippings.*

1 Make a roux *by adding flour to melted butter and whisking until golden brown. This will be your thickener.*

Make the gravy: Melt the butter in a small saucepan over medium-high heat until foaming. Add the flour and quickly whisk it into the butter until it's completely incorporated. Cook, whisking constantly, until the roux smells toasty and darkens slightly to a light caramel color, about 2 minutes. Watch carefully, as you don't want it to get too dark. Remove from the heat and set aside.

3 Whisk *the roux into the gravy a little at a time to thicken it just the way you like it.*

Pour the reserved turkey drippings into a clear, heatproof container, preferably a fat separator cup. (Don't rinse the roasting pan.) Let sit until the fat rises to the top, and then pour out 1 cup of the juices (or remove and discard the fat with a ladle and measure 1 cup of the juices). Combine the juices with the turkey or chicken broth.

Set the roasting pan on top of the stove over two burners on medium heat. Add the Pinot Noir and simmer, scraping the pan with a wooden spoon to release any stuck-on bits, until the wine has reduced by half, about 5 minutes. Add the broth mixture and simmer to meld the flavors, about 5 minutes. Whisk in the roux a little at a time until you have reached your desired thickness (you may not want to use it all). Adjust the seasoning with salt and pepper to taste. Strain through a fine sieve and transfer to a serving vessel.

Make ahead
The brine should be prepared 2 days before the Thanksgiving dinner. The turkey should be brined the day before. The roux may be prepared on Thanksgiving day and left at room temperature; whisk to recombine before using.

Sweet Potato Gratin with Caramelized Onions

Serves twelve.

2 oz. (4 Tbs.) unsalted butter; more for the baking dish
2 lb. yellow onions, thinly sliced (about 6 cups)
½ tsp. kosher salt; more to taste
½ tsp. freshly ground black pepper; more to taste
2 cups heavy cream
3 sprigs fresh thyme
½ Tbs. freshly grated orange zest (from 1 orange)
⅛ tsp. cayenne
4 lb. sweet potatoes (about 5 medium)
1 cup (4 oz.) pecan halves, toasted
2 Tbs. fresh breadcrumbs
2 Tbs. freshly grated Parmigiano-Reggiano

Cook the onions: Heat the butter in a heavy-based 12-inch skillet over medium heat until it begins to foam. Add the onions, reduce the heat to medium low, and cook slowly, stirring occasionally, until the onions are soft and nicely browned, 30 to 40 minutes. Season with the ½ tsp. each salt and pepper. Remove from the heat and set aside to cool slightly.

Assemble the gratin: Meanwhile, put the heavy cream, thyme, orange zest, and cayenne in a 2- to 3-qt. saucepan. Bring to a boil, remove from the heat, and steep for 15 minutes. Remove and discard the thyme sprigs.

While the cream is steeping, peel and cut the sweet potatoes crosswise into ⅛-inch-thick slices (use a mandolin if you have one).

Position a rack in the center of the oven and another rack directly below. Heat the oven to 350°F.

Lightly butter a 9x13-inch baking dish. Arrange about one-third of the sliced sweet potatoes in a double layer on the bottom of the dish, slightly overlapping the slices in each layer. Season lightly with salt and pepper. Spread half of the onions over the potatoes and drizzle about one third of the cream (⅔ cup) over the onions. Arrange another third of the potatoes in two more overlapping layers and season lightly with more salt and pepper. Spread the remaining onions over the potatoes and drizzle another third of the cream over the onions. Use the remaining sweet potato slices to make two final layers. Press down on the layers with your hands to compact and flatten them. Season lightly with salt and pepper, and drizzle the remaining cream over the potatoes, trying to cover them as much as possible.

Put a foil-lined baking sheet on the lower rack to catch any drips. Cover the gratin tightly with foil and bake on the center rack until the potatoes are almost tender but still offer a little resistance when pierced with a fork or skewer, about 1 hour. Remove the foil and bake until the sweet potatoes are completely tender and the top is lightly browned and bubbly, 30 to 40 minutes.

While the gratin is baking, put the pecans, breadcrumbs, and Parmigiano in a food processor and pulse until coarsely chopped.

Raise the oven temperature to 375°F. Cover the top of the gratin with the pecan mixture and return the baking dish to the oven. Bake until the top is lightly browned, about 10 minutes.

Make ahead

The onions can be made up to 3 days in advance. Transfer them to a bowl, cover with plastic, and refrigerate.

The gratin can be baked up to 1 day ahead to the point of adding the breadcrumb topping. Reheat at 375°F until bubbling and hot throughout, about 20 minutes, and then add the topping and bake 10 minutes more.

Sausage-Maple Bread Stuffing

Yields about 12 cups; serves twelve.

1½ lb. dense, chewy bread, cut into ¾-inch cubes (about 13 cups)
5 oz. (10 Tbs.) unsalted butter, softened
⅓ cup chopped fresh thyme leaves (from about 1 oz. thyme sprigs)
⅓ cup chopped fresh sage leaves (from about ¾ oz. sage sprigs)
¾ tsp. poultry seasoning
3 cups medium-diced yellow onion (2 medium)
3 cups medium-diced celery (6 large stalks)
7½ cups low-salt chicken broth
2 bay leaves
1 smoked ham hock (about 1 lb.)
1 lb. bulk pork breakfast sausage
⅓ cup maple syrup
1½ tsp. freshly ground black pepper
Kosher salt

Lay the bread cubes in a single layer on two baking sheets. Leave out to dry completely at room temperature, tossing once or twice, for about 2 days.

Position a rack in the center of the oven and heat the oven to 375°F.

In a heavy-based, 8-qt. stockpot or Dutch oven, melt 5 Tbs. of the butter over medium heat until it begins to foam. Stir in the thyme, sage, and poultry seasoning and cook just enough to coat the herbs and season the butter, 30 to 60 seconds. Stir in the onions and celery and cook, stirring occasionally, until soft and fragrant, about 15 minutes. Add the chicken broth, bay leaves, and ham hock and bring to a boil over high heat. Reduce the heat to medium low and simmer until the liquid reduces by one-third, about 30 minutes.

Meanwhile, put the sausage on a rimmed baking sheet and break it into quarter-size chunks. Roast until cooked through, about 15 minutes. Let cool, and then chop the sausage into smaller bits.

Add the sausage to the broth and simmer just to allow the flavors to meld, about 5 minutes. Remove the ham hock and bay leaves. Discard the bay leaves and set the hock aside to cool. Stir the dried bread, several cups at a time, into the broth until all of the broth is absorbed and the bread cubes are well moistened. Stir in the maple syrup, pepper, and the remaining 5 Tbs. butter.

When the hock is cool enough to handle, pick off the meat, chop it into small pieces, and add to the stuffing. Season to taste with salt if necessary (depending on the sausage and ham hock, both of which are salty, there may already be enough).

Transfer the stuffing to a 9x13-inch baking dish and bake uncovered at 375°F until heated through and crisp on top, about 20 minutes if freshly made, or about 30 minutes if made ahead.

Make ahead

The bread can be dried weeks in advance, bagged, frozen, and then thawed when ready to use. The stuffing can be made (but not baked) up to 2 days ahead and refrigerated, covered.

wine choices

Look for medium-bodied reds and whites

Young, fruity white wines with crisp acidity and little oak, and red wines with forward fruit, medium acidity, and soft tannins are ideal mates to the sweet, tangy, and zesty flavors of this menu.

Look for crisp Sauvignon Blancs, fruity off-dry Rieslings, and lightly oaked Viogniers. I like the 2006 Babich Sauvignon Blanc, Marlborough, New Zealand ($14), the 2006 Mönchhof Estate Riesling, Germany ($15), and the 2006 Zaca Mesa Viognier, Santa Ynez Valley ($18).

For reds, look for Pinot Noirs, Gamays, or lightly oaked Merlots, such as the 2005 Edna Valley Pinot Noir ($18), the 2005 Chateau de la Chaize Brouilly ($16), or the 2005 Penfolds Koonunga Hill Cabernet Merlot, Australia ($14).

—Tim Gaiser, contributing editor

Broccoli with Eggs & Lemony Parmesan Breadcrumbs

Serves twelve.

3 large eggs
2 cups fresh breadcrumbs
½ lb. (1 cup) unsalted butter
½ Tbs. sweet Hungarian paprika
1 tsp. plus ½ cup kosher salt
½ tsp. freshly ground white pepper
½ cup tightly packed, freshly grated Parmigiano-Reggiano
½ cup chopped fresh flat-leaf parsley
2 Tbs. finely grated lemon zest (from 2 to 3 lemons)
1 Tbs. fresh lemon juice
Two 1-lb. heads broccoli

Position a rack in the center of the oven and heat the oven to 375°F.

Put the eggs in a small saucepan and cover with cold water. Bring to a boil, turn off the heat, and cover the pan. Let sit, covered, for 10 minutes. Immediately pour off the hot water and run the eggs under a steady stream of cold water. Peel the eggs right away. Coarsely chop the eggs and set them aside.

Spread the breadcrumbs on a rimmed baking sheet and toast them in the oven until lightly browned, about 5 minutes.

Melt 8 Tbs. of the butter in a heavy-based 10-inch skillet over medium heat. Add the breadcrumbs, paprika, 1 tsp. of the salt, and the pepper and cook, stirring, for about 1 minute, just to meld the flavors. Remove from the heat and stir in the chopped eggs, Parmigiano, parsley, lemon zest, and lemon juice.

In a large pot, bring 1 gallon of water and the remaining ½ cup of the salt to a boil. Trim off the bottom of the broccoli stems, cut each broccoli head lengthwise in half, and then cut each half lengthwise into six spears. Add the broccoli to the boiling water and cook until crisp-tender, about 5 minutes.

Drain the broccoli well and arrange in a snug single layer on a rimmed baking sheet. Melt the remaining 8 Tbs. butter in the micro-wave or in a small saucepan over medium heat. Top the broccoli with the breadcrumb mixture and then drizzle on the melted butter. Bake until the broccoli is heated through and the topping is crisp, about 20 minutes. Transfer the broccoli to a serving platter and then scatter any topping that fell off back over the broccoli.

Make ahead
A day ahead, you can parcook the broccoli and combine the eggs with the parsley, the seasoned breadcrumbs with the Parmigiano, and the lemon juice with the zest. (Store everything separately in the fridge.) Then you can combine the topping ingredients, assemble the dish while the turkey roasts, and bake it while the turkey rests.

Classic Mashed Potatoes

Yields about 12 cups; serves twelve.

6 lb. russet potatoes, peeled and cut into 2-inch chunks
⅓ cup kosher salt; more to taste
2 cups heavy cream, half-and-half, or whole milk
½ lb. (1 cup) unsalted butter, cut into 1-inch pieces
¼ tsp. freshly ground white pepper; more to taste

Put the potatoes in an 8-qt. stockpot. Add the salt and enough water to cover the potatoes by about 2 inches. Cover and bring to a boil over medium-high heat. Reduce the heat to medium low and simmer, uncovered, until the potatoes are tender but not falling apart, 15 to 20 minutes.

Meanwhile, heat the heavy cream (or half-and-half or milk) in the microwave or in a medium saucepan over medium heat until hot but not boiling. Keep hot.

Drain the potatoes and return them to the pot over low heat. Add the butter, about two-thirds of the hot cream, and the white pepper. With a potato masher, mash the potatoes to your desired consistency, adding the remaining cream if they seem dry. Season with more salt and white pepper to taste.

To keep them warm, transfer the mashed potatoes to a heatproof bowl, cover them tightly with foil, and set the bowl over a saucepan of barely simmering water.

Ris Lacoste is the former executive chef at 1789 Restaurant in Georgetown, Washington, DC. ◆

Cranberry Sauce with Vanilla, Maple Syrup & Cassis

Yields about 4 cups.

6 cups (about 1½ lb.) fresh or frozen cranberries, picked over and rinsed
⅔ cup granulated sugar
⅓ cup fresh orange juice (from 1 orange)
⅓ cup crème de cassis (black-currant liqueur)
¼ cup maple syrup
1 Tbs. finely grated orange zest (from 1 orange)
Half a vanilla bean, split and scraped

Put 3 cups of the cranberries and all the remaining ingredients in a 3- or 4-qt. saucepan. Bring to a boil over medium-high heat, reduce the heat to medium, and cook, stirring occasionally, until the cranberries have popped and broken down and the juices look slightly syrupy, 5 to 7 minutes. Stir in the remaining 3 cups cranberries and cook until these have popped, 3 to 5 minutes more. Remove from the heat, discard the vanilla bean, and let cool to room temperature. Cover and refrigerate if not serving right away.

Make ahead
The cranberry sauce can be made up to one week in advance and kept covered in the refrigerator. Return to room temperature before serving.

An Essential Guide to Roasting Vegetables

I f there's someone in your life who doesn't like vegetables, here's how to turn things around: Roast the vegetables. Trust me, roasting browns them nicely on the outside, concentrating and sweetening their flavor in a way that even avowed veggie haters find hard not to like—and that goes for even the most unpopular of vegetables, like turnips and Brussels sprouts. But what's especially great about roasting is that it's fairly quick and hands-off, and much of the prep can be done ahead of roasting time. You can cut up the vegetables (except potatoes and sweet potatoes) in the morning, if you like, so by the time you're ready to roast, all you have to do is toss them with oil and seasonings, spread them on a pan, and check on them occasionally as they roast.

Easy ways to add flavor

Roasting gives vegetables enough extra flavor that they're terrific to eat as is—maybe brightened with a dash of lemon juice. This is perfect for a casual dinner, but for fancier occasions I've come up with several simple ways to add even more flavor. I toss the vegetables with a Moroccan-style spice rub or a lemony oil infused with rosemary and thyme before roasting, as both can stand up to the high heat of the oven. But I reserve flavorings that would burn in a hot oven to add after roasting. These include a Japanese toasted sesame salt called *gomasio* and a pan-Asian gingery lemon-soy splash. For a touch of the Middle East, I make a toasted garlic and coriander oil, and for a taste of France, the caramelized shallot butter is a personal favorite.

In general, when flavoring roasted vegetables (particularly after roasting), you want to avoid liquids because they'll soften any crisp edges that develop during roasting. The ginger-soy splash here is a compromise: I love the flavors enough to sacrifice a little crispness—plus it's really not much liquid.

A reliable technique and great tips— plus exciting flavoring ideas for your favorite vegetables

BY JENNIFER ARMENTROUT

Four tips for successful roasting

As I developed my basic roasted vegetable technique, I came up with a few pointers:

Roast in a very hot oven (475°F). The vegetables cook quickly—many of those in the chart at right take only 15 to 20 minutes—but they still have a chance to brown nicely on the outside by the time they become tender inside.

Cut evenly. It's very important that you cut the vegetables in pieces of about the same size. Unevenly sized pieces won't roast and brown in the same amount of time, and you'll end up with both over-roasted and underroasted vegetables.

Line the pan. To prevent sticking, line the pan with a sheet of parchment; otherwise, when you have to pry stuck vegetables off the baking sheet, it's the tasty brown bottoms that are left on the pan.

Position vegetables near the pan's edges. If the vegetable pieces cover the pan sparsely, arrange them more toward the edges of the pan. Pieces near the edge brown better.

Roasted green beans with Caramelized Shallot Butter

master recipe

Basic Roasted Vegetables

This method is for roasting one type of vegetable per baking sheet. For roasting a combination of vegetables see the box at far right.

1 lb. vegetable (see chart at right for choices)
1 to 3 Tbs. extra-virgin olive oil
½ tsp. kosher salt; more to taste
Freshly ground black pepper
Fresh lemon juice (optional)

Position a rack in the center of the oven and heat the oven to 475° F. Line a heavy-duty rimmed baking sheet with parchment. Prepare the vegetable according to the instructions in the chart at right. In a medium bowl, toss the vegetable with enough of the olive oil to coat generously, the salt, and a few grinds of pepper. If using a flavoring before roasting (see p. 56), toss it with the vegetable now.

Turn the vegetable out onto the baking sheet and arrange the pieces so that they are evenly spaced and lying on a cut side (if that applies). If the pieces cover the baking sheet sparsely, arrange them toward the edges of the baking sheet for the best browning. Roast according to the instructions in the chart.

Return the vegetables to the bowl in which you tossed them with the oil, or put them in a clean serving bowl. If they seem a bit dry, drizzle them with a little oil. Season to taste with salt, pepper, and lemon juice or another flavoring (see p. 57), if using.

How to prep and

Sweet potatoes

3 to 4 servings per pound

Prep: Peel and cut into 1-inch pieces.

How to roast: Roast until lightly browned on bottom, 10 minutes. Flip and roast until tender, 5 to 10 minutes.

Cauliflower

3 to 4 servings per pound

Prep: Trim and cut into 1- to 1½-inch florets.

How to roast: Roast, stirring every 10 minutes, until tender and lightly browned, 20 to 25 minutes total.

Asparagus

(medium or large, not small) 3 to 4 servings per pound

Prep: Rinse, pat dry, and snap off tough bottom ends.

How to roast: Roast for 5 minutes, flip, and roast until tender and a bit shriveled, 5 to 8 minutes.

Fennel

3 to 4 servings per pound

Prep: Quarter lengthwise. Trim the base and core, leaving just enough of the core intact to hold the layers together. Cut into ¾- to 1-inch wedges.

How to roast: Roast until the pieces begin to brown on the edges, 15 minutes. Flip and roast until tender and nicely browned, 10 minutes.

roast 15 vegetables

Turnips

3 to 4 servings per pound

Prep: Peel and cut into ³/₄- to 1-inch pieces.

How to roast: Roast until browned on bottom, 10 to 15 minutes. Flip and roast until tender, about 5 minutes.

Beets

4 servings per pound

Prep: Trim, peel, and cut into ³/₄- to 1-inch-thick wedges.

How to roast: Roast 15 minutes, flip, roast until tender, 10 to 15 minutes.

Green beans

4 servings per pound

Prep: Trim stem ends.

How to roast: Roast until tender, a bit shriveled, and slightly browned, about 15 minutes. No need to flip.

Brussels sprouts

3 to 4 servings per pound

Prep: Trim, halve lengthwise.

How to roast: Arrange cut side down on baking sheet. Roast until tender and browned, about 15 minutes. No need to flip.

Rutabaga

3 to 4 servings per pound

Prep: Peel and cut into ¹/₂- to ³/₄-inch pieces.

How to roast: Roast until browned on bottom, 13 to 15 minutes. Flip and roast until tender, 5 to 10 minutes.

Butternut squash

4 servings per pound

Prep: Peel and cut into ³/₄- to 1-inch pieces.

How to roast: Roast until browned on bottom, 15 minutes. Flip and roast until tender, 5 to 10 minutes.

Potatoes

(red, yellow, russet)
2 to 3 servings per pound

Prep: Peel or scrub well and dry. Cut into 1-inch pieces.

How to roast: Roast until browned on bottom, 10 to 15 minutes. Flip and continue to roast until tender, 5 minutes.

Parsnips

2 to 3 servings per pound

Prep: Peel, halve crosswise, halve or quarter thick end lengthwise, then cut all crosswise into 2-inch lengths.

How to roast: Roast until browned on bottom, about 10 minutes. Flip and roast until tender, about 5 minutes.

Mushrooms

(cremini or small white)
3 to 4 servings per pound

Prep: Wipe clean and trim stems flush with cap.

How to roast: Roast stem side down until brown on bottom, 20 to 25 minutes. Flip and roast until browned on top, 5 to 10 minutes.

Carrots

3 to 4 servings per pound

Prep: Peel. (If thick, cut in half crosswise to separate thick end from thin end; halve thick end lengthwise.) Cut crosswise into 1-inch lengths.

How to roast: Roast until lightly browned on bottom, 12 to 15 minutes. Flip and roast until tender and slightly shriveled, 3 to 5 minutes.

Broccoli crowns

2 to 3 servings per pound

Prep: Trim and peel the stem; slice it into ¹/₄-inch-thick disks. Where the stem starts to branch out, split the florets though the stem so that each piece is 1¹/₂ to 2 inches wide.

How to roast: Roast until the floret tops begin to brown, 8 to 10 minutes. Stir and continue to roast until tender, 3 to 6 minutes.

Roasting a medley of vegetables

Because they'll probably have different cooking times, it's best to roast a variety of vegetables (for a total of 1 pound) separately. You can roast them on different sections of the same baking sheet or, even better, on a separate baking sheet for each vegetable—this makes it easier to remove each from the oven when it's done. You can then combine them after roasting.

Add zing to your roasted

Pair with beets, butternut squash, carrots, cauliflower, fennel, mushrooms, parsnips, potatoes, and sweet potatoes.

Pair with butternut squash, carrots, cauliflower, parsnips, potatoes, sweet potatoes, and turnips.

Rosemary-Thyme-Lemon Oil

Yields enough for 1 batch of roasted vegetables.

Zest of 1 large lemon, removed in long strips with a vegetable peeler
2 Tbs. extra-virgin olive oil; more as needed
1 tsp. chopped fresh rosemary
1 tsp. chopped fresh thyme

In a small saucepan, combine the lemon zest and oil. Set over medium-low heat and cook until the lemon zest bubbles steadily for about 30 seconds. Remove from the heat and let cool briefly, about 3 minutes. Stir in the herbs and let sit at least 20 minutes before using.

Substitute the flavored oil for the plain olive oil in the master recipe and toss with the vegetables and salt and pepper before roasting. Once the vegetables are on the baking sheet, pick out and discard the lemon zest.

If the vegetables seem a little dry after roasting, toss them with additional oil before serving.

Moroccan-Style Spice Rub

Yields about 5 tsp., enough for 5 batches of roasted vegetables.

2 tsp. ground cumin
1 tsp. ground coriander
½ tsp. chili powder
½ tsp. sweet paprika, preferably Hungarian
½ tsp. ground cinnamon
¼ tsp. ground allspice
¼ tsp. ground ginger
⅛ tsp. cayenne
Pinch ground cloves

In a small bowl, mix all of the spices. In addition to the oil, salt, and pepper in the master recipe, toss 1 tsp. of the spice blend with a batch of vegetables before roasting.

Roasted fennel with Rosemary-Thyme-Lemon Oil

Roast a bigger batch

If you need more servings than a single batch yields, you can easily roast more vegetables by doubling or tripling the recipe on p. 54. Just don't crowd the vegetables on the baking sheet—they won't brown as well if they're packed too closely. Ideally, there should be at least ½ inch between them. Use another baking sheet if necessary and swap the sheets' positions in the oven about halfway through the roasting time so that the vegetables will roast evenly.

Before roasting

vegetables with these delicious flavorings

Pair with asparagus, broccoli, Brussels sprouts, green beans, parsnips, sweet potatoes, and turnips.

Pair with asparagus, Brussels sprouts, butternut squash, carrots, fennel, green beans, mushrooms, parsnips, potatoes, and sweet potatoes.

Pair with beets, broccoli, carrots, cauliflower, and mushrooms.

Pair with asparagus, beets, broccoli, cauliflower, fennel, green beans, mushrooms, and turnips.

Sesame Salt (*gomasio*)

Yields about 2 Tbs., enough for 3 batches of roasted vegetables.

2 Tbs. sesame seeds
½ tsp. sea salt

In a small dry skillet, toast the sesame seeds over medium heat, stirring almost constantly, until light golden-brown, 3 to 5 minutes. Add the salt and cook, stirring, for about 30 seconds. Transfer to a small bowl and cool completely.

Put the salted seeds in a clean spice grinder and pulse a few times to grind coarsely—you should still see a few whole seeds in the mixture. Toss about 2 tsp. sesame salt with a batch of vegetables after roasting.

Caramelized Shallot Butter

Yields about ¼ cup, enough for 3 batches of roasted vegetables.

3½ Tbs. unsalted butter, softened
1 large shallot, finely diced (⅓ cup)
½ tsp. chopped fresh thyme
½ tsp. finely grated lemon zest
Kosher salt and freshly ground black pepper

Heat 1 Tbs. of the butter in a small saucepan or skillet over medium-low heat until melted. Add the shallot and cook, stirring frequently, until deeply browned, 8 to 10 minutes. Remove from the heat and stir in the thyme. Cool completely.

In a small bowl, combine the shallot mixture with the remaining 2½ Tbs. butter and the lemon zest. Stir to blend well. Lightly season to taste with salt and pepper.

Scrape the butter onto a small piece of plastic wrap, mold into a log shape, and wrap in the plastic. Refrigerate until ready to use. Toss about one-third of the butter (a generous tablespoon) with a batch of vegetables after roasting.

Ginger-Lemon-Soy Splash

Yields enough for 1 batch of roasted vegetables.

1-inch piece fresh ginger
1 tsp. fresh lemon juice
½ tsp. soy sauce

Line a small bowl with a piece of cheesecloth or set a small fine strainer in the bowl. Peel and finely grate the ginger. Put the grated ginger in the cheesecloth or strainer and extract the ginger juice by gathering the cloth around the ginger and squeezing or by pressing the ginger in the sieve with a small spoon. Transfer ½ tsp. ginger juice to another small bowl (discard the rest or save for another use). Stir in the lemon juice and soy sauce. Toss with a batch of vegetables after roasting.

Toasted Garlic & Coriander Oil

Yields enough for 1 to 1½ batches of roasted vegetables.

1½ Tbs. extra-virgin olive oil
1 Tbs. finely chopped garlic (2 large cloves)
2 tsp. ground coriander
1 tsp. fresh lemon juice
Kosher salt and freshly ground black pepper

In a small saucepan, combine the oil and garlic. Set over medium-low heat and cook until the smaller pieces of garlic turn light golden-brown, about 3 minutes. Stir in the coriander and cook for about 20 seconds. Immediately remove from the heat and transfer to a small heatproof bowl to prevent overcooking. Keep warm.

Sprinkle the roasted vegetables with the lemon juice, season to taste with salt and pepper, and arrange on a serving platter. Spoon the toasted garlic oil over the vegetables.

Jennifer Armentrout is Fine Cooking's senior food editor and test kitchen manager. ◆

After roasting

Go Nuts:
Add Pecans to

BY KAREN BARKER

Every Thanksgiving, my husband and I throw a potluck celebration with friends, and since I'm a pastry chef, I'm always the designated baker. Though we make a different menu every year, certain elements of the meal always remain the same, and this means that there's a pecan pie—or some other dessert that includes toasty, buttery pecans—on the menu. To me, it makes sense to serve pecans at Thanksgiving because they're native to North America, and I naturally equate them with the harvest season. But I definitely wouldn't limit my use of pecans to autumn; their distinctly sweet flavor and soft, meaty texture make them a great ingredient in many desserts, no matter what time of year.

Pecan savvy: what to look for

In the fall, I occasionally see in-shell pecans in stores, but it's pretty time-consuming (and messy) to hand-shell them. So I prefer shelled pecans, which are usually vacuum-packed in cans, jars, or cellophane bags to protect against humidity and oxidation. You might also find pecans sold in bulk, but make sure they're fresh, since they can become rancid if they've been sitting around in storage for too long. Taste one—if it's rancid, the nut will have an unpleasant, bitter flavor. A fresh pecan, on the other hand, will be faintly sweet and buttery. Look for plump ones that are uniform in color and size.

Keeping pecans fresh

Once you've bought pecans, date them (or any stored nut) so that they're used in a timely fashion. In-shell pecans can be stored in a cool, dry place for 6 to 12 months. An open package of shelled nuts should be resealed or transferred to an airtight container. They will keep for several weeks in the refrigerator or up to one year in the freezer. While this preserves freshness, refrigerated or frozen nuts can turn flabby in texture. That's why I often lightly toast them (even if a recipe doesn't call for toasting), which brings back their crunch, accentuates their flavor, and tempers their astringency. Toast pecans in the oven at 350°F for 5 to 8 minutes. (Set a timer—the nuts can burn easily.)

Pecan pairings

Pecans marry well with a wide range of ingredients. In the upside-down cake shown at right, pecans act as an earthy foil to the bright, sunny pineapple. Since apple season and the pecan harvest coincide, I combine the two ingredients in a cinnamon-accented crisp. The traditional southern combo of bourbon, brown sugar, and buttermilk comes together in a nut-studded poundcake. And finally, I love pecan pie, but I often find it too cloying. In my version, chocolate and espresso moderate the pie's sugary nature. When I make this pie at Thanksgiving, it's always the first dessert to disappear.

Apple Crisp with Pecans & Orange

Bourbon-Glazed Brown Sugar Pecan Poundcake

Pecan Pineapple Upside-Down Cake

Chocolate Espresso Pecan Pie

More Than Just Pie

Pecan Pineapple
Upside-Down Cake

Pecan Pineapple Upside-Down Cake

Serves ten to twelve.

7 oz. (14 Tbs.) unsalted butter at room temperature; more for the pan
½ cup plus 2 Tbs. light or dark brown sugar
Six to eight ¼-inch-thick fresh pineapple rings (see From Our Test Kitchen, p. 78)
¼ to ⅓ cup pecan halves
½ cup lightly toasted pecan pieces
5½ oz. (1¼ cups) cake flour
1 tsp. baking powder
½ tsp. freshly grated nutmeg
¼ tsp. baking soda
¼ tsp. kosher salt
1 cup granulated sugar
2 large eggs, at room temperature
1 tsp. pure vanilla extract
½ cup plus 2 Tbs. buttermilk

Position a rack in the center of the oven and heat the oven to 350°F. Butter a 10x2-inch round cake pan or 10-inch cast-iron skillet.

Combine 6 Tbs. of the butter with the brown sugar in a small saucepan and cook over medium heat, whisking until the butter is melted, the sugar is dissolved, and the mixture is smooth, 1 to 2 minutes. Remove from the heat and immediately pour the mixture in the bottom of the prepared pan, tilting to evenly cover the surface.

Set one pineapple ring in the center of the pan. Surround it with several other rings, packing them tightly or even overlapping them slightly. Cut the remaining rings in quarters or sixths and fill in the spaces around the perimeter of the pan. Set a pecan half, curved side down, in the center of each pineapple ring. If you like, fill in any additional spaces with pecan halves, curved sides down. (You may not need all the pecans.)

Finely grind the toasted pecan pieces in a food processor but don't overprocess or you'll make pecan butter. In a small bowl, sift together the cake flour, baking powder, nutmeg, and baking soda. Add the salt and ground pecans, mix well, and reserve.

In a stand mixer fitted with the paddle attachment, beat the remaining 8 Tbs. butter with the granulated sugar on medium speed until fluffy, 2 to 3 minutes. Beat in the eggs one at a time, pausing to scrape the bowl. Mix in the vanilla. On low speed, alternate adding the dry ingredients and the buttermilk in five additions, beginning and ending with the dry ingredients, scraping the bowl once or twice, and mixing until the batter is smooth. Pour the batter over the fruit and spread it evenly with a spatula.

Bake until the cake is golden brown and springs back when pressed lightly in the center with a fingertip, 40 to 45 minutes.

Transfer the cake to a rack and cool in the pan for 15 minutes. Run the tip of a paring knife around the edge of the cake. Cover with a serving plate, and gripping both the cake and the plate, invert the two. Carefully lift off the cake pan, rearranging the fruit if necessary. Allow the cake to cool completely before serving.

Place the fruit carefully for a pretty cake

Position one pineapple ring in the center of the pan. Surround it with several other rings, packing them tightly—it's fine if they overlap slightly. Cut the remaining rings in quarters or sixths and fill in the spaces around the perimeter of the pan.

Set a pecan half, curved side down, in the center of each pineapple ring. If you like, fill in any additional spaces with pecan halves, curved sides down.

Apple Crisp with Pecans & Orange
Serves eight.

About 1 tsp. softened butter for the baking dish

FOR THE TOPPING:
4½ oz. (1 cup) unbleached all-purpose flour
⅓ cup old-fashioned rolled oats
¼ cup plus 2 Tbs. lightly packed light brown sugar
¼ cup plus 2 Tbs. granulated sugar
½ tsp. ground cinnamon
¼ tsp. kosher salt
4 oz. (½ cup) cold unsalted butter, cut into 8 pieces
1 cup lightly toasted, coarsely chopped pecans

FOR THE FILLING:
3 lb. Granny Smith apples (6 large or 8 medium), peeled, cored, and sliced ¼ inch thick
½ cup granulated sugar

2 Tbs. fresh orange juice (from 1 orange)
1 Tbs. finely grated orange zest (from 1 orange)
1½ tsp. unbleached all-purpose flour
¾ tsp. ground cinnamon
⅛ tsp. kosher salt

Position a rack in the center of the oven and heat the oven to 350°F. Lightly butter a 9x9x2-inch pan or other 10-cup ovenproof baking dish.

Make the topping: In a food processor, pulse the flour and the oats until the oats are finely ground. Add the brown sugar, granulated sugar, cinnamon, and salt and pulse until just combined. Add the butter and pulse in short bursts until the mixture just starts to form crumbs and has a streusel-like consistency. When squeezed together with light pressure, the mixture should just clump. Add the pecans and pulse just to blend; you don't want to chop the nuts

further. (You can make and refrigerate this topping up to 2 days ahead, or freeze for up to 2 months. Bring to room temperature before using.)

Assemble and bake the crisp: In a large bowl, combine all of the filling ingredients and gently toss until well combined. Transfer the mixture to the prepared baking dish. Press down to compact slightly into an even layer. Sprinkle the topping in a thick, even layer all over the filling.

Bake until the topping is golden brown, the juices are bubbling around the edges, and the apples are soft when pierced with the tip of a knife, 55 to 60 minutes. Transfer to a rack to cool for 20 to 30 minutes before serving. The crisp can be served warm or at room temperature, but it's best served the day it's made.

Bourbon-Glazed Brown Sugar Pecan Poundcake

Serves twelve.

FOR THE CAKE:
12 oz. (1½ cups) unsalted butter, at room temperature; more for the pan
½ cup fine, dry, plain breadcrumbs (store-bought are fine)
15¾ oz. (3½ cups) unbleached all-purpose flour
1 tsp. baking powder
¼ tsp. baking soda
¼ tsp. kosher salt
3 cups lightly packed light brown sugar
5 large eggs, at room temperature
2 tsp. pure vanilla extract
¾ cup buttermilk
¼ cup bourbon
2¼ cups toasted, coarsely chopped pecans

FOR THE GLAZE:
⅓ cup granulated sugar
⅓ cup bourbon

Make the cake: Position a rack in the center of the oven and heat the oven to 350°F. Butter a 10-inch (12-cup) Bundt pan and dust it with the breadcrumbs, shaking out and discarding the excess crumbs.

Sift together the flour, baking powder, and baking soda into a medium bowl. Add the salt and mix with a rubber spatula.

In a stand mixer fitted with the paddle attachment, beat the butter on medium speed, gradually adding the brown sugar until the mixture is light and fluffy, about 3 minutes. Add the eggs one at a time, mixing just enough to incorporate and pausing to scrape the bowl once or twice. Add the vanilla and mix until just combined.

In a measuring cup, combine the buttermilk with the bourbon. With the mixer running on low speed, alternate adding the flour mixture and the buttermilk mixture in five additions, beginning and ending with the dry ingredients, stopping occasionally to scrape the bowl. Mix until just combined. Add the toasted pecan pieces and mix until the nuts are just incorporated.

Pour the batter into the prepared pan and smooth the top with a spatula. Bake until the cake is golden brown and a cake tester or skewer comes out clean, 65 to 70 minutes. Transfer the cake to a rack and cool in the pan for 15 minutes.

Meanwhile, make the glaze: Combine the sugar and bourbon in a small saucepan or skillet. Cook over medium-low heat until the mixture comes to a simmer and the sugar dissolves, 3 to 5 minutes. Turn the cake out of the pan onto a cooling rack. With a pastry brush, brush the warm glaze over the entire surface of the cake. Allow to cool completely. This cake can be made up to 2 days ahead.

Chocolate Espresso Pecan Pie

Serves eight to ten.

FOR THE CRUST:
6 oz. (1⅓ cups) unbleached all-purpose flour; more for rolling out the crust
1 tsp. granulated sugar
¼ tsp. plus ⅛ tsp. kosher salt
2 oz. (4 Tbs.) chilled unsalted butter, cut into ½-inch pieces
2 oz. (4 Tbs.) vegetable shortening, chilled and cut into ½-inch pieces (put it in the freezer for 15 minutes before cutting)

FOR THE FILLING:
3 oz. unsweetened chocolate, coarsely chopped
2 oz. (4 Tbs.) unsalted butter
4 large eggs
1 cup light corn syrup
1 cup granulated sugar
¼ tsp. kosher salt
2 Tbs. instant espresso powder (or instant coffee)
2 Tbs. coffee liqueur (Kahlúa or Caffé Lolita)
2 cups lightly toasted, coarsely chopped pecans
About ½ cup perfect pecan halves

Pecan halves make a decorative border

Arrange the pecan halves in a ring around the perimeter of the pie shell interior, keeping the points of the pecans facing in and the backs just touching the pie shell.

Carefully pour the filling over the pecans until the shell is three-quarters full. The pecans will rise to the top as the pie bakes.

Make the crust: Pulse the flour, sugar, and salt in a food processor just to blend. Add the butter and shortening and pulse several times until the mixture resembles coarse cornmeal, 8 to 10 pulses. Transfer the mixture to a medium bowl. Tossing and stirring quickly with a fork, gradually add enough cold water (2 to 4 Tbs.) that the dough just begins to come together. It should clump together easily if lightly squeezed but not feel wet or sticky. With your hands, gather the dough and form it into a ball. Flatten the ball into a disk and wrap it in plastic. Chill the dough for 2 hours or up to 2 days before rolling. The dough can also be frozen for up to 2 months; thaw it overnight in the refrigerator before using.

Remove the dough from the refrigerator and let it sit at room temperature until pliable, 10 to 15 minutes. On a lightly floured surface with a lightly floured rolling pin, roll the dough into a 1/8-inch-thick, 13-inch-diameter round. Be sure to pick up the dough several times and rotate it, reflouring the surface lightly to prevent sticking. I use a giant spatula or the bottom of a removable-bottom tart pan to move the dough around. (See From Our Test Kitchen, p. 78, for tips on rolling out piecrust.)

Transfer the dough to a 9-inch Pyrex pie pan and trim the edges so there's a 1/2-inch overhang. Fold the overhang underneath itself to create a raised edge and then decoratively crimp or flute the edge. (Save the scraps for patching the shell later, if necessary). Chill until the dough firms up, at least 45 minutes in the refrigerator or 20 minutes in the freezer.

Position a rack in the center of the oven and heat the oven to 350°F. Line the pie shell with parchment and fill with dried beans or pie weights. Bake until the edges of the crust are light golden brown, 25 to 30 minutes. Carefully remove the parchment and beans or weights. If necessary, gently repair any cracks with a smear of the excess dough. Transfer the shell to a rack to cool.

Make the filling: Melt the chocolate and butter in the microwave or in a small metal bowl set in a skillet of barely simmering water, stirring with a rubber spatula until smooth.

In a medium mixing bowl, whisk the eggs, corn syrup, sugar, and salt. Dissolve the instant espresso in 1 Tbs. hot water and add to the egg mixture, along with the coffee liqueur and the melted chocolate and butter. Whisk to blend.

Evenly spread the toasted pecan pieces in the pie shell. To form a decorative border, arrange the pecan halves around the perimeter of the pie shell, on top of the pecan pieces, keeping the points of the pecans facing in and the backs just touching the crust (see photo above). Carefully pour the filling over the pecans until the shell is three-quarters full. Pour the remaining filling into a liquid measuring cup or small pitcher. Transfer the pie to the oven and pour in the remaining filling. (The pecans will rise to the top as the pie bakes.)

Bake the pie until the filling puffs up, just starts to crack, and appears fairly set, 45 to 55 minutes. Transfer it to a rack and allow it to cool completely (at least 4 hours) before serving.

tip: This pie tastes best if cooled and then refrigerated for several hours or overnight. I like to serve it lightly chilled with a dollop of very lightly sweetened whipped cream.

Karen Barker is the pastry chef and co-owner of the award-winning Magnolia Grill restaurant in Durham, North Carolina. ◆

A New Wave of Spinach Salads

Reinvent this classic with bold flavors and crunchy textures from around the world

BY JOANNE WEIR

Fresh Asian accents

Inspired by Italy

Bold Indian flavors

Classic flavors

When was the last time you heard a kid ask for a second helping of spinach? Everyone knows Popeye's favorite green is good for you, but it doesn't win too many popularity contests. And in fairness, when it's overcooked, spinach can acquire a strong, acidic flavor and leave your mouth feeling dry. But if you cook it gently or don't cook it at all, spinach has a clean, delicate flavor altogether contrary to its reputation. So around my house, I fight spinach's bad rap by tossing it in a vibrant salad with lots of tasty toppings and robustly flavored vinaigrettes.

The classic salad with eggs and bacon is delicious, of course (you'll find my version on p. 67), but I like to pique my diners' interest with fresh new twists, incorporating eclectic flavors and textures from international cuisines ranging from Italian to Asian to Indian. Take my Italian-inspired salad, for instance: I toss the spinach with sautéed mushrooms and Parmigiano and arrange everything on top of garlic-rubbed crostini, so it's more like a spinach-salad bruschetta. Heady Indian spices like curry powder and ground cumin add zip to a salad with apples and dried apricots. And I whisk together a vinaigrette of rice vinegar, soy sauce, sesame oil, and fresh ginger

to give a zesty Asian accent to a spinach salad with chicken and cashews.

Texture is as important as flavor. In my salads, I always add at least one ingredient that has a bit of crunch to create some textural contrast. Here, too, I like to span the globe and think beyond toasted nuts and croutons. Crispy pappadams (Indian flatbreads), fried wonton wrappers, and even fried Asian noodles are all great crunchy additions that help give a global flair and a little sophistication to my spinach salads.

Start with fresh, clean, dry spinach. At the market you can usually choose among large bundled spinach, bulk young spinach, or washed and bagged (or boxed) baby spinach. I prefer bundled young spinach because it tends to be more tender and have a cleaner flavor than the large, tough leaves—and it's not as dirty. Bagged spinach is convenient and works fine, but it can be hard to assess how fresh it is, so it generally doesn't last as long, unless you luck out on a really fresh batch. No matter what kind of spinach you buy, make sure you wash it carefully to remove all the dirt (I give even bagged spinach a rinse) and dry it thoroughly, since oil-based dressings don't cling well to wet leaves.

Photos: Scott Phillips

Asian

Spinach Salad with Chicken, Cashews, Ginger & Fried Wontons

Serves six as a first course, four as a main course.

Instead of cooking chicken breasts, you can use leftover roasted or rotisserie chicken. You'll need 3½ cups.

FOR THE VINAIGRETTE:
2 Tbs. rice vinegar
1 Tbs. soy sauce
1 Tbs. peanut oil
2 tsp. finely grated or minced fresh ginger
1 tsp. granulated sugar
1 tsp. Asian sesame oil
1 medium clove garlic, minced (1 tsp.)
Pinch crushed red pepper flakes
Kosher salt and freshly ground black pepper

FOR THE CHICKEN:
1 Tbs. peanut oil
3 bone-in, skin-on split chicken breasts (about 1 lb. total)
Kosher salt and freshly ground black pepper

FOR THE SALAD:
½ cup cashew pieces (about 3 oz.)
1½ cups peanut oil
2 oz. wonton wrappers (about 8 wrappers), cut into ⅛-inch strips
10 cups loosely packed baby spinach leaves, washed and dried (about 10 oz.)
2 scallions, thinly sliced on the diagonal

Position a rack in the center of the oven and heat the oven to 375°F.

Make the vinaigrette: In a small bowl, whisk together the vinaigrette ingredients, seasoning to taste with the salt and pepper.

Cook the chicken: Heat the peanut oil in an ovenproof 10-inch skillet over medium-high heat. Generously season the chicken breasts with salt and pepper. When the oil is shimmering, add the chicken breasts skin side down and cook until light golden, 1 to 2 minutes. Turn the chicken breasts so they are skin side up and transfer the pan to the oven. Bake until the chicken is just cooked through, 12 to 14 minutes. Transfer the chicken to a cutting board and let cool. Remove and discard the skin and bones. Cut each breast diagonally into thin slices and set aside.

Make the salad: While the chicken cools, scatter the cashews on a baking sheet and bake in the oven until golden and fragrant, 7 to 9 minutes. Let cool.

Pour the peanut oil into a small saucepan and heat over medium-high heat until the oil reaches 375°F. Use a candy thermometer to monitor the temperature, or test the oil temperature by dipping the end of one wonton strip into the oil. If it's hot enough, it should sizzle on contact.

Fry half of the strips until light golden, 30 to 60 seconds. Remove with a slotted spoon and drain on paper towels. Season with a light sprinkle of salt. Fry the remaining wonton strips, drain, and season with salt. (The wontons can be fried up to 2 hours ahead.)

In a large bowl, toss the vinaigrette with the spinach, chicken, and scallions and season to taste with salt. Divide the salad among four or six plates, garnish each with the fried wontons and cashews, and serve immediately.

Italian

Garlic Crostini with Spinach, Mushroom & Parmigiano Salad

Serves six as a first course, four as a main course.

FOR THE VINAIGRETTE:
2 Tbs. extra-virgin olive oil
1 Tbs. fresh lemon juice (from about half a lemon)
1 tsp. finely grated lemon zest (from about half a lemon)
1 small shallot, minced (1½ Tbs.)
1 medium clove garlic, minced
Kosher salt and freshly ground black pepper

FOR THE SALAD & CROSTINI:
Six ½-inch-thick slices coarse-textured Tuscan-style bread
2 cloves garlic, cut in half lengthwise
Kosher salt
2 Tbs. extra-virgin olive oil; more for drizzling
10 oz. small fresh button mushrooms, stems discarded, caps halved (about 2½ cups)
Freshly ground black pepper
6 cups loosely packed baby spinach leaves, washed and dried (about 6 oz.)
Parmigiano-Reggiano for shaving

Make the vinaigrette: In a small bowl, whisk together the vinaigrette ingredients, seasoning to taste with the salt and pepper.

Make the salad: Position a rack 6 inches from the broiler element and heat the broiler on high. Arrange the bread slices on a baking sheet and broil until crispy and light golden on top, 1 to 2 minutes. Flip and broil the other sides until golden, about 1 minute. Rub one side of the toasted bread with the cut sides of the garlic. Sprinkle each slice with a small pinch of salt and set aside.

Heat the oil in a 10-inch skillet over medium-high heat. When the oil is shimmering, add the mushrooms and stir to coat in the oil. Let the mushrooms cook undisturbed until the liquid they release evaporates and they're deep golden brown, 5 to 7 minutes. Sprinkle with ½ tsp. salt, stir, and continue cooking, stirring occasionally, until most sides are nicely browned, 3 to 5 minutes more. Season to taste with more salt and pepper. Remove from the heat and let cool slightly.

Toss the spinach and vinaigrette in a large bowl. Put the bread slices on four or six plates and drizzle each slice with a little olive oil. Divide the spinach among the plates, arranging it on the top of the bread but leaving part of the bread exposed. Top with the mushrooms. Using a cheese shaver or vegetable peeler, shave a few thin slivers of Parmigiano over the top. Serve immediately.

Indian

Spinach Salad with Apples, Dried Apricots & Pappadam Croutons

Serves six as a first course, four as a main course.

FOR THE VINAIGRETTE:
¼ cup extra-virgin olive oil
½ tsp. curry powder
¼ tsp. ground cumin
1 medium clove garlic, minced (about 1 tsp.)
2½ Tbs. fresh lemon juice (from 1 large lemon)
Kosher salt and freshly ground black pepper

FOR THE SALAD:
½ cup whole almonds (about 3 oz.)
Four 7-inch round plain, cumin-seed, or black-peppercorn pappadams (see From Our Test Kitchen, p. 78, for more information)

Classic

Warm Spinach Salad with Eggs, Bacon & Croutons

Serves six as a first course, four as a main course.

2 large eggs
Kosher salt
4½ Tbs. extra-virgin olive oil
2 cloves garlic, crushed and peeled
3 to 4 oz. rustic, coarse-textured bread, crust removed, cut into ¾-inch cubes (to yield 3 cups)
3 Tbs. sherry vinegar
1 Tbs. Dijon mustard
Freshly ground black pepper
3 slices bacon, cut into ¾-inch squares
1 small shallot, minced (1½ Tbs.)
10 cups loosely packed baby spinach leaves, washed and dried (about 10 oz.)

Put the eggs in a small saucepan of water and bring to a boil over medium-high heat. Boil for 4 minutes. Turn off the heat and let cool in the water. When the eggs are cool, crack and peel them. Chop the eggs, season to taste with salt, and reserve.

Position a rack in the center of the oven and heat the oven to 375°F. Heat 1½ Tbs. of the olive oil in a small sauce-pan over medium-high heat. Add the garlic and cook, stirring occasionally, until it starts to turn gold, about 1 minute. Discard the garlic.

Arrange the bread in a single layer on a baking sheet. Drizzle with the garlic-infused oil, sprinkle with a little salt, and toss. Bake, shaking the bread cubes once, until golden and crispy, 8 to 10 minutes. Remove from the oven and let cool.

In a small bowl, whisk together the remaining 3 Tbs. olive oil, the sherry vinegar, and the mustard. Season with salt and pepper to taste.

In a 10-inch skillet, cook the bacon over medium-high heat, stirring frequently, until golden brown and crisp, 3 to 5 minutes. With a slotted spoon, transfer the bacon to a plate lined with paper towels. Add the shallot to the pan and cook, stirring, until softened, about 1 minute. Let the pan cool slightly and add the vinaigrette to the pan, whisking well to blend the ingredients.

Toss the warm vinaigrette and the spinach together in a large bowl. Transfer to a platter and garnish with the chopped eggs, bacon, and croutons. Serve immediately.

Joanne Weir is a cooking teacher, cookbook author, and star of the PBS show Joanne Weir's Cooking Class. ◆

10 cups loosely packed baby spinach leaves, washed and dried (about 10 oz.)
1 small red apple (preferably Gala, Cortland, or McIntosh), cored and thinly sliced
1 small tart green apple (preferably Granny Smith or Pippin), cored and thinly sliced
¾ cup dried apricots (about 5 oz.), thinly sliced

Position a rack in the center of the oven and heat the oven to 375°F.

Make the vinaigrette: In a small saucepan or skillet, heat the olive oil, curry powder, cumin, and garlic over medium-low heat until sizzling and very fragrant, 1 to 2 minutes. Set aside until cool. Whisk in the lemon juice and season to taste with salt and pepper.

Make the salad: Scatter the almonds on a baking sheet and bake in the oven until lightly browned and fragrant, 8 to 12 minutes. Remove from the oven and let cool. Chop coarsely.

Turn off the oven, position a rack 6 inches from the broiler element and heat the broiler on high. Arrange the pappadams in a single layer on a baking sheet and broil until they bubble and crisp on one side, 15 to 30 seconds. Don't let them take on more than a light golden color. Turn the pappadams over and continue to broil until bubbly and crisp on the other side, about 5 seconds. Remove from the oven and let cool—they will continue to crisp. Break each pappadam into several pieces.

In a large bowl, toss the spinach, apples, apricots, and almonds with enough of the dressing to coat lightly. Divide the salad among four or six plates, garnish with the pappadam pieces, and serve immediately.

Linguine with Clam Sauce

Fresh clams and perfectly firm pasta are the keys to this simple Italian dish

BY PERLA MEYERS

If you've ever ordered a plate of linguine with clam sauce in Naples, Venice, or any Italian town overlooking the Mediterranean, you're surely a fan of this simple dish, with its intense, clean flavors. But return home and start to look for this classic in local restaurants and, like me, you're apt to be disappointed.

Linguine with clam sauce should be packed with flavor—nicely garlicky and a little spicy—with firm (but not chewy) pasta. Most of all, it should taste of fresh, delicious clams with the unmistakable tang of the sea. This is a simple dish, with familiar ingredients that are easy to find. Yet the simpler the dish, the harder it is to duplicate, because every ingredient has to be perfectly fresh and properly prepared. This is not the place for short cuts. But don't worry—I'll help you recreate the best linguine with clam sauce you've ever had.

Start with selecting the clams (see sidebar at right). The ones used in Italy and around the Mediterranean are small, meaty, and juicy, but this variety is not available in the United States. You're most likely to find Atlantic hard-shell clams in your market. The smallest of these, generally less than 2½ inches across, are called littlenecks, and

they are the tenderest. Medium ones, up to 3 inches across, are called cherrystones. The largest quahogs, called chowder clams, are too tough for this sauce. When making this dish for two to four people, I use the more expensive littlenecks, but when I plan to serve six or eight, I choose cherrystones because they're large, and each clam goes a long way.

Next, choose a brand of pasta that will remain al dente. I prefer the imported De Cecco, Rustichella d'Abruzzo, and Due Pastori brands. These take longer to cook but will retain a firm texture. The pasta water is very flavorful, so be sure to save some before draining the pasta. If you find yourself with too little clam juice, add about ½ cup of this reserved cooking water to the broth.

To ensure heat in every bite, I infuse olive oil with crushed red pepper flakes. Don't skip this simple, fast step, as it imparts a subtle spiciness throughout the dish.

This is a great classic that should be cooked and enjoyed for what it is. If it can make you feel as if you're eating at a seaside restaurant in Italy, so much the better.

Buying clams

When shopping for clams, you'll want to head for a market with rapid turnover. Since clams are such an important part of this dish, it'll be worth the extra time it takes to get to a good seafood market.

Look for intact, tightly closed (or just slightly gaping) shells, and a sea-like smell. Clams are sold alive, so don't store them in plastic or they'll suffocate. As soon as you get home, put them in a bowl, cover with a wet towel, and refrigerate. Just before cooking, look for any shellfish that are open and tap them on the counter. If they don't close, discard them. Also discard any clams that remain closed after cooking.

If you are not preparing this dish the day you buy the clams, it's smart to wash and cook them in the wine and herb broth, remove them from their shells, and refrigerate; they will keep for two or three days.

Linguine with Clam Sauce

Serves two to three.

24 littleneck clams
6 Tbs. extra-virgin olive oil
½ tsp. crushed red pepper flakes
⅓ cup dry white wine
5 Tbs. finely chopped fresh flat-leaf parsley, plus a few whole leaves for garnish
3 large cloves garlic, minced
Kosher salt
8 oz. linguine or spaghettini (I like De Cecco, Due Pastori, and Rustichella d'Abruzzo brands)
Freshly ground black pepper

Scrub the clams under cold water and set aside. In a heavy 3-qt. saucepan, heat 3 Tbs. of the oil over medium heat. Add the pepper flakes and cook briefly to infuse the oil, about 20 seconds. Immediately add the wine, 2 Tbs. of the chopped parsley, and half of the minced garlic. Cook for 20 seconds and add the clams.

Cover and cook over medium-high heat, checking every 2 minutes and removing each clam as it opens. It will take 5 to 6 minutes total for all the clams to open. Transfer the clams to a cutting board and reserve the broth. Remove the clams from the shells

and cut them in half, or quarters if they're large. Return the clams to the broth. Discard the shells.

Bring a large pot of well-salted water to a boil over high heat. Add the pasta and cook until it's almost al dente, 6 to 9 minutes. Don't overcook.

While the pasta is cooking, heat the remaining 3 Tbs. olive oil in a 10- or 12-inch skillet over medium heat. Add the remaining 3 Tbs. chopped parsley and the rest of the garlic and cook until the garlic is just soft, about 1 minute. Set the skillet aside.

When the pasta is done, reserve about ¼ cup of the pasta

cooking water and then drain the pasta. Add the pasta, the clams, and the broth the clams were cooked in to the skillet. Return to low heat, toss the pasta in the sauce, and simmer for another minute to finish cooking it, adding a little of the pasta water if you prefer a wetter dish.

Taste for salt and add a large grind of black pepper. Serve immediately, garnished with the parsley leaves.

Perla Meyers teaches cooking at workshops around the country and has cooked in restaurants throughout Italy, France, and Spain. ◆

Cinnamon Buns
In Less Than an Hour

Photos: Scott Phillips

A biscuit dough is the shortcut secret to this sweet breakfast treat

BY KATHY KINGSLEY

I f I could order up the perfect breakfast, it would definitely include warm, homemade cinnamon rolls swirled with a spiced filling and drizzled with a sweet white icing. As much as I love these rich, fragrant buns, I often don't have the time or haven't planned far enough in advance to make the yeast-leavened dough called for in most recipes. But several years ago, I discovered a shortcut method that makes light, tender buns in about 45 minutes—no lie.

The idea came to me during the time I owned and operated a bakery in Connecticut called Great Cakes. Our famous yeast-risen cinnamon rolls sold out quickly every Sunday morning, and week after week, we continued to get special orders for these delectable treats. One Sunday, after all the buns had been sold, I was baking biscuits and used some of the dough to make an impromptu cinnamon bun—we were always experimenting with new methods. It worked, but it wasn't great. That's when I began tinkering with the ingredients to see if I could come up with a biscuit-type dough that would work for a quick cinnamon bun.

I started with traditional biscuit dough, which contains flour, buttermilk, cold butter, and baking powder. After much experimentation, I increased the amount of butter in the original recipe to give the dough more flavor and a softer texture. I also added cottage cheese, which I had read is sometimes used in German baking recipes to make richer and more tender pastries. Increasing the amount of the baking powder made the buns rise more—I like them puffy. The baking powder also reacts with the buttermilk to neutralize its sourness. Rolling the dough and shaping it into pinwheel spirals proved easy, and the resulting buns were tender, golden, and flavorful, with a filling redolent of cinnamon and not overly sweet. And because I can't help trying out new variations, I came up with a version with an apple-butter filling. (For yet another variation, go to FineCooking.com for Coconut Almond Spice Buns.)

With this recipe, you won't need a lot of time, and you won't have to plan ahead to enjoy warm, homemade cinnamon buns—now that's a real breakfast treat, indeed.

reader review

A *Fine Cooking* reader gave both versions of the Fastest Cinnamon Buns a real-world test. Here are the results:

This was a great recipe for me to try, because it brought me out of my comfort zone. But the instructions were very clear, and both versions of the recipe came out perfectly—and looked just like the photos. Plus, baking these buns made the house smell wonderful.

—Jill Caseria
Newtown, Connecticut

Fastest Cinnamon Buns

Yields 12 buns.

Cooking spray for the pan

FOR THE DOUGH:
¾ cup cottage cheese (4% milk fat)
⅓ cup buttermilk
¼ cup granulated sugar
2 oz. (4 Tbs.) unsalted butter, melted
1 tsp. pure vanilla extract
9 oz. (2 cups) unbleached all-purpose flour; more for rolling
1 Tbs. baking powder
½ tsp. table salt
¼ tsp. baking soda

FOR THE FILLING:
¾ oz. (1½ Tbs.) unsalted butter, melted
⅔ cup packed light or dark brown sugar
1½ tsp. ground cinnamon
½ tsp. ground allspice
¼ tsp. ground cloves
1 cup (4 oz.) chopped pecans

FOR THE GLAZE:
2½ oz. (scant ⅔ cup) confectioners' sugar
2 to 3 Tbs. cold whole or low-fat milk
1 tsp. pure vanilla extract

Heat the oven to 400°F. Grease the sides and bottom of a 9- or 10-inch springform pan with cooking spray.

Make the dough: ▣ In a food processor, combine the cottage cheese, buttermilk, sugar, melted butter, and vanilla. Process until smooth, about 10 seconds. Add the flour, baking powder, salt, and baking soda and pulse in short bursts just until the dough clumps together (don't overprocess). The dough will be soft and moist.

Scrape the dough out onto a lightly floured surface and knead it with floured hands 4 or 5 times until smooth. With a rolling pin, roll the dough into a 12x15-inch rectangle.

Make the filling: Brush the dough with the melted butter, leaving a ½-inch border unbuttered around the edges. In a medium bowl, combine the brown sugar, cinnamon, all-

spice, and cloves. Sprinkle the mixture over the buttered area of the dough and pat gently into the surface. Sprinkle the nuts over the sugar mixture.

▣ Starting at a long edge, roll up the dough jelly-roll style. Pinch the seam to seal, and leave the ends open.

▣ With a sharp knife, cut the roll into 12 equal pieces. Set the pieces, cut side up, in the prepared pan; they should fill the pan and touch slightly, but don't worry if there are small gaps.

Bake until golden brown and firm to the touch, 20 to 28 minutes. Set the pan on a wire rack to cool for 5 minutes. Run a spatula around the inside edge of the pan and remove the springform ring. Transfer the rolls to a serving plate.

Make the glaze: ▣ In a small bowl, mix the confectioners' sugar, 2 Tbs. milk, and vanilla to make a smooth glaze. It should have a thick but pourable consistency, so add up to 1 Tbs. more milk if necessary. Drizzle the glaze over the rolls. Let stand 15 minutes and serve.

Variation:
Apple-Butter Cinnamon Buns

Instead of using the cinnamon-pecan filling in the main recipe, mix ¾ cup apple butter, 1½ Tbs. melted butter, and 1 tsp. ground cinnamon in a small bowl. Omit the melted butter from the main recipe and spread the dough rectangle with the apple mixture, leaving a ½-inch border around the edges. Sprinkle with ¾ cup (3 oz.) finely chopped walnuts, if desired. Roll, cut, bake, and ice as directed. Because this filling is wetter, the buns may need to bake for 30 minutes.

Kathy Kingsley has been baking for two decades. Her latest cookbook is Chocolate Therapy. ◆

1. Don't overprocess the dough, but be sure the cottage cheese is fully incorporated.

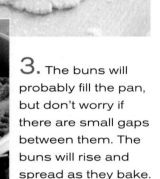

2. Leave a ½-inch border around the edge of the dough, so the filling won't spill out when you roll it up.

3. The buns will probably fill the pan, but don't worry if there are small gaps between them. The buns will rise and spread as they bake.

4. Make the glaze pourable so that it can seep down into each bun and infuse it with sweet vanilla goodness.

tip: For an extra-sweet touch, reserve some of the glaze to pass at the table, so people can drizzle a little more on each bun.

How to Make Hearty Bean & Vegetable Soups

BY MOLLY STEVENS

Learn the best method for making deeply flavored winter soups with your choice of ingredients

Every fall my soup pot gets a workout. But of all the soups and stews I concoct to keep my friends and family warm, everyone's favorites are the hearty bean and vegetable soups. Endlessly variable, this winning combination delivers delicious, nourishing soups that please almost any appetite. And happily for me, they're easy on the cook, too. The straightforward method on pp. 75–77 shows you how to make a satisfying bean soup using ingredients you like. Beans' gentle, earthy character makes them a perfect backdrop for a range of flavors, from bold and spicy to rich and mellow. So by simply varying the ingredients, you can create a winter's worth of comforting soups.

Another reason to add bean and vegetable soups to your repertoire is convenience. Make a big pot on the weekend (they take some time, but it's mostly unattended simmering), then refrigerate the leftovers and reheat them for easy meals throughout the week. Like many slow-cooked dishes, these soups taste even better the next day or the day after that. And you can easily freeze them for longer storage.

The best soups start with dried beans

Certainly canned beans speed up the process, but this is one of those instances where the extra step of starting with dried beans makes a big difference. First of all, they yield better flavor and texture: Freshly cooked beans are plumper, creamier, and truer to their natural flavor than canned. Dried beans also retain their shape better and are less apt to turn mushy. Another advantage of cooking your own beans is that you end up with a rich-tasting bean broth that goes right back into the soup.

Minestrone

Soak the beans first. This allows them to soften gently and plump up, shortening the cooking time and helping the beans cook evenly. Although many recipes call for soaking beans overnight, four hours is plenty. I often soak the beans in the morning of the day I plan to make soup.

Next, cook the beans alone. Give the beans a quick rinse, put them in a large pot with a garlic clove and bay leaf for extra flavor, and simmer gently in enough water to cover. I've found that it's best to add salt about three-quarters of the way through simmering. This is not so early as to slow down the cooking (which salt is known to do), but not too late to season the beans effectively. Instead of adding vegetables to the simmering beans, I prefer to cook the beans separately and add them to the soup later. If you cook them together, it's easy for the vegetables to overcook before the beans are ready.

Choose any vegetables and seasonings you like

It's always a good idea to think of flavor affinities before you start assembling ingredients. If you're leaning toward Mediterranean, you might select fennel, rosemary, and garlic, while a Latin American-inspired soup could include cumin, coriander, and chiles (see some of my favorite combinations at right). I also like to keep things seasonal, relying on the hearty vegetables available in fall and winter, such as cabbage, parsnips, carrots, and cauliflower.

No matter what type of soup I make, I find that a bit of cured or seasoned pork (such as bacon, pancetta, or sausage), while not absolutely necessary, adds depth and an irresistibly savory edge to the soup. I cook it in a little olive oil to create a flavor base. Then I remove it, set it aside to add back later, and add the aromatics followed by the vegetables and broth.

Finish with a flourish. After you've added the beans back to the soup pot and let everything simmer together, you have a final opportunity to personalize and add flavor to your soup. Stir in some lemon juice, vinegar, or hot sauce for a splash of acidity or heat. For a burst of freshness and color, toss in a handful of chopped herbs. And if you like, finish each serving with a drizzle of good olive oil or flavored oil, a handful of croutons, or even a sprinkling of grated cheese.

French farmers' soup

Classic combinations

Try one of these traditional combos or create your own hearty soup following the steps starting on the next page.

MEXICAN BLACK BEAN SOUP

Beans: black beans
Meat: chorizo or bacon
Aromatics: onion and celery
Seasonings: garlic, jalapeño, cumin, and coriander
Vegetables: carrots and tomatoes
Finishing touches: lime juice and fresh cilantro

MIDDLE-EASTERN CHICKPEA SOUP

Beans: chickpeas
Meat: omit
Aromatics: onions and celery
Seasonings: garlic, cumin, coriander, and red pepper flakes
Vegetables: potatoes, cauliflower, and carrots
Finishing touches: lemon juice, parsley, and a drizzle of chile oil

FRENCH FARMERS' SOUP

Beans: flageolets or baby lima beans
Meat: bacon
Aromatics: shallots and leeks
Seasonings: thyme
Vegetables: carrots, celery root, and turnips
Finishing touches: white-wine or Champagne vinegar, parsley, and croutons

CABBAGE AND WHITE BEAN SOUP

Beans: cannellini, great northern, or navy beans
Meat: fresh Italian sausage
Aromatics: onion and celery
Seasonings: rosemary and garlic
Vegetables: cabbage and potatoes
Finishing touches: parsley

MINESTRONE

Beans: cranberry beans
Meat: pancetta
Aromatics: onion and celery
Seasonings: garlic, rosemary, thyme, red pepper flakes, and tomato paste
Vegetables: chard or escarole, fennel, and tomatoes
Finishing touches: basil, grated Parmigiano-Reggiano, and a drizzle of olive oil

Six steps to a hearty bean & vegetable soup

Yields 9 to 10 cups; serves six.

What you'll need

Read carefully through all the steps and then choose and assemble the ingredients for each step before you start cooking.

- **8 oz. (1¼ cups) your choice of dried beans**
- **1 medium clove garlic**
- **1 bay leaf**
- **¾ tsp. kosher salt; more as needed**
- **2 Tbs. extra-virgin olive oil or unsalted butter**
- **¼ lb. bacon, pancetta, or sausage (optional)**
- **1½ cups your choice of aromatics**
- **4 tsp. your choice of spices and herbs or other seasonings**
- **1 Tbs. tomato paste (optional)**
- **3 cups your choice of vegetables**
- **5 to 6 cups homemade or store-bought low-salt chicken broth or homemade vegetable broth**
- **Freshly ground black pepper**
- **Your choice of finishing ingredients (see step 6)**

Quick-soak beans

Don't have at least four hours to soak beans? You can quick-soak them. In a saucepan, add enough cold water to cover the beans by 2 inches, bring quickly to a boil, remove from the heat, and let soak for one hour. The results tend to be less consistent than those you'd get from a cold-water soak, but it's a good trick in a pinch.

1 Soak the beans

Sort through your beans, discarding any little stones or clumps of dirt, and then give them a quick rinse. Transfer to a large bowl, add enough cold water to cover the beans by 3 inches, and soak for 4 to 12 hours.

Dried bean choices

Choose one (1¼ cups; 8 oz.)

Baby lima beans

Black beans (turtle beans)

Cannellini

Chickpeas (garbanzo beans)

Cranberry beans (borlotti or Roman beans)

Flageolets

Great northern beans

Kidney beans (red, pink, or white)

Navy beans

Pinto beans

Yellow-eye beans

Substituting canned beans

If you don't have time to soak and cook the beans, you can use canned beans, though the flavor of your soup won't be as rich. You'll need two 15-ounce cans to make the 3 cups cooked beans needed (you may have leftover beans). Rinse and drain before using.

2 Cook the beans

Drain and rinse the beans and transfer them to a 3- or 4-qt. saucepan. Add 1 medium garlic clove (smashed and peeled), 1 bay leaf, and 6 cups of cold water. Partially cover to limit evaporation and simmer gently, stirring every 20 to 30 minutes, until the beans are tender and almost creamy inside, without being mealy or mushy (see below for approximate cooking times). The beans' cooking time will vary depending on how long they've

soaked and how old they are. The older the beans, the longer they take to cook. But the longer you soak them, the shorter the cooking time. So the safest way to determine when the beans are done is to taste them as they cook.

Season with ¾ tsp. kosher salt when the beans are about three-quarters done. If at any time the liquid doesn't cover the beans, add 1 cup fresh water.

Drain the beans, reserving the cooking liquid, and discard the bay leaf (the garlic clove can stay). If you cook the beans in advance, refrigerate the beans and the cooking liquid separately until you make the soup (you can cook the beans one day ahead).

BEAN COOKING TIMES
(Times are approximate.)

Baby lima, flageolet, yellow-eye: ¾ to 1 hour

Black, cannellini, cranberry, great northern, kidney, navy, pinto: 1 to 1½ hours

Chickpeas: 1¼ to 2 hours

3 Create the flavor foundation

This important step consists of three consecutive sub-steps that create the soup's flavor base.

Heat 2 Tbs. extra-virgin olive oil or unsalted butter in a 4- to 5-qt. soup pot or Dutch oven over medium heat.

Add the meat
(optional; see choices below)

To give the soup a more savory, meaty flavor add some bacon (or pancetta) or fresh (or smoked) sausage. Cook, stirring often, until the fat is rendered and the meat begins to brown, 5 to 8 minutes. Pour the meat and fat into a small strainer set over a bowl, and set the meat aside. Spoon 2 Tbs. of fat back into the pot, and return it to medium heat. If you're not using any meat, skip to the aromatics.

Add aromatics
(see choices below)

Add your choice of aromatics and season with a pinch of kosher salt and freshly ground black pepper.

Cook, stirring frequently, until they begin to soften but not brown, 4 to 6 minutes.

Add seasonings
(see choices below)

Stir in your choice of seasonings and cook until fragrant, 1 minute.

By simply varying the ingredients, you can create a winter's worth of comforting soups.

Meat choices
(optional)
Choose one (¼ lb.)

Bacon or thinly sliced pancetta: cut into ½-inch pieces

Bulk pancetta: cut into small dice

Fresh Italian sausage or fresh chorizo: out of its casing and crumbled

Smoked or cured sausage (such as andouille, chorizo, or kielbasa): cut into ½-inch pieces

Aromatic choices

Choose at least two and up to four in any combination, for a total of 1½ cups

Celery: chopped
Leeks: chopped
Onions: chopped
Shallots: chopped

Tomato paste

Some of the pink and red beans can turn a muddy shade when cooked, but you can add 1 Tbs. tomato paste along with the seasonings (at right) to deepen the shade and make it more appealing. Tomato paste also adds a concentrated sweetness welcome in any bean soup, not just those made with dark beans.

Seasoning choices

HERBS & OTHER SEASONINGS
Choose up to three for a total of 1 Tbs., unless otherwise noted:

Dried herbes de Provence (no more than ¾ tsp.)

Fresh chiles: minced
Fresh garlic: minced
Fresh ginger: minced
Fresh marjoram: chopped
Fresh rosemary: chopped
Fresh sage: chopped
Fresh thyme: chopped

SPICES
Choose up to three for a total of 1 tsp., unless otherwise noted:

Crushed red pepper flakes (no more than ¼ tsp.)

Ground coriander

Ground cumin

Ground fennel seed

Hot or sweet paprika (smoked or plain)

4 Add vegetables & broth

Add the vegetables, stirring to incorporate with the seasonings and aromatics, and then add 2 cups of the broth, partially cover, and simmer until the vegetables are just barely tender, 10 to 20 minutes.

Vegetable choices

Choose up to three for a total of 3 cups

Canned diced tomatoes: drained (save the juice to add to the broth)

Carrots: peeled and cut into ¼-inch-thick half moons

Cauliflower: cut into ½-inch florets

Celery root: peeled and cut into ½-inch dice

Escarole: coarsely chopped

Fennel: coarsely chopped

Green cabbage: thinly sliced

Parsnips: peeled and cut into ½-inch dice

Red or white potatoes: peeled and cut into ½-inch dice

Swiss chard: stems chopped and leaves sliced

Turnips: peeled and cut into ½-inch dice

Broth choices

Choose one (5 to 6 cups, added in two steps)

Homemade or store-bought low-salt chicken broth

Homemade vegetable broth

5 Add beans & more liquid

Add the beans and then add 3 cups of chicken or vegetable broth and 1 cup of the reserved bean-cooking liquid. If you have less than 1 cup bean liquid left from cooking the beans or if you're adding the juice from canned tomatoes, adjust the broth for a total of 4 cups liquid.

Return the cooked meat to the pot, if using. Stir to combine and simmer, partially covered, for 10 minutes to meld the flavors.

6 Give the soup a finishing touch

Taste the soup and adjust the seasoning with salt and pepper. Finish your soup with an acid, if it needs brightening, a sprinkle of fresh herbs, and a final topping once the soup is ladled into bowls. You may want to reserve some of the herbs to sprinkle on top of each serving as well. The soup will keep in the fridge for three or four days, tightly covered. Or you can freeze it for up to three months. (If making ahead, wait to add the finishing touches until ready to serve.)

Finishing choices (optional)

ACIDS (optional)
Choose one (1 to 2 tsp.):

Fresh lemon or lime juice

Hot sauce: just a splash

Red-wine, white-wine, sherry, or Champagne vinegar

FRESH HERBS
Choose up to two for a total of ⅓ cup:

Basil: chopped

Chives: thinly sliced

Cilantro: chopped

Parsley: chopped

TOPPINGS

A drizzle of good-quality olive oil, toasted sesame oil, chile oil, or herb-infused oil per serving

A small handful of croutons per serving

1 Tbs. freshly grated Parmigiano-Reggiano per serving

Molly Stevens, a contributing editor to Fine Cooking, *is an award-winning cookbook author and cooking teacher.* ◆

Choose "easy-strip" thyme for faster picking

"Hard-to-strip" thyme

"Easy-strip" thyme

If you asked me to choose my least favorite kitchen task, I wouldn't have to think hard—as much as I love the flavor, the tediousness of picking little fresh thyme leaves off their stems drives me crazy. So when I discovered that our Thanksgiving menu calls for about ½ cup of chopped thyme, I wasn't too happy. Fortunately, our test kitchen intern, Will, returned from the store with beautiful bunches of what I like to call "easy-strip" thyme.

Let me explain: There are many varieties of thyme. Besides their flavor differences, some varieties have thin, weak stems; some have tough, woody stems; and still other varieties have both—the mature stems are woody while the new growth is weak. The fastest way to strip thyme leaves off the stem is to pinch the end of the stem and zip your fingers down the stem, pulling off the leaves in one fell swoop. With thin-stemmed thyme, this method usually breaks the stem and you practically have to pick the leaves off one by one, but with woody-stemmed varieties—easy-strip thyme—it works like a charm.

So the next time you buy thyme, choose the woodiest-looking bunch (it's not actually labeled "easy-strip"—that's just what I call it). When zip-stripping the thyme, start at the top end for a single sprig, and the bottom end for a multibranched sprig.

Pineapple Rings
1-2-3

The easiest way to prepare the glistening, caramelized fresh pineapple rings that top our Pecan Pineapple Upside-Down Cake on p. 60 is to buy a peeled and cored fresh pineapple from the grocery store and just slice it into rings. But if your market carries only whole fresh pineapples, here's how to trim one down into picture-perfect rings.

How to select a ripe pineapple

Look for a fresh, dark-green top and taut, shiny skin. Pick it up. It should feel heavy for its size and give a little when pressed, but there shouldn't be any large, very soft spots. It should have a light, sweet pineapple fragrance, especially at its base. A pineapple with a heavy, cloying fragrance may be overripe.

Contrary to popular belief, a pineapple with greenish skin may actually be ripe; skin color varies with variety. You may also have heard that the ease with which a leaf can be pulled free is a sign of ripeness, but this isn't necessarily so.

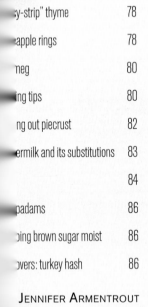

y-strip" thyme	78
apple rings	78
neg	80
ing tips	80
ng out piecrust	82
ermilk and its substitutions	83
	84
padams	86
ing brown sugar moist	86
overs: turkey hash	86

JENNIFER ARMENTROUT

1 Cut off the top and bottom and stand it on a cut end. Slice off the skin, cutting deeply enough into the pineapple to remove the eyes, too. You'll lose some edible flesh this way, but it's the best way to get nice round rings.

2 Cut the pineapple into ¼-inch-thick slices and then trim any pointy edges off each slice to round it off.

3 Remove the core from each slice with a small round cutter or a paring knife.

Photos: Scott Phillips

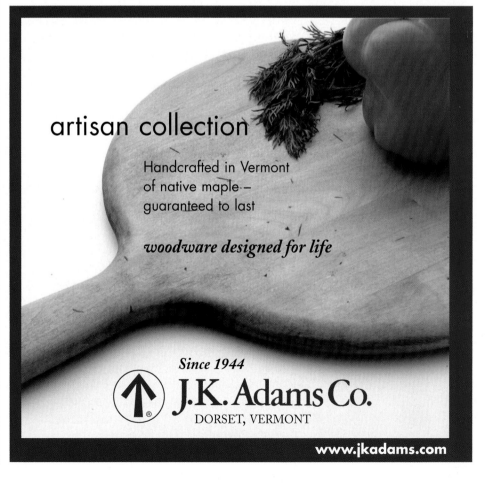

There's no substitute for
freshly grated nutmeg

Good cooks know there's a big difference between freshly ground spices and their pre-ground counterparts, and this is particularly true in the case of nutmeg. See for yourself: Open the jar of ground nutmeg that's probably in your cupboard (and may be several years old—come on, admit it), and compare it to some freshly grated. The freshly grated smells sweet, fragrant, almost citrusy, and, well, fresh. The pre-ground smells sharp and musky by comparison.

This isn't to say that there's no place for pre-ground nutmeg in the pantry alongside the whole nutmeg—it's convenient, after all—but I like to think of them as different spices. If a recipe calls for pre-ground nutmeg, go ahead and use it (provided it's not more than six months old). But when a recipe like the Pecan Pineapple Upside-Down Cake on p. 60 calls for freshly grated nutmeg, please don't be tempted to substitute—the results won't be nearly as nice.

A favorite nutmeg grater

Truthfully, you don't really need a special nutmeg grater—the side of a box grater with the little crown-shaped protrusions does the job. But as someone who loves gadgets that are truly useful, I've grown fond of this little number from Microplane because it's more than just a grater. It has two sides that lock together for storage. One side holds whole nutmegs, so when you want fresh nutmeg you don't have to hunt for the grater and the spice; they're already together. The other side is a little box with a flat grater attachment. The box collects the nutmeg as it's grated, and then you can either slide back the grater part to collect the nutmeg for measuring, or you can turn the whole thing over and use it as a sprinkler (the nutmeg falls back through the grater holes). Look for it in kitchenwares shops, or see p. 92 for a mail-order source.

---

plan ahead for juicy turkey

Space-saving brining tips

The hardest thing about brining a turkey is finding the space to store it in its brine. Author Ris Lacoste ("Plan Ahead for a Delicious Thanksgiving," p. 44) likes to brine her turkey in a 5-gallon pot, but with your refrigerator stuffed full of food around Thanksgiving time, you might be challenged to fit a large pot in there as well. And if you don't own such a large pot or bucket, you have a double conundrum. Here are a couple of alternative space-saving approaches to brining:

Use roasting or brining bags. Brining the turkey in a jumbo plastic bag uses less space and less brine than a pot does. Look in kitchen shops for turkey brining bags (see p. 92 for a mail-order source), and follow the instructions on the package. Or use the plastic turkey-cooking bags found in the plastic wrap and foil section of the supermarket. Just double up the bags (for leak protection) and add the turkey, breast side down. Put the bagged turkey in a roasting pan or bowl (again, for leak protection) and add enough brine to fill the inner bag about halfway up the turkey. Then tightly close the opening of each bag with a twist-tie, eliminating as much air as possible from the inner bag to force the brine to surround the turkey, and refrigerate.

Brine in a cooler. Using a clean cooler means the turkey won't be in the fridge at all—nice if you're really crunched for space. The challenge here is that you need to add ice to keep the turkey cold, but you don't want the melting ice to dilute your brine too much. To offset the ice-melt, use 1/2 cup extra kosher salt in your brine. Make sure the brine is refrigerator-cold before pouring it over the turkey in the cooler. Add enough ice to submerge the turkey in brine—you'll need 5 to 10 pounds, depending on the cooler. Store the cooler in the coldest location you can think of. If that happens to be outdoors, put it in a place where animals can't get to it, like a screened porch or your car.

—Allison Ehri Kreitler,
test kitchen associate

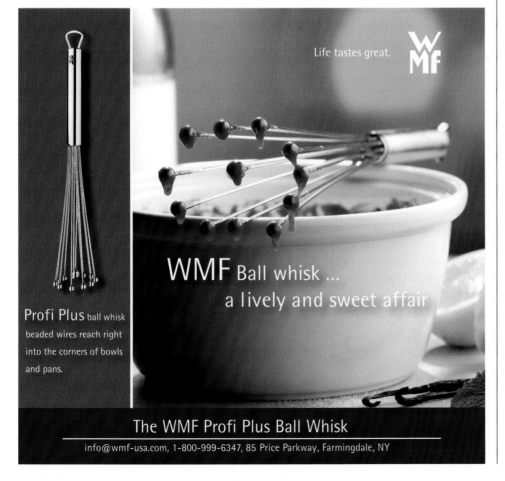

Here's how to roll out
perfect piecrust

There's no denying it: Piecrusts are one of the hardest things for a home cook to master. When it comes to rolling them out, experience counts for a lot, but good techniques are crucial, too. Here are some of our best pointers for rolling out lovely, even rounds of dough.

Start with dough at the right temperature

If it's too warm and soft, it'll stick like crazy to the rolling pin and the work surface, forcing you to add too much flour as you work it. Dough that's too cold and hard resists rolling and cracks if you try to force it. Press the dough lightly to check its rolling readiness—your fingertips should leave an imprint but shouldn't easily sink into the dough.

Go easy on the flour

Even dough that's at the perfect temperature needs a little extra flour to keep it from sticking, but try not to use more than you really need—the more extra flour you work into the dough as you roll it, the drier and tougher the crust will be.

Try an alternative rolling surface

Beyond the usual lightly floured countertop, other options for rolling surfaces include a pastry cloth (our current favorite, shown at right, especially when paired with a cloth rolling pin cover), a silicone rolling mat (brand name Roul'Pat; see p. 92 for sources), and sheets of parchment, waxed paper, or plastic wrap. Choose whichever one you like best.

Use the fewest possible passes of the rolling pin

Overworked dough equals tough crust, so the less you have to work it during rolling, the better.

Roll around the clock

Start with the rolling pin in the center of your dough disk. Roll toward 12 o'clock, easing up on the pressure as you near the edge (this keeps the edge from getting too thin). Pick up the pin and return it to center. Roll toward 6 o'clock, as shown at top right. Repeat this motion toward 3 and then 9 o'clock, always easing up the pressure near the edges and then picking up the pin rather than rolling it back to center. Continue to roll around the clock, aiming for different "times" (like 1, 7, 4, 10) on each round until the dough is the right width and thickness, as shown at bottom right.

Turn the dough and check often for sticking. After each round of the clock, run a bench knife underneath the dough, as shown at center right, to make sure it's not sticking, and reflour the surface if necessary. When you do this, give the dough a quarter turn—most people inevitably use uneven pressure when rolling in one direction versus another, so the occasional turn helps average it out for a more even thickness.

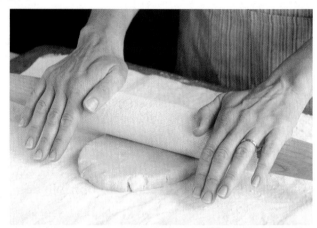

Can't find any buttermilk?

Cultured buttermilk lends moistness and a light tanginess to the Pecan Pineapple Upside-Down Cake on p. 60 and the Bourbon-Glazed Brown Sugar Pecan Poundcake on p. 62. Like regular milk, buttermilk comes in whole, low-fat, and nonfat varieties, and author Karen Barker likes to use whole buttermilk for these desserts. It's readily available in the south-eastern United States, where she lives, because it's a popular ingredient in that region. But in other areas, the selection is usually limited to low-fat and nonfat buttermilk.

Fortunately, all buttermilks are interchange-able in baking. With higher fat buttermilk, the results may be slightly richer, but because most baked goods get plenty of fat from butter or oil, the difference is hard to detect.

In some places, buttermilk of any kind can be hard to find. If you live in one of these areas, try one of the following substitutions—the results won't be quite the same as with buttermilk, but they all work in a pinch.

Try one of these substitutions:

Dried buttermilk powder

You can't reconstitute it to make buttermilk, but it's a handy baking ingredient. You add the powder to the dry ingredients and water to the wet ingredients before mixing (check the package for specifics). At the market, look for dried buttermilk either in the baking section or near other powdered milk.

Soured milk

Add 1 Tbs. lemon juice or white vinegar to 1 cup whole, low-fat, or nonfat milk and let stand at room temperature for 10 minutes.

Yogurt

Substitute whole-milk or low-fat plain yogurt, thinned if necessary with milk or water to the consistency of buttermilk.

ingredient

Tofu

firm

silken

If ever there was a food with an image problem, it would have to be tofu. Though it's been popular in Asia for centuries, many Westerners still think of it as something only vegetarians eat. Why choose bland tofu if you can have a juicy steak instead? Here's why: Tofu is just too good for you to ignore. It's a taste worth acquiring.

What it is

Tofu (a.k.a. dofu or soybean curd) is made from soybeans, water, and a coagulant, such as calcium sulfate, nigari (a natural sea salt extract), magnesium chloride (also an extract of sea salt), calcium chloride (derived from a mineral ore), vinegar, or lemon or lime juice. It has a soft texture that's vaguely similar to cheese, but its mild, plain flavor is not at all cheesy.

As a soyfood, it's full of low-fat, cholesterol- and saturated-fat-free protein, and it's high in calcium and vitamins. Not only is it good for your heart, it may also protect against cancer and osteoporosis.

How to buy & store it

Blocks of tofu come in different firmnesses, from silken to extra-firm; the firmness influences the way you use it (see next column). It's available plain or flavored, smoked, and even baked. Fresh tofu comes packaged in water, and there's also shelf-stable tofu available in aseptic packages. We tend to prefer the fresh-water-packed tofu; most grocery stores carry it in a refrigerator case in the produce section. Be sure to check the expiration date before buying.

Store unopened fresh tofu in the fridge. After opening, keep leftover tofu covered and submerged in fresh water. Change the water daily, keep it cold, and the tofu should last for about a week. Throw it out when it begins to smell sour.

If you have leftover firm or extra-firm tofu, you can drain and freeze it, which actually gives it a meatier texture. Frozen, well-wrapped tofu stays good for three to five months.

How to use it

You can eat tofu raw or cooked. Plain tofu is very mild, so it can be flavored in any way imaginable.

Silken tofu is smooth and custardy. It blends into a lush, creamy texture that's good for dressings, dips, creamy desserts like cheesecake and puddings, and smoothies, like the one below. Soft tofu isn't as smooth as silken, but it also blends well into dips, sauces, and soups. Crumbled, it makes a pleasing addition to tossed salads. Or try sautéing crumbled soft tofu as an addition to or substitution for scrambled eggs.

Both firm and extra-firm tofu are dense and hold their shape better than silken and soft tofu do. Their porous texture allows them to absorb marinades really well. Cut them into cubes or slices and try grilling, broiling, sautéing, or stir-frying them, as in our recipe for Seared Baby Bok Choy with Tofu & Shiitakes on p. 98a.

Even extra-firm tofu is still fragile, though, so to keep its shape as intact as possible when sautéing and stir-frying, cook it separately or wait to add it until near the end and cook no longer than five minutes. We especially like to fry firm tofu in a little oil to give it a golden crust that's a great contrast to its inner texture. You can also crumble and sauté firm tofu for an unusual addition to chili or meat sauces.

Before using, all water-packed tofu needs draining. Cut a slit in the packaging, turn upside down over the sink, and drain as much as possible before fully opening. That's all you need to do with silken tofu, since it'll fall apart with any more handling. Rinse and pat dry soft, firm, and extra-firm tofu. They're ready to go at this point, but you might want to further dry and increase their firmness by pressing them: Sandwich the tofu between paper or cloth towels and put it on a plate or something else to contain the water. Set a heavy skillet or pot on top and refrigerate for as little as 10 minutes or up to an hour, depending on how much drier and firmer you want the tofu to be.

Strawberry-Orange-Vanilla Breakfast Smoothie

Serves one.

Not only do we like this for breakfast, but we've also been known to whip one up in the test kitchen when we need a little pick-me-up during a busy day of recipe testing and food styling. You'll be surprised to taste how smooth, creamy, and tangy it is, especially considering that it contains no yogurt or other dairy products.

8 frozen strawberries
About ¼ lb. plain silken tofu
⅓ cup orange juice
2 Tbs. honey; more to taste
½ tsp. pure vanilla extract

Combine all of the ingredients in a blender and blend until smooth. Serve in a chilled glass.

What's a pappadam?

Indian pappadams are tortilla-size, paper-thin, crisp wafers with a lovely nutty flavor. Made from lentil, chickpea, or rice flour, they're available plain or accented with cumin, pepper, garlic, or chile. Usually served as a snack or as part of a meal, they add an unusual flourish to the Spinach Salad with Apples, Dried Apricots & Pappadam Croutons on p. 66.

Look for them in Indian markets and in supermarkets with Indian food sections. Also spelled papad, papadum, pappadum, and poppadum, they come dried and need to be cooked briefly by frying, toasting, microwaving, or broiling (as in the salad recipe). If you can't find them at a market, see p. 92 for a mail-order source or try an Indian restaurant. They'll sell them already cooked, so if you're making the spinach salad, skip the broiling step. Well-wrapped cooked pappadams stay crisp for at least a day.

—A.E.K.

Keeping brown sugar moist

It seems like every time I need brown sugar, the package in my pantry has completely dried out and become a rock-like mass. Frustrated by this constant problem, I decided to try several methods of keeping brown sugar moist to see if one is better than the rest.

My mom always put a slice of apple in with her brown sugar, but it would eventually shrivel up. I tried keeping a piece of bread in my sugar, but it got moldy. Next I tried a damp paper towel on top of the sugar, but that caused it to become soggy in some spots and crystallized in others.

Call me a slow learner, but I finally found the solution. Now I leave the sugar in its original bag and close the top loosely with tape, a rubber band, or a clip. Then I put it in a zip-top plastic bag and tuck in a damp paper towel. This way, the paper towel doesn't touch the sugar and make it soggy, but it keeps the air around the bag of sugar humid enough that there's no rock formation going on. I just change the towel every once in a while, and my brown sugar stays soft and moist for months. *—A.E.K.*

leftovers

Turkey hash
for breakfast, lunch, or dinner

Thanksgiving leftovers are as much a part of the holiday tradition as the turkey itself. You probably already have a few favorites when it comes to using up the bird, but if you're looking for something new this year, try this hash. If hash for breakfast isn't your thing, pair it with a salad for lunch or dinner.

Turkey & Sweet Potato Hash
Serves four.

3 oz. bacon, sliced crosswise into ⅓-inch-wide pieces (about 3 slices)
1 small yellow onion, small diced
2 cups medium-small-diced (about ⅓ inch) sweet potatoes (1 medium potato)
1 cup leftover turkey broth (p. 47) or low-salt chicken broth
2 Tbs. unsalted butter
2 cups leftover white and dark roasted turkey meat with skin (p. 48), roughly chopped
1 heaping Tbs. chopped fresh parsley
1 Tbs. maple syrup
2 tsp. chopped fresh rosemary
½ tsp. freshly ground black pepper; more to taste
A few dashes Tabasco or other hot sauce; more to taste
Kosher salt

Cook the bacon in a 10-inch skillet (preferably cast iron) over medium-high heat until crisp, about 4 minutes. Use a slotted spoon to transfer the bacon to a medium bowl. Pour off and discard all but 1 Tbs. fat. Add the onion and cook, stirring occasionally, until softened, about 2 minutes. Add the sweet potatoes, broth, and butter to the onions. Simmer, uncovered, until the sweet potatoes are just barely tender, about 6 minutes.

Meanwhile mix the turkey, parsley, maple syrup, rosemary, pepper, and Tabasco with the bacon.

When the potatoes are barely tender, add the turkey mixture to the skillet. Cook over medium-high heat, firmly patting the hash down and then occasionally flipping, scraping the bottom of the pan with a metal spatula and patting down again, until the broth has completely evaporated and the hash is nicely browned, about 8 minutes (reduce the heat if the hash is browning too quickly). Season to taste with salt, pepper, and hot sauce.

—A.E.K. ◆

Help!
Thanksgiving Is Driving Me Crazy

BY KIMBERLY Y. MASIBAY

No doubt about it, Thanksgiving is a high-pressure meal. It's enough to make any cook feel shaky. All those dishes! All those guests! Though we probably can't help you with Aunt Louise's meddling or Uncle Lenny's bad jokes, we can definitely teach you how to get your turkey, mashed potatoes, gravy, and vegetables to behave themselves.

A juicy turkey with crisp brown skin

the problem: After many years of dry turkey, last-year, I gave brining a try. It really helped with juiciness, but the skin wasn't as browned and crisp as usual. Can't I have both?

the solution:

With a little tinkering, you certainly can have a turkey with juicy meat and crisp skin—and brining is a great start. Turkey, especially the white meat, is prone to drying out because it's very lean and also because white meat cooks faster than dark meat, so the breast ends up overcooked by the time the legs and thighs are done. When you soak a turkey in salty water, or brine, the meat's tightly wound protein strands loosen and form a spongy matrix that sops up brine, and the meat becomes packed with extra moisture, which helps the white meat stay juicy until the dark meat is fully cooked.

All that extra juiciness, though, can potentially interfere with the molecular reactions that turn turkey skin brown and tasty. Brining leaves extra moisture on the surface of the turkey, which prevents the skin from getting hot enough for browning reactions to occur. Browning reactions, which alter the amino acids and sugars present in the skin, require hot, dry conditions.

But brining and browning aren't mutually exclusive. Simply pat the turkey's skin dry before it goes into the oven, preferably a very hot oven—the hotter the oven, the more quickly the skin will dry out completely and the browning can begin. Once you've got the browning underway, you can lower the oven temperature for the remaining cooking time.

Greener green beans

the problem: Green beans always turn a disappointing dull color when I cook them. Am I cooking them wrong?

the solution:

You're not necessarily cooking them wrong; you're just cooking them too long. Green beans get their vibrant color from the pigment chlorophyll. But chlorophyll, unfortunately, loses its luster in the presence of acids, and when a green bean cooks, its cells breakdown, allowing natural acids to escape and react with the bean's chlorophyll. To curtail color loss, simply limit the cooking time. You could toss the beans in a hot sauté pan or wok for a few minutes and serve them crisp-tender. Or if you prefer your beans cooked through, steam or boil for up to five minutes and promptly drain them. If you serve them immediately, their color should still be pretty.

That said, color isn't everything. Slow-cooked green beans have a depth of flavor that more than makes up for their lack of good looks. If you do go the quick-cooking route, though, just be sure you don't dull the beans' brilliance by dressing them too early with an acidic sauce—wait until right before serving.

Deodorizing Brussels sprouts

the problem: I'd like to serve Brussels sprouts, but can I prepare them without stinking up the house?

the solution:

Sure, just don't overcook them. Brussels sprouts, as well as other potentially malodorous vegetables like kale and collard greens, are members of the cabbage family. These plants contain sulfur compounds called isothiocyanates in their cells. During cooking, these compounds break down, forming other compounds, some of them terribly stinky; hydrogen sulfide, for example, smells like rotten eggs. The longer these sulfur compounds cook, the more they break down and the stinkier they get, so to minimize offensive odors, you have to minimize cooking. Try a fast cooking method such as sautéing, steaming, stir-frying, or blanching, and cook just until the Brussels sprouts are crisp-tender—they'll taste great.

But if you and your family really love Brussels sprouts, no one's likely to object to their odor, so go ahead and roast them or make your favorite gratin recipe—just throw open a few windows to air out the kitchen. And, honestly, as long they're not cooked to mush, the sprouts really shouldn't smell too bad.

Lump-free gravy

the problem: How can I keep lumps from forming in my gravy?

the solution:

When you make gravy, what you're doing, essentially, is dissolving tasty pan drippings in liquid and thickening the mixture with flour (or another starch). And how you add the flour makes all the difference. If you add the flour directly to the simmering liquid, you'll get lumps. Such lumps form because hot liquid causes the starch molecules on the surface of the flour to almost instantly gelatinize—that is, the starches swell, burst, and become sticky. The gelatinized starch forms a waterproof coating around the lump. Squeeze open one of these lumps, and you'll find dry flour inside.

To prevent lumps, you need to keep the grains of flour from touching one another. You can accomplish this by mixing the flour into cool liquid and then stirring this slurry into the warm or hot liquid that you want to thicken. Or if there's fat in the pan with the drippings, you can cook equal parts flour and fat together to make a roux. In a roux, fat coats the starch granules so that they won't stick together when they encounter hot liquid.

Fluffiest mashed potatoes

the problem: My mashed potatoes are never as light and fluffy as I'd like. What's the secret?

the solution:

Actually, there are three secrets: the right taters, the right technique, and the right tool.

1. The taters: High-starch varieties, such as russet and Idaho, give the fluffiest results because of the way their starch behaves during cooking. The microscopic starch granules in these potatoes' cells separate and swell as they sponge up moisture that's naturally present in the potato; as a result, the cooked potatoes' texture seems dry and fluffy. The starches in medium- or low-starch varieties such as Yukon Gold and red potatoes, on the other hand, tend to stick together, giving them a denser, moister texture that becomes creamy (or even sticky) when mashed.

2. The technique: Dry out the potatoes, and add the fat before the liquid. Waterlogged potatoes will give you a gummy mash, so if you cook the potatoes by peeling and boiling them, then you should return the potatoes to the pan after you've drained them and mash them over low heat, letting the potatoes dry out for a few minutes.

Or use a cooking method that prevents the potatoes from sopping up too much water in the first place: steaming, for example, or boiling the potatoes whole in their skins. Then, after you've mashed them, stir in the butter—the fat will coat the starches and help prevent them from absorbing additional moisture when you add the milk, cream, or other liquid.

3. The tool: Use a ricer, a potato masher, or a food mill, because any tool that you need to plug in (e.g., a food processor or electric mixer) is likely to overwork the potatoes, causing the starch granules to burst, release their sticky contents, and turn your mashed potatoes into a gluey mess.

Kimberly Y. Masibay is an editor at large for Fine Cooking. ◆

Cottage Cheese

BY LAURA GIANNATEMPO

A creamy, tangy addition to mixed salads and a perfect accompaniment to fresh fruit, cottage cheese is also used to tenderize baked goods in lieu of sour cream (as in the fast cinnamon rolls on p. 70). To find out which brands are best to buy, 11 *Fine Cooking* staffers participated in a blind tasting of 10 widely available cottage cheeses: five made with whole milk and five made with low-fat milk. While results were far from unanimous, our panel gravitated toward a moister, looser style of cottage cheese. Unsurprisingly, whole-milk cheeses had higher overall scores than low-fat ones. Read on to find out our favorites in each category.

Whole-milk *Listed in order of preference; prices may vary.*

1 Breakstone's
$3.39 (16 oz.)

Rich and creamy with a good sweet-and-sour balance (it reminded some of sour cream) and a pleasant, lingering flavor, this cottage cheese got top marks. We also liked its smooth, creamy texture with uniform curds.

2 Horizon
$3.99 (16 oz.)

This cottage cheese had huge curds that looked a bit like small pebbles. Despite its unusual appearance, it had a rich milk flavor, a good salt balance, and a nice yogurt-like tanginess. And the intimidating curds ended up being quite soft to the bite.

3 Friendship
$2.69 (16 oz.)

If you're a fan of a drier style of cottage cheese, look no further. This one's for you, though it was too dry and heavy for some panelists. And while several thought it tasted fresh and pleasantly tangy, for others it was a bit too sour and salty.

4 Organic Valley
$4.49 (16 oz.)

The mild, uninteresting flavor and watery, mushy texture of this cottage cheese didn't make it a favorite. "It tastes like it could be low-fat," said one taster. The chewy texture and uneven size of the curds didn't help either.

5 Cabot
$2.69 (16 oz.)

This cottage cheese didn't win much praise with its soupy texture and unevenly sized curds. The flavor was clean but bland with a slightly bitter finish. It would also benefit from a little more salt.

Low-fat *Listed in order of preference; prices may vary.*

1 Friendship
$2.69 (16 oz.)

The pronounced milk flavor, good salt balance, and pleasant tanginess of this cottage cheese won us over and made us almost forget it was low-fat. The texture was on the dry side, but the flavor was by far the best of the bunch.

2 Breakstone's
$3.27 (16 oz.)

This cottage cheese had a decent milk flavor and a pleasant "watermelon-like" hint of sweetness. But it was the thin, watery texture and soft, mushy curds that threw us off.

3 Light n' Lively
$3.27 (24 oz.)

The good looks and creamy texture of this cottage cheese are undeniable, but we found it disappointing in the flavor department. It was too salty and had a vaguely grassy quality and a slightly processed aftertaste.

4 Organic Valley
$4.99 (16 oz.)

This loose, watery cottage cheese had a strange slippery texture and soft curds that fell apart easily. Its flavor, too, was unimpressive. Bland and waterlogged, it still managed to be both too sour and too salty.

5 Horizon
$3.99 (16 oz.)

Too "lean-tasting," this cottage cheese didn't deliver the full milk flavor we expect, even from low-fat cheeses. Just like its whole-milk counterpart, it had huge, pebble-like curds, but these were dry and rubbery. ◆

Photos: Scott Phillips

The most useful tool in your kitchen...

ASSIC APPLE PIE SECRETS OF GREAT GRAVY 4 STEPS T

JST TANGY CRANBERRY SAUCE FLUFFY MASHED POTA

DING F CY ROAS

RIGHT PECAN

NUS FOR THE BIG MEAL NEW WINES FOR NKSGIVIN

ASTED BUTTERNUT SQUASH STUFFED TURKEY BREAST

ESTNUTS BREAD STUFFING THE WAY YOU WANT IT MA

EET POTATO BUTTERMILK DINNER ROLLS POACHED PEA

Search

Thanksgiving recipes

GO!

the New FineCooking.com

Thousands of trusted recipes and reliable cooking advice for stress-free holidays

The Taunton Press
Inspiration for hands-on living®

Cinnamon Buns, *p. 70*

Kathy Kingsley calls for a 9- or 10-inch springform pan to make the cinnamon buns. Cooking.com (800-663-8810) carries a wide range of brands in both sizes, ranging in price from $9.95 to $41.20.

Roasted Vegetables, *p. 53*

The only equipment you'll need for these vegetables is a heavy-duty rimmed baking sheet. If you don't have one, try Analon's commercial bakeware line (they call it a 13 x18-inch jelly roll pan); it's $14.99 at PotsAndPans.com (800-450-0156). For convenience, you can get 100 sheets of parchment sized to fit your baking sheet for $18.95 from King Arthur Flour (KingArthurFlour.com; 800-827-6836).

Pecan Desserts, *p. 58*

Shelled pecans are widely available in supermarkets, but in-shell pecans can be slightly harder to find. For our photo shoot, we ordered both kinds from the Green Valley Pecan Company (PecanStore .com; 800-327-3226), where a 1-pound bag of shelled pecan halves is $7, and a 5-pound bag of in-shell pecans is $18.

Spinach Salads, *p. 64*

One of Joanne Weir's spinach salads calls for pappadams, which are thin, crunchy Indian flatbreads made from lentil, chickpea, or rice flour. Joanne likes the Shakti brand (Pappadum.com), which she buys locally. Kalustyans.com (800-352-3451) also carries several brands; we liked the Madras brand at $3.99 for a 200-gram pack. You can also find packaged pappadams in stores that sell Indian food and spices, or you can buy them freshly made at your local Indian restaurant. (For more on pappadams, see *From Our Test Kitchen,* p. 78.)

Bean and Vegetable Soups, *p. 73*

If you're in the market for a Dutch oven for soup-making, visit ChefsResource.com (866-765-2433) for many Staub and Le Creuset Dutch ovens in 4- to 5-quart sizes.

In Season, *p. 24*

You can mail-order several varieties of sage plants from the Sandy Mush Herb Nursery in Leicester, North Carolina (SandyMushHerbs.com; 828-683-2014). The Thyme Garden Herb Company in Alsea, Oregon (ThymeGarden.com; 541-487-8671), offers several varieties of organically grown sage plants.

Wine, *p. 36*

While wines from Oregon and Washington are widely available, some of the other bottles featured here may be harder to find outside their production area. Well-stocked wine stores, however, usually carry a good selection of American wines. Tim Gaiser also recommends using the search engine Wine-Searcher.com, which can locate practically any wine and provide you with retailer contact information.

Equipment, *p. 28*

Soy milk can be made only from canned or dried soybeans, which you can buy at most health-food stores or in bulk online (10 pounds for $8 at FairviewFarms.com; 888-526-9296). Don't use edamame, which is the Japanese name for green vegetable soybeans. These are the immature, green form of edible soybeans.

From Our Test Kitchen, *p. 78*

If you're looking for a brining bag for your turkey, try a Grill Friends' brining bag, $7.99 each at LaPrimaShops.com (866-983-7467). Microplane's Grate-N-Shake spice grater sells for $9.95 at US.Microplane.com (800-555-2767). To buy a Roul'Pat, visit DemarleUSA.com (888-353-9726). They come in two sizes: 16½ x 24½ inches for $44 and 31½ x 23 inches for $57. ◆

Millie's Pierogi *p. 97* Handmade pierogi, made fresh and shipped fresh to your door! Cabbage, potato-cheese, cheese, prune, or blueberry fillings.
www.milliespierogi.com

Petaluma Coffee and Tea Co. *p. 96* Specialty coffee roaster since 1989. Featuring a wide selection of fair-trade coffees and gourmet teas. We ship nationwide for retail, wholesale, and corporate accounts. 800-929-JAVA
www.petalumacoffee.com

Sunnyland Farms *p. 96* The widest selection of top-quality nuts, dried fruits, and other specialty foods for creating delicacies at home or for giving to friends.
www.sunnylandfarms.com

Trenton Bridge Lobster Pound *p. 96* Your one-stop shopping for the freshest lobster, clams, and other shellfish shipped overnight to your door.
www.trentonbridgelobster.com

Trois Petits Cochons, Inc. *p. 93* Artisanal charcuterie. By using all-natural, high-quality ingredients, and by crafting small, handmade batches, the excellent quality of our pates, terrines, and mousses is guaranteed.
www.3pigs.com

Upton Tea Imports *p. 96* Visit our Web site to order or request a copy of our extensive catalog, listing tea accessories and over 380 varieties of garden-fresh, loose tea. 800-234-8327
www.uptontea.com

Ingredients

Bulk Foods *p. 97* Offering a wide selection of spices, nuts, dried fruits, and other ingredients.
www.bulkfoods.com

Colavita USA *p. 11* Extra-virgin olive oil unmatched for flavor and freshness, vinegars, pastas, and sauces. Colavita's authentic Italian products are available at food stores everywhere and visit our web site, where Fine Cooking readers receive a 10% discount with the code
www.colavita.com

Magic Seasoning Blends *p. 81* Chef Paul Prudhomme's all-natural magic seasoning blends, sauces and marinades, pepper sauce, smoked meats, cookbooks, gift packs, sweet potato pecan pie, and much more! 800-457-2857
www.chefpaul.com

Rafal Spice Co. *p. 96* All the spices, herbs, teas, coffees, and food specialties you'll need for all your special and everyday recipes! Order now and be prepared. 800-228-4276
www.rafalspicecompany.com

San Francisco Herb Co. *p. 96* We are an importer offering a complete line of quality spices and culinary herbs sold by the pound. Buy direct and save. Since 1973. 800-227-4530
www.sfherb.com

Sugarcraft, Inc. *p. 96* Sugarcraft Inc., Hamilton, Ohio. We carry baking, cake decorating, candy, and cookie supplies, etc. We import specialty items!
www.sugarcraft.com

The Catfish Institute *p. 25* Always fresh, healthy, mild and flaky, U.S. Farm-Raised Catfish suits any recipe.
www.catfishinstitute.com

The Spice Hunter *p. 3*
www.spicehunter.com

Kitchen Design & Tableware

Butter Bell *p. 13*
www.butterbell.com

Plum Pudding Kitchen *p. 15* Your online source for "irresistibly Italian" Vietri dinnerware, flatware, glassware, and much more. Let us help you set a special table! 888-940-7586
www.plumpuddingkitchen.com

Poggi Bonsi *p. 7* Direct importers of artisan Italian ceramics, olive wood utensils and cutting boards, and Umbrian kitchen towels.
www.poggibonsigifts.com

Replacements, Ltd. *p. 97* World's largest inventory: old and new china, crystal, sterling, silver-plate, and stainless. All manufacturers, fine and casual. 10 million pieces, 200,000 patterns. Buy and sell. 800-REPLACE
www.replacements.com

The Bowl Mill *p. 93* One-piece hardwood bowls made on 19th-century lathes in Vermont, ranging from 8" to 20" in diameter featuring maple, yellow birch, and cherry. 800-828-1005
www.bowlmill.com

Totally Bamboo *p. 96* Featuring over 150 products, Totally Bamboo is the industry pioneer of bamboo cutting boards and kitchen design. Order all of our fine products directly online!
www.totallybamboo.com

Zak Designs *p. 23* Zak Designs is the source for your kitchen. Incorporating great designs with color and function, Zak creates modern and innovative tabletop and kitchen prep collections.
www.laprimashops.com

Kitchen Tools & Utensils

Bella Copper *p. 97* The world's leading heat diffuser/defroster plate provides superior heat conduction for more even cooking and faster defrosting. Available in solid copper or pure silver. A gourmet kitchen essential. 805-215-3241
www.bellacopper.com

Chef Tools.com *p. 23* "Let's get you cooking" is our motto, and we mean it. If we don't have it, ask and we'll get it! Walter Kraus, owner.
ww.cheftools.com

Component Design Northwest *p. 19* CDN offers more than 60 different cooking thermometers and timers for the casual or gourmet chef. Find CDN products at gourmet specialty stores or online. 800-338-5594
www.cdn-timeandtemp.com

DeBuyer Industries *p. 7* French manufacturer since 1830, de Buyer offers professional high-quality cooking and pastry utensils for lovers of flavor and gastronomy.
www.debuyer.com

Gel Pro *p. 23* Stand in comfort! Let's Gel was started with one simple goal, to make the time you spend standing in your kitchen more comfortable. 866-GEL-MATS
www.gelmats.com

Helen's Asian Kitchen *p. 9* Since 1957, Harold Import Company has been a leading supplier of kitchenware products to the specialty retail trade, offering almost 3000 items. Our products are available in thousands of stores worldwide. What can HIC offer your business?
www.helensasiankitchen.com

House On the Hill *p. 97* Over 400 molds for springerle, speculaas, gingerbread, marzipan, fondant and cake decorating. Order now for holiday cookie baking. Catalog on request.
www.houseonthehill.net

Kerekes *p. 97* Your complete online source for professional chef's tools, cookware, bakeware, and cake decorating supplies used by top chefs at the finest restaurants and kitchens.
www.bakedeco.com

Kitchen Resource *p. 15* Kitchen Resource exclusive brand distributor of innovative, high quality small appliances, cookware, bakeware and gadgets from Bosch, B/R/K, Cloer, L'Equip and Lurch.
www.kitchenresource.com

Messermeister *p. 2* Messermeister markets one of the most extensive selections of innovative cutlery and related accessories for the professional and home chef.
www.messermeister.com

Polder Home Tools *p. 97* Polder makes products for everyday use with a focus on innovation and exclusive features. For 31 years we shown home chef's 'where life meets style'.
www.polder.com

RSVP International *p. 19* Supplier of innovative, high quality kitchen basics to kitchen specialty stores nationwide. We are best known for our Endurance® brand of quality stainless steel products.
www.rsvp-intl.com

WMF of America *p. 81* WMF is the only brand that can make cooking, dining, and drinking an event. WMF is the singular choice.
www.wmf-usa.com

J.K. Adams Company *p. 79* J.K. Adams, has been the premiere Vermont manufacturer of handcrafted, heirloom-quality, woodware, for the kitchen and table since 1944.
www.jkadams.com

Schools, Travel & Organizations

Culinary Business Academy *p. 93* Extensive and comprehensive personal chef business knowledge and training from the world's recognized leader in the personal chef industry. Nobody offers what we offer. 800-747-2433
www.culinarybusiness.com

Le Cordon Bleu *p. 93* Master the culinary arts. Earn the Grand Diplome in approximately nine months. Three- to five-week intensive courses and online hospitality programs are also available. 800-457-2433
www.cordonbleu.edu

Zingerman's Bakehouse *p. 96* Long known for their full flavored, traditionally-made breads, and pastries, Zingerman's Bakehouse now offers BAKE!; a hands-on teaching bakery in Ann Arbor.
www.zingermansbakehouse.com

Wines, Beverages & Accessories

Covington Cellars *p. 97* Award winning boutique Washington winery offers wine samples of our limited production wines that sell out fast! An excellent addition to any cellar!
www.covingtoncellars.com

Johnson Estate Winery *p. 13* The Oldest Estate Winery in New York. We grow 12 different varieties of grapes on 200 acres. Wines including classis vinifera and American Heirloom wines as well we port, sherry, and ice wines. Open 10am-6pm daily.
www.johnsonwinery.com

The California Wine Club *p. 7* A true California wine adventure. Award-winning wines from California's best artisan wineries since 1990. A fun and unique gift.
www.cawineclub.com

Woodbridge Winery *p. 99* For 25 years, we have aged our wines in small oak barrels and handcrafted each vintage. Woodbridge: Taste our small winery tradition™.
www.woodbridgewines.com

Recipe	Page	Calories total	from fat	Protein (g)	Carb (g)	Fats (g) total	sat	mono	poly	Chol. (mg)	Sodium (mg)	Fiber (g)	Notes
In Season	24												
Pork Tenderloin w/ Sage & Marsala Sauce		300	120	28	5	14	6	6	1	95	200	0	based on 4 servings
Thanksgiving Menu	44												
Herb-Butter Roasted Turkey w/ Pinot Noir Gravy		780	420	74	7	47	21	14	7	270	1650	0	based on 12 servings
Sausage-Maple Bread Stuffing		430	190	17	42	22	9	7	2.5	65	800	3	based on 12 servings
Classic Mashed Potatoes		470	270	5	46	30	19	8	1	95	560	5	based on 12 servings
Cranberry Sauce w/ Vanilla, Maple Syrup & Cassis		100	0	0	25	0	0	0	0	0	0	2	based on 12 servings
Broccoli w/ Eggs & Lemony Parmesan Breadcrumbs		200	150	5	8	17	10	4.5	1	95	370	3	based on 12 servings
Sweet Potato Gratin w/ Caramelized Onions		360	230	4	31	25	12	9	2.5	65	150	5	based on 12 servings
Roasted Vegetables	53												
Roasted Fennel w/ Rosemary-Thyme-Lemon Oil		100	60	1	8	7	1	5	0.5	0	200	4	based on 4 servings
Roasted Butternut Squash w/ Moroccan-Style Rub		70	30	1	10	3.5	0	2.5	0	0	140	3	based on 4 servings
Roasted Asparagus w/ Sesame Salt		50	40	2	3	4	0.5	2.5	0.5	0	250	1	based on 4 servings
Roasted Green Beans w/ Caramelized Shallot Butter		100	60	2	9	7	2.5	3.5	0.5	10	190	4	based on 4 servings
Roasted Carrots w/ Ginger-Lemon-Soy Splash		70	30	1	10	3.5	0.5	2.5	0	0	260	3	based on 4 servings
Roasted Broccoli w/ Toasted Garlic & Coriander Oil		140	100	3	8	12	1.5	8	1	0	360	3	based on 3 servings
Pecan Desserts	58												
Apple Crisp w/ Pecans & Orange		480	200	4	70	23	9	9	3.5	30	60	6	based on 8 servings
Bourbon-Glazed Brown Sugar Pecan Poundcake		790	370	9	91	42	17	16	6	150	170	3	based on 12 servings
Chocolate Espresso Pecan Pie		650	380	8	66	42	12	18	8	110	120	5	based on 10 servings
Pecan Pineapple Upside-Down Cake		360	180	3	43	20	9	7	2	70	115	1	based on 12 servings
Spinach Salads	64												
Warm Spinach Salad w/ Eggs, Bacon & Croutons		190	120	5	13	14	2.5	9	1.5	75	460	2	based on 6 servings
Spinach Salad w/ Chicken, Cashews & Ginger		230	120	17	15	13	2.5	6	3	35	510	3	based on 6 servings
Garlic Crostini w/ Spinach & Mushroom Salad		180	90	5	20	10	1.5	7	1.5	0	360	3	based on 6 servings
Spinach Salad w/ Apples, Apricots & Pappadams		250	130	7	32	15	1.5	10	2.5	0	190	7	based on 6 servings
Linguine with Clam Sauce	68												
Linguine w/ Clam Sauce		670	270	31	63	30	4	20	4	50	330	4	based on 3 servings
Cinnamon Buns	70												
Fastest Cinnamon Buns		300	120	5	40	13	4.5	6	2.5	15	290	2	per bun
Apple-Butter Cinnamon Buns		260	100	6	35	11	4.5	2	3.5	15	290	1	per bun
Bean & Vegetable Soups	73												
Mexican Black Bean Soup		320	120	18	33	14	4	7	1.5	15	660	10	based on 6 servings
Middle-Eastern Chickpea Soup		270	90	13	35	10	1.5	5	3	0	260	8	based on 6 servings
French Farmers' Soup		300	80	16	40	9	2	5	1.5	5	470	9	based on 6 servings
Cabbage & White Bean Soup		270	80	15	34	9	2	5	1.5	5	360	8	based on 6 servings
Minestrone		280	130	15	25	15	3.5	8	2	15	730	8	based on 6 servings
Test Kitchen	78												
Breakfast Smoothie		270	30	7	54	3.5	0	0.5	2	0	10	2	based on 1 serving
Turkey & Sweet Potato Hash		330	140	24	20	16	7	5	2.5	80	540	2	based on 4 servings
Quick & Delicious	98a												
Sesame Chicken w/ Ginger & Snow Peas		310	170	26	10	19	2.5	9	6	65	800	2	based on 4 servings
Hoisin Pork w/ Napa Cabbage		290	130	26	12	15	2	8	3.5	65	1190	3	based on 4 servings
Curried Coconut Shrimp		350	240	20	10	27	14	7	3.5	170	610	3	based on 4 servings
Spicy Beef w/ Peanuts & Chiles		350	210	27	8	23	5	12	5	45	1040	1	based on 4 servings
Seared Baby Bok Choy w/ Tofu & Shiitakes		400	290	15	16	33	3	19	9	0	700	3	based on 2 servings
Stir-Fried Noodles w/ Beef & Vegetables		390	220	14	29	24	3.5	12	7	20	1320	2	based on 4 servings
Orange Chicken w/ Scallions		430	160	36	30	18	2	9	5	85	830	1	based on 3 servings

The nutritional analyses have been calculated by a registered dietitian at Nutritional Solutions in Melville, New York. When a recipe gives a choice of ingredients, the first choice is the one used. Optional ingredients with measured amounts are included; ingredients without specific quantities are not. When a range of ingredient amounts or servings is given, the smaller amount or portion is used. When the quantities of salt and pepper aren't specified, the analysis is based on ¼ teaspoon salt and ⅛ teaspoon pepper per serving for entrées, and ⅛ teaspoon salt and ¹⁄₁₆ teaspoon pepper per serving for side dishes.

Finally! Holiday cooking made foolproof...

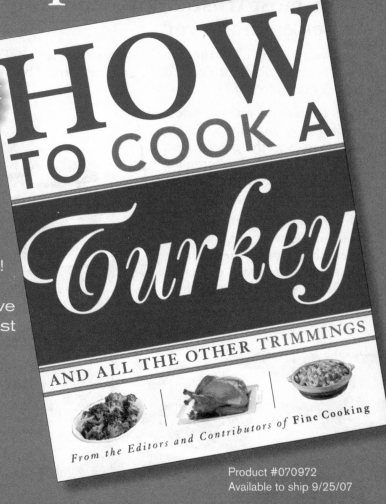

Seared Baby Bok Choy with Tofu & Shiitakes

Serves two.

½ lb. extra-firm tofu
⅓ cup low-salt chicken broth
1½ Tbs. minced jarred jalapeño slices
2 tsp. Asian sesame oil
1 tsp. granulated sugar
3 Tbs. canola oil
½ lb. baby bok choy (about 2), split in half lengthwise
1 tsp. kosher salt
1½-inch piece fresh ginger, peeled and thinly sliced (about 2 Tbs.)
2 cloves garlic, thinly sliced (about 1 Tbs.)
3½ oz. fresh shiitakes, stemmed

Drain and cut the tofu into ¾-inch-thick slices. Cut each slice crosswise into ½-inch-wide sticks (you should have fat, rectangular sticks). Put the tofu on paper towels and set aside. In a small bowl, mix the broth, jalapeño, sesame oil, and sugar.

Set a 12-inch skillet over medium-high heat until hot, about 1 minute. Add 1½ Tbs. of the canola oil and once it's shimmering hot, add the bok choy, cut side down. Sprinkle with ½ tsp. of the salt and cook, without touching, until browned, about 2 minutes. Continue to cook, tossing, until the bok choy stems start to soften and wilt, about 2 minutes more. Transfer to a plate.

Add the remaining 1½ Tbs. canola oil and the ginger to the skillet and cook, stirring, until golden, about 1 minute. Add the garlic and let it sizzle for 10 seconds. Add the tofu and shiitakes, sprinkle with the remaining ½ tsp. salt, and cook, stirring occasionally, until the mushrooms brown and soften, about 3 minutes.

Return the bok choy to the pan, add the broth mixture, and cook, tossing, until the sauce evenly coats the vegetables and the bok choy is tender, about 2 minutes. Serve immediately.

Note: For more on tofu, see From Our Test Kitchen, p. 78.

Hoisin Pork with Napa Cabbage

Serves four.

1 lb. pork tenderloin, cut into ¼-inch-thick strips (about 3 inches long)
1 tsp. kosher salt; more to taste
3 Tbs. hoisin sauce (I like Lee Kum Kee brand)
2 Tbs. soy sauce
1 Tbs. balsamic vinegar
3 Tbs. canola or peanut oil
2 tsp. minced garlic
6 cups napa cabbage, cut into 1½-inch pieces (about ¾ lb.)
1 red bell pepper, cored, thinly sliced, and cut into 2- to 3-inch lengths
¼ cup thinly sliced fresh chives

In a large bowl, season the pork with ½ tsp. of the salt. In a small bowl, mix the hoisin sauce, soy sauce, and vinegar.

Heat 2 Tbs. of the oil in a 12-inch nonstick skillet or large stir-fry pan over medium-high heat until shimmering hot. Add the pork and cook, stirring, until it browns and loses most of its raw appearance, about 2 minutes. Transfer to a plate.

Add the remaining 1 Tbs. oil to the skillet. Add the garlic, and once it begins to sizzle, add the cabbage and pepper. Sprinkle with the remaining ½ tsp. salt and cook, stirring, until the cabbage starts to wilt, about 2 minutes.

Add the hoisin mixture, the pork, and half of the chives and cook, tossing, until heated through, about 1 minute. Let sit for 2 minutes off the heat (the cabbage will exude some liquid and form a rich broth), toss well again, and serve sprinkled with the remaining chives.

Curried Coconut Shrimp

Serves four.

½ cup coarsely shredded
   coconut, preferably
   unsweetened
3 Tbs. canola or peanut oil
1 medium yellow onion,
   finely diced
2 Tbs. coarsely chopped
   ginger
1 tsp. kosher salt; more to
   taste
2 tsp. Madras hot curry
   powder
¾ cup canned diced
   tomatoes with their juices
¾ cup coconut milk
Freshly ground black pepper
1 lb. shrimp (26 to 30 or 21
   to 25 per lb.), peeled and
   deveined
⅓ cup chopped fresh cilantro
2 Tbs. fresh lime juice

In a 12-inch skillet over medium heat, toast the coconut,
tossing often, until lightly
browned, 2 to 5 minutes.
Transfer to a plate.

Heat 1½ Tbs. of the oil in
the skillet over medium heat
until shimmering hot. Add the
onion and ginger, sprinkle
with ½ tsp. of the salt, and
cook, stirring, until softened,
3 to 5 minutes. Add the curry
powder and cook, stirring, for
1 minute. Add the tomatoes
and coconut milk and cook,
stirring, until the mixture
reduces slightly, 3 to 5 minutes. Transfer to a blender
and purée. Season to taste
with salt and pepper.

Toss the shrimp with the
remaining ½ tsp. salt and
several grinds of pepper.
Rinse and dry the skillet.
Set over medium-high heat
until hot, 1 minute. Add the
remaining 1½ Tbs. oil and
once it's shimmering hot, add
the shrimp. Cook without
touching for about 2 minutes,
allowing the shrimp to brown
nicely. Flip and cook until they
turn almost completely pink
(but are not quite cooked
through), about 1½ more
minutes.

Add the curry sauce and
simmer, stirring, until the
shrimp are cooked through
and the sauce is hot, 1 to
2 minutes. Stir in half of
the cilantro and half of the
lime juice. Season to taste
with more salt, pepper, and
the remaining lime juice.
Serve sprinkled with the
toasted coconut and the
remaining cilantro.

Stir-Fried Noodles with Beef & Vegetables

Serves four.

3 oz. bean threads
   (cellophane noodles) or
   thin rice noodles (see note
   below)
¼ cup canola or peanut oil
3 Tbs. soy sauce
1½ Tbs. Asian sesame oil
1½ Tbs. rice vinegar
1 Tbs. light brown sugar
½ lb. flank steak
Kosher salt
1 small zucchini (about 6 oz.),
   halved and thinly sliced
   crosswise into half circles
1 cup matchstick-cut or
   grated carrot (1 large
   carrot)
1 small yellow onion, halved
   and thinly sliced crosswise
   into half circles
1 Tbs. toasted sesame seeds

Bring a 3-qt. pot of water to a
boil. Add the bean threads or
rice noodles, remove from the
heat, and let sit until just softened (they should still be
plenty toothy), about 3 minutes. Drain in a colander and
rinse well under cool, running
water. Toss with 1 Tbs. of the
canola or peanut oil, and
spread out on a tray or large
plate lined with paper towels.

In a small bowl, mix the
soy sauce, sesame oil, rice
vinegar, and brown sugar.

Trim the beef of excess fat
and slice it thinly across the
grain. Cut the slices into
2-inch pieces. Season the
beef with salt.

Heat 1½ Tbs. of the canola
or peanut oil in a 12-inch nonstick skillet or large stir-fry pan
over medium-high heat until
shimmering hot. Add the beef
and cook, stirring, until it loses
most of its raw appearance,
about 1 minute. Transfer to a
large plate.

Add the remaining 1½ Tbs.
oil and the vegetables to the
pan. Cook, stirring, until they
start to soften, about 2 minutes. Reduce the heat to
medium and add the beef
and the noodles. Stir the soy
mixture and drizzle it over
all. Cook, tossing until everything is evenly coated with the
sauce and the vegetables are
cooked through, about 3 minutes. Serve immediately, sprinkled with the sesame seeds.

Note: Traditionally, the
noodles for this Korean
favorite are made of sweet-
potato starch, though bean
threads or thin rice noodles
are also fine.

Spicy Beef with Peanuts & Chiles

Serves four.

- **1 lb. flank steak, thinly sliced on the diagonal against the grain**
- **2 Tbs. soy sauce**
- **2 tsp. fish sauce**
- **¼ tsp. kosher salt; more to taste**
- **2 Tbs. fresh lime juice**
- **1 Tbs. light brown sugar**
- **¼ cup salted peanuts**
- **2 large shallots, coarsely chopped**
- **2 Thai or serrano chiles, stemmed and coarsely chopped (don't seed)**
- **3 Tbs. canola or peanut oil**
- **⅓ cup coarsely chopped fresh cilantro**
- **3 Tbs. chopped fresh basil**

Toss the steak with 1 Tbs. of the soy sauce, 1 tsp. of the fish sauce, and the salt. Combine the remaining 1 Tbs. soy sauce and 1 tsp. fish sauce with 1 Tbs. of the lime juice and the brown sugar and set aside.

Pulse the peanuts, shallots, and chiles in a food processor until finely chopped. Transfer to a small bowl.

Set a 12-inch skillet over medium-high heat until hot, about 1 minute. Add 1½ Tbs. of the oil and once it's shimmering, add the beef. Cook, stirring, until the beef just loses its raw appearance, about 2 minutes. Transfer to a plate.

Reduce the heat to medium, add the remaining 1½ Tbs. oil and the shallot mixture, sprinkle with salt, and cook, stirring, until the shallots are soft, about 2 minutes.

Return the beef to the pan. Stir the soy mixture and add it, along with half of the cilantro and basil, and cook, stirring to let the flavors meld, 2 minutes. Season to taste with salt and serve sprinkled with the remaining lime juice, cilantro, and basil.

Sesame Chicken with Ginger & Snow Peas

Serves four.

- **1 to 1¼ lb. boneless, skinless chicken breasts (2 to 3), very thinly sliced on the diagonal**
- **2 Tbs. soy sauce**
- **1 Tbs. Asian sesame oil**
- **1 Tbs. plus 1 tsp. rice vinegar**
- **2 Tbs. ketchup**
- **8 scallions**
- **6 oz. snow peas, trimmed (about 1½ cups)**
- **2 Tbs. minced fresh ginger**
- **3 Tbs. canola oil**
- **2 Tbs. lightly toasted sesame seeds**

In a large bowl, toss the chicken with 1 Tbs. of the soy sauce, 1½ tsp. of the sesame oil, and 1 tsp. of the rice vinegar.

In a 1-cup liquid measuring cup or another bowl, combine ¼ cup water with the ketchup and the remaining 1 Tbs. soy sauce, 1 Tbs. vinegar, and 1½ tsp. sesame oil.

Trim the scallions and separate the dark-green tops from the light-green and white bottoms. Slice the tops into 2-inch pieces and the bottoms into thin rounds. Combine both in a medium bowl with the snow peas and ginger.

Heat 1½ Tbs. of the oil in a 12-inch nonstick skillet or large stir-fry pan over medium-high heat until shimmering hot. Add the chicken and cook, stirring occasionally, until it loses most of its raw appearance, 1 to 2 minutes. Transfer to a large plate.

Add the remaining 1½ Tbs. oil and the scallions, snow peas, and ginger, and cook, stirring occasionally, until the ginger and scallions start to brown, about 2 minutes.

Return the chicken to the pan and add the ketchup mixture and half of the sesame seeds. Cook, stirring, until the chicken is cooked through and the snow peas are crisp-tender, 2 to 3 minutes. Transfer to a platter, sprinkle with the remaining sesame seeds, and serve.

Tip: Before cutting the chicken, freeze it for 10 minutes so that it firms up, making it easier to slice thinly.

Tony Rosenfeld is a contributing editor to Fine Cooking. ◆

A flash in the pan: speedy stir-fries

BY TONY ROSENFELD

As seductive as picking up the telephone and ordering in on a busy weeknight may be, you can throw together the following stir-fries quicker than it takes a delivery person to get to your doorstep. Even better, these dishes are just as good as anything you'll find in a to-go carton. If you've ever made a stir-fry, you already know the preparation drill: Make sure to get all of your slicing and dicing done first, because once you start cooking, things move quickly (see below for more tips). So put down that phone and start chopping, because dinner is on the way.

for the best stir-fries

Cut the ingredients uniformly so that they will cook evenly.

Use a stir-fry pan if you have one. (See Equipment, p. 28, for more on stir-fry pans.) If not, use a heavy skillet with a large surface area, which will give the ingredients enough space to sear properly.

Make sure your pan is hot before cooking so the ingredients will brown but not stick.

Orange Chicken with Scallions

Serves two to three.

- 1 large navel orange
- 1 Tbs. soy sauce
- 1 Tbs. rice vinegar
- 2 tsp. light brown sugar
- ⅛ tsp. crushed red pepper flakes
- 1 lb. boneless, skinless chicken breasts, cut into 1-inch cubes
- ¾ tsp. kosher salt
- 2 large egg whites
- ⅓ cup cornstarch
- 3 to 4 Tbs. canola or peanut oil
- 4 scallions, trimmed and thinly sliced (keep whites and greens separate)

Using a vegetable peeler, shave the zest from the orange in long, wide strips. If necessary, remove any large patches of bitter white pith from the zest strips with a paring knife. Juice the orange into a small bowl and mix with the soy sauce, rice vinegar, brown sugar, and red pepper flakes.

Sprinkle the chicken with ½ tsp. of the salt. In a mini chopper or food processor, process the egg whites, cornstarch, and the remaining ¼ tsp. salt until smooth. In a medium bowl, toss the chicken with the cornstarch batter.

Heat 2 Tbs. of the oil in a 12-inch nonstick skillet or large stir-fry pan over medium-high heat until shimmering hot. Using tongs, transfer about half the chicken to the pan. Reduce the heat to medium and cook, flipping every minute or so, until the chicken browns and crisps all over and is firm to the touch, 3 to 4 minutes. With clean tongs, transfer to a paper-towel-lined plate. Add the remaining 1 Tbs. oil to the skillet (or 2 Tbs. oil if the pan seems very dry) and repeat the cooking process with the remaining chicken; transfer to the plate.

Put the orange zest strips in the skillet and cook, stirring, until they darken in spots, 15 to 30 seconds. Stir the orange juice mixture and add it to the pan. Let it boil for about 10 seconds and then add the chicken and the scallion whites. Cook, stirring often, until the sauce reduces to a glaze and the chicken is just cooked through—check by cutting into a thicker piece—1 to 2 minutes. If the chicken isn't cooked through but the glaze is cooking away, add a couple tablespoons of water and continue cooking. Serve sprinkled with the scallion greens.

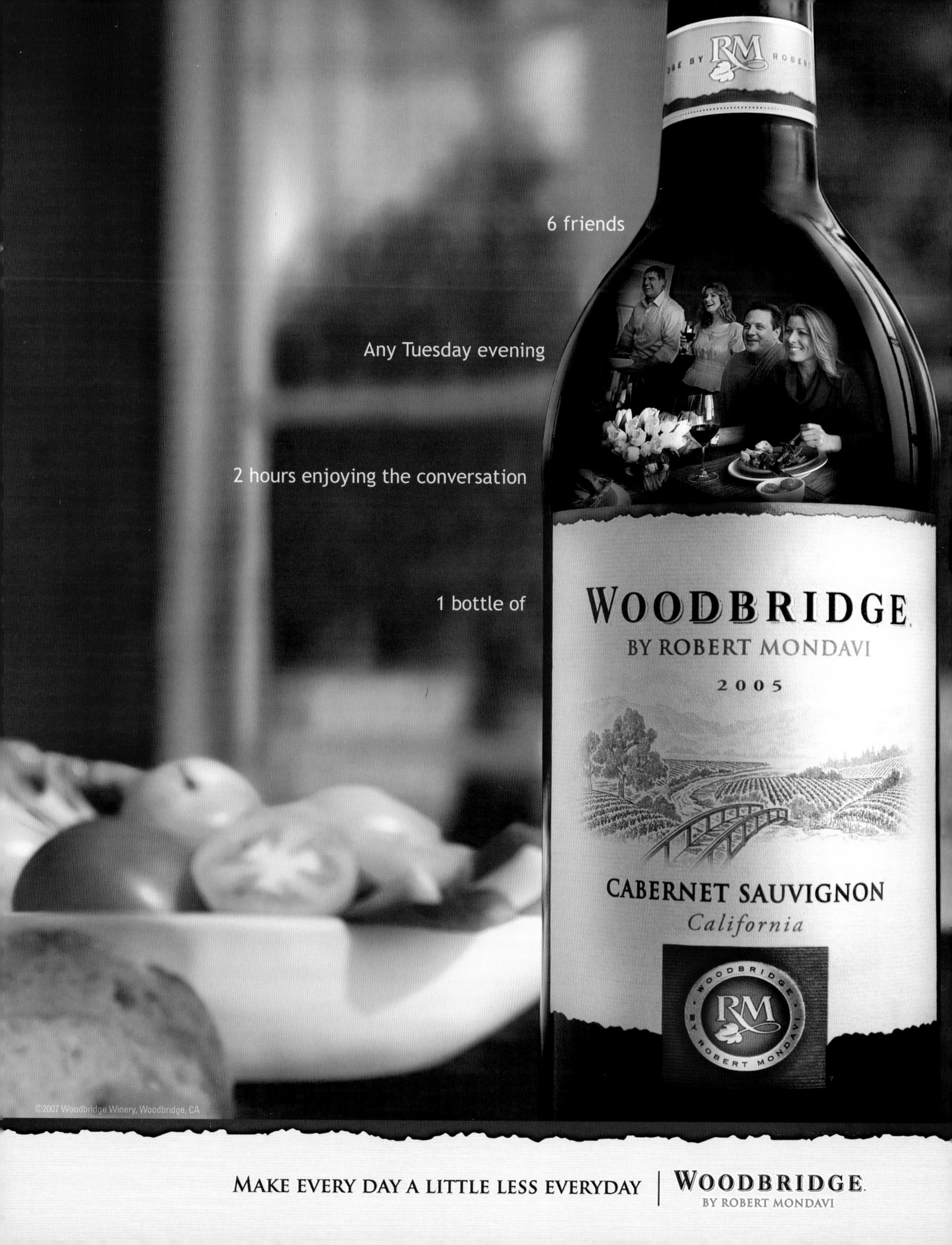

6 friends
Any Tuesday evening
2 hours enjoying the conversation
1 bottle of
WOODBRIDGE
BY ROBERT MONDAVI
2005
CABERNET SAUVIGNON
California
RM
©2007 Woodbridge Winery, Woodbridge, CA
MAKE EVERY DAY A LITTLE LESS EVERYDAY
WOODBRIDGE
BY ROBERT MONDAVI

what's inside

74

54

67

20

72

62

98a

50

26

52

69

onus: How to make the best waffles, pancakes, muffins & eggs

fine Cooking

DECEMBER 2007   NO. 89

FOR PEOPLE WHO LOVE TO COOK

beef tenderloin:
easiest holiday roast

delicious cookies for any occasion

how to cook a crown roast of pork

making crispy potato pancakes

Thai for dinner tonight

gingerbread desserts

vw.finecooking.com

95 CAN $7.95

Fennel & Rosemary Beef Tenderloin with Creamy Mustard Sauce

74470 56529 1

12

WE'VE GONE FROM THE FIRE TO THE FRYING PAN.

The same professional performance of the Viking range is also available in Viking cookware. Handcrafted in Belgium from an exclusive 7-ply material, Viking cookware offers the exceptional cleanability of stainless steel and the even heat distribution of aluminum.

6 friends

Any Tuesday evening

2 hours enjoying the conversation

1 bottle of

WOODBRIDGE
BY ROBERT MONDAVI
2005

CABERNET SAUVIGNON
California

MAKE EVERY DAY A LITTLE LESS EVERYDAY | WOODBRIDGE
BY ROBERT MONDAVI

44   46

fine Cooking

DECEMBER 2007   ISSUE 89

BONUS FOLDOUT

30a Breakfast Basics
How to make the best eggs, pancakes, muffins & granola

Light, Crisp Waffles

ON THE COVER

102a Quick & Delicious
Quick prep, easy roast

Fennel & Rosemary Beef Tenderloin with Creamy Mustard Sauce

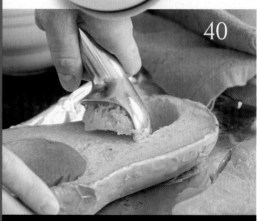

20

28

UP FRONT

6   Index

8   Menus

10 Letters

14 Contributors

16 Links

18 Artisan Foods
    Miette Confiserie

20 Great Finds
    Stocking stuffers for cooks

22 In Season
    Leeks

26 Ask the Expert
    Serving cheese

28 Equipment
    ❖ **Pizza cutter**
    ❖ **Stand mixer**
    ❖ **Baking peel**
    ❖ **Silicone pan update**

36 Enjoying Wine
    Sherry

40 Readers' Tips

40

36

visit our web site: **www.finecooking.com**

56 60 66 70

FEATURES

44 Surprise Your Guests
with Homemade Crackers
**An easy dough makes baking these
crackers a breeze**
by Lynne Sampson

46 Roasts to Boast About
**For a special holiday dinner, learn how to stuff,
cook, and sauce an impressive pork or beef roast**
by Allison Ehri Kreitler

52 Crispy Potato Pancakes
**A chef shares her tricks for making this classic
holiday side—and a few great ways to jazz it up**
by Arlene Jacobs

56 Sprouting Up
**Bring out the fresh, nutty flavor of Brussels
sprouts by roasting, braising, or sautéing**
by Martha Holmberg

60 Move Over, Gingerbread Man
**Spice up the season with four amazing desserts
inspired by the most familiar of holiday flavors**
by Julia M. Usher

66 WEEKNIGHT COOKING
Thai on the Fly:
A Quick Curry for Any Night
**A simple method gives you a repertoire
of comforting, aromatic dishes**
by Nancie McDermott

70 A Cookie for Every Occasion
**Baker Abby Dodge shares her seven favorite
cookies for the holiday**
Text by Lisa Waddle;
Recipes by Abigail Johnson Dodge

78

86

IN THE BACK

78 From Our
Test Kitchen
❖ Molasses
❖ Nonstick
baking liners
❖ Cooking
with bourbon
❖ Homemade
curry paste
❖ Royal icing

86 Food Science
Cocoa vs. chocolate

90 Where To Buy It

92 2007 Index

102 Nutrition
Information

80

84

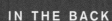

index

50 *Beef Tenderloin with Wild Mushroom Stuffing & Port Wine Sauce*

75 *Macadamia Double-Decker Brownie Bars*

57 *Roasted Brussels Sprouts with Dijon, Walnuts & Crisp Crumbs*

recipes

◆ QUICK
   Under 45 minutes

◆ MAKE AHEAD
   Can be completely
   prepared ahead but
   may need reheating
   and a garnish to serve

◆ MOSTLY MAKE AHEAD
   Can be partially
   prepared ahead but will
   need a few finishing
   touches before serving

◆ VEGETARIAN
   May contain eggs
   and dairy ingredients

Cover Recipe

Fennel & Rosemary Beef
Tenderloin with Creamy
Mustard Sauce, 102a

Appetizers

◆ Leek Tart with Bacon
   & Gruyère, 23
◆◆ Seeded Crackers, 45

Beverages

◆◆ Classic Hot Cocoa, 88
◆◆ Rich Hot Chocolate, 88

Light Main Dishes

◆◆ Classic Potato Pancakes
   (Latkes), 53
◆ Leek Tart with Bacon
   & Gruyère, 23
◆◆ Potato Pancakes Stuffed
   with Duxelles, 54
◆ Sweet Potato & Chile Hash
   with a Fried Egg, 30a

Turkey & Chicken

◆ Green Curry with Chicken
   & Eggplant, 69
Roasted Chicken Legs with
   Lemon & Green Olives, 102a

Beef, Pork & Lamb

Beef Tenderloin with Wild
   Mushroom Stuffing &
   Port Wine Sauce, 50
Crown Roast of Pork with
   Fennel-Apple Stuffing &
   Cider-Bourbon Sauce, 48
Fennel & Rosemary Beef
   Tenderloin with Creamy
   Mustard Sauce, 102a

◆ Rack of Lamb with Ancho-
   Honey Glaze, 102a
◆ Red Country-Style Curry with
   Beef, Shiitakes & Edamame,
   67
Roasted Sausages & Grapes,
   102a
Spice-Crusted Roast Pork
   Tenderloin, 102a

Seafood

◆ Orange-Roasted Salmon with
   Yogurt-Caper Sauce, 102a
◆ Red Curry with Shrimp
   & Sugar Snap Peas, 68
◆ Roasted Cod with Lemon-
   Parsley Crumbs, 102a

Side Dishes

Arroz Verde (Green Rice), 10
◆ Brussels Sprouts Braised
   with Pancetta, Shallot,
   Thyme & Lemon, 59
◆◆ Classic Potato Pancakes
   (Latkes), 53
◆◆ Potato Pancakes Stuffed
   with Duxelles, 54
◆ Roasted Brussels Sprouts
   with Dijon, Walnuts & Crisp
   Crumbs, 57
◆◆ Sautéed Shredded Brussels
   Sprouts with Fresh Herbs
   & Crisp Shallots, 58

Condiments,
Sauces & Stuffings

◆◆◆ Duxelles, 54
◆◆ Eggnog Crème Anglaise, 63
◆◆◆ Green Curry Paste, 83
◆◆◆ Red Curry Paste, 83

Desserts

◆◆ Ginger-Spice Ice Cream, 64
◆◆ Ginger-Molasses
   Cheesecake, 65
◆◆ Gingerbread-Pear Cobbler, 61
◆◆ Steamed Coriander-
   Gingerbread Cake with
   Eggnog Crème Anglaise, 62

Cookies & Icings

◆◆ Bourbon Balls, 80
◆◆ Cardamom-Honey Cutouts, 72
◆◆ Dark Chocolate Crackles, 71
◆◆ Ginger-Spiced Slice & Bake
   Cookies, 74
◆◆ Macadamia Double-Decker
   Brownie Bars, 75
◆◆ Maple-Walnut Tuiles, 76
◆◆ Peanut Butter & Chocolate
   Sandwiches, 77
◆◆◆ Royal Icing, 85
◆◆ Rugelach, 73
◆◆ Vanilla Slice & Bake Cookies,
   74

Breakfast

◆◆ Basic Buttermilk Pancakes, 30a
◆◆ Blueberry Muffins, 30a
◆◆ Classic Hot Cocoa, 88
◆◆ Crispy Sweet Pecan Granola,
   30a
◆◆ Honey-Almond Granola, 30a
◆◆ Light, Crisp Waffles, 30a
◆◆ Rich Hot Chocolate, 88
◆ Sweet Potato & Chile Hash
   with a Fried Egg, 30a

Help for the holidays

While most people look forward to this time of year, for cooks there's an added anticipation to the holidays. It comes from the chance to immerse yourself in the kitchen, making traditional dishes while also showing off a bit by pulling together impressive dinners or baking scrumptious cookies to give as gifts. If all that extra kitchen time begins to sound like just another obligation, though, don't despair. In this issue of *Fine Cooking* we've included a collection of roasted dishes, from pork to beef to fish, that lend themselves to make-ahead prep. Then when it's party time, you can let the oven do the rest of the work. Even better, roasts practically guarantee leftovers, which always come in handy. And because you can't go all out all the time, we've also included some suggestions for smaller, casual get-togethers. Be sure to check recipe yields; you may need to double or halve recipes depending on your needs.

Casual entertaining

Mostly make-ahead

You can marinate the pork tenderloin up to four hours ahead and bake the steamed gingerbread up to a week ahead, as it only gets better with age.

Spice-Crusted Roast Pork Tenderloin, *p. 102a*

Roasted Potatoes

Applesauce

Steamed Coriander-Gingerbread Cake with Eggnog Crème Anglaise, *p. 62*

Easy Mediterranean

A meal in itself, served over a bed of couscous. You could also add a green salad to start.

Roasted Chicken Legs with Lemon and Green Olives, *p. 102a*

Couscous

Rugelach, *p. 73*

Brunch for friends & family

Check out the breakfast pull-out in this issue for even more brunch ideas.

Sweet Potato & Chile Hash with Fried Egg, *p. 30a*

Blueberry Muffins, *p. 30a*

Hot Cocoa, *p. 88*

Visit FineCooking.com to find recipes for applesauce, roasted potatoes, and couscous, as well as other side dishes.

Three holiday feasts

Each of these menus stars a different delicious roast.
To make things easier, prepare the starters and desserts ahead.

Elegant beef tenderloin

Rosemary and Sea Salt Crackers, *p. 45,* served with a selection of cheeses and grapes

Beef Tenderloin with Wild Mushroom Stuffing, *p. 50*

Classic Potato Pancakes, *p. 53*

Roasted Brussels Sprouts with Dijon, Walnuts & Crisp Crumbs, *p. 57*

Ginger-Molasses Cheesecake, *p. 65*

Dramatic crown roast of pork

Leek Tart with Bacon & Gruyère, *p. 23*

Crown Roast of Pork with Fennel-Apple Stuffing, *p. 48*

Brussels Sprouts Braised with Pancetta, Shallot, Thyme & Lemon, *p. 59*

Ginger-Spice Ice Cream, *p. 64,* served with Maple-Walnut Tuiles, *p. 76*

Quick rack of lamb

Seeded Crackers, *p. 45,* with your favorite dip

Rack of Lamb with Ancho-Honey Glaze, *p. 102a*

Potato Pancakes Stuffed with Duxelles, *p. 54*

Sautéed Shredded Brussels Sprouts with Fresh Herbs & Crisp Shallots, *p. 58*

Gingerbread Pear Cobbler, *p. 61*

Saving your favorites

I am one of those people who gets *really* excited about Christmas. I decorate the house, make lots of cookies, have parties, and play annoying Christmas carols throughout the month of December. I actually like the chaos of Christmas shopping and the ritual of wrapping presents. I love to sit on the floor with a mug of hot cider, surrounded by paper and ribbons and boxes, and watch Rudolf or Frosty on TV. All this amazes my husband, a.k.a. The Grinch. Once he trucks the tree into the house, he's pretty much done with Christmas. Well, he'll be happy to know, this year he doesn't even have to worry about getting me a present. I've already got the best one I could have: the entire archive of *Fine Cooking* recipes.

So I'm hoping you're now saying, "Oh boy! Oh boy! Where do I get that? I've got to have it." You get it—and a whole lot more—if you visit the new FineCooking .com and become a member. Actually, we've upgraded the entire Web site, and there are exciting new features for everyone, whether you want to become a member or not. Personally, I like the idea of being a member, because not only can I access all of those recipes, but I'll get to talk to our expert authors, see the entire current issue online, watch a whole new series of how-to videos, and try out a cool new interactive feature

> ## I can save and organize all my favorite recipes in my virtual recipe file, called MyFineCooking.

called Create Your Own Recipe. Best of all, I can save and organize all my favorite recipes in my virtual recipe file, called MyFineCooking.

My own MyFineCooking file is going to get pretty big pretty quickly. I'll start with some of the *FC* recipes I've made the most over the years—Arroz Verde, Chicken Under a Brick, Easy Pizza Dough, and Slow-Sautéed Green Beans, to name a few. Then I'll add some of our favorite family recipes, like my mom's pumpkin bread and her great spaghetti sauce (Letty's Sghetti). And then I'll have to go through all my back issues of *FC* to grab those recipes that have the sticky notes and the stains all over them. And this December issue alone has a ton of new recipes that I made a mental note to make at home after we tasted them in the test kitchen.

In fact, if the editor is allowed to have a favorite issue of the year, then I have to say, this one is it. I like everything about it, from the handsome cover to those delicious holiday roasts to that cool breakfast foldout. And I think I may have found my favorite cookie ever—contributing editor Abby Dodge's chocolate crackle cookie (be sure to make them with really good chocolate).

Happy holidays, and remember to go save your favorites on FineCooking.com.

—Susie Middleton, editor

Add to favorites:

Arroz Verde (Green Rice)
Serves six to eight.

- ½ cup tightly packed fresh cilantro sprigs (about ½ oz.)
- 1 cup tightly packed fresh stemmed spinach leaves (about 1½ oz.)
- 1¼ cups low-salt chicken broth
- 1¼ cups milk
- 1 tsp. salt
- 3 Tbs. unsalted butter
- 1 Tbs. olive oil
- 1½ cups long-grain rice
- ¼ cup finely minced onion
- 1 clove garlic, minced

Put the cilantro, spinach, and broth in a blender and blend until the vegetables are puréed. Add the milk and salt and blend a bit more until well combined.

In a medium (3-quart) heavy-based saucepan (with a good lid), heat the butter and olive oil over medium heat. When the butter is melted, add the rice and cook, stirring about every 30 seconds, until it just begins to brown, 3 to 4 minutes. Add the onion and garlic and cook 1 minute, stirring constantly. Add the contents of the blender, stir well, turn the heat to high, and bring to a boil. Cover the pan, turn the heat to low, and cook for 20 minutes. Stir the rice carefully to avoid crushing it, cover, and cook another 5 minutes. Take the pan off the heat and let the rice steam in the covered pot for 10 minutes. Serve hot.

—Jim Peyton (Fine Cooking #35)

No room for gunk

I've been a *Fine Cooking* subscriber for many years, and I love your magazine. I've never written to any magazine to express an idea or opinion, but your review of the Chef'n Switchit silicone spoon/spatula in *Fine Cooking* #87 (Equipment, p. 22) has compelled me to write. I agree with everything Lisa Waddle said about the tool, but in my opinion, she missed the best part—it's sanitary. There's no joint between the handle and the scraper/spoon where gunk can get stuck or mold can grow. I love these tools and have purchased them to give as gifts whenever I've found them, for no other reason than I want my friends to have the best spatula in the world.

—*Erin Maffit, via email*

Corn's finest hour

I've made many recipes from *Fine Cooking*, but tonight I made one of the most wonderful meals of my life, from the August/September issue (*Fine Cooking* #87). We had Grilled Tandoori-Style Chicken Thighs and Corn Sauté with Ginger, Garlic & Fresh Cilantro. My husband could not stop raving about the dinner. He's a huge corn-on-the-cob fan, so I wasn't sure he'd be OK with corn *off* the cob. He said it was "corn's finest hour." I had a large jalapeño on hand, so I substituted a quarter of it for the serrano; it was the perfect level of heat. But "Serves four as a side dish"—I think not. We devoured every kernel.

The chicken thighs were wonderfully tender and flavorful. I gave them a little less time than the author's suggested 4 to 5 minutes per side on the grill: 4 minutes one side, 2 minutes on the other side, and 3 minutes on the grill with the heat off. They were unbelievable. Thanks so much.

—*Ellen Siegler,*
Charlotte, North Carolina

Keep brown sugar moist in a Ball jar

Having read several suggestions lately for how to keep brown sugar moist, I felt compelled to write. The tip in your latest issue (*Fine Cooking* #88, Test Kitchen, p. 86)—keeping the sugar in its original bag inside a zip-top bag with a moist paper towel—is probably a good one. However, for a number of years I have been transferring what's left after the box is opened to a pint-size Ball jar (Ball being the brand name of those screw-top jars available in most supermarkets and most often used for canning). The sugar stays moist in the tightly sealed jar for months, and you needn't think about it periodically to wet your paper towels. The advantage to this solution is twofold: You can always count on its being usable, no matter how long it's been on the pantry shelf, and you can see at a glance just how much is left in the jar. Though I haven't tried other screw-top jars, I would think something like a mayonnaise jar would work just as well if it has a tight-fitting lid.

—*Dorothy Miller, via email*

What about wine from Illinois?

In your article on all-American wines (Enjoying Wine, *Fine Cooking* #88) I found a serious omission. I am from Illinois, and I feel your author, Mr. Gaiser, must be unaware of the fine wines being produced in the numerous wineries in the southern counties of my state.

—*Harold Osborn, via email*

Editors' reply: We knew we'd be hearing from people in states we couldn't include. There are many wonderful wines produced throughout the United States, and we wish we could have mentioned more of them. It was a tough call, but for space reasons, we had to limit ourselves to six states. We're sorry Illinois wasn't among them. ◆

fine Cooking

EDITOR
Susie Middleton

ART DIRECTOR
Annie Giammattei

SPECIAL ISSUES EDITOR
Joanne McAllister Smart

SENIOR FOOD EDITOR/TEST KITCHEN MANAGER
Jennifer Armentrout

SENIOR EDITOR **Rebecca Freedman**

ASSOCIATE EDITORS
Laura Giannatempo, Lisa Waddle

MANAGING WEB EDITOR **Sarah Breckenridge**

SENIOR COPY/PRODUCTION EDITOR
Enid Johnson

ASSOCIATE ART DIRECTOR **Pamela Winn**

TEST KITCHEN ASSOCIATE/FOOD STYLIST
Allison Ehri Kreitler

RECIPE TESTER **Dabney Gough**

EDITORIAL ASSISTANT **Kim Landi**

EDITORS AT LARGE
Maryellen Driscoll, Kimberly Y. Masibay

TEST KITCHEN INTERN **Will Moyer**

EDITORIAL INTERN **Sharon Anderson**

CONTRIBUTING EDITORS
Pam Anderson, Abigail Johnson Dodge,
Tim Gaiser, Sarah Jay, Tony Rosenfeld,
Molly Stevens

PUBLISHER **Maria Taylor**

ASSISTANT PUBLISHER **Karen Lutjen**

VICE PRESIDENT, CIRCULATION
Dennis O'Brien

SENIOR SINGLE COPY SALES MANAGER
Jay Annis

SENIOR NATIONAL ACCOUNT MANAGER
Judy Caruso

ADVERTISING SALES ASSOCIATE
Stacy Purcell

Fine Cooking: (ISSN: 1072-5121) is published seven times a year by The Taunton Press, Inc., Newtown, CT 06470-5506. Telephone 203-426-8171. Periodicals postage paid at Newtown, CT 06470 and at additional mailing offices. GST paid registration #123210981.

Subscription Rates: U.S. and Canada, $29.95 for one year, $49.95 for two years, $69.95 for three years (GST included, payable in U.S. funds). Outside the U.S./Canada: $36 for one year, $62 for two years, $88 for three years (payable in U.S. funds). Single copy, $6.95. Single copy outside the U.S., $7.95.

Postmaster: Send address changes to *Fine Cooking*, The Taunton Press, Inc., 63 South Main St., P.O. Box 5506, Newtown, CT 06470-5506.

Canada Post: Return undeliverable Canadian addresses to *Fine Cooking*, c/o Worldwide Mailers, Inc., 2835 Kew Drive, Windsor, ON N8T 3B7, or email to mnfa@taunton.com.

Printed in the USA.

While working as a chef at the Herbfarm restaurant in Seattle, **Lynne Sampson** ("Crackers," p. 44) baked rye crackers almost every day and learned just how simple it is to make (better) what typically comes out of a box. Lynne is now a professional baker and freelance writer based in eastern Oregon's Wallowa Mountains. Her baking recipes appear regularly in *The Oregonian*.

Allison Ehri Kreitler

("Stuffed Roasts," p. 46), *Fine Cooking*'s test kitchen associate and food stylist, has recently embarked upon an exciting project for any serious cook: an elaborate home kitchen renovation. She's crossing her fingers that it's finished by the holidays, so she can serve her family one of the stuffed roasts she's developed for this issue. Before joining the staff of *Fine Cooking* almost three years ago, Allison worked as a freelance food stylist, recipe tester, and writer for several national food magazines.

Arlene Jacobs ("Potato

Pancakes," p. 52) loves to come up with inventive new recipes, but she still has a soft spot for the simple, tried-and-true dishes of her childhood. Here, she delivers both: her family's traditional recipe for crispy potato pancakes, as well as a few creative ways to jazz them up. Arlene is a restaurant consultant, freelance recipe developer, cooking instructor, and food writer.

Martha Holmberg

("Brussels Sprouts," p. 56), *Fine Cooking*'s former publisher, moved to Portland, Oregon, three years ago, but we still reel her in to write for us. In this issue, she shares her tricks for cooking Brussels sprouts so that they're perfectly nutty and sweet. Martha is editor of the *The Oregonian* newspaper's food section, which recently won first prize

from The Association of Food Journalists. She's also the editor of the *Oregonian*'s new quarterly food and wine magazine, *Mix*.

Julia M. Usher

("Gingerbread," p. 60) grew up baking and decorating gingerbread cookies during the holidays. But cutout cookies aren't the only sweets showing up at her holiday parties these days. "I love the challenge of coming up with new spins on a theme," she says. The former chef and owner of AzucArte, a bakery in St. Louis, Julia is now a freelance recipe developer, food stylist, and food writer, who splits her time between St. Louis and Maine. She is working on her first cookbook, to be published in the fall of 2009.

Nancie McDermott

("Thai Curries," p. 66) fell in love with Thai cuisine while volunteering with the Peace Corps in Thailand, where she lived for three years. She's an expert on Thai and other Southeast Asian cooking and has written numerous books on these cuisines, including *Real Thai, Real Vegetarian Thai,* and *Quick & Easy Thai*. She also teaches classes at cooking schools around the country. Her latest books, *300 Best Stir-Fry Recipes* and *Southern Cakes,* were published this year.

Because we work so far ahead, this issue's deadlines had contributing editor **Abigail Johnson Dodge** ("Cookies," p. 70) baking and eating holiday cookies in June. Not that she or her family complained. Abby's sixth cookbook, *The World on a Plate,* comes out next summer. It will focus on international cooking for children and adults, linking cultures through recipes, photographs, maps, and tips. Her most recent book is *The Weekend Baker.* ◆

Abigail Johnson Dodge

Julia M. Usher

Martha Holmberg

The Taunton Press

Inspiration for hands-on living®

INDEPENDENT PUBLISHERS SINCE 1975

Founders, **Paul and Jan Roman**

President
Suzanne Roman

EVP & CFO
Timothy Rahr

EVP & Publisher, Magazine Group
Jon Miller

SVP, Operations
Thomas Luxeder

SVP, Creative & Editorial
Susan Edelman

SVP, Technology
Jay Hartley

SVP, Group Publisher, Home
Paul Spring

VP, Human Resources
Carol Marotti

VP & Controller
Wayne Reynolds

VP, Fulfillment
Patricia Williamson

VP, Finance
Kathy Worth

VP, Circulation
Dennis O'Brien

THE TAUNTON PRESS

Books: *Marketing:* Melissa A. Possick, Audrey Locorotondo. *Publicity:* Nicole Salvatore, Janel Noblin. *Editorial:* Helen Albert, Peter Chapman, Steve Culpepper, Pamela Hoenig, Courtney Jordan, Carolyn Mandarano, Nicole Palmer, Jennifer Russell, Erica Sanders-Foege. *Art:* Alison Wilkes, Nancy Boudreau, Amy Griffin, Sandra Mahlstedt, Wendi Mijal, Lynne Phillips, Carol Singer. *Manufacturing:* Thomas Greco, Laura Burrone.

Business Office: Holly Smith, Gayle Hammond, Patricia Marini. *Legal:* Carolyn Kovaleski. *Magazine Print Production:* Philip Van Kirk, Nicole Chappuis, Jennifer Kaczmarcyk.

Circulation: David Pond, Andrew Corson, Catherine Hansen.

Distribution: Paul Seipold, Walter Aponte, Frank Busino, David DeToto, Leanne Furlong, Deborah Greene, Frank Melbourne, Reinaldo Moreno, Raymond Passaro, Darian Pettway, Michael Savage, Alice Saxton, David Rodriguez.

Finance/Accounting: *Finance:* Brett Manning. *Accounting:* Patrick Lamontagne, Lydia Krikorian, Michelle Mendonca, Judith O'Toole, Elaine Yamin, Carol Diehm, Dorothy Blasko, Susan Burke, Lorraine Parsons, Larry Rice, James Tweedle, Priscilla Jennings.

Fulfillment: Diane Goulart. *Fulfillment Systems:* Jodi Klein, Kim Eads, Nancy Knorr, Thomas Kuzebski. *Customer Service:* Kathleen Baker, Bonnie Beardsley, Deborah Ciccio, Katherine Clarke, Alfred Dreher, Paula Ferreri, Eileen McNulty, Patricia Parks, Deana Parker, Patricia Pineau, Betty Stepney. *Data Entry:* Melissa Youngberg, Anne Champlin, Mary Ann Colbert, Caryne-Lynne Davis, Maureen Pekar, Debra Sennefelder, Andrea Shorrock, Marylou Thompson, Barbara Williams, Christine Palmer.

Human Resources: Linda Ballerini, Christine Lincoln, Dawn Ussery.

Photos, from top: Joyce Ravid, Bryan Meyers, Scott Phillips

TAUNTON MAGAZINES
*Fine Woodworking • Fine Homebuilding
Threads • Fine Gardening • Fine Cooking*

Our magazines are for people who are passionate about their pursuits. Written by practicing experts in the field, Taunton Press magazines provide authentic, reliable information supported by instructive and inspiring visuals.

TAUNTON BOOKS
Our books are filled with in-depth information and creative ideas from the finest authors in their fields. Whether you're practicing a craft or engaged in the creation of your home, Taunton books will inspire you to discover new levels of accomplishment.

WWW.TAUNTON.COM
Our website is a place where you can discover more about the interests you enjoy, converse with fellow enthusiasts, shop at our convenient on-line store or contact customer service.

EMPLOYMENT INFORMATION
To inquire about career opportunities, please e-mail us at tauntonjobs@taunton.com or visit our website www.taunton.com. You may also write to The Taunton Press, Human Resources, 63 S. Main St., Box 5506, Newtown, CT 06470.

CUSTOMER SERVICE
We are here to answer any questions you might have and to help you order our magazines, books and videos. Just call us toll-free at 800-477-8727.

The Taunton Press, Inc., Taunton Direct, Inc., Taunton Trade, Inc., and Taunton Interactive, Inc., are all subsidiaries of Taunton, Inc.

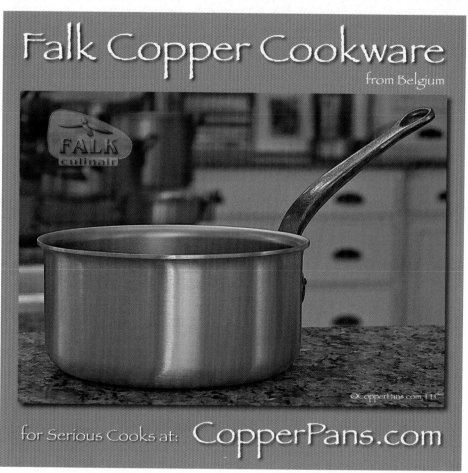

links

on the web
Experience the all-new **FineCooking.com**

Find something new on our homepage every day, from seasonal editors' picks to quick weeknight meals, international cuisines to test-kitchen-perfected classics.

Browse and search recipes by ingredient, course, cuisine, and more.

Rate and review recipes.

Save and organize your favorite recipes, menus, and articles.

See the experts in action in our new video channel: all our how-to videos in one place.

Learn more about seasonal produce and specialty foods in our new ingredients channel.

free email newsletter

Sign up at FineCooking .com to get great recipes, tips, techniques, and videos delivered directly to your inbox twice a month.

special collections

Holiday Entertaining Menus

Have a house full of guests for the holidays? We've got menus for every occasion, including:

Welcome-home-and-relax dinner
Rustic chicken with mushrooms, Gruyère polenta, butterscotch baked pears

Hearty fuel-for-shopping lunch
Spicy chicken & white bean chili with toppings and cornbread

Showstopping holiday dinner
Slow-roasted beef tenderloin with red-wine sauce, potatoes mousseline, creamed spinach

Celebratory brunch
Salmon hash with dilled crème fraîche, broiled grapefruit, Champagne cocktails

Thai Hot & Sour Shrimp Soup

Exploring Thai Food

Discover the authentic ingredients and iconic dishes of Thailand, plus quick curries for weeknight dinners.

The Essential Thai Pantry Guide

Recipes include:

Pad Thai

Coconut Rice Pudding with Mango

Hot & Sour Shrimp Soup

Beef, Chicken & Pork Satay

Roast Lemongrass Chicken

Salmon Hash with Dilled Crème Fraîche

Photos: Scott Phillips, except far right, second from top, courtesy of Laura Werlin; third from top, Joyce Ravid

Only on FineCooking.com

In every issue, you'll find bonus recipes from our feature articles online. This month's extras:

From "Sprouting Up" (on p. 56 of this issue) comes another delicious Brussels sprouts side dish.

Roasted Brussels Sprouts with Brown Butter & Lemon

From "Thai on the Fly" (p. 66) a quick weeknight one-dish meal.

Green Curry with Cod & Green Beans

Become a FineCooking.com member

Members get full access to our
complete online recipe database—
more than a decade of *Fine Cooking* **recipes—plus these member-only exclusives:**

Ask the Expert

Post a question in our new forum and get a personal answer from the pros within 48 hours.

Susie Middleton, editor of *Fine Cooking,* takes on planning and timing your holiday dinner.
November 1 to November 21

Laura Werlin, *Fine Cooking* contributor and author of *The New American Cheese,* discusses serving cheese for holiday dinners and parties.
November 26 to December 9

Abigail Johnson Dodge, *Fine Cooking* contributing editor and author of *The Weekend Baker,* takes questions on holiday cookie baking.
December 3 to December 16

Create Your Own Recipe

This interactive feature lets you **build your own recipe** step by step, choosing ingredients, seasonings, and garnishes. Start out by creating your own bean and vegetable soup or bread stuffing; many more recipes are coming soon.

Web-Only Feature:

Comforting Quick Breads
by Carolyn Weil

Mini loaves make perfect holiday gifts. Our recipes include chocolate chip banana bread, pumpkin-spice bread, and cranberry-orange streusel loaf.

View the current issue online

Miette Confiserie, Caitlin Williams and Megan Ray's colorful candy store, offers unusual candies from Europe and the United States, including handmade sweets from local artisans.

From Retro Cakes to
Whimsical Candies

BY LAURA GIANNATEMPO

When the dot-com bubble burst in the Bay Area at the turn of the millennium, Megan Ray got bit by the baking bug and couldn't shake it off. She'd always loved to bake, but it wasn't until she was laid off that she got serious about it. She started Miette Pâtisserie without fanfare, selling cakes at the Berkeley farmers' market. Business was good and a couple of years later, with partner Caitlin Williams (also a dot-com casualty), she grabbed the opportunity to open a cake store in San Francisco's then-new Ferry Building.

From day one, they had a clear vision for their cakes' aesthetics: retro yet simple and modern, with a playful "girlie" sensibility. They were also strict about using only the freshest ingredients—organic and sustainably produced when-

ever possible—from nearby family farms and mills.

Miette was such a hit that customers clamored for another store in the city. But instead of replicating the pâtisserie, Megan and Caitlin recently opened Miette Confiserie, a charming candy store in the Hayes Valley district, complete with huge glass candy jars, lollipop trees, and candy bouquets. The shelves abound with rare, nostalgic, and humorous candies from small bakeries and candy stores all over the United States and Europe, along with sweets handmade by Bay Area artisans and in the bakery's own kitchen, from candied popcorn and cotton candy to rich, crunchy, ultrathin chocolate-and-nut-coated toffee. *For more information, visit MietteCakes.com.* ◆

Chocolate-covered toffee with toasted almonds is one of the candy store's best sellers.

Co-owner Caitlin Williams packages toffee fresh from Miette's kitchen.

Make every day a holiday with illy

Treat yourself or the coffee lover in your life to the joy of starting each day with authentic Italian espresso or cappuccino at home. With the illy a casa℠ espresso membership program, coffee lovers receive everything they need to make the consistently flawless espresso served in the world's finest cafés and restaurants.

Give an illy a casa℠ espresso membership featuring the Francis Francis X5 holiday introductory kit.

Yours for $150 or 3 payments of $50 (a $753 value).*

Members receive the striking, state-of-the-art Francis Francis X5 espresso machine, 2 illy cappuccino cups, a professional steaming pitcher, and 6 stainless demitasse stirrers.** As a member, purchase any 4 cans of illy each month for 12 months, and enjoy convenient home delivery. Make every day feel like a holiday. Spread the joy with illy.

30-day risk-free trial

Order by 12/31/07. **1 877 4MY ILLY** (1-877-469-4559) **illyusa.com/PFCN7**
Use offer code **PFCN7**

Good Things Come in Small Packages

Stocking stuffers that'll make any cook's holiday

BY REBECCA FREEDMAN

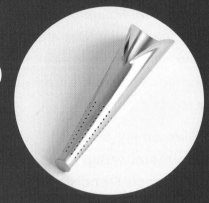

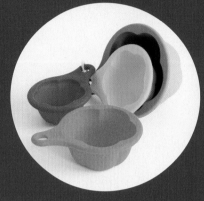

Perfect for tea for one: Scoop up tea with the wide end of this infuser; then set the narrow end into a mug of hot water. *$9 at BroadwayPanhandler.com.*

These silicone measuring cups are flexible; just push the cups out to remove sticky or packed ingredients, like brown sugar. *$18 at LaPrimaShops.com.*

Breakfast in bed? Try these clever egg cups—the top holds one egg, while a second stays warm hidden in the base. *$7.50 for two at SurLaTable.com.*

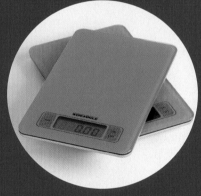

For Asian food novices, beginner chopsticks make eating easier and more fun. *$3 at Pfaltzgraff.com.*

Cuisipro's Accutec rasps come with a cover that'll catch and save the zest you grate. *From $12 at Amazon.com.*

The Page scale is super compact, so it's ideal for small kitchens. *About $45 at LeifheitGoods.com.*

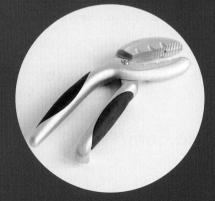

Seafood lovers will appreciate these lobster crackers, which slide on a hinge to widen for large claws. *$25 at ChefCentral.com.*

No more searching for that one missing measuring spoon; this magnetic set stays together in a drawer. *$8 at Amazon.com.*

A glow-in-the-dark meat thermometer takes the guesswork out of nighttime barbecuing. *$7 at Store.BbqProShop.com.* ◆

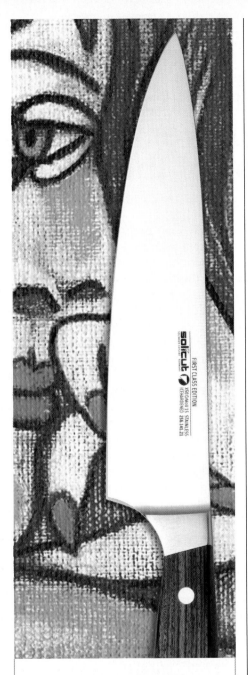

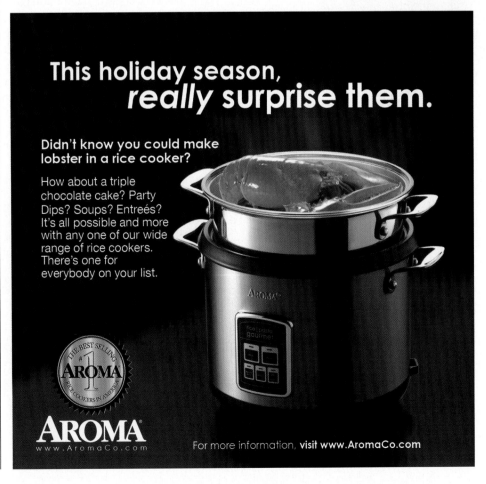

Versatile leeks,
supporting player or star of the show

BY RUTH LIVELY

There are a million reasons why I love leeks: They're sweet and mildly oniony, they're easy to prep, and they cook quickly. But most of all, I love leeks because they promise good eating. Unfortunately, these members of the onion family are easily overlooked on this side of the Atlantic. In France, where I spend several months each year, leeks are a day-in, day-out vegetable, a real kitchen workhorse. So I've grown accustomed to using them not only as an aromatic base for soups, stews, and braises or as a supporting player to other vegetables but also as a stand-alone vegetable (see sidebar, opposite page).

Leeks' delicate flavor and gentle sweetness work well with both tangy, vibrant vinaigrettes and with the richness of cream and cheese. Bacon, pancetta, and prosciutto are also good additions to any leek dish. And when I'm not serving them alone, I like to pair leeks with other cold-season vegetables like winter squash, celery root, fennel, parsnips, beets, and of course, potatoes for a classic leek and potato soup. Leeks are excellent braised, roasted, and sautéed. Steaming is also a good method for cooking leeks before you toss them with a vinaigrette or finish them in the oven or on the grill.

For braising, roasting, and grilling, I prefer to cut cleaned and trimmed leeks in half lengthwise, but I usually slice them crosswise for sautés and salads.

Buying and storing

Leeks are available year-round, but they're at their best from early fall through winter and into spring. When buying leeks, look for firm, undamaged stalks and fresh-looking, brightly colored tops—the darker the tops, the older and tougher the leeks. The edible parts of leeks are the white and light-green portions (the dark-green leafy tops are usually cut off and discarded or used to flavor broths), so ideally, you want leeks with as much white stalk as possible. Wrapped in a damp paper towel and stored in a plastic bag in the refrigerator, leeks will last at least a week.

Clean them carefully

Since leeks are grown with soil piled all around them, there is plenty of opportunity for dirt and grit to settle between their onion-like layers. The easiest way to clean a leek is to trim the root end and the dark green tops and cut it in half lengthwise (or, if you want to retain the appearance of whole leeks in your dish, just cut about two-thirds of the way through the stalk, as shown at right). Hold the leek root-end-up under cold running water and riffle the layers as if they were a deck of cards. Do this on both sides a couple of times until all the dirt has been washed out.

Photos: Scott Phillips

Leek Tart with Bacon & Gruyère

Serves six as a main course, twelve as an appetizer.

Paired with a green salad and a glass of crisp white wine, this tart is perfect for lunch or a light dinner. I also like to cut it into thin wedges and serve it as an appetizer along with aperitifs. It's delicious warm or at room temperature.

FOR THE TART SHELL:

9 oz. (2 cups) unbleached all-purpose flour
1 Tbs. chopped fresh thyme
¼ tsp. table salt
¼ tsp. freshly ground black pepper
5½ oz. (11 Tbs.) cold unsalted butter, cut into ½-inch cubes
5 to 6 Tbs. ice-cold water

FOR THE FILLING:

3 thick slices bacon, cut into small dice
1 oz. (2 Tbs.) unsalted butter
3 large leeks (white and light green parts only), cleaned and sliced crosswise ¼ inch thick to yield about 4 cups
1 Tbs. unbleached all-purpose flour
2 large eggs
⅓ cup heavy cream
⅓ cup whole milk
¾ tsp. kosher salt
⅛ tsp. freshly grated nutmeg
Freshly ground black pepper
⅔ cup grated Gruyère (or Emmentaler)

Make the tart shell: In a food processor, pulse the flour, thyme, salt, and pepper to blend thoroughly. Add the butter and pulse until the butter pieces are about the size of rice grains (about eight 1-second pulses). Add the ice water 1 Tbs. at a time through the feed tube while pulsing in short bursts until the dough starts coming together. It may still look crumbly, but if you press it with your fingers, it should become compact. (Don't add more water than absolutely necessary to get the dough to cling together.) Turn the dough out onto a clean work surface and, using your hands, gather and press the dough into a rough ball, blotting up the stray crumbs. Transfer the dough to a piece of waxed paper, shape it gently into a disk, and wrap it tightly to keep it from drying out. Refrigerate for at least 45 minutes. (The dough can be made up to 2 days ahead.)

Position a rack in the center of the oven and heat the oven to 450°F.

Unwrap the dough, set it on a lightly floured surface, and if necessary, let sit until pliable. Roll the dough out to a 14-inch circle about ⅛ inch thick.

Transfer the dough to an 11-inch fluted tart pan with a removable bottom and press it carefully into the corners and up the sides

of the pan. Let the edges of the dough hang over the rim of the pan and then roll the rolling pin over the top of the pan to cut away the excess dough. Prick the surface of the dough all over with a fork, line it with parchment, and fill it with pie weights or dried beans. Put the pan on a rimmed baking sheet and bake until the edges of the tart shell are dry and flaky (but not browned), about 10 minutes. Remove the weights and parchment; the center should still be moist and raw. Prick the bottom again and return the shell to the oven. Bake until the bottom surface is completely dry, 5 to 7 minutes more. Remove from the oven and let cool. Lower the oven temperature to 375°F.

Make the filling: In a 12-inch skillet, cook the bacon over medium heat until it's crisp and golden brown, about 5 minutes. With a slotted spoon, transfer the bacon to a dish and set aside. Discard all but about 2 tsp. of the bacon fat. Set the skillet over medium-low heat, add the butter, let it melt, and then add the leeks. Stir to coat them with the fat, cover, and cook, stirring occasionally, until soft, 8 to 10 minutes. Stir the flour into the leeks and cook uncovered, stirring, for about 2 minutes to cook off the raw-flour flavor. Set aside and let cool slightly.

In a medium bowl, lightly whisk the eggs. Add the cream, milk, salt, nutmeg, and several grinds of pepper and whisk until blended. Add the bacon and leeks to the mixture and stir to combine.

To assemble the tart, scatter ⅓ cup cheese over the cooled tart shell and pour in the egg mixture. Spread the leeks evenly. Scatter the remaining ⅓ cup cheese evenly over the top. Bake until the custard is set and the top is light golden brown, about 35 minutes. Let cool on a rack for at least 30 minutes before serving.

Store leftovers in the refrigerator, covered. Reheat for 10 to 15 minutes at 350°F.

Tasty ideas starring leeks

For rich braised leeks, brown halved leeks in butter or olive oil; then deglaze the pan with white wine. Add a little chicken broth, cover, and simmer until tender. Finish with chopped fresh thyme.

Toss together a zesty salad. Steam thin leek slices until barely tender and then toss with soy sauce, rice vinegar, lime or lemon juice, and toasted sesame seeds.

Make a comforting leek gratin. Steam leek halves until barely tender and then layer them in a buttered baking dish with white sauce and sautéed bacon bits. Top with Gruyère and breadcrumbs and bake until brown and bubbling.

For a hearty side or vegetarian main course, toss halved leeks in olive oil, salt, and pepper and roast until tender and lightly browned. Serve on top of hot, creamy polenta with a generous dab of Gorgonzola.

Ruth Lively cooks, writes, and gardens in New Haven, Connecticut. ◆

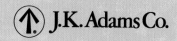

Laura Werlin is an expert on American cheese and the author of four books on the topic, including her brand-new *Laura Werlin's Cheese Essentials*.

Serving Cheese

It's not hard to put together a cheese selection; just follow some basic guidelines

I recently received a set of three differently shaped cheese knives. Which should be used for which cheese?

—*Hilary Drake, Stamford, Connecticut*

You'll find that each knife is specially shaped to handle a certain texture of cheese. A **skeleton knife** has a 3- to 5-inch blade with large holes cut out of the middle. Because there's far less surface area on the blade for creamy cheese to stick to, this type of knife is great for soft cheeses like Brie. A **forked knife** is an all-purpose cheese knife and can be used for most cheeses, from mozzarella to Cheddar. Think of the forked tip as a toothpick and use it to pick up a piece of cheese you've just cut and transfer it to your plate. Just don't eat from it. The **triangular-shaped knife** is short and stubby, ideal for digging chunks out of hard cheeses like Parmigiano-Reggiano. You won't get nice, neat slices with this type of knife, but that's not the goal.

In future issues we'll tackle yeast, chocolate, and eating local. Send your questions on these topics to Ask the Expert, *Fine Cooking*, PO Box 5506, Newtown, CT 06470-5506, or by email to fcqa@taunton.com.

How many cheeses should I include on a cheese board? What guidelines should I follow on what types of cheeses to choose?

—*Sylvie Molnar, Bainbridge Island, Washington*

First, think about when you're serving the cheese. For an after-dinner cheese course, you need no more than three cheeses and preferably just one or two. If you're serving cheese as an hors d'oeuvre, one great cheese can be enough. Go for a perfectly ripe Camembert or a wedge of Gruyère. As for amount, plan on a little less than 1 ounce per person. Third, let your main course determine the specific cheeses. If you're serving fish, then go for a selection of lighter style cheeses, like goat cheese, Brie, and creamy blue cheeses. If you're serving meat, plan on just one or two cheeses, such as an American cloth-wrapped Cheddar, an aged Gouda, or a crumbly-style blue cheese like Stilton. Aim for variety in terms of texture or the type of milk the cheese is made from.

What are some good complements to a selection of cheeses, besides crackers and bread?

—*Noreen Wooten, Dumfries, Virginia*

Don't reinvent the wheel when it comes to pairing cheese with other foods. Fresh goat cheese has a natural affinity to olives. A salty and pungent blue cheese is great with sweet things such as honey, dried figs, and jams. Compotes, toasted nuts, and other dried fruit are great with all but the mildest cheeses. Although apples and cheese may be one of the oldest pairings around, it's actually not the best. The high acidity of the apples makes them taste sour next to many cheeses. ◆

Storing tips

❖ Take your cheeses out of the refrigerator at least one hour before serving.

❖ Keep cheese in the drawer of your refrigerator, where the humidity and temperature are the highest.

❖ Wrap firmer cheeses and blue cheeses in waxed paper followed loosely by plastic wrap, which allows the cheese to breathe without letting plastic touch its surface.

❖ Store soft and creamy cheese unwrapped in a plastic container and poke a few small holes in the lid, to keep the cheese from suffocating.

RIZO
DESIGN TOSHIYUKI KITA

Single Touch. Multi-function.

RIZO. Cooking Made Easy.

ZOJIRUSHI

Zojirushi America Corporation

Contact us at: (800)733-6270   www.zojirushi.com

RIZO™ Micom Rice Cooker & Warmer NS-XAC05 / NS-XBC05

Capacity: 3 cups / 0.5 liter **Color:** RIZO Stainless (XR) / RIZO White (WR) / RIZO Yellow (YR)
Accessories: Steaming Plate, Measuring Cup, Nonstick Rice Spatula, Spatula Stand

what's new

Measure & prep

This set of five small nesting bowls makes mise en place easy. Made of flexible silicone, each also serves as a measuring cup, with measurements printed inside and a raised ridge denoting half measurements. The set, with bowls from 1/8 cup to 2 cups, costs $20 and is part of Food Network's new line of cookware and bakeware, available exclusively at Kohl's stores.

Surgical precision

Lives may not depend on your coring an apple just right or cutting a neat slice of pizza, but it's nice to know that the same expertise that goes into making surgical tools is behind this latest line of kitchen gadgets. Made by California-based Van Vacter Products, the tools all feature thick black handles similar to those on a motorbike, for a comfortable, nonslip grip. Each tool is specific to a task—an avocado knife, a cheese grater—and has well-thought-out features. The pizza knife ($20), for example, has a second wheel that trails behind the cutter to break through any remaining cheese or crust. Needless to say, all the tools are scalpel sharp. You can buy them at CoolFoodTools.com.

Prep bowls	28
Pizza cutter	28
Squeeze bottles	28
Baking peel	30
Oven rack guard	30
New stand mixer	30
Bar cart	32
Wooden utensils	32
Ratchet corkscrew	32
Baking sheet	34
Nonstick muffin tins	34
Silicone & metal pan	34

BY LISA WADDLE

Dress your plate

Plastic squeeze bottles are the not-so-secret garnishing weapon of professional chefs, who use them to drizzle desserts with melted chocolate, dot sauces on a dinner plate, or squiggle dressings over a salad. Here's a stylish update to the standard mustard-style bottle, featuring angled silicone tips in two diameters. Each bottle holds 2 cups and comes with a cap, making it easy to store your sauce or dressing in the fridge. Sold at Williams-Sonoma stores for $10 (narrow green tip) and $11 (wide gray tip).

Photos except where noted: Scott Phillips

Beyond the peel

Baking peels can be intimidating to use, but here's a version that makes moving all types of dough easier. Called the Super Peel, it combines a baker's peel with a pastry cloth, resulting in a hand-held conveyor belt that can transport pizza onto a baking stone or move cutout cookies to a cookie sheet. While traditional peels require a jerk action to slide pizza or bread into the oven (which can dislodge toppings or deflate delicate doughs), the Super Peel is gentler because you hold the peel with one hand and with the other move a plastic clip that rotates the cloth. The pastry cloth must be floured, but it proved to be nonstick with pie crust, bread, pizza, and cookies. Made of maple, with a reversible pastry cloth, the Super Peel is $34 at SuperPeel.com.

Don't get burned

When I worked in a professional bakery, my arms were striped with burn marks from brushing against hot oven racks as I retrieved cookie sheets. So I was jazzed to see this Cool Touch oven rack guard from JAZ Innovations. Made of the same heat- and flame-resistant fiber used in the protective clothing for firefighters, the padded fabric strips are 18 inches long and wrap around the front of the oven rack, snapping into place. They resist heat up to 500°F (you need to remove them when you run the broiler), and yes, they do work. I intentionally touched them during testing, and while they got warm, they weren't nearly hot enough to burn my arm. They're $20 for two, and you can buy them at JazInnovations.com.

Newest stand mixer

Cuisinart has introduced its first stand mixer, designed to give other high-end models a run for their money. Available in 5.5-quart ($350) and 7-quart ($450) bowl capacities, the mixer boasts 12 speeds and comes with the standard attachments—paddle, whisk, and dough hook.

Contributing editor and baking guru Abigail Johnson Dodge put the 7-quart mixer through its paces in her kitchen and found the large machine "surprisingly lightweight." It did a great job with tasks big (whipping 4 cups of cream) and small (whipping a single cup), thanks to the tapered bowl, which allows the attachments to reach all the way to the bottom and sides. The disadvantage of that shape, Abby found, is that its height and narrow base make it awkward to scrape the sides and scoop out or pour batter from the bowl.

At 800 watts for the 5.5-quart and 1,000 watts for the 7-quart, the Cuisinarts are among the most powerful stand mixers available and easily handled stiff bread dough without hopping around the counter. Unique to the Cuisinart: a 15-minute countdown timer that turns off the mixer after the selected time has elapsed (more of a novelty than a necessity, Abby thought) and a "fold" speed, a slower option that did a good job of incorporating flour into cake batter.

If you're looking to make a design statement with your mixer, this is your machine. Standing 14½ inches tall (21 inches with the mixer head tilted up) and 15 inches wide, it is slightly smaller than other stand mixers, yet its overall design gives it an impressive appearance. It comes in white or brushed chrome and has three ports for attachments (avail-

Cuisinart 7-quart stand mixer

able separately), including a pasta maker, a blender, and a 3-cup food processor. You can get more information and buy the mixers at Cuisinart.com.

Honey-Almond Granola

Yields 9 to 10 cups.

The larger clumps of this honey-sweet version are easily eaten out of hand.

Cooking spray
4 cups old-fashioned (not quick-cooking) rolled oats
1 cup oat bran
2 cups whole almonds, coarsely chopped
1 cup nonfat dry milk powder
¾ cup vegetable oil
¾ cup honey
1 Tbs. pure vanilla extract
½ tsp. pure almond extract
½ tsp. table salt
1 cup raisins (optional)

Position racks in the upper and lower thirds of the oven and heat the oven to 325°F. Spray two rimmed baking sheets with cooking spray. In a large bowl, mix the oats, oat bran, and almonds. In a smaller bowl, whisk the dry milk powder, oil, honey, vanilla, almond extract, and salt. Pour the mixture (it will be gloppy) over the oats and stir, with your hands or a spoon, until well combined.

　Divide the mixture between the two oiled baking sheets and spread in an even layer. Bake for 20 minutes, stir the granola, and switch the positions of the pans. Bake until the oats are golden brown and the almonds look well toasted, another 10 to 20 minutes; don't overcook. The oats may feel soft but will crisp as they cool. Let cool completely in the pans. When completely cool, stir in the raisins, if using.

—Robin Asbell

Crispy Sweet Pecan Granola

Yields 4 to 5 cups.

The looser texture of this granola makes it perfect for sprinkling over a bowl of yogurt.

Cooking spray
3 cups old-fashioned (not quick-cooking) rolled oats
1 cup pecan halves, roughly chopped
2 tsp. ground cinnamon
¼ tsp. table salt
½ cup packed light brown sugar
2 Tbs. canola oil
1 Tbs. pure vanilla extract

Position racks in the upper and lower thirds of the oven and heat the oven to 300°F. Spray two rimmed baking sheets with cooking spray. In a large bowl, mix the oats, pecans, cinnamon, and salt. In a small saucepan, combine the brown sugar and ¼ cup water. Bring to a simmer over medium heat, stirring until the sugar is melted. Stir in the oil and vanilla. Remove from the heat and pour over the oat mixture. Stir with a spoon until well mixed.

　Divide the mixture between the two oiled baking sheets and spread in an even layer. Bake for 15 minutes, stir the granola, and switch the positions of the pans. Bake until the oats are golden brown and the nuts look well toasted, another 10 to 15 minutes. The oats may feel soft but will crisp as they cool. Let cool completely in the pans.

—Robin Asbell

Tips for great granola

❖ Spread the granola in a single layer on the baking sheet for even toasting.

❖ Don't bake granola in a hot oven until completely crisp, or it will taste burned. It should come out a little soft and will firm as it cools.

❖ For added crispness in the honey granola, turn off the oven, leave the door ajar, and let the granola cool in the oven.

❖ Store cooled granola in an airtight container; it will keep for at least three weeks.

Easy fried eggs

A fried egg makes a great topper for any hash, including the southwestern-style hash at left. Fried eggs are easier to cook if not crowded in the pan; if you're frying a lot, keep them warm by undercooking them slightly and holding them on an oiled baking sheet in a 200°F oven.

Sunny side up

Crack an egg into a cup. Heat about 2 tsp. butter or oil in a small nonstick skillet over medium heat. When the fat is hot, slip in the egg, season it with salt and pepper, and turn the heat to medium low or low. Cook until done to your liking, 1 to 2 minutes, basting the egg white with the fat to help it set.

Over easy

Begin cooking as you would for sunny-side-up eggs but rather than basting the egg, flip it gently with a spatula after the first side has set and continue to cook for another minute or until done to your liking.

Sweet Potato & Chile Hash with a Fried Egg

Serves six.

The adobo sauce found in a can of chipotle chiles in adobo (available in most supermarkets) gives the hash's mayonnaise garnish a spicy-smoky flavor. You can also flavor it with a medium-hot, not-too-chunky salsa.

FOR THE CHILE MAYONNAISE:
½ cup mayonnaise
3 Tbs. adobo sauce or salsa
1 Tbs. fresh lime juice
Kosher salt and freshly ground black pepper to taste

FOR THE HASH:
1 lb. sweet potatoes, peeled and cut into ½-inch cubes (3½ to 4 cups)
6 Tbs. olive oil; more as needed
1 small onion, diced (about 1 cup)
2 small fresh poblano or 4 Anaheim chiles (or other medium-hot chiles), diced (about ¾ cup)
One-half red bell pepper, diced (about ½ cup)
2 Tbs. finely chopped garlic
1 to 2 jalapeños, finely chopped
2 Tbs. chopped fresh cilantro
1 Tbs. fresh lime juice
2 tsp. chopped fresh oregano
2 tsp. kosher salt; more to taste
Freshly ground black pepper
6 eggs
6 sprigs fresh cilantro

Make the chile mayonnaise: In a bowl, combine the mayonnaise, adobo sauce or salsa, and lime juice. Season with a little salt and pepper. Whisk until smooth. Taste and adjust the seasonings; set aside.

Make the hash: Cook the diced sweet potatoes in boiling salted water until firm-tender, about 3 minutes. Drain well and set aside.

In a large nonstick skillet, heat 3 Tbs. of the oil over medium heat. Cook the onion, chiles, and bell pepper, stirring frequently, until all are well softened and the onion is golden brown, about 20 minutes. Stir in the garlic and jalapeño and cook for 1 minute. Transfer to a plate.

Return the skillet to the stove, and heat the remaining 3 Tbs. oil over medium-high heat. Add the sweet potatoes and cook, tossing frequently, until the edges begin to brown, adjusting the heat as necessary, about 10 minutes. Return the onion and pepper mixture to the pan and cook until warmed through. Stir in the cilantro, lime juice, oregano, and salt; season with pepper to taste. Transfer to a warmed plate or bowl; cover and keep warm.

Add more oil to the pan if needed. When the oil is hot, fry the eggs in batches, as directed at right. You can serve them sunny side up or over easy, but the yolks should still be runny.

Divide the hash among six plates, top each portion with a fried egg, a dollop of the chile mayo, and a cilantro sprig. Serve at once.

—*Karen & Ben Barker*

The best batter for crispy waffles

As for most waffle batters, the wet ingredients are mixed quickly with the dry.

Then whipped egg whites are folded in to make the batter—and the waffles—ultralight.

Light, Crisp Waffles

Yields four or five 8-inch waffles.

A required rest in the oven not only adds to the crispiness of the waffles but also allows you to make a big batch, so everyone can eat at once.

**3½ oz. (¾ cup) bleached
   all-purpose flour
1 oz. (¼ cup) cornstarch
½ tsp. table salt
½ tsp. baking powder
¼ tsp. baking soda
¾ cup buttermilk
¼ cup milk
6 Tbs. vegetable oil
1 large egg, separated
1 Tbs. granulated sugar
½ tsp. pure vanilla extract**

Heat the oven to 200°F and heat the waffle iron. Mix the flour, cornstarch, salt, baking powder, and baking soda in a medium bowl. Measure the buttermilk, milk, and vegetable oil in a Pyrex measuring cup; mix in the egg yolk and set aside.

In another bowl, beat the egg white almost to soft peaks. Sprinkle in the sugar and continue to beat until the peaks are firm and glossy. Beat in the vanilla.

Pour the buttermilk mixture into the dry ingredients and whisk until just mixed. Drop the whipped egg white onto the batter in dollops and fold in with a rubber spatula until just incorporated.

Pour the batter onto the hot waffle iron (½ to ⅔ cup depending on your waffle iron) and cook until the waffle is crisp and nutty brown (follow the manufacturer's instructions for timing at first and then adjust to your liking). Set the waffle directly on the oven rack to keep it warm and crisp. Repeat with the remaining batter, holding the waffles in the oven (don't stack them). When all the waffles are cooked, serve immediately.

—Pam Anderson

VARIATIONS:

Chocolate Chip Waffles
Stir ½ cup coarsely chopped chocolate chips (or ½ cup mini chocolate chips) into the batter.

Cornmeal Waffles
Substitute ½ cup cornmeal for ½ cup of the flour (keep the cornstarch).

Cranberry-Orange Waffles
Stir ½ cup coarsely chopped dried cranberries and 2 tsp. finely grated orange zest into the batter.

Whole-Grain Waffles
Add ¼ cup wheat germ to the dry ingredients.

Waffle-iron tips

❖ Grease your waffle iron (even a nonstick one) the first few times you use it. Use vegetable shortening and a pastry brush or cooking spray.

❖ Use wooden or rubber utensils—not metal—to preserve the integrity of nonstick surfaces.

❖ Start with about ½ cup batter for the smallest irons and ⅔ cup for bigger ones; increase as necessary to fill out waffles.

❖ Don't open the waffle iron prematurely; if your iron doesn't have a beeper or light, watch the steam; it will decrease as the waffle cooks.

❖ The very first waffle is usually a throwaway; adjust the amount of batter and the iron's settings until you get the results you like.

Blueberry Muffins

Yields 12 muffins.

This muffin batter is also delicious with the flavoring variations that follow the recipe. Be sure to add the fruit before the batter is fully mixed to avoid overmixing.

Vegetable oil or cooking spray for the pan
1 lb. (3½ cups) unbleached all-purpose
    flour
4 tsp. baking powder
½ tsp. baking soda
½ tsp. table salt
1⅓ cups granulated sugar
5 oz. (10 Tbs.) unsalted butter, melted and
    cooled slightly
1 cup whole milk, at room temperature
1 cup crème fraîche or sour cream, at
    room temperature
2 large eggs, at room temperature
1 large egg yolk, at room temperature
2 tsp. finely grated lemon zest
1½ cups fresh (washed, dried, and picked
    over) or frozen (no need to thaw)
    blueberries

Position a rack in the center of the oven and heat the oven to 350°F. Lightly oil (or spray with cooking spray) the top of a standard 12-cup muffin tin and then line with paper or foil baking cups. (Spraying the pan keeps the muffin tops from sticking to the pan's surface.)

Overfilling the muffin cups gives you those great big bakery-style muffin tops.

In a large bowl, sift together the flour, baking powder, baking soda, and salt; mix well. In a medium bowl, whisk the sugar, butter, milk, crème fraîche or sour cream, eggs, egg yolk, and zest until well combined.

Pour the wet ingredients into the dry and fold gently with a rubber spatula just until the dry ingredients are mostly moistened; the batter will be lumpy, and there should still be quite a few streaks of dry flour. Sprinkle the blueberries on the bat-

ter and fold them in until just combined. (The batter will still be lumpy; don't try to smooth it out or you'll overmix.)

If you have an ice cream scoop with a "sweeper" in it, use it to fill the muffin cups. Otherwise, use two spoons to spoon the batter in, distributing all of the batter evenly. The batter should mound higher than the rim of the cups by about ¾ inch.

Bake until the muffins are golden brown and spring back lightly when you press the middle, 30 to 35 minutes. (The muffin tops will probably meld together.) Let the muffin tin cool on a rack for 15 to 20 minutes. Use a table knife to separate the tops, and then invert the pan and pop out the muffins.

—*Joanne Chang*

VARIATIONS:

Cranberry-Orange Muffins
In place of the lemon zest and blueberries in the batter, add orange zest and chopped fresh cranberries.

Banana-Walnut Muffins
Don't add any zest to the batter. Instead add 1½ cups thinly sliced ripe banana and ¾ cup coarsely chopped toasted walnuts.

pancakes

Perfect pancakes every time

The ideal time to flip a pancake is after bubbles cover the surface but before they all pop. Once flipped, the second side should cook for about half as long as the first.

Pour the batter from the tip of a spoon to get a nice round shape. Thick batter may need some spreading.

Before flipping, take a peek to be sure they're nicely browned on the bottom; that color means lots of flavor.

Basic Buttermilk Pancakes

Yields twelve 4-inch pancakes.

Buttermilk gives these pancakes their light texture and slightly tangy flavor. If you don't have any on hand, you can substitute 2 to 2¼ cups whole milk instead. You'll get the best results if all of your ingredients are close to room temperature.

10 oz. (2¼ cups) unbleached all-purpose flour
4 tsp. granulated sugar
1½ tsp. baking powder
½ tsp. baking soda
½ tsp. table salt
2½ cups buttermilk
2 large eggs
1 oz. (2 Tbs.) butter, melted
Vegetable oil for the pan or griddle

In a large bowl, whisk together the flour, sugar, baking powder, baking soda, and salt. In a medium bowl, whisk together the buttermilk, eggs, and melted butter.

Pour the wet ingredients into the dry ingredients. With as few strokes as possible, mix just until the batter is evenly moistened but still a little lumpy. Let the batter rest for at least 5 minutes, during which time it should smooth out.

Very lightly oil a griddle and heat it over medium heat until the droplets from a sprinkle of water dance briefly before disappearing. Drop about 2 Tbs. of batter onto the griddle. Use the spoon to gently spread this fairly thick batter. Be sure to leave space between the pancakes for flipping. Cook the pancakes until they're covered in bubbles on top and nicely browned on the bottom. Flip and cook the other side until the bottom is nicely browned and the center of the pancake feels firm when poked.

Pancakes are best made to order; if you must, you can keep them warm spread on a baking sheet lined with a kitchen towel in a 200°F oven.

—*Kathleen Stewart*

THE BEST OF Fine Cooking

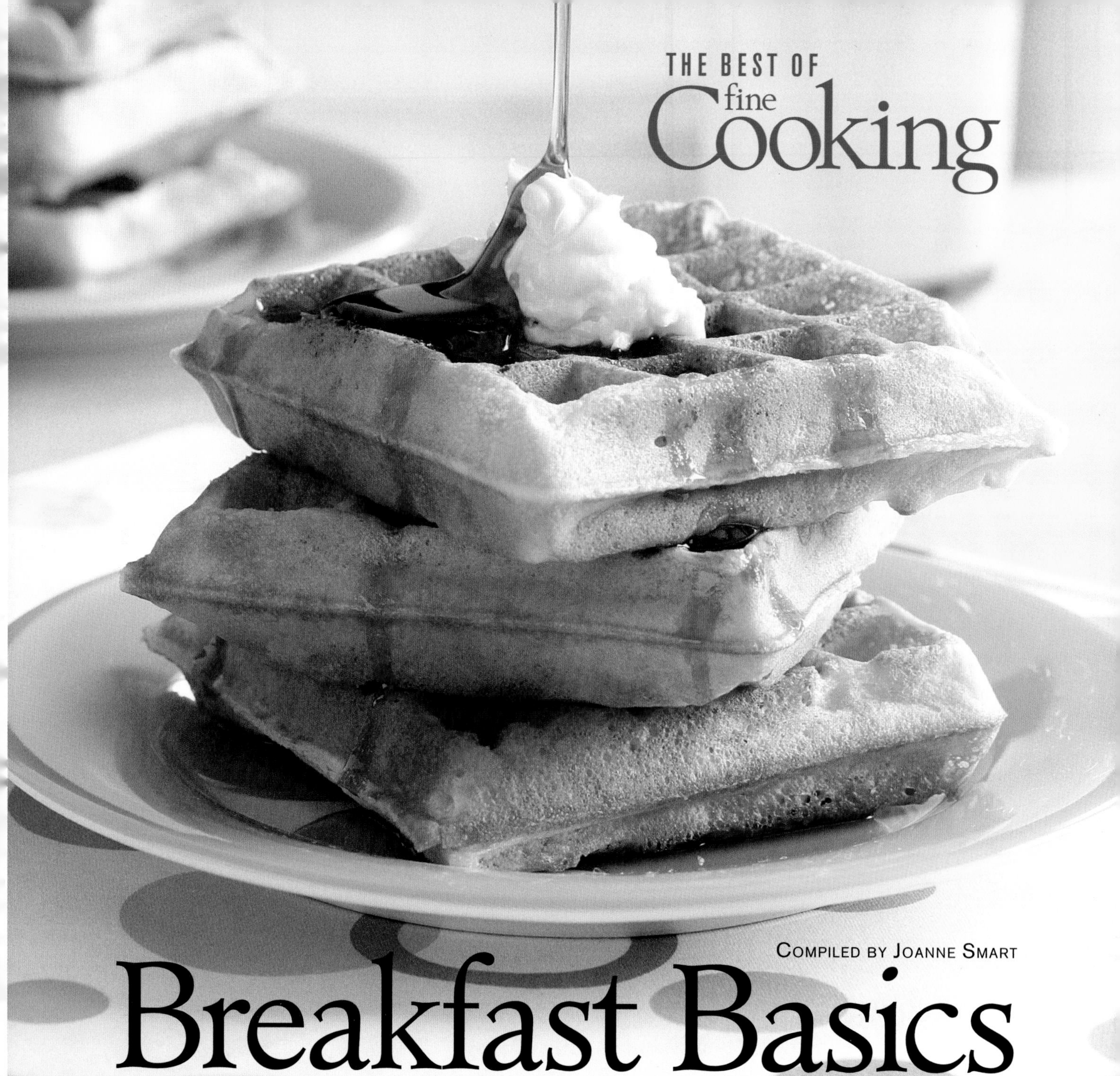

Compiled by Joanne Smart

Breakfast Basics

There's never been a better time than right now to perfect your pancakes and finesse your fried egg flip. That's because, given the season, there's a good chance a special-occasion breakfast is in order, one that calls for dusting off the waffle maker or greasing muffin tins. In this special pullout, you'll find not only delicious recipes from past issues of *Fine Cooking* but also helpful tips to ensure the best results. Happy holidays.

What's inside:

- How to make the lightest, crispiest waffles ever
- Easy fried eggs, plus a great hash
- Perfect pancakes every time
- How to make magnificent muffins
- Granola, sweet & crunchy

Keeping your favorite cook happy

Whether you're looking for a small hostess gift or a more extravagant splurge for that special someone, kitchen tools are thoughtful and practical. Here are some we wouldn't mind getting ourselves.

A wheel splurge

Here's an idea for the cook on your list who's been very good: beautiful rolling work and storage carts made of laminated bamboo, similar to the intricate cutting boards we've seen everywhere of late. The Kitchen Cart, at $1,075, has a storage cabinet and drawer, removable cutting board, and side racks for towels or condiments. The Bar Cart (left), at $1,125, is similar in style but with a wine cubby to accommodate 18 bottles and a hanging stemware rack. Both are 36 inches high, with locking casters, making them useful wherever you need an extra work or serving surface. You can buy them at TotallyBamboo.com.

Beautiful & functional

If you're looking for a present for the cook who has everything, why not replace an essential tool with a piece of art? These wooden tools are just two of 60 spoons, spatulas, and paddles crafted of cherry and maple by Pennsylvania-based Mark Hamm. Beyond their good looks, the tools feel wonderful in the hand, with a silky-smooth finish and nice balance. Each piece is shaped for a specific task, such as the Stir-Fry Tool ($11), at left, and the Sauté Stirrer ($17). Setting the tools apart are the details: Several include a notch in the handle, to allow the spoon to sit on the edge of a pan, and many can be ordered in right- or left-hand versions. See the complete line and purchase at CPBasils.com.

Ratchet it up

I love this new Wine Ratchet from Built NY Inc. Unlike the ubiquitous lever openers, the Ratchet puts a little effort back into popping a cork. Acting and sounding much like the ratchet wrench that inspired it, this corkscrew is cranked into a cork with a repeated twist of the wrist. At the base of the screw is a metal washer with teeth that grab onto the cork; then you just pull to uncork. Particularly nice is the inclusion of two interchangeable screws—a thicker, wire-type screw for older, longer corks and a thinner, auger-type screw for shorter and synthetic corks. Cost is $100, at BuiltNY.com.

New baking essentials

As you gear up for your holiday baking, having the best tools can make all the difference. Here are some updates to essential equipment no baker should be without.

CIA shares its secrets

Drawing on its 60-year history as a training ground for chefs, the Culinary Institute of America has come out with a line of cookware and bakeware designed by its teaching chefs. We like the nonstick cookie sheet; it's made of heavy-duty steel and comes in a light platinum color, which helps prevent overbrowning. One side is angled to create a secure handle, while the three flat edges make it easy to slide the cookies off. At 14x17³⁄₄ inches, it's slightly larger than other baking sheets. Be sure it's not too big for your oven; you want to leave 2 inches of room on each side of a cookie sheet so that air can circulate. The sheet is $30 at CIACook.com.

Release me

We've liked the Doughmakers line of shiny aluminum pans for cookies, cakes, and pies since they came out several years ago, and now they've added muffin pans. The 12-cup standard size (pictured above), 6-cup jumbo, and 24-cup mini-muffin pans all feature the line's heavy-gauge aluminum and patented textured surface—called a "pebble pattern" —that leads to wonderful browning and no sticking (even without any Teflon or silicone lining). It also means they are easy to clean. Each is $26, and you can find a retailer near you at Doughmakers.com.

update

Silicone meets metal

First our kitchens were rocked by all-silicone bakeware, brilliantly stick-resistant and colorful but floppy. Then came another generation of silicone pans, thicker and sturdier yet failing to conduct heat as well as the old reliable metal. Now, Kaiser Bakeware has united silicone and metal for the best of both materials. The La Forme Perfect collection consists of steel bakeware lined with silicone. Cakes and breads released cleanly from the heavy-duty pans with only a light spray of oil or butter, and they also browned evenly and developed a nice crust. Absent are the bright colors of other silicone bakeware; this dark-gray lining matches the pan. Cost is $37 for a 10-inch loaf pan; $50 for a 9-cup Bundt; $64 for a 10-inch springform with a regular and a tube base. Buy them at KaiserBakeware.com. ◆

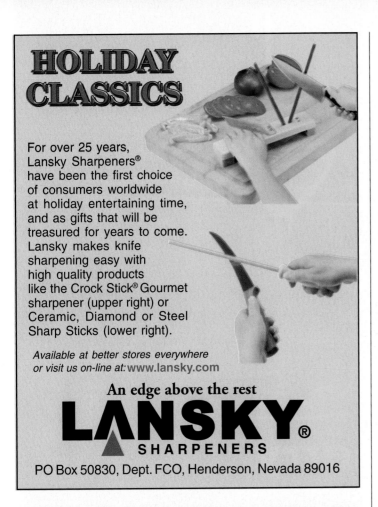
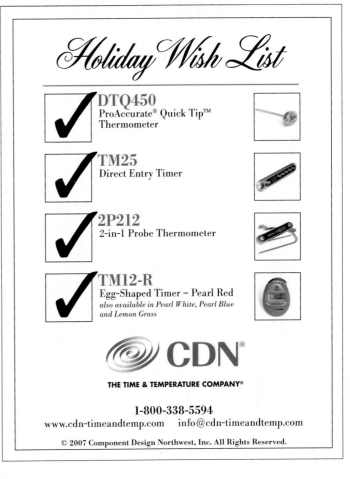

Discovering Sherry

BY TIM GAISER

Think beyond dessert—sherry can be a perfect aperitif or an ideal match for dinner

If the word sherry makes you think of cheap cooking wine or granny's ultra-sweet after-dinner libation, you might want to reconsider. While most people associate sherry with sweetness, many high-quality sherries are anything but sweet. In fact, they're excellent dry wines that are perfectly suitable for a variety of foods, not just dessert.

The name sherry derives from Jerez de la Frontera, the town and region in the southern part of Spain where the wine is made. Sherry is a product of the region's hot, arid climate. It's not uncommon for temperatures to climb above 100°F in Jerez during the growing season, and hot winds keep the climate bone dry. If it weren't for the chalk-laden soil, called *albariza*, it would be impossible to grow wine grapes. Albariza soil, however, dries to a hard protective shell during the hot summer months, trapping moisture beneath the surface and allowing vine roots access to water.

A fortified wine

Made primarily from Palomino grapes, sherry is a fortified wine, which means that a neutral spirit is added during production. In the case of sherry, that spirit is a colorless, odorless brandy called *aguardiente*. Unlike port and sweet Madeira, the other major fortified wines, in which fortification takes place during fermentation and leaves residual sugar in the wine, sherry is fortified after fermentation, when the wine is completely dry. Dessert sherries are then sweetened with boiled, reduced grape juice or sweetened wine.

Aged with an unusual system

Sherries are aged a minimum of two years in oak barrels, called butts, using the traditional solera system, a technique of blending in which older wine is refreshed by younger wine of the same type to maintain consistency of style. A solera is a series of barrels in which each successive vintage is held separately. Wine is bottled from the oldest barrels, which are then topped with wine from the next-oldest barrels, and so forth. By law, the barrels can never be emptied by more than one third at a time. Some soleras are well over a hundred years old and contain thousands of barrels of wine. Wines from an older solera indicate the year of its founding on the label, even though each bottle contains only a few scant drops of the oldest wine in the solera.

How do you store sherry?

Like other fine wines, sherry should be stored in a dark place at a temperature between 55° and 60° F. Fino and manzanilla sherries are very delicate. Once opened, they lose their freshness within a day or two. That's why I highly recommend purchasing these sherries in half-bottles and only from wine shops that stock them regularly. The richer sherries, such as olorosos and sweet sherries, will keep for several days when opened. In general, it's always best to use a clamp-on bottle stopper in place of the original cork to prevent air from seeping into the bottle.

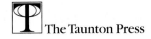

Sherry Styles

There are several styles of sherry, based on how strongly they're fortified and on whether and how long they've been exposed to air.

Fino

One of the driest and most elegant styles of sherry, fino is fortified to about 15% alcohol, allowing a frothy layer of yeast called "flor" to develop on the surface after fermentation. Flor is a vital component of fino, protecting it from contact with air and giving it a characteristic tangy quality. A deep straw color, fino sherries have a nutty, minerally flavor with suggestions of pressed flowers and preserved citrus.

What to pair it with: Enjoy it chilled with fresh shell fish, any kind of tapas, and lighter appetizers.

Bottles to try:
NV Lustau Solera Reserva Puerto Fino, $14 (750 ml)

NV González Byass Tio Pepe Fino, $9 (375 ml)

Manzanilla

This is a special fino produced in and around the coastal town of Sanlúcar de Barrameda. The region's higher humidity results in a thicker layer of flor that gives manzanilla remarkable delicacy, elegance, and a slightly briny flavor.

What to pair it with: Enjoy it chilled with fish and shell fish, chicken, or tapas like olives, marcona almonds (a type of Spanish almonds), and jamón serrano (Spanish prosciutto).

Bottles to try:
NV Hidalgo Manzanilla "La Gitana," $10 (500 ml)

NV Lustau Manzanilla "Papirusa," $12 (750 ml)

Amontillado

This is a type of sherry whose flor layer dies after a certain period of time, allowing the wine to oxidize, that is, to come in contact with air and develop raisiny, caramel-like flavors. Stylistically, amontillados fall between finos and dry olorosos, displaying a medium-golden amber color and a smooth, dry character, with flavors of bitter chocolate, coffee, raisins, and a distinctive nuttiness.

What to pair it with: Serve it slightly chilled as an aperitif with olives, almonds, and hard cheeses. Amontillado is also a classic accompaniment to rich soups.

Bottles to try:
NV Lustau Solera Reserva Dry Amontillado "Los Arcos," $14 (750 ml)

NV Hartley & Gibson Amontillado, $12 (750 ml)

Oloroso

Oloroso, which means scented, is a rich, deeply colored wine that's fortified to a higher alcohol level (about 18%) to prevent flor from developing. It's aged and oxidized longer than amontillados (three years or longer), so it develops rich flavors of raisins, dates, prunes, roasted nuts, and caramel. Traditional olorosos are dry, but sweet olorosos are produced as well.

What to pair it with: Serve dry olorosos at cellar temperature (55° to 60°F) as an apéritif with nuts, olives, and dried figs, or with roasted or braised meats, hearty sides, and rich cheeses.

Bottles to try:
Osborne Dry Oloroso "Bailén," $18 (750 ml)

NV Lustau Solera Reserva Dry Oloroso "Don Nuño," $18 (750 ml)

Palo Cortado

Palo cortado is a rare style of sherry that loses its layer of flor, as does an amontillado, but develops more of an oloroso richness while maintaining some of fino's delicate nuance.

What to pair it with: Serve it slightly chilled as an aperitif or with roast beef or lamb.

Bottle to try:
NV Lustau Solera Reserva Palo Cortado "Peninsula," $22 (750 ml)

Sweet sherries

There are several kinds of sweet sherry, including medium-sweet cream sherry, the dessert-sweet East India sherry (both sweet olorosos), and the Pedro Ximenez and Moscatel varietal sherries. Sweet sherries usually display caramel and dried fruit flavors.

What to pair them with: Enjoy cream sherries as an aperitif, chilled or over ice. The sweeter East India and varietal sherries are good with chocolate desserts or sipped solo in place of dessert.

Bottles to try:
NV Harveys Bristol Cream, $12 (750 ml)

NV Lustau East India Sherry, $21 (750 ml)

NV Osborne Pedro Ximenez 1827, $14 (750 ml)

NV Lustau Solera Reserva Moscatel Superior "Emilín," $22 (750 ml) ◆

Contributing editor Tim Gaiser is a master sommelier and wine educator. ◆

readers' tips

Winning tip

Freeze spoons for defatting stocks

When I'm making a soup or a stock, I toss a few slotted metal spoons into the freezer. After letting the stock cool a bit, I skim the top with one of the frozen spoons. The fat congeals on the back of the metal spoon, while the stock slides through. You generally get only one pass per spoon, because once they warm up they don't attract the fat.

—*Tara Hearn, Victoria, British Columbia*

Freeze lemongrass to have on hand

Many recipes that call for lemongrass require only part of a large stalk. Instead of wasting the pricey herb, I found a way to extend its life. I buy three or four stalks at a time, cut away the woody exterior, and grind the stalks in a food processor. I store this ground lemongrass in zip-top bags in the freezer and have found that it keeps for a long time. I can take out just a tablespoon or so to use for that night's recipe.

—*Linda Rittelmann, Baltimore, Maryland*

Ice cream scoop works for squash, too

Squash is so plentiful in the fall that I cook with it a lot. I prefer to roast butternut and acorn squash, because roasting intensifies their natural flavor. I've found that an ice cream scoop is excellent at removing the squash from the shell after baking.

—*Brian Wigley, via email*

Making cookie logs perfectly square

To make logs of refrigerator cookies in a square shape, I line an aluminum foil or plastic wrap box with plastic wrap and then press the dough inside. I put the dough-filled box in the fridge to chill. The result is a uniform, precisely shaped log.

—*Lorelee Kimbley, Calgary, Alberta*

Turn a mistake into rave reviews

I recently made a batch of the blondies (from *Fine Cooking* #82) but made the mistake of baking them too long. The result was a batch of hard, inedible bars. I hated to waste the ingredients, so I put these "mistakes" into a food processor and ground them up. This gave me a supply of toffee-like crunch that I sprinkled on ice cream, yogurt, and fresh fruit—to rave reviews. (And the second batch of blondies I baked came out perfect.)

—*Kathleen Delaney, Arlington Heights, Illinois*

Photos: Scott Phillips

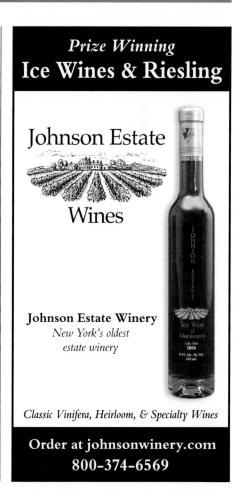

Don't lose small fruit when dipping

We like to give holiday gifts of chocolate-dipped dried fruits but always seemed to lose a number of dried apricots in the dipping pan. We came up with the idea of skewering each apricot with a toothpick and then dipping it into the chocolate. We then poke the toothpick into a piece of styrofoam covered with waxed paper or parchment and leave the apricot there until the chocolate hardens.

—*Anne and Pat Costello, Newton, Massachusetts*

Flat-freezing vegetables without sticking

When you flat-freeze vegetables, they sometimes stick to the pan's surface. I line a jellyroll pan or baking sheet with a linen dishtowel and spread the produce on the towel in a single layer. I freeze the produce until hard and then transfer it to storage bags. The towel absorbs any excess water and prevents the fruits or vegetables from sticking to the pan.

—*Susan Asanovic, Wilton, Connecticut*

Dry out clay baker with baking soda

I use my clay baker quite often but find that when I pull it out of the cupboard it often has mold in it, because the porous clay holds moisture. I solved this problem by sprinkling the inside of the baker with baking soda before putting it away and storing it with the lid off. When I'm ready to cook, I quickly rinse it out, and I'm all set to go.

—*Anne Tufts, Agassiz, British Columbia*

STAFF CORNER

Grated garlic adds a nice finish

When making pasta sauce that includes sautéed garlic, I often boost the flavor by grating a little bit of raw garlic (about half a clove) right into the sauce during the last few minutes of simmering. (I use a rasp-style grater so the garlic is very fine.) Because of the brief cooking, you don't get a raw garlic flavor, but that extra bit adds a deliciously rich undertone, especially in cream sauces.

—*Joanne Smart, special issues editor*

Nondairy alternative for ganache

I have been working with chocolate for many years and am considered an excellent truffle maker. Several years ago, I pondered how to make my famous candy for my vegan son and lactose-intolerant daughter. After trying various soymilk and rice milk combinations, which didn't taste good, I hit upon coconut cream as a substitute for heavy cream. It works beautifully and has about the same consistency. It imparts a subtle coconut flavor and is a great way to offer a treat to those with special dietary needs.

—*Maria Brandriff, Hamden, Connecticut*

Sieve keeps small cookie cutters from getting lost

My small round cookie cutters often fell down the drain into the garbage disposal at cleaning time, until I came up with an easy solution. Since I already had my sieve out to sift flour for the recipe, I put the sieve in the sink and then put the cutters in the sieve as I was done with them. This also eased cleaning. After I scrubbed each cutter, I put it back in the sieve and rinsed them all at once.

—*Laura Rose, Naugatuck, Connecticut*

Hold cutting board in place

I keep a large maple cutting board on my stone countertop all the time. To prevent the board from sliding around on the smooth surface, I position four inexpensive rubber hose washers (which you can buy at most hardware stores) under the board near the corners. The rubber prevents any movement and keeps the board solidly in place. This works for plastic cutting boards, too.

—*James Knodell, Seattle, Washington* ◆

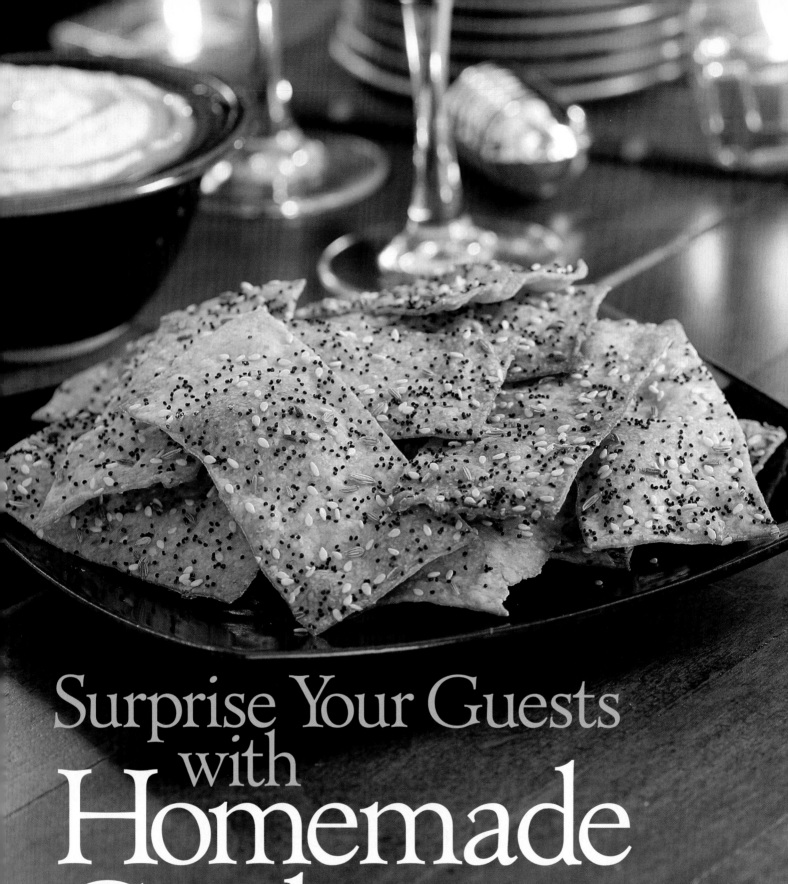

Surprise Your Guests
with
Homemade Crackers

An easy dough
makes baking these
crackers a breeze

Photos: Scott Phillips

BY LYNNE SAMPSON

The more I entertain, the more I realize that it's the small details that make the biggest impression. Take these homemade crackers. Unfussy and quick to make, even for the most pastry-challenged, they bake beautifully into crisp, light flatbread-style snacks. Perfect with wine and cheese at a cocktail party or with crocks of soup at an after-ski gathering, these crackers always have my guests begging for the recipe. Who would have guessed that a simple cracker could be such a hit?

The dough needs no yeast, no kneading, and no elaborate mixing. In a single bowl, a blend of all-purpose and whole-wheat flour with only salt, water, and a splash of olive oil comes together quickly. You'll have a dough that will smooth and stretch easily as you roll it nice and thin for the snappiest, brownest crackers. I don't trim the dough before cutting it into rectangles, because I love how the slightly ragged edge gives them a rustic charm. Plus, that way, there's no wasted dough. A light coating of water with a pastry brush helps the topping adhere and also sweeps away any excess flour that would dull the crackers' surface as they bubble, curl, and brown.

Seeded Crackers

*Yields about 3¹/₂ dozen
2x4-inch crackers.*

The dough can be refrigerated for two days or frozen for up to a month, and then thawed for two hours at room temperature.

FOR THE TOPPING:
1 Tbs. sesame seeds
2 tsp. poppy seeds
2 tsp. fennel or caraway seeds
¾ tsp. kosher salt

FOR THE DOUGH:
**6¾ oz. (1½ cups) unbleached
all-purpose flour; more for rolling**
2 oz. (scant ½ cup) whole-wheat flour
1 tsp. table salt
3 Tbs. extra-virgin olive oil

Position a rack in the lower third of the oven and heat the oven to 450°F.

Make the topping: In a small bowl, stir the sesame seeds, poppy seeds, and fennel or caraway seeds. Fill another small bowl with water and set it aside along with a pastry brush and the kosher salt.

Make the dough: In a large bowl, whisk the all-purpose flour, whole-wheat flour, and table salt. Add the olive oil and ½ cup water to the flour; stir with a rubber spatula until it collects into a soft, crumbly ball of dough. Use the spatula or your hands to press the dough against the sides of the bowl to gather all the stray flour.

Set the dough on a lightly floured work surface and portion it into thirds. Pat each portion into a square. Set two squares aside and cover with a clean towel. Roll the remaining dough into a rectangle about ¹/₁₆ inch thick and 7 or 8 inches wide by 14 or 15 inches long. Whenever you feel resistance, lift up one edge of the dough and sprinkle more flour underneath before you continue rolling.

With a pastry brush, brush the dough lightly with water and sprinkle about a third of the seed mix evenly over the surface. Sprinkle with ¼ tsp. of the kosher salt. With a dough scraper, pizza cutter, ravioli cutter, or sharp knife, cut the dough in half lengthwise and then cut across to make rectangles roughly 2 by 4 inches. Don't bother trimming the edges; rustic edges add character. Transfer to an unlined baking sheet. Bake until nicely browned, about 10 minutes. Let cool on a wire rack.

While each batch is baking, clean your work surface as needed and repeat the rolling and cutting with the remaining portions of dough. Store the cooled crackers in a zip-top plastic bag. They'll keep for up to a week.

VARIATION
Rosemary & Sea Salt Crackers

Add 2 Tbs. chopped fresh rosemary to the dry ingredients in the dough. Skip the seed topping and instead sprinkle each batch of crackers with ¼ tsp. fine sea salt.

Roll the dough into a very thin rectangle; the thinner the dough, the snappier the crackers.

Cut the dough into smaller rectangles and don't worry about trimming the outer edges.

Lynne Sampson is a food writer living in Joseph, Oregon. ◆

Crown Roast of Pork with Fennel-Apple
Stuffing & Cider-Bourbon Sauce

BY ALLISON EHRI KREITLER

Roasts to Boast About

For a special holiday dinner, learn
how to stuff, cook, and sauce an
impressive pork or beef roast

Beef Tenderloin with Wild Mushroom
Stuffing & Port Wine Sauce

The holidays present a wonderful excuse to show off in the kitchen. So at this time of year—for at least one night—why not pull out all the stops and make something really fancy: a stuffed crown roast of pork or a stuffed beef tenderloin, served with an elegant sauce. Though these roasts are sophisticated in both flavor and appearance, you don't have to sacrifice your whole evening for the sake of a fabulous presentation. A few make-ahead strategies ensure that you can both impress your guests and enjoy the party.

A stuffed beef tenderloin comes together more easily than you'd think. I make a rich, earthy mushroom filling ahead of time and freeze it in a log shape. Then when I butterfly the tenderloin (a few simple cuts, and it opens like a book), all I have to do is lay the log down the center of the roast, fold the roast back up and tie it neatly. You can do this a day ahead. Cooking is simple, too. Instead of searing the meat on the stovetop, which is cumbersome, I oven-sear it by starting the roasting at a high temperature.

A crown roast of pork is a real showstopper, yet it's even easier to stuff than a beef tenderloin. Since you buy the roast already tied (see the sidebar on p. 48), all you have to do is treat the center of the roast like a bowl and fill it up. As with the beef, I start the pork in a very hot oven to brown it, but I wait to stuff it until partway through roasting. This helps the pork cook more evenly. And the stuffing for the pork—which has a delicious all-American flavor profile of bacon, apples, and cider—can be mostly made ahead, too.

A robust sauce is the finishing touch. In a restaurant, a rich meat stock, which takes many hours to make, is the backbone of a good sauce. To give my sauces intense flavor in less time, I punch them up with bold ingredients like port, porcini, bourbon, and cider and simmer to concentrate their flavors. If you like, make your sauce ahead, so all it will need is reheating and a few final touches.

Crown Roast of Pork with Fennel-Apple Stuffing & Cider-Bourbon Sauce

Serves ten to fourteen.

FOR THE SAUCE:
- 1 quart apple cider
- 2 cups bourbon
- 2 cups low-salt chicken broth
- ⅓ cup sour cream
- 1 Tbs. cider vinegar; more to taste
- Kosher salt and freshly ground black pepper

FOR THE STUFFING:
- 1 lb. Tuscan bread (or similar crusty artisan-style bread), cut into ½-inch cubes (8 to 9 cups)
- 8 oz. bacon (8 to 10 slices), cut crosswise into ½-inch-wide strips
- 2½ oz. (5 Tbs.) unsalted butter
- 2 medium-small yellow onions, cut into small dice (about 2 cups)
- 1 medium fennel bulb, cut into medium dice (about 3 cups)
- 1 tsp. kosher salt; more to taste
- ½ tsp. freshly ground black pepper; more to taste

- 4 medium Granny Smith apples, peeled, cored, and cut into ½-inch pieces (about 4 cups)
- 2 Tbs. bourbon
- 2 Tbs. apple cider
- 2 Tbs. chopped fresh marjoram
- 1 Tbs. chopped fresh sage
- 2 tsp. fennel seeds, lightly chopped or pulsed in a spice grinder
- ½ tsp. ground allspice
- 2 to 2½ cups low-salt chicken broth

FOR THE ROAST:
- 16-rib crown roast of pork (8½ to 9½ lb.), chine bone removed and bones frenched; see sidebar below for more information
- Kosher salt and freshly ground black pepper

Follow steps 1 through 5, starting at right.

Buying a crown roast of pork

Butchers can cut a crown roast of pork in more than one way, so I found it helpful to have photos of what I did (and didn't) want my roast to look like.

Do: Ask the butcher to remove the chine bone (part of the backbone) in order to bend the roast into the "crown" but not to cut into the meat of the roast (see top photo). A roast trimmed like this will stay juicy and look pretty, too, which is important because a crown roast is all about dramatic presentation. (The timing for the recipe here is based on a roast trimmed this way.) Also, instead of weight, some butchers want to know the number of ribs you'd like. I call for about 16 ribs, which makes for a nice crown.

Don't: Buy a roast with the chine bone still attached. The chine, which runs perpendicular to the ribs, makes carving the roast difficult, so if the chine is left on, butchers usually cut through it between each rib to facilitate carving. The problem is that these cuts often continue too far into the meat, partially dividing each chop (see bottom photo) and making the roast more likely to dry out because more surface area of the meat is exposed.

1 Make the sauce reduction

Put the cider, bourbon, and chicken broth in a 3- to 4-quart (preferably 8-inch-wide) saucepan and bring to a boil over high heat. Reduce the heat to maintain a very brisk simmer and cook until the sauce has reduced to 1¼ cups, about 1 hour. Set aside until the roast is done. (The sauce can be made to this point and refrigerated up to 2 days ahead.)

wine pick

Look for a big, well-oaked yet balanced Burgundy-style Chardonnay to go with the robust sweet-tart flavors of the crown roast of pork. The Matanzas Creek Winery 2005 Chardonnay from Sonoma Valley ($30) makes a stunning pairing.

2 Make the stuffing base

Put the bread on a rimmed baking sheet and let it sit out to dry overnight.

Cook the bacon in a 12-inch skillet over medium-high heat, stirring occasionally, until just crisp, 5 to 6 minutes. With a slotted spoon, transfer the bacon to a large mixing bowl. Pour off and discard all but about 1 Tbs. of the bacon fat. Add 3 Tbs. of the butter to the skillet and melt over medium heat. Add the onions, fennel, salt, and pepper and cook, stirring occasionally with a wooden spoon, until just softened and lightly browned, 10 to 12 minutes. Transfer to the bowl with the bacon.

Melt the remaining 2 Tbs. butter in the skillet over medium-high heat. Add the apples and cook, tossing or stirring occasionally, until nicely browned on a few sides but still firm, 4 to 6 minutes. Mix the bourbon with the apple cider and 3 Tbs. water. Carefully add it to the pan, scraping with a wooden spoon to loosen the brown bits stuck to the pan. Cook until the deglazing liquid has reduced and coats the apples, about 1 minute. Add the apples to the bowl. Add the marjoram, sage, fennel seeds, and allspice and stir to combine. (The stuffing base can be prepared to this point and refrigerated for up to 12 hours.)

3 Stuff & cook the roast

Let the roast sit out at room temperature for 1 hour. If the stuffing base was refrigerated, let it sit at room temperature, too.

Position a rack in the bottom third of the oven and heat the oven to 500°F. Season the roast all over with salt and pepper. Put the roast on an oiled flat rack set in a roasting pan or heavy-duty rimmed baking sheet. Cover the bones tightly with aluminum foil. Roast the pork for 30 minutes.

Meanwhile, stir the dried bread into the stuffing base. Pour 2 cups of the chicken broth over the mixture and stir to combine. If the bread immediately sucks up the liquid, add the remaining 1/2 cup broth. The bread should be moist but not soggy. Season to taste with salt and pepper.

Take the roast out of the oven and reduce the oven temperature to 325°F. Remove the foil from the bones and loosely fill the center of the roast with stuffing, mounding it half

way up to the top of the bones (don't worry if the roast doesn't hold very much stuffing; just put in as much as you can). Cover the bones and stuffing tightly with aluminum foil. Set a timer for 1 hour and return the roast to the oven. Wrap the remaining stuffing in a double layer of aluminum foil and set aside.

When the timer goes off, put the wrapped stuffing seam side up in the oven next to the roast. Set a timer for 30 minutes.

When the timer goes off, remove the foil from the roast and open the package of stuffing so the top can crisp up. Set a timer for 15 minutes. When it goes off, start checking for doneness: Insert an instant-read thermometer into the meat between two bones without hitting the bones. The roast is done when the thermometer reads 155° F. Check the temperature in two or three places. The total roasting time will be 2½ to 3 hours.

Slide a wide spatula under the roast to keep the stuffing in and transfer it to a carving board or serving platter. Tent loosely with foil and let rest for 30 minutes. Meanwhile, continue to bake the package of stuffing until the top is crisp and then turn off the oven. Leave the stuffing in the oven until ready to serve.

4 Finish the sauce

Shortly before serving, reheat the sauce in a small saucepan over low heat. Remove the sauce from the heat and whisk in the sour cream and vinegar. Season the sauce to taste with salt, pepper, and additional vinegar. Transfer the sauce and the additional stuffing to serving bowls.

5 Plate & serve

Remove the strings from the roast. At the table, carve the roast into chops by cutting between the ribs into the stuffing. Serve the sauce and additional stuffing on the side.

Beef Tenderloin with Wild Mushroom Stuffing & Port Wine Sauce

Serves eight to ten.

Don't be scared off by the liver in this stuffing. It's really there just to bind the stuffing and add a rich background note; you won't even notice it.

FOR THE SAUCE:
1¼ oz. (2½ Tbs.) unsalted butter
1 large shallot, finely chopped
   (about ¼ cup)
One 750 ml bottle tawny port
   (about 3¼ cups)
2 sprigs fresh thyme
2½ cups low-salt chicken broth
1 oz. dried porcini mushrooms
2 tsp. all-purpose flour
1 tsp. good-quality balsamic vinegar;
   more to taste
Kosher salt and freshly ground black
   pepper

FOR THE STUFFING:
1 Tbs. dried currants
2 Tbs. canola oil
1 small chicken liver, fat trimmed
   and lobes separated (1½ to 2 oz.)
½ lb. mixed fresh shiitake, oyster,
   and hen-of-the-woods mushrooms,
   stemmed and sliced ¼ inch thick
   (use all 3 varieties if you can find
   them; otherwise, try to use at least 2)
1 tsp. kosher salt; more to taste
¼ tsp. freshly ground black pepper;
   more to taste
1 small shallot, finely chopped
   (a heaping 1 Tbs.)
2 medium cloves garlic, finely chopped
   (about 2 tsp.)
¼ cup low-salt chicken broth
1 oz. (2 Tbs.) unsalted butter, cut
   into 4 pieces and softened at
   room temperature
1 Tbs. chopped fresh parsley
1½ tsp. Cognac or Armagnac
1 tsp. fresh lemon juice
½ tsp. chopped fresh thyme
¼ tsp. finely grated lemon zest

FOR THE ROAST:
4-lb. beef tenderloin roast, preferably
   center-cut (see sidebar opposite for
   more information)
Kosher salt and freshly ground black
   pepper

Follow steps 1 through 5, starting at right.

1 Make the sauce reduction

Melt 1 Tbs. of the butter in a 3- to 4-quart (preferably 8-inch-wide) saucepan over medium-low heat. Add the shallot and cook until softened, about 5 minutes. Add the port and the thyme sprigs and bring to a boil over high heat. Reduce the heat to maintain a brisk simmer and cook until the port has reduced to a syrupy texture, about 30 minutes—you should have about ½ cup including the shallot.

Meanwhile, bring the chicken broth to a simmer in a small saucepan. Off the heat, add the porcini and let them soak for 15 minutes. With a slotted spoon, transfer the porcini to a small bowl. Strain the soaking liquid through a fine sieve lined with a paper towel or coffee filter.

Add the soaking liquid and half of the porcini (about ⅓ cup) to the port reduction (save the remaining porcini for the stuffing). Bring the sauce to a boil over high heat. Reduce the heat to maintain a brisk simmer and cook until it has reduced to 1⅓ cups, about 15 minutes. Strain the sauce through a fine strainer, pressing on the solids. You should have about 1 cup sauce. Set aside until the roast is done. (The sauce can be made to this point and refrigerated up to 2 days ahead. If not making the stuffing ahead, refrigerate the remaining soaked porcini separately.)

wine pick

A hearty red wine with developed tannins, a mineral undertone, and bright fruit pairs well with the earthy-mushroom and port elements of the beef tenderloin. The Waterstone 2004 Cabernet Sauvignon from Napa Valley ($29) would be perfect.

2 Make the stuffing

Soak the currants in hot water for 10 minutes. Drain and put them in a food processor. Add the reserved soaked porcini. Heat 1 Tbs. of the oil in a 10-inch skillet over medium heat. Pat the chicken liver dry and cook on both sides until browned on the outside and just a little pink inside, 3 to 4 minutes total. Transfer to a plate, let cool slightly, and then add to the food processor. Process until finely chopped.

Heat the remaining 1 Tbs. oil in the skillet over medium-high heat. Add the mushrooms, salt, and pepper. Cook, stirring occasionally, until they look wilted and shrunken, 2 to 3 minutes. Add the shallot and garlic and continue to cook, stirring, until the mushrooms are tender and beginning to brown, 3 to 4 more minutes. Add the chicken broth and scrape the bottom of the pan with a wooden spoon to loosen any brown bits. If the liquid doesn't evaporate right away, boil until it does. Remove the pan from the heat and let cool slightly.

Add the sautéed mushrooms, butter, parsley, Cognac or Armagnac, lemon juice, thyme, and lemon zest to the liver mixture in the food processor. Pulse to form a chunky paste and season to taste with additional salt and pepper. Scrape the stuffing onto a large piece of plastic wrap and shape it into a log a few inches longer than the roast. Tightly roll the stuffing up in the plastic wrap and twist the ends to form a very tight log. Twisting the ends of the plastic will compress the stuffing so that it's just a bit shorter than the roast. Freeze until firm, about 2 hours and up to 2 days.

3 Stuff & cook the roast

Trim the silverskin and excess fat from the tenderloin. Butterfly the tenderloin by slicing it lengthwise almost but not completely in half, so that you can open it like a book. Unwrap the stuffing and center it along one half of the roast. Fold the roast back up to its original shape and tie at 1- to 2-inch intervals with butcher's twine. (The roast can be stuffed and refrigerated up to 1 day in advance.)

Let the roast sit at room temperature for 1 hour (2 hours if the stuffing is frozen solid). Position a rack in the bottom third of the oven and heat the oven to 500°F. Let the remaining 1½ Tbs. butter for the sauce soften at room temperature.

Season the roast generously with salt and pepper and put it on a flat rack set in a roasting pan or heavy-duty rimmed baking sheet. Roast for 15 minutes and then reduce the oven temperature to 325°F. Continue to roast the beef until a meat thermometer inserted into the center of the meat (not the stuffing) registers 125°F for rare or 130°F for medium rare, 30 to 45 minutes more. Move the roast to a carving board and let it rest, loosely tented with foil, for 15 minutes.

4 Finish the sauce

While the roast rests, bring the sauce to a simmer in a small saucepan over medium-low heat. Mix the softened butter with the flour to form a paste and whisk it into the sauce. Simmer the sauce to thicken slightly and cook off any raw flour taste, about 3 minutes. Whisk in the vinegar. Season to taste with salt, pepper, and additional vinegar.

5 Plate & serve

Remove the strings from the roast and slice it into 8 to 10 medallions. Put a medallion on each plate and drizzle the sauce around the beef.

Buying a beef tenderloin

Beef tenderloin is a widely available cut of meat. Try to get a center-cut piece (often referred to as a Châteaubriand) because it's evenly thick from end to end, which makes for easy stuffing and even cooking. However, a 4-pound center-cut piece comes from a very large tenderloin, which can be hard to find. If you have this problem, then it's fine to use the butt end (the fatter end) of the tenderloin. Just note that there's another piece of meat attached to the side of the butt end, so when you're butterflying the meat, cut through this extra piece first and then into the longer tenderloin piece (see top left photo).

Make sure to tell your butcher that you don't need your roast tied, and ask him to remove the "chain"—a slender, fatty piece of meat that runs along the entire side of the tenderloin. A good butcher should sell you a solid, nicely trimmed piece of meat without any gouges or slashes; the tenderloin is a pricey cut, so don't settle for a piece that's not in good condition.

Allison Ehri Kreitler is Fine Cooking's *test kitchen associate and food stylist.* ◆

Crispy
Potato Pancakes

A chef shares her tricks for making this classic holiday side—and a few great ways to jazz it up

BY ARLENE JACOBS

During the frosty Montreal winters of my childhood, I'd often come home to find my mother at the stove frying up a batch of potato pancakes. The aromas and gentle sizzling sounds rising from the pan were always familiar and soothing. These pancakes, which some of you might know as "latkes," are a traditional food for Hanukkah, the Jewish festival of lights. After years of trial and error, our family recipe has been perfected and lovingly passed along from generation to generation.

The pancakes are easy to make—you whip up a batter with grated potatoes and a few other ingredients and then pan-fry it in spoonfuls. When properly prepared, the finished pancakes are crisp around the edges and soft and chewy in the center, and eating them is sheer pleasure. But there are a few tricks to getting them right, so if you've never made potato pancakes before, look to the following guidelines to help get you started.

Use starchy potatoes, like russets. The starch acts like glue, helping hold the pancakes together. Plus, starchy potatoes have a lower water content than waxy potatoes—and less water means a crispier pancake.

Grate the potatoes in a food processor. Before food processors were invented, cooks grated the potatoes on a box grater. This was tedious and often caused unpleasant knuckle scraping. Fortunately, a food processor can do the grating much faster.

Next, you'll salt the potatoes, which both seasons and draws water from them (this helps the pancakes brown when frying). Then return the potatoes to the food processor, process them until finely minced, and combine them with a few other ingredients to create a batter: egg and flour, which are both good binders, baking powder for lightness, a little oil for richness, and salt and pepper to season.

Fry only a few pancakes at a time in a 10-inch skillet. Limit the number of pancakes in the pan to three or four, so you can turn them quickly as soon as they're golden. I like to use a flexible slotted metal spatula for turning the pancakes, because it slides under them easily and lets the oil drain from them. As you finish each batch, transfer the pancakes to a baking sheet in a low oven while you fry the rest. (For more frying tips, see the sidebar at right.)

Once you've got the basic technique, you can create your own flavor or size variations. Such variations are by no means traditional, but potatoes are so versatile that it's fun to give the pancakes a twist. Try adding herbs or spices to the batter or changing the size of the pancakes. One of my favorite ways to vary the classic recipe is to "stuff" the pancakes with different fillings, as in the recipe for Potato Pancakes Stuffed with Duxelles on p. 54. For more ideas, see the sidebar on p. 55.

Frying right

Pan-frying these pancakes is a snap, but a few helpful tips can ensure the best—and crispiest—results.

❖ For an even, golden color, add enough oil to maintain a ⅛-inch depth before cooking each new batch, and wait a minute for it to come up to temperature.

❖ Don't crowd the pancakes in the pan, or they'll run together. Also, too much batter in the pan will drop the oil's temperature.

❖ For extra-crisp pancakes, press on them with a spatula several times during cooking. You'll get thinner pancakes with less-chewy insides.

❖ After a few batches, you'll see bits of potato batter accumulating in the oil. If they look like they're burning, clean the oil by passing it through a strainer into a clean bowl. Wipe out the skillet with a paper towel and return the clean oil to the skillet.

Photos: Scott Phillips

Classic Potato Pancakes (Latkes)

Yields 18 to 20 pancakes.

2½ lb. russet (Idaho) potatoes (4 medium), peeled, cut in quarters lengthwise, and reserved in cold water
2½ tsp. kosher salt; more to taste
About ¾ cup corn oil
1 medium yellow onion, diced (about 1¼ cups)
1 large egg
2 Tbs. all-purpose flour
1 tsp. baking powder
⅛ tsp. freshly ground black pepper
Sour cream and applesauce, for serving (optional)

Heat the oven to 250°F.

Set a colander in the sink. Grate the potatoes in a food processor fitted with a medium (4 mm) grating disc. Transfer them to the colander and sprinkle with 2 tsp. of the salt. Toss and let drain for 10 minutes, tossing occasionally.

Meanwhile, replace the processor's grating disc with the chopping blade. Add 1 Tbs. of the oil and the onion, egg, flour, baking powder, pepper, and the remaining ½ tsp. salt to the food processor bowl.

In batches, squeeze the liquid from the shredded potatoes with your hands. Put the potatoes in the food processor with the other ingredients and process for 10 seconds. Stop the machine, scrape the bowl with a rubber spatula, and process until the mixture is finely chopped, 10 to 15 seconds more. Transfer the mixture to a large bowl.

Have ready a large plate lined with paper towels. In a 10-inch skillet, heat ⅛ inch of the remaining oil over medium heat until the surface of the oil shimmers very slightly. With a soupspoon, carefully ladle four mounds of the potato mixture into the oil and spread them slightly with the back of the spoon until they are about 3½ inches in diameter. (The oil should be bubbling gently around the pancakes.) Cook until the pancakes are a deep golden color, 2 to 3 minutes. Lift the pancakes with a slotted metal spatula and carefully turn them over. Continue to cook until the second side is a deep golden color, about 2 minutes more. Using the spatula, transfer the pancakes to the paper-towel-lined plate and blot well with more paper towels. Sprinkle lightly with salt. Use the spatula to transfer the pancakes to a baking sheet; keep them warm in the oven while you finish the rest. Continue to add oil between batches as needed to maintain the ⅛-inch level of the oil. Serve with the sour cream and applesauce on the side, if using.

Making them ahead

If you're preparing several batches for a crowd, fry the pancakes, let them cool, and freeze them on baking sheets. Once they're frozen, transfer them to freezer bags. You can reheat the pancakes on rimmed baking sheets in a 350°F oven for 10 to 15 minutes.

Potato Pancakes Stuffed with Duxelles

Yields 9 to 10 pancakes.

**2½ lb. russet (Idaho) potatoes
   (4 medium), peeled, cut in quarters
   lengthwise and reserved in cold water**
2½ tsp. kosher salt; more to taste
About ¾ cup corn oil
**1 medium yellow onion, diced
   (about 1¼ cups)**
1 large egg
2 Tbs. all-purpose flour
1 tsp. baking powder
⅛ tsp. freshly ground black pepper
1 recipe Duxelles (see below)
2 Tbs. thinly sliced fresh chives

Heat the oven to 250°F.

Set a colander in the sink. Grate the potatoes in a food processor fitted with a medium (4 mm) grating disc. Transfer the potatoes to the colander and sprinkle with 2 tsp. of the salt. Toss and let the potatoes drain for 10 minutes, tossing occasionally.

Meanwhile, replace the processor's grating disc with the chopping blade. Add 1 Tbs. of the oil and the onion, egg, flour, baking powder, pepper, and the remaining ½ tsp. salt to the food processor bowl.

In batches, squeeze the liquid from the shredded potatoes with your hands. Put the potatoes in the food processor with the other ingredients and process for 10 seconds. Stop the machine, scrape the bowl with a rubber spatula, and process until the mixture is finely chopped, 10 to 15 seconds more. Transfer the mixture to a large bowl.

Have ready a large plate lined with paper towels. In a 10-inch skillet, heat ⅛ inch of the remaining oil over medium heat until the surface of the oil shimmers very slightly. With a soupspoon, carefully ladle three or four mounds of the potato mixture into the oil and spread them slightly with the back of the spoon until they are about 3½ inches in diameter. (The oil should be bubbling gently around the pancakes.) On top of each pancake, drop a heaping spoonful of the duxelles and flatten slightly. Top with an additional spoonful of the potato mixture and flatten gently once again. With the tip of your spatula, gently coax the sides of the tops and bottoms of the pancakes together.

Cook until the pancakes are a deep golden color, 2 to 3 minutes. Lift the pancakes with a slotted metal spatula and carefully turn them over. Continue to cook until the second side is a deep golden color, about 2 minutes more. Using the spatula, transfer the pancakes

Stuffing the pancakes,

1 Drop a spoonful of the duxelles on top of each pancake and use the spoon to flatten slightly.

to the paper-towel-lined plate and blot well with more paper towels. Sprinkle lightly with salt. Use the spatula to transfer the pancakes to a baking sheet; keep them warm in the oven while you finish the rest. Continue to add oil between batches as needed to maintain the ⅛-inch level of the oil. Serve the pancakes sprinkled with the chives.

Duxelles

Yields about ¾ cup.

Duxelles is a mixture of finely chopped mushrooms, shallots, and sometimes herbs that is cooked slowly in butter until it becomes thick.

**6 oz. white button mushrooms, cleaned and thinly
   sliced (about 2 cups)**
**10 oz. shiitake mushrooms, stems removed
   and discarded, caps cleaned and thinly sliced
   (about 3 cups)**
2 large shallots, peeled and thinly sliced
4 Tbs. unsalted butter
¾ tsp. kosher salt
⅛ tsp. freshly ground black pepper

Put the mushrooms and shallots in a food processor fitted with the chopping blade. Pulse until finely chopped. The mushrooms and shallots should be in about ⅛-inch pieces—don't overprocess.

Melt the butter in a 10-inch skillet over medium heat. Add the mushroom mixture, salt, and pepper and cook, stirring. When the mushrooms begin to release their moisture, turn the heat to low and cook, stirring occasionally, until the liquid has evaporated and the duxelles look dry, 20 to 25 minutes. Let cool.

Mushrooms are 90% water; the long, slow cooking of duxelles will evaporate the water and concentrate the mushroom flavor. Save any leftover duxelles in the freezer—it's great in omelets, stuffed under the skin of a roasted chicken, or stuffed in baby squash or cherry tomatoes.

step by step

2 Top the duxelles with an additional spoonful of the potato mixture and flatten once again.

3 Use the tip of your spatula to coax the tops and bottoms of the pancakes together.

Give potato pancakes a twist

Though it's nontraditional, you can easily give a new spin to potato pancakes by varying their flavor or size. Once you've mastered the basic cooking technique, try one of the ideas below, or come up with your own version.

Serve oversize stuffed potato pancakes with a salad for a terrific lunch. Follow the stuffed potato pancake recipe at left but form larger pancakes.

Try other stuffings, like shredded Gruyère and caramelized onions, goat cheese and fresh herbs, prosciutto and shredded Fontina, or ratatouille.

Add chopped fresh herbs like thyme, rosemary, tarragon, chives, or dill (or a mix) to the potato mixture before frying (2 to 3 Tbs. per recipe). Add the herbs toward the end of processing the potatoes; too much chopping can mute the herbs' flavor.

Spice them up. Add ½ tsp. curry or chili powder, 1 clove of finely minced garlic, or ½ tsp. caraway, fennel, or celery seed to the potato batter before frying.

Top the pancakes with a finishing touch. I love them topped with smoked salmon or salmon caviar with a dollop of sour cream and sliced chives.

Make them mini and serve them as a passed hors d'oeuvre, along with sour cream and applesauce.

Arlene Jacobs is a restaurant consultant, recipe developer, food writer, and teacher. ◆

Sprouting Up

Bring out the fresh, nutty flavor of Brussels sprouts by roasting, braising, or sautéing

BY MARTHA HOLMBERG

No one is indifferent about Brussels sprouts—people either love them or hate them. Those in the "hate 'em" camp undoubtedly adopted that attitude after eating overcooked, cabbagy versions during childhood. (I've tasted a few sprouts that way myself, so I can't blame the haters.) A subset of non-sprout-lovers has had the opposite problem—undercooked Brussels sprouts. I've noticed that lots of chefs focus too much on the sprouts' leaves and lovely color and not enough on cooking them all the way through.

So the problem with Brussels sprouts is, paradoxically, overcooking and undercooking. Which is understandable, because a nice fresh sprout is a tight little ball of densely layered leaves. With most cooking methods, the outer layers will indeed be overcooked by the time the heart is tender.

The trick to cooking sprouts perfectly is to deal with their density. To maximize their nuttiness and downplay their membership in the cabbage clan, it's best to cut sprouts into the size and shape that works best with your cooking method. I find that quartered sprouts work best for roasting, slices are ideal for braising, and shredded sprouts make a delicious sauté. Cutting the sprouts also lets them better integrate other flavors; great matches include butter, nuts, onions, shallots, bacon, fresh herbs, and citrus.

No matter how you decide to cut, cook, and flavor your sprouts, they'll need their ends trimmed first with a sharp paring knife. Then be sure to pull off any tough-looking, damaged, or yellow leaves to expose the prettier surface below.

Photos: Scott Phillips

roast

quarters are best

for roasting. The oven's heat penetrates the quarters well; plus, they have a lot of surface area to come in contact with the roasting pan, so they get browned for deeper flavor.

Roasted Brussels Sprouts with Dijon, Walnuts & Crisp Crumbs

Serves six to eight.

The mustard-Worcestershire seasoning is a tangy counterpoint to the sprouts, which—despite people's remembrances from childhood—are essentially sweet and nutty. You can fry the crumb topping up to 2 hours before serving.

¼ cup plus 1 Tbs. extra-virgin olive oil
2 Tbs. Dijon mustard
1 tsp. Worcestershire sauce
½ tsp. caraway seeds, toasted lightly
    and crushed
¾ tsp. kosher salt; more to taste
Freshly ground black pepper
2 lb. Brussels sprouts, ends trimmed,
    cut through the core into quarters
1 Tbs. unsalted butter
1 cup coarse fresh breadcrumbs
½ cup chopped walnuts

Position racks in the top and bottom thirds of the oven and heat the oven to 400°F. Line two rimmed baking sheets with parchment.

In a large bowl, whisk ¼ cup of the olive oil with the mustard, Worcestershire sauce, caraway seeds, ½ tsp. of the salt, and about 10 grinds of pepper.

Add the Brussels sprouts and toss to thoroughly distribute the mustard mixture. Spread the sprouts in an even layer on the two baking sheets.

Roast until the cores of the sprouts are just barely tender and the leaves are browning and crisping a bit, 20 to 25 minutes (if your oven heat is uneven, rotate the pans midway through cooking).

While the sprouts are roasting, make the topping: Line a plate with two layers of paper towel. Heat the remaining 1 Tbs. oil with the butter in a medium (10-inch) skillet over medium-high heat. When the butter has stopped foaming, add the breadcrumbs all at once; toss to coat with the fat. Reduce the heat to medium, add the walnuts and the remaining ¼ tsp. salt, and cook, stirring constantly, until the crumbs are browned and slightly crisp and the nuts are golden, 4 to 6 minutes. (The crumbs will start to sound "scratchy" as they get crisp.) Dump the breadcrumb mixture onto the paper towels to drain the excess fat.

Transfer the sprouts to a serving bowl and season to taste with salt and pepper if necessary. Sprinkle the crumbs over the sprouts just before serving.

Sautéed Shredded Brussels Sprouts with Fresh Herbs & Crisp Shallots

Serves six.

You can fry the shallots several hours ahead, but don't top the sprouts with them until moments before serving, so the shallots stay crunchy.

FOR THE SHALLOTS:
3 to 4 cups vegetable oil, for frying
5 to 6 oz. shallots (5 to 6 medium), peeled and cut into ¹⁄₁₆-inch-thick rounds and separated into rings
Kosher salt

FOR THE SPROUTS:
1½ lb. Brussels sprouts
2 Tbs. vegetable oil
Kosher salt and freshly ground black pepper
1 small clove garlic, minced
⅔ cup low-salt chicken broth or water
1 Tbs. unsalted butter
2 Tbs. chopped mixed fresh herbs (I like tarragon, parsley, and chives)

Fry the shallots: Arrange a double layer of paper towels on two plates for draining the shallots. Pour about ¾ inch of oil into a 3-quart saucepan and attach a candy thermometer to the side of the pan. Heat over medium-high heat until the thermometer reads 350°F. (It's important to use a deep pan and fairly shallow oil so there's no danger of the oil boiling over as you fry.) Add about a quarter of the shallots and fry, stirring almost constantly with a slotted metal spoon or a skimmer, until pale brown (the color of a brown grocery bag—any darker and the shallots will be bitter), about 60 seconds. With the slotted spoon, quickly scoop out the shallots and drain on the first plate of paper towels. They'll crisp up as they cool. Repeat with the remaining shallots in three more batches, transferring each batch to the first plate when done. Allow the oil to return to 350°F before each batch. If burned bits accumulate in the oil, scoop them out before adding a new batch.

Transfer all the fried shallots to the second plate so they can drain on fresh paper. Season generously with salt and set aside. (The fried shallots may be prepared several hours ahead. Once cool, transfer to an airtight container.)

sauté

Shred and cook the sprouts: Trim each sprout and cut in half through the core. Set a half (cut side down) securely on the cutting board and with a sharp knife, cut it into crosswise slices. Start at the core end and slice quite finely (¹⁄₁₆ to ⅛ inch), because the core is very dense. As you move toward the top of the sprout, make your slices wider (¼ inch). Transfer the cut sprouts to a bowl, tossing them a few times to encourage the leaf sections to separate.

In a large (12-inch) skillet, heat the oil over high heat until very hot. Add the sprouts and toss with tongs to coat with oil (don't worry if the skillet seems full; the sprouts will wilt). Season generously with salt and pepper. Reduce the heat to medium high and cook the sprouts, tossing frequently, until they wilt and brown slightly, 3 to 5 minutes. Add the garlic and toss to distribute. Pour in the broth and continue to cook until the sprouts are just tender and the liquid has evaporated, another 3 to 5 minutes. Remove from the heat, toss with the butter and half of the herbs. Season to taste with salt and pepper. Pile the sprouts into a bowl, sprinkle with the remaining herbs and top with all of the fried shallots; serve immediately.

shredding is perfect for a quick, high-heat sauté. This cutting method gives you the "leafiest" texture because most of the shreds aren't attached to the core, so they can separate and fluff up.

<u>Find</u> a recipe for Brussels sprouts with brown butter and lemon at **finecooking.com**

Brussels Sprouts Braised with Pancetta, Shallot, Thyme & Lemon

Serves six to eight.

¼ lb. pancetta, cut into ¼-inch dice (about ½ cup)
1 Tbs. olive oil
½ cup small-diced carrot (2 small)
⅓ cup minced shallot (2 to 3 medium)
⅛ tsp. crushed red pepper flakes
2 lb. Brussels sprouts, trimmed, cut lengthwise through the core into ¼-inch-thick slices
Kosher salt and freshly ground black pepper
14-oz. can low-salt chicken broth
1 bushy 3-inch sprig fresh thyme
2 Tbs. chopped oil-packed sun-dried tomato
1 Tbs. unsalted butter
1 tsp. lightly packed finely grated lemon zest

In a 12-inch skillet over medium heat, cook the pancetta in the olive oil, stirring frequently, until the pancetta has rendered much of its fat and is nicely browned, 4 to 5 minutes. Increase the heat to medium high, stir in the carrot, shallot, and red pepper flakes and cook to soften the vegetables, 1 to 2 minutes. Add the sprouts, season lightly with salt and pepper, stir to coat with the fat, and cook, stirring, until the sprouts wilt slightly and a few brown lightly, 2 to 3 minutes.

Add the broth and thyme, cover with the lid slightly ajar, and adjust the heat to a lively simmer. Cook the sprouts until they're just barely tender, 4 to 6 minutes. Remove the lid, increase the heat to medium high and cook, stirring frequently, until all the liquid has evaporated and the sprouts are quite tender (but not mushy), about 3 minutes. Off the heat, gently stir in the sun-dried tomato, butter, and lemon zest. Season to taste with salt and pepper.

slicing is great for braising. The liquid surrounds the sprouts and cooks them evenly and relatively quickly, and the flavors of the braising liquid and other ingredients integrate deliciously with the slices.

Selecting and storing sprouts

Brussels sprouts are a cool-weather vegetable, growing best in areas with sunny days and cool, foggy nights. Sprouts may get a bad rap in some quarters, but growers certainly think of sprouts as a noble vegetable, giving them names like Valiant and Prince Marvel (though I also found a variety called Bubbles). The best specimens have seen some frost, which intensifies their sweetness. Look for sprouts from early fall through spring, and choose tight heads with little decay or yellowing, though most sprouts will have a few outer leaves that aren't perfect. You'll often see sprouts whose outer leaves have been munched by insects, but that doesn't seem to affect the quality of the inner sprout. Sprouts that are loose and ruffly have most likely been grown in too much heat. Their flavor won't be as intensely sweet and nutty, and their leaves will dry out more quickly, so those aren't your best choice.

If you're lucky, you can find the whole stalk, which is gorgeous in a sculptural way but a pain to store once you get it home. I often buy them on the stalk at the farmers' market and then admire them on the counter for a while before I cut off the sprouts and put them in a plastic bag in the crisper drawer. I've had good luck storing sprouts in the fridge for up to a couple of weeks; keep them in the coldest part and be sure they're not too moist or they'll get moldy. The longer they're stored, the more the outer leaves will yellow, so just peel them off before cooking.

Martha Holmberg, the former publisher of Fine Cooking, *is the food editor of* The Oregonian *newspaper in Portland.* ◆

Move Over, Gingerbread Man

Spice up the season with four amazing desserts inspired by the most familiar of holiday flavors

BY JULIA M. USHER

If you're like me, the slightest hint of the holidays brings back a flood of food memories. My favorite is a steaming loaf of gingerbread fresh from the oven and slathered with whipped cream—just like the one my great-grandmother used to bake. But as much as I crave gingerbread's familiar flavor and the warm, fuzzy feelings it stirs up, I often find myself growing weary of loaves and cutout cookies long before Saint Nick arrives on Christmas Eve.

So what do I do to spice things up? I take other popular desserts and infuse them with the holiday spirit using gingerbread's defining ingredients: molasses and the spice trio of ginger, cinnamon, and cloves. For the holiday sweets in these pages, I sifted through my recipe files and selected desserts with the same rustic simplicity that had endeared me to gingerbread in the first place and then gave them a gingerbread twist. So, for example, my pear cobbler has a gingerbread biscuit topping that adds an element of surprise to this classic crowd-pleaser. I drizzle a luscious eggnog crème anglaise over a moist steamed coriander-gingerbread cake, and I make a creamy cheesecake doubly delicious by adding molasses and spices in both the gingersnap crust and the filling. (Cheesecake, by the way, is a real boon during the holiday rush because it has to be made ahead so it can chill overnight.) Finally, a velvety ginger-spice ice cream is an unexpected and delicious treat—especially if you serve it with the cobbler.

Molasses

Gingerbread's defining ingredients

Ground cloves

Ground cinnamon

Ground ginger

Use mild molasses

I use mild molasses—not blackstrap—for these desserts. Blackstrap molasses is intense and somewhat bitter, so I usually reserve it for savory dishes that are a better match for its strength. For more on molasses, see From Our Test Kitchen, p. 78.

Gingerbread-Pear Cobbler

Yields one 10x15-inch cobbler; serves twelve to sixteen.

Though best eaten warm from the oven—and even better with whipped cream or ice cream—this cobbler can be made a day ahead.

1 Tbs. softened unsalted butter for the pan

FOR THE PEAR LAYER:
5¼ lb. ripe pears (about 12 medium), peeled, cored, and cut into ⅛- to ¼-inch-thick slices (Bosc or Anjou pears work well)
¾ cup granulated sugar
2 Tbs. fresh lemon juice (from 1 lemon)
1½ tsp. minced lemon zest (from 1 lemon)
2 Tbs. minced crystallized ginger (about 1 oz.)
1½ Tbs. unbleached all-purpose flour
1 oz. (2 Tbs.) unsalted butter, at room temperature, cut into small pieces

FOR THE GINGERBREAD BISCUIT LAYER:
9 oz. (2 cups) unbleached all-purpose flour
5½ Tbs. granulated sugar
1 Tbs. ground ginger
2½ tsp. baking powder
2 tsp. ground cinnamon
¾ tsp. ground cloves
½ tsp. table salt
¼ tsp. baking soda

3 oz. (6 Tbs.) vegetable shortening
1¼ oz. (2½ Tbs.) unsalted butter, at room temperature
2 large eggs
6 Tbs. whole milk
⅓ cup molasses
¾ tsp. pure vanilla extract

FOR THE TOPPING:
½ cup sliced almonds
2 Tbs. granulated sugar

Position a rack in the center of the oven and heat the oven to 400°F. Lightly butter a 10x15x2-inch baking dish.

Make the pear layer: In a large bowl, gently toss the sliced pears with the sugar, lemon juice, and lemon zest. Make sure the lemon juice completely coats the pears to keep them from browning. Sprinkle the crystallized ginger and flour over the top. Stir until evenly incorporated, breaking apart any ginger pieces that may be stuck together. Spread the pear mixture evenly in the bottom of the prepared pan and dot with the softened butter pieces.

Make the biscuit layer: In a medium bowl, stir the flour, sugar, ginger, baking powder, cinnamon, cloves, salt, and baking soda with a fork. With the fork, work in the shortening and the softened butter until the size of small peas.

In a small bowl, whisk the eggs, milk, molasses, and vanilla extract. Make a well in the center of the dry ingredients and pour the egg mixture into the well. Stir just until the dry ingredients are completely blended. Dollop the batter by heaping tablespoonfuls onto the pears to create a cobbled effect, taking care to space the dollops about 1 inch apart. (Though the batter will cover only about half of the pear layer, don't spread it out. It will rise and spread to cover most of the pears as it bakes. If you run out of space to dollop the batter before it's all used, distribute what remains among the existing dollops.)

Apply the topping and bake: Sprinkle the nuts and sugar evenly over the cobbler. Bake until the pears are tender and the topping is golden brown, 35 to 40 minutes. If needed, rotate the pan midway through the baking to allow the top to brown evenly. Let rest at least 20 minutes before serving. Serve warm.

Storing: Once completely cool, wrap the cobbler in plastic and store it at room temperature for up to 24 hours. For longer storage, refrigerate for up to one week. To reheat, remove the plastic, cover loosely with foil, and set in a 300°F oven until warmed through, 20 to 25 minutes.

Steamed Coriander-Gingerbread Cake with Eggnog Crème Anglaise

*Yields two 9-inch cakes;
each serves eight to ten.*

Though the steaming process leaves it deliciously moist straight from the oven, I prefer this cake one or two days later, after the spices have had a chance to meld.

Cooking spray for the cake pans
1 lb., 1 oz. (3¾ cups) unbleached all-purpose flour
1 Tbs. baking soda
1 Tbs. ground ginger
1½ tsp. ground cinnamon
1½ tsp. ground cloves
1¼ tsp. table salt
6 oz. (generous 1 cup) pitted dates, chopped into ¼-inch pieces
2 Tbs. plus 1 tsp. whole coriander seeds
6 oz. (12 Tbs.) unsalted butter, at room temperature
¾ cup granulated sugar
1½ cups molasses
3 large eggs, at room temperature
3 oz. (¾ cup) walnut halves, toasted and coarsely chopped
1 recipe Eggnog Crème Anglaise (at right)

Bring a large kettle of water to a boil—you'll need 1½ cups for the cake batter and about 2 quarts for the steaming pan.

Position one rack in the center of the oven and another beneath it in the lowest slot. Set a 10x15x2-inch baking pan or Pyrex dish on the lower rack and fill the pan halfway with boiling water. Heat the oven to 350°F. Lightly coat two 9x2-inch round cake pans with cooking spray and line the bottoms with parchment. Apply another light coat of cooking spray to the parchment.

Prep the ingredients: Sift the flour, baking soda, ginger, cinnamon, cloves, and salt into a large bowl. Stir to combine. Put the chopped dates in a small bowl with 3 Tbs. of the flour mixture. Pull apart any date pieces that may be stuck together and toss to evenly coat with the flour.

Crush the coriander seeds with a mortar and pestle or in a spice grinder. Alternatively, seal the seeds in a zip-top plastic bag and use a rolling pin to crush them finely.

Mix the batter: Put the softened butter in the bowl of a stand mixer fitted with a paddle attachment. Cream the butter on medium speed until very soft and smooth. Gradually add the sugar and continue to beat on medium speed until light and fluffy, about 2 minutes. Stop the mixer and scrape down the sides of the bowl with a spatula. Add the molasses and beat again on medium speed just until evenly incorporated. Add the eggs

one at a time, mixing for about 10 seconds after each addition and scraping down the bowl as needed between additions. The batter will look broken.

Measure out 1½ cups boiling water. Turn the mixer to very low speed or, if you prefer, do all remaining mixing by hand. Alternate adding the flour mixture and the boiling water in five additions, beginning and ending with the flour. Mix just until each addition is incorporated, as overmixing will lead to a tougher cake—it's fine if the batter looks slightly lumpy. Stir in the reserved date-flour mixture, crushed coriander seeds, and chopped walnuts. The batter will be quite loose.

Bake the cakes: Divide the batter equally between the two prepared cake pans. Set both pans on the center rack and bake until a toothpick inserted in the center of each cake comes out clean, 40 to 55 minutes. Let the cakes cool in their pans about 10 minutes and then invert them onto cooling racks and peel off the parchment paper. (Allow the water-filled baking pan to cool in the oven until it can be safely moved without spilling hot water.)

Serve the cakes warm or at room temperature. Cut each cake into 8 to 10 slices and serve each piece with 2 to 3 Tbs. of Eggnog Crème Anglaise (see the recipe at right).

Storing: If baking ahead, wrap the cakes tightly in plastic while they are still slightly warm to the touch. (Any trapped steam will condense, adding moisture to the cakes.) Store the cakes up to a week at room temperature. To reheat, remove the plastic, put the cakes on a cookie sheet, and cover them loosely with foil. Heat them in a 300°F oven until warmed through, 15 to 20 minutes.

You can freeze the cakes, wrapped in plastic and then foil, for up to two months.

Eggnog Crème Anglaise

Yields about 2¼ cups, enough sauce for two 9-inch cakes.

Spiked with bourbon, rum, and grated nutmeg, this holiday-inspired cream sauce will quickly get you in the spirit. It thickens to a rich, velvety consistency as it chills, so for the most luxurious texture, make it a day ahead.

2 cups heavy cream
½ cup granulated sugar
4 large egg yolks
⅛ tsp. table salt
1 Tbs. dark rum
1 Tbs. bourbon
1 tsp. freshly grated nutmeg
1 tsp. pure vanilla extract

Set a medium metal bowl in a large bowl of ice water and have a fine sieve at the ready.

Combine the cream and sugar in a 3-quart saucepan. Set the pan over medium heat, stirring occasionally to encourage the sugar to dissolve. Heat the mixture through but do not allow it to boil. Remove from the heat.

Put the egg yolks and salt in a small heatproof bowl and gently whisk to break up the yolks. Gradually whisk in ½ cup of the warm cream mixture. Pour the yolk mixture into the cream remaining in the saucepan and whisk to combine.

Cook over medium-low heat, stirring constantly with a clean wooden or heat-proof plastic spoon until the custard thickens slightly, enough to coat the back of the spoon and hold a line drawn through it with a finger, 4 to 8 minutes. An instant-read thermometer should register 170° to 175°F. Do not let the sauce overheat or boil, or it will curdle. Immediately strain the sauce through the sieve into the bowl set in the ice-water bath (see the sidebar, above right).

Gently whisk in the rum, bourbon, nutmeg, and vanilla extract. Stir the sauce occasionally until cool, 20 to 30 minutes. Transfer it to another container, if you like, and cover the surface of the sauce with plastic to prevent a skin from forming. Wrap the container tightly with more plastic and refrigerate a minimum of 2 hours, until velvety and slightly thick.

Storing: The sauce can be stored in the refrigerator in a tightly sealed container for 2 to 3 days. Cover the surface of the sauce with plastic wrap to prevent a skin from forming.

A water bath stops the cooking

Crème anglaise is a delicate, sweet egg-based sauce that's prone to curdling if overheated. So as soon as it begins to thicken, you'll need to stop the cooking by putting the bowl in an ice-water bath. (You'll have to do this when making the ice cream on p. 64 as well.) Be sure to set up the water bath before you start cooking the crème anglaise, so you won't have to scramble at the last minute and take the risk of scrambling your sauce, too.

When it comes to ground spices, freshness is key

Before you bake any of these desserts, check your ground spices for freshness. An old spice can mean the difference between a pleasantly spicy dessert and one that's downright bland.

Grinding whole spices is the best way to ensure that they're fresh. But it can be time-consuming, especially when you're juggling baking with tree-trimming, gift-wrapping, and all the other little tasks of the season. So bottled ground spices are fine if time is short. To make sure they're as fresh as possible when you buy them and that they stay fresh, follow these simple steps:

❖ **Inspect the expiration date on spice bottles** and choose those with the most distant dates, ideally six months away or more.

❖ **Throw away old spices.** Discard bottled spices if they have been open longer than six months.

❖ **Store spices properly.** Though you might be tempted to store spices (ground or whole) in pretty containers above your stovetop, where they're handy, they will stay fresh longer in a cool, dark cabinet or a corner of your refrigerator.

Ginger-Spice Ice Cream

Yields a generous 1 quart; serves eight.

To learn how to make the twisty cookie garnish on the bowls of ice cream below, see From Our Test Kitchen, p. 78.

4 large egg yolks
¾ cup plus 1 Tbs. granulated sugar
1½ cups heavy cream
1½ cups whole milk
1½ tsp. ground ginger
1 tsp. ground cinnamon
¼ tsp. ground cloves
2 Tbs. molasses
1 tsp. pure vanilla extract
Pinch table salt

Set a medium metal bowl in a large bowl of ice water and have a fine sieve at the ready.

Whisk the egg yolks with ¼ cup of the sugar in a medium heatproof bowl. Combine the remaining ½ cup plus 1 Tbs. sugar with the heavy cream and milk in a 3-quart saucepan. Set over medium heat and stir occasionally until the milk is hot but not simmering. Whisk about ½ cup of the hot milk into the yolks and then whisk the yolk mixture back into the milk.

Reduce the heat to medium low and cook, stirring constantly with a clean wooden spoon or rubber spatula, until you see wisps of steam and the custard thickens slightly, 3 to 4 minutes. An instant-read thermometer should register 170° to 175°F. Don't let the custard overheat or boil, or it will curdle. Immediately strain the custard through the sieve into the bowl set in the ice-water bath to halt the cooking process (see sidebar, p. 63).

Sprinkle the ginger, cinnamon, and cloves over the custard while it's still warm and whisk well to distribute evenly. Wait 10 minutes and then whisk in the molasses, vanilla, and salt. Cover the surface of the custard with plastic to prevent a skin from forming and let it cool to room temperature. Take the bowl out of the water bath and cool thoroughly in the refrigerator (ideally overnight) before freezing.

Stir the chilled custard to evenly distribute any molasses or spices that may have settled to the bottom. Freeze in an ice cream maker according to the manufacturer's instructions. With most ice cream makers, the custard will reach its thickest consistency after churning 30 to 35 minutes. However, the ice cream can still be somewhat soft at this point. If you prefer a firmer consistency, transfer it to a covered storage container and freeze until it reaches the desired consistency.

Storing: Tightly covered, this ice cream will keep fresh and freezer-burn-free for about a week.

Ginger-Molasses Cheesecake

Yields one 10-inch cheesecake;
serves sixteen to twenty.

I use gingersnaps from the store because
their crunchiness makes them ideal for grinding to a fine crumb. Serve with a sprinkle of
candied nuts—pecans would be great.

FOR THE CRUST:

2 cups finely crushed gingersnap cookies
(about 8½ oz.; crush in a food processor
or in a zip-top bag with a rolling pin)
2 Tbs. granulated sugar
2½ oz. (5 Tbs.) unsalted butter, melted; plus
1 tsp. melted butter for the pan

FOR THE GINGER-MOLASSES FILLING:

Five 8-oz. packages cream cheese, at room
temperature
1¾ cups granulated sugar
1 Tbs. unbleached all-purpose flour
1 Tbs. ground ginger
1½ tsp. ground cinnamon
½ tsp. ground cloves
¼ tsp. table salt
4 large eggs, at room temperature
3 large egg yolks, at room temperature
¼ cup molasses
2 Tbs. heavy cream, at room temperature
1 tsp. pure vanilla extract

Position one rack in the center of the oven
and another directly beneath it. Heat the
oven to 350°F.

Make the crust: Mix the crushed gingersnaps and sugar in a small bowl. Using a fork
or your hands, gradually work in the melted

butter, mixing until all the crumbs
are moistened. Use your fingers and the bottom of a straight-sided, flat-bottomed metal
measuring cup or drinking glass to press the
mixture firmly into a 10x3-inch springform pan
to create a uniform ⅛- to ¼-inch-thick crust
that covers the bottom and goes 1 to 1½
inches up the sides. Bake the crust on the
middle oven rack until it's fragrant and warm
to the touch, 5 to 7 minutes. Let the pan cool
on a rack while you prepare the filling.

Make the filling: Put the softened cream
cheese in the bowl of a stand mixer fitted
with a paddle attachment. Beat on medium
speed until very smooth and entirely free
of lumps. Gradually add the sugar. Scrape
down the sides of the bowl and continue mixing until the sugar has dissolved, 1 to 2 minutes. (Smear a small amount of the mixture
between your fingertips; there should be no
grittiness if the sugar has dissolved.)

In a small bowl, mix the flour, ginger, cinnamon, cloves, and salt. Sprinkle the mixture
evenly over the cream cheese and mix on low
speed until blended.

Add the eggs and yolks, one at a time,
beating on medium speed until just combined. Scrape down the sides of the bowl
after every other addition. (Beat no more than
necessary to mix in each egg or you'll incorporate too much air, making the cheesecake
dry and porous as opposed to dense and
creamy.) Add the molasses, cream, and
vanilla and mix until well combined.

Assemble and bake the cheesecake:
Brush the inside rim of the pan above the
crust with the remaining 1 tsp. melted butter,
without disturbing the crust. Pour the batter
into the pan—it should fill the pan to a little
above the crust. Put the pan on the middle
oven rack and position a foil-lined baking
sheet directly beneath it to catch any butter
drips. Bake until the top of the cake is golden
brown and the center just barely jiggles when
the side of the pan is gently tapped, 1 hour
and 10 to 20 minutes. It's fine if the cake
develops a few cracks on the surface. Turn
off the oven, open the door, and let the
cheesecake cool in the oven for 15 minutes.

Set the cake on a rack until completely
cool, at least 4 hours. Cover the cake loosely
with plastic, put a few air vents in the plastic,
and refrigerate it overnight in the pan. When
ready to serve, slowly release the pan sides.
If any of the cake edge appears stuck, gently
loosen it with a sharp paring knife before
continuing to release the pan.

For the cleanest servings, use a sharp
chef's knife and wipe it clean with a warm,
damp cloth between slices.

Storing: Cover the cake loosely with
plastic and refrigerate. It's best if eaten
within a day or two, as the crust will soften.

Julia M. Usher is a baker, freelance writer,
and the former chef/owner of AzucArte,
a bakery in St. Louis. ◆

Thai on the Fly
A Quick Curry for Any Night

A simple method gives you a repertoire of comforting, aromatic dishes

BY NANCIE MCDERMOTT

When I traveled to Thailand for the first time in 1975, I knew next to nothing about Thai food. It wasn't meant to be a culinary trip after all: I was serving in the Peace Corps, and all I knew was that I wanted to see Asia. But when I got to Thailand there was no escaping the pull of the deeply flavored local cuisine. Thai curries, in particular, captivated me with their heady spiciness and complex harmony of flavors. These rich stews—simmered in broth and, often, coconut milk and finished with a combo of salty, sweet, and hot ingredients like fish sauce, sugar, and fresh chiles—are distinctively flavored with a spicy, powerfully aromatic mix called curry paste (see sidebar on p. 69). They're among the most popular dishes in Thailand, often prepared for special occasions but also savored daily at small curry shops that line busy town streets.

The good news is that you don't have to go to Thailand to eat a good Thai curry. You don't even have to go to a Thai restaurant. Thai curries are easy enough to make at home—even on a busy night—without having to hunt far and wide for exotic ingredients. The four steps at right give you a basic method for making any Thai curry. And while many Thai cooks and restaurants make curry paste from scratch (for a recipe, see p. 83), you can use store-bought curry paste to speed things up, and you can replace traditional ingredients like palm sugar or Thai basil with more readily available ones, like brown sugar and Italian basil. So after one stop at your local supermarket, cooking a fabulous curry takes just about half an hour. It's no surprise that in my house Thai curries are high on the list of go-to weeknight dishes.

A meal in a bowl. Another reason I love making curries on a weeknight is that they're a perfect one-dish supper. With beef, chicken, seafood, or even tofu and a variety of vegeta-bles, a Thai curry over rice (or noodles) makes a fantastic, satisfying meal.

Not all curries have coconut milk. Thai cooks use coconut milk in many curry dishes, but they also enjoy curries made with just broth. These curries, like the one at right, are called "country-style" or "jungle" curries because they're rustic and simple enough to make anywhere, anytime, using just meat, vegetables, curry paste, and broth or water. (In Thailand, skipping the coconut milk makes things a lot easier because home cooks make it from scratch, painstakingly squeezing grated coconut flesh.) Because no coconut milk is added to thicken the broth, these curries have the texture of hearty soups rather than stews.

1 *Heat a little vegeta-ble oil, add the curry paste, and stir, pressing the paste against the bottom of the pan. This will coat it with hot oil and make it "bloom," releasing complex aromas and flavors.*

2 *Add meat and vegetables to the pan and stir to coat them with the curry paste. If you're using fish or vegetables that cook quickly, add them later.*

Red Country-Style Curry with Beef, Shiitakes & Edamame
Serves four.

When I make this curry with store-bought curry paste and no lime leaves, I like to serve it with lime wedges on the side to squeeze over all.

1 lb. flank steak
5 oz. fresh shiitake mushrooms
2 Tbs. vegetable oil
3 Tbs. jarred or homemade red curry paste (see recipe, p. 83)
2¾ cups low-salt chicken broth
5 wild lime leaves, torn or cut into quarters (optional)
1½ cups frozen shelled edamame (soy beans), thawed
3 Tbs. fish sauce
1 Tbs. palm sugar or light brown sugar
¼ tsp. kosher salt; more to taste
A handful of fresh Thai or Italian basil leaves
Hot cooked rice or rice noodles for serving
1 long, slender fresh red chile (such as red jalapeño or serrano), thinly sliced on the diagonal (optional)

Slice the beef across the grain ¼ inch thick and then cut the slices into 1½- to 2-inch-long pieces.

Trim and discard the stems from the shiitakes; slice the caps ¼ inch thick (you should have 1½ to 2 cups).

Heat the oil in a 2- to 3-quart saucepan over medium heat until a bit of curry paste just sizzles when added to the pan. Add all the curry paste and cook, pressing and stirring with a wooden spoon or heatproof spatula to soften the paste and mix it in with the oil, until fragrant, about 2 minutes.

Increase the heat to medium high, and add the beef. Spread it in an even single layer and cook undisturbed until it just begins to lose its pink color, about 1 minute. Turn the beef and continue cooking, stirring occasionally to coat it with the curry paste, until most of the beef no longer looks raw, 1 to 2 minutes.

Stir the shiitakes into the beef. Add the chicken broth and stir again. Add half the lime leaves (if using), and bring to a simmer. Simmer gently, stirring occasionally, until the shiitakes are tender and the beef is cooked through, about 5 minutes.

Add the edamame, stir well, and cook for about 1 minute, just to blanch them. Add the fish sauce, sugar, and salt and stir to combine. Remove from the heat. Tear the basil leaves in half (or quarters if they are large), and stir them into the curry, along with the remaining lime leaves (if using). Let rest for 5 minutes to allow the flavors to develop. Season to taste with salt.

Serve hot or warm with rice or noodles, garnished with the chile slices (if using).

3 *Pour in the broth and the coconut milk, if using, and simmer to cook the ingredients through and to build flavor.*

4 *After adding any quick-cooking ingredients, like shrimp, finish with fish sauce, brown sugar, salt, and torn basil leaves.*

Red Curry with Shrimp & Sugar Snap Peas

Serves four.

2 Tbs. vegetable oil
2 Tbs. jarred or homemade red curry paste (see recipe, p. 83)
15-oz. can unsweetened coconut milk
1 cup low-salt chicken broth, fish broth, or water
1 lb. shrimp (21 to 25 per lb.), peeled and deveined
2 cups sugar snap peas (7 to 8 oz.), trimmed
5 wild lime leaves, torn or cut into quarters (optional)
2 Tbs. fish sauce
1 Tbs. palm sugar or light brown sugar
½ tsp. kosher salt
A handful of fresh Thai or Italian basil leaves
Hot cooked rice or rice noodles for serving
1 long, slender fresh red chile (such as red jalapeño or serrano), thinly sliced on the diagonal (optional)

Heat the oil in a 2- to 3-quart saucepan over medium heat until a bit of curry paste just sizzles when added to the pan. Add all the curry paste and cook, pressing and stirring with a wooden spoon or heatproof spatula to soften the paste and mix it in with the oil, until fragrant, about 2 minutes.

Add the coconut milk and broth and bring to a simmer. Simmer, stirring often, for 5 minutes, allowing the flavors to develop.

Increase the heat to medium high and let the curry come to a strong boil. Add the shrimp, sugar snap peas, and half the lime leaves (if using), and stir well. Cook, stirring occasionally, until the shrimp curl and turn pink, about 2 minutes. Add the fish sauce, sugar, and salt and stir to combine. Remove from the heat.

Tear the basil leaves in half (or quarters if they are large), and stir them into the curry, along with the remaining lime leaves (if using). Let rest for 5 minutes to allow the flavors to develop.

Serve hot or warm with rice or noodles, garnished with the chile slices (if using).

Find a recipe for Green Curry with Cod & Green Beans at finecooking.com

Substitutions are quicker

In these recipes, traditional ingredients like palm sugar and Thai basil can be replaced with easier-to-find items like light brown sugar and Italian basil. Wild lime leaves have no good substitution, though, so leave them out if you can't find them. We made these curries with both traditional ingredients and substitutions and found that the latter still produce delicious results.

reader review

A *Fine Cooking* reader gave the Green Curry with Chicken & Eggplant a real-world test. Here are the results:

I liked the fact that this dish tasted like the curries I get in some of my favorite Thai places. Making the extra effort to get the lime leaves, palm sugar, and Thai basil made the dish fantastic for me. It reminded me that the ingredients really matter. Each flavor was so distinct that it really popped, and each bite held a little different experience as a result. This curry was very good, and it was fast and easy to make.

—John Lagan,
Sandy Hook, Connecticut

Green Curry with Chicken & Eggplant

Serves four.

Green curry paste tends to be spicier than red curry paste (see sidebar at right). If you use homemade curry paste, it may be hotter than the jarred paste, depending on the chiles you use. Use 1½ Tbs. if you'd like a slightly milder curry.

1 lb. boneless, skinless chicken thighs (4 large)
2 small Japanese eggplants or 2 very small Italian eggplants (about 4 oz. each)
2 Tbs. vegetable oil
1½ to 2 Tbs. jarred or homemade green curry paste (see recipe, p. 83)
15-oz. can unsweetened coconut milk
1 cup low-salt chicken broth
5 wild lime leaves, torn or cut into quarters (optional)
2 Tbs. fish sauce
1 Tbs. palm sugar or light brown sugar
¼ tsp. kosher salt
A handful of fresh Thai or Italian basil leaves
Hot cooked rice or rice noodles for serving
1 long, slender fresh red chile (such as red jalapeño or serrano), thinly sliced on the diagonal (optional)

Trim the chicken and cut it into bite-size chunks. Trim the eggplant, cutting away stems and bottoms. Quarter each lengthwise, and then slice crosswise at 1-inch intervals.

Heat the oil in a 2- to 3-quart saucepan over medium heat until a bit of curry paste just sizzles when added to the pan. Add all the curry paste and cook, pressing and stirring with a wooden spoon or heatproof spatula to soften the paste and mix it in with the oil, until fragrant, about 2 minutes.

Increase the heat to medium high and add the chicken. Spread it in a single layer and cook undisturbed until it starts to brown around the edges, 1 to 2 minutes. Stir and continue cooking until most of the chicken is lightly browned, 1 to 2 minutes.

Add the coconut milk and chicken broth and stir well, scraping the bottom of the pan to release the browned bits. Add the eggplant and half the lime leaves (if using) and bring to a simmer.

Simmer, adjusting the heat as needed and stirring occasionally, until the chicken is completely done and the eggplant is tender, 8 to 10 minutes.

Add the fish sauce, sugar, and salt and stir. Remove from the heat. Tear the basil leaves in half (or quarters if they are large), and stir them into the curry, along with the remaining lime leaves (if using). Let rest for 5 minutes to allow the flavors to develop.

Serve hot or warm with rice or noodles, garnished with the chile slices (if using).

Nancie McDermott is a cooking teacher and cookbook author specializing in Southeast Asian cuisines. ◆

The skinny on curry paste

Curry pastes, an essential ingredient in Thai curries, are intensely flavored combinations of herbs and spices chopped fine and then ground into a thick, sturdy paste. The standard ingredient list includes fresh or dried chiles, lemongrass, galangal, wild lime peel, cilantro root, coriander and cumin seeds, and shrimp paste. (See From Our Test Kitchen, p. 78, for more on some of these ingredients.)

There are two main types of curry paste: red, made with dried hot red chiles that are usually soaked before grinding, and green, made with fresh hot green chiles. While all curry pastes are spicy, the red ones tend to be milder than the green ones. The heat level, however, will vary with the brand of paste you buy, or if you're making your own, with the type of chiles you use (see below).

Buy it or make your own

You can find jarred red and green curry paste in the Asian section of most supermarkets. Store it in the refrigerator for up to two weeks after opening.

Jarred pastes are ideal for busy weeknights, but if you have a little more time, try making curry paste from scratch (see the recipe on p. 83 in From Our Test Kitchen). It'll require a trip to an Asian market for a few ingredients, but it's worth it: Homemade curry paste will give your curries a more complex, nuanced flavor. And what's great is that you can make curry paste on a weekend, refrigerate or freeze it, and use it later to whip up a quick curry.

A Cookie
for Every

TEXT BY LISA WADDLE

RECIPES BY
ABIGAIL JOHNSON DODGE

Occasion

**Dark Chocolate
Crackles**

**Cardamom-Honey
Cutouts**

Rugelach

**Vanilla Slice & Bake
Cookies**

**Macadamia Double-
Decker Brownie Bars**

Maple-Walnut Tuiles

**Peanut Butter &
Chocolate Sandwiches**

Baker Abby Dodge shares her seven favorite cookies for the holidays

Just about everyone I know has a tradition surrounding the making—or at least eating—of certain cookies at this time of year. Inevitably, we all wind up making those familiar recipes that have been handed down through the generations. For me, I feel compelled to make my grandmother's walnut biscotti, though, to be honest, they're not particularly exciting.

This year I decided once and for all to revamp my cookie arsenal, to really find some showstoppers I could make for parties, for gifts, and for the office. As luck would have it, I wound up with a secret weapon in my search for extraordinary cookies: *Fine Cooking*'s contributing editor and baking guru Abigail Johnson Dodge. It just so happens that for this December issue, we asked Abby to pull out all the stops and develop seven fabulous cookies, each of which would suit a different occasion or taste. And, wow, did Abby deliver.

"I started by imagining my audience: who was I serving and what would the event be?" Abby said of her strategy. "I thought

about a cookie swap, and I knew I wanted a recipe that would make a big batch, that everyone in the family would love, but that wasn't boring. That's how I came up with the Vanilla Slice & Bake cookies, which can also be spiked with crystallized ginger. They're very different cookies than, say, the Maple Walnut Tuiles, which are a bit more impressive—perfect for a dinner party.

Abby didn't hold back on the ingredients in these cookies, and the flavors are really spectacular because of that. The nuance of a little orange in her Dark Chocolate Crackles really makes the cookie. And her Cardamom Honey Cutouts are nothing like any rolled cookie you've ever made before. And though macadamia nuts are pricey, their rich flavor, along with coconut and cocoa, make Abby's Macadamia Double-Decker Brownie Bars a slam-dunk.

Who knows, one of these cookies may turn out to be your newest cookie tradition, to bake and eat at every holiday. As for me, I think Grandma's biscotti are an endangered species.

When it has to be chocolate

Dark Chocolate Crackles

Yields about 5 dozen cookies.

11¼ oz. (2½ cups) unbleached
  all-purpose flour
1 tsp. baking soda
¼ tsp. table salt
8 oz. (1 cup) unsalted butter, at
  room temperature
2 cups firmly packed light brown
  sugar
2 oz. (⅔ cup) natural,
  unsweetened cocoa, sifted
  if lumpy
2 tsp. finely grated orange zest
1 tsp. pure vanilla extract
3 large eggs
8 oz. bittersweet chocolate,
  melted and cooled until
  barely warm
¾ cup (4 oz.) chopped chocolate
  (white, bittersweet, or
  semisweet)
    ⅓ cup granulated sugar;
    more as needed

Position a rack in the center of the oven and heat the oven to 350°F. Line three large cookie sheets with parchment or nonstick baking liners.

In a medium mixing bowl, whisk together the flour, baking soda, and salt. In the bowl of a stand mixer fitted with the paddle attachment (or in a large mixing bowl with a hand mixer), beat the butter, brown sugar, cocoa, orange zest, and vanilla on medium speed until well combined, about 4 minutes. Add the eggs one at a time, beating briefly between additions. Add the cooled chocolate and mix until blended, about 1 minute. Add the dry ingredients and mix on low speed until almost completely blended, about 1 minute. Add the chopped chocolate and mix until blended, about 15 seconds.

Shape the dough into 1¼-inch balls with a small ice-cream scoop or two tablespoons. (The balls of dough may be frozen for 1 month. Thaw them overnight in the refrigerator before proceeding with the recipe.)

Pour the granulated sugar into a shallow dish. Dip the top of each ball in the sugar and set the balls sugar side up about 1½ inches apart on the prepared cookie sheets. Bake one sheet at a time until the cookies are puffed and cracked on top, 11 to 12 minutes. Let the cookies cool on the sheet for 5 minutes before transferring them to a rack to cool completely.

tip: These cookies are fragile when hot, so be sure to let them cool on the cookie sheet for 5 minutes.

Decorating party

Cardamom-Honey Cutouts

Yields 6 dozen 2 1/2-inch round cookies.

13 1/2 oz. (3 cups) unbleached all-purpose flour; more for rolling
1 tsp. ground cardamom
1/2 tsp. table salt
1/4 tsp. baking soda
8 oz. (1 cup) unsalted butter, at room temperature
3/4 cup granulated sugar
1/4 cup honey
1 large egg
1 tsp. pure vanilla extract

In a medium mixing bowl, combine the flour, cardamom, salt, and baking soda. Whisk until well blended.

In the bowl of a stand mixer fitted with the paddle attachment (or in a large mixing bowl with a hand mixer), beat the butter and sugar on medium speed until well blended and slightly fluffy, about 3 minutes. Scrape down the bowl and the beater. Add the honey, egg, and vanilla. Continue mixing on medium speed until well blended, about 1 minute. Add the flour mixture and mix on low speed until the dough is well blended and comes together in moist clumps, 30 to 60 seconds.

Divide the dough roughly in half. On a piece of plastic wrap, shape each dough half into a smooth 5-inch disk. Wrap well in the plastic. Refrigerate until chilled and firm enough to roll out, 1 to 1 1/2 hours. (The dough may be refrigerated for up to 3 days or frozen for 1 month. Thaw overnight in the refrigerator before proceeding with the recipe.)

Bake the cookies: Position a rack in the center of the oven and heat the oven to 350°F. Line two or more cookie sheets with parchment or nonstick baking liners. Working with one disk at a time, roll the dough on a floured work surface to about 3/16 inch thick. Dust with additional flour as needed. Choose one or more cookie cutters of any shape that are about 2 1/2 inches wide and cut out shapes. Arrange the cookies about 1 inch apart on the lined cookie sheets. Gather the scraps and gently press together. Re-roll and cut. Repeat with the remaining dough.

Bake one sheet at a time until the cookies' edges develop a 1/4-inch-wide light-brown rim, 11 to 13 minutes (rotate the sheet halfway through baking for even browning). Let the cookies cool on the sheet for about 10 minutes and then transfer them to a rack to cool completely.

For decorating tips and ideas, see From Our Test Kitchen, p. 78)

tip: If you cut the cookies into larger or smaller shapes, you'll need to adjust the baking time. Just be sure to bake until the edges turn light brown.

Hostess gift

Rugelach

Yields about 40 cookies.

These buttery, flaky cookies feature a jewel-like filling of jam and a dusting of chopped pistachios.

FOR THE DOUGH:
10½ oz. (2⅓ cups) unbleached all-purpose flour
¼ cup granulated sugar
½ tsp. table salt
8 oz. (1 cup) cold unsalted butter, cut into 10 pieces
8 oz. cold cream cheese, cut into 10 pieces

FOR THE FILLING:
6 Tbs. raspberry or apricot jam

FOR THE TOPPING:
1 large egg
1 Tbs. water
¼ cup finely chopped salted pistachios (1¼ oz.)

Make the dough: Put the flour, sugar, and salt in a large (11-cup or larger) food processor. Pulse briefly to blend the ingredients. Scatter the butter and cream cheese pieces over the dry ingredients. Pulse until the dough begins to come together in large (about 1-inch) clumps.

Divide the dough into four pieces and on a lightly floured surface, knead each until smooth. Shape each into a flat 6x3-inch rectangle and wrap in plastic wrap. Refrigerate until well chilled, about 1½ hours. (The dough may be refrigerated for up to 3 days or frozen for 1 month before proceeding with the recipe.)

Shape and fill the cookies: Working with one piece of dough at a time, roll the dough on a piece of lightly floured plastic wrap into a rectangle slightly larger than 5 x13 inches (if refrigerated overnight, let sit at room temperature until pliable enough to roll). Dust with additional flour as needed. Using a sharp knife, trim off the ragged edges to make a 5x13-inch rectangle. Position the dough with one long edge facing you. Using a metal spatula (offset is best), spread evenly with 1½ Tbs. of the jam. Using the plastic wrap as an aid, roll up the dough jelly roll-style beginning with one long side. Wrap in plastic and refrigerate until firm, at least 1 hour. Repeat with remaining dough and jam. (The logs can be wrapped well and frozen for up to 1 month. Thaw overnight in the refrigerator before proceeding with the recipe.)

Top and bake the cookies: Position racks in the top and bottom thirds of the oven and heat the oven to 350°F. Line two cookie sheets with parchment or nonstick baking liners. In a small bowl, mix the egg and water with a fork until blended.

Unwrap one roll and set on a cutting board. Using a serrated knife and a ruler, cut the roll into 1¼-inch-wide pieces. Arrange cookies seam side down 1 inch apart on the cookie sheets. Repeat with the remaining rolls. Lightly brush the tops with the egg mixture (you won't need it all) and sprinkle with the chopped pistachios. Bake until the rugelach are golden brown, 28 to 30 minutes, swapping the cookie sheets' positions about halfway through. Let cool on the sheets for about 20 minutes. Transfer to a rack to cool completely.

tip: Make a half-batch of dough if your food processor is small.

Cookie swap

Vanilla Slice & Bake Cookies

Yields about 8 dozen cookies.

15 oz. (3⅓ cups) unbleached all-purpose flour
¾ tsp. baking powder
½ tsp. table salt
9 oz. (18 Tbs.) unsalted butter, at room temperature
1½ cups granulated sugar
1 large egg
1 large egg yolk
1½ tsp. pure vanilla extract

In a medium mixing bowl, combine the flour, baking powder, and salt. Whisk until well blended.

In the bowl of a stand mixer fitted with the paddle attachment (or in a large mixing bowl with a hand mixer), beat the butter and sugar on medium speed until fluffy and well blended, about 3 minutes. Scrape down the bowl and the beater. Add the egg, egg yolk, and vanilla. Continue mixing on medium until well blended, about 1 minute. Add the flour mixture and mix on low speed until the dough is well blended and forms moist clumps, about 1 minute.

Gently knead the dough by hand in the bowl until smooth. Shape it into two square or round logs, each about 10 inches long, and wrap in plastic wrap. Refrigerate until chilled and very firm, about 4 hours. (The dough may be refrigerated for up to 3 days or frozen for 1 month. Thaw overnight in the refrigerator before proceeding with the recipe.)

Position a rack in the center of the oven and heat the oven to 350°F. Line two or three cookie sheets with parchment or nonstick baking liners.

Using a thin-bladed, sharp knife and a ruler, mark off ³⁄₁₆-inch-wide slices on the top of the log. Using the same knife, cut straight down to form cookies. Arrange the cookies about 1 inch apart on the lined cookie sheets. Bake one sheet at a time until the cookies' edges are golden

brown, 11 to 13 minutes (for even browning, rotate the sheet after about 5 minutes). Let the cookies cool on the sheet for about 10 minutes and then transfer them to a rack to cool completely.

FLAVOR VARIATION:

Ginger-Spiced

Add to the flour mixture:

¾ cup finely chopped crystallized ginger
2 tsp. ground ginger
1 tsp. ground cinnamon
Pinch of ground black pepper

Note: The crystallized ginger may cause the dough to crumble as you slice the cookies; just press them back together.

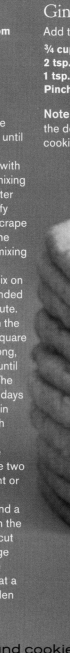

tip: For perfectly round cookies, shape the dough into logs, wrap in plastic, and insert into empty paper towel tubes.

Office celebration

Macadamia Double-Decker Brownie Bars

Yields 48 bars.

These gorgeous two-layer bars have a brownie base topped with a gooey nut-and-coconut-studded topping.

FOR THE BROWNIE LAYER:
Cooking spray
6 oz. (12 Tbs.) unsalted butter, cut into large chunks
1½ cups granulated sugar
2¼ oz. (¾ cup) unsweetened cocoa powder (natural or Dutch processed)
¼ tsp. table salt
2 large eggs
1 tsp. pure vanilla extract
3½ oz. (¾ cup) unbleached all-purpose flour

FOR THE MACADAMIA LAYER:
½ cup firmly packed light brown sugar
1½ oz. (⅓ cup) unbleached all-purpose flour
⅔ cup light corn syrup
1½ oz. (3 Tbs.) unsalted butter, melted
1½ tsp. pure vanilla extract
2 large eggs
1½ cups roughly chopped salted macadamia nuts
⅓ cup sweetened coconut flakes

Position a rack in the center of the oven and heat the oven to 325°F. Line the bottom and sides of a 9x13-inch baking pan with foil, leaving some overhang on the sides, and spray with cooking spray.

Make the brownie layer: In a medium saucepan over medium heat, whisk the butter until it is melted. Remove the pan from the heat and add the sugar, cocoa powder, and salt. Whisk until well blended, about 1 minute. Add the eggs and vanilla and whisk until smooth. Add the flour and stir with a rubber spatula until blended. Scrape into the prepared pan and spread evenly. Bake until the top is shiny and dry-looking and the brownie springs back very slightly when pressed with a fingertip, about 20 minutes. (The brownie should not be completely baked.) Remove from the oven and put on a rack.

While the brownie layer is baking, make the macadamia topping: In a large mixing bowl, combine the brown sugar and flour. Whisk until well blended, breaking up any large clumps. Add the corn syrup, melted butter, and vanilla. Whisk until blended, about 1 minute. Add the eggs and whisk just until combined, about 30 seconds. (Don't overmix or the batter will be foamy.) Add the nuts and

tip: Dipping the knife in warm water and wiping it dry between cuts will keep the gooey topping from sticking to the knife.

coconut and stir with a rubber spatula until evenly blended.

Pour the macadamia topping over the warm, partially baked brownie layer. Using a spatula, carefully spread the mixture into an even layer. Return the pan to the oven and bake until the top is golden brown, 37 to 40 minutes. Transfer the pan to a rack to cool completely. (At this point, the entire pan can be wrapped in plastic wrap, then foil, and frozen for up to 1 month.)

Using the foil as handles, lift the rectangle from the pan and invert onto a work surface. Carefully peel away the foil. Flip right side up. Using a sharp knife, cut into 2x2-inch squares and then cut each square into triangles.

Sophisticated dinner party

Maple-Walnut Tuiles

Yields about 20 cookies.

To give them their curved form, the tuiles are draped over a rolling pin when they're hot from the oven. So measure your rolling pin and figure out how many 4-inch cookies you'll be able to drape over it at once. That's how big your batch of cookies should be. But you don't have to shape them if you don't want to—they're just as delicious flat.

Cooking spray (if baking on parchment)
2 large egg whites
¼ cup granulated maple sugar or firmly packed light brown sugar
Pinch table salt
¼ cup pure maple syrup (preferably Grade B)
1½ oz. (3 Tbs.) unsalted butter, melted and cooled slightly
½ tsp. pure vanilla extract
3 oz. (⅔ cup) unbleached all-purpose flour
2 Tbs. finely chopped walnuts

Position a rack in the center of the oven and heat the oven to 350°F. Line four cookie sheets with nonstick baking liners or parchment paper sprayed with cooking spray. If shaping the tuiles, have a rolling pin at the ready.

In a medium mixing bowl, combine the egg whites, sugar, and salt. Whisk until blended and a bit foamy, about 1 minute. Add the maple syrup, melted butter, and vanilla and whisk until blended. Add the flour and continue to whisk until smooth and blended.

Drop the batter by scant tablespoonfuls onto the prepared cookie sheets, positioning them about 4 inches apart (you should be able to fit 4 to 5 to a cookie sheet, but bake only as many as you can drape over your rolling pin, if you plan to shape them). Spread each round of batter into a 4-inch circle with the back of a spoon (use a circular motion to spread the batter outward from the center.)

Sprinkle about ¼ tsp. of the walnuts over each cookie. Bake until the cookies are browned around the edges and in spots toward the center, 7 to 9 minutes. The cookies will inevitably be slightly uneven and, therefore, will have a few darker-brown spots. Not to worry —they'll still taste good. Don't underbake or the cookies won't be crisp.

Working quickly, move the cookie sheet to a rack. Using a metal spatula, lift off the hot cookies one by one and, if shaping, immediately drape them over the rolling pin. Let cool until set, about 1 minute. Carefully remove the tuiles from the rolling pin and set them on a rack to cool completely. If not shaping, immediately transfer them to a rack.

tip: It's worth seeking out the granulated maple sugar, as it elevates these cookies into something truly special.

To leave out for Santa

Peanut Butter & Chocolate Sandwiches

Yields about 30 sandwich cookies (or 60 single cookies).

These soft, flourless cookies house a bittersweet filling, for a taste combination that appeals to the kid in all of us.

FOR THE PEANUT BUTTER COOKIES:
2½ cups smooth peanut butter, at room temperature
1½ cups firmly packed light brown sugar
1 tsp. baking soda
2 large eggs
2 tsp. pure vanilla extract

FOR THE CHOCOLATE FILLING:
10 oz. bittersweet chocolate, coarsely chopped (about 2 cups)
4 oz. (8 Tbs.) unsalted butter, cut into 4 pieces

Make the cookies: Position a rack in the center of the oven and heat the oven to 350°F. Line four cookie sheets with parchment or nonstick baking liners.

In the bowl of a stand mixer fitted with the paddle attachment (or in a large mixing bowl with a hand mixer), beat the peanut butter, brown sugar, and baking soda on medium speed until well blended, about 1 minute. Add the eggs and vanilla and mix on low speed until just blended, about 25 seconds.

Shape level tablespoonfuls of the dough into balls about 1 inch in diameter. (The balls of dough may be frozen for 1 month. Thaw them overnight in the refrigerator before proceeding with the recipe.) Arrange the balls 1½ inches apart on the prepared baking sheets. Do not press down. Bake one sheet at a time until the cookies are puffed and crackled but still moist-looking, about 11 minutes. Transfer the cookie sheet to a rack to cool about 10 minutes. Using a spatula, move the cookies to the rack and let cool completely. Repeat with the remaining cookies.

Make the filling: Melt the chocolate and the butter in the microwave or in a medium heatproof bowl set in a

tip: Substitute semisweet chocolate for the bittersweet in the filling for a sweeter kick.

skillet with 1 inch of barely simmering water, stirring with a rubber spatula until smooth. Remove from the heat and set aside until cool and slightly thickened, 20 to 30 minutes.

Assemble the sandwiches: Turn half of the cooled cookies over so they are flat side up. Spoon 2 tsp. of the chocolate filling onto the center of each cookie. Top with the remaining cookies, flat side down. Press gently on each cookie to spread the filling almost to the edge. Set on the rack until the filling is firm, 20 to 30 minutes.

Abigail Johnson Dodge, author of The Weekend Baker, *is a contributing editor to* Fine Cooking. ◆

Molasses
What it all boils down to

The gingerbread desserts on pp. 60–65 owe much of their deep, complex sweetness to molasses. True molasses is a by-product of sugar cane processing. Sugar cane juice is boiled, crystallized, and then centrifuged to separate the crystallized cane sugar from the liquid. That leftover liquid is molasses; it can be refined and processed as is, or it may be boiled up to two more times to produce different grades of sweetness and intensity. Three basic grades exist, but producers use several different terms to refer to them.

Light, mild, Barbados, or robust molasses has been boiled only once. It has a high sugar content and a mild flavor, and it can be used directly on foods as a syrup. Some brands of single-boil molasses haven't even had any sugar removed from them—they're simply refined sugar cane juice

that's been reduced to a syrup. A widely distributed brand of this type is Grandma's Original, and it's what we used to test the gingerbread dessert recipes.

Dark, full, or cooking molasses has been boiled twice. It's slightly bitter and less sweet than single-boil molasses. It's typically used for baking and cooking.

Blackstrap molasses has been boiled three or more times. It has the deepest, most intense flavor of the three. It is generally used for animal feed, although some people prize it for its nutritional value.

The preservative sulphur dioxide is often added to molasses. It alters the flavor somewhat, so use unsulphured molasses when you can.

—*Dabney Gough, recipe tester*

Molasses	78
Twisty tuile garnish	78
Cooking with bourbon	80
Bourbon balls	80
Nonstick baking liners	81
Making your own curry paste	82
Red curry paste	83
Decorating cookies	84
Royal icing	85

A twist on tuiles

To make the twisty tuile garnish shown with the Ginger-Spice Ice Cream on p. 64, we modified the recipe for Maple-Walnut Tuiles on p. 76. Here's how to do it: First make a stencil from a moisture-resistant paper plate by cutting off its border with scissors so that it can lie flat and then cutting out a 5x½-inch rectangle from the center of the plate with scissors or a utility knife.

1 Next, line a baking sheet with parchment or a nonstick baking liner. Have ready a few wooden spoons to shape the tuiles after

they're baked. Lay the stencil on the baking sheet and thinly spread some of the batter over the top of the stencil with a small offset spatula. Lift the stencil and repeat until you've made two tuiles per spoon (depending on handle length, a wooden spoon can usually shape two tuiles, so bake only as many tuiles in a batch as you have spoons to shape them). Don't use the nuts from the tuile recipe. Bake at 350°F until golden brown, 3 to 5 minutes.

2 Remove the pan from the oven and, working very quickly,

drape the tuiles over the spoon handles and loosely twist them around the handles like candy-cane stripes. Let them sit for 1 minute to set the shape and then slide them off onto a rack to cool completely. If you find that they harden before you can get them twisted, make fewer per batch or try shaping them in the oven (but remember, they'll be hot). Use twisty tuiles not just on ice cream but as a cute garnish for mousses and puddings, too.

—*Allison Ehri Kreitler,
test kitchen associate*

Photos: Scott Phillips

IT'S HARD TO LET GO

Messermeister blends ergonomic perfection with exacting performance. The elite edge is crafted using an exclusive 3-step hand-finishing process that allows you to slice, dice, chop, split, trim, pare, carve and julienne with precision and delight. The revolutionary bolsterless edge enables continuous cutting along the full length of the edge and the contoured handle and polished spine create a knife so comfortable, some chefs call it sensual. It's a feeling that you'll want to hold on to forever.

Messermeister

THE KNIFE FOR LIFE™

Cooking with bourbon

When it comes to cooking and baking with liquor, bourbon is one of our favorites. Its smoky caramel and vanilla flavor adds a special nuance to savory and sweet dishes alike. It pairs particularly well with brown sugar, pecans, vanilla, chocolate, mint, apples, pears, peaches, ham, and pork. It's great in sauces, marinades, brines, glazes, cakes, pies, truffles, and cookies. In this issue, it's an important ingredient in the Crown Roast of Pork with Fennel-Apple Stuffing & Cider-Bourbon Sauce on p. 48, in the Eggnog Crème Anglaise on p. 63, and in the Bourbon Balls below.

Bourbon whiskey, which gets its name from Bourbon County, Kentucky, is distilled from a grain mash that's at least 51% corn (but usually 65% to 80%) and may also contain barley, rye, and sometimes wheat (as in Maker's Mark brand). The distilled liquor is then aged in new charred oak barrels from which it gets its color and smoky, caramelly undertones.

Save expensive single-barrel bourbons like Blanton's or Eagle Rare and small-batch bourbons like Knob Creek or Basil Hayden's for sipping. For cooking, a regular bourbon such as Jim Beam, Wild Turkey, Old Crow, or Heaven Hill is fine.

—A.E.K

Bourbon Balls

Yields 3½ to 4 dozen.

For some of us, it wouldn't be Christmas without these rich, potent treats. I like to make them with chocolate or vanilla cake scraps that I've saved in the freezer, but you can also use a store-bought pound cake, since saving scraps takes some forethought. But if you happen to have scraps, or even a leftover cake layer, here's your chance to use them.

1 cup heavy cream
¼ cup bourbon
½ tsp. pure vanilla extract
12 oz. bittersweet chocolate, chopped (about 2½ cups)
8 oz. pecans, toasted and cooled (about 2 cups)
8 oz. plain homemade or store-bought pound cake (thawed if frozen), cut into cubes (about 2½ cups)
⅔ cup cocoa powder, preferably Dutch processed
⅓ cup confectioners' sugar

In a small saucepan, bring the cream just to a boil over medium-high heat. Remove from the heat and stir in the bourbon and vanilla. Sprinkle the chocolate evenly over the cream and let sit without stirring for 5 minutes.

Meanwhile, pulse the pecans in a food processor until coarsely chopped. Add the pound cake and pulse until the nuts and cake are finely chopped.

Stir the chocolate and the cream until smooth. Pour the chocolate over the pecan and pound cake mixture in the food processor and pulse until combined. Transfer to a medium bowl and refrigerate, stirring occasionally, until firm enough to scoop, about 1 hour.

Sift the cocoa powder and confectioners' sugar together into a medium bowl. Line a rimmed baking sheet with waxed paper or parchment. Scoop out a heaping tablespoon of the bourbon-chocolate mixture and roll it in your hands to form a ball. Transfer the bourbon ball to the cocoa-sugar mixture, roll it around to coat, and transfer to the baking sheet. Repeat with the remaining bourbon-chocolate mixture. Sift some of the remaining cocoa-sugar mixture over the bourbon balls just to dust them. Refrigerate the bourbon balls until firm, about 2 hours. For a nice presentation, you can put them in mini muffin cups. —A.E.K.

The care & keeping of nonstick baking liners

If you bake lots of cookies, a couple of nonstick silicone baking liners are handy to have because they're reusable and they reduce the need for parchment. Often referred to generically by the name of the leading brand—Silpat (see Where to Buy It, p. 90), they rely on their silicone surface to maintain their nonstick quality, so it's important to treat them with care.

To clean a Silpat, wipe it down with a soft, damp sponge and let it air dry. In the test kitchen, we wash it last and drape it over everything else in the dish rack. You may use a diluted solution of mild dishwashing liquid if you like, but remember that an oily feeling on the mat even after cleaning is normal. Silpats are not dishwasher-safe.

Never use knives, scrapers, brushes, or scrubbers on the mats—they will damage the surface.

Store Silpats flat or rolled but not folded. If you store your baking sheets flat, just lay your Silpats in one of them. We store ours by rolling them in paper towels and securing the roll with tape. An empty paper towel tube is another good way to keep them from unrolling.
—D.G

Homemade Thai curry paste

For many cooks (those not living in Southeast Asia, anyway), the hardest part about making Thai curry paste is finding a few of the ingredients. Some of what you need is waiting for you at your supermarket, but for the ingredients below, you may need to visit an Asian market. If there's not one in your area, see p. 90 for mail-order sources.

A. Lemongrass
(*tah-krai*)

With a floral lemony scent and a delicate citrus-like flavor, lemongrass shows off in a wide array of Thai dishes. It's standard in curry pastes and valued in traditional medicines as well. It's becoming more mainstream, so some supermarkets carry it, but Asian markets are a better bet for the freshest lemongrass. Look for sturdy, fibrous, pale-green stalks.

To use, trim away the top portion of each stalk, leaving a 4-inch-long section, including the base. Pull off any dry, tired outer leaves before chopping or slicing as needed.

To keep lemongrass fresh, wrap stalks loosely in a plastic bag and refrigerate them for five to seven days. To freeze lemongrass, trim the tops, wrap well to make them airtight, and freeze for up to six weeks. Use directly from the freezer without thawing. Avoid dried and powdered lemongrass, as they retain none of the flavor or aroma you need.

B. Galangal
(*kah*)

This cousin of ginger is prized for its extraordinary citrus-like flavor in soups and its burst of herbal heat in curry pastes. In its fresh form, its color ranges from delicate ivory to warm brown, depending on its exact variety and age. Round and plump with lots of thumb-like protrusions, it's always encircled with small dark rings along the rounded chunks.

Peel and chop it before grinding with other curry paste ingredients. Store fresh galangal loosely wrapped in plastic in the refrigerator for five to seven days. Or slice it thinly, arrange in a single layer in a zip-top plastic bag, press out the air, seal tightly, and freeze for up to six weeks (use frozen galangal slices without thawing them).

You may also find dried galangal in large, woody-looking slices of wildly varying sizes. These work wonderfully in Thai dishes. Before chopping, soak them in warm water for 20 to 30 minutes or until pliable. Avoid ground galangal powder, as it lacks the intense flavor and aroma of fresh.

C. Shrimp paste
(*ka-pi*)

Profoundly redolent of all things oceanic, shrimp paste is an essential and treasured source of flavor and texture in curry pastes and in *nahm prik*, the beloved genre of hot chile dipping sauces. Made from tiny shrimp which are boiled, peeled, salted, dried, and then ground to a fine, sturdy, and very aromatic paste, it ranges in color from purplish-red to brown, with a firm but moist texture. It packs a powerful scent and super-salty flavor, but it melds into curry paste without a trace of its original intensity.

Look for it in small plastic jars and keep it tightly closed until you need it. If it's sealed with a layer of wax, simply break the wax and discard it. Store it at room temperature, tightly sealed, for up to six months.

D. **Dried lime peel**
(*piew mah-kroot*)

Essential in most curry pastes, the intensely aromatic and flavorful dried peel of the wild lime (also known as kaffir lime) delivers the vibrant citrus notes of limes and lemons with amazing depth. Drying sometimes turns the peel from vivid green to dull brown, but the intense flavor remains.

Soak the peel in warm water for about 20 minutes or until it's pliable and chop very finely before grinding with other curry paste ingredients. Store unused peel in an airtight container for up to six months.

You may find frozen whole wild limes as well. Keep them frozen, and cut off strips of peel, including some white pith, as needed without thawing the lime. In place of wild lime, you can substitute lime or lemon zest, using the zest only, without the pith.

E. **Cilantro root**
(*rahk pahk chee*)

Milder in flavor and aroma than their leafy tops, cilantro roots provide a delicate herbal note and a plush, moist texture to curry pastes, bringing pungent ingredients like chiles, garlic, and galangal into a harmonious, flavor-packed whole. Look for cilantro bunches sold with their roots still attached. They may be tiny or up to several inches long. Use the root and about 1 inch of the stem portion attached to each root. Wash well and chop finely before grinding with other curry paste ingredients.

To store, rinse well and put the roots in a jar of water with the leafy tops protruding from the jar. Keep at room temperature for one or two days, or cover loosely with a plastic produce bag and refrigerate for three or four days.

You may also find frozen cilantro root in Asian markets. If you can't find any cilantro root, substitute chopped cilantro stems with a few leaves mixed in.

—*Nancie McDermott, contributor*

Red Curry Paste
Yields 1 scant cup.

Thai curry paste is traditionally made using a sturdy granite mortar and pestle, but a food processor works fine. This curry paste will have a softer texture than the fudge-textured curry pastes you find in stores because of the water you add to help the blades move.

½ cup small dried hot red chiles (such as Thai bird chiles or chiles de arbol)
1 large dried red New Mexico chile (optional)
1 Tbs. coriander seeds
1 tsp. cumin seeds
5 whole black peppercorns
3 stalks fresh lemongrass
¼ cup chopped shallots
2 Tbs. chopped garlic
1 Tbs. chopped fresh or frozen galangal or fresh ginger
1 Tbs. coarsely chopped cilantro root (root plus about 1 inch of stem) or chopped cilantro stems and leaves
1 tsp. finely chopped dried wild lime peel (soak in warm water before chopping) or lime zest
1 tsp. kosher salt
1 tsp. shrimp paste (optional)

Open the chiles, breaking off their stems and shaking out and discarding most of their seeds. Break the pods into pieces. (Large chiles will be somewhat pliable, while small ones will be brittle.) Combine the chile pieces in a medium bowl and add warm water to cover them. Set aside to soak for about 30 minutes.

Meanwhile, put the coriander seeds in a small, dry skillet over medium-high heat. Cook, shaking the pan, until they darken to a golden brown color and become fragrant, 2 to 3 minutes. Transfer to a small plate.

Let the skillet cool for a few minutes and then toast the cumin seeds in the same way until nicely browned and fragrant, 1 to 2 minutes. Transfer to the plate with the coriander seeds.

Put the coriander, cumin, and peppercorns in a small spice grinder and finely grind. Transfer to a plate and set aside.

Chop off and discard the grassy tops of the lemongrass, leaving about 4 inches, including the rounded base and root end. Discard any dry or discolored outer leaves and trim off the root end to leave a smooth base just under the plump bulb. Slice crosswise into thin rounds and then chop coarsely; transfer to a medium bowl.

Drain the chiles well and add them to the bowl of chopped lemongrass along with the shallots, garlic, galangal, cilantro root, dried lime peel or lime zest, salt, and shrimp paste (if using). Add the ground spices and stir gently to combine.

Transfer to a food processor, add 1 or 2 Tbs. cold water, and process to an almost-smooth paste. If the paste hasn't come together, add more water, 1 Tbs. at a time. Scrape the paste into a jar, cover tightly, and refrigerate for up to 5 days, or freeze in 1- to 2-tablespoon-size portions for up to 1 month.

—*Nancie McDermott*

Green Curry Paste Variation
To make green curry paste, use ½ cup finely chopped unseeded fresh hot green chiles (such as Thai bird chiles or serranos), instead of the dried red chiles. (You won't need to soak them.)

How to decorate cookies with royal icing

A blend of egg whites and confectioners' sugar, royal icing hardens to a durable, rock-hard consistency when allowed to dry. Start by making a batch of icing (recipe, opposite) and then coloring it however you like. You can split the batch up and make lots of colors, or you can leave it white.

To outline a cookie

Spoon some of the icing into a pastry bag fitted with a very small plain tip and outline the rim of a cookie with the icing. (Practice first on a piece of cardboard or waxed paper. If the icing is too thick to pipe evenly, put it back in the bowl and stir in water, a drop or two at a time, until it pipes easily but still retains its shape.) Scatter sprinkles or sparkling sugar over the icing, if you like. Set the iced cookies aside to dry.

To coat an entire cookie with icing

Have ready a small clean artist's brush (one that you use only for food). If you want to use colors, set out a bowl for each color, portion the icing into the bowls, and stir drops of food coloring into each until the desired shade is reached. Outline the rim of a cookie with the icing as described at left and let harden slightly. Dampen the brush in water and spread a small amount of additional icing in an even layer within the cookie's border. Decorate the cookie with sprinkles, sparkling sugar, or edible dragées, if you like. Set the cookie aside to dry.

Once the icing is completely dry and hard, store the cookies in airtight containers at room temperature for two to three days or in the freezer for longer storage.

—*Abby Dodge, contributing editor*

Risk-free royal icing

Royal icing carries a very slight risk of salmonella infection from the raw egg whites used to make it. If you want to eliminate that risk completely, use pasteurized whites, which are available either dried or fresh. Look for **dried egg white powder** or **meringue powder** (dried egg white powder plus sugar and stabilizers) in the baking section of the market. You'll need to reconstitute the powder before making the icing, as described in the recipe below.

Fresh pasteurized egg whites are kept in the dairy case near the other eggs and egg products. Depending on your store, you may find cartons of whole in-shell pasteurized eggs (look closely at all the cartons because they're packaged just like regular eggs and are sometimes hard to notice), or you may find containers of liquid egg whites. Use fresh pasteurized egg whites just as you would use regular egg whites.

—Jennifer Armentrout, test kitchen manager

Royal Icing
Yields about 3 cups.

**2 Tbs. powdered egg whites
or meringue powder
plus 6 Tbs. warm water
OR 3 large egg whites
16 oz. (4 cups)
confectioners' sugar
Food coloring (optional)**

If using the powdered egg whites or meringue powder and warm water, combine them in the bowl of a stand mixer or in a large mixing bowl. Let stand, whisking frequently, until the powder is dissolved, about 5 minutes. If using fresh egg whites, just put them in the bowl.

With the whisk attachment on a stand mixer or with a hand mixer, begin mixing on medium speed until frothy. Add the confectioners' sugar and continue beating until blended. Increase the speed to high and beat until the mixture is thick and shiny, about 3 minutes for fresh eggs and 5 minutes for powdered. Stir in food coloring (if using). Put a damp paper towel directly on the icing to keep a skin from forming. If not using within 2 hours, cover the bowl with plastic and refrigerate.

*—Abby Dodge,
contributing editor* ◆

Baking: chocolate vs. cocoa powder

BY NICOLE REES

These days, it's easy to get your hands on amazing chocolate from all over the world—chocolate that, until recently, was considered way too good for baking. Now it's not unusual to use top-notch chocolate in everything from brownies to birthday cakes. True, it's always good to use the best ingredients you can find, but if you're thinking that excellent chocolate is the key to intensely flavored chocolate desserts, think again. When it comes to delivering deep, dark chocolate flavor, plain old cocoa powder is hard to beat.

Cocoa and chocolate: What's the difference?

Cocoa is by no means a lesser product than chocolate. On the contrary, it's a purer form of chocolate.

Chocolate has two main components—cocoa solids (where the flavor comes from) and cocoa butter (where the rich texture comes from). Cocoa powder has very little cocoa butter in it; it's mainly cocoa solids. In other words, you can think of cocoa powder as chocolate with most of its cocoa butter removed. Cocoa powder generally contains just 10 to 12% cocoa butter, while pure unsweetened chocolate contains about 55%.

So, ounce for ounce, cocoa powder packs a bigger punch of chocolate flavor, because you're getting more cocoa solids and less cocoa butter.

When to use cocoa and when to use chocolate

When I create a recipe for a chocolate dessert, flavor isn't the only attribute I consider—texture is also important.

The finished texture of a dessert is strongly influenced by the types of fat in the recipe, be it butter, oil, cocoa butter from chocolate, or a combination.

In creamy desserts, chocolate's usually best. Some desserts need the silkiness that only cocoa butter can provide. Cocoa butter is an unusual fat because it melts at a temperature very close to our body temperature. Chocolate that's hard and solid at room temperature feels rich on the tongue. In puddings, ganache, and mousses, the luxurious mouth-feel of cocoa butter really shines, so for these desserts, chocolate (yes, the best you can find) is almost always preferable to cocoa powder. That doesn't mean cocoa powder is a no-no for such recipes. In fact, adding a tablespoon or two to puddings or mousses along with the chocolate can boost the flavor without altering how the custard sets up.

In cakes, the choice is more complicated. Cakes made with cocoa and cakes made with chocolate can differ remarkably in flavor and texture. And those differences have a lot to do with the other fats used in the recipe.

Cakes made with cocoa powder and oil are tender and intensely flavored. Consider devil's food cake, for example. Its deep flavor, dark color, and moist texture come from pairing cocoa powder with oil. The flavor is intense because there's no milk or butter to dilute the pure chocolate flavor of the cocoa solids. (My favorite devil's food cake recipe calls for about a third as much cocoa as flour: ¾ cups unsweetened cocoa powder to every

Cocoa: Dutched or Natural?

Recipes that use cocoa often specify either natural or Dutch-process cocoa. Dutch-process cocoa has been treated with alkali, which increases the pH and mellows sharp flavors. You may find that Dutch-process cocoa tastes flat compared to natural cocoa, so it's important to use a good brand. It's best to keep both kinds of cocoa on hand for baking cakes, because the success of recipes that call for one or the other depends on the batter having a specific pH. If you have a strong preference for one type of cocoa, though, it's fine to substitute a portion of it into any recipe, even cakes.

Photos: Scott Phillips

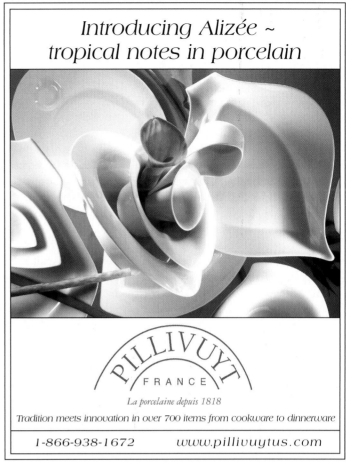

food **science**

2½ cups flour.) And the texture is moist because vegetable oil is liquid at room temperature (and even when cool), unlike butter and cocoa butter, which are solid. You can serve devil's food cake refrigerator-cold, and it will still be exceptionally tender.

Chocolate cake made with chocolate, on the other hand, is temperature-sensitive. If you've ever been served a slice of cold chocolate cake that was dry and crumbly, it may well have been made with chocolate. Remember, cocoa butter is hard even at cool room temperature. The cake's flavor suffers, too, because the cocoa butter is what carries the chocolate flavor, and the colder it is, the longer it takes to melt on your tongue and release the flavor.

This is not to say that cakes made with chocolate are unpleasant; you just need to remember to serve them at room temperature. And, the fact is, the cocoa butter can make for a pleasantly firm cake, especially if the recipe contains at least 4 ounces of unsweetened chocolate—think of a rich Bundt cake with a dense, springy crumb.

In brownies, cocoa yields chewy results, while chocolate gives a fudgy texture. Chocolate lovers can be snobby about brownies, but the fact is that cocoa powder makes for fabulously rich, chewy brownies. Brownies are chewy when they're high in sugar, fat, and eggs but low in flour. The last variable to their final texture is the nature of the fat used in the recipe—specifically how hard the fat is at the temperature the brownies are to be served. Butter is soft at room temperature, so brownies made with cocoa plus butter (or oil) have a noticeably soft, chewy texture. And the flavor is intensely chocolatey with a wonderful lingering buttery flavor. By contrast, brownies made with chocolate plus butter are often firmer, almost fudgy, because cocoa butter is harder than butter at room temperature. The more chocolate the recipe contains, the fudgier the brownies will be.

> A cake made with 4 ounces of unsweetened chocolate should pack the same flavor punch as a cake made with ¾ cup cocoa powder.

Compare hot cocoa and hot chocolate

Here's an easy way to experience the difference between cocoa and chocolate. The first recipe, at right, uses cocoa powder (with milk) and it's plenty chocolatey (front cup). The second recipe is made with chocolate. The cocoa butter makes it taste richer, but the chocolate flavor is more muted at first.

Classic Hot Cocoa
Yields 2⅔ cups; serves three or four.

This is the hot cocoa from my childhood, chocolatey but not rich enough to spoil dinner. I think mini marshmallows are essential, but you can skip them if you wish.

⅓ cup unsweetened natural cocoa powder
3 to 4 Tbs. granulated sugar
Pinch table salt
2½ cups whole milk
Mini marshmallows (optional), for garnish

Put the cocoa powder, sugar, and salt in a medium saucepan. Pour in ¼ cup of the milk and whisk constantly until the mixture is smooth and free of lumps. Pour in the remaining milk and whisk to combine. Set the pan over medium to medium-high heat. Cook, whisking frequently, until hot, 4 to 5 minutes. For best flavor, do not let the cocoa boil. Serve hot, topped with mini marshmallows, if you like.

Rich Hot Chocolate
Yields 3¼ cups; serves four.

This hot chocolate tastes rich enough to be dessert—forget the marshmallows. To vary the flavor, infuse the milk with orange zest or fresh mint leaves before adding the chocolate.

2½ cups whole milk
3 Tbs. granulated sugar (chocolates vary in sugar level, so feel free to add another tablespoon if necessary)
Pinch table salt
3½ oz. bittersweet chocolate, finely chopped (about ¾ cup)

Put the milk, sugar, and salt in a medium saucepan set over medium-high heat. Cook, whisking frequently, until the sugar is melted, about 2 minutes. Continue to cook until the milk nearly reaches a boil, stirring occasionally, about 2 more minutes. Turn off the heat and add the chopped chocolate to the pan. Whisk constantly until the chocolate is melted and the mixture is smooth.

Frequent Fine Cooking *contributor Nicole Rees is a food scientist and baker.* ◆

To really appreciate fine Italian art,
all you have to do is turn on your stove.

The finest Italian Cappuccino at home.

Mukka Express
L'Arte del Cappuccino

BIALETTI
CASA.ITALIA.

Crackers, *p. 44*

Dough scrapers (from $6.99) and pizza cutters or pastry wheels (from $2.90) for cutting the crackers are all available at CooksWares.com (800-915-9788). The site also sells rolling pins ranging in price from $10.99 to $49.99.

Potato Pancakes, *p. 52*

A slotted spatula, like a fish spatula with a curved lip, is the perfect tool for turning potato pancakes. Try one like Wüsthof's, $29.95 at CutleryAndMore.com.

Gingerbread Desserts, *p. 60*

You'll need two 9-inch cake pans to make Julia Usher's Steamed Coriander-Gingerbread Cake; they're available at KingArthurFlour.com (800-827-6836) for $12.95 apiece. The company also carries packages of forty-eight 9-inch parchment rounds ($7.95). If you're looking for a 10x3-inch springform pan for the Ginger-Molasses Cheesecake, try Wilton's version, $13.99 at CandylandCrafts.com (877-487-4289).

Thai Curries, *p. 66*

Visit TempleOfThai.com for dried lime peel and MyThaiMart.com for cilantro root. Both sites sell Thai chiles, Thai basil, and wild lime leaves (look for kaffir lime leaves) along with the ingredients you need to make curry paste from scratch, including fresh galangal, lemongrass, and shrimp paste. You can buy jarred curry paste, coconut milk, and fish sauce at these sites too, but they're also available at well-stocked supermarkets.

Holiday Cookies, *p. 70*

For a heavy-duty 9x13-inch baking pan for the double-decker bar cookies ($21.95), visit KitchenConservatory.com (866-862-2433). Look for Silpat nonstick baking liners ($19.95) and cooling racks (from $15) at ChefsResource.com (866-765-2433). Grade B maple syrup is available at Whole Foods markets and Trader Joe's, or order it from Green Mountain Sugar House (gmsh.com; 800-643-9338) where prices

Wine, *p. 36*

Tim Gaiser recommends sipping sherry from a sherry glass. He likes Riedel's reasonably priced Ouverture sherry glasses made of lead-free crystal. A set of four is available at Amazon.com for $31.68.

Marcona almonds are sold at Whole Foods markets and specialty stores. You can also find them online at Tienda.com (800-710-4304), where a 5-ounce jar is $8.95; or buy them in larger quantities from TheSpanishTable .com ($18.99 for 1.1 pounds).

start at $27.95 per quart. The store also carries 1-pound bags of granulated maple sugar for $8.95.

In Season, *p. 22*

For her leek tart, Ruth Lively calls for an 11-inch fluted tart pan with a removable bottom. Look for one at CooksDream.com (866-285-2665) where they sell for $9.98.

From Our Test Kitchen, *p. 78*

For this issue, we bought liquid egg whites from Eggology.com (888-669-6557). The store locator will point you to a store in your area, or you can purchase in bulk directly from the site. For dried egg white powder ($5.25 for 4 ounces) and meringue powder ($5.50 for 8 ounces), visit KitchenKrafts .com (800-776-0575). The site also carries a wide range of cookie decorating supplies, such as sanding sugars, dragées, and food coloring, as well as cookie cutters and piping (pastry) bags.

For Thai ingredients like curry paste, galangal, lemongrass, and more, see the source under Thai Curries.

Breakfast Basics, *p. 30a*

Cooking.com (800-663-8810) sells several brands of 12-cup muffin pans, starting at $11.95. To scoop muffin batter into the pans, try using two spoons or a #20 ice cream scoop with a "sweeper" that pushes the batter out. To find a similar scoop, go to Instawares.com (800-892-3622) and search for a #20 food disher (from $6.86 to $9.54).

If you're in the market for a new waffle maker, here are a few good options:

❖ Villaware's classic round waffle maker: It performs well and is compact ($59.95 at Williams-Sonoma.com; 877-812-6235).

❖ The Waring restaurant-style Belgian waffle maker: A flip waffler that turns out light, crisp Belgian waffles ($79.95 at SurLaTable.com; 800-243-0852).

❖ Chef's Choice Five-of-Hearts WafflePro: Yes, it's heart shaped, but it makes a very delicious, very crisp waffle very quickly ($49 at ChefsCorner.com; 877-372-4535). ◆

Now...holiday cooking as easy as 1-2-3!

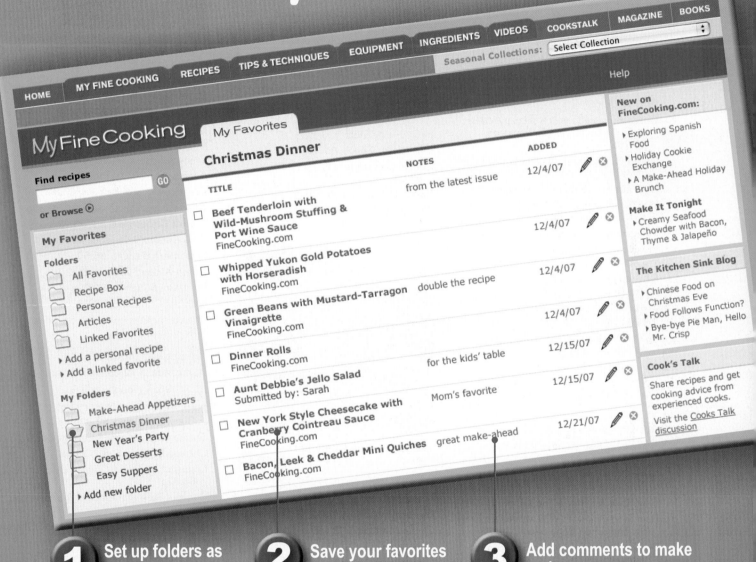

1 Set up folders as you want them.

2 Save your favorites for quick reference.

3 Add comments to make recipes your own.

the New FineCooking.com

Thousands of trusted recipes and reliable cooking advice for stress-free holidays

The Taunton Press
Inspiration for hands-on living®

Recipes, listed by title only, from *Fine Cooking* issues 83–89. For a free printout of the full 2007 index, call customer service at 800-888-8286. For a full searchable index, visit www.finecooking.com.

APPETIZERS

Bacon-Wrapped Stuffed Apricots, 86:39

Farmers' Market Crudités with Buttermilk Herb Dip, 86:26a

Gravlax, 86:66

Grilled Bruschetta with Rosemary-White Bean Purée & Heirloom Tomatoes, 86:26a

Grilled Goat Cheese Crostini with a Tangle of Marinated Roasted Peppers, 87:42

Leek Tart with Bacon & Gruyère, 89:23

Mini Tuna Burgers with Mint-Caper Aïoli on Pita Triangles, 86:38

Pancetta & Pineapple Skewers, 86:38

Prosciutto-Wrapped Melon with Mint & White Balsamic Vinegar, 86:64

Roasted Red Pepper & Walnut Dip with Pomegranate Molasses, 85:75

Seeded Crackers, 89:45

Shrimp Skewers, 86:37

Smoky Eggplant & White Bean Dip with Pita Crisps, 83:82a

Tomato & Olive Pizzettas with Fennel Seeds & Aged Goat Cheese, 86:39

Wild Mushroom Toasts, 85:40

BEEF, VEAL & LAMB

Argentine Spice-Rubbed Flank Steak with Salsa Criolla, 86:26a

Asian-Style Beef Barbecue in Lettuce Packages, 84:78a

Beef Stew with Red Wine & Carrots, 84:39

Beef Tenderloin with Wild Mushroom Stuffing & Port Wine Sauce, 89:50

Braised Lamb Shanks with Garlic & Vermouth, 84:35

Broiled Lamb Skewers with Baby Arugula & Lemon Vinaigrette, 85:84a

Chili-Rubbed Rib-Eye Steak with Corn & Green Chile Ragoût, 87:78a

Fennel & Rosemary Beef Tenderloin with Creamy Mustard Sauce, 89:102a

Grilled Flank Steak with Sesame Sauce & Grilled Scallions, 87:53

Grilled Herb-Crusted Leg of Lamb with Fresh Mint Sauce, 86:26a

Lamb Chops with Lemon, Thyme & Mustard Butter, 84:78a

Lamb Shank & Sweet Pepper Ragù, 83:61

Middle Eastern Style Lamb Pita "Pizza," 84:68

Rack of Lamb with Ancho-Honey Glaze, 89:102a

Red Country-Style Curry with Beef, Shiitakes & Edamame, 89:67

Short Rib & Porcini Mushroom Ragù, 83:60

Spicy Beef with Peanuts & Chiles, 88:98a

Steak Adobo, 87:46

Steak, Egg & Blue Cheese Salad, 83:82a

Steak & Eggs Rancheros, 86:68

Steak with Red Onion, Wine & Port Sauce, 87:45

Steak with Three-Chile Sauce, 87:47

Stir-Fried Noodles with Beef & Vegetables, 88:98a

BEVERAGES

Classic Hot Cocoa, 89:88

Double-Chocolate Malted Milk Shake, 87:66

Rich Hot Chocolate, 89:88

Strawberry-Orange-Vanilla Breakfast Smoothie, 88:84

Grilled Garlic Bread, 87:41

BREADS & SANDWICHES

Apple-Butter Cinnamon Buns, 88:72

Blueberry Muffins, 89:30a

Caramelized Onion Biscuits, 85:50

Cheese Biscuits, 85:50

Cinnamon-Rhubarb Muffins, 85:63

Cream Shortcake Biscuits, 87:61

Farmers' Market Quesadillas, 87:78a

Fastest Cinnamon Buns, 88:72

Flaky Buttermilk Biscuits, 85:49

Fresh Herb Biscuits, 85:50

Grilled Garlic Bread, 87:41

Grilled Goat Cheese Crostini with a Tangle of Marinated Roasted Peppers, 87:42

Grilled Portabella Sandwiches with Tomatoes, Mozzarella & Basil, 86:78a

Quesadillas with Roasted Poblanos & Onions (Rajas), 86:21

Smoky Black Bean & Cheddar Burrito with Baby Spinach, 85:84a

Fastest Cinnamon Buns, 88:72

BREAKFAST

Apple-Butter Cinnamon Buns, 88:72

Basic Buttermilk Pancakes, 89:30a

Blueberry Muffins, 89:30a

Caramelized Onion Biscuits, 85:50

Cheese Biscuits, 85:50

Cinnamon-Rhubarb Muffins, 85:63

Classic Hot Cocoa, 89:88

Cream Shortcake Biscuits, 87:61

Crispy Sweet Pecan Granola, 89:30a

Fastest Cinnamon Buns, 88:72

Flaky Buttermilk Biscuits, 85:49

Fresh Herb Biscuits, 85:50

Honey-Almond Granola, 89:30a

Light, Crisp Waffles, 89:30a

Rich Hot Chocolate, 89:88

Strawberry-Orange-Vanilla Breakfast Smoothie, 88:84

Sweet Potato & Chile Hash with a Fried Egg, 89:30a

CHICKEN, DUCK & TURKEY

Buttermilk Country Fried Chicken with Cucumber Salad, 83:82a

Chicken with Vinegar & Onions, 84:37

Chinese Chicken Salad, 86:58

Chinese Five-Spice-Crusted Duck Breasts, 83:82a

Coconut Rice with Chicken & Snow Peas, 83:40

Crispy Cheddar & Jalapeño Coated Chicken Breasts, 84:51

Crispy Chicken Breasts with Lemon & Capers, 84:50

Crispy Orange-Sesame Chicken Breasts, 84:52

Green Curry with Chicken & Eggplant, 89:69

Grilled Five-Spice Chicken Thighs with Soy-Vinegar Sauce & Cilantro, 87:31

Grilled Rosemary Chicken Thighs with Sweet & Sour Orange Dipping Sauce, 87:32

Grilled Tandoori-Style Chicken Thighs, 87:33

Grilled Thai Chicken Breasts with Herb-Lemongrass Crust, 86:26a

Herb-Butter Roasted Turkey with Pinot Noir Gravy, 88:48

Herbed Chicken Breasts with a Crispy Black Olive & Parmigiano Crust, 84:52

Indonesian Grilled Chicken Thighs with Mango-Peanut Salsa, 87:33

Jerk Chicken Drumsticks, 84:78a

Lemony Chicken Caesar Salad with Garlic-Parmesan Toasts, 83:42

Lime Chicken with Poblano Sour Cream, 84:78a

Orange Chicken with Scallions, 88:98a

Roast Chicken with Rosemary-Lemon Salt, 83:39

Roasted Chicken Legs with Lemon & Green Olives, 89:102a

Roasted Chicken Thighs with Late-Summer Vegetables & Pan Sauce, 87:78a

Roasted Cornish Game Hens with Wildflower Honey & Orange, 85:42

Sesame Chicken with Ginger & Snow Peas, 88:98a

Soft Chicken Tacos with the Works, 83:42

Spicy Fried Chicken, 86:78a

Spinach Salad with Chicken, Cashews, Ginger & Fried Wontons, 88:65

Turkey & Sweet Potato Hash, 88:86

Steak & Eggs Rancheros, 86:68

EGGS

Egg Salad with Smoked Salmon, Capers & Dill, 86:78a

Frittata with Asparagus, Herbs & Scallions, 83:62

Frittata with Kale, Onions & Chorizo, 83:62

Frittata with Mushrooms, Leeks & Goat Cheese, 83:62

Frittata with Potatoes, Onions & Pancetta, 83:62

Frittata with Sausage, Mushrooms & Onions, 83:62

Garlic & Herb Fried Eggs on Toasts with Prosciutto Crisps, 85:84a

Steak, Egg & Blue Cheese Salad, 83:82a

Steak & Eggs Rancheros, 86:68

Sweet Potato & Chile Hash with a Fried Egg, 89:30a

Sear-Roasted Halibut with Roasted Red Pepper Purée, 85:84a

FISH & SHELLFISH

Angel Hair Pasta with Sautéed Cherry Tomatoes, Lemon & Tuna, 87:78a

Braised Cod with Fennel, Potatoes & Littlenecks, 84:61

Braised Red Snapper Puttanesca, 84:59

Colossal Shrimp with Watercress & Tomato Salad, 84:78a

Curried Coconut Shrimp, 88:98a

Gravlax, 86:66

Grilled Corn, Shrimp & Chorizo Salad, 87:43

Grilled Fish Steaks, 86:41

Grilled Salmon Bundles with Saffron, Tomatoes & Olives, 86:78a

Hot Garlicky Shrimp with Asparagus & Lemon, 85:59

Linguine with Clam Sauce, 88:69

Linguine with Shrimp & Chorizo, 83:82a

Mini Tuna Burgers with Mint-Caper Aïoli on Pita Triangles, 86:38

Orange-Roasted Salmon with Yogurt-Caper Sauce, 89:102a

Red Curry with Shrimp & Sugar Snap Peas, 89:68

Roasted Cod with Lemon-Parsley Crumbs, 89:102a

Salmon Braised in Pinot Noir, 84:60

Sear-Roasted Halibut with Roasted Red Pepper Purée, 85:84a

Seared Tuna with Fennel Seeds & Caper Brown Butter, 83:82a

Shrimp Skewers, 86:37

Shrimp with Fennel, Tomato & Pernod Sauce, 85:58

Spicy Seared Chipotle Shrimp with Zucchini & Chorizo, 85:57

Summer Bouillabaisse with Smoky Rouille, 87:78a

Thai Seafood Salad, 87:57

Tuna Teriyaki with Scallion Salad, 84:78a

LIGHT MAIN DISHES

Classic Potato Pancakes (Latkes), 89:53

Corn Sauté with Canadian Bacon, Potatoes & Peppers, 87: back cover

Farmers' Market Quesadillas, 87:78a

Feta & Dill Galette with Lemony Spinach Salad, 87:78a

Garlic Crostini with Spinach, Mushroom & Parmigiano Salad, 88:66

Leek Tart with Bacon & Gruyère, 89:23

Potato Pancakes Stuffed with Duxelles, 89:54

Seared Baby Bok Choy with Tofu & Shiitakes, 88:98a

Spinach Salad with Apples, Dried Apricots & Pappadam Croutons, 88:66

Spinach Salad with Chicken, Cashews, Ginger & Fried Wontons, 88:65

Sweet Potato & Chile Hash with a Fried Egg, 89:30a

Thai Seafood Salad, 87:57

Warm French Lentil Salad with Smoked Sausage, 84:back cover

Warm Spinach Salad with Eggs, Bacon & Croutons, 88:67

PASTA & PASTA SAUCES

Angel Hair Pasta with Sautéed Cherry Tomatoes, Lemon & Tuna, 87:78a

Baked Fettucine with Asparagus, Lemon, Pine Nuts & Mascarpone, 84:26a

Baked Rigatoni with Cauliflower in a Spicy Pink Sauce, 84:26a

Baked Ziti with Tomato, Mozzarella & Sausage, 84:26a

Campanelle with Broccoli Raab, Sausage & Olives, 84:26a

Cavatappi with Roasted Peppers, Capocollo & Ricotta, 84:26a

Classic Macaroni & Cheese, 84:26a

Create-Your-Own Pasta Salad with Grilled Eggplant, 87:67

Lamb Shank & Sweet Pepper Ragù, 83:61

Linguine with Clam Sauce, 88:69

Linguine with Shrimp & Chorizo, 83:82a

Neapolitan Rib & Sausage Ragù, 83:59

No-Cook Tomato Sauce, 87:39

No-Cook Tomato Sauce with Basil Pesto, 87:39

No-Cook Tomato Sauce with Cheese, 87:39

No-Cook Tomato Sauce with Tapenade, 87:39

Orecchiette with Caramelized Onions, Green Beans, Fresh Corn & Jalapeño, 86:45

Orzo & Grilled Vegetable Salad with Feta, Olives & Oregano, 86:78a

Pan-Fried Gnocchi with Bacon, Onions & Peas, 85:84a

Penne with Asparagus, Olives & Parmigiano Breadcrumbs, 85:84a

Rigatoni with Summer Squash, Spicy Sausage & Goat Cheese, 86:44

Short Rib & Porcini Mushroom Ragù, 83:60

Spaghetti with Portabellas, Sage & Walnuts, 84:26a

Spaghetti with Spicy Shrimp, Cherry Tomatoes & Herbed Breadcrumbs, 86:44

Warm Pasta Salad with Grilled Tomatoes, Zucchini & Pecorino, 86:26a

PORK & SAUSAGES

Crown Roast of Pork with Fennel-Apple Stuffing & Cider-Bourbon Sauce, 89:48

Deviled Pork Chops, 84:78a

Fried Ham with Redeye Gravy, 85:76

Frittata with Kale, Onions & Chorizo, 83:62

Frittata with Sausage, Mushrooms & Onions, 83:62

Grilled Asian Pork Tenderloin with Peanut Sauce, 86:78a

Grilled Corn, Shrimp & Chorizo Salad, 87:43

Hoisin Pork with Napa Cabbage, 88:98a

Linguine with Shrimp & Chorizo, 83:82a

Neapolitan Rib & Sausage Ragù, 83:59

Oven-Glazed Ham with Cherry-Pomegranate Glaze & Sauce, 85:47

Oven-Glazed Ham with Maple, Tea & Cardamom Glaze & Sauce, 85:47

Oven-Glazed Ham with Tangerine Marmalade Glaze & Sauce, 85:47

Pork Lo Mein with Seared Scallions & Shiitakes, 87:54

Pork Tenderloin with Sage & Marsala Sauce, 88:26

Roasted Sausages & Grapes, 89:102a

Spice-Crusted Roast Pork Tenderloin, 89:102a

Warm French Lentil Salad with Smoked Sausage, 84:back cover

RICE & NOODLES

Arroz Verde (Green Rice), 89:10

Coconut Rice with Chicken & Snow Peas, 83:40

Rice Pilaf with Sage, Parmigiano & Prosciutto, 84:44

Rice Pilaf with Spiced Caramelized Onions, Orange, Cherry & Pistachio, 84:42

Saffron Rice Pilaf with Red Pepper & Toasted Almonds, 84:41

Southwestern Rice Pilaf, 84:43

Stir-Fried Noodles with Beef & Vegetables, 88:98a

SALADS

Arugula & Fennel Salad with Orange & Fennel Seed Dressing & Toasted Hazelnuts, 86:50

Arugula Salad with Pears, Prosciutto & Aged Gouda, 87:78a

Butter Lettuce with Poppy Seed & Tarragon Crème Fraîche Dressing, 86:48

Carrot Salad with Walnut Oil & Honey, 85:54

Chinese Chicken Salad, 86:58

Chopped Tomato & Cucumber Salad with Mint & Feta, 86:26a

Colossal Shrimp with Watercress & Tomato Salad, 84:78a

Create-Your-Own Pasta Salad with Grilled Eggplant, 87:67

Egg Salad with Smoked Salmon, Capers & Dill, 86:78a

Feta & Dill Galette with Lemony Spinach Salad, 87:78a

Garden Lettuces with Garlic Chapons, 85:41

Garlic Crostini with Spinach, Mushroom & Parmigiano Salad, 88:66

Grilled Corn, Shrimp & Chorizo Salad, 87:43

Grilled Southwestern Potato Salad, 86:26a

Lemony Chicken Caesar Salad with Garlic-Parmesan Toasts, 83:42

Mâche with Spicy Melon & Pink-Peppercorn Dressing, 86:51

Mixed Green Salad with Red-Wine & Dijon Vinaigrette, 86:47

Orzo & Grilled Vegetable Salad with Feta, Olives & Oregano, 86:78a

Spinach Salad with Apples, Dried Apricots & Pappadam Croutons, 88:66

Spinach Salad with Chicken, Cashews, Ginger & Fried Wontons, 88:65

Steak, Egg & Blue Cheese Salad, 83:82a

Thai Seafood Salad, 87:57

Tuna Teriyaki with Scallion Salad, 84:78a

Warm French Lentil Salad with Smoked Sausage, 84:back cover

Warm Pasta Salad with Grilled Tomatoes, Zucchini & Pecorino, 86:26a

Warm Spinach Salad with Eggs, Bacon & Croutons, 88:67

SEASONINGS, CONDIMENTS, DRESSINGS & SAUCES

Baby Carrots Pickled in Champagne & Sherry Vinegars, 85:54

Basic Vinaigrette, 87:67

Caramelized Shallot Butter, 88:57

Cranberry Sauce with Vanilla, Maple Syrup & Cassis, 88:52

Duxelles, 89:54

Eggnog Crème Anglaise, 89:63

Garam Masala, 83:70

Garlic-Cumin Vinaigrette with Feta & Herbs, 87:51

Ginger-Lemon-Soy Splash, 88:57

Green Curry Paste, 89:83

Homemade Crema (Mexican Sour Cream), 84:70

Honey-Mustard Sherry Vinaigrette, 83:72

Lemon, Dill & Cucumber Sauce, 86:42

Moroccan-Style Spice Rub, 88:56

Olive, Orange & Anchovy Vinaigrette, 87:50

Pickled Cauliflower with Carrots & Red Bell Pepper, 87:64

Pimentón Vinaigrette, 86:37

Red Curry Paste, 89:83

Rhubarb & Dried-Cherry Chutney, 85:11

Roasted Red Pepper Relish with Pine Nuts, Currants & Marjoram, 87:51

Rosemary-Thyme-Lemon Oil, 88:56

Sea Salt, Chile & Lime Butter, 86:42

Sesame Salt, 88:57

Spiced Pickled Beets, 87:65

Sun-Dried Tomato, Olive & Caper Relish, 86:42

Tarragon-Scented Mayonnaise with Cornichons & Capers, 86:42

Three-Herb Butter, 88:47

Toasted Breadcrumbs, 84:48

Toasted-Breadcrumb Salsa Verde, 87:50

Toasted Garlic & Coriander Oil, 88:57

Browned Cauliflower with Anchovies, Olives & Capers, 83:21

SIDE DISHES

Basic Roasted Vegetables, 88:54

Braised Bok Choy with Sherry & Prosciutto, 84:54

Broccoli with Eggs & Lemony Parmesan Breadcrumbs, 88:51

Browned Cauliflower with Anchovies, Olives & Capers, 83:21

Brussels Sprouts Braised with Pancetta, Shallot, Thyme & Lemon, 89:59

Cabbage & Carrot Stir-Fry with Toasted Cumin & Lime, 83:47

Carrot Salad with Walnut Oil & Honey, 85:54

Chopped Tomato & Cucumber Salad with Mint & Feta, 86:26a

Classic Mashed Potatoes, 88:52

Classic Potato Pancakes (Latkes), 89:53

Corn & Mushroom Sauté with Leeks & Pancetta, 87:37

Corn Sauté with Canadian Bacon, Potatoes & Peppers, 87:back cover

Corn Sauté with Ginger, Garlic & Fresh Cilantro, 87:37

Corn, Sweet Onion & Zucchini Sauté with Fresh Mint, 87:36

Create-Your-Own Pasta Salad with Grilled Eggplant, 87:67

Crispy Smashed Roasted Potatoes, 83:45

Green Bean Stir-Fry with Shredded Coconut, 83:49

Grilled Asparagus & Onions with Balsamic Vinegar & Blue Cheese, 86:26a

Grilled Corn on the Cob with Thyme & Roasted Red Pepper Butter, 86:26a

Grilled Eggplant, 87:49

Grilled Eggplant with Garlic-Cumin Vinaigrette with Feta & Herbs, 87:51

Grilled Eggplant with Olive, Orange & Anchovy Vinaigrette, 87:50

Grilled Eggplant with Roasted Red Pepper Relish with Pine Nuts, Currants & Marjoram, 87:51

Grilled Eggplant with Toasted-Breadcrumb Salsa Verde, 87:50

Grilled Southwestern Potato Salad, 86:26a

Ham Bone Collards, 85:76

Maple Pan-Roasted Baby Carrots, 85:53

Mushroom Stir-Fry with Onions & Tomatoes, 83:48

New Potatoes with Butter, Shallots & Chervil, 85:42

Orzo & Grilled Vegetable Salad with Feta, Olives & Oregano, 86:78a

Pan-Seared Artichokes with Sherry Vinegar & Thyme, 85:19

Potato Pancakes Stuffed With Duxelles, 89:54

Potato Stir-Fry with Mint & Cilantro, 83:49

Rice Pilaf with Sage, Parmigiano & Prosciutto, 84:44

Rice Pilaf with Spiced Caramelized Onions, Orange, Cherry & Pistachio, 84:42

Roasted Asparagus with Lemon & Olive Oil, 85:42

Roasted Brussels Sprouts with Dijon, Walnuts & Crisp Crumbs, 89:57

Roasted Eggplant with Chiles, Peanuts & Mint, 84:55

Roasted Parsnips with Cinnamon & Coriander, 84:19

Saffron Rice Pilaf with Red Pepper & Toasted Almonds, 84:41

Sausage-Maple Bread Stuffing, 88:50

Sautéed Shredded Brussels Sprouts with Fresh Herbs & Crisp Shallots, 89:58

Southwestern Rice Pilaf, 84:43

Stir-Fried Cauliflower with Green Peas & Ginger, 83:back cover

Stir-Fried Napa Cabbage with Garlic, Fresh Chile & Basil, 84:56

Stir-Fried Snow Peas with Shiitakes & Ginger, 84:57

Sweet Potato Gratin with Caramelized Onions, 88:50

Warm French Lentil Salad with Smoked Sausage, 84:back cover

Warm Pasta Salad with Grilled Tomatoes, Zucchini & Pecorino, 86:26a

SOUPS, STEWS, & STOCKS

Cabbage and White Bean Soup, 88:74

Curried Lentil Soup, 83:82a

French Farmers' Soup, 88:74

Ginger Chicken Soup, 85:84a

Green Gazpacho, 87:19

Mexican Black Bean Soup, 88:74

Middle-Eastern Chickpea Soup, 88:74

Minestrone, 88:74

Summer Bouillabaisse with Smoky Rouille, 87:78a

Summer Corn Chowder with Scallions, Bacon & Potatoes, 87:55

Tomatillo Gazpacho, 86:78a

Turkey Broth, 88:47

Tuscan Peasant Soup with Rosemary & Pancetta, 83:10

Velvety Carrot Soup with Ginger, 85:55

Desserts & Pastry

Classic Crème Brûlée, 84:46

Chocolate Espresso Pecan Pie, 88:62

Balsamic-Macerated Strawberries with Basil, 86:back cover

Cakes

Bourbon-Glazed Brown Sugar Pecan Pound Cake, 88:62

Brandy & Rum Glazed Pound Cake, 83:68

Butter Pound Cake, 83:67

Chocolate Chip Pound Cake, 83:69

Ginger-Molasses Cheesecake, 89:65

Lemon-Coconut Pound Cake, 83:69

Pecan Pineapple Upside-Down Cake, 88:60

Steamed Coriander-Gingerbread Cake with Eggnog Crème Anglaise, 89:62

Cookies & Squares

Bourbon Balls, 89:80

Cardamom-Honey Cutouts, 89:72

Dark Chocolate Crackles, 89:71

Fried Chocolate-Hazelnut Wontons with Orange Dipping Sauce, 84:65

Ginger-Spiced Slice & Bake Cookies, 89:74

Lemon Cheesecake Squares, 86:53

Macadamia Double-Decker Brownie Bars, 89:75

Maple-Walnut Tuiles, 89:76

Peanut Butter & Chocolate Sandwiches, 89:77

Rugelach, 89:73

Vanilla Slice & Bake Cookies, 89:74

Crisps, Crumbles & Cobblers

Apple Crisp with Pecans & Orange, 88:61

Gingerbread-Pear Cobbler, 89:61

Plum Cobbler with Almonds, Lemon Zest & Ginger, 86:61

Raspberry-Peach Cobbler with Cornmeal Biscuits, 86:61

Rhubarb Brown Sugar Crumble, 85:63

Triple Berry Cobbler with Pecans & Cinnamon, 86:61

Custards, Mousses & Ice Cream

Bourbon-Chocolate Mousse, 85:back cover

Classic Crème Brûlée, 84:46

Ginger-Spice Ice Cream, 89:64

Phyllo "Chips" with Vanilla Ice Cream & Strawberry Mash "Dip," 84:63

Vanilla Ice Cream with Espresso-Caramel Sauce, 85:43

Fruit Desserts

Balsamic-Macerated Strawberries with Basil, 86:back cover

Marinated Peaches, 87:59

Peaches & Cream Dessert, 87:59

Peaches & Cream Parfait, 87:60

Peaches & Cream Shortcakes, 87:61

Pies & Tarts

Apple Brown-Butter Jalousie, 83:56

Chocolate Espresso Pecan Pie, 88:62

Free-Form Pear Tarts with Almond & Cinnamon, 84:64

Mixed-Berry Jalousie, 83:56

Strawberry-Rhubarb Pie, 85:62

Fillings, Compotes & Icings

Honey Whipped Cream, 87:59

Lemon Curd, 86:53

Royal Icing, 89:85

Strawberry-Rhubarb Compote with Vanilla & Cardamom, 85:61 ◆

Messermeister *p.79* Messermeister markets one of the most extensive selections of innovative cutlery and related accessories for the professional and home chef.
www.messermeister.com

Norton Professional Sharpening *p.7* Norton, the leading worldwide manufacturer of professional culinary sharpening stones for over a century, offers cutlery sharpening kits for home cooks that are easy to use and store.
800-848-7379
www.nortonstones.com

Solicut *p.21* Founded nearly 60 years ago in Solingen, Germany-Solicut is an award winning manufacturer of hand finished, drop-forged knives sold in 25 countries around the world.
www.solicut.com

Gifts

Bialetti Casa Italia *p.89* Italian Stovetop Coffeemakers and Cookware. Made in Italy. Visit our website to Purchase our Products Online or for Retailer Information.
www.bialetti.com

Earthy Delights *p.101* The food lover's source for wild mushrooms, truffles, aged Balsamic Vinegar, fine culinary oils, exotic ingredients and a wide selection of Specialty Food Gifts.
www.earthy.com

Gourmet Foods

Avocado of the Month Club *p.100* Your online source for gourmet avocados you won't find in grocery stores. Delicious premium avocados delivered straight to your front door—order today!
805-277-7452
www.aotmc.com

Earthy Delights *p.101* The food lover's source for wild mushrooms, truffles, aged Balsamic Vinegar, fine culinary oils, exotic ingredients and a wide selection of Specialty Food Gifts.
www.earthy.com

Ghirardelli Chocolate Co. *p.103* Ghirardelli's Premium Chocolate is made from the finest cocoa beans and pure ingredients blended to create a smooth, creamy texture and deep, intense chocolate taste.
www.ghirardelli.com

Grannys Kettle Korn *p.101* Like nothing you've ever tasted. A delicious and wholesome gift for Holidays, Birthdays or any occasion. Popped the day of shipment to insure freshness.
www.grannyskorn.com

Illy Espresso USA, Inc. *p.19* Full selection of expertly roasted coffee, home-delivery coffee subscription programs, artist cup collections, and exceptional accessories and gifts. Free shipping on coffee orders over $50.
www.illyusa.com/pfcn7

John Wm. Macy's Cheesesticks *p.81* Enrich any occasion with our all-natural sourdough CheeseSticks, CheeseCrisps and SweetSticks, made with fine aged cheeses and choice seasonings, then baked twice to "the perfect crunch!"
www.cheesesticks.com

La Tienda *p.101* A window to the best of Spain. America's most comprehensive inventory of quality Spanish food selected by a knowledgeable and dedicated family. Immediate delivery.
800-828-1005
www.tienda.com

Ladd Hill Orchards *p.100* Premium, Oregon-grown fresh or dried chestnuts and chestnut flour Gluten free. Certified organic by guaranteed organic certification agency.
www.laddhillchestnuts.com

Millie's Pierogi *p.101* Handmade pierogi, made fresh and shipped fresh to your door! Cabbage, potato-cheese, cheese, prune, or blueberry fillings.
www.milliespierogi.com

Sunnyland Farms *p.101* The widest selection of top-quality nuts, dried fruits, and other specialty foods for creating delicacies at home or for giving to friends.
www.sunnylandfarms.com

Trenton Bridge Lobster Pound *p.100* Your one-stop shopping for the freshest lobster, clams, and other shellfish shipped overnight to your door.
www.trentonbridgelobster.com

Upton Tea Imports *p.101* Visit our Web site to order or request a copy of our extensive catalog, listing tea accessories and over 380 varieties of garden-fresh, loose tea.
800-234-8327
www.uptontea.com

Ingredients

CTL Foods, Inc. *p.21* Your on-line source for the same premium malted milk powder, previously only available to restaurants and frozen treat establishments. Available in 1 lb, 2 1/2 lbs, 15 lbs or 50 lbs sizes.
www.ctlcolfax.com

Colavita USA *p.39* Extra-virgin olive oil unmatched for flavor and freshness, vinegars, pastas, and sauces. Colavita's authentic Italian products are available at food stores everywhere and visit our web site, where Fine Cooking readers receive a 10% discount with the code
www.colavita.com

Magic Seasoning Blends *p.21* Chef Paul Prudhomme's all-natural magic seasoning blends, sauces and marinades, pepper sauce, smoked meats, cookbooks, gift packs, sweet potato pecan pie, and much more!
800-457-2857
www.chefpaul.com

Rafal Spice Co. *p.100* All the spices, herbs, teas, coffees, and food specialties you'll need for all your special and everyday recipes! Order now and be prepared.
800-228-4276
www.rafalspicecompany.com

Rodelle *p.96* Rodelle Vanilla has been used by professional bakers for 70 years. We use only the highest quality ingredients to ensure the excellence of Rodelle Vanilla.
www.rodellevanilla.com

San Francisco Herb Co. *p.100* We are an importer offering a complete line of quality spices and culinary herbs and teas sold by the pound. Buy direct and save. Since 1973.
800-227-4530
www.sfherb.com

The Spice Hunter *p.33* With over 140 herbs and spices, The Spice Hunter will provide you plenty of inspiration to create. For recipes and more, please visit our website.
www.spicehunter.com

Sugarcraft, Inc. *p.101* Sugarcraft Inc., Hamilton, Ohio. We carry baking, cake decorating, candy, and cookie supplies, etc. We import specialty items!
www.sugarcraft.com

Kitchen Design & Tableware

The Bowl Mill *p.13* One-piece hardwood bowls made on 19th-century lathes in Vermont, ranging from 8" to 20" in diameter featuring maple, yellow birch, and cherry.
www.bowlmill.com

Plum Pudding Kitchen *p.31* Your online source for "irresistibly Italian" Vietri dinnerware, flatware, glassware, and much more. Let us help you set a special table!
888-940-7586
www.plumpuddingkitchen.com

Poggi Bonsi *p.35* Direct importers of artisan Italian ceramics, olive wood utensils and cutting boards, and Umbrian kitchen towels.
www.poggibonsigifts.com

Replacements, Ltd. *p.101* World's largest inventory: old and new china, crystal, sterling, silver-plate, and stainless. All manufacturers, fine and casual. 10 million pieces, 200,000 patterns. Buy and sell.
800-REPLACE
www.replacements.com

Totally Bamboo *p.101* Featuring over 150 products, Totally Bamboo is the industry pioneer of bamboo cutting boards and kitchen design. Order all of our fine products directly online!
www.totallybamboo.com

Kitchen Tools & Utensils

Bella Copper *p.100* The world's leading heat diffuser/defroster plate provides superior heat conduction for more even cooking and faster defrosting. Available in solid copper or pure silver. A gourmet kitchen essential.
805-215-3241
www.bellacopper.com

Chef Tools.com *p.87* "Let's get you cooking" is our motto, and we mean it. If we don't have it, ask and we'll get it! Walter Kraus, owner.
www.cheftools.com

Component Design Northwest *p.35* CDN offers more than 60 different cooking thermometers and timers for the casual or gourmet chef. Find CDN products at gourmet specialty stores or online.
800-338-5594
www.cdn-timeandtemp.com

DeBuyer Industries *p.96* French manufacturer since 1830, de Buyer offers professional high-quality cooking and pastry utensils for lovers of flavor and gastronomy.
www.debuyer.com

Gel Pro *p.29* STAND IN COMFORT! Let's Gel was started with one simple goal, to make the time you spend standing in your kitchen more comfortable.
866-GEL-MATS
www.gelmats.com

Helen's Asian Kitchen *p.7* Since 1957, Harold Import Company has been a leading supplier of kitchenware products to the specialty retail trade, offering almost 3000 items. Our products are available in thousands of stores worldwide. What can HIC offer your business?
www.helensasiankitchen.com

House On the Hill *p.100* Over 400 molds for springerle, speculaas, gingerbread, marzipan, fondant and cake decorating. Order now for holiday cookie baking. Catalog on request.
www.houseonthehill.net

J.K. Adams Company *p.15* J.K. Adams, has been the premiere Vermont manufacturer of handcrafted, heirloom-quality, woodware for the kitchen and table since 1944.
www.jkadams.com

Kerekes *p.100* Your complete online source for professional chef's tools, cookware, bakeware, and cake decorating supplies used by top chefs at the finest restaurants and kitchens.
www.bakedeco.com

Kitchen Resource *p.37* Kitchen Resource exclusive brand distributor of innovative, high quality small appliances, cookware, bakeware and gadgets from Bosch, B/R/K, Cloer, L'Equip and LURCH.
www.kitchenresource.com

Messermeister *p.79* Messermeister markets one of the most extensive selections of innovative cutlery and related accessories for the professional and home chef.
www.messermeister.com

Polder Home Tools *p.101* Polder makes products for everyday use with a focus on innovation and exclusive features. For 31 years we have shown home chefs 'where life meets style'.
www.polder.com

SealSaver *p.29* SealSaver is an innovative food storage system that preserves the freshness of foods up to five times longer than conventional storage methods. Easy and convenient!
www.sealsaverfood.com

Schools, Travel & Organizations

Culinary Business Academy *p.13* Extensive and comprehensive personal chef business knowledge and training from the world's recognized leader in the personal chef industry. Nobody offers what we offer.
800-747-2433
www.culinarybusiness.com

Le Cordon Bleu *p.31* Master the culinary arts. Earn the Grand Diplome in approximately nine months. Three- to five-week intensive courses and online hospitality programs are also available.
800-457-2433
www.cordonbleu.edu

The Osthoff Resort *p.101* Professional French style cooking school for the home chef offering one-day, weekend, and five-day courses immersing participants in the ambiance of a French culinary school.
www.osthoff.com

Zingerman's Bakehouse *p.101* Long known for their full flavored, traditionally-made breads, and pastries, Zingerman's Bakehouse now offers BAKE!; a hands-on teaching bakery in Ann Arbor.
www.zingermansbakehouse.com

Wines, Beverages & Accessories

The California Wine Club *p.11* A true California wine adventure. Award-winning wines from California's best artisan wineries since 1990. A fun and unique gift.
www.cawineclub.com

Covington Cellars *p.101* Award winning boutique Washington winery offers wine samples of our limited production wines that sell out fast! An excellent addition to any cellar!
www.covingtoncellars.com

Johnson Estate Winery *p.41* The Oldest Estate Winery in New York. We grow 12 different varieties of grapes on 200 acres. Wines including classis vinifera and American Heirloom wines as well we port, sherry, and ice wines. Open 10am-6pm daily.
www.johnsonwinery.com

Woodbridge Winery *p.3* For 25 years, we have aged our wines in small oak barrels and handcrafted each vintage. Woodbridge: Taste our small winery tradition™.
www.woodbridgewines.com

cook's market

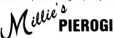

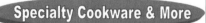

 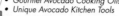 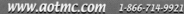

Recipe	Page	Calories total	from fat	Protein (g)	Carb (g)	Fats total	sat	mono	poly	Chol. (mg)	Sodium (mg)	Fiber (g)	Notes
Letters	10												
Arroz Verde (Green Rice)		210	70	4	30	8	4	3	1	15	320	1	based on 8 servings
In Season	22												
Leek Tart with Bacon & Gruyère		270	170	7	20	19	11	5	1	85	200	1	based on 12 servings
Breakfast Basics	30a												
Light, Crisp Waffles		290	160	5	25	18	3	4	10	45	380	1	per waffle
Honey-Almond Granola		290	150	8	30	17	1.5	9	6	0	90	4	per ½ cup
Crispy Sweet Pecan Granola		230	110	4	29	12	1	7	3.5	0	65	4	per ½ cup
Sweet Potato & Chile Hash w/ a Fried Egg		430	300	9	28	33	6	16	10	225	970	4	based on 6 servings
Buttermilk Pancakes		140	35	5	21	4	2	1	0.5	40	260	1	per pancake
Blueberry Muffins		410	170	7	54	19	12	5	1	95	320	1	per muffin
Crackers	44												
Seeded Crackers		30	10	1	4	1	0	1	0	0	75	0	per cracker
Rosemary & Sea Salt Crackers		30	10	1	4	1	0	0.5	0	0	90	0	per cracker
Roasts	46												
Crown Roast of Pork w/ Fennel-Apple Stuffing		580	200	42	34	22	9	9	2	105	880	4	based on 14 servings
Beef Tenderloin w/ Wild Mushroom Stuffing		530	210	41	16	24	9	9	2	140	640	1	based on 10 servings
Potato Pancakes	52												
Classic Potato Pancakes (Latkes)		130	80	1	12	9	1.5	2.5	5	10	170	1	based on 20 servings
Potato Pancakes Stuffed w/ Duxelles		160	100	2	13	12	2.5	3	5	15	210	1	based on 10 servings
Brussels Sprouts	56												
Roasted Brussels Sprouts w/ Brown Butter & Lemon		170	130	4	10	15	6	7	1	20	170	4	based on 6 servings
Brussels Sprouts Braised w/ Pancetta, Shallot & Thyme		140	80	7	12	8	3	4	1	15	460	4	based on 8 servings
Roasted Brussels Sprouts w/ Dijon & Walnuts		200	130	5	14	15	2.5	7	4.5	5	270	5	based on 8 servings
Sautéed Shredded Brussels Sprouts w/ Crisp Shallots		140	80	5	14	9	2	3.5	3	5	270	4	based on 6 servings
Gingerbread Desserts	60												
Coriander-Gingerbread Cake w/ Crème Anglaise		430	180	6	57	20	11	5	3	125	380	2	based on 20 servings
Eggnog Crème Anglaise		60	50	1	3	5	3	1.5	0	40	15	0	per 1 Tbs.
Gingerbread-Pear Cobbler		340	110	4	57	12	4.5	4	2	35	170	5	based on 16 servings
Ginger-Molasses Cheesecake		390	240	7	33	26	16	8	1.5	145	290	0	based on 20 servings
Ginger Spice Ice Cream		310	180	4	28	20	12	6	1	170	80	0	based on 8 servings
Thai Curries	66												
Green Curry w/ Chicken & Eggplant		480	350	25	13	39	23	7	5	75	980	3	w/o rice or noodles
Red Curry w/ Shrimp & Sugar Snap Peas		430	280	24	18	31	21	4.5	4	170	1240	4	w/o rice or noodles
Red Country-Style Curry w/ Beef, Shiitakes & Edamame		350	160	33	15	18	4.5	7	3.5	45	1370	3	w/o rice or noodles
Cookies	70												
Dark Chocolate Crackles		110	45	2	16	5	3	1.5	0	20	45	1	per cookie
Vanilla Slice & Bake Cookies		50	20	1	6	2.5	1.5	0.5	0	10	15	0	per cookie
Ginger-Spiced Slice & Bake Cookies		50	20	1	8	2.5	1.5	0.5	0	10	15	0	per cookie
Macadamia Double-Decker Brownie Bars		130	70	1	16	8	3	3.5	0	25	35	1	per bar
Maple-Walnut Tuiles		50	20	1	8	2	1	0.5	0	5	20	0	per cookie
Cardamom-Honey Cutouts		50	25	1	7	2.5	1.5	0.5	0	10	20	0	per cookie
Peanut Butter & Chocolate Sandwiches		250	150	7	21	17	6	7	3	20	160	2	per sandwich cookie
Rugelach		100	60	1	9	7	4	2	0	20	50	0	per cookie
Test Kitchen	78												
Bourbon Balls		110	70	2	9	8	3	3.5	1	10	30	2	per bourbon ball
Red Curry Paste		10	0	0	2	0	0	0	0	0	75	1	per 1 Tbs.
Green Curry Paste		10	0	0	2	0	0	0	0	0	70	0	per 1 Tbs.
Royal Icing		40	0	0	9	0	0	0	0	0	0	0	per 1 Tbs.
Food Science	86												
Classic Hot Cocoa		140	50	6	20	6	3.5	1.5	0	15	135	2	based on 4 servings
Rich Hot Chocolate		260	110	7	31	12	8	4	0	15	85	3	based on 4 servings
Quick & Delicious	102a												
Roasted Sausages & Grapes		340	170	14	31	19	7	8	2.5	40	1100	2	based on 6 servings
Roasted Chicken Legs w/ Lemon & Green Olives		440	260	40	3	29	7	14	6	140	500	1	based on 6 servings
Fennel & Rosemary Beef Tenderloin w/ Mustard Sauce		310	170	30	2	19	8	8	1	100	300	0	based on 8 servings
Rack of Lamb w/ Ancho-Honey Glaze		420	230	28	19	25	11	11	2	110	370	1	based on 6 servings
Orange-Roasted Salmon w/ Yogurt-Caper Sauce		340	160	40	2	18	3	8	5	110	300	0	based on 6 servings
Roasted Cod w/ Lemon-Parsley Crumbs		210	60	28	7	7	4	1.5	0.5	80	410	0	based on 6 servings
Spice-Crusted Roast Pork Tenderloin		330	110	47	5	12	3.5	6	1.5	125	300	1	based on 6 servings

The nutritional analyses have been calculated by a registered dietitian at Nutritional Solutions in Melville, New York. When a recipe gives a choice of ingredients, the first choice is the one used. Optional ingredients with measured amounts are included; ingredients without specific quantities are not. When a range of ingredient amounts or servings is given, the smaller amount or portion is used. When the quantities of salt and pepper aren't specified, the analysis is based on ¼ teaspoon salt and ⅛ teaspoon pepper per serving for entrées, and ⅛ teaspoon salt and ¹⁄₁₆ teaspoon pepper per serving for side dishes.

Quick Prep, Easy Roast

BY MOLLY STEVENS

Even the most enthusiastic cook occasionally balks at the prospect of preparing an elaborate holiday meal. When this happens to me, I respond by firing up the oven for any one of these lively and reliable roasts. Roasting is easy on the cook, because it requires only a minimal amount of time and toil to assemble and season, and then the oven concentrates the flavors. The roasting time depends entirely on the size and shape of whatever you're cooking. For instance, the Fennel & Rosemary Beef Tenderloin cooks for 40 to 50 minutes, while the Orange-Roasted Salmon is ready in less than 20 minutes. Either way, roasting leaves you free to make a salad, set the table, or to just relax and enjoy the appetizing aromas filling your kitchen. Each of these recipes serves at least six, making them ideal for effortless yet elegant entertaining, or for a Sunday night supper that leaves you with delicious leftovers for a weekday meal.

Fennel & Rosemary Beef Tenderloin with Creamy Mustard Sauce

Serves six to eight.

- **1 Tbs. extra-virgin olive oil**
- **1 Tbs. finely chopped fresh rosemary**
- **1½ tsp. ground fennel seed**
- **1 tsp. kosher salt; more to taste**
- **½ tsp. freshly cracked black pepper**
- **2½- to 3-lb. beef tenderloin roast, excess fat trimmed**
- **½ cup crème fraîche**
- **2 Tbs. Dijon mustard**
- **2 tsp. fresh lemon juice**

Position a rack in the center of the oven and heat the oven to 375°F.

In a small bowl, combine the olive oil, rosemary, fennel seed, salt, and pepper. Stir to make a paste. Pat the beef dry with paper towels and rub the paste all over the surface of the meat. If necessary, tie the roast at 1½-inch intervals. (The roast can be seasoned and refrigerated up to 4 hours in advance.)

Put the roast on a rack on a small, rimmed baking sheet or in a shallow roasting pan. Roast until an instant-read thermometer inserted in the center reads 120°F for rare, 125° to 130°F for medium rare, or 135°F for medium, 40 to 50 minutes.

Meanwhile, in a small bowl, whisk together the crème fraîche, mustard, and lemon juice. Season lightly with salt to taste.

Transfer the roast to a carving board (preferably with a well for collecting juices) and let it rest, uncovered, for 10 to 15 minutes before carving it into ⅓- to ½-inch-thick slices. Serve the beef, passing the mustard sauce at the table (it is also excellent cold, spread on leftover roast beef sandwiches).

Spice-Crusted Roast Pork Tenderloin

Serves six.

- **4 tsp. extra-virgin olive oil; more as needed for the baking sheet**
- **¼ cup plain low-fat or whole-milk yogurt**
- **1 tsp. Dijon mustard**
- **2 cloves garlic, minced**
- **¾ tsp. kosher salt**
- **Fresh coarsely ground black pepper**
- **Two 1½-lb. pork tenderloins, trimmed**
- **¾ cup fresh breadcrumbs (from a baguette or other white artisan-style bread)**
- **1½ tsp. mustard seeds**
- **1½ tsp. coriander seeds**
- **1½ tsp. cumin seeds**
- **1½ tsp. sesame seeds**

Position a rack in the center of the oven and heat the oven to 450°F. Lightly oil a heavy-duty rimmed baking sheet.

In a small bowl, stir together 2 tsp. of the olive oil and the yogurt, mustard, garlic, salt, and several grinds of pepper. Spread this mixture over the entire surface of the tenderloins with your hands or a rubber spatula. (The pork can be slathered with the yogurt mixture and refrigerated for up to 4 hours ahead.)

In a shallow baking dish, combine the breadcrumbs and the mustard, coriander, cumin, and sesame seeds.

Roll the tenderloins in the breadcrumb mixture, patting so that the crumbs and spices adhere to the meat. Put the tenderloins on the baking sheet, gather up any remaining crumbs and spices, and pat them onto the top of the pork. Drizzle the remaining 2 tsp. olive oil over the top.

Roast the tenderloins for 10 minutes and then lower the oven temperature to 325°F. Continue roasting until an instant-read thermometer inserted in the center of each tenderloin reads 140°F, 25 to 30 minutes longer. Transfer the pork to a carving board and let it rest for 10 minutes before carving it into ½-inch-thick slices. Be sure to serve all the crumb coating that falls off during carving.

Serving suggestion:

The rather lean pork tenderloins deserve something a bit rich and creamy alongside, such as risotto, buttery mashed potatoes, a creamy gratin, or puréed winter squash. I sometimes like to serve this with a little tangy chutney on the side, too.

Roasted Cod with Lemon-Parsley Crumbs

Serves six.

- **1 cup panko breadcrumbs**
- **3 Tbs. melted unsalted butter**
- **3 Tbs. finely chopped fresh flat-leaf parsley**
- **2 tsp. finely grated lemon zest**
- **Kosher salt and freshly ground black pepper**
- **Six 1- to 1½-inch-thick cod fillets (about 6 oz. each)**

Position a rack in the center of the oven and heat the oven to 425°F.

In a medium bowl, combine the panko, butter, parsley, and lemon zest. Add a pinch of salt and a grind of pepper and stir to evenly distribute the ingredients.

Line a heavy-duty rimmed baking sheet with parchment. Arrange the cod fillets on the baking sheet and season all over with salt and pepper.

Divide the panko topping among the fillets, pressing lightly so it adheres. Roast until the breadcrumbs are browned and the fish is mostly opaque (just cooked through), with a trace of translucence in the center (cut into a piece to check), 10 to 12 minutes, depending on the thickness of the fillets. Serve immediately.

Tip: If you get thinner tail pieces of cod, you might want to fold them over to double the thickness so they don't cook too quickly and dry out.

Molly Stevens is a contributing editor and the author of All About Braising, *a winner of the James Beard Foundation award for best single-subject cookbook.* ◆

Orange-Roasted Salmon with Yogurt-Caper Sauce

Serves six.

2 Tbs. extra-virgin olive oil; more for the baking sheet
Six 1-inch-thick, skin-on center-cut salmon fillets (about 6 oz. each), pin bones removed
1½ tsp. finely grated orange zest
¾ tsp. kosher salt; more to taste
Freshly ground black pepper
¾ cup plain whole-milk yogurt
2 Tbs. finely chopped fresh flat-leaf parsley
1½ Tbs. capers, drained, rinsed, and chopped
1 Tbs. fresh orange juice

Position a rack in the center of the oven and heat the oven to 400°F. Lightly oil a heavy-duty rimmed baking sheet.

Arrange the salmon skin side down on the baking sheet, drizzle with 1 Tbs. of the olive oil, and sprinkle with 1 tsp. of the orange zest, the salt, and a few grinds of black pepper. Gently rub the seasonings into the fish. Let sit at room temperature while the oven heats.

Combine the yogurt in a small bowl with the remaining 1 Tbs. of olive oil, ½ tsp. orange zest, and the parsley, capers, and orange juice. Stir to combine. Season to taste with salt and black pepper. The sauce can be made up to several hours ahead and kept refrigerated.

Roast the salmon until just cooked through, with a trace of bright pink in the center (cut into a piece to check), 10 to 15 minutes. Serve immediately, drizzled with the yogurt sauce.

Rack of Lamb with Ancho-Honey Glaze

Serves six.

2 racks of lamb (each 1¼ to 1½ lb. with 7 to 8 ribs), trimmed, or frenched
Kosher salt and freshly ground black pepper
⅓ cup honey
2 Tbs. red-wine vinegar
1½ tsp. ground cumin, preferably toasted
1 tsp. ancho chile powder
½ cup orange juice
1 clove garlic, minced
1 Tbs. finely chopped mint, parsley, basil, or cilantro (optional)

Position a rack in the center of the oven and heat the oven to 425°F. Line a small roasting pan or rimmed baking sheet with foil (to make it easier to clean the glaze from the pan).

If necessary, trim the lamb so that only a thin layer of fat remains, being careful not to remove all the fat. Arrange the lamb bone side down in the roasting pan, interlocking the bone ends if necessary to make them fit. Season each rack generously with salt and pepper.

In a small bowl, combine the honey, vinegar, cumin, ancho chile powder, and a pinch each of salt and pepper. Brush the surface of the meat with about half (¼ cup) of the glaze.

Roast, brushing the lamb after 10 minutes and then again every 5 minutes with the glaze that has begun to caramelize on the roasting pan, until an instant-read thermometer inserted close to but not touching the bones reads 125°F for rare or 130° to 135°F for medium rare, about 20 minutes for rare and 25 minutes for medium rare.

Meanwhile, pour the remaining glaze into a small saucepan, add the orange juice and garlic, and bring to a simmer over medium-high heat. Simmer until reduced to a slightly syrupy glaze, about 7 minutes. Add the herbs, if using.

Let the lamb rest for about 5 minutes. Cut between the bones to carve the racks into chops and drizzle each chop with a little of the glaze before serving.

Serving suggestion:

Honey-spiced lamb is a traditional Moroccan festival meal. This simplified version makes the most of the way sweet honey balances the richness of the lamb. Serve herb-flecked couscous or rice pilaf alongside.

Roasted Chicken Legs with Lemon & Green Olives

Serves six.

6 chicken leg quarters (drumsticks and thighs connected; 4 to 5 lb.)
3 Tbs. extra-virgin olive oil; more as needed
1 tsp. dried thyme
1 tsp. kosher salt
¼ tsp. crushed red pepper flakes
1 small lemon, scrubbed, halved lengthwise, seeded, and sliced into ⅛-inch-thick half moons (discard the ends)
Heaping ½ cup unpitted green olives, preferably picholine or lucques

Position a rack in the center of the oven and heat the oven to 450°F.

If portions of the backbone are still attached to the chicken quarters, cut them off and discard. Pat the chicken dry with paper towels. In a small bowl, combine the olive oil, thyme, salt, and red pepper flakes. Using your fingers, rub all of the seasoned oil over all the chicken pieces, carefully separating the skin from the meat and rubbing the oil under the skin as well. Arrange the legs skin side up (not overlapping) on a heavy-duty rimmed baking sheet. Roast the chicken for 20 minutes.

Meanwhile, put the lemon slices and olives in a small bowl. When the chicken has roasted for 20 minutes, take the pan out of the oven and spoon a little of the fat from the pan over the lemons and olives (or use a little fresh olive oil). Scatter the lemons and olives on the baking sheet around but not on top of the chicken, trying to keep the lemon slices away from the edge of the pan where they might burn.

Continue to roast until the chicken juices run clear when pierced with a knife and an instant-read thermometer inserted in a thigh registers 170°F, another 20 to 25 minutes. Transfer the chicken, olives, and lemon slices to a platter and serve.

Note: Be sure to tell your guests that the olives have pits, and encourage them to eat the roasted lemon slices, rind and all. They add a nice sour-bitter counterpoint to the rich chicken meat. If Meyer lemons are in season, by all means use them here.

Roasted Sausages & Grapes

Serves six.

1¾ to 2 lb. hot or sweet Italian sausage links (or a combination)
2 lb. seedless red grapes, stemmed
2 Tbs. sherry vinegar
Kosher salt and freshly ground black pepper
¼ cup chopped fresh flat-leaf parsley

Position a rack in the center of the oven and heat the oven to 425°F.

Cut the sausages in half on a sharp angle and arrange them on a large rimmed baking sheet or in a shallow roasting pan. Add the grapes to the pan. Sprinkle the vinegar over the sausages and grapes, season with salt and a generous amount of black pepper, and toss so that everything is evenly seasoned.

Roast, turning with a spatula after 15 minutes, until the sausages are browned and cooked through (cut into one to check), 35 to 40 minutes total. Scatter the parsley over the top, stir to mingle all the juices, being careful not to crush the grapes, and serve.

Serving suggestion:

A side dish of creamy polenta or risotto is just right to balance the sweetness of the roasted grapes and the richness of the sausages.

Tip: I like to use a mix of hot and sweet sausages for a more interesting dish. The result depends a lot on the quality of the sausages.

Photos: Scott Phillips

60% CACAO. 100% IMPRESSIVE.

BAKE WITH OUR DEEP, INTENSE CHOCOLATE FOR PURE PLEASURE IN EVERY BITE.

GHIRARDELLI® INDIVIDUAL CHOCOLATE LAVA CAKES

Yield - 6 servings

Center: 1/2 bar (2 oz) 60% Cacao Bittersweet
          Chocolate Baking Bar
1/4 cup heavy cream

Cake: Nonstick cooking spray
1 bar (4 oz) 60% Cacao Bittersweet Chocolate
  Baking Bar
8 Tbsp. (1 stick) unsalted butter
2 whole eggs
2 egg yolks
1/3 cup sugar
1/2 tsp. vanilla extract
1/4 cup cake flour
Raspberries and whipped cream for garnish

To make centers, melt chocolate and cream in double boiler. Whisk gently to blend. Refrigerate about 2 hours or until firm. Form into 6 balls; refrigerate until needed.

To make cake, heat oven to 400°F. Spray six 4-ounce ramekins or custard cups with cooking spray. Melt chocolate and butter in double boiler; whisk gently to blend. With an electric mixer, whisk eggs, yolks, sugar, and vanilla on high speed about 5 minutes or until thick and light. Fold melted chocolate mixture and flour into egg mixture just until combined. Spoon cake batter into ramekins. Place a chocolate ball in the middle of each ramekin.

Bake about 15 minutes or until cake is firm to the touch. Let it sit out of the oven for about 5 minutes. Run a small, sharp knife around inside of each ramekin, place a plate on top, invert and remove ramekin. Garnish with raspberries and a dollop of whipped cream.

MOMENTS OF TIMELESS PLEASURE.™

Visit your local grocery store for a complete range of delectable Ghirardelli baking chips, bars and cocoa.   www.ghirardelli.com

what's inside

48

57

54

102a

68

77

88

73

50

2007 Index

Covering issues 83–89. Page numbers followed by a letter indicate a fold-out guide.

A

Aidells, Bruce
"The Most Delicious Glazed
Ham," 85:44–47
Anderson, Pam
"Chicken Thighs Take a Turn on
the Grill," 87:30–33
appetizers
Baby Carrots Pickled in
Champagne & Sherry Vinegars,
85:54
Bacon-Wrapped Stuffed Apricots,
86:39
Farmers' Market Crudités with
Buttermilk Herb Dip, 86:26a
grilled, 86:36–39
Grilled Bruschetta with
Rosemary-White Bean Puree &
Heirloom Tomatoes, 86:26a
Grilled Goat Cheese Crostini with
a Tangle of Marinated Roasted
Peppers, 87:42
Leek Tart with Bacon & Gruyere,
89:23
Mini Tuna Burgers with Mint-
Caper Aioli on Pita Triangles,
86:38
Pancetta & Pineapple Skewers,
86:38
Prosciutto-Wrapped Melon
with Mint & White Balsamic
Vinegar, 86:64
Roasted Red Pepper & Walnut
Dip with Pomegranate Molasses,
85:75
Rosemary & Sea Salt Crackers,
89:45
Seeded Crackers, 89:45
Shrimp Skewers, 86:37
Smoky Eggplant & White Bean
Dip with Pita Crisps, 83:82a
Tomato & Olive Pizzettas with
Fennel Seeds & Aged Goat
Cheese, 86:39
Wild Mushroom Toasts, 85:40
apples
Apple Brown-Butter Jalousie,
83:56
Apple Crisp with Pecans &
Orange, 88:61
appliances
space-saving, 84:26
apricots
Bacon-Wrapped Stuffed Apricots,
86:39
Armentrout, Jennifer
"An Essential Guide to Roasting
Vegetables," 88:53–57
artichokes
about, 85:18
how to prep, 85:19
Pan-Seared Artichokes with
Sherry Vinegar & Thyme, 85:19
suggestions for using, 85:19
Artisan Foods column
From Retro Cakes to Whimsical
Candies, 89:18
Handcrafting Salumi in San
Francisco, 85:32
Handmade Sea-Salt Caramels,
83:24
Raw-Milk Cheese from Tennessee,
88:18
Rich & Creamy German-Style
Wheat Beers, 86:32–33

arugula
Arugula & Fennel Salad with
Orange & Fennel Seed Dressing
& Toasted Hazelnuts, 86:50
Arugula Salad with Pears,
Proscuitto & Aged Gouda,
87:78a
Broiled Lamb Skewers with Baby
Arugula & Lemon Vinaigrette,
85:84a
Asian chile sauces
sources, 86:73
asparagus
Baked Fettucine with Asparagus,
Lemon, Pine Nuts &
Mascarpone, 84:26a
frittata with asparagus, herbs &
scallions, 83:62
Grilled Asparagus & Onions
with Balsamic Vinegar & Blue
Cheese, 86:26a
Hot Garlicky Shrimp with
Asparagus & Lemon, 85:59
Penne with Asparagus, Olives
& Parmigiano Breadcrumbs,
85:84a
avocados
keeping the flesh green, 85:34
mashing with a potato ricer, 85:34
Soft Chicken Tacos with the
Works, 83:42

B

bacon
Bacon-Wrapped Stuffed Apricots,
86:39
freezing in portions, 87:29
Pan-Fried Gnocchi with Bacon,
Onions & Peas, 85:84a
baking pans
for edge lovers, 84:22
preventing rust on, 88:42
baking pans, 9x13-inch
sources, 89:90
baking peel
with pastry cloth, 89:30
baking sheets
from CIA, 89:34
bar cookies
Lemon Cheesecake Squares,
86:53
Macadamia Double-Decker
Brownie Bars, 89:75
Barber, Dan
"Carrots, Pure & Simple,"
85:51–55
Barker, Karen
"Go Nuts: Add Pecans to More
Than Just Pie," 88:58–63
"Rhubarb's Greatest Hits,"
85:60–63
basil
rating prepared basil pesto, 83:74
basting brushes
silicone, 83:28
batter
measuring level with Popsicle
stick, 87:29
beans
Grilled Bruschetta with
Rosemary-White Bean Puree &
Heirloom Tomatoes, 86:26a
Smoky Eggplant & White Bean
Dip with Pita Crisps, 83:82a

Tuscan Peasant Soup with
Rosemary & Pancetta, 83:10
beef
Argentine Spice-Rubbed Flank
Steak with Salsa Cruda, 86:26a
Asian-Style Beef Barbecue in
Lettuce Packages, 84:78a
Beef Stew with Red Wine &
Carrots, 84:39
Beef Tenderloin with Wild
Mushroom Stuffing & Port
Wine Sauce, 89:50
buying a beef tenderloin, 89:51
Chili-Rubbed Rib-Eye Steak with
Corn & Green Chile Ragout,
87:78a
choosing chuck for stew, 84:67
Fennel & Rosemary Beef
Tenderloin with Creamy
Mustard Sauce, 89:102a
Grilled Flank Steak with Sesame
Sauce & Grilled Scallions,
87:53
Red Country-Style Curry with
Beef, Shiitakes & Edamame,
89:67
Short Rib & Porcini Mushroom
Ragu, 83:60
Spicy Beef with Peanuts & Chiles,
88:98a
Steak & Eggs Rancheros, 86:68
Steak Adobo, 87:46
Steak with Red Onion, Wine &
Port Sauce, 87:45
Steak with Three-Chile Sauce,
87:47
Stir-Fried Noodles with Beef &
Vegetables, 88:98a
beer
ales, 87:20
from High Point Brewing
Company, 86:32–33
German-style wheat beers from
an American microbrewery,
86:32–33
how to store, 87:20
ideal temperature for serving,
87:20
lagers, 87:21
pouring technique, 87:21
beets
Spiced Pickled Beets, 87:65
berries
Mixed-Berry Jalousie, 83:56
beverages
Classic Hot Cocoa, 89:88
Double-Chocolate Malted Milk
Shake, 87:66
Rich Hot Chocolate, 89:88
Strawberry-Orange-Vanilla
Breakfast Smoothie, 88:84
biscuit cutters
sources, 85:78
biscuits
Caramelized Onion Biscuits,
85:50
Cheese Biscuits, 85:50
Flaky Buttermilk Biscuits, 85:49
Fresh Herb Biscuits, 85:50
black beans
Smoky Black Bean & Cheddar
Burrito with Baby Spinach,
85:84a
blenders
KitchenAid, improved, 84:22

Bloom, Carole
"Peaches & Cream," 87:58–61
bok choy
about, 84:54
Braised Bok Choy with Sherry &
Prosciutto, 84:54
Seared Baby Bok Choy with Tofu
& Shiitakes, 88:98a
bottles with sticky contents
using oil to open, 84:28
bourbon
Bourbon Balls, 89:80
Bourbon-Chocolate Mousse, 85:
back cover
cooking with, 89:80
bowls
insulated, 88:32
mix-and-measure, 85:24
box wine
for cooking, 84:28
bread
Apple-Butter Cinnamon Buns,
88:72
Banana-Walnut Muffins, 89:30a
Blueberry Muffins, 89:30a
Cranberry-Orange Muffins,
89:30a
drying in oven, 83:36
Fastest Cinnamon Buns, 88:72
Garlic Crostini with Spinach,
Mushroom & Parmigiano Salad,
88:66
Grilled Bruschetta with
Rosemary-White Bean Puree &
Heirloom Tomatoes, 86:26a
Grilled Corn, Shrimp & Chorizo
Salad, 87:43
Grilled Garlic Bread, 87:41
Grilled Goat Cheese Crostini with
a Tangle of Marinated Roasted
Peppers, 87:42
Rosemary & Sea Salt Crackers,
89:45
Sausage-Maple Bread Stuffing,
88:50
Seeded Crackers, 89:45
Toasted Breadcrumbs, 84:48
bread pan, 85:26
brining
bags for, sources, 88:92
broccoli
Broccoli with Eggs & Lemony
Parmesan Breadcrumbs, 88:51
broccoli raab
Campanelle with Broccoli Raab,
Sausage & Olives, 84:26a
brown sugar
keeping it moist, 88:86
Brussels sprouts
Brussels Sprouts Braised with
Pancetta, Shallot, Thyme &
Lemon, 89:59
reducing cooking odor of, 88:89
Roasted Brussels Sprouts with
Dijon, Walnuts & Crisp
Crumbs, 89:57
Sauteed Brussels Sprouts with
Fresh Herbs & Crisp Shallots,
89:58
selecting and storing, 89:59
Bucheron cheese
sources, 86:73
Bundt pans
better way to grease, 83:73
for pound cakes, 83:68
reinforced silicone, 83:28

sources, 83:76
burritos & quesadillas
  Farmers' Market Quesadillas, 87:78a
  Quesadillas with Roasted Poblanos & Onions (Rajas), 86:21
  Smoky Black Bean & Cheddar Burrito with Baby Spinach, 85:84a
butter
  Caramelized Shallot Butter, 88:57
  mix flavored butter in plastic bag, 84:29
  Sea Salt, Chile & Lime Butter, 86:42
  Three-Herb Butter, 88:47
buttermilk
  Basic Buttermilk Pancakes, 89:30a
  cultured vs. old-fashioned, 88:22
  Farmers' Market Crudités with Buttermilk Herb Dip, 86:26a
  Flaky Buttermilk Biscuits, 85:49
  saving leftover, 85:36
  substitutes for, 88:83

C

cabbage
  Cabbage & Carrot Stir-Fry with Toasted Cumin & Lime, 83:47
  shredding method, 83:71
  Tuscan Peasant Soup with Rosemary & Pancetta, 83:10
Caggiano, Biba
  "The Best Ragus," 83:58–61
cake pans
  sources, 89:90
cake platter
  improvised, 84:28
cakes
  Bourbon-Glazed Brown Sugar Pecan Pound Cake, 88:62
  Brandy & Rum Glazed Pound Cake, 83:68
  Butter Pound Cake, 83:67
  Chocolate Chip Pound Cake, 83:69
  Ginger-Molasses Cheesecake, 89:65
  Lemon Cheesecake Squares, 86:53
  Lemon-Coconut Pound Cake, 83:69
  Pecan Pineapple Upside-Down Cake, 88:60
  pound cakes
    made with all-purpose flour vs. cake flour, 83:69
  Steamed Coriander-Gingerbread Cake with Eggnog Creme Anglaise, 89:62
Canadian bacon
  about, 87:63
  Corn Saute with Canadian Bacon, Potatoes & Peppers, 87:back cover
candies
  Bourbon Balls, 89:80
cannellini beans
  rated, 86:72
canning
  basics, 87:64
caramels, sea-salt
  handmade, 83:24
carrots
  Baby Carrots Pickled in Champagne & Sherry Vinegars, 85:54
  baby, sources, 85:78

Cabbage & Carrot Stir-Fry with Toasted Cumin & Lime, 83:47
Carrot Salad with Walnut Oil & Honey, 85:54
Maple Pan-Roasted Baby Carrots, 85:53
Pickled Cauliflower with Carrots & Red Bell Pepper, 87:64
Velvety Carrot Soup with Ginger, 85:55
cauliflower
  Baked Rigatoni with Cauliflower in a Spicy Pink Sauce, 84:26a
  Browned Cauliflower with Anchovies, Olives & Capers, 83:21
  for soup, 83:21
  how to cut up, 83:20
  Pickled Cauliflower with Carrots & Red Bell Pepper, 87:64
  pureed, 83:21
  Stir-Fried Cauliflower with Green Peas & Ginger, 83:back cover
  with pasta, 83:21
Cheddar
  evaluating at a tasting party, 83:52
  sources, 83:77
cheese
  American originals, 83:18
  classic cheese for classic dishes, 83:34
  complements to, 89:26
  knives for, 89:26
  listeria risk, 83:23
  made from raw milk, 88:18
  melting categories, 83:32
  Mexican anejo, 87:47
  Mexican cotija, 87:47
  Mexican Oaxaca, 87:47
  putting together a selection, 89:26
  rules for melting, 83:32
  Steak, Egg & Blue Cheese Salad, 83:82a
  storing tips, 89:26
  what happens when it melts, 83:34
cheese board
  olivewood, 83:18
cheesecakes
  Ginger-Molasses Cheesecake, 89:65
  Lemon Cheesecake Squares, 86:53
  using cheese knife to cut, 84:28
Cheney, Dina
  "How to Host a Tasting Party," 83:50–54
cherry pitters
  to contain the mess, 87:22
chervil
  about, 85:73
chicken
  Buttermilk Country Fried Chicken with Cucumber Salad, 83:82a
  Chicken with Vinegar & Onions, 84:37
  Chinese Chicken Salad, 86:59
  Coconut Rice with Chicken & Snow Peas, 83:40
  Crispy Cheddar & Jalapeno Coated Chicken Breasts, 84:51
  Crispy Chicken Breasts with Lemon & Capers, 84:50
  Crispy Orange-Sesame Chicken Breasts, 84:52
  Ginger Chicken Soup, 85:84a
  Green Curry with Chicken & Eggplant, 89:69

Grilled Five-Spice Chicken Thighs with Soy-Vinegar Sauce & Cilantro, 87:31
Grilled Rosemary Chicken Thighs with Sweet & Sour Orange Dipping Sauce, 87:32
Grilled Tandoori-Style Chicken Thighs, 87:33
Grilled Thai Chicken Breasts with Herb-Lemongrass Crust, 86:26a
Herbed Chicken Breasts with a Crispy Black Olive & Parmigiano Crust, 84:52
Indonesian Grilled Chicken Thighs with Mango-Peanut Salsa, 87:33
Jerk Chicken Drumsticks, 84:78a
Lemony Chicken Caesar Salad with Garlic-Parmesan Toasts, 83:42
Lime Chicken with Poblano Sour Cream, 84:78a
making kebabs from thighs, 87:32
method for crisp oven chicken, 84:50
Orange Chicken with Scallions, 88:98a
Roast Chicken with Rosemary-Lemon Salt, 83:39
Roasted Chicken Legs with Lemon & Green Olives, 89:102a
Roasted Chicken Thighs with Late-Summer Vegetables & Pan Sauce, 87:78a
Roasted Cornish Game Hens with Wildflower Honey & Orange, 85:42
roasted, how to handle leftovers, 83:40
roasted, ideas for using leftovers, 83:43
Sesame Chicken with Ginger & Snow Peas, 88:98a
Soft Chicken Tacos with the Works, 83:42
Spicy Fried Chicken, 86:78a
Spinach Salad with Chicken, Cashews, Ginger & Fried Wontons, 88:65
tips for moist meat and crisp skin, 83:39
chile powder
  Espelette
    sources, 86:73
  sources, 87:72
chiles
  cleaning hands after handling, 86:34
  Farmers' Market Quesadillas, 87:78a
  guide to hot chiles, 84:66
  poblanos, about, 86:20
  sources, 87:72
  three ways to add chile flavor, 87:44
chipotle
  ground, sources, 87:72
chipotles en adobo
  sources, 85:78
chocolate
  "pearl" decorations for desserts, 88:20
  Bourbon-Chocolate Mousse, 85:back cover
  Chocolate Espresso Pecan Pie, 88:62
  cups for desserts, 88:20
  Dark Chocolate Crackles, 89:71
  evaluating at a tasting party, 83:53

Peanut Butter & Chocolate Sandwiches, 89:77
Rich Hot Chocolate, 89:88
vs. cocoa powder, 89:86
chocolate, dark
  sources, 83:77
chopping
  tips for chopping sticky foods, 83:73
chopsticks
  for beginners, 89:20
chorizo
  frittata with kale, onions & chorizo, 83:62
  Grilled Corn, Shrimp & Chorizo Salad, 87:43
  Linguine with Shrimp & Chorizo, 83:82a
  sources, 85:78
  Spicy Seared Chipotle Shrimp with Zucchini & Chorizo, 85:57
cilantro root
  sources, 89:90
citrus
  zest, julienned or chopped, 87:63
  zest, to flavor sugar, 85:34
clams
  how to buy, 88:68
  Linguine with Clam Sauce, 88:69
clay baker
  keeping dry in storage, 89:42
cleaning mitts
  for stainless steel, 86:28
clogs
  Dansko
    sources, 84:72
cobblers
  favorite fruit combinations, 86:61
  Gingerbread-Pear Cobbler, 89:61
  putting together a fruit cobbler, 86:60–63
  Sour Cream Cobbler Dough, 86:62
cocoa
  Classic Hot Cocoa, 89:88
  Dutched or natural?, 89:86
  vs. chocolate, 89:86
coconut
  Coconut Rice with Chicken & Snow Peas, 83:40
  Green Bean Stir-Fry with Shredded Coconut, 83:49
coconut cream
  vegan alternative to cream in ganache, 89:42
cod
  Braised Cod with Fennel, Potatoes & Littlenecks, 84:61
  Roasted Cod with Lemon-Parsley Crumbs, 89:102a
colanders
  for scooping pasta, 86:24
collards
  Ham Bone Collards, 85:76
Conant, Scott
  "Quick Pastas with a Kick," 86:43–45
condiments
  Sea Salt, Chile & Lime Butter, 86:42
  Tarragon-Scented Mayonnaise with Cornichons & Capers, 86:42
condiments & seasonings
  Caramelized Shallot Butter, 88:57
  Cranberry Sauce with Vanilla, Maple Syrup & Cassis, 88:52
  Ginger-Lemon-Soy Splash, 88:57
  Homemade Crema (Mexican Sour Cream), 84:70
  Moroccan-Style Spice Rub, 88:56

Pickled Cauliflower with Carrots
& Red Bell Pepper, 87:64
Red Curry Paste, 89:83
Rhubarb & Dried-Cherry
Chutney, 85:11
Roasted Red Pepper Relish
with Pine Nuts, Currants &
Marjoram, 87:51
Rosemary-Thyme-Lemon Oil,
88:56
Sesame Salt, 88:57
Spiced Pickled Beets, 87:65
Three-Herb Butter, 88:47
Toasted Garlic & Coriander Oil,
88:57
cookies
Cardamom-Honey Cutouts, 89:72
Dark Chocolate Crackles, 89:71
Ginger-Spiced Slice & Bake
Cookies, 89:74
how to make square logs of
refrigerator dough, 89:40
Macadamia Double-Decker
Brownie Bars, 89:75
Maple-Walnut Tuiles, 89:76
Peanut Butter & Chocolate
Sandwiches, 89:77
Rugelach, 89:73
Vanilla Slice & Bake Cookies,
89:74
Cooking Without Recipes
"How to Make a Memorable Fruit
Cobbler," 86:60–63
"How to Make Hearty Bean &
Vegetable Soups," 88:73–77
"Versatile Frittata, for Breakfast,
Lunch, or Dinner," 83:62–65
cookware
care tips for nonstick, 84:23
cooling racks
sources, 89:90
corn
Corn & Mushroom Saute with
Leeks & Pancetta, 87:37
Corn Saute with Canadian Bacon,
Potatoes & Peppers,
87:back cover
Corn Saute with Ginger, Garlic
& Fresh Cilantro, 87:37
Corn, Sweet Onion & Zucchini
Saute with Fresh Mint, 87:36
Grilled Corn on the Cob with
Thyme & Roasted Red Pepper
Butter, 86:26a
on the cob, keeping warm, 86:35
Orecchiette with Caramelized
Onions, Green Beans, Fresh
Corn & Jalapeno, 86:45
shopping for, 87:62
Summer Bouillabaisse with Smoky
Rouille, 87:78a
Summer Corn Chowder with
Scallions, Bacon & Potatoes,
87:55
tidy way to cut, 87:36
corn cob holders
ways to store, 86:35
Cornish game hens
about, 85:73
Roasted Cornish Game Hens with
Wildflower Honey & Orange,
85:42
cottage cheese
rated, 88:90
crabmeat
Thai Seafood Salad, 87:57
cranberries
Cranberry Sauce with Vanilla,
Maple Syrup & Cassis, 88:52
cream
Honey Whipped Cream, 87:59

creme brulee
Classic Creme Brulee, 84:46
making it, step by step, 84:46–47
mini blow torch for, 84:47
variations on the classic, 84:46
crinkle cutters
for pickles, 87:24
crisps
Apple Crisp with Pecans &
Orange, 88:61
crumbles
Rhubarb Brown Sugar Crumble,
85:63
cucumbers
Buttermilk Country Fried
Chicken with Cucumber Salad,
83:82a
Chopped Tomato & Cucumber
Salad with Mint & Feta, 86:26a
Green Gazpacho, 87:19
growing, 87:19
Lemon, Dill & Cucumber Sauce,
86:42
recipe ideas, 87:19
seed sources, 87:72
varieties, 87:18
curries
Green Curry with Chicken &
Eggplant, 89:69
Red Country-Style Curry with
Beef, Shiitakes & Edamame,
89:67
Red Curry with Shrimp & Sugar
Snap Peas, 89:68
curry leaves
about, 83:70
sources, 83:76
curry paste
about, 89:69
major components of, 89:82
Red Curry Paste, 89:83
cutting boards
how to hold in place, 89:42

D

deep frying
reusing oil, 87:28
DeSerio, Tasha
"A Taste of Spring," 85:38–43
"Dressing Up Grilled Eggplant,"
87:48–51
dessert embellishments, 88:20
Dodge, Abigail Johnson
"A Cookie for Every Occasion,"
89:70–77
"How to Make a Memorable Fruit
Cobbler," 86:60–63
double-boiling
with clear bowl, 83:37
dough scrapers
sources, 89:90
duck
Chinese Five-Spice-Crusted Duck
Breasts, 83:82a
Dutch ovens
sources, 83:76, 84:72, 88:92
using parchment with, 84:15

E

edamame
Red Country-Style Curry with
Beef, Shiitakes & Edamame,
89:67
egg cups, 89:20
eggplant
Create-Your-Own Pasta Salad
with Grilled Eggplant, 87:67
Green Curry with Chicken &
Eggplant, 89:69

Grilled Eggplant, 87:49
Grilled Eggplant with Garlic-
Cumin Vinaigrette with Feta
& Herbs, 87:51
Grilled Eggplant with Olive,
Orange & Anchovy Vinaigrette,
87:50
Grilled Eggplant with Roasted
Red Pepper Relish with Pine
Nuts, Currants & Marjoram,
87:51
Grilled Eggplant with Toasted-
Breadcrumb Salsa Verde, 87:50
Japanese, about, 84:55
Roasted Eggplant with Chiles,
Peanuts & Mint, 84:55
scoring for cooking, 86:34
Smoky Eggplant & White Bean
Dip with Pita Crisps, 83:82a
eggs
Egg Salad with Smoked Salmon,
Capers & Dill, 86:78a
frittata with asparagus, herbs
& scallions, 83:62
frittata with kale, onions
& chorizo, 83:62
frittata with mushrooms, leeks
& goat cheese, 83:62
frittata with potatoes, onions
& pancetta, 83:62
frittata with sausage, mushrooms
& onion, 83:62
Garlic & Herb Fried Eggs on
Toasts with Prosciutto Crisps,
85:84a
how to boil perfectly, 83:71
liquid whites, sources, 89:90
pasteurized whites, 89:85
powdered whites, 89:85
powdered whites, sources, 89:90
preventing green ring around yolk
in hard-cooked, 83:22
Steak & Eggs Rancheros, 86:68
Steak, Egg & Blue Cheese Salad,
83:82a
Sweet Potato & Chile Hash with
a Fried Egg, 89:30a
Ehri, Allison
"Appetizers, Hot Off the Grill,"
86:36–39
"Quick-Braised Fish," 84:58–61
Enjoying Wine column
All-American Wines, 88:36–40
Breaking Out of Your Wine Rut,
83:26
Buying a Mixed Case (or Two)
for Your Summer Cookout,
86:22–23
Discovering Sherry, 89:36–38
Discovering the Wines of Greece,
85:20–22
Wine Lingo, Demystified,
84:20–21

F

faucets
hands-free, 84:23
fennel
Arugula & Fennel Salad with
Orange & Fennel Seed Dressing
& Toasted Hazelnuts, 86:50
Shrimp with Fennel, Tomato &
Pernod Sauce, 85:58
fenugreek leaves
about, 83:70
sources, 83:76
feta
Feta & Dill Galette with Lemony
Spinach Salad, 87:78a

fiddleheads
about, 85:72
sources, 85:78
fish
Braised Cod with Fennel, Potatoes
& Littlenecks, 84:61
Braised Red Snapper Puttanesca,
84:59
Grilled Fish Steaks, 86:41
grilled, toppings for, 86:40–42
how to fillet, 84:69
keep fresh with gel ice, 83:37
method for quick-braising, 84:58
Salmon Braised in Pinot Noir,
84:60
Sear-Roasted Halibut with
Roasted Red Pepper Puree,
85:84a
steaks vs. fillets, 86:65
tips for grilling, 86:41
five-spice powder
sources, 87:72
flour
all-purpose flour vs. cake flour for
pound cakes, 83:69
flower petals
candied, as dessert
embellishments, 88:20
food processors
cleaning safely, 83:37
cleaning with hard cheese, 87:29
Food Science column
A Simple Guide to Handling
Fruits and Vegetables Safely,
86:70–71
Baking: Chocolate vs. Cocoa
Powder, 89:86–88
Help! Thanksgiving Is Driving
Me Crazy, 88:88–89
The Art of Grilling, Demystified,
87:68–69
The Rules of Melting Cheese,
83:32
frittatas
with asparagus, herbs & scallions,
83:62
with kale, onions & chorizo,
83:62
with mushrooms, leeks & goat
cheese, 83:62
with potatoes, onions
& pancetta, 83:62
with sausage, mushrooms
& onion, 83:62
fruit
dipping dried, 89:42

G

galettes
Feta & Dill Galette with Lemony
Spinach Salad, 87:78a
ganache
how to retain the sheen, 83:22
vegan alternative to cream in,
89:42
Gand, Gale
"Playful Desserts," 84:62–65
garlic
as freshly grated finish in sauces,
89:42
garlic presses
for making anchovy paste, 87:28
reviewed, 84:24–25
garnishes
how to make twisty tuiles, 89:78
gelatin
vegetarian alternative to, 87:16
gelato
about, 87:71

ginger
cutting into fine julienne, 84:67
Ginger Chicken Soup, 85:84a
Ginger-Molasses Cheesecake, 89:65
Ginger-Spice Ice Cream, 89:64
Ginger-Spiced Slice & Bake Cookies, 89:74
Gingerbread-Pear Cobbler, 89:61
Steamed Coriander-Gingerbread Cake with Eggnog Creme Anglaise, 89:62
glazes
for ham
Cherry-Pomegranate Glaze & Sauce, 85:47
Maple, Tea & Cardamom Glaze & Sauce, 85:47
Tangerine Marmalade Glaze & Sauce, 85:47
gnocchi
Pan-Fried Gnocchi with Bacon, Onions & Peas, 85:84a
goat cheese
frittata with mushrooms, leeks & goat cheese, 83:62
Grilled Goat Cheese Crostini with a Tangle of Marinated Roasted Peppers, 87:42
Rigatoni with Summer Squash, Spicy Sausage & Goat Cheese, 86:44
Tomato & Olive Pizzettas with Fennel Seeds & Aged Goat Cheese, 86:39
gold powder
edible, as dessert embellishment, 88:20
Goldstein, Joyce
"Versatile Frittata, for Breakfast, Lunch, or Dinner," 83:62–65
Gouda
aged, 87:63
Arugula Salad with Pears, Proscuitto & Aged Gouda, 87:78a
granola
Crispy Sweet Pecan Granola, 89:30a
Honey-Almond Granola, 89:30a
tips for making, 89:30a
gravy
keep warm in teapot, 88:43
lump-free, 88:89
green beans
Green Bean Stir-Fry with Shredded Coconut, 83:49
keeping them bright, 88:88
Orecchiette with Caramelized Onions, Green Beans, Fresh Corn & Jalapeno, 86:45
grilling
direct vs. indirect heat, 87:68
flavors from charcoal and gas, 87:69
lid up or down?, 87:69
preventing foods from sticking, 87:69
grilling for a crowd
grilling checklist, 86:26a
strategies for feeding a crowd, 86:26a
grills
cleaning, 86:69
Gruyere
Leek Tart with Bacon & Gruyere, 89:23

H

halibut
Sear-Roasted Halibut with Roasted Red Pepper Puree, 85:84a
Summer Bouillabaisse with Smoky Rouille, 87:78a
ham
bone-in vs. boneless, 85:45
butt vs. shank, 85:45
city vs. country, 85:45
Fried Ham with Redeye Gravy, 85:76
grades, 85:45
Ham Bone Collards, 85:76
Oven-Glazed Ham with a Pan Sauce, 85:46
sources, 85:78
hand-washing
for food safety, 84:68
herbs
chopping techniques, 87:62
freezing in broth, 85:36
freezing whole, 85:36
Holmberg, Martha
"Sprouting Up," 89:56–59

I

ice cream
chocolate, rated, 87:70
Ginger-Spice Ice Cream, 89:64
Phyllo Chips with Vanilla Ice Cream & Strawberry Mash "Dip," 84:63
sandwiches, tip for making, 86:34
scoops, rated, 87:26
scoops, sources, 89:90
Vanilla Ice Cream with Espresso-Caramel Sauce, 85:43
ice makers
portable, 87:25
icings
how to decorate with royal icing, 89:84
Royal Icing, 89:85
Indian vegetable stir-fries
improvising your own, 83:48

J

Jacobs, Arlene
"Crispy Potato Pancakes," 89:52–55
jalapenos
reducing the spiciness of, 83:back cover
jalousie
Apple Brown-Butter Jalousie, 83:56
Mixed-Berry Jalousie, 83:56
jars
canning, 87:24
plastic, for freezing, 87:24

K

kale
frittata with kale, onions & chorizo, 83:62
Karmel, Elizabeth
"Grilled Bread for Satisfying Sides, Starters & Mains," 87:40–43
kebabs
with chicken thighs, 87:32
Kingsley, Kathy
"Cinnamon Buns in Less Than an Hour," 88:70–72
kitchen carts, 89:32
kitchen scales
compact, 89:20
kitchens
outdoor, how to plan for, 86:55
outdoor, in Vermont, 86:54–57
outdoor, working details, 86:55
Kleiman, Evan
"Great Tomatoes Don't Need Cooking to Become a Great Sauce," 87:38–39
knife care, 85:71
knife sharpeners
electric sharpeners, 85:70
finding the one that's right for you, 85:64–71
how often to use, 85:66
professional services, 85:71
pull-over sharpeners, 85:68
pull-through sharpeners, 85:68
sharpening stones, 85:66–67
sources, 85:66
V-stick sharpeners, 85:69
knives
protecting with potholders, 83:37
Kreitler, Allison Ehri
"Roasts to Boast About," 89:46–51

L

Lacoste, Ris
"Plan Ahead for a Delicious Thanksgiving," 88:44–52
"The Secrets to Fluffy and Flavorful Rice Pilaf," 84:40–44
ladles
comfortable, dripless, 88:29
lamb
Braised Lamb Shanks with Garlic & Vermouth, 84:35
Broiled Lamb Skewers with Baby Arugula & Lemon Vinaigrette, 85:84a
Grilled Herb-Crusted Leg of Lamb with Fresh Mint Sauce, 86:26a
Lamb Chops with Lemon, Thyme & Mustard Butter, 84:78a
Lamb Shank & Sweet Pepper Ragu, 83:61
Middle Eastern Style Lamb Pita "Pizza," 84:68
Rack of Lamb with Ancho-Honey Glaze, 89:102a
lattice strips for pie
cutting evenly, 85:36
Lauterbach, Barbara
"Chinese Chicken Salad," 86:58–59
leeks
buying and storing, 89:22
Corn & Mushroom Saute with Leeks & Pancetta, 87:37
how to clean, 89:22
Leek Tart with Bacon & Gruyere, 89:23
ways to use, 89:23
lemon
cutting wedges that don't squirt, 88:43
lemongrass
Grilled Thai Chicken Breasts with Herb-Lemongrass Crust, 86:26a
how to freeze, 89:40
sources, 86:73
lemons
Lemon Cheesecake Squares, 86:53
Lemon Curd, 86:53
lentils
Curried Lentil Soup, 83:82a
du Puy, sources, 84:72
Warm French Lentil Salad with Smoked Sausage, 84:back cover

lime peel, dried
sources, 89:90
Little Flower Candy Co.
for sea-salt caramels, 83:24
loaf pans
of silicone and metal, 89:34
lobster crackers, 89:20

M

mache
Mache with Spicy Melon & Pink Peppercorn Dressing, 86:51
malted milk powder
about, 87:66
sources, 87:72
mangos
slicer for, 84:23
maple syrup, grade B
sources, 89:90
marbles
as warning when simmering water level too low, 84:29
Masibay, Kimberly
"A Sweet Treat That's Easy to Make," 83:55–57
"Creme Brulee," 84:45–47
McDermott, Nancie
"Fresh from the Sea, a Thai Classic," 87:56–59
"Thai on the Fly: A Quick Curry for Any Night," 89:66–69
measuring cups
silicone, 89:20
measuring spoons
magnetic, 89:20
meat
cooked, storing safely in refrigerator, 87:16
meat tenderizers
for docking dough, 87:28
meat thermometers
glow in the dark, 89:20
melons
finding the ripest, 86:64
Mache with Spicy Melon & Pink Peppercorn Dressing, 86:51
Prosciutto-Wrapped Melon with Mint & White Balsamic Vinegar, 86:64
Mexican cheeses
sources, 87:72
Meyers, Perla
"Linguine with Clam Sauce," 88:68–69
microgreens
about, 86:18
microwave-safe dishes
how to determine, 83:12
Middleton, Susie
"Crowd-Pleasing Crispy Potatoes," 83:44–45
"Endless Summer Corn Sautes," 87:34–37
Miette Confiserie
handcrafted candies, 89:18
milk shake mixers
do you need one?, 87:66
sources, 87:72
mini blowtorch
for creme brulee, 84:47
sources, 84:72
molasses
about, 89:78
morels
about, 85:72
sources, 85:78
mortars and pestles
reviewed, 88:34
what to look for, 88:34

mousse
  Bourbon-Chocolate Mousse,
    85:back cover
muffin pans
  easy-release, 89:34
  metal and silicone, 86:28
  sources, 89:90
muffins
  Banana-Walnut Muffins, 89:30a
  Blueberry Muffins, 89:30a
  Cranberry-Orange Muffins,
    89:30a
  Rhubarb Muffins, 85:63
mushrooms
  cleaning with melon baller, 83:36
  Corn & Mushroom Saute with
    Leeks & Pancetta, 87:37
  cremini vs. portabella, 83:73
  Duxelles, 89:54
  frittata with mushrooms, leeks &
    goat cheese, 83:62
  frittata with sausage, mushrooms
    & onion, 83:62
  ground, for dredging flour, 83:37
  Mushroom Stir-Fry with Onions
    & Tomatoes, 83:48
  Potato Pancakes Stuffed with
    Duxelles, 89:54
  Short Rib & Porcini Mushroom
    Ragu, 83:60
  Wild Mushroom Toasts, 85:40
  wild, sources, 85:78
mussels
  Thai Seafood Salad, 87:57

N
napa cabbage
  about, 84:56
  Hoisin Pork with Napa Cabbage,
    88:98a
  Stir-Fried Napa Cabbage with
    Garlic, Fresh Chile & Basil,
    84:56
nonstick baking liners (Silpat)
  care and keeping of, 89:81
  sources, 88:92, 89:90
  storing, 85:36
  to keep cupcakes from sliding,
    85:36
noodles
  Stir-Fried Noodles with Beef &
    Vegetables, 88:98a
nutcracker
  new style, 85:24
Nutella
  Fried Chocolate-Hazelnut
    Wontons with Orange Dipping
    Sauce, 84:65
nutmeg
  freshly grated, 88:80
  grater for, 88:80
nuts
  how to contain while chopping,
    85:36

O
oil bottles
  wrapping to catch drips, 84:29
olive oils, extra-virgin
  evaluating at a tasting party,
    83:54
  sources, 83:77
onions
  Mushroom Stir-Fry with Onions
    & Tomatoes, 83:48
  Rice Pilaf with Spiced
    Caramelized Onions, Orange,
    Cherry & Pistachio, 84:42

slicing crosswise vs. lengthwise,
  85:73
Sweet Potato Gratin with
  Caramelized Onions, 88:50
oven rack guards, 89:30
ovens
  wall-mounted with door that
    lowers, 87:22

P
pancakes
  Basic Buttermilk Pancakes,
    89:30a
  tips for making, 89:30a
pancetta
  Corn & Mushroom Saute with
    Leeks & Pancetta, 87:37
  frittata with potatoes, onions &
    pancetta, 83:62
  Pancetta & Pineapple Skewers,
    86:38
pans
  carbon-steel crepe, 83:29
  ceramic brazier
    sources, 83:76
  electric crepe, 83:29
  stir-fry
    what to look for, 88:33
paper planks
  for grilling, 86:27
pappadams
  about, 88:86
  sources, 88:92
parchment
  easier way to line pans with, 84:29
  rounds, sources, 89:90
  sources, 88:92
  use with Dutch ovens, 84:15
parfaits
  Peaches & Cream Parfait, 87:60
paring knives
  colorful, 86:26
Parmigiano-Reggiano
  make matchsticks with julienne
    peeler, 87:29
parsnips
  braising suggestions, 84:19
  growing, 84:18
  mashing suggestions, 84:19
  prepping, 84:18
  Roasted Parsnips with Cinnamon
    & Coriander, 84:19
  roasting suggestions, 84:19
  storing, 84:18
pasta
  Angel Hair Pasta with Sauteed
    Cherry Tomatoes, Lemon &
    Tuna, 87:78a
  Baked Fettucine with Asparagus,
    Lemon, Pine Nuts &
    Mascarpone, 84:26a
  Baked Rigatoni with Cauliflower
    in a Spicy Pink Sauce, 84:26a
  Baked Ziti with Tomato,
    Mozzarella & Sausage, 84:26a
  Campanelle with Broccoli Raab,
    Sausage & Olives, 84:26a
  Cavatappi with Roasted Peppers,
    Capocollo & Ricotta, 84:26a
  Classic Macaroni & Cheese,
    84:26a
  colander for scooping, 86:24
  Create-Your-Own Pasta Salad
    with Grilled Eggplant, 87:67
  Linguine with Clam Sauce, 88:69
  Linguine with Shrimp & Chorizo,
    83:82a
  made of farro, 86:24

Orecchiette with Caramelized
  Onions, Green Beans, Fresh
  Corn & Jalapeno, 86:45
Orzo & Grilled Vegetable Salad
  with Feta, Olives & Oregano,
  86:78a
Pan-Fried Gnocchi with Bacon,
  Onions & Peas, 85:84a
Penne with Asparagus, Olives
  & Parmigiano Breadcrumbs,
  85:84a
Rigatoni with Summer Squash,
  Spicy Sausage & Goat Cheese,
  86:44
Spaghetti with Portabellas, Sage
  & Walnuts, 84:26a
Spaghetti with Spicy Shrimp,
  Cherry Tomatoes & Herbed
  Breadcrumbs, 86:44
summer pasta with a kick,
  86:43–45
tool for measuring amounts, 86:24
tortelloni like homemade, 86:24
trofie, about, 86:24
pastries
  Apple Brown-Butter Jalousie,
    83:56
  Mixed-Berry Jalousie, 83:56
pastry brushes
  silicone, 83:28
peaches
  Marinated Peaches, 87:59
  Peaches & Cream Dessert, 87:59
  Peaches & Cream Parfait, 87:60
  Peaches & Cream Shortcakes,
    87:61
pears
  Arugula Salad with Pears,
    Proscuitto & Aged Gouda,
    87:78a
  Free-Form Pear Tarts with
    Almond & Cinnamon, 84:64
  Gingerbread-Pear Cobbler, 89:61
peas
  Stir-Fried Cauliflower with Green
    Peas & Ginger, 83:back cover
pecans
  Apple Crisp with Pecans &
    Orange, 88:61
  Bourbon-Glazed Brown Sugar
    Pecan Pound Cake, 88:62
  Chocolate Espresso Pecan Pie,
    88:62
  Pecan Pineapple Upside-Down
    Cake, 88:60
  sources, 88:92
peelers
  square, to nestle in palm, 83:28
peppers
  Cavatappi with Roasted Peppers,
    Capocollo & Ricotta, 84:26a
  Grilled Goat Cheese Crostini with
    a Tangle of Marinated Roasted
    Peppers, 87:42
  Roasted Red Pepper & Walnut
    Dip with Pomegranate Molasses,
    85:75
pesto
  rating prepared basil pesto, 83:74
Peyton, Jim
  "Steaks, Mexican Style,"
    87:44–47
phyllo
  Phyllo Chips with Vanilla Ice
    Cream & Strawberry Mash
    "Dip," 84:63
pickled peppers
  ways to use leftovers, 87:67
pickles
  Pickled Cauliflower with Carrots
    & Red Bell Pepper, 87:64

Spiced Pickled Beets, 87:65
piecrust
  rolling perfect, 88:82
pies
  blind bkaing shell, 88:43
  Chocolate Espresso Pecan Pie,
    88:62
  keeping pumpkin filling from
    shrinking, 88:22
  Strawberry-Rhubarb Pie, 85:62
pimenton
  sources, 86:73
pineapple
  how to cut rings, 88:78
  how to select, 88:78
  Pancetta & Pineapple Skewers,
    86:38
  Pecan Pineapple Upside-Down
    Cake, 88:60
pizza cutter, 89:28
poblanos
  about, 86:20
  how to roast, 86:21
  Lime Chicken with Poblano Sour
    Cream, 84:78a
  Quesadillas with Roasted
    Poblanos & Onions (Rajas),
    86:21
  sources for seedlings, 86:73
  suggestions for using, 86:21
pomegranate
  products, 85:74
    sources, 85:78
  Roasted Red Pepper & Walnut
    Dip with Pomegranate Molasses,
    85:75
pork
  buying a crown roast of pork,
    89:48
  Crown Roast of Pork with
    Fennel-Apple Stuffing & Cider-
    Bourbon Sauce, 89:48
  Deviled Pork Chops, 84:78a
  Grilled Asian Pork Tenderloin
    with Peanut Sauce, 86:78a
  Hoisin Pork with Napa Cabbage,
    88:98a
  Neapolitan Rib & Sausage Ragu,
    83:59
  Pork Lo Mein with Seared
    Scallions & Shiitakes, 87:54
  Pork Tenderloin with Sage &
    Marsala Sauce, 88:26
  Spice-Crusted Roast Pork
    Tenderloin, 89:102a
portabellas
  Grilled Portabella Sandwiches
    with Tomatoes, Mozzarella
    & Basil, 86:78a
  removing the gills, 86:69
  Spaghetti with Portabellas, Sage
    & Walnuts, 84:26a
portable burners
  compared, 88:32
potato pancakes
  tips for frying, 89:52
potatoes
  Classic Mashed Potatoes, 88:52
  Classic Potato Pancakes, 89:53
  Crispy Smashed Roasted Potatoes,
    83:45
  frittata with potatoes, onions
    & pancetta, 83:62
  New Potatoes with Butter,
    Shallots & Chervil, 85:42
  Potato Pancakes Stuffed with
    Duxelles, 89:54
  potato pancakes with a twist,
    89:55
  Potato Stir-Fry with Mint &
    Cilantro, 83:49

ricer *vs.* masher, 88:29
secret to fluffy mashed, 88:89
pots
cast iron, to keep things cool, 87:28
poultry
new USDA doneness
temperature, 83:71
prep bowls
silicone, 89:28
produce
how to minimize risk of
contamination, 86:70–71
how to select, 86:70
prosciutto
Garlic & Herb Fried Eggs on
Toasts with Prosciutto Crisps,
85:84a
Prosciutto-Wrapped Melon
with Mint & White Balsamic
Vinegar, 86:64
Rice Pilaf with Sage, Parmigiano
& Prosciutto, 84:44
smoked, 85:30
Pyrex pan
to protect cookbook, 88:43

Q

quenelles
how to make, 84:70

R

ramps
about, 85:72
sources, 85:78
ranges
with stepped-up back burners,
88:28
rasps
with covers, 89:20
red snapper
Braised Red Snapper Puttanesca,
84:59
Rees, Nicole
"Pound Cake, Perfected,"
83:66–69
refrigerators
with glass door, 86:28
with variable cold and freezer
spaces, 83:29
Reinhart, Peter
"How to Make Flaky, Buttery
Biscuits," 85:48–50
relishes
Sun-Dried Tomato, Olive &
Caper Relish, 86:42
Reusing, Andrea
"Getting to Know Asian
Vegetables," 84:53–57
reviews
A Passion for Ice Cream, by Emily
Luchetti, 84:32
Baking, from My Home to Yours, by
Dorie Greenspan, 84:32
Eggs, by Michel Roux, 84:30
Jamie's Italy, by Jamie Oliver,
84:31
Joy of Cooking, by Marion
Rombauer Becker, Ethan
Becker, and Irma S. Rombauer,
84:31
*One Spice, Two Spice: American
Food, Indian Flavors,* by Floyd
Cardoz, 84:31
The Cake Book, by Tish Boyle,
84:32
The Improvisational Cook, by Sally
Schneider, 84:30
rhubarb
growing, 85:60

Rhubarb & Dried-Cherry
Chutney, 85:11
Rhubarb Brown Sugar Crumble,
85:63
Rhubarb Muffins, 85:63
roots for growing, sources,
85:78
selecting, storing, prepping,
85:60
Strawberry-Rhubarb Compote
with Vanilla & Cardamom,
85:61
Strawberry-Rhubarb Pie, 85:62
rice
Coconut Rice with Chicken &
Snow Peas, 83:40
Rice Pilaf with Sage, Parmigiano
& Prosciutto, 84:44
Rice Pilaf with Spiced
Caramelized Onions, Orange,
Cherry & Pistachio, 84:42
Saffron Rice Pilaf with Red
Pepper & Toasted Almonds,
84:41
Southwestern Rice Pilaf, 84:43
rice cookers, Fuzzy-Logic
reviewed, 83:30
rice pilaf
best type of rice for, 84:41, 84:44
method for cooking, 84:41
Ried, Adam
"Knife Sharpeners: Find the One
That's Right for You," 85:64–71
roasting pans
sources, 83:76
roasting racks
sources, 83:76
rosemary
Grilled Rosemary Chicken Thighs
with Sweet & Sour Orange
Dipping Sauce, 87:32
Rosenfeld, Tony
"A New Take on Crispy Coated
Chicken," 84:48–52
"Grilling for a Crowd," 86:26a
"Roast Chicken for Today and
Tomorrow," 83:38–43
"Scallions: More Than a
Garnish," 87:52–55
"Sear & Sauce for Fast Shrimp
Sautés," 85:56–59

S

saffron
Grilled Salmon Bundles with
Saffron, Tomatoes & Olives,
86:78a
Saffron Rice Pilaf with Red
Pepper & Toasted Almonds,
84:41
sage
about, 88:24
fried, as garnish or snack, 88:26
plants, sources, 88:92
Pork Tenderloin with Sage
& Marsala Sauce, 88:26
ways to add to everyday cooking,
88:26
salad greens
about, 86:49
best way to store, 86:67
how to wash, 86:49, 86:71
salads
Arugula & Fennel Salad with
Orange & Fennel Seed Dressing
& Toasted Hazelnuts, 86:50
Arugula Salad with Pears,
Proscuitto & Aged Gouda,
87:78a

Butter Lettuce with Poppy Seed
& Tarragon Creme Fraiche
Dressing, 86:48
Carrot Salad with Walnut Oil
& Honey, 85:54
Chinese Chicken Salad, 86:59
Chopped Tomato & Cucumber
Salad with Mint & Feta,
86:26a
Colossal Shrimp with Watercress
& Tomato Salad, 84:78a
Create-Your-Own Pasta Salad
with Grilled Eggplant, 87:67
Feta & Dill Galette with Lemony
Spinach Salad, 87:78a
Garden Lettuces with Garlic
Chapons, 85:41
Garlic Crostini with Spinach,
Mushroom & Parmigiano Salad,
88:66
Grilled Corn, Shrimp & Chorizo
Salad, 87:43
Grilled Southwestern Potato
Salad, 86:26a
Lemony Chicken Caesar Salad
with Garlic-Parmesan Toasts,
83:42
Mache with Spicy Melon & Pink
Peppercorn Dressing, 86:51
making fresh green salads,
86:46–51
Mixed Green Salad with Red-
Wine & Dijon Vinaigrette,
86:47
Orzo & Grilled Vegetable Salad
with Feta, Olives & Oregano,
86:78a
Spinach Salad with Apples,
Dried Apricots & Pappadam
Croutons, 88:66
Spinach Salad with Chicken,
Cashews, Ginger & Fried
Wontons, 88:65
Steak, Egg & Blue Cheese Salad,
83:82a
Thai Seafood Salad, 87:57
tips for dressing a green salad,
86:51
Warm French Lentil Salad with
Smoked Sausage, 84:back cover
Warm Pasta Salad with Grilled
Tomatoes, Zucchini & Pecorino,
86:26a
Warm Spinach Salad with Eggs,
Bacon & Croutons, 88:67
salame
spiced with mole ingredients,
85:30
salmon
cold-smoked, explained, 86:66
Egg Salad with Smoked Salmon,
Capers & Dill, 86:78a
Gravlax, 86:66
gravlax, explained, 86:66
Grilled Salmon Bundles with
Saffron, Tomatoes & Olives,
86:78a
hot-smoked, explained, 86:66
Orange-Roasted Salmon with
Yogurt-Caper Sauce, 89:102a
organic, 84:15
Salmon Braised in Pinot Noir,
84:60
turning a steak into a medallion,
86:65
salumi, 85:30
from the Fatted Calf in San
Francisco, 85:32
sambal oelek
sources, 87:72

Sampson, Lynne
"Surprise Your Guests with
Homemade Crackers,"
89:44–45
sandwiches
Grilled Portabella Sandwiches
with Tomatoes, Mozzarella &
Basil, 86:78a
Saran, Suvir
"Spice Up Your Vegetable Stir-
Fries, Indian Style," 83:46–49
saucepans
for induction cooking, 86:30
large, reviewed, 86:30–31
sauces
barbecue, how to keep from
sticking to grill, 87:16
Cranberry Sauce with Vanilla,
Maple Syrup & Cassis, 88:52
Eggnog Creme Anglaise, 89:63
for ham
Cherry-Pomegranate Glaze &
Sauce, 85:47
Maple, Tea & Cardamom
Glaze & Sauce, 85:47
Tangerine Marmalade Glaze
& Sauce, 85:47
for pasta
Lamb Shank & Sweet Pepper
Ragu, 83:61
Neapolitan Rib & Sausage
Ragu, 83:59
No-Cook Tomato Sauce,
87:39
No-Cook Tomato Sauce
with Basil Pesto, 87:39
No-Cook Tomato Sauce
with Cheese, 87:39
No-Cook Tomato Sauce
with Tapenade, 87:39
Short Rib & Porcini
Mushroom Ragu, 83:60
Lemon Curd, 86:53
Lemon, Dill & Cucumber Sauce,
86:42
Sea Salt, Chile & Lime Butter,
86:42
Sun-Dried Tomato, Olive &
Caper Relish, 86:42
Tarragon-Scented Mayonnaise
with Cornichons & Capers,
86:42
Toasted-Breadcrumb Salsa Verde,
87:50
sausage
Baked Ziti with Tomato,
Mozzarella & Sausage, 84:26a
Campanelle with Broccoli Raab,
Sausage & Olives, 84:26a
frittata with sausage, mushrooms
& onion, 83:62
Linguine with Shrimp & Chorizo,
83:82a
Neapolitan Rib & Sausage Ragu,
83:59
Rigatoni with Summer Squash,
Spicy Sausage & Goat Cheese,
86:44
Roasted Sausages & Grapes,
89:102a
Sausage-Maple Bread Stuffing,
88:50
Spicy Seared Chipotle Shrimp
with Zucchini & Chorizo,
85:57
Warm French Lentil Salad with
Smoked Sausage, 84:back cover
scallions
Grilled Flank Steak with Sesame
Sauce & Grilled Scallions,
87:53

Pork Lo Mein with Seared Scallions & Shiitakes, 87:54
Summer Corn Chowder with Scallions, Bacon & Potatoes, 87:55
scallops
  Thai Seafood Salad, 87:57
scoops
  ice cream, 87:26
scrubber, 85:28
seven-spice pepper
  about, 86:18
shallots
  judging size, 84:67
sherry
  about, 89:36
  glasses for, 89:36
  storing, 89:36
  styles of, 89:38
sherry vinegar
  about, 83:72
  sources, 83:76
shiitakes
  Pork Lo Mein with Seared Scallions & Shiitakes, 87:54
  Red Country-Style Curry with Beef, Shiitakes & Edamame, 89:67
  Seared Baby Bok Choy with Tofu & Shiitakes, 88:98a
  Stir-Fried Snow Peas with Shiitakes & Ginger, 84:57
shortcakes
  Cream Shortcake Biscuits, 87:61
  Peaches & Cream Shortcakes, 87:61
shrimp
  best shrimp for sautéing, 85:58
  Colossal Shrimp with Watercress & Tomato Salad, 84:78a
  Curried Coconut Shrimp, 88:98a
  doneness test, 85:59
  Grilled Corn, Shrimp & Chorizo Salad, 87:43
  Hot Garlicky Shrimp with Asparagus & Lemon, 85:59
  Linguine with Shrimp & Chorizo, 83:82a
  Red Curry with Shrimp & Sugar Snap Peas, 89:68
  Shrimp Skewers, 86:37
  Shrimp with Fennel, Tomato & Pernod Sauce, 85:58
  Spaghetti with Spicy Shrimp, Cherry Tomatoes & Herbed Breadcrumbs, 86:44
  Spicy Seared Chipotle Shrimp with Zucchini & Chorizo, 85:57
  techniques for sautéing, 85:56
  Thai Seafood Salad, 87:57
side dishes
  Basic Roasted Vegetables, 88:54
  Braised Bok Choy with Sherry & Prosciutto, 84:54
  Broccoli with Eggs & Lemony Parmesan Breadcrumbs, 88:51
  Brussels Sprouts Braised with Pancetta, Shallot, Thyme & Lemon, 89:59
  Cabbage & Carrot Stir-Fry with Toasted Cumin & Lime, 83:47
  Carrot Salad with Walnut Oil & Honey, 85:54
  Chopped Tomato & Cucumber Salad with Mint & Feta, 86:26a
  Classic Mashed Potatoes, 88:52
  Classic Potato Pancakes, 89:53
  Corn & Mushroom Saute with Leeks & Pancetta, 87:37

Corn Saute with Canadian Bacon, Potatoes & Peppers, 87:back cover
Corn Saute with Ginger, Garlic & Fresh Cilantro, 87:37
Corn, Sweet Onion & Zucchini Saute with Fresh Mint, 87:36
Create-Your-Own Pasta Salad with Grilled Eggplant, 87:67
Crispy Smashed Roasted Potatoes, 83:45
Green Bean Stir-Fry with Shredded Coconut, 83:49
Grilled Asparagus & Onions with Balsamic Vinegar & Blue Cheese, 86:26a
Grilled Corn on the Cob with Thyme & Roasted Red Pepper Butter, 86:26a
Grilled Eggplant, 87:49
Grilled Eggplant with Garlic-Cumin Vinaigrette with Feta & Herbs, 87:51
Grilled Eggplant with Olive, Orange & Anchovy Vinaigrette, 87:50
Grilled Eggplant with Roasted Red Pepper Relish with Pine Nuts, Currants & Marjoram, 87:51
Grilled Eggplant with Toasted-Breadcrumb Salsa Verde, 87:50
Grilled Southwestern Potato Salad, 86:26a
Ham Bone Collards, 85:76
Maple Pan-Roasted Baby Carrots, 85:53
Mushroom Stir-Fry with Onions & Tomatoes, 83:48
New Potatoes with Butter, Shallots & Chervil, 85:42
Orzo & Grilled Vegetable Salad with Feta, Olives & Oregano, 86:78a
Potato Pancakes Stuffed with Duxelles, 89:54
Potato Stir-Fry with Mint & Cilantro, 83:49
Rice Pilaf with Sage, Parmigiano & Prosciutto, 84:44
Rice Pilaf with Spiced Caramelized Onions, Orange, Cherry & Pistachio, 84:42
Roasted Asparagus with Lemon & Olive Oil, 85:42
Roasted Brussels Sprouts with Dijon, Walnuts & Crisp Crumbs, 89:57
Roasted Eggplant with Chiles, Peanuts & Mint, 84:55
Roasted Parsnips with Cinnamon & Coriander, 84:19
Saffron Rice Pilaf with Red Pepper & Toasted Almonds, 84:41
Sausage-Maple Bread Stuffing, 88:50
Sauteed Brussels Sprouts with Fresh Herbs & Crisp Shallots, 89:58
Southwestern Rice Pilaf, 84:43
Stir-Fried Cauliflower with Green Peas & Ginger, 83:back cover
Stir-Fried Napa Cabbage with Garlic, Fresh Chile & Basil, 84:56
Stir-Fried Snow Peas with Shiitakes & Ginger, 84:57
Sweet Potato Gratin with Caramelized Onions, 88:50

Warm Pasta Salad with Grilled Tomatoes, Zucchini & Pecorino, 86:26a
silicone
  basting brush, 83:28
  Bundt pan, reinforced, 83:28
  pastry brush, 83:28
silver powder
  edible, as dessert embellishment, 88:20
sinks
  with cooking element, 85:28
  with small dishwasher, 85:28
Sinskey, Maria Helm
  "Delicious Finishes for Grilled Fish," 86:40–42
slotted spatulas
  sources, 89:90
snow peas
  about, 84:57
  Coconut Rice with Chicken & Snow Peas, 83:40
  Sesame Chicken with Ginger & Snow Peas, 88:98a
  Stir-Fried Snow Peas with Shiitakes & Ginger, 84:57
soppressata, 85:30
soups, stews & stocks
  Beef Stew with Red Wine & Carrots, 84:39
  Cabbage & White Bean Soup, 88:74
  choosing beef chuck for stew, 84:67
  Curried Lentil Soup, 83:82a
  French Farmers' Soup, 88:74
  Ginger Chicken Soup, 85:84a
  Green Gazpacho, 87:19
  Mexican Black Bean Soup, 88:74
  Middle-Eastern Chickpea Soup, 88:74
  Minestrone, 88:74
  Summer Bouillabaisse with Smoky Rouille, 87:78a
  Summer Corn Chowder with Scallions, Bacon & Potatoes, 87:55
  Tomatillo Gazpacho, 86:78a
  Turkey Broth, 88:47
  Tuscan Peasant Soup with Rosemary & Pancetta, 83:10
  Velvety Carrot Soup with Ginger, 85:55
sources
  American wines, 88:92
  Asian chile sauces, 86:73
  Asian condiments, 84:72
  baby carrots, 85:78
  baking pans, 9x13-inch, 89:90
  biscuit cutters, 85:78
  brining bags, 88:92
  Bucheron cheese, 86:73
  Bundt pans, 83:76
  cake pans, 89:90
  canned chipotles en adobo, 85:78
  ceramic brazier pans, 83:76
  champagne vinegars, 84:72
  Cheddar, sharp, 83:77
  chile powder, 87:72
  chiles, 87:72
  chocolate, dark, 83:77
  chocolate-covered espresso beans, 85:78
  chorizo, 85:78
  cilantro root, 89:90
  cooling racks, 89:90
  creme brulee set, 84:72
  cucumber seeds, 87:72
  curry leaves, 83:76
  Dansko clogs, 84:72

Delouis Fils champagne vinegar, 84:72
demerara sugar, 87:72
dough scrapers, 89:90
du Puy lentils, 84:72
Dutch ovens, 83:76, 84:72, 88:92
egg whites, liquid, 89:90
egg whites, powdered, 89:90
Espelette chile powder, 86:73
extra-virgin olive oil, 83:77
fenugreek leaves, 83:76
fish spatulas, 86:73
five-spice powder, 87:72
Gouda, aged, 87:72
Greek wines, 85:78
ground chipotle, 87:72
hams, 85:78
ice cream scoops, 89:90
lemongrass, 86:73
lime peel, dried, 89:90
Madagascar vanilla beans, 84:72
malted milk powder, 87:72
maple syrup, grade B, 89:90
Mexican cheeses, 87:72
milkshake mixer, 87:72
mini blowtorch, 84:72
muffin pans, 89:90
nonstick baking liners (Roul'Pat), 88:92
nonstick baking liners (Silpat), 89:90
pappadams, 88:92
parchment, 88:92
parchment rounds, 89:90
pecans, 88:92
pimenton, 86:73
poblano seedlings, 86:73
pomegranate molasses, 85:78
pomegranate syrup, 85:78
pomegranate vinegar, 85:78
rhubarb roots, 85:78
roasting pans, heavy-duty, 83:76
roasting racks, 83:76
sage plants, 88:92
sambal oelek, 87:72
sherry vinegar, 83:76, 86:73
slotted fish spatula, 84:72
slotted spatulas, 89:90
soy beans for milk, 88:92
spatulas, giant, 83:76
springform pans, 89:90
tart pans with removable bottoms, 89:90
Thai basil, 89:90
Thai bird chiles, 86:73
Thai chiles, 89:90
tomato seed, 87:72
tomatoes, canned San Marzano, 83:76
tongs, locking, 87:72
vanilla beans, 83:76
vanilla beans, Madagascar, 85:78
waffle makers, 89:90
wild lime leaves, 89:90
wild mushrooms, 85:78
soymilk
  beans for, source, 88:92
  making at home, 88:33
spatulas
  for fish
    sources, 84:72, 86:73
  oversize, five things to do with, 86:27
  to remove ramekins from water bath, 84:29
spatulas, giant
  sources, 83:76
spices
  Garam Masala, 83:70
  Indian, 83:70

spinach
Feta & Dill Galette with Lemony Spinach Salad, 87:78a
Garlic Crostini with Spinach, Mushroom & Parmigiano Salad, 88:66
Spinach Salad with Apples, Dried Apricots & Pappadam Croutons, 88:66
Spinach Salad with Chicken, Cashews, Ginger & Fried Wontons, 88:65
Warm Spinach Salad with Eggs, Bacon & Croutons, 88:67
spoon rest
clip on, 85:24
spoon/spatula
silicone, 87:22
spoons
freezing for defatting stocks, 89:40
spring menu, 85:38–43
springform pans
sources, 89:90
squash
Farmers' Market Quesadillas, 87:78a
Rigatoni with Summer Squash, Spicy Sausage & Goat Cheese, 86:44
squeeze bottles
for garnishing, 89:28
squid
Thai Seafood Salad, 87:57
stand mixers
new from Cuisinart, 89:30
steamer inserts
silicone, 86:26
steel
for honing, not sharpening, 85:65
Stevens, Molly
"Bistro Cooking at Home," 84:33–39
"How to Make Hearty Bean & Vegetable Soups," 88:73–77
stir-fries
Curried Coconut Shrimp, 88:98a
Hoisin Pork with Napa Cabbage, 88:98a
Orange Chicken with Scallions, 88:98a
Seared Baby Bok Choy with Tofu & Shiitakes, 88:98a
Sesame Chicken with Ginger & Snow Peas, 88:98a
Spicy Beef with Peanuts & Chiles, 88:98a
Stir-Fried Noodles with Beef & Vegetables, 88:98a
tips for, 88:98a
stocking stuffers for a cook, 89:20
strawberries
Balsamic-Macerated Strawberries with Basil, 86:back cover
Phyllo Chips with Vanilla Ice Cream & Strawberry Mash "Dip," 84:63
Strawberry-Orange-Vanilla Breakfast Smoothie, 88:84
Strawberry-Rhubarb Compote with Vanilla & Cardamom, 85:61
Strawberry-Rhubarb Pie, 85:62
stuffing
frying leftover, 88:43
Sausage-Maple Bread Stuffing, 88:50
sugar
demerara, sources, 87:72
sugar snap peas
Red Curry with Shrimp & Sugar Snap Peas, 89:68

Suzuki, Meg
"Lemon Cheesecake, To Go, 86:52–53
sweet potatoes
Sweet Potato & Chile Hash with a Fried Egg, 89:30a
Sweet Potato Gratin with Caramelized Onions, 88:50
Turkey & Sweet Potato Hash, 88:86

T

tacos
Soft Chicken Tacos with the Works, 83:42
tart pans with removable bottoms
sources, 89:90
tarts
Free-Form Pear Tarts with Almond & Cinnamon, 84:64
Leek Tart with Bacon & Gruyere, 89:23
preventing soggy shells, 88:42
tea infuser, 89:20
Thai basil
sources, 89:90
Thai bird chiles
sources, 86:73
Thai chiles
sources, 89:90
Thanksgiving
a plan-ahead meal, 88:44–52
questions answered, 88:88–89
thermometers
holding in place, 85:34
instant-read, calibrating, 84:68
laser, 84:22
thyme
"easy-strip," 88:78
timers
digital, for refrigerator items, 86:26
tofu
about, 88:84
how to buy and store, 88:84
how to use, 88:84
Seared Baby Bok Choy with Tofu & Shiitakes, 88:98a
Strawberry-Orange-Vanilla Breakfast Smoothie, 88:84
tomatillos
Tomatillo Gazpacho, 86:78a
tomatoes
Angel Hair Pasta with Sauteed Cherry Tomatoes, Lemon & Tuna, 87:78a
canned San Marzano sources, 83:76
Chopped Tomato & Cucumber Salad with Mint & Feta, 86:26a
Grilled Bruschetta with Rosemary-White Bean Puree & Heirloom Tomatoes, 86:26a
Mushroom Stir-Fry with Onions & Tomatoes, 83:48
No-Cook Tomato Sauce, 87:39
No-Cook Tomato Sauce with Basil Pesto, 87:39
No-Cook Tomato Sauce with Cheese, 87:39
No-Cook Tomato Sauce with Tapenade, 87:39
seed sources, 87:72
Spaghetti with Spicy Shrimp, Cherry Tomatoes & Herbed Breadcrumbs, 86:44
Summer Bouillabaisse with Smoky Rouille, 87:78a

Warm Pasta Salad with Grilled Tomatoes, Zucchini & Pecorino, 86:26a
tomatoes, sun-dried
Sun-Dried Tomato, Olive & Caper Relish, 86:42
tongs
with attached LED light, 86:27
tuna
Angel Hair Pasta with Sauteed Cherry Tomatoes, Lemon & Tuna, 87:78a
Mini Tuna Burgers with Mint-Caper Aioli on Pita Triangles, 86:38
Seared Tuna with Fennel Seeds & Caper Brown Butter, 83:82a
Tuna Teriyaki with Scallion Salad, 84:78a
turkey
brining tips, 88:80
brining vs. crisp skin, 88:88
Herb-Butter Roasted Turkey with Pinot Noir Gravy, 88:48
Turkey & Sweet Potato Hash, 88:86
twist-ties
to truss chicken legs, 84:29

U

Usher, Julia M.
"Move Over, Gingerbread Man," 89:60–65

V

vacuum-sealers for food
tested, 87:23
vanilla beans
Madagascar, sources, 84:72, 85:78
sources, 83:76
vegetables
Basic Roasted Vegetables, 88:54
four tips for roasting, 88:54
guide to roasting, 88:53–57
how to freeze without sticking, 89:42
how to roast a medley, 88:55
tip for grilling, 86:35
vinaigrettes
Garlic-Cumin Vinaigrette with Feta & Herbs, 87:51
Honey-Mustard Sherry Vinaigrette, 83:72
how to prevent breaking, 83:22
Mixed Green Salad with Red-Wine & Dijon Vinaigrette, 86:47
Olive, Orange & Anchovy Vinaigrette, 87:50
Pimenton Vinaigrette, 86:37
vinegar
balsamic
Balsamic-Macerated Strawberries with Basil, 86:back cover
champagne
rating, 84:71
sources, 84:72
sherry, about, 83:72
sherry, sources, 86:73
white balsamic, about, 86:64

W

Waddle, Lisa
"A Kitchen That Goes All Out," 86:54–57
waffle makers
sources, 89:90

waffles
Chocolate Chip Waffles, 89:30a
Cornmeal Waffles, 89:30a
Cranberry-Orange Waffles, 89:30a
Light, Crisp Waffles, 89:30a
tips for making, 89:30a
Whole-Grain Waffles, 89:30a
wall ovens
with French doors, 88:28
washes in baking
egg vs. milk, 88:22
Wayte, Annie
"The Art of Making Green Salads," 86:46–51
Weir, Joanne
"A New Wave of Spinach Salads," 88:64–67
wild lime leaves
sources, 89:90
wine
search engine for locating, 88:92
wine (see also Enjoying Wine column)
alternatives to popular varietals, 83:26
American wines, 88:36
appellation explained, 88:36
from Greece, 85:20–22
how much to buy for a party, 86:22
putting together a mixed case, 86:22–23
tasting terms, 84:21
what makes a good summer wine, 86:22
white, chilled but not opened, 86:18
wine label jargon, 84:20
wine decanters
what kind to look for, 84:15
wine ratchet, 89:32
wontons
Fried Chocolate-Hazelnut Wontons with Orange Dipping Sauce, 84:65
wooden utensils
beautifully handcrafted, 89:32

Y

yogurt
as buttermilk substitute, 86:35
yogurt maker
reviewed, 85:26

Z

zucchini
Corn, Sweet Onion & Zucchini Saute with Fresh Mint, 87:36
Spicy Seared Chipotle Shrimp with Zucchini & Chorizo, 85:57
Warm Pasta Salad with Grilled Tomatoes, Zucchini & Pecorino, 86:26a